AN EXEGETICAL SUMMARY OF
LUKE 1–11

AN EXEGETICAL SUMMARY OF
LUKE 1–11

Second Edition

Richard C. Blight

SIL International

Second Edition
© 2007, 2008 by SIL International

Library of Congress Catalog Card Number: 2008924474
ISBN: 978-155671-211-1

Printed in the United States of America

All Rights Reserved
No part of this publication may be reproduced, stored in a retrieval system, or transmitted in any form or by any means without the express permission of SIL International. However, brief excerpts, generally understood to be within the limits of fair use, may be quoted without written permission.

Copies of this and other publications
of SIL International may be obtained from

International Academic Bookstore
SIL International
7500 West Camp Wisdom Road
Dallas, TX 75236-5699, USA

Voice: 972-708-7404
Fax: 972-708-7363
academic_books@sil.org
www.ethnologue.com

PREFACE

Exegesis is concerned with the interpretation of a text. Exegesis of the New Testament involves determining the meaning of the Greek text. Translators must be especially careful and thorough in their exegesis of the New Testament in order to accurately communicate its message in the vocabulary, grammar, and literary devices of another language. Questions occurring to translators as they study the Greek text are answered by summarizing how scholars have interpreted the text. This is information that should be considered by translators as they make their own exegetical decisions regarding the message they will communicate in their translations.

The Semi-Literal Translation

As a basis for discussion, a semi-literal translation of the Greek text is given so that the reasons for different interpretations can best be seen. When one Greek word is translated into English by several words, these words are joined by hyphens. There are a few times when clarity requires that a string of words joined by hyphens have a separate word, such as "not" (μή), inserted in their midst. In this case, the separate word is surrounded by spaces between the hyphens. When alternate translations of a Greek word are given, these are separated by slashes.

The Text

Variations in the Greek text are noted under the heading TEXT. The base text for the summary is the text of the fourth revised edition of *The Greek New Testament,* published by the United Bible Societies, which has the same text as the twenty-sixth edition of the *Novum Testamentum Graece* (Nestle-Aland). Dr. J. Harold Greenlee researched the variants and has written the notes for this part of the summary. The versions that follow different variations are listed without evaluating their choices.

The Lexicon

The meaning of a key word in context is the first question to be answered. Words marked with a raised letter in the semi-literal translation are treated separately under the heading LEXICON. First, the lexicon form of the Greek word is given. Within the parentheses following the Greek word is the location number where, in the author's judgment, this word is defined in the *Greek-English Lexicon of the New Testament Based on Semantic Domains* (Louw and Nida 1988). When a semantic domain includes a translation of the particular verse being treated, **LN** in bold type indicates that specific translation. If the specific reference for the verse is listed in *A Greek-English Lexicon of the New Testament and Other Early Christian Literature* (Bauer, Arndt, Gingrich, and Danker 1979), the outline location and page number is given. Then English equivalents of the Greek word are given to show how it is translated by commentators who offer their own translations of the whole text and, after a semicolon, all the versions in the list of abbreviations for translations. When reference is made to "all versions," it refers to only the versions in the list of translations. Sometimes further comments are made about the meaning of the word or the significance of a verb's tense, voice, or mood.

The Questions

Under the heading QUESTION, a question is asked that comes from examining the Greek text under consideration. Typical questions concern the identity of an implied actor or object of an event word, the antecedent of a pronominal reference, the connection indicated by a relational word, the meaning of a genitive construction, the meaning of figurative language, the function of a rhetorical question, the identification of an ambiguity, and the presence of implied information that is needed to understand the passage correctly. Background information is also considered for a proper understanding of a passage. Although not all implied information and background information is made explicit in a translation, it is important to consider it so that the translation will not be stated in such a way that prevents a reader from arriving at the proper interpretation. The question is answered with a summary of what commentators have said. If there are contrasting differences of opinion, the different interpretations are numbered and the commentaries that support each are listed. Differences that are not treated by many of the commentaries often are not numbered, but are introduced with a contrastive 'Or' at the beginning of the sentence. No attempt has been made to select which interpretation is best.

In listing support for various statements of interpretation, the author is often faced with the difficult task of matching the different terminologies used in commentaries with the terminology he has adopted. Sometimes he can only infer the position of a commentary from incidental remarks. This book, then, includes the author's interpretation of the views taken in the various commentaries. General statements are followed by specific statements, which indicate the author's understanding of the pertinent relationships, actors, events, and objects implied by that interpretation.

The Use of This Book

This book does not replace the commentaries that it summarizes. Commentaries contain much more information about the meaning of words and passages. They often contain arguments for the interpretations that are taken and they may have important discussions about the discourse features of the text. In addition, they have information about the historical, geographical, and cultural setting. Translators will want to refer to at least four commentaries as they exegete a passage. However, since no one commentary contains all the answers translators need, this book will be a valuable supplement. It makes more sources of exegetical help available than most translators have access to. Even if they had all the books available, few would have the time to search through all of them for the answers.

When many commentaries are studied, it soon becomes apparent that they frequently disagree in their interpretations. That is the reason why so many answers in this book are divided into two or more interpretations. The reader's initial reaction may be that all of these different interpretations complicate exegesis rather than help it. However, before translating a passage, a translator needs to know exactly where there is a problem of interpretation and what the exegetical options are.

Acknowledgments

Ronald L. Trail wrote four volumes of the *Exegetical Summaries*. Because of this experience he did an excellent job of editing this volume.

Matthew E. Carlton took time to read this volume and offer many valuable suggestions while writing his next book, *The Translator's Reference Translation of the Gospel of Luke*.

J. Harold Greenlee has spent most of his life teaching and writing about New Testament Greek. He wrote five volumes of the *Exegetical Summaries*. Since retiring he has provided textual comments for a number of the summaries, including this one.

ABBREVIATIONS

COMMENTARIES AND REFERENCE BOOKS

Asterisks indicate books that translators may find especially helpful as they study the text of Luke. A dagger indicates that a knowledge of Greek is required.

AB*	Fitzmyer, Jospeph A. *The Gospel According to Luke.* 2 vols. Garden City, N.Y.: Doubleday, 1981 and 1985.
Alf	Alford, Henry. *The Four Gospels.* The Greek Testament, vol. 1. 1874. Reprint. Chicago: Moody, 1968.
Arn*	Arndt, William F. *Luke.* St. Louis: Concordia, 1984.
BAGD	Bauer, Walter. *A Greek-English Lexicon of the New Testament and Other Early Christian Literature.* Translated and adapted from the fifth edition, 1958 by William F. Arndt and F. Wilbur Gingrich. Second English ed. revised and augmented by F. Wilbur Gingrich and Frederick W. Danker. Chicago: University of Chicago Press, 1979.
Bai	Bailey, Kenneth E. *Poet & Peasant and Through Peasant Eyes.* Reprint (2 vols. in 1). Grand Rapids: Eerdmans, 1983.
BECNT*	Bock, Darrell L. *Luke.* 2 vols. Baker Exegetical Commentary on the New Testament. Grand Rapids: Baker Books, 1994 and 1996.
Blm	Blomberg, Craig. *Interpreting the Parables.* Downer Grove, Ill.: InterVarsity Press, 1990.
BNTC	Leaney, A. R. C. *A Commentary on the Gospel According to St. Luke.* 2d ed. Black's New Testament Commentary. London: Adam and Charles Black, 1966.
Crd	Creed, John Martin. *The Gospel According to St. Luke.* London: MacMillan, 1930.
EGT	Bruce, Alexander Balmain. *The Synoptic Gospels.* Expositor's Greek Testament, vol. 1. 1910. Reprint. Grand Rapids: Eerdmans, 1997.
Gdt	Godet, F. *A Commentary on the Gospel of St. Luke.* 2 vols. 1870. Reprint. Edinburgh: T. & T. Clark, 1957.
Hlt	Hiltgren, Arland J. *The Parables of Jesus.* Grand Rapids: Eermans, 2000.
Hu	Hultgren, Arland J. *The Parables of Jesus.* Grand Rapids: Eerdmans, 2000.
ICC*	Plummer, Alfred. *A Critical and Exegetical Commentary on the Gospel According to S. Luke.* The International Critical Commentary. Edinburgh: T. & T. Clark, 1896.
Kst	Kistemaker, Simon J. *The Parables of Jesus.* Grand Rapids: Baker, 1950.

ABBREVIATIONS

LN*	Louw, Johannes P., and Eugene A. Nida. *Greek-English Lexicon of the New Testament Based on Semantic Domains*. New York: United Bible Societies, 1988.
Lns*	Lenski, R. C. H. *The Interpretation of St. Luke's Gospel*. Minneapolis: Augsburg, 1946.
MGC	Pate, C. Marvin. *Luke*. Moody Gospel Commentary. Chicago: Moody Press, 1995.
My	Meyer, Heinrich August Wilhelm. *Critical and Exegetical Handbook to the Gospels of Mark and Luke*. [American Edition.] New York: Funk and Wagnalls, 1884.
NAC	Stein, Robert H. *Luke*. New American Commentary. Nashville, Tenn.: Broadman, 1992.
NIBC	Evans, Craig A. *Luke*. New International Biblical Commentary. Peabody, Mass.: Hendrickson, 1990.
NIC	Geldenhuys, Norval. *Commentary on the Gospel of Luke*. New International Commentary on the New Testament. Grand Rapids: Eerdmans, 1951.
NICNT	Green, Joel B. *The Gospel of Luke*. New International Commentary on the New Testament. [Replacement.] Grand Rapids: Eerdmans, 1997.
NIGTC*†	Marshall, I. Howard. *The Gospel of Luke*. The New International Greek Testament Commentary. Grand Rapids: Eerdmans, 1978.
NIVS	Barker, Kenneth, ed. *The NIV Study Bible*. Grand Rapids: Zondervan, 1985.
NTC*	Hendriksen, William. *Exposition of the Gospel According to Luke*. New Testament Commentary. Grand Rapids: Baker, 1978.
Pnt	Pentecost, J. Dwight. *The Parables of Jesus*. Grand Rapids: Zondervan, 1982.
Rt	Robertson, Archibald Thomas. *The Gospel According to Luke*. Word Pictures in the New Testament, vol. 2. Nashville, Tenn.: Broadman, 1930.
Su	Summers, Ray. *Commentary on Luke*. Waco, Texas: Word, 1972.
TG*	Bratcher, Robert G. *A Translator's Guide to the Gospel of Luke*. London, New York: United Bible Societies, 1982.
TH*	Reiline, J., and J. L. Swellengrebel. *A Handbook on The Gospel of Luke*. New York: United Bible Societies, 1971.
TNTC	Morris, Leon. *Luke*. Revised Edition. Tyndale New Testament Commentaries. Grand Rapids: Eerdmans, 1988.
WBC*	Nolland, John. *Luke*. 3 vols. Word Biblical Commentary. Dallas: Word Books, 1989 and 1993.

GREEK TEXT AND TRANSLATIONS

GNT	The Greek New Testament. Edited by B. Aland, K. Aland, J. Karavidopoulos, C. Martini, and B. Metzger. Fourth ed. London, New York: United Bible Societies, 1993.
CEV	The Holy Bible, Contemporary English Version. New York: American Bible Society, 1995.
GW	God's Word. Grand Rapids: World Publishing, 1995.
HCSB	Holman Christian Standard Bible. Nashville, Tennessee: Holman Bible Publishers, 2000.
KJV	The Holy Bible. Authorized (or King James) Version. 1611.
NASB	New American Standard Bible. La Habra, Calif.: Lockman Foundation, 1995.
NCV	New Century Version. Dallas: Word Publishing, 1991.
NET	The NET Bible. New English Translation, New Testament. Version 9.206. WWW.BIBLE.COM: Biblical Studies Press, 1999.
NIV	The Holy Bible, New International Version. Grand Rapids: Zondervan, 1984.
NLT	The Holy Bible, New Living Translation. Wheaton, Ill.: Tyndale House, 1996.
NRSV	The Holy Bible: New Revised Standard Version. New York: Oxford University Press, 1989.
REB	The Revised English Bible. Oxford: Oxford University Press and Cambridge University Press, 1989.
TEV	Good News Bible, Today's English Version. Second ed. New York: American Bible Society, 1992.

GRAMMATICAL TERMS

act.	active		mid.	middle
fut.	future		opt.	optative
impera.	imperative		pass.	passive
imperf.	imperfect		perf.	perfect
indic.	indicative		pres.	present
infin.	infinitive		subj.	subjunctive

EXEGETICAL SUMMARY OF LUKE 1–11

DISCOURSE UNIT: 1:1–2:52 [BECNT]. This unit functions as the preface of the book and the topic is the introduction of John and Jesus.

DISCOURSE UNIT: 1:1–4 [AB, BECNT, NAC, NICNT, NIGTC, Su, TNTC, WBC; CEV, GW, HCSB, NASB, NCV, NET, NIV, NLT, NRSV, REB, TEV]. The topic is the prologue [AB, NAC, NICNT], the preface [BECNT, NIGTC, Su, TNTC; NET], the introduction [NASB, NIV, NLT, TEV], Luke writes to Theophilus [GW], dedication to Theophilus [HCSB, NRSV], dedicatory preface [WBC], Luke writes about Jesus' life [NCV]. There is no heading for this introductory unit [CEV, REB]. This unit is one long sentence in the Greek text. It follows the type of introduction used by Greek writers of that time [AB, Arn, Crd, Gdt, ICC, Lns, NIGTC, NTC, TH].

1:1 Since^a many have-undertaken^b to-compile^c an-account^d about the events^e (which) happened/have-been-fulfilled^f among us,

LEXICON—a. ἐπειδήπερ (LN 89.3) (BAGD p. 284): 'since' [AB, Arn, BAGD, LN, Lns, NTC; NRSV], 'inasmuch as' [BAGD, BECNT, NIGTC, WBC; NASB], 'forasmuch as' [KJV], not explicit [HCSB, NCV, NLT]. Instead of 'since' here in 1:1, some have made explicit the reciprocal relationship of *conclusion* at the beginning of 1:3: 'so' [CEV, GW, NET, REB, TEV], 'therefore' [NIV].

b. aorist act. indic. of ἐπιχειρέω (LN 68.59) (BAGD p. 305): 'to undertake' [AB, Arn, BECNT, LN, NTC; HCSB, NASB, NET, NIV, NRSV, REB], 'to set one's hand to' [BAGD], 'to take in hand' [Lns, WBC; KJV], 'to do one's best' [TEV], 'to try' [BAGD, LN; CEV, NCV], 'to attempt' [BAGD, NIGTC; GW], not explicit [NLT].

c. aorist mid. (deponent = act.) infin. of ἀνατάσσομαι (LN 62.3) (BAGD p. 61): 'to compile' [AB, BAGD, BECNT, LN, NIGTC; HCSB, NASB, NET], 'to arrange' [LN, WBC], 'to put together' [LN], 'to draw up' [Arn, NIGTC, NTC; NIV, REB], 'to set down' [NRSV], 'to set forth in order' [KJV], 'to write' [NLT, TEV], 'to tell' [CEV], 'to recount' [Lns]. The phrase 'to compile an account' is translated 'to write about' [GW], 'to report on' [NCV].

d διήγησις (LN **33.11**) (BAGD p. 195): 'account' [Arn, BAGD, BECNT, LN; NASB, NET, NIV, NLT, NRSV, REB], 'orderly account' [AB; NRSV], 'report' [LN; TEV], 'narrative' [BAGD, Lns, NTC, WBC; HCSB], 'story' [CEV], 'declaration' [KJV], not explicit [GW, NCV]. In the context of 'have undertaken', which is literally 'to set one's hand to' [BAGD], this refers to a written account [NET].

e. πρᾶγμα (LN **13.105**) (BAGD 1. p. 697): 'event' [AB, BAGD, LN, NIGTC; HCSB, NET, NLT, NRSV, REB], 'thing' [BECNT, NTC, WBC; KJV, NASB, NCV, NIV, TEV], 'matter' [Lns], 'what' [CEV, GW]. It refers to historical facts [NIC].

LUKE 1:1

f. perf. pass. participle of πληροφορέω (LN **13.106**) (BAGD 1.a. p. 670): 'to happen' [LN; NCV], 'to take place' [**LN**; GW, NLT, REB, TEV], 'to be accomplished' [BAGD, WBC; NASB], 'to be brought to full measure' [NIGTC], 'to be brought to completion' [Lns], 'to be fulfilled' [BECNT, LN, NTC; HCSB, NET, NIV, NRSV], 'to come to fulfillment' [AB], '(what God) has done' [CEV], 'to be surely believed' [KJV], '(the things concerning which) there is full assurance' [Arn].

QUESTION—What relationship is indicated by ἐπειδήπερ 'since'?

1. It indicates the grounds for Luke's decision to write (1:3) [AB, BAGD, BECNT, EGT, Lns, MGC, NIC, NICNT, NIGTC, NTC, TH, WBC; CEV, GW, KJV, NASB, NET, NIV, REB, TEV]: *since* many have undertaken to compile an account..., (v. 3) it seemed good to me also to write about this in an orderly way. Luke is not criticizing the many who had written before, but he perhaps wishes to write a more complete account than others had done [NTC]. This makes the point that his undertaking is quite regular. However, the following statements show that he is doing more than writing a useless repetition of what has already been done [Lns]. The existence of many accounts showed that there was a large demand for information that still wasn't adequately met and therefore his attempt was not superfluous [EGT]. Not only did others provide an incentive to write, but their writings provided resources for Luke to investigate in producing his own account [NIGTC].

2. This conjunction is omitted by some and instead of this verse being the reason for his decision to write in 1:3, the participial clause of 1:3 is the only explicit grounds [NCV, NLT]: '*since* I myself have studied everything carefully from the beginning...it seemed good for me to write it out for you' [NCV].

QUESTION—Who were the 'many' who had complied accounts?

It refers to the writers Luke researched in 1:3 [TH]. The Gospel of Mark was written previously and probably was one of the sources Luke used [Arn, MGC, NIBC, NIGTC, NTC, Su], and also Matthew [Arn]. The reference to many writers brings out the importance of what Luke will write about [NAC, NICNT, WBC]. The number is unknown, but it was probably quite a few even though their accounts have not been preserved [Arn, Lns], and it was not an exaggeration [EGT]. 'Many' is used in a formal manner of beginning a document and it does not have to be taken to literally mean a large number [AB, NAC, NICNT, NIGTC], so that it could be translated 'others' [NAC].

QUESTION—What is the sense of 'have undertaken', which some translate as 'have tried' or 'have attempted'?

The verb can be used in a formal way to introduce a literary document. It can have a neutral sense, with Luke using it of his own effort ('it seemed good to me also' in 1:3), or it could have the sense of attempting to do something but not succeeding, perhaps suggested by Luke referring to his writing in an orderly way after extensive research (1:3), and claiming to offer assurance of its truth (1:4) [AB]. It does not imply that some failed [Arn, BECNT, ICC,

Lns, NAC, NICNT, NIGTC, NTC, TH, WBC; NET], since in 1:3 he puts himself in the same class with them [Lns, NAC, WBC]. The word points to the difficulty of compiling the account and it suggests neither success nor failure [Lns, NIGTC]. Luke might have approved of their work, but realized that that no one had made as complete an account as he wished to make [NTC]. It gives a gentle hint that finality had not yet been reached [EGT]. It implies that Luke is writing his account because some had done inadequate work [TG].

QUESTION—Does πεπληροφορημένων mean here 'have happened', 'have been fulfilled', or something else?

1. It means to have taken place or happened [LN, TG; CEV, GW, NCV, NLT, REB, TEV]: the events that have taken place. These are the events concerning the beginning of the Christian movement and its spread [TG].
2. It means to have been brought to completion [ICC, Lns, Rb, WBC; NASB]: the events that have been accomplished. These events are not still in progress, they have been fully completed by Jesus' death and resurrection and they now stand as they are for all time [Lns]. This refers to the matters that have been carried through to an end [ICC]. This does not say that Scripture has been fulfilled, but refers to the events themselves being fulfilled or accomplished. Luke is thinking of matters that have been brought to a successful completion, perhaps referring to the obstacles overcome in Jesus' life, or to Jesus' achieving enthronement in heaven [WBC].
3. It means to have been fulfilled [AB, BECNT, MGC, NAC, NIC, NICNT, NIGTC, NIVS, NTC, Su, TNTC; HCSB, NET, NIV, NRSV]. This refers to the prophecies in the OT that have been fully accomplished [NIVS, NTC]: the events that have been fulfilled as planned. God's promises to provide a Savior had been fulfilled [NIGTC, Su]. The passive participle 'have been fulfilled' implies that God has fulfilled his plans [BECNT].
4. It means to have fullness of knowledge and thus concerns the things that have become widely known among Christians [EGT].
5. It means to have fullness in regard to conviction and thus 'to be surely believed' [Arn; KJV]. The meanings 'to convince' and 'to lead to sure belief' for this verb are also found in Rom. 4:21 and 14:5, while the noun form is found in 1 Thess. 1:5. The following phrase 'among us' better goes with this meaning than with the other interpretations, so in this verse the meaning is 'to draw up an account of the things concerning which there is full assurance among us' [Arn].

QUESTION—Who are 'us' in the phrase 'among us'?

1. Since 'us' includes both the eyewitnesses and those who received their accounts, it refers to the Christian church regarded as a corporate body [BECNT, BNTC, Gdt, ICC, NAC, NICNT, NIGTC, NTC, Su, TH; TEV]. They are the people living at the time of fulfillment [Su]. This is different from the 'us' in 1:2 [AB, NIGTC, NTC, Su]. These things happened in the midst of the church and the church also retained the saving effects of them

[NIGTC]. Second generation Christians felt themselves to be a part of the Christians of the fulfillment time [Su]. It refers to all Christians as being affected by salvation-history [AB].
2. It refers to the Christians to whom the accounts were delivered by the eyewitnesses, so that this is the same as the people referred to by 'us' in 1:2 [Lns].
3. It refers to Luke and his fellow Christians, most of whom had not been eyewitnesses to those events that had occurred, but all were firmly convinced that the events were historical [Arn].

1:2 just-as[a] the (ones who) from (the) beginning[b] were eyewitnesses and (then) became servants[c] of-the word delivered[d] to-us,

LEXICON—a. καθώς (LN 64.14) (BAGD 1. p. 391): 'just as' [AB, Arn, BAGD, LN, NTC, WBC; HCSB, NASB, NIV, NRSV], 'according as' [NIGTC], 'even as' [BECNT; KJV], 'like' [NET], not explicit [CEV, GW, NCV, NLT, REB, TEV].

b. ἀρχή (LN 67.65) (BAGD 1.b. p. 112): 'beginning' [Arn, BAGD, BECNT, LN, NIGTC, NTC, WBC; CEV, GW, KJV, NASB, NCV, NET, NRSV, TEV], 'the first' [NIV]. This noun is also translated as an adjective modifying the eyewitnesses: 'the original (eyewitnesses)' [AB; HCSB, REB], 'the early (disciples)' [NLT]. It is the beginning of a duration of time [LN]. This refers to the beginning of Jesus' ministry [Lns, NAC, NIC, NIGTC, TH, TNTC, WBC; NET], of the Christian movement [TG]. In regard to the eyewitnesses and servants of the word, the beginning refers to the time when John baptized Jesus [Arn, NAC]. However, this does not imply that the events in the first two chapters do not come from eyewitnesses also [NAC]. This stresses the reliability of the witnesses since they knew the whole story of Jesus [Lns].

c. ὑπηρέτης (LN 35.20) (BAGD p. 842): 'servant' [Arn, BAGD, BECNT, LN, NIGTC, WBC; GW, HCSB, NASB, NET, NIV, NRSV, REB], 'helper, assistant' [BAGD], 'minister' [AB, NTC; KJV], 'disciple' [NLT], 'those who proclaim (the message)' [TEV], not explicit [CEV]. The phrase 'servants of the word' is translated 'who…served God by telling people his message' [NCV].

d. aorist act. indic. of παραδίδωμι (LN 33.237) (BAGD 3. p. 615): 'to deliver' [BECNT; KJV], 'to instruct, to teach' [BAGD, LN], 'to pass on' [AB, BAGD; GW], 'to hand down' [Arn, NTC; HCSB]. This verb is also translated with 'the account about the events' of 1:1 as its subject: 'to be handed down' [NIGTC; NASB, NIV, REB], 'to be handed on' [WBC; NRSV], 'to be passed on' [NET], 'to circulate' [NLT]. The reciprocal verb is also used with 'we' as subject: 'to learn' [NCV], 'to be told' [CEV]. This includes both oral and written transmission [Arn, NICNT, NTC, Su]. It means to pass on information in order to save it from oblivion [NICNT].

QUESTION—What relationship is indicated by καθώς 'just as'?
1. It indicates a comparison of the accounts [AB, BAGD, BECNT, ICC, LN, NIGTC, NTC; HCSB, KJV, NASB, NET, NIV, NRSV]: many have complied accounts about the events which are *just the same as* the accounts eyewitnesses delivered to us. This compares two types of accounts, that which was written (1:1) and that which was taught by the eyewitnesses (1:2) [NET]. Those who wrote were faithful to the manner and form of their authorities [Lns]. They wrote what was told by the eyewitnesses [CEV, NCV, TEV]. This affirms the reliability of the written accounts [AB, Lns, NIGTC], even though Luke will put the material together in a better way [AB].
2. It indicates a comparison of the many writers with the eyewitnesses [NICNT]: just as the eyewitnesses passed on to us the message, so the many writers compiled narratives of those events.
3. It indicates a comparison of the eyewitnesses with Luke [WBC]: just as they transmitted the message to us, I will write it for you. The likeness is between Luke's activity and the activity of the eyewitnesses, both being concerned with communicating the knowledge of the matters under discussion [WBC].

QUESTION—How are the servants connected with the word in the genitive construction 'servants of the word'?
They served God by telling people his message [NCV]. They were preachers of the gospel [Arn, TH], men who proclaimed the message [AB, TG, TNTC; TEV]. Being servants of the word, they unreservedly gave themselves to the cause of telling the gospel message [BECNT, NIGTC, WBC].

QUESTION—Are the eyewitnesses and the servants of the word the same group of people?
1. They are the same group of people [AB, BECNT, EGT, MGC, NAC, NIC, NICNT, NIGTC, NTC, Su, TH, TNTC, WBC; NET]. They were eyewitnesses who became servants of the message [WBC]. This refers to the original disciples who were at first eyewitnesses and then became servants of the word [AB, Arn, Su, TH]. This refers primarily to the apostles [EGT, MGC, NIC, NIGTC, Su], but not exclusively to them [NAC, NIGTC, WBC]. It could include the seventy disciples (10:1–12) [NAC], and Mary, the brothers of Jesus, other women, and others [NTC].
2. They are two groups of people [Lns]. The one article that combines the eyewitnesses and the servants of the word makes them one class of authorities, but this does not mean that all of the servants of the word were eyewitnesses from the beginning of Jesus' ministry [Lns].

QUESTION—What did they deliver to us?
They delivered the traditions [BECNT, NAC, NIGTC; REB], the accounts [NET], the reports [NLT], or the message of what they knew [WBC]. Although grammatically the object is πραγμάτων 'events' (1:1), it was the information about the events that they delivered [TH, WBC].

QUESTION—Who does 'us' refer to?
Those who take 'us' in 1:1 to refer to the corporate body of the church recognize that here 'us' is more restricted since the eyewitnesses were not part of the 'us' who received the accounts. Luke and his generation are distinguished from the eyewitnesses and ministers of the word [AB, Gdt, Lns, NAC, NIGTC, NTC, Su, TG, TH]. This refers to the writer and all contemporary Christians [TG, TH]. It excludes the many writers mentioned in 1:1 [NAC]. Or, it refers to Luke and the many who have written accounts of the events that had been taught them (1:1) [Arn].

1:3 **it-seemed-good to-me-also, having-investigated[a] everything carefully from-(the)-beginning/for-a-long-time,[b] to-write in-an-orderly-way[c] to-you, most-excellent[d] Theophilus.**

LEXICON—a. perf. act. part. of παρακολουθέω (LN **27.38**) (BAGD 3. p. 619): 'to investigate' [Arn, BAGD, **LN**, WBC; HCSB, NASB, NIV, NLT, NRSV, REB], 'to diligently check out' [LN], 'to study' [NCV, TEV], 'to make a study of' [CEV], 'to follow' [BECNT; GW, NET], 'to trace' [AB, Lns], 'to trace the course' [NTC], 'to have perfect understanding' [KJV], It refers to personal investigation, not just reading what had been written [TG].

b. ἄνωθεν (LN **67.90**) (BAGD 2.a. and possibly 2.b. p. 77): 'from the beginning' [AB, Arn, BAGD (2.a.), BECNT, NTC; GW, NASB, NCV, NET, NIV, NLT], 'from their beginning' [TEV], 'from the start' [Lns], 'from the very first' [HCSB, KJV, NRSV], 'from way back' [WBC], 'the whole course' [REB], 'for a long time' [BAGD (2.b), **LN**], not explicit [CEV].

c. καθεξῆς (LN **61.7**) (BAGD p. 388): 'in an orderly way' [Lns], 'in an orderly manner' [**LN**], 'in an orderly fashion' [Arn], 'in order' [KJV], 'in sequence' [**LN**], 'in orderly sequence' [BAGD; HCSB], 'in consecutive order' [NASB], 'systematically' [AB], 'exactly' [CEV]. This adverb is also translated as a noun phrase: 'an orderly account' [BECNT, NTC; GW, NET, NIV, NRSV, TEV], 'an orderly narrative' [REB], 'a well-ordered account' [WBC], 'a careful summary' [NLT]; or as a verb phrase: 'to arrange in order' [NCV]. This means a chronological account [Gdt, ICC, TG]. The book shows that he did not mean chronological exactness, although it is broadly so, but he means an orderly and clear narrative [Arn, NIGTC; NET]. It refers to an orderly account which includes topical order as well as a general chronological order [BECNT, Lns, NIC, NTC; NET]. It was written in a logical and literary order [AB, NAC, NTC].

d. κράτιστος (LN **87.55**) (BAGD 2. p. 449): 'most excellent' [BAGD, BECNT, LN, NTC, WBC; KJV, NASB, NCV, NET, NIV, NRSV], 'most noble' [Arn], 'most honorable' [HCSB, NLT], 'Honorable' [CEV]. 'your Excellency' [AB, Lns; GW, REB, TEV].

QUESTION—What relationship is indicated by the use of the participle 'having investigated'?
1. It indicates reason [ICC, NTC; HCSB, NCV, NET, NIV, TEV]: *because* I have investigated everything carefully, it seemed good to me to write about it in an orderly way. It is a second and even stronger reason for his writing, the first reason being given in 1:1 [ICC; probably NTC; NASB, NET, NIV, TEV]. This shows his qualifications for writing this account [NTC].
2. It indicates a temporal sequence [Lns; NRSV]: *after* investigating, it seemed good to me to write about it to you. This may imply that it is also a reason for concluding that he should write.

QUESTION—To what does ἄνωθεν 'the beginning' refer?
1. This refers to the events researched by Luke—from the beginning of Jesus' history [Arn, BECNT, EGT, Lns, NAC, TG, TNTC, WBC]. It refers to the events in 1:1 [WBC]. The beginning chapters show that he went back to the events surrounding Jesus' birth [Lns]. His research went back to the angel's promise of John's birth [Arn, BECNT, EGT, ICC, NAC].
2. This refers to the time spent in Luke's research—he had investigated for a long time [LN (67.90), NIGTC]. Luke had investigated all of the facts for a long time and this stresses the care he had put into his research [NIGTC].

QUESTION—What is the significance of the word κἀμοί 'to me also'?
The 'also' means 'I, as well as others' [BAGD]. This goes with 'it seemed good to me to write' and it means 'I, too, resolved to write' [Lns; HCSB, KJV, NASB, NET, NIV, NRSV, REB]. Since he said 'it seemed good to me *also*', he is not criticizing the earlier writings [ICC; NET]. The attempts of others encouraged Luke to write [ICC]. Luke is writing from a more advantageous position than the others who have already written [AB]. Another view is that it means 'I also have followed everything closely from the beginning' [GW].

QUESTION—Who was Theophilus?
All who comment on his identity think that he was a real man who is unknown except for the mention of his name here and in Acts 1:1. Addressing him as 'your excellency' indicates that he was high in rank or position [AB, Arn, Su, TG, TNTC, WBC]. It is not known whether he was prominent because of his wealth or office [Lns]. Perhaps he was a Roman official who had the responsibility of knowing the truth about Christians who were accused of being enemies of Rome [Su]. Some take 1:1–4 as Luke's dedication of this book to Theophilus [AB, WBC; NRSV]. He could have been Luke's literary patron who paid for the cost of publishing—copying—the book [AB, EGT, MGC, NIGTC, TNTC]. Others do not take this as a dedication, but as a personal address to Theophilus, telling him that the reason for writing it especially to him was so that he may know the certainty of what he had been taught [Lns, WBC]. As well as addressing

Theophilus, Luke wrote this book for a wider readership [BECNT, NICNT, NIGTC]. Luke also wrote for an audience which knew little of Christianity and he presented Jesus so that any reader could accept him as the Messiah, their Lord and Savior [NIGTC].

1:4 in-order-that[a] you-may-know the certainty[b] of-(the)-things[c] about which you-were-taught/informed.[d]

    LEXICON—a. ἵνα (LN 89.59): 'in order that' [Arn, NTC], 'so that' [AB, LN, WBC; HCSB, NASB, NET, NIV, NRSV, TEV], 'in order to, for the purpose of' [LN], 'so as to' [REB], 'to help' [NCV], 'that' [BECNT, Lns; KJV], 'in this way' [GW], 'I have done this to (let you know)' [CEV], 'to (reassure)' [NLT].

    b. ἀσφάλειαν (LN **31.41**): 'certainty' [Arn, BECNT, **LN**, Lns; HCSB, KJV, NIV], 'exact truth' [NTC; NASB], 'full truth' [TEV], 'the truth' [WBC; CEV, NLT, NRSV], 'authentic (knowledge)' [REB] '(know) for certain' [NET], 'assurance' [AB], '(to be) certainly true' [LN], '(to be) true' [GW, NCV].

    c. λόγος (LN 33.260) (BAGD 1.b.β. p. 478): 'thing' [Arn, BECNT, LN; HCSB, KJV, NASB, NET, NIV, NRSV], 'matter' [LN, NTC; REB], 'message' [LN], 'teaching' [BAGD, LN, Lns], 'report' [WBC]. The phrase 'things about which' is translated 'what' [CEV, GW, NCV], 'everything which' [TEV], 'of all' [NLT].

    d. aorist pass. indic. of κατηχέω (LN **33.190, 33.225**) (BAGD 2.a. p. 423): 'to be taught' [BAGD, **LN** (33.225); NASB, NCV, NET, NIV, NLT, TEV], 'to be instructed' [Arn, BECNT, LN (33.225); HCSB, KJV, NRSV], 'to receive instruction' [NTC], 'to be informed' [**LN** (33.190), Lns; REB], 'to be told' [GW], 'to have heard' [WBC; CEV].

QUESTION—What relationship is indicated by ἵνα 'in order that'?

    It indicates purpose [AB, Arn, BECNT, Lns, NAC, NICNT, NIVS, NTC; CEV, HCSB, NASB, NET, NIV, NRSV, REB, TEV]: I write an orderly account *in order that* you may know the certainty of what you were taught/informed.

QUESTION—Does κατηχέω mean 'to be taught' or 'to be informed'?

    The verb can mean either 'to be taught', perhaps implying that Theophilus was a Christian, or 'to be informed', perhaps implying that he was not a Christian [LN, NIGTC, TG], and this in turn determines whether Theophilus is included or excluded in the references to 'us' in this passage [LN (33.225)].

    1. It means to be taught [BAGD, BECNT, EGT, NAC, NIBC, NIGTC, NTC, Su; all versions except CEV, GW, REB]. This is taken to refer to instruction in Christian things and implies that Theophilus was a Christian [AB, NIBC, NIGTC; NET]. He probably had received formal Christian instruction [NIGTC]. Even though it could mean that he was taught, this does not prove that he was a Christian at this time [BECNT, TH]. He had been instructed in Christian teachings but it is not certain if he was a

Christian who needed to gain confidence in what he had been taught in view of Jewish and Gentile attacks upon the truth, or if he needed to come to know the truth so as to obtain salvation [NTC].
2. It means to be informed [Lns, TNTC, WBC; CEV, GW, REB]. This simply means that he had learned about these things. Some think that it implies that he was not yet a Christian [Lns, WBC]. He was a Gentile who had been informed about Christian doctrine but had not yet become certain about its truth [Lns]. He is not called 'brother', so he may have been an interested outsider who knew something about the faith [TNTC].

QUESTION—Why did Theophilus need to know the certainty of these matters?

There may have been many accounts in circulation and Luke wanted him to be able to determine which accounts were reliable and which were doubtful [NIGTC]. Luke wanted him to be assured of the truth of the initial instruction he had received [AB]. Theophilus had not yet become a believer [Lns].

DISCOURSE UNIT: 1:5–2:52 [AB, NAC, NICNT, NIGTC, Su, TNTC, WBC; REB]. The topic is the infancy narrative [AB, NAC, TNTC,], the infancy prologue [WBC], the birth and childhood of Jesus [NICNT, NIGTC], the annunciation and the early years of Jesus [Su], the coming of Christ [REB].

DISCOURSE UNIT: 1:5–2:40 [BECNT]. The topic is the infancy narrative about the forerunner and about the fulfillment.

DISCOURSE UNIT: 1:5–56 [AB]. The topic is the events before the birth of John the Baptist and of Jesus.

DISCOURSE UNIT: 1:5–25 [AB, BECNT, NAC, NICNT, NIGTC, Su, TNTC, WBC; CEV, GW, HCSB, NASB, NCV, NET, NIV, NLT, NRSV, TEV]. The topic is Zechariah and Elizabeth [NCV], the birth announcement of John the Baptist [NET], John the Baptist's birth foretold [AB, NAC, NICNT, NIGTC, Su, TNTC, WBC; NASB, NIV, NLT, NRSV, TEV], the announcement to Zechariah [BECNT], the angel Gabriel appears to Zechariah [GW], an angel tells about the birth of John [CEV], Gabriel predicts John's birth [HCSB]. This Gospel is about Jesus Christ, and it begins with the events leading up to the birth of John the Baptist in order to show how God prepared for Christ's coming [NIC].

1:5 There-was in the days of-King Herod of Judea a-certain priest (by the) name-of Zechariah of (the) division[a] of-Abijah, and his wife (was) of the daughters[b] of-Aaron and her name (was) Elizabeth.

LEXICON—a. ϕημερία (LN 11.47) (BAGD p. 330): 'division' [BAGD, BECNT, LN; GW, HCSB, NASB], 'division of the priesthood' [REB], 'priestly division' [NTC, WBC; NET, NIV], 'priestly order' [NLT, NRSV, TEV], 'priestly course' [AB], 'course' [KJV], 'priestly group' [CEV], 'group' [NCV], 'work group' [**LN**], 'class' [Arn], 'day class' [Lns].

b. θυγάτηρ (LN 10.31) (BAGD 2.b.α. p. 364): 'daughter' [Arn, BECNT, WBC; HCSB, KJV, NASB], 'female descendant' [BAGD, LN], 'descendant' [AB, NTC; GW, NET, NIV, NRSV], 'descent' [REB], 'line' [NLT], 'family' [CEV, NCV, TEV]. These were the women descendants of the first Jewish high priest, Aaron, the brother of Moses [Lns]. John was therefore of priestly descent through both parents [BECNT, EGT, ICC, My, NICNT, Su, TNTC, WBC].

QUESTION—What geographic area is designated by 'Judea'?

1. Judea means the land of the Jews and it includes all of Palestine [AB, Arn, BECNT, ICC, Lns, NAC, NIC, NTC, TG, TH]. It is not as restricted as 'Judea' in 1:65, but includes Judea proper, Galilee, Samaria, and much of Perea and Coele-Syria as well [AB].
2. The narrower sense of the Roman province of Judah is intended here and this is sustained in 1:65 and 2:4 (also 3:1; 5:17; 21:21), although Luke used the broader sense of all Palestine in 4:44; 6:17; 7:17 [WBC].

QUESTION—What is meant by the 'division of Abijah'?

It means that Zechariah belonged to a group of priests which was known as the division of Abijah [LN (10.31)]. The division was named after the priest Abijah [GW]. It was the eighth of the twenty-four divisions that resulted when the priests were organized and divided into divisions (1 Chron. 24:10), and twice a year each division served for a week in the temple at Jerusalem [AB, Arn, BECNT, NIGTC, NTC, Su, TH]. Although only four divisions returned from the Babylonian captivity, they were again divided into twenty-four divisions and the old names of the divisions were restored [Lns, WBC].

1:6 And they-were both righteous[a] in-the-opinion-of[b] God, walking[c] in all the commandments[d] and regulations[e] of-the Lord blameless.[f]

LEXICON—a. δίκαιος (LN 88.12) (BAGD 1.b. p. 195): 'righteous' [Arn, BAGD, LN, Lns, NTC, WBC; HCSB, KJV, NASB, NET, NLT, NRSV], 'upright' [AB; NIV], 'upright and devout' [REB], 'good people' [CEV]. The phrase 'were righteous in the opinion of God' is translated 'had God's approval' [GW], 'truly did what God said was good' [NCV], 'lived good lives in God's sight' [TEV]. This is not an absolute sinlessness, but a way of saying they were faithful and pious [NIVS; NET]. They conformed to God's will as expressed in the law [AB]. They were righteous in the sense described by the clause which follows [BECNT, EGT, NTC, Su, TH]. Since barrenness was considered to be a reproach (1:25), this information about their blameless life is given to prevent a reader from thinking that they were childless as a result of sin [AB, NIGTC; NET]. This is also mentioned to show that God rewards piety [NIGTC]. See this word at 1:17; 2:25; 5:32; 14:14; 15:7; 18:9; 20:20; 23:47, 50.

b. ἐναντίον (LN **90.20**) (BAGD 1.b. p. 262): 'in the opinion of' [LN], 'in the sight of' [AB, BAGD, **LN**, NTC; HCSB, NASB, NET, NIV, TEV], 'in the eyes of' [NLT], 'in the judgment of' [BAGD, LN], 'before' [Arn,

Lns, WBC; KJV, NRSV], not explicit [CEV, GW, NCV, REB]. Being righteous is not limited to conforming to the Jewish legal requirements, it means that God approved of their heart condition [Lns].
 c. pres. mid./pass. (deponent = act.) participle of πορεύομαι (LN **41.11**) (BAGD 2.c. 692): 'to walk' [Arn, BAGD, Lns, WBC; KJV, NASB], 'to conduct oneself' [BAGD], 'to live' [AB, BAGD, **LN**; HCSB, NRSV], 'to behave, to go about doing' [LN], 'to follow' [BECNT; KJV, NET], 'to do' [NCV], 'to observe' [NTC; NIV, REB], 'to obey' [CEV, NLT, TEV]. This verb means to live or behave in a customary manner [LN].
 d. ἐντολή (LN 33.330): 'commandment' [AB, Arn, LN, Lns, NTC, WBC; HCSB, KJV, NASB, NET, NIV, NLT, NRSV, REB], 'command' [GW, TEV], 'order' [LN], 'what the Lord commanded' [NCV]. The phrase 'all the commandments and regulations' is translated 'all that he had commanded' [CEV].
 e. δικαίωμα (LN 33.334) (BAGD 1. p. 198): 'regulation' [BAGD, LN; GW, NIV, NLT, NRSV], 'requirement' [AB, BAGD, LN, NTC; HCSB, NASB], 'ordinance' [Arn, WBC; KJV, NET, REB], 'legal ordinance' [Lns], 'law' [NCV, TEV]. See d. above for CEV.
 f. ἄμεμπτος (LN **88.317**) (BAGD p. 45): 'blameless' [BAGD, LN, Lns, NTC, WBC; KJV, NIV], 'without blame' [**LN**; HCSB], 'without fault' [NCV]. This adjective is also translated as an adverb: 'blamelessly' [AB, Arn; NASB, NET, NRSV, REB]; and as a verb phrase: 'to please God' [CEV], 'to follow perfectly' [GW], 'careful to obey' [NLT], 'to obey fully' [TEV]. They were not sinless and this adjective describes them as having a practical righteousness of being faithful and pious [NET]. This adjective is explained in the preceding clause: they were blameless in respect to the commandments and regulations of the Lord [BECNT, ICC, Lns, My, TH].

QUESTION—Should καί 'and' at the beginning of this sentence be translated into English?
 This conjunction is omitted by all versions except KJV. Although it is Greek style to begin many sentences and clauses with 'and', English style properly omits it in translation [NET].

QUESTION—Who considered them to be blameless?
 1. The were blameless in God's estimation [NTC, TH; CEV]: they were righteous before God and he considered them to be blameless.
 2 They were blameless in the estimation of people [EGT, Lns]. They were righteous before God and blameless before people [Lns].

QUESTION—How do the terms 'commandments' and 'regulations' differ?
 1. They are synonyms [Alf, EGT, ICC, NAC, TH; CEV, NCV]. The synonyms simply reinforce each other [TH].
 2. They have different areas of meaning [Arn, Gdt, Lns]. 'Commandments' refer to the demands of God's will and 'regulations' refer to legal ordinances [Lns]. Commandments refer to the moral law, such as the Ten Commandments, and the regulations refer to particular Levitical

ceremonial ordinances [Gdt]. The commandments refer to general principles of conduct while regulations refer to specific rules [Arn].

QUESTION—Who does the phrase 'the Lord' refer to?

It refers to God [AB, Lns, NIGTC, TG, TH, WBC], or to Yahweh [AB]. 'Lord' is used to refer to God in the context of OT references and OT background [NIGTC]. In the infancy chapters of 1–2, 'Lord' is used of God 25 times and twice for Jesus (1:43 and 2:11). Elsewhere in the book, 'Lord' without the article refers to God and '*the* Lord' refers to Jesus [WBC].

1:7 **And/yet there-was not a-child to-them, because Elizabeth was barren, and both were advanced in their days.**

QUESTION—At the beginning of this sentence, does καί mean 'and' or 'yet'?

1. It introduces another fact about Zechariah and Elizabeth [BECNT, BNTC, Lns, TH; KJV, NLT, TEV]: they were righteous before God *and* they were childless. This is another pertinent fact about them [Lns], which is relevant to what follows [TH]. It does not imply that having no children was a disgrace or a punishment from God [TH].
2. It indicates a contra-expectation [AB, NICNT, NIGTC, NTC, TNTC, WBC; all versions except KJV, NLT, TEV]: they were righteous before God, *and yet* they were childless. This assumes that children were an expected blessing from God for righteous people [AB, NIGTC, WBC]. In Deut. 7:14 there is a promise that one of the blessings of obedience was fertility, so people unjustly deduced that any individual case of barrenness was a sign that God was displeased with that woman [NTC].

QUESTION—What does καί 'and' in the last clause connect to?

1. It is coordinate with 'there was not a child to them' [AB, ICC, Lns, TH, WBC; HCSB, NIV, TEV]: they were childless *and* they were now advanced in age. It is not logical to take this clause as another reason for never having had a child [ICC, WBC], rather it gives a reason why they had no hope for a child the future [ICC].
2. It is coordinate with 'because Elizabeth was barren' [NIC, NIGTC; CEV]: they were childless because Elizabeth was barren *and because* they were now advanced in age. This is the second reason they did not have a child [NIGTC].

1:8 **And it-happened**[a] **in his serving-as-priest**[b] **in the order**[c] **of-his division before**[d] **God,**

LEXICON—a. aorist mid. (deponent = act.) indic. of γίνομαι (LN 13.107) (BAGD I.3.f. p. 159): 'to happen' [BAGD, LN, WBC; HCSB, NASB], 'to come to pass' [Arn, Lns; KJV], 'once' [AB, NTC; NIV, NRSV, REB], 'one day' [CEV, NLT, TEV]. Many times in Luke's text, and in English, γίνομαι is redundant [NET], or meaningless [NIGTC]. Often it is best to leave it untranslated [BAGD, BECNT, NIGTC, TH; GW, NCV, NET]. It occurs 69 times in Luke. After giving the background information, using this word is the normal way to begin a narrative [TG].

b. pres. act. infin. of ἱερατεύω (LN **53.85**) (BAGD p. 371): 'to serve as priest' [Arn, BAGD, BECNT, NTC, WBC; CEV, HCSB, NCV, NET, NIV, NRSV], 'to do one's work as a priest' [LN], 'to act as priest' [Lns], 'to perform one's priestly service' [NASB], 'to execute the priest's office' [KJV], 'to serve' [AB; GW], 'to serve in the Temple' [NLT], 'to do one's work as a priest in the Temple' [TEV], 'to take part in the temple service' [REB].
c. τάξις (LN **61.3**) (BAGD 1. p. 803): 'order' [BAGD, LN, Lns; KJV], 'the appointed order' [NTC; NASB], 'the appointed time' [Arn], 'the turn' [AB, WBC; REB], 'course' [BECNT]. This noun is also translated as a verb: 'to be on duty' [CEV, GW, HCSB, NCV, NET, NIV, NLT, NRSV], 'to take one's turn' [TEV]. It means that his division was having its regular week of priestly service [Lns].
d. ἔναντι with genitive object (LN **83.33**) (BAGD 1. p. 261): 'before' [AB, Arn, BAGD, BECNT, LN, Lns, NTC, WBC; HCSB, KJV, NASB, NCV, NET, NIV, NRSV], 'in (God's) presence' [GW], not explicit [CEV, NLT, REB, TEV].

QUESTION—What is meant by 'serving as priest before God'?
God was especially connected with the temple [Lns, TH], and when a priest served in the temple, he was in front of God [Gdt], and under his observation [TH]. For 'serving as a priest before God' some merely translate that he was serving God [CEV, NLT] or that he was taking his turn 'at the altar' or 'in the Temple worship' [TG].

1:9 in-accordance-with[a] the custom of-the priesthood[b] he-was-chosen-by-lot[c] to-burn-incense having-entered into the temple of-the Lord,

LEXICON—a. κατά with genitive object (LN 89.8) (BAGD II. 5.a.α. p. 407): 'in accordance with' [BAGD, LN], 'according to' [AB, Arn, BAGD, BECNT, Lns, NTC, WBC; all versions except GW, NLT, REB], 'in conformity with, corresponding to' [BAGD], 'as was' [NLT], 'by' [GW, REB].
b. ἱερατεία (LN 53.86) (BAGD p. 371): 'priesthood' [Arn, BECNT, LN, Lns, NTC, WBC; HCSB, NET, NIV, NRSV], 'priestly office' [BAGD; NASB], 'priest's office' [KJV], 'priests' [AB; CEV, NCV, NLT, TEV]. This noun is also translated as an adjective: 'priestly (custom)' [GW, REB].
c. aorist act. indic. of λαγχάνω (LN **30.106**) (BAGD 2. p. 462): 'to be chosen by lot' [BAGD, NTC; all versions except CEV, GW, KJV], 'to be selected by lot' [**LN**], 'to obtain by lot' [Arn, Lns], 'to be chosen' [CEV, GW]. The phrase 'he was chosen by lot' is translated 'his lot was' [KJV], 'it fell to his lot' [AB], 'the lot fell to him' [BECNT, WBC].

QUESTION—What relationship is indicated by κατά 'in accordance with'?
It indicates correspondence with the following custom [AB, BNTC, Crd, EGT, ICC, Lns, My, NICNT, NIGTC, NTC, TH; all versions]: he was chosen by lot *in accordance with* the custom followed by priests. Twice a

24   LUKE 1:9

day it was the custom to cast lots in order to determine which priest would offer the incense with the whole burnt offering [BECNT].
QUESTION—What was involved in being chosen by lot to burn incense?
Only one priest was to burn incense at the altar of incense located in the first room of the Sanctuary, which was called the 'Holy Place', and this privileged priest was chosen by lot from the division on duty. His duty was to clean the altar and add fresh incense [AB]. An assistant first placed burning coals on the altar and then withdrew before the chosen priest came to put incense on the coals [Arn]. The priest's task was to place incense on the heated altar of incense and then prostrate himself before it in prayer [NIGTC]. There were around 18,000 [NAC, NIGTC, NTC], or 8,000 [WBC], priests, so no priest was allowed the honor of offering incense more than once in his lifetime [Lns, NIGTC, NTC]. The custom was to cast lots to see which of the priests of the division would have the privilege of entering the Holy Place to burn incense [Lns]. The lot may have involved drawing names or using some mechanical method [Su].
QUESTION—How are the nouns related in the genitive construction 'the temple of the Lord'?
It means the temple where God dwelt in the Holy of Holies [TH]. Entering the temple of the Lord implies that the priest entered in order to serve the Lord [TH]. He entered the front room, the Holy Place [AB, WBC].
QUESTION—What relationship is indicated by the use of the participle 'having entered'?
It indicates a coordinate circumstance to the preceding clause [Crd, EGT, ICC] and being in the aorist tense it refers to a separate event preceding the event of the main verb [NIGTC, TH]: *upon* entering the temple of the Lord, he burned incense. The purpose for choosing him was to have him burn incense in the temple and the fact that he entered the temple to do so is apparent [TH], and even superfluous [EGT]. The choosing by lot occurred before he entered the temple [ICC, Lns, TH; CEV, GW, HCSB, NASB, NCV, NET, NIV, NRSV, REB]: he was chosen by lot to enter the temple and burn incense.

1:10 **and all the multitude of-the people were praying outside at-the hour of-the incense-offering.**
QUESTION—What relationship is indicated by καί 'and'?
1. It indicates an accompanying circumstance with the preceding clause [TH; CEV, TEV]: he entered the temple to burn incense *while* the multitude prayed outside. This mention of the crowd gives the setting for 1:21 and following [NIGTC, TH].
2. This verse is a parenthetical comment in the narrative [NET; probably GW, NCV, NLT, NRSV which make this an independent sentence].
QUESTION—Who comprised the multitude of people and where were they?
It was usual for a crowd of spectators of the daily sacrifices to be outside the sanctuary, a building which was divided into the holy place and the holy of

holies [NIGTC; NET]. They were outside the temple building, but still inside the temple precincts [AB, EGT, ICC, My, TH]. The crowd was outside, occupying the court of the men and the court of the women [Lns, MGC, NTC]. Some translate this to indicate a large crowd: 'multitude' [KJV, NASB], 'whole crowd' [NET, NLT, TEV], 'great many' [NCV]. However, this does not necessarily mean that there was a large multitude, since it could be a rhetorical exaggeration [AB], and 'multitude' is used in comparison with the solitary priest inside [ICC]. Some translate without an emphasis on the number: 'assembled worshippers' [NIV], 'whole assembly' [NRSV], 'the people' [CEV, GW, REB].

1:11 And there-appeared to-him an-angel of-(the)-Lord (who) stood on (the) right of-the altar of-the incense.
QUESTION—What relationship is indicated by δέ 'and'?
   This introduces the next thing that happened [Lns]. After placing incense on the altar and prostrating himself to pray, Zechariah then saw the angel [NIGTC].
QUESTION—How did the angel appear to Zechariah?
   This was not a subjective vision, but an objective appearance of the angel [Alf, My, NIGTC, TH]. He did not see the angel approach, the angel was suddenly there [Lns]. The angel probably appeared in the form of a human being [Arn].
QUESTION—How are the nouns related in the genitive construction ἄγγελος κυρίου 'an angel of the Lord'?
   It means an angel who was sent by God, or an angel who served God [TG].
QUESTION—What is meant by standing 'on the right of the altar of incense'?
   Being at the right side is at a place of honor [AB, BECNT, NICNT, NIGTC, TH], and therefore stresses the dignity of the angel [TH]. It may indicate that the angel was bringing good news [AB, NIGTC]. The altar was across the room from the entrance of the building and was centered in front of the veil that separated the room from the inner room, the Holy of Holies.
   1. The angel stood to the right of the altar as viewed from the entrance of the building, so that the angel was to Zechariah's right [Alf, Gdt, Lns]. It is to be expected that this would be described from Zechariah's point of view [Gdt].
   2. The angel stood to the right of the altar as viewed from the veil looking towards the entrance to the building, so that the angel was to Zechariah's left [BECNT, EGT, ICC, NICNT, NIVS, NTC, Su, TG, TH, TNTC, WBC].

1:12 And Zechariah was-greatly-distressed[a] seeing (the angel) and fear[b] fell upon him. 1:13 But/and the angel said to him, Do- not -be-afraid, Zechariah, because your prayer was-heard,[c] and your wife Elizabeth will-bear a-son to-you and you-will-call his name John.
LEXICON—a. aorist pass. indic. of ταράσσω (LN 25.244) (BAGD 2. p. 805): 'to be greatly distressed' [LN], 'to be perturbed' [Arn], 'to be confused'

[CEV], 'to be alarmed' [AB; TEV], 'to be disturbed' [Lns], 'to be troubled' [BAGD, NTC, WBC; GW, KJV, NASB], 'to be startled' [HCSB, NCV, NIV, REB], 'to be visibly shaken' [NET], 'to be terrified' [BAGD; NRSV], 'to be frightened' [BAGD], 'to be afraid' [BECNT]. The phrase 'was greatly distressed and fear fell upon him' is translated 'was overwhelmed with fear' [NLT]. See this word at 24:38.

b. φόβος (LN 25.251) (BAGD 2.a.α. p. 863): 'fear' [BAGD, LN], 'fright, alarm' [BAGD]. The phrase 'fear fell upon him' [Arn, BECNT, Lns, WBC; KJV] is also translated 'fear overwhelmed him' [NRSV], 'became overwhelmed with fear' [NTC], 'fear came over him' [AB], 'fear gripped him' [NASB], 'was gripped with fear' [NIV], 'was overcome with/by fear' [GW, HCSB, REB], 'was seized with fear' [NET], 'was frightened' [NCV], 'was afraid' [CEV], 'felt afraid' [TEV].

c. aorist pass. indic. of εἰσακούω (LN 24.60) (BAGD 2.b. p. 232): 'to be heard' [Arn, BAGD, BECNT; HCSB, KJV, NASB, NIV, NRSV, REB], 'to be listened to, to be heeded' [LN]. This passive verb is also translated actively with God as subject: 'to hear' [CEV, GW, NCV, NET, NLT, TEV]. The passive implies that the prayer has been heard by God [NET]. That it was heard implies the request will be heeded and granted [LN, Lns, TH].

QUESTION—What is the difference between ταράσσω 'to be greatly distressed' and φόβος 'fear'?

'To be greatly distressed' describes his state of mind as being perturbed and φόβος 'fear' falling upon him is the specific reaction [EGT].

QUESTION—In 1:13, does δέ mean 'but' or 'and'?
1. It contrasts Zechariah's fear with what his response should have been [Lns, NTC, TH; all versions except GW]: Zechariah was terrified, *but* the angel said, 'Do not be afraid'.
2. It indicates sequence [AB, Arn]: Zechariah was terrified. *And then* the angel said, 'Do not be afraid'.

QUESTION—What relationship is indicated by διότι 'because' in the clause 'because your prayer was heard'?
1. It indicates the reason he should not be afraid [BECNT, Lns, WBC; KJV, NASB, NET, NLT, NRSV]: do not be afraid, *because* your prayer was heard.
2. The presence of the angel was the cause of Zechariah's fear (not an unanswered prayer), and since the angel is there to tell him that his prayer had been heard, Zechariah has nothing to fear from the angel [TH]: do not be afraid of me, *because* I am here to tell you the welcome news that your prayer will be answered.

QUESTION—What prayer had been heard??
1. This refers to Zechariah's personal prayers for a son [Alf, Arn, BECNT, EGT, Gdt, Lns, NAC, NTC, Su, TG, TH]. This does not refer to a prayer offered while he was offering the incense, but to previous prayers for a son [BECNT]. The requests had been made during the years when

childbirth could be expected and the aorist tense 'was heard' indicates that the prayer had just now been effectively listened to so as to answer it [Lns]. This was the time that all of those prayers would be answered [Alf]. His prayers for a son were going to be answered and this son would prepare Israel for the coming Messiah [TH].

2. It refers to his prayer in the temple in his role as a priest and that prayer concerned the nation's deliverance by the Messiah [ICC, MGC, My, NIC, NIGTC, TNTC; NET]. Although it is just possible that this refers to Zechariah's prayers at other occasions, it is doubtful that Zechariah and his wife felt it was still worth praying for a son, and if this refers to his prayer offered in the holy place, it is not likely that it would be a personal request [NIGTC]. The aorist tense of 'was heard' probably refers to a specific prayer for Israel's redemption offered at the time of burning the incense [My, TNTC] and this was to be answered with the addition that he would have a son [TNTC]. The aorist tense indicates that the prayer had been heard when it was uttered [ICC]. The answer would refer to his being the father of a son who would play a part in the beginning of God's salvation [NIGTC].

1:14 And he-will-be a-joy^a to-you and gladness^b and many will-rejoice because-of^c his birth.

LEXICON—a. χαρά (LN 25.123) (BAGD 1. p. 875): 'joy' [AB, Arn, BAGD, BECNT, LN, Lns, NTC, WBC; all versions except CEV, GW, TEV], 'gladness, great happiness' [LN]. The phrase 'he will be a joy to you and gladness' is translated 'his birth will make you very happy' [CEV], 'how glad and happy you will be' [TEV], 'he will be your pride and joy' [GW].

b. ἀγαλλίασις (LN 25.132) (BAGD p. 3): 'gladness' [BECNT, WBC; KJV, NASB, NCV, NET, NLT, NRSV], 'delight' [AB; HCSB, NIV, REB], 'exultation' [BAGD, Lns, NTC]. This noun is also translated as a verb: 'to exalt' [Arn]. See a. above for CEV, GW, TEV.

c. ἐπί (LN 89.27): 'because of' [LN; NCV, NIV], 'on account of' [Arn], 'at' [AB, BECNT, WBC; HCSB, KJV, NASB, NET, NLT, NRSV], 'that (he was born)' [GW], 'over (his birth)' [NTC], 'over (his being)' [Lns], 'when (he is born)' [TEV], not explicit [CEV, REB].

QUESTION—What is the difference between 'joy' and 'gladness'?
They are synonyms [NICNT, TH; CEV, TEV]. In LN (25.125) 'joy' is described as a state of joy while in LN (25.132) 'gladness' is described as a state of *intensive* joy and gladness. Or 'joy and gladness' is a doublet which intensifies the experience of joy [TH], and this means that they will be 'very happy' [CEV].

QUESTION—What is the cause of this joy and rejoicing?
Zechariah and Elizabeth will have this great joy because they will at last have a son, and they will rejoice in what kind of a person he will be [EGT, Lns]. John's birth will cause many to rejoice [TH] because of the fact of his birth (1:58), and also later when he is man they will be glad that he was born

to become such a prophet (1:15–17) [Lns, NTC]. 'Birth' is focused on the event of being born and refers to the fact that John has come on the scene [NAC, WBC]. Because of John's birth, many will rejoice over John's entire ministry, as confirmed by the next verse [BECNT, MGC]. They will rejoice particularly because John will be great in the sight of the Lord [NICNT].

1:15 Because he-will-be great[a] in the-opinion-of[b] the Lord,

LEXICON—a. μέγας (LN 87.22) (BAGD 2.b.α. p. 498): 'great' [AB, Arn, BAGD, BECNT, LN, Lns, NTC, WBC; all versions except CEV, NCV], 'important' [LN], 'a great servant' [CEV], 'a great man' [NCV]. This means great in regard to rank and dignity [BAGD, TH], or to status [LN]. See this word at 1:32; 7:28; 9:46; 22:24.

b. ἐνώπιον (LN 90.20) (BAGD 3. p. 270): 'in the opinion of' [BAGD, LN], 'in the sight of' [AB, LN, Lns, NTC; HCSB, KJV, NASB, NET, NIV, NRSV, REB, TEV], 'in the eyes of' [NLT], 'in the judgment of' [BAGD, LN], 'as far as (the Lord) is concerned' [GW], 'before' [Arn, BECNT, WBC], 'for' [NCV], not explicit [CEV]. The word ἐνώπιον here and the word ἐναντίον 'in the opinion of' in 1:6 are both included in the same semantic domain 90.20 of LN.

QUESTION—What relationship is indicated by γάρ 'because'?

It indicates the reason that Zechariah and many others will rejoice [Arn, BECNT, Gdt, Lns, NIGTC, TH]. The reason extends through 1:15–17 [TH].

QUESTION—In what way will John be great before the Lord?

John will be a great servant of the Lord [CEV], a great man for the Lord [NCV]. He will be great in rank and dignity [TH], and importance [TG]. His greatness is described in the following verses which tell of his dedication to his task and God's empowerment to accomplish it [NIGTC].

and wine[a] and strong-drink[b] in-no-way will-he-drink,

LEXICON—a. οἶνος (LN 6.197) (BAGD p. 562): 'wine' [AB, Arn, BAGD, BECNT, LN, Lns, NTC, WBC; all versions].

b. σίκερα (LN 6.200) (BAGD p. 750): 'strong drink' [BAGD, BECNT, NTC; KJV, NET, NRSV, REB, TEV], 'fermented drink' [NIV], 'beer' [AB, LN, WBC; CEV, HCSB, NCV], 'liquor' [GW, NASB], 'hard liquor' [NLT], 'intoxicating drink' [Lns], 'other intoxicants' [Arn]. Distilled alcoholic drinks were unknown and this refers to an intoxicating drink made from grain [LN], or any other drink made by fermentation [TG]. It could be prepared from such things as corn, fruit, dates, and palms [My]. 'Wine and beer' is a stereotyped combination in the OT [NICNT, WBC].

QUESTION—What is the significance of this clause?

This gives directions for John's manner of life [CEV, NET, NIV, NLT, NRSV, REB, TEV]: he must never drink wine and strong drink. Abstaining will be a mark of his consecration to God [EGT, MGC, NAC, NICNT]. Some think this marks him as a Nazarite [AB, Arn, Gdt, ICC, My, NIVS, Rb, TH], as were Samson and Samuel [NIVS], or someone who has taken a vow of devotion to God and shows this by abstaining from the products of the grapevine (Numbers 6:1–4) [TH]. Another view is that it does not indicate that he was a Nazarite, but refers to the abstinence demanded of priests while on duty (Lev. 10:9) [Lns, NIGTC]. This restriction points to a special consecration to John's prophetic office [BECNT].

and he-will-be-filled[a] **(with the) Holy Spirit still**[b] **in/from his mother's womb,**

LEXICON—a. fut. pass. indic. of πίμπλημι (LN 59.38) (BAGD 1.a.β. p. 658): 'to be filled' [AB, Arn, BAGD, BECNT, Lns, NTC; all versions except CEV], 'to be filled completely' [LN]. This passive verb is translated actively with the Holy Spirit as the subject: 'to be with (him)' [CEV]. See this word at 1:41, 67.

b. ἔτι (LN 67.128) (BAGD 1.a.γ. p. 315): 'still, yet' [BAGD, LN]. The phrase ἔτι ἐκ 'still in/from' is translated 'while still in' [BAGD; HCSB], 'while yet in' [NASB], 'from' [AB; REB, TEV], 'even from' [Arn, BECNT, Lns, NTC; KJV, NCV, NIV], 'even before (his birth)' [GW, NET, NLT, NRSV], 'from the time (he is born)' [CEV].

QUESTION—What is meant by being filled with the Holy Spirit?
It means that the power of the Holy Spirit will be with him [TG; CEV] and that the Holy Spirit will control him [Lns, MGC, TG], and inspire him [ICC, NTC]. The Holy Spirit will enable him to prophesy [TH]. Instead of being stimulated with wine, he will have his stimulation from the Holy Spirit [AB, Alf, ICC, NTC, Su]. In Luke and Acts, this has two meanings: being empowered or controlled by the Holy Spirit (1) as an ongoing state or (2) for a specific task or role [NICNT]. Here it refers to an ongoing state as shown by his being filled from birth [BECNT, NICNT].

QUESTION—Does ἔτι ἐκ mean 'while in his mother's womb' or 'from leaving his mother's womb'?
1. The time commences before his birth [AB, Arn, BECNT, Gdt, Lns, MGC, My, NAC, NIGTC, TH, WBC; GW, HCSB, NASB, NET, NLT, NRSV]: even *while in* his mother's womb. This is supported by the baby leaping in the womb at 1:41 at Mary's greeting [AB, BECNT, MGC, NAC].
2. The time commences at his birth [Alf, ICC; CEV, NCV, NIV, REB, TEV]: even from his birth.

1:16 **and many of-the sons**[a] **of-Israel he-will-turn-back**[b] **to (the) Lord the God of-them.**

LEXICON—a. υἱός (LN **11.58**) (BAGD 1.b.α. p. 833): 'son, descendant' [BAGD, LN]. The phrase τῶν υἱῶν Ἰσραήλ 'the sons of Israel' [Arn, BECNT, Lns, NTC, WBC; HCSB, NASB] is also translated 'the children of Israel' [AB; KJV], 'the people of Israel' [**LN**; CEV, NCV, NET, NIV, NRSV, TEV], 'people in Israel' [GW], 'Israelites' [NLT, REB]. 'Sons' refers to descendants [TH].

b. fut. act. indic. of ἐπιστρέφω (LN 31.61) (BAGD 1.a. p. 301): 'to turn back' [CEV, NASB], 'to turn' [AB, Arn, BAGD, BECNT, Lns, NTC; HCSB, KJV, NET, NLT, NRSV], 'to bring back' [GW, NIV, REB, TEV], 'to restore' [WBC], 'to help someone return' [NCV], 'to cause to change belief, to cause to turn to' [LN]. This refers to a change of direction in life [BECNT], a turning from idolatry and sin to serving God [NIGTC]. Israel was estranged from God and needed a prophet to call them back to righteousness to serve God [Gdt, ICC]. It is a term for Christian conversion [NAC, NIGTC], but here 'the Lord' is identified as their God and the call is to turn to God and live the way God expects his people to live [BECNT].

QUESTION—What does the phrase 'of them' modify?

It modifies 'God' [AB, Arn, BECNT, NTC, WBC; CEV, GW, HCSB, NASB, NCV, NET, NLT, NRSV, REB, TEV]: the Lord, their God. 'Lord' refers to Yahweh, the OT proper name for God [Lns, My].

1:17 And he will-precede[a] before him in (the) spirit/Spirit and power of-Elijah,

LEXICON—a. fut. mid. (deponent = act.) indic. of προέρχομαι (LN **15.141**) (BAGD 2. p. 705): 'to precede, to go prior to, to go beforehand' [LN], 'to go before' [Arn, BAGD; HCSB], 'to go ahead' [WBC]. The phrase αὐτὸς προελεύσεται ἐνώπιον 'he will precede before' is translated 'he will precede' [NLT], 'he will go ahead of' [LN; CEV, GW, TEV], 'he will go before' [AB, BECNT, Lns, NTC; KJV, NCV, NRSV], 'he will go on before' [NIV], 'he will go as a forerunner before' [NASB, NET], 'he will go before (him) as forerunner' [REB]. This has a temporal relationship rather than spatial and means to come prior to someone else [LN].

QUESTION—Who does 'he' and 'him' refer to and what does it mean?

John will go ahead of the Lord their God [Arn, BECNT, ICC, NAC, NICNT, Rb, WBC; CEV, GW, NASB, NCV, NET, NIV, NLT, TEV]. John will be the forerunner to prepare the way for the Lord their God (1:16) [BECNT, NIGTC]. The pronoun 'him' is the same as 'the Lord, their God' in 1:16, that is, Yahweh [ICC, NIGTC, Rb] since the Messiah has not yet been mentioned [ICC, Rb]. John will prepare people for God's work through Jesus [BECNT]. Or, since John will be the forerunner of the Messiah [Arn, Lns, Rb], this refers to God coming in the person of the Messiah [ICC, Lns]. John will be the forerunner of the Messiah, who is identical with the Lord, their God [Lns]. Luke used his readers' knowledge of John being the forerunner of Jesus to refer to Jesus as Lord here [Arn, NAC], but only three other places in chapters 1–2 (1:43, 76; 2:11) refer 'Lord' to Jesus [NAC].

QUESTION—What is meant by 'the spirit and power of Elijah'?

1. This refers to Elijah's spirit [Arn, BECNT, BNTC, EGT, ICC, Lns, NIGTC, NTC, Rb, TG, WBC; all versions]. John will have the same spirit and power that Elijah had [CEV, GW, NLT], he will go in spirit and power like that of Elijah's [NCV, TEV], he will be possessed by the spirit and power of Elijah [REB]. John's character and power are compared with Elijah's and this comparison focuses on John's powerful messages [BECNT]. John said that he was not actually Elijah, but Jesus called him

Elijah in spirit (Mark 9:12) [Rb]. As a preacher of repentance, John had the same spirit and power that Elijah had [ICC]. He was like Elijah in his mission and in being a fearless prophet [TG].
2. This refers to God's Holy Spirit [BAGD (6.a. p. 677), Gdt, My, NAC, TH]. It refers to God's Spirit and God's power [My]. John will be under the influence of the divine Spirit as was Elijah [TH].

to-turn-back^a (the) hearts of-(the)-fathers to (their) children
LEXICON—a. aorist act. infin. of ἐπιστρέφω (LN **25.95**) (BAGD p. 301): 'to turn back' [NASB, NET], 'to turn' [AB, Arn, BAGD, BECNT, Lns, NTC, WBC; HCSB, KJV, NIV, NLT, NRSV], 'to change' [GW]. The phrase 'to turn back the hearts of the fathers to their children' is translated 'he will cause fathers to be well-disposed to their children' [LN], 'he will make peace between parents and their children' [GW], 'to reconcile father and child' [REB], 'he will bring fathers and children together again' [TEV], 'parents will be more thoughtful of their children' [CEV]. The idiom ἐπιστρέφω καρδίας ἐπί 'to turn back the hearts to' means 'to make well disposed toward, to make friendly toward, to cause someone to become acceptable' [LN]. See this word at 1:16.
QUESTION—What relationship is indicated by the use of the infinitive 'to turn back'?
  1. It indicates the purpose of the preceding clause [Lns; probably translations using 'to': KJV, NASB, NET, NIV, NRSV, REB]: he will precede in the spirit and power of Elijah *in order to* turn back the hearts of the fathers to their children.
  2. It indicates the result of the preceding clause [CEV]: he will precede in the spirit and power of Elijah *and because of him* the hearts of the fathers will be turned back to their children.
QUESTION—What is meant by 'to turn back the hearts of the fathers to their children' in the light of the following line about the disobedient and the righteous?
  1. In a family, parents and children will be reconciled with one another [BECNT, NIGTC, NTC, Su, TG; NCV, REB, TEV]. Those who are prepared by John will live in peace and righteousness with one another [NIGTC]. The text in Malachi 4:5 has two lines concerning restoring good family relationships: 'He will turn the hearts of parents to their children and the hearts of children to their parents' [NRSV]. It is stated as one line here: 'he will make peace between parents and their children' [NCV], 'he will reconcile father and child' [REB], 'he will bring fathers and children together again' [TEV].
  2. Righteous parents will be reconciled to their disobedient children when the children become obedient [Alf, NAC; CEV, GW]. The second line in Malachi 'and the hearts of children to their parents' [NRSV] is implied and covered by the second line here about turning the disobedient to the wisdom of the righteous [Alf]. This is chiastic correspondence in which

fathers are the righteous and children are the disobedient [NAC]. 'Parents will be more thoughtful of their children' [CEV], 'he will change parent's attitudes toward their children' [GW].
3. Disobedient fathers will be converted to the beliefs of their righteous children [Arn, Lns, NICNT]. John will find some godly children and his work will be to turn their fathers to God also. Not explicit, but understood from the following parallel line is the thought that if there are godly fathers, his work will also be to turn their disobedient children to God [Lns].
4. The people of the present disobedient generation will be changed so that the Jewish patriarchs (the fathers) will approve of them [Gdt, NIC]. The fathers are the pious ancestors of the Israelites [NIC]. The patriarchs Abraham and Jacob have turned away from their guilty descendants, but will turn again toward them in satisfaction as they see the change produced by John [Gdt].
5. Disobedient fathers will receive children's hearts and become righteous [BNTC].

and (the) disobedient to/by-means-of (the) way-of-thinking/wisdom[a] of-(the)-righteous,[b]

LEXICON—a. φρόνησις (LN **26.15,** 32.30) (BAGD 1. p. 866): 'way of thinking' [BAGD, **LN** (26.15); NCV, TEV], 'the ways' [REB], 'attitude' [NASB], 'frame of mind' [NTC], 'wisdom' [BECNT, LN (32.30), WBC; GW, KJV, NET, NIV, NLT, NRSV], 'sensibleness' [Lns], 'understanding' [AB, Arn; HCSB]. This noun is also translated as verb phrase: 'to think as they ought' [CEV].

b. δίκαιος (LN 88.12) (BAGD 1.b. p. 195): 'righteous'. See translations of this word at 1:6. This word also occurs at 2:25; 5:32; 14:14; 15:7; 18:9; 20:20; 23:47, 50.

QUESTION—How is this clause related to the previous one?

This is a general statement of the previous specific expression and 'disobedient' is not limited to either fathers or children but to anyone whose characteristic is disobedience to God [ICC, My]. The verb 'to turn back' from the previous clause should be supplied here [Gdt, ICC, NIGTC, Su, TH].

QUESTION—Does ἐν mean 'to' or 'by means of'?
1. The preposition ἐν means 'to' [AB, Alf, BECNT, Crd, Gdt, ICC, My, NIC, NICNT, NIGTC, Su, TG, TH; all versions]: and to turn the disobedient *to* the way of thinking/wisdom of the righteous. The preposition means 'into' or 'into the state of' [NIGTC]. He will turn the disobedient *so as to be in* the wisdom of the righteous [ICC]. It means that he will cause those who do not obey God to return to the principles of those who obey God's commandments [TG].
2. The preposition ἐν means 'by means of' [Lns]: and to turn back the disobedient *by means of* the wisdom of the righteous. Different from ἐπί

'to' in the previous statement 'turn back the hearts of the fathers *to* their children', here ἐν is 'by means of' and means that John will use the wisdom of righteous people to convert disobedient people [Lns].

QUESTION—Does φρόνησις mean 'way of thinking' or 'wisdom'?

1. It means 'way of thinking' [BAGD, LN (26.15), NTC, TG, TH; CEV, NASB, NCV, REB, TEV]. It refers to the principles they hold [TG]. The clause is translated 'he will turn the disobedient to the attitude of the righteous' [NASB], 'he will bring those who are not obeying God back to the right way of thinking' [NCV], 'to convert the rebellious to the ways of the righteous' [REB], 'he will cause disobedient people to accept the way of thinking of the righteous' [LN (25.94)], 'he will turn disobedient people back to the way of thinking of the righteous' [TEV], 'to turn…the disobedient to the frame of mind of the righteous' [NTC], 'because of John…people who now disobey God will begin to think as they ought to' [CEV].
2. It means 'wisdom' [AB, BECNT, Gdt, Lns, NAC, Su; GW, KJV, NET, NIV, NLT, NRSV]. It is the wise obedience that characterizes the upright [Su]. The clause is translated 'he will change disobedient people so that they will accept the wisdom of those who have God's approval' [GW], 'he will change disobedient minds to accept godly wisdom' [NLT], 'to turn…disobedient ones by means of sensibleness of righteous ones' [Lns].

to-prepare[a] for-(the)-Lord a-people (who) have-been-made-ready.[b]

LEXICON—a. aorist act. infin. of ἑτοιμάζω (LN 77.3) (BAGD p. 316): 'to prepare' [Arn, BAGD, LN; GW, NLT, REB], 'to make ready' [AB, BECNT, LN, Lns, NTC; HCSB, KJV, NASB, NCV, NET, NIV, NRSV], 'to get ready' [CEV, TEV], 'to establish' [WBC].

b. perf. pass. participle of κατασκευάζω (LN **77.6**) (BAGD 1. p. 418): 'to be made ready' [BAGD, LN], 'to be ready' [Arn], 'to be prepared' [BAGD, BECNT, LN, WBC; HCSB, KJV, NASB, NET, NIV, NRSV], 'to be thoroughly prepared' [**LN**], 'to be well prepared' [NTC], 'to be entirely prepared' [Lns], 'to be fit for (the Lord)' [AB; REB], not explicit [CEV, GW, NCV, NLT, TEV].

QUESTION—What relationship is indicated by the use of the infinitive form of ἑτοιμάσαι 'to prepare'?

1. It indicates the result of the preceding infinitive clause 'to turn back' [CEV, GW, NIV, NLT]: to turn back the hearts of the fathers to their children and the disobedient to the way of thinking/wisdom of the righteous; *thus* he will prepare a people for the Lord.
2. It indicates the purpose of the preceding infinitive clause [NTC; NASB, NCV]: to turn back the hearts of the fathers to their children and the disobedient to the way of thinking/wisdom of the righteous *in order to* prepare a people for the Lord.
3. It is a second purpose or ultimate purpose for John to precede the Lord [AB; NET, NRSV, REB]: he will precede the Lord, *in order to* turn back

the hearts of the fathers to their children and the disobedient to the way of thinking/wisdom of the righteous, and *in order to* prepare a people for the Lord.

QUESTION—According to the lexicon, the verbs ἑτοιμάζω 'to prepare, to make ready' and κατασκευάζω 'to make ready, to prepare' are virtually synonymous. What is meant by '*to prepare* for the Lord a people having been made ready'?

1. 'For the Lord' tells John's motive as he prepares the people [Gdt, Lns, My, NICNT, NTC, Su, TH; NET]: *doing this for the Lord*, John will prepare the people so that they will be made ready. John will prepare the people as described in the previous verse [Lns]. They will be ready to serve the Lord [TH], they will be fit for the Lord's use [NTC], they will be in the right moral state to set up the Messianic kingdom [My], they will have everything that the Lord will require when he comes [Lns]. The people will be made ready for the Lord's coming [NICNT]. The Messiah is not in view here, it the coming of the Lord God who will directly inaugurate his kingdom [NICNT]. 'Lord' refers to Yahweh, but Yahweh is identical to the Messiah, the Son of God [Lns]. The people will be made ready in the sense that they will be disposed to receive the Messiah [Gdt, Su].
2. 'For the Lord' tells for whom the people are made ready, and this tells the result of John's action on the people [KJV, NASB, NIV, NRSV, TEV]: John will prepare the people *so that* they are made ready for the Lord. They will be ready for the Lord in the sense of being fit for him [REB].
3. 'For the Lord' tells for whom the people are made ready, and the two verbs are translated as one verb [AB; CEV, GW, NCV, NLT]: John will get the people ready *for* the Lord. They will be made ready for the Lord in the sense they will be ready for the coming of the Lord [NCV, NLT], they will be fit for the Lord [AB].

1:18 **And Zechariah said to the angel, By what will-I-know this? Because[a] I am old and my wife (is) advanced in her days.**

LEXICON—a. γάρ: 'because', 'for' [Arn, Lns, NTC, WBC; HCSB, KJV, NASB, NET, NRSV], not explicit [AB, BECNT; CEV, GW, NCV, NIV, NLT, REB, TEV].

QUESTION—What is meant by the question 'by what will I know this'?

Zechariah is asking for a sign as proof that he will really have a son as the angel said [BECNT, Gdt, MGC, My, NAC, NIC, NICNT, NIGTC, NIVS, Rb, TH, TNTC]. If having a son depends on him and his wife, it is impossible [Lns]. He could not believe the angel [NTC, TH, TNTC]. He knew that in the past God had provided signs, for example, to Gideon (2 Kings 20:8–11) and Hezekiah (Isa. 7:11) [AB, NTC].

QUESTION—What relationship is indicated by γάρ 'because' and what is the argument here?

It indicates reason [Lns, NTC; HCSB, KJV, NASB, NET, NRSV]. This 'because' includes two implied steps in the argument: *I have need for a sign to believe this, because* my wife and I are very old *and such old people cannot have children* [Gdt, NIGTC, NTC, TH].

1:19 **And answering the angel said to-him, I am Gabriel the (one who) stood before God and I-was-sent to-speak to you and to-announce-the-good-news**[a] **(of) these-things to-you.**

LEXICON—a. aorist mid. infin. of εὐαγγελίζω (LN **33.215**) (BAGD 1. p. 317): 'to announce good news' [BAGD, WBC], 'to tell the good news, to announce the gospel' [LN]. The phrase εὐαγγελίσασθαί σοι ταῦτα 'to announce the good news of these things to you' is translated 'to announce to you the good news of these things' [WBC], 'to announce to thee as glad tidings these things' [Lns], 'to tell you this good news' [**LN**; CEV, GW, HCSB, NCV, NIV, TEV], 'to bring you this good news' [Arn, BECNT, NTC; NASB, NET, NLT, NRSV, REB], 'to show thee these glad tidings' [KJV], 'to announce this to you' [AB]. See this word at 2:10; 3:18: 4:18, 43; 7:22; 8:1; 9:6; 16:16; 20:1.

QUESTION—What is meant by 'the one who stood before God'?

The angel described his customary position [Su]. It means that he stood in God's presence [NIC, NIGTC; HCSB, NCV, NET, NIV, NLT, NRSV, TEV], in attendance on God [TH; REB]. This indicates that he was God's servant [ICC, NTC, TH; CEV, GW], who stood ready to receive and execute God's commands [Lns, MGC, Su]. It indicates that he has great authority [TG] and dignity [TNTC]. He had direct access to God and this implies that his message is to be accepted [BECNT].

1:20 **And behold**[a] **you-will-be silent/mute**[b] **and not being-able to-speak until that day these-things happen, because you-did- not -believe my words, which will-be-fulfilled in their time.**

LEXICON—a. ἰδού (LN 91.13) (BAGD 1.b.β. p. 371): 'behold' [Arn, BAGD, BECNT; KJV, NASB], 'lo' [Lns], 'look' [BAGD, LN], 'listen' [LN; HCSB, NCV], 'pay attention' [LN], 'mark well' [NTC], 'now' [AB; NET, NIV, NLT, NRSV, REB], not explicit [WBC; CEV, GW, TEV]. This particle is the imperative of the verb 'to see' and it is used as a demonstrative particle [TH]. It is a call for attention to emphasize the following statement [LN, TG, TH]. The phrase 'and behold' introduces something new [BAGD, ICC, NTC], or unexpected [TH]. The word ἰδού is used quite frequently, occurring at 1:31, 36, 38, 44, 48; 2:10, 25, 34, 48; 5:12, 18; 6:23; 7:12, 25, 27, 34, 37; 8:41; 9:30, 38, 39; 10:3, 19, 25; 11:31, 32, 41; 13:7, 11, 16, 30, 32, 35; 14:2; 15:29; 17:21, 23; 18:28, 31; 19:2, 8, 20; 22:10, 21, 31, 38, 47; 23:14, 15, 29, 50; 24:4, 13, 49.

b. pres. act. participle of σιωπάω (LN 33.117, **33.118**) (BAGD 2.a. p. 753): 'to be silent' [BECNT, LN (33.117), Lns; NASB, NET, NIV], 'to become silent' [HCSB], 'to remain silent' [NTC], 'to be reduced to silence' [WBC], 'to keep quiet' [LN (33.117)], 'to not be able to speak' [**LN (33.118)**], 'to be unable to speak' [TEV], 'to lose all power of speech' [REB], 'to be mute' [AB; NRSV], 'to be dumb' [Arn; KJV], not explicit or uniting this phrase with the following 'not being able to speak' [CEV, GW, NCV, NLT]. 'To be silent' means to lose the ability to speak [BAGD].

QUESTION—What is meant by ἔσῃ σιωπῶν 'you will be silent/mute' and how does this effect the relationship with the following clause 'and not being able to speak'?

1. It means to be silent [Alf, Gdt, ICC, TH] and the following phrase explains the reason he will be silent [Alf, Gdt]: you will be silent, *and the reason is* that you will not be able to speak. The explanation shows that his silence will not be a voluntary act [Gdt, ICC, TH].
2. It means to be mute [AB, Arn, BAGD, BECNT, LN (33.118), Lns, MGC, NICNT, NIGTC, Rb, WBC; CEV, GW, KJV, NCV, NLT, NRSV]: you will be silent, *that is,* you will not be able to speak. Here the specific meaning of the generic verb 'to be silent' is to lose the ability to speak [NIGTC, NTC]. The two clauses are synonymous and together emphasize the fact that he will not be able to speak [BECNT, Lns, NICNT, Rb].

QUESTION—What is the purpose of adding the last clause 'which will be fulfilled in their time'?

It implies that the angel's words deserve to be believed because they will happen at the proper time [Crd]. 'Their time' is the time the words become a reality [Su], the time determined by God [AB].

1:21 And the people were expecting Zechariah and they-were-amazed[a] at his delay in the temple.

LEXICON—a. imperf. act. indic. of θαυμάζω (LN 25.213) (BAGD 1.a.α. p. 352): 'to be amazed' [LN; GW, HCSB], 'to be astonished' [BAGD], 'to be surprised' [NCV, REB], 'to wonder (at/why)' [AB, BAGD, BECNT, LN, Lns, NTC; CEV, NASB, NET, NIV, NLT, NRSV, TEV], 'to marvel' [Arn, LN, WBC; KJV]. Zechariah's remaining inside the sanctuary longer than normal was something to be concerned about [MGC, NAC, TNTC]. See this word at 1:63; 2:18, 33; 4:22; 7:9; 8:25; 11:14, 38; 20:26; 24:12, 41.

1:22 And having-come-out he-was- not -able to-speak to-them, and they-knew that he-has-seen a-vision[a] in the temple, and[b] he was motioning to-them and he-remained mute.[c]

LEXICON—a. ὀπτασία (LN 33.488) (BAGD 1. p. 576): 'vision' [AB, Arn, BAGD, LN, Lns, NTC, WBC; all versions]. The phrase 'he had seen a vision' is translated 'he had a supernatural encounter' [BECNT]. This refers to an event that is not physically present but which appears to the mind [Lns]. It is a communication from God [BAGD, LN]. The word 'vision' corresponds to 'an angel appeared to him' in 1:11 [TG].

b. καί (LN 89.23): 'and' [Arn, BECNT, Lns; NASB], 'because' [LN; NET], 'for' [AB, NTC; KJV, NIV], not explicit [WBC; CEV, GW, HCSB, NCV, NLT, NRSV, REB, TEV].
c. κωφός (LN 33.106) (BAGD 1. p. 105): 'mute' [BAGD, LN, WBC; NASB], 'dumb' [Arn, BAGD, LN, Lns; REB], 'speechless' [AB; HCSB, KJV], 'deaf and mute' [BECNT]. This noun is also translated as a verb phrase: 'to be unable to talk/speak' [NTC; GW, NCV, NET, NIV, NLT, NRSV], 'to be unable to say a word' [TEV], 'to not say a thing' [CEV]. This word can indicate both deafness and muteness [AB, BECNT, NIGTC]. The last question at 1:62 shows that the need to communicate to Zechariah by motions causes many to think that Zechariah was both deaf and mute [AB, Alf, BECNT, BNTC, Crd, MGC, NAC, NICNT, NIGTC, TG, WBC; NET].

QUESTION—How is the clause 'and they knew that he has seen a vision in the temple (and...)' connected to its context?
1. It functions as a conclusion to the preceding clause [Arn, Lns, WBC; CEV, GW, HCSB, NCV, NRSV, REB, TEV]: he was not able to speak to them, *and so* they knew he had seen a vision. The last clause is translated 'And he on his part kept motioning to them and continued to remain dumb' [Lns].
2. It functions as a conclusion to the following clause [AB, LN, NTC; KJV, NET, NIV, NLT]: they knew he had seen a vision, *because* he was motioning to them and remained mute. Καί 'and' explains how they knew he had seen a vision [NET].

QUESTION—How did he motion to them?
He nodded to them [BAGD (p. 187), NIGTC], or made signs with his hands [CEV, TEV]. He used his hands to sign the customary spoken blessing [BECNT]. He wanted to let them know it was time for them to leave without the usual blessing [Lns]. He was trying to indicate what had happened to him [NTC].

1:23 And it-happened[a] when the days of his service were completed,[b] he-went to his house.
LEXICON—a. aorist act. indic. of γίνομαι (LN 13.107): 'to happen'. See translations of this word at 1:8.
b. aorist act. indic. of πίμπλημι (LN **67.70**) (BAGD 1.b.β. p. 658): 'to be completed' [**LN**, NTC, WBC; HCSB, NIV, REB], 'to be fulfilled' [Lns], 'to come to an end' [BAGD, LN], 'to be ended' [BECNT; NASB, NET, NRSV], 'to be finished' [Arn; NCV], 'to be accomplished' [KJV], 'to be over' [AB; CEV, GW, NLT, TEV].

1:24 And after these days Elizabeth his wife became-pregnant and she-was-hiding[a] herself (for) five months saying,
LEXICON—a. imperf. act. indic. of περικρύβω (LN **28.79**) (BAGD p. 648): 'to hide' [Arn, BAGD, BECNT, **LN**, Lns, WBC; KJV], 'to conceal' [BAGD, LN], 'to keep secret' [LN]. The phrase 'to hide herself' is translated 'to

not go out in public' [GW], 'to not leave the house' [CEV, TEV], 'to not go out of the house' [NCV], 'to keep herself in seclusion' [NTC; HCSB, NASB, NET], 'to remain in seclusion' [AB; NIV, NRSV], 'to go into seclusion' [NLT], 'to live in seclusion' [REB]. It indicates that she concealed her pregnancy [Su].

QUESTION—Which part of Elizabeth's pregnancy were covered by the five months and why did she hide herself?

This refers to the first five months of her pregnancy [AB, Alf, Arn, Crd, Gdt, ICC, My, NIC, NICNT, NTC, WBC]. Luke gives no reason for hiding herself, but there are some guesses. She made this a time of contemplation and rejoicing concerning her pregnancy [BECNT, Su]. Since barrenness was considered a reproach (1:25), perhaps she decided not to appear in public until it was evident that she was pregnant [AB, Arn, Gdt, NICNT, NTC]. It would be indelicate for her to explain that they were wrong [Arn]. One commentator thinks this refers to the last five months of her pregnancy and regards this as a customary retirement when pregnancy shows [Lns]. The reason for her seclusion is not known, but this explains why Mary did not know that Elizabeth was pregnant [BECNT, NAC].

1:25 Thus[a] (the) Lord has-done to-me in (the) days in-which he-looked-with-favor[b] to-take-away my disgrace[c] among people.[d]

LEXICON—a. οὕτως (LN 61.9): 'thus' [BECNT, LN, Lns; KJV], 'so, in this way' [LN], 'this is the way' [NTC; NASB], 'in this manner' [Arn], 'this' [NIV, REB], 'this is what' [NET, NRSV], 'this is how' [AB, WBC], 'look what' [NCV], 'what (the Lord has done for me)' [CEV], not explicit [GW, HCSB, NLT, TEV].

b. aorist act. indic. of ἐπεῖδον (LN **30.45**) (BAGD p. 284): 'to look with favor' [NTC; NASB], 'to look favorably on' [NRSV], 'to concern oneself with someone' [BAGD, LN], 'to take notice of, to consider, to pay attention to' [LN], 'to take note' [Arn], 'to see fit' [AB], 'to see to it' [Lns], 'to look' [BECNT, WBC], 'to look upon' [KJV], 'to show favor' [NIV, REB], 'to be gracious to' [NET], 'to help' [TEV], 'to be kind' [NLT], not explicit [CEV, GW, NCV]. She refers to the Lord watching over her [BECNT].

c. ὄνειδος (LN **87.73**) (BAGD p. 570): 'disgrace' [AB, BAGD, LN, NTC, WBC; GW, HCSB, NASB, NET, NIV, NRSV, TEV], 'reproach' [Arn, BAGD, BECNT, Lns; KJV], 'shame' [NCV], 'disgrace of having no children' [NLT], 'disgrace of childlessness' [REB]. This noun is also translated as a verb with 'people' as the subject: 'to look down on' [CEV]. Barrenness was commonly considered to be a matter of shame and reproach [AB, Alf, BECNT, Gdt, TH]. People considered barrenness to be a punishment from God [TNTC].

d. ἄνθρωπος (LN 9.1): 'person, human being, individual' [LN]. The plural form is translated 'people' [AB, LN, NTC, WBC; CEV, HCSB, NCV, NET, NIV, NRSV], 'men' [Arn, BECNT, Lns; KJV, NASB], not explicit

[NLT, REB]. This noun is also translated as an adjective: 'public (disgrace)' [GW, TEV].

DISCOURSE UNIT: 1:26–38 [AB, BECNT, NAC, NICNT, NIGTC, Su, TNTC, WBC; CEV, GW, HCSB, NASB, NCV, NET, NIV, NLT, NRSV, TEV]. The topic is a birth announcement of Jesus the Messiah [NET], Jesus' birth foretold [AB, NAC, NICNT, NIGTC, Su, TNTC, WBC; NASB, NIV, NLT, NRSV, TEV], an angel appears to Mary [NCV], the angel Gabriel comes to Mary [GW], an announcement to Mary [BECNT], an angel tells about the birth of Jesus [CEV], Gabriel predicts Jesus' birth [HCSB].

1:26 Now in the sixth month the angel Gabriel was-sent by/from[a] God to a-city of-Galilee which (has the) name Nazareth **1:27** to a-virgin[b] (who) was-engaged to-a-man whose name (was) Joseph of (the) house[c] of-David, and the name of-the virgin (was) Mary.

LEXICON—a. ἀπό (LN 90.7, 90.15): 'by' [AB, BECNT, LN (90.7); HCSB, NET, NRSV, REB], 'from' [Arn, LN (90.15), Lns, WBC; KJV, NASB]. The passive verb 'was sent' is also translated actively, thus omitting this preposition: 'God sent' [CEV, GW, NCV, NIV, NLT, TEV]. The translation 'by' (agent LN 90.7) emphasizes the agent who sent Gabriel, while the translation 'from' (source LN 90.15) emphasizes the place from which Gabriel came, leaving implicit the fact that it was God who sent him. [NET].

b. παρθένος (LN 9.39) (BAGD 1. p. 627): 'virgin' [AB, Arn, BAGD, BECNT, LN, NTC, WBC; all versions except REB, TEV], 'girl' [REB], 'young woman' [LN; TEV], 'maiden' [Lns]. This refers to a female past puberty who was not yet married and was still a virgin [LN]. The noun means a young, unmarried girl and it is implied that she was a virgin [NIGTC]. Although the general meaning is 'girl', the specific meaning of 'virgin' is intended here [TH]. The normal meaning of the word is 'virgin' [AB, MGC, NTC, Su]. That Mary was a virgin is stressed both here and at 1:34 [NAC, NICNT, WBC] to emphasize the magnitude of the miracle [WBC]. Or, in this verse the focus is not on the virginity of this unmarried girl of marriageable age. It is not until 1:34 where she says 'I do not know a man' that the fact that she was a virgin is brought out [TG]. Mary was probably a teenager [TG]. A Jewish girl could be betrothed at twelve [NICNT, NIGTC], or thirteen [WBC], and a year later she would move to the bridegroom's home to begin normal married life [WBC].

c. οἶκος (LN 10.24) (BAGD 3. p. 561): 'house' [Arn, BECNT, Lns, NTC, WBC; HCSB, KJV, NRSV], 'lineage, family line' [LN], 'family' [CEV, NCV], 'descendants' [BAGD; NASB], 'a descendent of' [AB; GW, NET, NIV, NLT, REB, TEV]. This refers to persons related by birth through successive generations [LN]. See this word at 1:33.

QUESTION—Who was of the lineage (house) of David?
  1. Joseph was of the lineage of David [AB, Alf, BECNT, Crd, EGT, Gdt, MGC, My, NAC, NIC, NICNT, NIGTC, NTC, Su, TH, WBC; CEV, GW,

NCV, NET, NLT]: a man whose name was Joseph, who was of the house of David. David is mentioned because of Joseph being descended from David, thus showing that Jesus is of the house of David (1:32) through his legal father [MGC, NAC, NIGTC, WBC]. This point about Joseph is important in the following account of Jesus' birth in Bethlehem, the city of David [Su]. Mary is reintroduced into the narrative in the following clause [BECNT, NAC], by the repetition of the word 'virgin' [TH].
2. Mary was of the lineage of David [Arn, Lns]: the angel appeared to a virgin of the house of David. The main person in this account is Mary and this information is about her [Arn, Lns].

1:28 **And having-approached toward her he-said, Hail,[a] (one who) has-been-favored,[b] the Lord (is) with[c] you.**

TEXT—Following εἰσελθών 'having approached', some manuscripts read ὁ ἄγγελος 'the angel'. GNT does not mention this variant. Ὁ ἄγγελος 'the angel' is read by KJV.

TEXT—Following σοῦ 'you', some manuscripts read εὐλογημένη σὺ ἐν γυναιξίν 'blessed (are) you among women'. GNT rejects this reading with an A decision, indicating that the text is certain. This reading is followed by KJV.

LEXICON—a. pres. act. impera. of χαίρω (LN 33.22) (BAGD p. 874): 'hail' [AB, BAGD, LN; KJV], 'greetings' [Arn, BECNT, LN, Lns, NTC; NASB, NCV, NET, NIV, NLT, NRSV, REB], 'peace be with you' [TEV], 'rejoice' [WBC; HCSB]. This is also translated outside the quote: 'greeted and said' [CEV, GW].

b. perf. pass. participle of χαριτόω (LN **88.66**) (BAGD p. 879): 'to be favored' [AB, BAGD, BECNT, Lns; GW, HCSB, NASB, NET, NLT, NRSV], 'to be highly favored' [Arn, NTC; KJV, NIV], 'to be most favored' [REB], 'to be shown kindness' [**LN**], 'to be blessed' [NCV], 'to be truly blessed' [CEV], 'to be privileged' [WBC]. This passive is also translated in the active voice with the Lord as subject: 'to greatly bless' [TEV]. The perfect participle indicates that Mary was the recipient of God's grace [NET]. The passive implies that God had favored her [AB, Arn, Lns, NIGTC] to be the mother of the Son of the Most High [AB]. God was satisfied with Mary and intended to bless her [Arn].

c. μετά (LN 89.108) (BAGD A.II.1.c.β. p. 509): 'with' [AB, Arn, BAGD, BECNT, LN, Lns, NTC; all versions]. It is a figurative use of 'with' and means that the Lord will help her [BAGD]. This assures Mary of God's presence to help and protect her [BECNT, NICNT].

QUESTION—Where was the angel before he approached Mary?
When the angel came from God to Nazareth (1:26), he entered Mary's home [Arn, BECNT, Lns, NIGTC, TH; GW], and went into the room where she was [TG]. Perhaps he walked in through the door [Lns, NTC].

QUESTION—What is meant by 'Hail'?
1. This is a greeting [AB, Arn, BAGD, BECNT, Crd, LN, Lns, NAC, NIGTC, NTC, TH; CEV, GW, KJV, NASB, NCV, NET, NIV, NLT, NRSV, REB]: greetings, favored one. It is a formalized greeting and implies a wish of happiness for the person greeted [LN (33.22)]. It was the normal form of greeting [NAC].
2. This is a command to rejoice about being favored by God [BNTC, NICNT, WBC; HCSB]: rejoice, favored one.

1:29 But[a] at the words she was-greatly-perplexed[b] and kept-pondering[c] of-what-sort this greeting might-be.
LEXICON–a. δέ: 'but' [AB, Lns; NASB, NCV, NET, NRSV, REB], 'and' [KJV], not explicit [NTC, WBC; CEV, GW, NIV, NLT, TEV].
b. aorist pass. indic. of διαταράσσω (LN **25.246**) (BAGD p. 189): 'to be greatly perplexed' [BECNT], 'to be much perplexed' [NRSV], 'to be quite perplexed' [AB], 'to be perplexed' [BAGD; NASB], 'to be deeply troubled' [**LN**; HCSB, REB, TEV], 'to be thoroughly troubled' [WBC], 'to be greatly troubled' [NTC; NET, NIV], 'to be troubled' [KJV], 'to be very much upset' [Lns], 'to be confused' [BAGD; CEV], 'to be confused and disturbed' [NLT], 'to be disturbed' [Arn], 'to be greatly perturbed' [Lns], 'to be startled' [GW], 'to be very startled' [NCV].
c. imperf. mid./pass. (deponent = act.) indic. of διαλογίζομαι (LN **30.10**) (BAGD 1. p. 186): 'to ponder' [AB, BAGD; NASB, NRSV], 'to wonder' [NTC, WBC; CEV, HCSB, NCV, NET, NIV, REB, TEV], 'to consider' [Arn, BAGD], 'to carefully consider' [**LN**], 'to reason' [BAGD], 'to reason thoroughly' [LN], 'to try to figure out' [GW], 'to try to think' [NLT], 'to cast in one's mind' [KJV], 'to argue with oneself' [Lns].
QUESTION—Why would the angel's message cause Mary's reaction?
Zechariah had been frightened by the appearance of the angel, but here it is the message that caused Mary's distress [BECNT, TH, TNTC]. She could not understand why she should be addressed by an angel [NAC], especially in such exalted terms [NIGTC, TNTC], and selected for this honor [EGT]. The angel's greeting was cryptic [WBC]. Since the angel will now tell her to stop being afraid, her distress included fear [Lns, NIGTC].

1:30 And the angel said to-her, Do- not -fear Mary, for you-found favor[a] with God. **1:31** And behold[b] you-will-conceive in (your) womb and will-bear a-son and you-will-call his name Jesus.
LEXICON—a. χάρις (LN **88.66**, 25.89) (BAGD 2.b. p. 877): 'favor' [Arn, BAGD, BECNT, LN (25.89), Lns, NTC, WBC; GW, HCSB, KJV, NASB, NET, NIV, NRSV], 'kindness' [LN (88.66)], 'grace' [BAGD; NCV]. The phrase 'you found favor with God' is translated 'have been favored by God' [AB], 'God is pleased' [CEV] 'God has decided to bless' [NLT], 'God has been gracious' [REB, TEV]. That Mary found favor with God means that God had graciously chosen her to do something special [BECNT]. See this word at 2:40.

b. ἰδού: 'behold'. See this word at 1:20.

QUESTION—Is the phrase 'and you will call his name Jesus' prophetic or does it function as a command?
1. It is a continuation of the prophecy in the future tense [BNTC, Lns, NAC, NTC, WBC; all versions except NIV, NLT, REB]: you will conceive and you will bear a son and you will name him Jesus. These things are going to occur without human will and consent [Lns].
2. It commands Mary to name her son Jesus [AB, BECNT, ICC; NIV, NLT, REB]: you will conceive and you will bear a son and you are to name him Jesus. This does not continue the prophecy, but it is a command [BECNT, ICC]. The future tense is equivalent to an imperative here [AB].

1:32 This-one will-be great[a] and he-will-be/will-be-called[b] (the) Son of-(the)-Most-High[c] and (the) Lord God will-give him the throne of-David his ancestor,[d]

LEXICON—a. μέγας (LN 87.22) (BAGD 2.b.a. p. 498): 'great'. See translations of this word at 1:15. This is different from the greatness of John and it is explained in the rest of the verse [ICC, NIGTC]. He will be great in terms of his holiness, power, and influence [Gdt]. This word also occurs at 1:15; 7:28; 9:46; 22:24
  b. fut. pass. indic. of καλέω (LN 33.131) (BAGD 1.a.δ. p. 399): 'to be called' [Arn, BECNT, LN, Lns, NTC, WBC; all versions], 'to be hailed as' [AB], 'to be named' [BAGD, LN]. Often the focus is not on the name of the person, but what the name says about him, and the passive may be translated 'to be' [BAGD]. See this word at 1:35, 76.
  c. ὕψιστος (LN **12.4**) (BAGD 2.b.α. p. 850): 'Most High' [AB, BAGD, BECNT, **LN**, NTC, WBC; all versions except CEV, KJV, TEV], 'Most High God' [TEV], 'God Most High' [CEV], 'the Highest' [Arn, Lns; KJV]. The title 'Son of the Most High' is equivalent to 'the Son of God', which is more commonly used [BECNT, NAC, NICNT, NIGTC]. See this word at 1:35, 76; 6:35.
  d. πατήρ (LN 10.20) (BAGD 1.b.): 'ancestor' [BAGD, LN; CEV, GW, NCV, NLT, NRSV, REB, TEV], 'father' [AB, Arn, BECNT, Lns, NTC, WBC; KJV, NASB, NET, NIV]. Both Mary and Joseph were descendants of David [NIVS].

QUESTION—What is meant by 'he will be called'?
1. This is the equivalent of 'to be' [BAGD, EGT, NAC, NTC]: and he will be the Son of the Most High.
2. This means that he will be recognized to be the Son of the Most High [Gdt, WBC]. He will be universally recognized as such because he is such in fact [Gdt].
3. This refers to the title that God will give him [NIGTC, TG, TH]: and he will be given the title 'Son of the Most High'. The passive form indicates that this is a name given to the Messiah by God [NIGTC, TG, TH]. This name indicates his true being [NIGTC].

4. This means all three of the above [Arn].

QUESTION—What is meant by God giving Jesus the throne of his ancestor David?

This means that God will grant to him the right to sit on the throne [WBC]. He will reign over Israel as his ancestor David once did [TH]. This implies that he will be king [Arn], the Messiah [Arn, NAC, NIGTC, TH].

1:33 and he-will-rule over the house^a of-Jacob into the ages^b and of-his kingdom there-will-be no end.

LEXICON—a. οἶκος (LN 10.24) (BAGD 3. p. 561): 'house'. See this word at 1:27.
  b. εἰς τοὺς αἰῶνας (BAGD 2.b. p. 27) (LN 67.95): 'to the eons' [Lns], 'forever' [AB, BECNT, LN, NTC, WBC; all versions], 'always' [LN], 'forever and ever, eternally' [LN] 'to all eternity' [BAGD], 'to eternity' [Arn].

QUESTION—What is meant by 'the house of Jacob'?

This designation is common in the OT and appropriate in the context of ruling over the whole twelve tribes [WBC]. It is a traditional way of speaking of the nation of Israel [AB, BECNT, NAC, NIGTC, TG, TH; NET].

1:34 And Mary said to the angel, How will- this -be, since^a I do- not -know^b a-man?

LEXICON—a. ἐπεί (LN 89.32) (BAGD 2 p. 284): 'since' [AB, Arn, BAGD, BECNT, Lns, NTC, WBC; HCSB, NASB, NCV, NET, NIV, NRSV], 'because' [BAGD, LN], 'seeing' [KJV], not explicit [CEV, GW, NLT, REB, TEV].
  b. pres. act. indic. of γινώσκω (LN 23.61) (BAGD 5. p. 161): 'to know' [Arn, BAGD, BECNT, Lns; KJV], 'to have sexual intercourse with' [LN], 'to have sexual relationship with' [WBC; NET], 'to have relations with' [AB]. The clause 'I do not know a man' is translated 'I've never had sexual intercourse' [GW], 'I have not been intimate with a man' [HCSB], 'I am a virgin' [NASB, NCV, NIV, NLT, NRSV, TEV], 'I am still a virgin' [REB], 'I am not living with a husband' [NTC], 'I am not married' [CEV]. 'Know' is used here as an euphemism for having sexual relations [BAGD; NET].

QUESTION—What relationship is indicated by ἐπεί 'since' and what is the argument?

'Since' indicates the reason for Mary's perplexity [EGT, Gdt, Lns, NIGTC, NTC, Su, TNTC]. Although accepting the truth of the angel's statement, she was perplexed about how this could happen and asked for an explanation [Alf, Gdt, NICNT]. This question does not indicate the kind of doubt shown by Zechariah since there is no rebuke in the angel's answer [NAC]. Mary believed the message, but could not understand how it could happen [NICNT, NTC].

1. Mary assumed that her pregnancy could come about only in the normal manner of conception [Arn, BECNT, Lns, MGC, My, NIGTC, Su, TG, TH, WBC]: I don't understand how this can be, *since I can conceive only by sexual union and* I do not have a sexual relationship with a man. She assumed that the pregnancy would occur soon and before she could have a son normally through marriage with Joseph [Arn, BECNT, MGC, My, TG, TH].
2. Mary has correctly interpreted the angel's message to mean that her pregnancy would come about independent of sexual union [NAC, NIC, NTC, TNTC]: I don't understand how this can be, *although it must mean a virginal conception since* I do not have a sexual relationship with a man.

1:35 **And answering the angel said to-her, (The) Holy Spirit will-come upon^a you and (the) power of-(the)-Most-High^b will-overshadow^c you; therefore also the (one) being-born will-be-called/will-be^d holy^e (The) Son of-God.**

TEXT—Following γεννώμενον 'being born' some manuscripts add ἐκ σοῦ 'from you'. GNT rejects this addition with an A decision, indicating that the text is certain. This addition is read by KJV.

LEXICON—a. ἐπί (LN 90.57) (BAGD III.1.b.γ. p. 289): 'upon' [AB, Arn, BAGD, BECNT, Lns, NTC; all versions except CEV, GW, TEV], 'on' [LN; TEV], 'to' [LN; GW], 'down to' [CEV]. This preposition points to the one who experiences the action [LN]. It refers to a power which comes upon someone or influences that person [BAGD]. It suggests that he will come with power [BNTC].

b. ὕψιστος (LN 12.4) (BAGD 2.b.α. p. 850): 'Most High'. See this word at 1:32, 35, 76; 6:35.

c. fut. act. indic. of ἐπισκιάζω (LN **14.62**) (BAGD 3 p. 298): 'to overshadow' [Arn, BAGD, BECNT, **LN**, Lns, NTC, WBC; all versions except CEV, NCV, TEV], 'to cast a shadow upon' [BAGD, LN], 'to cast a shadow over' [AB], 'to come over' [CEV], 'to cover' [NCV], 'to rest upon' [TEV]. This is a figurative use of the verb and means that the Holy Spirit will cause Mary to conceive [BAGD, LN]. Some take this figure to refer to the cloud of light called the Shekinah Glory in which God manifested his presence above the ark of the covenant [Gdt, ICC, Lns, NICNT, NIGTC, Rb, WBC] and it denotes God's presence to protect [NIGTC]. But the reference to the Shekinah Glory is denied by others [NAC, NTC]. The figure refers to the Spirit hovering over the water in the account of creation (Gen. 1:2) and relates to the Spirit protecting and creating [NTC].

d. fut. pass. indic. of καλέω (LN 33.131) (BAGD 1.a.δ. p. 399): 'to be called, to be'. See translations of this word at 1:32, 76. This verb may be translated differently for the attribute 'holy' and for the title 'the Son of God': 'he *will be* holy and *will be called* the Son of God' [AB; NCV,

NET, NLT, NRSV], 'the *holy* One to be born *will be called* the Son of God' [HCSB].
  e. ἅγιος (LN 88.24) (BAGD 1.b.γ. p. 9): 'holy' [AB, Arn, BAGD, BECNT, LN, Lns, WBC; all versions], 'divine' [LN]. Besides indicating superior moral qualities, it refers to having divine qualities in contrast with what is human [LN]. It means that Jesus will originate from God and belong to him [TH]. He will be divine and dedicated to God [NIGTC]. It refers to Jesus being free from sin [ICC, NIVS], set apart for God's purposes [AB, NAC, Su], and dedicated to the service of God [TH].

QUESTION—How are the Holy Spirit and 'the power of the Most High' related?
  The clause 'the Holy Spirit will come upon you' is in synonymous parallelism with 'the power of the Most High will overshadow you' [AB, NAC, NICNT, NIGTC, NTC, TH]. This refers to the action of the Holy Spirit coming upon Mary and overshadowing her with power [NAC, NIC, NTC, Su]. The Holy Spirit will accomplish this by using his divine power [BECNT, NTC]. The all-encompassing presence of the Most High is the power of the Holy Spirit [Su].

QUESTION—How is the adjective 'holy' related to the phrase 'the Son of God'?
  1. 'Holy' modifies the implied subject 'child', and the object of 'will be called' is 'the Son of God' [Alf, Arn, Lns, My, NTC; GW, HCSB, KJV, NASB, NIV, REB, TEV]: the holy child to be born will be called the Son of God. Jesus was called 'Son of God' by many people, by his Father in heaven, by Gabriel, and by himself when he spoke of his Father [Lns].
  2. 'Holy' modifies 'the Son of God' [CEV]: the child to be born will be called the holy Son of God.
  3. 'Holy' is the object of 'will be called' and 'the Son of God' is in apposition to 'holy' [BECNT, BNTC, Crd, ICC, MGC, NICNT, NIGTC, WBC]: the child to be born will be called holy, the Son of God.
  4. Since 'holy' is not a title as is 'the Son of God', a distinction is made so that the verb is translated 'to be' with the first and 'will be called' with the second [AB, Gdt, NAC; NCV, NET, NLT, NRSV]: the child to be born will *be* holy and will *be called* the Son of God.

QUESTION—What is meant by the title 'Son of God'?
  This is similar to 'Son of the Most High' in 1:32 [AB, WBC], and it is a title of the Messiah [ICC, Rb]. At this point in the narrative, Luke uses this title to describe the Messiah, but it was not the same as saying that Jesus was divine [BECNT]. In 1:32 Jesus is 'Son' in his role as king, but here he is Son of God as a result of his conception [Arn, BNTC, NIGTC]. This title is not identical to 'Messiah', since 'Messiah' expresses his office while 'Son of God' expresses his very being [Lns]. The title 'Son of God' goes beyond messianic terms such as 'Son of David' since he is more than this, and 'Son of God' has other implications than just his mission [Gdt, NAC]. Here the full sense of one begotten by God is intended [EGT, NIGTC]. It recalls the

promised son Immanuel, 'God with us', in Isaiah 9:6 [BNTC]. This title signifies the divine origin of the child [Crd, Gdt].

1:36 **And behold**[a] **Elizabeth your relative,**[b] **she also has-conceived a-son in her old-age and this month is (the) sixth (for) her the (one) called barren; 1:37 because**[c] **every thing**[d] **will- not -be-impossible with God.**

LEXICON—a. ἰδού: 'behold'. See translations of this word at 1:20. Parallel with 1:20, this draws attention to what God is doing at the same time he is working in Mary. Although Mary did not ask for a sign, God gave her this sign to encourage her [BECNT].

b. συγγενίς (LN 10.7) (BAGD p. 772): 'relative' [AB, Arn, BAGD, BECNT, LN, Lns, NTC, WBC; all versions except KJV, REB], 'kinswoman' [BAGD, **LN**; REB], 'cousin' [KJV]. This word means a woman of the same kin [TH], but it does not indicate the degree of kinship [AB, EGT, Lns, NICNT, TG, TH]. It does not mean cousin [AB]. Although Elizabeth was a descendant of Aaron (1:5), this does not mean that Mary was a descendant of Aaron and not of David and Judah. An ancestor or relative of either could have married a descendant of the other ancestor [NTC]. If one of Mary's parents was descended from David and the other one was descended from Aaron, it would make Mary a kinswoman of Elizabeth who was also descended from Aaron [Gdt, TNTC]. She might have been a cousin or aunt of Mary [NIVS].

c. ὅτι (LN 89.33): 'because' [Arn, LN, Lns], 'since' [AB], 'for' [BECNT, NTC, WBC; all versions except CEV, GW, NCV], 'but' [GW], not explicit [CEV, NCV].

d. ῥῆμα (LN 13.115) (BAGD 1. p. 735): 'thing, matter, event' [BAGD, LN]. With the negative 'not', this is translated 'nothing' [AB, Arn, BAGD, BECNT, Lns, NTC, WBC; all versions except NCV, REB]. This negative phrase is also translated positively: 'God can do anything' [NCV], 'God's promises can never fail' [REB].

QUESTION—What relationship is indicated by ὅτι 'because' at the beginning of 1:37?

Primarily this explains the statement of Elizabeth being pregnant, but it also explains how it will be possible for Mary to become supernaturally pregnant [BECNT, NAC, NICNT, NIGTC, TH]. It gives the reason for what occurred in Elizabeth's case and now is to occur in Mary's case [Lns]. With the future tense, it refers specifically to Mary's pregnancy, not Elizabeth's [WBC].

QUESTION—Since ῥῆμα can mean 'thing' or have a more specific meaning of 'word' or 'saying', what does this statement mean?

1. This refers to a thing done by God [AB, Arn, BECNT, BNTC, Gdt, Lns, NTC, TG, TH; all versions except REB]: *nothing* will be impossible with God. Although ῥῆμα means 'spoken word' in 1:38, here it means 'thing' in accordance with Hebrew usage [NTC]. The word refers to all that God does in word and action [BECNT].

2. This refers to a statement made by God [Alf, ICC, My, Rb, Su; REB]: no *word* from God will be impossible. Nothing promised by God is impossible [ICC], 'God's promises can never fail' [REB]. Instead of taking οὐκ ἀδυνατήσει to mean 'will not be impossible', some take it to mean 'will not be powerless' [My, Su]. It means 'no word which God sends forth into the affairs of his creation will be powerless to execute its end' [Su].

1:38 **And Mary said, Behold**[a] **the servant**[b] **of-(the)-Lord. May-it-be-done to-me according-to your word. And the angel departed from her.**
LEXICON—a. ἰδού: 'behold'. See translations of this word at 1:20.
  b. δούλη (LN 87.83) (BAGD p. 205): 'servant' [BECNT, WBC; all versions except KJV, NASB], 'bondmaid' [BAGD], 'bondwoman' [Arn], 'bondslave' [NASB], 'slave maid' [Lns], 'slave woman' [LN], 'slave' [HCSB], 'handmaid' [AB, NTC; KJV]. Mary is God's willing property for him to command as he pleases [Lns], she is ready to serve the Lord [Su]. Her statement indicates that she fully accepts what God asks of her [BECNT].
QUESTION—What is the function of Mary's response ἰδού 'behold'?
  It is an exclamation and not a verb [ICC, Lns], showing the depth of her feelings [Lns]. It indicates that Mary is ready to serve the Lord or to listen to his words [Alf, NIGTC, TH]. She is saying: 'Here am I, the servant of the Lord' [NRSV], 'Yes, I am a servant of the Lord' [NET], or simply 'I am the servant of the Lord' [CEV, GW, NCV, NIV, NLT, REB, TEV].

DISCOURSE UNIT: 1:39–56 [AB, NAC, NICNT, NIGTC, Su, WBC]. The topic is the meeting of John the Baptist and Jesus [NAC], Mary's visit to Elizabeth [AB, NICNT, NIGTC, Su], a mutual greeting of the mothers [WBC].

DISCOURSE UNIT: 1:39–45 [BECNT, TNTC; CEV, GW, HCSB, NASB, NCV, NET, NIV, NLT, NRSV, TEV]. The topic is Mary and Elizabeth [NET], Mary visits Elizabeth [BECNT, TNTC; CEV, GW, HCSB, NASB, NCV, NIV, NLT, NRSV, TEV].

1:39 **And in these days Mary having-arisen**[a] **traveled into the hill-country**[b] **with haste to a-city of-Judah, 1:40 and she-entered into the house of-Zechariah and greeted Elizabeth.**
LEXICON—a. aorist act. participle of ἀνίστημι (LN 15.36) (BAGD 2.d. p. 70): 'to arise' [Arn, Lns; KJV, NASB], 'to rise up' [BECNT], 'to get up' [NCV, NET], 'to depart, to leave' [LN], 'to set out' [AB; HCSB, NRSV, REB], 'to set off' [WBC], 'to get ready' [NIV, TEV]. The phrase 'having arisen traveled with haste' is translated 'hurried to' [CEV, GW, NLT], 'hurried away to' [NTC]. 'Having arisen, she went' is Hebrew wording [AB, WBC]. The verb has a weakened sense of 'rise, stand up, get up' and indicates the beginning of an action that is expressed by another verb [BAGD]. This circumstantial participle 'having arisen' is not necessary

[Arn, Lns, NTC], but it is customarily used in narratives and Luke uses it sixty times [Lns].

b. ὀρεινός (LN 1.47) (BAGD p. 580): 'hill country' [AB, BAGD, BECNT, LN, Lns, NTC; all versions except GW, NCV, REB], 'the uplands' [REB], 'the hills' [NCV], 'mountain country' [Arn], 'mountain region' [GW]. It was not much more hilly than Galilee [NIGTC]. It was the hill country of Judea in contrast to level land that is found especially on the coast [Lns].

QUESTION—Was the city in Judah or Judea?

The GNT does not mention a textual difference here. The phrase τὴν ὀρεινὴν μετὰ σπουδῆς εἰς πόλιν Ἰούδα 'into the hill country, to a city of Judah' in this verse is similar to the phrase ἐν ὅλῃ τῇ ὀρεινῇ τῆς Ἰουδαίας 'the entire hill country of Judea' in 1:65. This refers to a region which originally had been allotted to the tribe of Judah [NTC]. The hill country takes in less territory than the province of Judea [Lns]. The phrase could well mean 'a city named Judah', although no city of such a name is known [Lns]. It was a town in Judea (ancient Judah) [AB]. 'Judah' is used only here and in Matt. 2:6, and refers to the same region as in Luke 1:65 [TH]. Although the text is Ἰούδα 'Juda', many translate with a word for the same location, 'Judea' [AB, BECNT; CEV, NCV, NIV, NLT, NRSV, TEV].

1:41 **And it-happened when Elizabeth heard Mary's greeting, the baby in her womb leaped,[a] and Elizabeth was-filled[b] (with the) Holy Spirit,**

LEXICON—a. aorist act. indic. of σκιρτάω (LN 15.243) (BAGD p. 756): 'to leap' [AB, Arn, BAGD, BECNT, LN, Lns, NTC, WBC; HCSB, KJV, NASB, NET, NIV, NLT, NRSV], 'to jump' [NCV], 'to kick' [GW], 'to move' [CEV, TEV], 'to stir' [REB]. This refers to an unborn child's movements in the womb [BAGD]. It was a strong, vigorous stirring of the baby in the womb [TH], but it wouldn't be a jump [TG]. At six months, the movement of the baby would not be unusual [NTC, TNTC], but this could have been an exceptionally strong movement [NIC, Su]. The reason for this movement was the joy of the baby (1:44) [BECNT, NICNT, NIGTC]. The movement at this time was a sign that Elizabeth's unborn baby acknowledged both the Lord Jesus and the mother of the Lord [AB, MGC].

b. aorist pass. indic. of πίμπλημι (LN 59.38) (BAGD 1.a.β. p. 658): 'to be filled' [AB, Arn, BECNT, Lns, NTC, WBC; all versions except CEV]. This passive voice is also translated actively with the Holy Spirit as subject: 'to come upon' [CEV]. This indicates that the Holy Spirit is enabling her to speak prophetically [NET]. See this word at 1:15, 67.

QUESTION—What is meant by Elizabeth's being filled with the Holy Spirit?

This filling was to be the source of her inspiration in what she says here [AB, Alf, EGT, Gdt, My, NAC, NIC, NIGTC, Su, TNTC; NET]. The Holy Spirit enabled Elizabeth to understand the significance of her baby's movement and inspired her speech [NICNT, NTC]. When the verb of filling is in the aorist tense (here and in 1:67), it refers to a sudden and momentary experience in which the Spirit inspires the person to speak prophetically [TH]. This is an extraordinary filling for this one time in order to enable her to prophesy [Lns].

1:42 and she-cried-out[a] with-a-loud cry and said, You have-been-blessed[b] among[c] women and the fruit[d] of your womb has-been-blessed. **1:43** And why (did) this (happen) to-me that the mother of-my Lord should-come to me? **1:44** Because behold when the sound of your greeting came into my ears, the baby leaped in my womb with joy.

TEXT—In 1:42, instead of κραυγῇ 'cry', some manuscripts read φωνῇ 'voice'. GNT does not mention this variant. Φωνῃ 'voice' is translated by CEV, GW, KJV, NASB, NCV, NET, NIV, REB, TEV (but probably all except KJV do so for stylistic rather than textual reasons).

LEXICON—a. aorist act. indic. of ἀναφωνέω (LN **33.77**) (BAGD p. 63): 'to cry out' [BAGD, LN], 'to cry' [Arn], 'to speak in a loud voice' [**LN**]. The phrase 'she cried out with a loud cry and said' is translated 'in a loud voice she said' [CEV], 'she said in a loud voice' [GW, TEV]. 'she cried out with/in a loud voice and said' [NASB, NCV], 'she called out in a loud voice' [WBC], 'she spoke out with a loud voice and said' [KJV], 'she exclaimed with/in a loud voice' [HCSB, NET, REB], 'exclaimed with a loud cry' [BECNT; NRSV], 'in a loud voice she cried out' [NTC], 'uttered in a loud voice' [AB], 'in a loud voice she exclaimed' [NIV], 'Mary gave a glad cry and exclaimed' [NLT], 'she lifted up her voice with a great shout and said' [Lns]. The crying out would be an indication of an inspired utterance [Alf, My, NAC, NIGTC, WBC]. It showed Elizabeth's surprise and joy at seeing Mary [Lns, NIGTC]. It showed her excitement [TNTC], her wonder, thanksgiving, and love [NTC].

b. perf. pass. participle of εὐλογέω (LN 88.69) (BAGD 3. p. 322): 'to be blessed' [AB, Arn, BAGD, BECNT, LN, Lns, NTC, WBC; all versions except CEV, NCV, REB]. This passive is also translated as active with God as the subject: 'God has blessed' [CEV, NCV], 'God's blessing is on' [REB]. The word means to receive special favor from God [BECNT]. This is a statement and means that God has blessed her [BECNT, Lns, TH]. It is an exclamation [Gdt]. She is blessed in that God chose her to be the mother of his son [Lns, Su], and that her child is the Messiah [WBC].

c. ἐν (LN 83.9): 'among' [AB, Arn, BECNT, LN, Lns, NTC; KJV, NASB, NET, NIV, NRSV]. The phrase 'among women' is translated 'more than any other woman' [CEV, NCV], 'above all women' [REB], 'above all other women' [NLT], 'most (blessed) of all women' [WBC; GW, HCSB, TEV]. 'Among' indicates that the participle is used in a comparative or superlative sense 'you are the most blessed among women' [AB, Alf, EGT, Gdt, Lns, NAC, NIGTC, NTC, Rb, TH, TNTC, WBC]. It means that God has blessed Mary more than any other woman [NAC, NTC, TG].

d. καρπός (LN 10.38) (BAGD 1.b. p. 404): 'fruit' [AB, Arn, BAGD, BECNT, Lns, NTC, WBC; KJV, NASB, NRSV, REB], 'child' [LN; NET], 'baby' [LN]. The phrase 'the fruit of the womb' is an idiom for the child of a woman [LN] and is a Hebraism (Gen. 30:2) [BECNT, TH]. The phrase is translated 'your child' [HCSB, NLT], 'the child you will have' [CEV, GW], 'the child you will bear' [NIV, TEV], 'the baby to which you will give birth' [NCV]. This figure of speech may refer to the embryo in Mary's womb [AB, My, NTC], or to the child she will later bear [Gdt, Su, TH]. The baby is blessed in that God favors him and is concerned about his life [Lns]. He is blessed to be born to such a blessed woman [Su].

QUESTION—What is the function of Elizabeth's question 'Why did this happen to me'?

It is a rhetorical question [Lns, TG] that expresses her surprise [TH]. Translated as a statement it is 'I don't deserve to have such a wonderful thing as this happen to me!' [TG]. It expresses her feeling of unworthiness to be honored by the visit of the mother of her Lord [BNTC, Crd, Lns, NIGTC]. It shows her humility [BECNT, MGC, Su], or her joyful surprise [NTC]. It indicates that she thinks she didn't deserve to have such a wonderful thing happen to her [BECNT, TG].

QUESTION—Up to now, 'Lord' has referred to Yahweh, but what did Elizabeth mean when she said 'the mother of my Lord'?

She used 'Lord' to refer to the Messiah [BECNT, Crd, Gdt, My, NIGTC, NTC, Su, TH, TNTC, WBC]. She was inspired to recognize the divine nature of Mary's baby [Alf]. She spoke of her submission to the unborn baby [NICNT] and sees the child as her superior [BECNT]. This can only be explained as being uttered by inspired prophecy [Alf, ICC, Lns, NTC, Rb].

QUESTION—In 1:44, what relationship is indicated by γάρ 'because'?

It indicates the reason Elizabeth knew that Mary was to be mother of the Lord [AB, Crd, EGT, My, NIGTC, NTC, TH]: *I know that you are the mother of my Lord because* at the sound of your voice, my baby leaped with joy.

QUESTION—What was the cause for Elizabeth's baby to jump for joy?

Presumably Mary had already conceived. Elizabeth's baby leaped for joy because he was filled with the Holy Spirit at that moment to recognize the presence of his Lord [Arn, Lns, NICNT, WBC].

1:45 **And blessed[a] (is) the[b] (one who) believed that/because there-will-be a-fulfillment to-the (things which) have-been-spoken to-her by (the) Lord.**

LEXICON—a. μακάριος (LN 25.119) (BAGD 1.b. p. 485): 'blessed' [AB, BAGD, BECNT, Lns, NTC, WBC; all versions except CEV, REB, TEV], 'happy' [BAGD, LN; REB, TEV], 'fortunate' [BAGD]. This adjective is also translated as a verb with God as subject: 'God has blessed' [CEV]. It refers to the enjoyment of favorable circumstances [LN]. It is the happy condition of someone whom God has favored [Lns]. See this word at 6:20; 7:23; 10:23; 11:27; 12:37, 43; 14:14; 23:29.

b. The feminine article ἡ 'she (who), the (one who)' refers to Mary in the third person and is translated 'you' in agreement with the second person references in 1:42–44 [CEV, GW, NLT, TEV]. This use of the third person for the second person is OT style [NIGTC]. An explanation for not using the second person address is that Elizabeth used the third person form as a generalized statement to make Mary an example of faith [BECNT].

QUESTION—Is there a difference between the passive verb εὐλογέω 'to be blessed' in 1:42 and the adjective μακάριος 'blessed' here in 1:45?

Both are translated 'blessed' [AB, BAGD, BECNT, Lns, NTC, WBC; all versions except REB, TEV]. The words are essentially synonymous [NAC]. However, some see a difference and translate the words differently or explain the differences [LN, Lns, NICNT, TH; REB, TEV]. The adjective 'blessed' here refers to a state of happiness and bliss, while the verb 'to be blessed' refers to a situation originating from God [TH]. The adjective expresses the happy condition of those who are favored by God [Lns]. The blessedness of the previous verbs was based on Mary's motherhood, but here she is blessed in the sense that she was fortunate because of her faith [NICNT].

QUESTION—Is the relationship indicated by ὅτι 'that' or 'because'?

1. It indicates the content of what Mary believed [BECNT, Gdt, NICNT, NIGTC, Su, TG, WBC; all versions except KJV]: blessed is the one who believed *that* there will be a fulfillment. It is anticlimactic to take this as 'because' since there is no need to confirm Mary's faith [WBC].

    1.1 The participle 'having believed' identifies the one who is blessed [BECNT, Gdt, NIGTC, TG, WBC; NASB, NET, NIV, NLT, NRSV, REB, TEV]: blessed is she *who believed that* the Lord will keep his promise.

    1.2 The participle 'having believed' is the reason she is blessed [NICNT, Su; CEV, GW, NCV]: she is blessed *because she believed that* the Lord will keep his promise.

2. It indicates the reason for calling Mary blessed [AB, Alf, Lns, MGC, NIC, NTC, TH, TNTC; HCSB, KJV]: blessed is the one who believed *because* there will be a fulfillment. The participle 'having believed' identifies the one who is blessed [Lns, NTC]. Mary believed what God had told her about her son and she was in a state of blessedness because the Lord would fulfill all that has been prophesied of her son [Lns]. The assurance that God would fulfill his promises is a better ground for calling her blessed than Mary's subjective faith in the fulfillment of the promises [NTC]. This affirms that it would be fulfilled, not that Mary believed it would [TNTC].

DISCOURSE UNIT: 1:46–56 [BECNT, TNTC; CEV, GW, HCSB, NASB, NCV, NET, NIV, NLT, NRSV, TEV]. The topic is the song of Mary [TNTC;

NIV], Mary's praise [HCSB], Mary's song of praise [BECNT; CEV, NET, NLT, NRSV, TEV], Mary praises God [GW, NCV], the Magnificat [NASB].

1:46 And Mary said, 1:47 My soul[a] magnifies[b] the Lord, and my spirit[c] rejoices/rejoiced[d] in God my savior,

TEXT—Instead of Μαριάμ 'Mary', some manuscripts read the alternative form Μαρία 'Mary', and some Latin manuscripts read *Elisabeth*. GNT reads Μαριάμ 'Mary' with an A decision, indicating that the text is certain.

LEXICON—a. ψυχή (LN 26.4) (BAGD 1.b.γ. p. 893): 'soul' [AB, Arn, BAGD, BECNT, Lns, NTC, WBC; all versions except CEV, NET, NLT], 'inner self, being, mind' [LN], 'heart' [CEV, TEV], 'I' [NLT]. 'My soul' means 'I' [AB, BNTC, NAC, NIGTC; NLT].
  b. pres. act. indic. of μεγαλύνω (LN 33.358) (BAGD 2. p. 497): 'to magnify' [Arn, BECNT, Lns, NTC, WBC; KJV, NRSV], 'to praise' [BAGD; CEV, GW, NCV, NLT, TEV], 'to exalt' [BAGD; NASB, NET], 'to extol' [BAGD], 'to glorify' [BAGD; NIV], 'to praise the greatness of' [LN], 'to declare/proclaim/tell the greatness of' [AB; HCSB, REB]. It means to make the Lord great and glorious by what one says [Lns]. Here it means to proclaim how great the Lord is [NTC]. It means to express praise and thanksgiving for the Lord's greatness and majesty [AB]. Mary does this by means of her song [WBC].
  c. πνεῦμα (LN 26.9) (BAGD 3.b. p. 675): 'spirit' [AB, Arn, BAGD, BECNT, LN, Lns, NTC, WBC; GW, HCSB, KJV, NASB, NET, NIV, NRSV, REB], 'inner being' [LN], 'heart' [NCV], 'soul' [TEV], 'My spirit' means 'I' [NAC; CEV, NLT].
  d. aorist act. indic. of ἀγαλλιάω (LN **25.133**) (BAGD p. 4): 'to rejoice' [Arn, BAGD, BECNT, **LN**, NTC; all versions except CEV, GW, TEV], 'to find delight' [AB], 'to be glad' [CEV, TEV], 'to find one's joy' [WBC; GW], 'to jubilate' [Lns]. See this word at 10:21.

QUESTION—Is there a difference intended between 'my soul' and 'my spirit'?
  1. There is no difference intended [AB, Arn, BECNT, Crd, EGT, ICC, MGC, My, NAC, NTC, Rb, Su, TNTC, WBC; NLT]. They are used synonymously [Crd, EGT, ICC, NTC, Su, WBC]. The change of wording is due to poetic parallelism [AB, NAC, NTC, TNTC, WBC]. The word 'I' can be substituted for both soul and spirit [AB, BECNT, NAC; NLT]. Both soul and spirit refer to the immaterial part of one's life, in contrast with the body [ICC]. They refer to the inner, higher self [Arn, ICC, My]. The inner spiritual nature of a person is referred to with the two different terms [Rb].
  2. There is a distinction between soul and spirit [LN, Lns, TG]. They are not separate parts of a person, but 'soul' refers to the aspect of thinking, while 'spirit' refers to the aspect of willing [TG]. Soul refers to the immaterial part of a person that animates the body, while spirit refers to the same immaterial part as it is directed towards God and is capable of receiving impressions from him [Lns]. Soul is 'the essence of life in terms of

thinking, willing, and feeling' [LN (26.4)] and spirit is 'the non-material, psychological faculty which is potentially sensitive and responsive to God' [LN (26.9)].

QUESTION—What is indicated by the aorist tense of ἠγαλλίασεν 'rejoiced' which follows μεγαλύνει 'magnifies' in the present tense?

1. It is translated in the present tense [AB, LN (25.133), NICNT, NTC, TH; all versions except HCSB, KJV, NET, REB]: my soul magnifies the Lord and my spirit *rejoices* in God. In parallelism with the first clause, 'rejoices' is to be understood as a timeless aorist [AB]. This difference in tenses is influenced by Hebrew poetry style and the tense change is not significant [TH]. This may be influenced by a Hebrew construction in which a normally past tense verb takes on a present value after a present participle, and Hebrew poetic parallelism requires the translation to make both verbs present tense [NICNT].
2. It is an ingressive aorist [Arn, BECNT; NET]: my soul magnifies the Lord and my spirit *has begun to rejoice* in God. Mary magnifies the Lord now that she has begun to find joy in her Savior God [BECNT]. Mary began to rejoice at the angel's announcement [NET].
3. The aorist indicates past tense [Lns, TNTC, WBC; HCSB, KJV, REB]: my soul magnifies the Lord and my spirit *rejoiced* in God. While the present tense 'magnifies' denotes a habitual act, the aorist tense 'rejoiced' points to the particular past event when the angel brought the message [TNTC]. Or, it is an ordinary historical aorist that points back to the moment before she spoke [Lns]. Or, the aorist tense 'has found gladness' refers to the past time when God enabled her to become pregnant with the Messiah [WBC].

1:48 **because he-looked**[a] **upon the humble-state**[b] **of-his servant. For behold from now (on) all generations**[c] **will-regard- me -as-blessed,**

LEXICON—a. aorist act. indic. of ἐπιβλέπω (LN **30.45**) (BAGD p. 290): 'to look upon' [Arn, BAGD, BECNT, Lns; NET], 'to pay attention to' [**LN**], 'to concern oneself with' [LN], 'to show concern for' [NCV], 'to consider' [BAGD], 'to take notice of' [NLT], 'to look favorably on' [GW], 'to look with favor on' [NTC; HCSB, NRSV, REB], 'to have regard for' [AB, WBC; NASB], 'to regard' [KJV], 'to care for' [BAGD; CEV], 'to be mindful of' [NIV], 'to remember' [TEV]. This verb is similar to ἐπεῖδον 'to look with favor' in 1:25 and here it means 'to look with concern or tenderness' [TG], or 'to look with loving care' [NICNT]. 'To look upon' implies that God intended to do something about it and will change Mary's humble situation [TH]. The aorist tense refers to the time when God sent the angel Gabriel to her [Lns]. 'Looked upon' refers to the loving care with which God selected Mary to bear the child [BECNT].

b. ταπείνωσις (LN **87.60**) (BAGD 2. p. 805): 'humble state' [NTC; NASB, NET, NIV], 'humble condition' [HCSB], 'humble station' [BAGD], 'low status' [**L N**], 'low estate' [KJV], 'afflicted state' [WBC], 'the humbleness' [Arn, Lns], 'the lowliness' [AB; NRSV], 'humility' [BAGD]. This noun is also translated as an adjective modifying 'servant': 'humble' [CEV, GW, NCV], 'lowly' [BECNT; NLT, REB, TEV]. The word probably implies the quality of humility [LN]. Mary meant the lowliness of her person, feeling that she was an insignificant maiden [My], engaged to just a carpenter [ICC, NTC, Rb], and poor [NICNT]. This refers to her low social state in the estimation of the world [Alf, BECNT, NAC, NICNT, NIGTC, TNTC], and perhaps also to her humble attitude towards God [NIGTC, TNTC].

c. γενεά (LN 11.4) (BAGD 3. p. 154): 'generation' [AB, Arn, BECNT, LN, Lns, NTC, WBC; HCSB, KJV, NASB, NET, NIV, NLT, NRSV, REB], 'people' [CEV, GW, NCV, TEV], 'age (the time of a generation)' [BAGD]. See this word at 1:50; 7:31; 9:41; 11:29, 50; 16:8; 17:25; 21:32.

QUESTION—What relationship is indicated by ὅτι 'because' at the beginning of this verse?

It indicates the reason for Mary's praise [AB, BECNT, Lns, NAC, NICNT, NIGTC]: my soul magnifies the Lord, and my spirit rejoices in God *because* he looked upon my humble state.

QUESTION—What relationship is indicated by γάρ 'for' in the phrase 'for behold'?

1. It indicates the grounds for saying that God looked upon her [BECNT, Lns]: it is true that he looked upon my humble state *since* from now on all people will call me blessed.
2. It indicates the result of God's looking on Mary's humble state [NAC, TH]: he looked upon my humble state *with the result that* from now on all people will call me blessed.

QUESTION—How did Mary know that all generations will regard her as blessed?

This is not a prophecy, it is a deduction brought about by accepting the angel's message [Lns]. 'All generations' does not mean everybody in all succeeding generations, but the believers in each succeeding generation [Lns].

1:49 because the Mighty-One did great-things for-me, and holy (is) his name, 1:50 and his mercy (is) to generations and generations, to-the (ones who) fear[a] him.

LEXICON—a. pres. act. participle of φοβέω (LN **53.58**) (BAGD 2.a. p. 863): 'to fear' [AB, Arn, BAGD, BECNT, Lns, NTC, WBC; all versions except CEV, NCV, TEV], 'to have reverence for' [BAGD, **LN**], 'to honor' [TEV], 'to worship' [LN; CEV], 'to worship and serve' [NCV]. It implies having awe that borders on fear [LN]. It is a reverent regard for God [NTC]. It means to recognize and reverence God's sovereignty [AB, Lns], and to reverently obey him [NAC].

QUESTION—What relationship is indicated by ὅτι 'because'?
1. It indicates the reason people will regard Mary as blessed [NICNT, NIGTC]: all generations will regard me as blessed *because* the mighty one did great things for me.
2. It is a second reason for Mary's rejoicing, parallel with the 'because' at the beginning of 1:48 [AB, BECNT, NICNT, TH]: my soul exalts the Lord, and my spirit rejoices in God *because* he looked upon the humble state of his servant, *and because* he did great things for me. This verse focuses on God's attributes, not on Mary, and thus explains why Mary praises God [BECNT].
3. Instead of functioning as a second reason for Mary's rejoicing, it functions as a synonymous parallel with the first clause of 1:48 [NAC].

QUESTION—Why is the phrase 'and holy is his name' inserted between the statements of God's might and his mercy?
1. This clause is more closely connected with the preceding clause in 1:49 [AB, BECNT, Lns, NICNT, NTC, TH; CEV, HCSB, NET, NIV, NLT, NRSV]. In calling God holy, Mary has in mind the great things God had done in causing her to become pregnant with the holy child to be born [Lns]. Mary was so impressed with the great things he had done for her that she uttered this exclamation [NTC]. She further describes the Mighty One as he who is holy [AB; NLT]. God's authority is a demonstration of an exalted, holy ruler [BECNT].
2. This clause goes with the following clause in 1:50 [Gdt, NAC, WBC; REB]. 'Fearing' him is a response to God's holiness [WBC].
3. This clause is a separate sentence, not closely connected with either the preceding or following clauses [ICC].

1:51 He displayed power[a] with his arm, he scattered[b] (the) proud in-(the)-thoughts of their heart.

LEXICON—a. κράτος (LN 76.6, **76.7**) (BAGD 2. p. 449): 'power' [BECNT, LN (76.6)], 'mighty deed' [BAGD, **LN** (76.7)], 'miracle' [LN (76.7)]. The anthropomorphism 'he displayed power with *his arm*' is translated 'he has done/performed mighty deeds with his arm' [NTC; NASB, NIV], 'he has done a mighty deed with his arm' [HCSB], 'the Lord has used his powerful arm' [CEV], 'he wrought strength with his arm' [Lns], 'he has shown strength with his arm' [KJV, NRSV], 'he has shown might with his arm' [WBC], 'he has exerted power through his arm' [Arn], 'he has shown the might of his arm' [REB], 'he has demonstrated power with his arm' [NET], 'he exercised power with his arm' [BECNT], 'he has displayed the might of his arm' [AB], 'his mighty arm does tremendous things' [NLT], 'he has stretched out his mighty arm' [TEV], 'he displayed his mighty power' [GW], 'he has done mighty deeds by his power' [NCV].

b. aorist act. indic. of διασκορπίζω (LN 15.136) (BAGD p. 188): 'to scatter' [Arn, BAGD, BECNT, LN, Lns, NTC, WBC; all versions except REB], 'to disperse' [BAGD], 'to put to rout' [AB], 'to rout' [REB].

QUESTION—In verses 1:51–53 there are six verbs in the aorist tense. How are these aorists used in these verses?

1. This is a historic use of the aorists [AB, Gdt, Lns, NIC, NTC, Su, WBC; probably all which translate in the past tense: GW, KJV, NCV, NET, NIV, NRSV, REB, TEV]: God did this in the past. Mary tells what the Lord has done for others in the past and especially what he has done for her by being merciful to her (1:48–49) [NTC]. Although basically historical, they also indicate actions that recur over and over [NTC]. The aorist is ingressive: God began to do this when he chose Mary [Gdt, NIC].

2. This is a futuristic use of the aorists telling what will happen in the future [Alf, Arn, BECNT, Crd, ICC, My, NAC, NIGTC, Su, TH, TNTC]: God will do this. Mary is referring to the effects of her being blessed rather than to past events [TH, TNTC]. She is interested in what the coming of Jesus will mean [BECNT]. It describes the future work of God's Son and Mary saw this as already accomplished [NAC]. This is equivalent to the Hebrew prophetic perfect tense which refers to events of the future as being already accomplished [NAC, TH].

3. This is a gnomic use of the aorists to express a general truth [EGT]: God always does this.

4. Combinations are involved. CEV translates 1:51 in the past tense and 1:52–53 in the present tense. NLT translates 1:51 in the present tense and 1:52–53 in the past tense.

QUESTION—What is meant by the anthropomorphism 'his arm'?

God's *arm* symbolizes his power [AB, BECNT, NTC, TG, TH, WBC], might [NAC], or force [Gdt].

QUESTION—How is κράτος 'power' used here?

1. This refers to God's attribute of power which he has displayed [AB, BECNT, Lns, NIGTC, TG, TH, WBC; CEV, GW, KJV, NET, NRSV, REB, TEV]: he has shown his power. 'He displayed power' is from a Hebrew idiom [WBC]. With the meaning 'power', the verb ἐποίησεν means he showed or displayed his power [TH].

2. This refers to the kind of deeds he did by his power [NIC, NIVS, NTC, TH; NASB, NCV, NIV]: he has done mighty deeds. With the meaning 'mighty deed', the verb ἐποίησεν means 'he did' mighty deeds [TH].

3. This includes both of the above [NLT]: 'his mighty arm does tremendous things'.

QUESTION—How does the first clause, 'he displayed power with his arm', relate to the following clauses?

The clause 'he displayed power with his arm' is explained by the following three clauses (1:51–53) [Lns, NICNT, NTC, TH]. Some mention that there are two groups of people described in various ways through these verses: one group is described as being proud, rulers, and rich, the other group is described as being humble and in hunger [Lns, NAC, NICNT, NIGTC, NTC, Su, WBC]. The powerful and privileged people oppose God and also other people, so when God punishes the proud, rulers, and rich, at the same time he cares for the humble and hungry [NICNT].

QUESTION—What is meant by scattering the proud?

God has repeatedly punished arrogant people by dispersing them in all directions [NTC]. This gives the picture of an opposing army being scattered [Gdt, NIC]. He has put his enemies to rout [AB]. This refers to their punishment [NAC, NIGTC].

1:52 He-brought-down[a] rulers from (their) thrones and lifted-up[b] (the) humble, 1:53 (the ones) hungering he-filled with-good-things and rich (ones) he-sent-away empty.

LEXICON—a. aorist act. indic. of καθαιρέω (LN 15.199) (BAGD 1. p. 386): 'to bring down' [BAGD, LN, NTC, WBC; NASB, NCV, NET, NIV, NRSV, REB, TEV], 'to put down' [AB; KJV], 'to throw down' [Lns], 'to drag' [CEV], 'to pull' [GW], 'to pull down' [Arn], 'to topple' [HCSB], 'to take' [NLT]. The active voice is also translated as passive: '(powers) were cast down' [BECNT]. This refers to overthrowing rulers who do not obey God's will [NIGTC].

b. aorist act. indic. of ὑψόω (LN **87.20**) (BAGD 2. p. 851): 'to lift up' [BAGD, NTC; NET, NIV, NRSV, TEV], 'to raise up' [NCV], 'to raise on high' [REB], 'to give high position to' [**LN**], 'to exalt' [AB, BAGD, BECNT, LN, Lns, WBC; KJV, NASB, NLT], 'to put in places of power' [CEV], 'to honor' [GW], 'to exalt' [Arn; HCSB]. 'Lift up' has the figurative meaning of raising them to a high position [ICC, TH].

QUESTION—What are the good things that God filled the hungry ones with?

The good things refer to good food to eat [CEV, GW]. The 'hungering ones' can be taken to refer to more than physical hunger and include those who are in want generally [NIGTC, TH]. The hungry ones can be hungry for food and also for what is more than physical, so the good things include all that they may need [Lns]. God cares for the physically hungry and also the spiritually hungry [NIVS, NTC]. After Jesus came, there were still political tyrannies and there was still physical poverty, so this has a spiritual meaning [Arn].

1:54 He-helped his servant Israel, to-remember[a] mercy, 1:55 just-as he-spoke to our fathers, to-Abraham and his offspring into the age.[b]

LEXICON—a. aorist pass. infin. of μιμνῄσκω (LN 29.7) (BAGD 1.c. p. 522): 'to remember' [Arn, BAGD, BECNT, LN], 'to be concerned about' [BAGD]. The phrase 'to remember mercy' is translated 'remembering his mercy' [NET], 'in remembrance of his mercy' [NTC, WBC; KJV, NASB, NRSV], 'mindful of his mercy' [AB; HCSB], 'remembering to be merciful' [NIV], 'remembering to show them mercy' [NCV], 'he has remembered to show mercy' [TEV], 'he remembered to help' [GW], 'he has not forgotten to show mercy' [REB], 'he has not forgotten his promise

to be merciful' [NLT], 'in order to remember mercy' [Lns], 'and is always merciful to his people' [CEV]. See this word at 1:72.
   b. αἰών (LN 67.95) (BAGD p.27): 'age' [BAGD] 'eon' [Lns]. The idiom εἰς τὸν αἰῶνα 'into the age' is translated 'forever' [AB, Arn, BECNT, LN, NTC, WBC; all versions].

QUESTION—What is meant by the phrase 'to remember mercy'?

1. The infinitive 'to remember' is due to Hebrew influence and denotes an act parallel with, or modifying, the previous verb so that this verse means 'he helped his servant Israel; he has remembered his mercy' [TH, WBC].

1.1 It indicates the reason for helping Israel [BECNT, EGT, NIGTC, TH; NET]: he helped Israel *because* he was merciful. This added infinitive has the sense 'and he remembered', but instead of giving the result of helping Israel, it indicates the cause [NIGTC]. Helping Israel is presented as fulfilling a promise made long ago, but not forgotten by God [EGT]. To speak of God *remembering* is an anthropomorphism that is common in the OT [WBC].

1.2 It defines God's helping Israel as a remembering of mercy [Lns, NICNT, NTC, WBC; probably KJV, NASB, NCV, NET, NIC, NLT, NRSV]: he helped his servant Israel in remembrance of his mercy. God remembered his promise to be merciful [NLT].

2. It is the infinitive of purpose [AB, Arn, ICC, Lns]: he helped Israel *in order to* remember mercy. 'To remember mercy' means to carry his mercy into effect [Lns]. It may be translated 'so as to remember mercy' and means to prove that he had not forgotten [ICC]. This is an allusion to Psalm 98:3 and means God remembered his mercy and faithfulness to Israel [AB].

QUESTION—How is the last phrase 'to Abraham and his offspring forever' connected?

1. It is in apposition to 'our fathers' and defines who are included in the word 'fathers' [AB, Crd, NAC, TH; CEV, GW, NCV, NET, NLT, NRSV]: just as he spoke (promised: CEV, GW, NCV, NET, NLT, NRSV) to our fathers, *that is,* to Abraham and his offspring forever. Many of the translations seem to attach the adverb 'forever' to the verb 'he spoke' [AB; KJV, NCV, NET, NRSV] and this is criticized as being meaningless [Gdt, NIGTC]. A few have adjusted the syntax to have 'forever' modify being merciful: 'for he promised our ancestors— Abraham and his offspring—to be merciful to them forever' [TH; NLT], 'He remembered to help his servant Israel forever. This is the promise he made to our ancestors, to Abraham and his descendants' [GW].

2. As an indirect object, it identifies the recipients of God's mercy [Alf, Arn, BECNT, Gdt, ICC, Lns, NIGTC, NTC, TNTC, WBC; NIV, REB, TEV]: to remember mercy…to Abraham and his offspring forever. The phrase 'just as he spoke to our fathers' is parenthetical [Alf, BECNT, Lns, NIGTC, NTC, TNTC, WBC]. The promise of mercy, which had been spoken to our fathers, was a promise of mercy for Abraham and his seed

in the gift of the Messiah and the effects of the promise would extend forever [Lns]. God would be merciful forever [Lns, NIGTC; NIV, REB, TEV], he would never forget to be merciful [Gdt]. This avoids the difficulty of making sense of 'speaking…forever' [Gdt, NIGTC].
3. This is the dative of advantage [EGT]: to remember mercy for the benefit of Abraham and his offspring.

1:56 And Mary remained with her about three months, and she-returned to her house.
QUESTION—Since this brings the account to Elizabeth's pregnancy to the ninth month, did Mary stay until John was born?
1. Mary probably stayed with Mary until John was born [Arn, ICC, My, NAC, NIGTC, WBC]. Mary would not have left when the birth was imminent [ICC]. Since Mary is not mentioned in the following accounts of the birth and circumcision of John, she must have left soon after the birth [WBC].
2. Mary probably left before John was born [AB, BECNT, BNTC, Crd, Lns, MGC, NAC, NIC, NTC, Su, TG, TNTC]. The phrases 'about three months' here and 'now the time to give birth was fulfilled' in 1:75 indicate that she left before John was born [AB]. Mary probably stayed until almost the day John was born, but felt that it would be best to leave before being criticized for being pregnant by the many visitors who would come to Elizabeth's house when they learned of John's birth [Lns, NIC, NTC, TNTC].

DISCOURSE UNIT: 1:57–2:52 [AB]. The topic is the birth and infancy of John and Jesus.

DISCOURSE UNIT: 1:57–80 [AB, NAC, NICNT, NIGTC, Su; GW]. The topic is the birth of John the Baptist.

DISCOURSE UNIT: 1:57–66 [BECNT, TNTC, WBC; CEV, HCSB, NASB, NCV, NET, NIV, NLT, NRSV, TEV]. The topic is the birth of John the Baptist [BECNT; CEV, NASB, NCV, NET, NIV, NLT, NRSV, TEV], the birth, circumcision, and naming of John [WBC], the birth and naming of John [TNTC; HCSB].

DISCOURSE UNIT: 1:57–58 [NICNT]. The topic is the birth of a son.

1:57 Now the time was-fulfilled[a] for-Elizabeth to-give-birth and she-bore a-son. 1:58 And her neighbors and relatives heard that (the) Lord had-magnified[b] his mercy to her and they-were-rejoicing with-her.
LEXICON—a. aorist pass. indic. of πίμπλημι (LN 67.70) (BAGD 1.b.β. p. 658): 'to be fulfilled' [Arn, Lns, NTC], 'to come to an end' [BAGD, LN], 'to be complete' [BECNT, LN]. The phrase 'the time was fulfilled' is translated 'when the time came' [GW], 'the time came' [AB; NET, NRSV, REB, TEV], 'when it was time' [NCV, NIV], 'now it was time' [NLT], 'the time had come' [HCSB, NASB], 'the time arrived' [WBC],

'the full time came' [KJV], 'when (Elizabeth's son was born)' [CEV]. This is a Hebraism that is repeated about Mary in 2:6 [BECNT]. The usual time from conception to delivery had ended [BECNT, EGT, My, NTC].
  b. aorist act. indic. of μεγαλύνω (BAGD 1. p. 497): 'to magnify' [BAGD, BECNT, Lns]. The phrase 'had magnified his mercy' is translated 'had shown great mercy' [AB, BAGD; KJV, NET, NIV, NRSV], 'had shown her his great mercy' [HCSB], 'had shown greatly his mercy' [WBC], 'had displayed his great mercy' [NASB], 'had made his mercy abound' [Arn], 'had been very kind' [GW, NLT], 'what great kindness the Lord had shown' [REB], 'how wonderfully good the Lord had been' [TEV], 'how kind the Lord had been' [NTC; CEV], 'how good the Lord was' [NCV]. God magnifies his mercy when he does notable merciful deeds [Lns].
QUESTION—How was the birth of Elizabeth's son an indication of the Lord's great mercy to her?
  In his mercy, God took away the cause of her grief about her barrenness [Lns] and allowed her to bear a son [BECNT]. The birth of Elizabeth's son removed the disgrace of being barren [AB]. This does not mean that now Elizabeth's pregnancy was revealed to others; rather it refers to the safe delivery that ended the pregnancy [WBC].

DISCOURSE UNIT: 1:59–66 [NICNT]. The topic is the circumcision and naming of the child.

1:59 And it-happened on the eighth day they-came to-circumcise the child and they-were-calling him by the name of his-father Zechariah. 1:60 And his mother having-answered said, No, but he-will-be-called John. 1:61 And they-said to her, There-is no-one from your relatives who is-called by-this name. 1:62 And they-were-motioning to-his father what he-might-wish him to-be-called.

TEXT—In 1:61, instead of ἐκ τῆς συγγενείας σου 'from your relatives', some manuscripts read ἐν τῇ συγγενείᾳ σου 'among your relatives', although GNT does not mention it.
QUESTION—What is significant about the eighth day?
  Circumcision on the eighth day was commanded in the Law of Moses (Lev. 12:3) and Philippians 3:5 indicates that only those who had been circumcised on the eighth day had unblemished Jewish credentials [WBC]. The eighth day means seven days after he was born [TH]. It was the corresponding day of the following week [Gdt].
QUESTION—Who are the 'they' who came to circumcise John?
  Only one person performed the rite and others were witnesses [EGT, NTC], so 'they' came to join in the ceremony [TH]. They are the neighbors and relatives of 1:58 who came to witness the ceremony of circumcision [AB, Gdt, Lns, NICNT, NIGTC, TH, WBC]. It was usual for the head of the house to perform the circumcision [NIGTC].

QUESTION—Why would they have to motion to Zechariah?
1. This implies that Zechariah was deaf as well as mute [AB, Alf, BECNT, BNTC, Crd, MGC, NAC, NICNT, NIGTC, TG, WBC; NET]. Since Zechariah had not heard what Elizabeth wanted to name their son, his agreement to call him John caused the people to be amazed [NAC, NICNT, NIGTC]. They were surprised at the firmness of his answer, or at the unusual name for his son [NIGTC]. Deafness was often associated with being mute [NAC]. The word κωφός can mean both deaf and mute and if he was not deaf, the people would not have bothered gesturing to him [BECNT].
2. This does not imply that Zechariah was deaf [Arn, Gdt, Lns, My, NTC, Su]. It was normal to use signs in communicating to someone who only communicated his messages through signs [Su]. People instinctively use signs with those who cannot speak [Gdt]. The account assumes that Zechariah was listening to the discussion, but to spare Elizabeth's feelings they called for his decision by using signs [My]. He had heard everything, so they just had to nod to him and motion for him to settle the discussion [Arn, Gdt, Lns].

1:63 And having-asked (for) a-tablet[a] he wrote saying, John is his name. And everyone was-amazed.[b] **1:64** And his mouth was-opened at-once and his tongue, and he-was-speaking praising God.

LEXICON—a. πινακίδιον (LN **6.60**) (BAGD p. 658): 'tablet' [LN; NASB], 'little tablet' [BAGD], 'writing tablet' [AB, Arn, Lns, NTC, WBC; all versions except NASB], 'wax tablet' [BECNT]. A writing tablet was normally made of wood [BAGD, LN]. Here it would have been a wax tablet [NET]. It was a flat piece of wood that had a film of wax that could be written into by means of a pointed object [Alf, BECNT, EGT, ICC, Lns, NAC, NIC, NIGTC, NIVS, NTC, Rb, TG, TH, TNTC, WBC]. Or, it was a piece of wood which was covered with parchment [BNTC].
b. aorist act. indic. of θαυμάζω (LN 25.213) (BAGD 1.a.α. p. 352): 'to be amazed'. See translations of this word at 1:21. This word also occurs at 2:18, 33; 4:22; 7:9; 8:25; 11:14, 38; 20:26; 24:12, 41.

QUESTION—When it says that Zechariah 'wrote saying', does this imply that he could now speak?
The verb 'saying' merely introduces the contents of what was written [AB, Arn, BAGD (p. 469), EGT, NAC, NTC, TH]. It is merely a Hebraism [BECNT, Gdt, WBC]. He did not speak until after writing the name [BECNT]. The word 'saying' is omitted in most translations [AB, NTC, WBC; all versions except KJV].

QUESTION—What happened when 'his mouth was opened and his tongue'?
This is a zeugma where two nouns, mouth and tongue, are construed with one verb, 'was opened', but only the noun 'mouth' suits the verb [AB, Arn, BECNT, BNTC, EGT, Lns, NIGTC, NTC, TH, WBC; NET]. The verb supplied with 'tongue' is: loosed [AB, Gdt, NTC, TH; KJV, NASB, NIV],

released [NET], set free [HCSB], freed [WBC; NRSV, REB]. Another approach is to combine the mouth and tongue in one phrase: 'he started speaking' [CEV], 'he was able to speak' [GW, TEV], 'he could talk/speak again' [NCV, NLT]. The redundancy emphasizes that Zechariah received a total return of speech [BECNT].

1:65 And fear came upon all the-ones living-around them, and in (the) entire hill-country of Judea everyone was-talking-about these matters, **1:66** and everyone (who) heard kept (these things) in their heart saying, What then will- this child -be? Because indeed (the) hand of-(the)-Lord was with him.

TEXT—In 1:66, instead of καὶ γάρ 'because indeed', some manuscripts read καί 'and'. GNT does not mention this variant. Καί 'and' is read by KJV.

TEXT—In 1:66, some manuscripts omit the imperfect tense ἦν 'was'. GNT includes this word with an A decision, indicating that the text is certain.

QUESTION—What is meant by the question 'What then will this child be' and to whom did they say this?

By asking 'what' instead of 'who' it shows that they wondered about John's role in preceding the Messiah [BECNT, NAC]. They wondered what these incidents might indicate with respect to the character of John and his future role [NTC, WBC]. They wondered what the child would grow into in regard to the kind of a man he would be and the kind of work he would do [Lns, TH]. They discussed this question among themselves [NIC].

QUESTION—Is the final clause a comment by Luke or a part of what the people were saying?

1. This begins a comment made by Luke as he wrote this account and the conjunction γάρ 'because' indicates the grounds for what everyone was saying [AB, Alf, Arn, BECNT, EGT, ICC, MGC, NAC, NICNT, NTC, Su, TG, WBC; GW, NASB, NCV, NET, NIV, NRSV, REB, TEV]: *they had reason to ask this because* the hand of the Lord was with him. The change in the tenses of the verbs from future ('what will this child be') to imperfect ('was with him') shows that this is an editorial comment and not part of the preceding quotation [Arn, NAC, NIGTC]. It is Luke's comment to explain the thought behind the people's question [Alf, EGT, NIGTC, Su]. Or, the people were right in having such high expectations for John because later events proved that they were right [NTC]. The people's question about John was kept alive because of the impression the growing child continued to make on them [WBC]. The imperfect tense indicates that the Lord was repeatedly with him [MGC].

2. This conjunction is part of the quotation attributed to the people [Lns; NLT]. This is what the people were saying long after the day of the circumcision when they looked back at his life [Lns].

QUESTION—What is meant by the anthropomorphism 'the *hand* of the Lord was with him'?

It refers to God's protection and direction that would stay with John [AB, NTC, TG]. It refers to God's presence, direction, and favor [NET], or to God's power which was present with John [BECNT, WBC]. The hand represents strength and this means that God was at work to do something special [BECNT].

DISCOURSE UNIT: 1:67–80 [BECNT, TNTC, WBC; CEV, HCSB, NASB, NCV, NET, NIV, NLT, NRSV, TEV]. The topic is the song of Zechariah [TNTC; NIV], Zechariah's praise [BECNT; CEV], Zechariah praises God [NCV], Zechariah's praise and prediction [NET], Zechariah's prophecy [HCSB, NASB, NLT, NRSV, TEV], Zechariah's recognition of John [WBC].

DISCOURSE UNIT: 1:67–79 [NICNT]. The topic is the prophecy of Zechariah.

1:67 And his father Zechariah was-filled[a] (with the) Holy Spirit and he-prophesied saying, **1:68** Praised[b] (be/is) (the) Lord the God of-Israel, because he-visited[c] (us) and accomplished redemption[d] for-his people,

LEXICON—a. aorist pass. indic. of πίμπλημι (LN 59.38) (BAGD 1.a.β. p. 658): 'to be filled'. See this word at 1:15, 41.

b. εὐλογητός (LN 33.362) (BAGD p. 322): 'praised, blessed' [BAGD], 'one to be praised' [LN]. With the implied verb, this is translated 'blessed be' [AB, Arn, BECNT, Lns, NTC, WBC; KJV, NASB, NET, NRSV], 'praise be to' [NIV], 'praise to' [REB], 'let us praise' [NCV, TEV], 'praise (the Lord)' [CEV, GW, HCSB, NLT]. This is a call to praise God [BECNT, NAC, TG], and means 'let all people speak well of God in the way he deserves' [Lns]. In English it is not natural to speak of people blessing God (causing good things to happen to God), and here it means that God should be thanked or praised [TG]. Or, it is to be taken as a statement, 'blessed is', instead of an exhortation [TH].

c. aorist mid. (deponent = act.) indic. of ἐπισκέπτομαι (LN 34.50, 85.11) (BAGD 3. p. 298): 'to visit' [BAGD, BECNT, LN (34.50), WBC; HCSB, KJV, NASB, NLT], 'to be present to help' [LN (85.11)], 'to look favorably on' [NRSV], 'to look upon' [Arn, Lns], 'to look after' [NTC], 'to take note of' [AB], 'to come to help' [NCV, NET], 'to come to the help of' [TEV], 'to come to take care of' [GW], 'to come' [CEV, NIV], 'to turn to' [REB]. There is a similar phrase in 7:16, 'God has come to help his people' [LN (85.11)]. When used of God, it means that he has come in order to bless and save them [NIGTC], to bestow grace upon them [BECNT, NICNT, TH], to help them [TG], or to bring deliverance of various sorts [AB, WBC]. It describes the coming redemption [TG] and salvation by the Messiah [BECNT, WBC].

d. λύτρωσις (LN 37.128) (BAGD 1. p. 483): 'redemption' [AB, BECNT, NTC, WBC; NASB], 'deliverance' [BAGD, LN], 'liberation' [LN]. The phrase 'to accomplish redemption' is a Hebraism [WBC] and is translated 'to have wrought ransoming' [Lns], 'to make a redemption' [Arn], 'to provide redemption' [HCSB], 'to redeem' [KJV, NET, NIV, NLT, NRSV], 'to set free' [GW, REB, TEV], 'to give freedom' [NCV], 'to save' [CEV]. See this word at 2:38.

QUESTION—What was accomplished by being filled with the Holy Spirit?

This was a filling for the purpose of uttering inspired prophecy [AB, Arn, BECNT, NICNT, NIGTC, NTC, TNTC, WBC]. The words 'and he prophesied' states the result of the filling [AB, Lns; NET]. This is the same kind of filling experienced by Elizabeth in 1:41 [AB, BECNT, Lns, NAC, NTC]. Under the Spirit's control, Zechariah praised God by using his memorized words of Scripture and song in the form of poetry [Su].

QUESTION—How are the aorist tenses of the verbs 'accomplished redemption' and 'raised up a horn of salvation' in 1:68–69 to be taken?

1. They describe what God has already done [AB, Gdt, Lns, Su, WBC; all versions]: praise the Lord because he has visited us and accomplished redemption and raised up a horn of salvation. This is what God has done through the conception and coming birth of the Messiah [AB, Lns]. The conception of Jesus includes the coming fulfillment of all of God's promises [WBC]. God's past work of redeeming Israel merges into the present events [Su].

2. They are prophetic aorists [BECNT, NAC, NIGTC, TH]: praise the Lord because he will visit us and will accomplish redemption and will raise up a horn of salvation. Although the conception of the Messiah had already taken place, this 'visitation' is concerned with what is yet to happen through the Messiah, and the visitation is also spoken of in the future tense in 1:78 [BECNT]. The time of salvation has already come in the events of 1:5–67 and although the redemption will be accomplished in the future work of the Messiah, its certainty is shown by a prophetic aorist [NAC]. God has begun his saving work through the birth of John and the conception of the Messiah, but the idea of 'visitation' is made specific in terms of 'redemption' and the content of the verbs look forward to the redemption yet to be accomplished [NIGTC].

QUESTION—What is meant by 'redemption'?

The background of this word is the setting free of a slave [LN]. This is the word used to describe God's setting his people free by his mighty acts in the Exodus [NIGTC, TG], and after that this terminology was applied to subsequent acts of deliverance [NIGTC]. The picture of release at a cost had become lost through usage and finally this word meant no more than deliverance [WBC]. There is no reference to paying money to set a slave free [TG]. The word is general and the character of deliverance is uncertain [NIGTC]. This is messianic deliverance in its political aspects and refers to a deliverance from enemies (1:74), but it is accompanied by spiritual reformation [BECNT, ICC, My]. Or, in this context deliverance is not political, but spiritual, and refers to deliverance from Satan and sin and to attaining salvation through Christ [Arn, NAC, NTC].

1:69 and he-has-raised-up a-horn^a of-salvation for-us in (the) house of-David his servant,

LEXICON—a. κέρας (LN 76.16) (BAGD 3. 429): 'horn' [BAGD, LN], and this has a figurative meaning of 'power' [BAGD, LN]. The clause ἤγειρεν κέρας σωτηρίας ἡμῖν 'he has raised up a horn of salvation for us' [Arn, Lns, NTC, WBC; HCSB, KJV, NASB, NET, NIV; similarly AB, BECNT] is also translated 'he has raised for us a strong deliverer' [REB], 'he has raised up a mighty Savior for us' [GW, NRSV], 'he has provided for us a mighty Savior' [TEV], 'God has given us a mighty Savior' [CEV], 'he has sent us a mighty Savior' [NLT], 'he has given us a powerful Savior' [NCV].

QUESTION—What is meant by saying God raised up a horn of salvation for us?

The κέρας 'horn' refers to the horn of a powerful fighting animal [Arn, NICNT, WBC] and is used metaphorically for strength and power [AB, Arn, BAGD (3. p. 429), Lns, MGC, NAC, NIC, NIVS, NTC, Rb, Su, TG, TNTC, WBC; NET]. The figure of a horn comes from the OT where an ox is able to defeat enemies with a thrust of its horns (Deut. 33:17) and a warrior with a horned helmet symbolizes power [BECNT]. The horn may be that of a ram, wild ox, or a bull [NTC]. To account for the singular form of the noun, one commentary refers it to the horn of the mystical one-horned unicorn [Lns]. It is used because kings were anointed with a horn filled with oil and also because horned animals are so powerful [EGT]. 'Horn of salvation' refers to the Savior's power to save [Lns], and means a strong or mighty Savior [NICNT, TNTC]. In a loose sense, the expression is a messianic title [AB].

1:70 just-as he-spoke through (the) mouth of-his holy prophets from (the) age,^a 1:71 salvation from our enemies and from (the) hand of-all those hating us,

LEXICON—a. αἰών (LN 67.25) (BAGD 1.a. p. 27): 'age' [BAGD, LN]. The idiom ἀπ' αἰῶνος 'from the age' is translated 'from the eon' [Lns], 'from the beginning' [BECNT], 'from of old' [WBC; NASB, NRSV] 'from long ago' [NET], 'from ancient times' [Arn], 'of old' [AB, NTC], 'of long ago' [NIV], 'who lived long ago' [NCV], 'which have been since before the world began' [KJV], 'in ancient times' [HCSB], 'ages long past' [BAGD], 'long ago' [LN; CEV, GW, TEV], 'age after age' [REB].

QUESTION—What does ἀπ' αἰῶνος 'from the age' modify?

1. It modifies 'prophets' [AB, BECNT, EGT, ICC, MGC, NIC, NTC, Su, TH; KJV, NCV, NIV; probably Arn, WBC; NASB, NET, NRSV]: he spoke through his prophets who lived long ago. 'From the age' does not mean that there were prophets from the beginning of time [ICC]. God's prophets were the holy ones of old, not from the beginning of time [AB]. The expression 'from the age' is hyperbolic and means 'from early times'

[BECNT, NIGTC]. The prophecies came from a long succession of prophets dating back from the early days of the nation [BECNT], beginning with Moses [BECNT, NTC]. It goes back to the covenant promises made to David [WBC], This does not mean that each of the prophets told the entire story, but collectively the story was told as prophesy after prophecy added to the story of the coming of the Deliverer [NTC]
2. It modifies 'he spoke' [Lns; CEV, GW, NLT, REB, TEV]: he spoke long ago through his prophets. This goes all the way back to when God spoke through the mouth of Adam [Lns].

QUESTION—How is 1:71 connected?
1. Verse 1:71 is in apposition to 1:68–69 and explains 'salvation' [AB, BECNT, BNTC, EGT, Gdt, ICC, Lns, MGC, My, NICNT, NIGTC, NTC, TG, TH, WBC; NASB, NIV], or 'redemption' [NTC]. Verse 1:70 is parenthetical [EGT, NAC, TG, TH; NASB, NIV], probably an addition made by Luke [NAC, WBC], and 1:71 resumes and develops the thought that was interrupted by 1:70 [EGT].
2. Verse 1:71 is translated as the beginning of what 'he spoke' (1:70) [CEV, GW, NCV, NET, NRSV, REB, TEV]: he said/promised that he would save us from our enemies.

QUESTION—What is meant by being saved 'from the hand' of those who hate us?

The word χείρ 'hand' is used figuratively to allude to their 'power' [BAGD (2.b. p. 880), BECNT, LN (**76.3**), Lns, TH; CEV, NCV, TEV]: salvation from the *power* of all those who hate us. Salvation is to be taken spiritually of salvation from Satan and other forces that would oppose both a person's and a nation's religious life [Arn; NET].

1:72 to-show mercy to our fathers and/even to-remember[a] his holy covenant,[b]

LEXICON—a. aorist pass. infin. of μιμνήσκω (LN 29.7) (BAGD 1.c. p. 522): 'to remember' [Arn, BAGD, BECNT, LN, Lns, NTC, WBC; all versions except CEV, REB], 'to call to mind' [REB], 'to be mindful of' [AB], 'to keep' [CEV]. The word does not imply that he had actually forgotten [LN]. That God 'remembers' the covenant is an anthropomorphism [Lns] and means that God has continually kept the covenant [TH], or that now after a long delay [Lns] God executes the covenant [Lns, NICNT, WBC], or that God fulfills what he has promised in the covenant [My, TG]. See this verb at 1:54.
b. διαθήκη (LN **34.44**) (BAGD p. 42): 'covenant' [AB, Arn, BAGD, BECNT, **LN**, Lns, NTC, WBC; all versions except CEV, GW, NCV], 'promise' [CEV, GW, NCV]. This refers to the contents of an agreement that specifies the reciprocal benefits and responsibilities of those involved [LN], although it is possible to take this as the act of making the covenant here [LN (34.43)]. The covenant is not an agreement between two

persons, but it is God's decree binding himself and the other person to what he has promised [TH]. The covenant is holy because it belongs to God [TH], because it is originated and executed by God [Lns], because it is special and set apart [BECNT, NIGTC], or because it is a solemn thing [NIGTC]. This refers to the covenant made with Abraham and the patriarchs [Lns, WBC], but it is not put in contrast with the Mosaic covenant [WBC].

QUESTION—What is the relationship signaled by the use of the infinitives 'to show mercy' and 'to remember'?

1. The infinitives indicate the purpose of salvation [Arn, ICC, Lns; NET]: God saved/will-save us from our enemies *in order to* show mercy and keep his covenant. It indicates the purpose of raising up a horn of salvation [ICC; NET].
2. The infinitives indicate the result of salvation [BECNT, Gdt, NIGTC; NRSV]: God saved/will-save us from our enemies *and thus* show his mercy and keep his covenant. By saving his people, God shows that he is keeping his promises to the fathers [NIGTC].
3. The infinitives explain and expand the thought of salvation [AB, EGT, WBC]: salvation from our enemies, *that is,* God showed/will-show mercy and keep his covenant.
4. This begins a new sentence parallel with the preceding verse [NICNT; CEV, GW, NCV, REB, TEV]. He continues to list reasons why praising God is appropriate [NICNT].

QUESTION—What is meant by 'to show mercy to our fathers'?

1. It means to be merciful to our fathers [AB, BECNT, BNTC, EGT, ICC, Lns, My, TG, TH, WBC; all versions except KJV, NRSV]. This is literally 'to do mercy *with* (μετά)' and μετά can indicate the one who experiences the event [LN (90.60)]. The expression is a Hebraism meaning 'to show mercy to' [AB, Lns, WBC], 'to deal mercifully with' [NTC].
2. It means to perform the act of mercy that was promised [Arn; KJV, NRSV].
3. If ἔλεος is translated 'mercy', it means 'the mercy promised to the fathers', not showing mercy to them, but ἔλεος actually expresses the idea of loyal behavior in accordance with the covenant so that this is speaking of God keeping faith with our fathers (who are thought of as being alive and waiting) [NIGTC].

QUESTION—How are the two clauses of this verse connected?

1. The second clause is in a coordinate relationship with the first [Arn, BECNT, Lns, NAC, NTC, WBC; KJV, NASB, NCV, NET, NIV, NRSV]: to show mercy *and* to remember his covenant. God's actions reflect both being merciful and being faithful to his covenant [BECNT]. The clauses are in synonymous parallelism and describe two aspects of the same idea [NAC].

2. The second clause indicates what showing mercy to the fathers means, that is, God remembered his covenant [WBC; NLT, REB]: to show mercy *by* remembering his covenant. This mercy to the fathers fulfills the covenant [WBC].

1:73 **(the) oath that he-swore to Abraham our father, to allow^a us 1:74 fearlessly, having-been-delivered from (the) hand of-enemies, to-serve^b him 1:75 in holiness and righteousness before him all our days.**

TEXT—In 1:74, instead of ἐκ χειρὸς ἐχθρῶν 'from (the) hand of enemies', some manuscripts read ἐκ χειρὸς τῶν ἐχθρῶν ἡμῶν 'from (the) hand of our enemies', other manuscripts read ἐκ χειρὸς πάντων τῶν ἐχθρῶν ἡμῶν 'from (the) hand of all our enemies', and some Coptic manuscripts read ἐκ τῶν ἐχθρῶν ἡμῶν 'from our enemies'. GNT reads ἐκ χειρὸς ἐχθρῶν 'from (the) hand of enemies' with a B decision, indicating that the text is almost certain. Either ἐκ χειρὸς ἐχθρῶν 'from (the) hand of enemies' or ἐκ χειρὸς τῶν ἐχθρῶν ἡμῶν 'from (the) hand of our enemies' would probably be translated 'from the hand of our enemies' by many versions.

TEXT—In 1:75, instead of πάσαις ταῖς ἡμέραις ἡμῶν 'all our days', some manuscripts read πάσαις ταῖς ἡμέραις τῆς ζωῆς ἡμῶν 'all the days of our life'. GNT does not mention this variant.

LEXICON—a. aorist act. infin. of δίδωμι (LN **13.142**) (BAGD p. 45): 'to allow' [BAGD, **LN**], 'to grant' [AB, Arn, BAGD, BECNT, LN, NTC, WBC; KJV, NASB, NET, NRSV], 'to give' [Lns; HCSB], not explicit [CEV, GW, NCV, NIV, NLT, REB, TEV]. This means to grant someone the opportunity to do something [LN]. It is God who allows this, not Abraham [TH].

b. pres. act. infin. of λατρεύω (LN 53.14) (BAGD p. 467): 'to serve' [Arn, BAGD, BECNT, Lns, NTC; all versions except REB], 'to worship' [AB, LN, WBC; REB]. This means to carry out religious duties [BAGD], to perform religious rites in worship [LN]. It is not just service performed in a temple, but it means the total service a person gives to God [AB, BECNT]. The emphasis of this word is on living one's whole life in dedication to God [WBC]. This verb means to worship and adore God, and the attitude that accompanies this is indicated in the following phrase [TH]. They can do this fearlessly, that is, without fear that their enemies will persecute them because of their worship [TG]. See this word at 2:37 and 4:8.

QUESTION—How is 1:73 related to the preceding verse?
1. This verse further defines the holy covenant (1:72) as being God's oath which he swore to Abraham [AB, Crd, Gdt, My, NIGTC, TH; GW, NET, NLT, REB]. That oath is found in Genesis 22:16–18 [AB, ICC, NAC, NIGTC, NTC, TH] and 26:3 [NIGTC, TH]. The specific oath is here understood in spiritual terms [NIGTC].

2. This adds another thing that God remembered [AB, Lns]: to remember his holy covenant and also the oath he swore to Abraham. As God remembered the covenant, he naturally remembered the oath with which he sealed that covenant [Lns]. The oath is referred to in a broad sense since it is not the promise of land but the promise of deliverance from enemies for the continual worship of God [AB].

QUESTION—At the end of 1:73, what is the function of the articular infinitive phrase τοῦ δοῦναι ἡμῖν 'the to allow us'?

1. It indicates the content of the oath (1:73) [AB, Arn, ICC, NAC, NIGTC, TH, WBC; CEV, GW, NCV, NET]: he swore an oath *to the effect that* he would allow us to serve him fearlessly.
2. It indicates the purpose of giving the oath [BECNT, My]: he swore an oath *in order to* allow us to serve him fearlessly.
3. It indicates God's purpose for redemption and salvation in 1:68–71 [Gdt, MGC, NIC, NTC]: God brought about redemption *in order to* allow us to serve him fearlessly.
4. It indicates God's purpose in remembering the covenant and oath [Lns]: he remembered the covenant and oath *in order to* allow us to serve him fearlessly.

QUESTION—In 1:74, what relationship is indicated by the use of the participial phrase 'having been delivered from the hand of our enemies'?

It is the first step of the oath that leads to serving God fearlessly [Gdt, Lns, NTC, TG, TH; CEV, GW, NCV, NIV, NLT, TEV]: he told our ancestors that he would rescue us from our enemies' power *and then* [Gdt, NTC, TG; CEV, NIV, TEV], or *so that* [Lns, TH; GW, NCV, NLT], we could serve him fearlessly. The act of serving God *fearlessly* logically follows from being delivered from the power of our enemies [NTC] and *fearlessly* refers to not being afraid that our enemies would persecute us for worshipping God [TG]. This participial clause is not an end in itself but is done to make it possible for us to serve the Lord without fear of our enemies [BECNT, TH]. The reference to 'fearlessly' is emphatic in this sentence [AB, BECNT, NAC; NET]. Another view is that the phrase is parenthetic and reiterates the negative description of salvation in 1:71 [WBC].

QUESTION—How are the qualities of holiness and righteousness related?

Holiness indicates their relationship to God, and righteousness is their relationship to people [EGT, MGC, NIGTC, Rb, TH]. Holiness is being dedicated to God and righteousness is obeying God's will [TH]. Holiness is a negative quality, that of the absence of stain, and righteousness is a positive quality, that of religious and moral virtues that make worship acceptable to God [Gdt]. Holiness is being separated from sin and being devoted to God, while righteousness is the devotion that is approved by God [Lns].

QUESTION—How is 'before him' in 1:75 connected?

1. It modifies the verb 'to serve' in 1:74 [AB, BECNT, ICC, Lns, NTC, TG, WBC; REB; probably CEV, GW, HCSB, NLT which do not translate

'before him']: to allow us to serve him in his presence. Because of the earlier 'him' in the phrase 'to serve him', it does not easily connect with it, so it can be translated as a separate phrase: 'to worship him in holiness and righteousness—in his presence all our days' [WBC]. They are to worship God with the realization that all service is done before him [BECNT].
2. It is connected with the phrase 'in holiness and righteousness' [Arn, TH; KJV, NASB, NCV, NET, NRSV, TEV]: to serve him in a state of holiness and righteousness before him.

1:76 And now you, child, will-be-called[a] a-prophet of-(the) Most-High.[b] Because you-will-go-on-before[c] before (the) Lord to-prepare his roads,[d]

TEXT—Instead of καὶ σὺ δέ 'and now you', some manuscripts read καὶ σύ 'and you', although GNT does not mention this variant. Καὶ σύ 'and you' is read by EGT, Gdt, and KJV.

TEXT—Instead of ἐνώπιον κυρίου 'before (the) Lord', some manuscripts read πρὸ προσώπου κυρίου 'before (the) face of (the) Lord'. GNT does not mention this variant. Πρὸ προσώπου κυρίου 'before (the) face of (the) Lord' is read by KJV.

LEXICON—a. fut. pass. indic. of καλέω (LN 33.131) (BAGD 1.a.δ. p. 399): 'to be called'. The clause 'you will be called a prophet' [Arn, Lns, NTC; CEV, GW, HCSB, KJV, NCV, NIV, NLT, TEV] is also translated 'you will be called the prophet' [NASB, NET, NRSV], 'you will be hailed as the prophet' [AB], 'you will be called Prophet (of the Most High) [BECNT, WBC; REB]'. See this verb at 1:32, 35.
  b. ὕψιστος (LN 12.4) (BAGD 2. p. 850): 'most high' [BAGD, LN]. See this word at 1:32, 35; 6:35; 8:28.
  c. fut. mid. (deponent = act.) indic. of προπορεύομαι (LN **15.143**) (BAGD p. 709): 'to go on before' [BAGD, **LN**], 'to go in front of, to precede' [LN]. The phrase 'to go on before' is translated 'to go on before' [NASB, NIV], 'to go ahead of' [CEV, GW, TEV], 'to go before' [AB, Arn, BECNT, Lns, NTC, WBC; HCSB, KJV, NCV, NET, NRSV], 'to be (the Lord's) forerunner' [REB], not explicit [NLT]. This verb is similar to the one in the angel's announcement in 1:17, 'he will precede before him in the spirit and power of Elijah' where the verb προέρχομαι has a *temporal* meaning of 'to precede, to go prior to some other person, to go beforehand' [LN (15.141)]. Here the verb has a *spatial* meaning of 'to move ahead of someone' [LN (15.143)]. He will go as a messenger to announce that the Lord is coming to save them [TG]. Or, this verb may be considered to be equivalent to the verb in 1:17 [TH].
  d. ὁδός (LN 1.99) (BAGD 1.a. p. 554): 'road, way' [BAGD, LN]. The phrase 'to prepare his roads' is translated 'to prepare his road for him' [TEV], 'to prepare his ways' [Arn, BECNT, Lns, WBC; HCSB, KJV, NASB, NET, NRSV], 'to prepare his way' [AB; GW, NCV, REB], 'to prepare the way for him' [NIV, NLT], 'to get everything ready for him'

[CEV]. Some translate the plural 'roads' as singular, 'road', but the plural form suggests that there are many elements included in that salvation [NET]. See this word at 3:4.

QUESTION—How is the beginning phrase καί δέ 'and now' to be understood?

Here the style of the hymn changes [NIGTC]. The long Greek sentence of 1:68–75 has ended and a new part of the hymn begins with a change from the previous aorist tenses to future tenses [AB, NAC], and with a shift of person from 'us' to 'you' [NICNT]. The καί indicates a change from the Lord's grace in sending the Messiah to John's work as a forerunner so that there is a contrast: 'but you also, child' [ICC]. The καί 'and' expresses a continuation, since John's work is not to be separated from the prophecies of the Messiah, and δέ 'now' shows the transition from the hymn to this last part directed specifically to John whose birth was the occasion for the hymn [TH]. The conjunction καί 'and' indicates an addition and δέ means that what is added is somewhat different, so this is translated 'and now' [Lns]. Some follow the alternate Greek text which lacks δέ 'now' [EGT, Gdt]. The phrase is translated 'and now' [Lns], 'and' [NTC; KJV, NET, NIV, NLT, NRSV, REB], 'now' [AB; NCV], not explicit [BECNT, WBC; CEV, GW, TEV].

QUESTION—What relationship is indicated by γάρ 'because'?

This indicates the reason why this child will have the title 'a prophet of the Most High' [Lns, NAC, NIGTC; KJV, NASB, NET, NIV, NLT, NRSV, REB].

QUESTION—Does 'Lord' refer to God as do most of the references in this chapter, or does it refer to Christ?

Although Christian readers would take 'Lord' to refer to Jesus, it is not clear whether Zechariah was thinking of God or of the Messiah (as Elizabeth did in 1:43) [NIGTC]. This may be a fortunate ambiguity [WBC].

1. It refers to the Lord God [BECNT, EGT, Lns, TG]. God is coming to save them [TG]. Throughout this chapter 'Lord' is the Greek word for Yahweh, so John is to go before Yahweh. However, the idea is that Yahweh comes to his people in the person of Jesus [Lns]. Salvation is tied to the Messiah, so when the Messiah comes, God comes [BECNT].
2. It refers to the Lord Christ [AB, Gdt, NAC, NICNT]. In the light of 1:43, 3:4, and 7:27, along with John's role as a forerunner, this is a reference to Jesus [NAC]. Since this book has been composed after Jesus' ministry, it is likely that 'Lord' was intended to refer to Jesus, and John's role as Jesus' forerunner is clear [AB]. There has been a subtle shift from a reference to Yahweh so that God's visitation is understood to be in the form of the coming Messiah. However, this identification was unknown to the characters in the account and so it is a title for Jesus only in the assessment of Luke [NICNT].

QUESTION—What is meant by the metaphor of preparing the Lord's roads?

The picture is that of preparing for a visit by a king by putting the roads in order so that it will make travel easy for him [Lns]. It refers to fixing up existing, but impassable, roads so that the Lord may come along them [TH]. The roads are those over which the Lord will come in order to bestow salvation [NTC]. The figure means to do what is necessary to make it possible for God to come to his people [TG]. This refers to a call to conversion and faith in Jesus as the Messiah [NTC].

1:77 to-give to-his people (the) knowledge of-salvation in/by (the) forgiveness of-their sins,

QUESTION—How is this verse connected to what precedes it?
1. It explains what is involved in 'preparing his roads' [Lns, NAC, NIC, NIGTC, NTC, TH, TNTC]: you will go on before the Lord to prepare his roads, *that is,* to give his people the knowledge of salvation. The preparation is accomplished by giving his people the knowledge of salvation [NIGTC].
2. This gives the second purpose of going on before the Lord [EGT, Gdt, ICC, Rb]: you will go on before the Lord in order to prepare his roads and *in order to* give his people the knowledge of salvation.

QUESTION—What relationship is indicated by ἐν 'in/by'?
1. It means 'in' and specifies what salvation consists of [BECNT, EGT, Gdt, ICC, NAC, NIGTC, TH, TNTC]: to give the knowledge of salvation, a salvation consisting in the forgiveness of their sins. Salvation is equated with forgiveness [TH]. Forgiveness of sins defines salvation [NAC].
2. It means 'by' and indicates the means of obtaining salvation [BNTC, NTC, TG; CEV, GW, HCSB, NCV, NLT, TEV]: to give the knowledge of salvation *which is obtained by* the forgiveness of their sins. John will tell people that they can be saved when their sins are forgiven [CEV]. They are saved through the forgiveness of their sins [GW]. Probably those which translate 'by/through forgiveness of sins' [KJV, NASB, NET, NIV, NRSV, REB] are in support of this interpretation, although some possibly could be in support of the next interpretation.
3. It means 'by' and indicates the means by which God will make salvation known [Arn, Crd, Lns]: by means of the forgiveness of sin he will give the knowledge of salvation. God's objective act of forgiving sin results in the subjective knowledge of salvation, that is, without having one's sins forgiven, no one can really know what salvation is [Lns]. John will make known the salvation that results from preaching the forgiveness of sins [Crd].

1:78 because-of (the) bowels[a] of-mercy of-our God, with which (the) rising[b] from on-high will-visit us,

TEXT—Instead of the future tense ἐπισκέψεται 'will visit', some manuscripts read the aorist tense ἐπεσκέψατο 'has visited'. GNT reads ἐπισκέψεται 'will visit' with a B decision, indicating that the text is almost certain. Ἐπεσκέψατο 'has visited' is read by Gdt, My, and KJV.

LEXICON—a. σπλάγχνα (LN 25.49) (BAGD 1.b. p. 763): 'bowels' [Lns], 'heart' [BAGD], 'compassion' [BAGD, LN]. Literally 'entrails', this word is used figuratively like the English word 'heart' to refer to the seat of the emotions, the source of love, sympathy, and mercy [BAGD]. The phrase σπλάγχνα ἐλέους 'bowels of mercy' is translated 'tender mercy' [Arn; KJV, NASB, NET, NIV, NLT, NRSV], 'tender mercies' [WBC], 'deep tender mercy' [BECNT], 'loving mercy' [NCV], 'tender compassion' [REB], 'merciful compassion' [AB; HCSB], 'love and kindness' [CEV], 'the merciful heart' [NTC]. These nouns are also translated as adjectives: '(God is) loving and merciful' [GW], '(God is) merciful and tender' [TEV]. The genitive construction 'a heart of mercy' means 'a merciful heart' [ICC].

b. ἀνατολή (LN 15.104, 14.42) (BAGD 3. p. 62): 'rising' [BAGD]. It refers especially to the upward movement of the sun, stars, or clouds [LN (15.104)]. The phrase 'the rising from on high will visit us' is idiomatic and is translated 'the dawn will break upon us from on high' [NET], 'the dawn from on high will break upon us' [NRSV], 'the dawn from heaven will break upon us' [REB], 'there will come upon us the dawn from on high' [Arn], 'the dawn from on high shall look upon us' [Lns], 'the Dawn from on High will take note of us' [AB], 'the Dawn from on high will visit us' [HCSB], 'the rising sun will come to us from heaven' [NIV], 'the rising sun from on high will visit us' [BECNT], 'the Sunrise from on high' [NASB], 'he will visit us: a sunrise out of heaven' [WBC], 'the Rising Sun will visit us from on high' [NTC], 'the light from heaven is about to break upon us' [NLT], 'the dayspring from on high' [KJV], 'a new day will dawn on us from above' [GW], 'a new day from heaven will dawn on us' [NCV], 'will shine upon us like the sun that rises in the sky' [CEV], 'he will cause the bright dawn of salvation to rise on us' [TEV].

QUESTION—What relationship is indicated by διά 'because of'?

1. It indicates the reason for the forgiveness of sins [Gdt, Lns, My, TG, TH]: the forgiveness of sins *because of* the tender mercies of our God.
2. It indicates the reason for giving the knowledge of salvation (1:77) [EGT, NAC, NIGTC, NTC, TNTC]: to give the knowledge of salvation by the forgiveness of sins *because of* the tender mercies of God.
3. It indicates the reason for the preceding sentence (1:76b–77) [BECNT, ICC, NICNT, WBC]. Some take it as being the reason for the main verb: 'you will go before the Lord…*because of* the tender mercies of our God' [ICC, WBC]. Since all of the above relationships are interrelated, some regard God's mercy as the reason for all the actions included above [BECNT, NICNT].
4. It indicates the reason for the following clause [GW, NET, NLT, NRSV]: *because of* the tender mercies of our God, the dawn from on high will visit us.
5. Only a loose connection can be found and there is no definite connection expressed [AB].

74 LUKE 1:78

QUESTION—What is meant by the figurative language of the rising from on high visiting us?

'Rising' is taken to refer to a light, and, by metonymy [NIGTC], to the rising sun [BECNT, Crd, Gdt, Lns, NIC, NIGTC, NTC, Su, TG, TH, TNTC, WBC; CEV, NASB, NIV; probably GW, NET, NRSV, REB, TEV which translate this as the rising of the dawn]. The picture is not exact since the sun does not rise from on high, so 'the rising' or 'the Sun' refers to the Messiah who comes from heaven [BECNT, Lns, MGC, NAC, NIC, NICNT, NTC, Su, TH, WBC]. As in 24:49, 'from on high' refers to heaven [AB]. Or, instead of referring to Christ, it refers to God's plan of salvation [Arn].

1:79 to-shine-on[a] those sitting in darkness and (in the) shadow of-death, to-direct our feet into (the) way of-peace.

LEXICON—a. aorist act. infin. of ἐπιφαίνω (LN **14.39**) (BAGD 1.b. p. 304): 'to shine on/upon' [AB, Arn, BECNT, **LN**, Lns, NTC, WBC; CEV, HCSB, NASB, NCV, NIV, REB, TEV], 'to illuminate' [LN], 'to give light to' [GW, KJV, NET, NLT, NRSV], 'to appear, to show itself' [BAGD]. Here 'to appear' is used in the metaphor as 'to shine forth, to give light' [TH].

QUESTION—What is meant by the phrase 'to shine on those sitting in darkness and in the shadow of death'

The Dawn from on High will illuminate the sinners referred to in 1:77, the people who sit in darkness and in the shadow of death [AB]. The light that shines on them refers to the Messiah's presence, teaching, and deeds of mercy and power which would change people from being filled with gloom and despair to being filled with the joy of salvation [NTC]. Darkness is intensified by the phrase 'the shadow of death' and this describes the hopelessness and despair caused by death which enveloped the people [Lns]. Darkness is a metaphor for a difficult situation that has no solution in sight [TH]. The darkness refers to the delusion, depravity, and despondency of people who have no human help in sight [NTC]. Humans are pictured as being locked up in ignorance while being on the edge of death and needing release and forgiveness, and shining refers to the coming of the Messiah to teach and minister to them [BECNT]. This verse continues the picture of the rising sun in 1:78 [NAC]. Both 'to shine on' and 'to direct' explain the mission of the Messiah and the purpose for his coming [BECNT, Lns, NTC, TG].

QUESTION—What is meant by directing our feet into the way of peace?

'To direct our feet' continues the imagery of the light [WBC]. The people who do not know God's way will find that the Messiah is a light by which they can see the road [BECNT]. By saying 'our feet' Zechariah shows that he regards himself to be one those sinners [AB, BECNT]. Salvation is described as peace, the OT idea of a person's total well-being that results from being in harmony with God [BECNT]. Here peace means spiritual prosperity, wholeness, and salvation, and this is the salvation that God's

Messiah will bring [TG]. This peace is reconciliation with God with the resulting comforting assurance of forgiveness and being adopted by God [NTC]. Peace calms our hearts and causes us to be strong to live for God [NTC]. This peace is described in 1:71, 74–75 [TH].

DISCOURSE UNIT: 1:80 [NICNT]. The topic is the growth of the child.

1:80 And (the) child was-growing and was-being-strengthened[a] in-spirit/Spirit, and he-was in the deserts[b] until (the) day of-his manifestation[c] to Israel.

LEXICON—a. imperf. pass. indic. of κραταιόω (LN 23.134) (BAGD p. 448): 'to be strengthened' [BECNT], 'to become strong' [AB, BAGD, LN, NTC, WBC; NASB, NCV, NET, NIV, NLT, NRSV, REB], 'to gain strength' [Lns], 'to wax strong' [Arn; KJV]. The phrase 'was being strengthened in spirit' is translated 'he became spiritually strong' [GW, HCSB], 'he developed in spirit' [TEV], 'God's Spirit gave him great power' [CEV].

b. ἔρημος (LN 1.86) (BAGD 2. p. 309): This plural form is translated 'deserts' [KJV, NASB], 'desert regions' [Lns, NTC], 'desert' [AB, BAGD, BECNT, LN; CEV, GW, NCV, NIV, TEV], 'wilderness areas' [WBC], 'wilderness' [Arn, BAGD, LN; HCSB, NET, NLT, NRSV, REB], 'lonely place' [LN]. This refers to a region that has sparse vegetation and is mostly uninhabited [LN]. It is in contrast with cultivated and inhabited country [BAGD]. These lonely places were not far from his home and he visited them frequently as a child and then constantly lived in them during his manhood [EGT]. The plural form 'deserts' does not refer to several places; it is an abstract plural that refers to one general location [BECNT] and is best translated in the singular [AB, BAGD, BECNT, LN, NIGTC; CEV, GW, NCV, NET, NIV, NRSV, REB, TEV]. Or, some take it to mean various desert places [EGT, Gdt, Lns, NTC, WBC; KJV, NASB]. See this word at 3:2; 4:1.

c. ἀνάδειξις (LN **28.54**) (BAGD p.53): 'manifestation' [BAGD, WBC], 'revelation' [LN], 'appearing' [BECNT], 'public appearance' [NTC; HCSB, NASB], 'showing' [KJV], 'presentation' [Lns], 'commissioning' [BAGD]. The phrase 'his manifestation' is translated 'he was manifested' [AB], 'his being manifested' [Arn], 'he was revealed' [NET], 'he appeared' [GW], 'he appeared publicly' [NIV, NRSV, REB, TEV], 'he made himself known' [**LN**], 'he began his public ministry' [NLT], 'he came out to preach' [NCV], 'he was sent' [CEV]. This was when God presented John to Israel for his work [Lns]. It refers to the beginning of his public ministry [TG], when God installed John into his office [Gdt]. John announced his inauguration into his office by manifesting himself to the people at God's command [ICC, My].

76 LUKE 1:80

QUESTION—What is meant by John 'being strengthened in spirit/Spirit'?
1. This refers to John's spirit and describes his spiritual development [Arn, EGT, Gdt, TG; all versions except CEV]. It refers to his religious, moral, and intellectual development [Gdt].
2. This refers to the Holy Spirit and tells the source of his strength [NICNT; CEV]. John was filled with the Holy Spirit from the time he was born and the Spirit fashioned John's life before God and prepared him for his prophetic ministry [NICNT].

DISCOURSE UNIT: 2:1–52 [NAC]. The topic is the birth of Jesus.

DISCOURSE UNIT: 2:1–21 [WBC]. The topic is the birth, circumcision, and naming of Jesus.

DISCOURSE UNIT: 2:1–20 [AB, NAC, NICNT, NIGTC; NASB]. The topic is the birth of Jesus [AB, NAC, NICNT, NIGTC], Jesus' birth in Bethlehem [NASB].

DISCOURSE UNIT: 2:1–7 [BECNT, NICNT, Su, TNTC; CEV, GW, HCSB, NCV, NET, NIV, NLT, NRSV, TEV]. The topic is the birth of Jesus [BECNT, NICNT, Su, TNTC; CEV, GW, HCSB, NCV, NIV, NLT, NRSV, TEV], the census and the birth of Jesus [NET].

2:1 And it-happened in those days a-decree was-sent-out from Caesar[a] Augustus to-register all the world. **2:2** This was (the) first census (while) Quirinius was-governor of-Syria.

LEXICON—a. Καῖσαρ (LN 93.208) (BAGD p. 396): 'Caesar' [AB, BAGD, BECNT, LN (93.208), Lns, NTC, WBC; HCSB, KJV, NASB], 'Emperor' [Arn; CEV, GW, NCV, NET, NIV, NRSV, TEV], 'the emperor' [REB], 'the Roman emperor' [NLT]. This Greek form is derived from the Latin word that was used both as a name and as a title for a Roman emperor [LN]. 'Caesar' was originally the proper name of Caesar Augustus, but later it was used as a title with the meaning Emperor, such as 'Emperor Tiberius' in 3:1 [BAGD]. Here it is a part of his name [TH].

QUESTION—What does 'those days' refer to?
The preceding chapter told of John's birth and ended at 1:80 with a one-sentence summary of John's growth until his public appearance. Now the narrative turns back to the period of time before 1:80. Some focus on the time of John's birth [EGT, Gdt, ICC, My, NIGTC, TG], or more exactly, about six months after John's birth [Crd]. Others focus on the days of Herod (1:5) [AB, NTC, TH], and also to all the other events related before 1:80 [EGT]. The reference covers the time it took to issue the decree in Rome until it reached Palestine and was carried out [Lns].

QUESTION—What was the purpose of registering the people?
People were required to register for a census (2:2), and this census would be used as a basis for collecting taxes [AB, Arn, BECNT, Crd, EGT, Gdt, Lns, My, NAC, NICNT, NIGTC, NTC, Rb, Su, TG, TH, WBC]. This journey

was for the purpose of registering for the tax, not paying it [Su]. Jews would not be registering for military service as was done in other countries [BECNT, NAC, NICNT].

QUESTION—How could 'all the world' register?

The expression is an exaggerated description used to refer to the whole Roman empire [Arn, BECNT, Crd, EGT, ICC, My, NIC, NIGTC, NTC, Su, TG, TH, WBC; NET]. To the Romans, their empire was the entire world and they considered the other parts of the earth to be relatively unimportant [Su]. 'All the world' is also translated 'all the people' [CEV], 'all the inhabited earth' [NASB], 'the Roman Empire' [GW], 'throughout the Roman Empire' [NLT, TEV], 'all the empire' [NET], 'the entire Roman world' [NIV], 'all the people in the countries under Roman rule' [NCV].

QUESTION—Why is this called the 'first' census?

1. It is called the first census since there had been none before it [AB, BAGD (1.b. p. 725), Lns, TH; REB]: this was the first time there was a census taken in Judea. 'First' looks back to when there was none at all and does not look forward to an additional census [BAGD]. Nothing like this had ever been decreed before [Lns].
2. It is called the first census to distinguish it from following censuses [BECNT, ICC, My, NIC, NTC, Rb, Su]: this was the first of the censuses that took place. The emperor ordered a regular system of censuses that would occur at equal intervals and this was the first of them [NTC]. It was the first of at least two censuses decreed by Quirinius [BECNT]. It is distinguished from the enrollment that took place in A.D. 6 that is mentioned in Acts 5:37 [ICC, My, Rb, Su, WBC].

2:3 And everyone was-traveling to-register, each to his-own city.

QUESTION—What is meant by a person's 'own city'?

1. His 'own city' means the home town of his most important ancestor [Arn, BECNT, ICC, Lns, NAC, NTC, Rb, WBC]. For Joseph, a descendant of David, it was Bethlehem where David had been born and brought up [Arn, BECNT]. Each man had to go to the town where his family register was kept [Lns, Rb, WBC], and this was regarded as his native town no matter where he was then living [Lns, Su].
2. Since 2:39 says that Joseph and Mary's own city was Nazareth, and it was unlikely that everyone had to return to their ancestral homes, it can be presumed that Joseph had some property in Bethlehem [NIGTC]. It does not necessarily mean the town where one was born, because someone could have a claim to property in another town [TH].

QUESTION—Did everyone have to travel to his own city?

This refers to everyone in Palestine, not everyone in the whole world [EGT]. 'Everyone' is used as a hyperbole [NAC]. It means all the people concerned, not every individual [TH]. This was unusual for a Roman census, but it would fit in with Jewish customs [Arn, BECNT].

LUKE 2:4–5

2:4 **And Joseph also went-up[a] from Galilee from (the) city of-Nazareth to Judea to (the) city of-David which is-called Bethlehem, because he was of (the) house and lineage of-David, 2:5 to-register with Mary, the (one who) was-engaged to-him, being pregnant.**

TEXT—In 2:5, following αὐτῷ 'to him' some manuscripts add γυναικί 'wife'. GNT does not mention this variant. Γυναικί 'wife' is added by KJV so as to read 'his espoused wife'.

LEXICON—a. aorist act. indic. of ἀναβαίνω (LN 15.101) (BAGD 1.a.α. p. 50): 'to go up' [AB, Arn, BAGD, BECNT, LN, Lns, NTC, WBC; HCSB, KJV, NASB, NET, NIV, REB], 'to ascend' [LN], 'to go' [GW, NRSV, TEV], 'to leave...to go to' [CEV, NCV], 'to travel' [NLT]. Bethlehem is about 1,000 feet higher than Nazareth, but the trip of 63 miles involved descending as well ascending. The emphasis is more on going than on ascending [TH; CEV, NCV, NLT, NRSV, TEV]. The verb 'to go up' was often used for journeys [BECNT] and is used naturally here since their destination was much higher [AB].

QUESTION—Why was Bethlehem called the city of David?

In the OT, the city of David is Jerusalem (2 Sam. 5:7) [NAC, NIGTC, WBC]. However, here the 'city of David' does not mean the city where David lived as king, or the city that he ruled, but it refers to Bethlehem, the city where David was born [Arn, NIGTC, NTC, TG, WBC]. In 1 Samuel 20:6, Bethlehem is referred to as David's hometown and it can be assumed that Joseph's family records were kept here [NTC]. What is of greatest importance here is that Bethlehem is named in Micah 5:2 and linked to the messianic fulfillment of God's covenant with David's royal line [NIGTC, TH, WBC]. The city of David is also translated 'David's ancient home' [NLT], 'the birthplace of King David' [TEV], 'David had been born there' [GW], 'King David's hometown' [CEV].

QUESTION—What is the difference between 'house' and 'lineage'?

1. The two words are synonymous [BECNT, NAC, NIGTC, TG, TH, WBC; CEV, GW, NCV, NLT, TEV] and the combination emphasizes the concept [BECNT, TH]. This is translated 'he was from David's family' [CEV], 'he was from the family of David' [NCV], 'a descendant of David' [TEV], 'a descendant of King David' [GW, NLT].

2. 'House' is a generic term that is narrowed by the addition of 'lineage' [Gdt, NTC; REB]. 'House' refers to all those related to David, including his brothers and their direct descendants [Gdt]. This is translated 'he was of the house of David by descent' [REB].

QUESTION—Why did Mary go with Joseph?

1. The phrase 'with Mary' belongs with the main verb 'went up' and not with 'to register' [AB, Arn, BECNT, Gdt, MGC, NIBC, NIGTC, TH; CEV, NLT, REB]: Joseph went up to Bethlehem to register and he went with Mary. This does not explicitly say that Mary had to come to be registered, although that may have been the case [BECNT]. Nothing is known about women being required to register in a census [AB].

2. The phrase 'with Mary' belongs with the verb 'to register' [EGT, My, NTC, WBC; GW, HCSB, KJV, NASB, NCV; probably NET, NIV, NRSV, TEV]: Joseph went up to Bethlehem to register along with Mary. Mary also needed to be there to register herself [WBC]. Mary was also of the house of David and probably was required to register in person. Even if it wasn't required, Joseph wanted her to be with him when the baby was born [Lns].

2:6 And it-happened while they were there the days were-fulfilled[a] (for) her to-give-birth, **2:7** and she-bore her firstborn[b] son, and she-swaddled[c] him and laid him in a-manger,[d] because there-was not a-place for-them in the inn.[e]

LEXICON—a. aorist act. indic. of πίμπλημι (LN 67.70) (BAGD 1.b.β. p. 658): 'to be fulfilled'. See translations of this word at 1:57.
  b. πρωτότοκος (LN **10.43**) (BAGD 1. p. 726): 'firstborn' [AB, Arn, BAGD, BECNT, **LN**, Lns, WBC; all versions except NCV, NLT, TEV], 'first' [NCV, NLT, TEV]. Some translate 'firstborn' as an attribute to 'son' [AB, Arn, BECNT, Lns, TH; CEV, GW, KJV, NASB, NCV, NET, NLT, NRSV, TEV]: her firstborn son. Others emphasize it by translating it in apposition to 'son': 'a son, her firstborn' [WBC; REB], 'her firstborn, a son' [NIV].
  c. aorist act. indic. of σπαργανόω (LN **49.6**) (BAGD p. 761): 'to swaddle', 'to wrap up in swaddling cloths' [BAGD], 'to wrap in swaddling clothes' [Arn, WBC; KJV, REB], 'to wrap in swathing clothes' [Lns], 'to wrap in cloths' [**LN**; NASB, NIV, TEV], 'to wrap snugly in cloth' [HCSB]. 'to wrap in strips of cloth' [GW, NET], 'to wrap snugly in strips of cloth' [NLT], 'to wrap in bands of cloth' [NRSV], 'to wrap in cloth bands' [AB], 'to wrap with pieces of cloth' [NCV], 'to wrap up' [BECNT], 'to dress in baby clothes' [CEV]. Babies were wrapped with strips of cloth to keep their limbs straight [BECNT, NAC, NIGTC]. This is what any mother in Israel would have done and it does not indicate poverty [AB, NAC, Su, WBC].
  d. φάτνη (LN **6.137**) (BAGD p. 854): 'manger' [AB, Arn, BAGD, **LN**, Lns, WBC; all versions except CEV, HCSB, NCV], 'feed trough' [BECNT], 'feeding trough' [HCSB], 'box where animals are fed' [NCV], 'bed of hay' [CEV]. It would be a feeding trough for the animals [BECNT, BNTC, NAC, NIGTC, TG]. It was probably a movable trough placed on the ground [Crd].
  e. κατάλυμα (LN **7.11**) (BAGD p. 414): 'inn' [Arn, BAGD, LN; all versions except NLT], 'the village inn' [NLT], 'lodge' [AB], 'lodging' [WBC], 'stopping place' [Lns], 'guest room' [BECNT]. The word 'lodging' has a broad range and can refer to a room in a private house as well as a room in an inn [NIGTC].

QUESTION—What is the significance of describing Mary's son as 'firstborn'?
'Firstborn' merely looks backward and means that no other child had been born before this son [Lns]. Being firstborn does not necessarily imply that Mary later had other sons since the firstborn child could be an only child [Arn, ICC, NAC, NIGTC, Rb, Su, TG, WBC]. Or, it implies that Mary had other children later [Alf, BNTC, Gdt, ICC, MGC, NIC, NTC, Rb, Su, TG], and the Gospels name four other men as Jesus' brothers and also refer to his sisters [Su]. 'Firstborn' refers to Jesus having the inheritance rights of a firstborn son, including regal rights [AB, BECNT, Lns, MGC, NICNT, WBC]. As firstborn, Jesus would inherit his birthright so that he would be of the house of David as Joseph was [NICNT]. Describing the son as being the 'firstborn' prepares for the following account of the dedication of Jesus as the firstborn in 2:22–24 [AB, Gdt, NAC, NIGTC].

QUESTION—Why did they place Jesus in the manger?
Since there was no room in the inn, it is implied that they were lodging in the stable [Gdt] and used a manger of soft hay for the baby's bed [Su]. Most take the stable to be connected to a public inn [AB, Alf, EGT, Gdt, MGC, My, NTC, Rb, Su; all versions]. Another view is that since the word κατάλυμα for 'inn' refers to a guest room in 22:11, it probably means a guest room in a private home or some type of public shelter, and the animal room they were in would be a stable or a cave next to the building [BECNT]. The inn was probably a crude overnight lodging place for caravans, the one lodging place in Bethlehem. The reason they had to stay in the stable was not because of a lack of a hotel room, but because of a lack of a suitable place for Mary to give birth to her baby [NAC]. Joseph must have had some relative in town and the 'stopping place' would be that relative's small house and the only accommodation would be a shed built at the side or lower level of the house [Lns, NICNT].

DISCOURSE UNIT: 2:8–21 [BECNT; CEV, NCV, NET]. The topic is the shepherds [CEV], the shepherds' visit [NET], the shepherds hear about Jesus [NCV], the reaction to the birth [BECNT].

DISCOURSE UNIT: 2:8–20 [NICNT, Su, TNTC; GW, HCSB, NIV, NLT, NRSV, TEV]. The topic is the visit to the shepherds [Su], the shepherds and the angels [TNTC; HCSB, NIV, NLT, NRSV, TEV], the angelic message and the shepherds [NICNT], angels announce the birth of Jesus [GW].

2:8 **And shepherds were in the same region living-outdoors[a] and watching[b] watches (during) the night over their flock.**

LEXICON—a. pres. act. participle of ἀγραυλέω (LN **85.64**) (BAGD p. 13): 'to live outdoors' [AB, BAGD, BECNT], 'to remain outdoors' [LN], 'to stay out in the fields' [**LN**, WBC; HCSB, NASB], 'to be in the fields' [GW, NCV], 'to be out in the fields' [NET, NLT, REB], 'to live in the fields' [NRSV], 'to live in the open fields' [NTC], 'to live out in the fields' [NIC], 'to abide in the field' [KJV], 'to spend (the night) in the fields'

[TEV], 'to stay under the open sky' [Arn]. 'to camp in the open' [Lns], 'in the fields' [CEV].
  b. pres. act. participle of φυλάσσω (LN **37.119**) (BAGD 1.a. p. 868): 'to watch, to guard, to defend' [BAGD]. The idiom φυλάσσω φυλακάς 'to watch watches' is translated 'to watch' [LN; NCV], 'to keep watch' [AB, Arn, WBC; HCSB, KJV, NASB, NIV, NRSV, REB], 'to take turns watching' [GW], 'to guard' [BAGD, **LN**; CEV, NLT], 'to keep guard' [BECNT, Lns; NET], 'to take care of' [TEV]. This refers to guarding a flock in order to prevent robbers from stealing sheep or wild animals from harming them [Arn, BECNT, LN, NIGTC]. Shepherds who kept their flocks in the open had to take turns during the night to guard the sheep [AB, BECNT, NIGTC]. The plural 'watches' means that the shepherds watched in turns so that only one had to keep awake at a time [Gdt, ICC, Rb, WBC; GW].

QUESTION—What is the significance of the singular form 'their flock'?
  It cannot be determined whether all the shepherds worked for one owner of a flock or whether shepherds worked for several owners and had brought their flocks together to form one flock at that time [NTC]. They probably brought their separate flocks together in the open for the night [NIC].

2:9 And an-angel of-(the)-Lord appeared[a] to-them and (the) glory[b] of-(the)-Lord shone-around[c] them, and they-were-afraid[d] (with) a-great fear.

TEXT—Instead of καὶ ἄγγελος 'and an angel', some manuscripts read καὶ ἰδοὺ ἄγγελος 'and behold, an angel' and some version manuscripts read ἄγγελος 'an angel'. GNT reads καὶ ἄγγελος 'and an angel' with a B decision, indicating that the text is almost certain. Καὶ ἰδοὺ ἄγγελος 'and behold, an angel' is read by KJV.

LEXICON—a. aorist act. indic. of ἐφίστημι (LN 17.5, 85.13) (BAGD 1.a. 330): 'to appear (to)' [BAGD, WBC; NET, NIV, TEV], 'to appear (among)' [NLT], 'to suddenly appear (to)' [GW, REB], 'to stand (before)' [HCSB, NCV, NRSV], 'to suddenly stand (before)' [NASB], 'to stand (by)' [AB, BAGD, LN (17.5)], 'to stand (near)' [BECNT], 'to step up' [Arn], 'to approach' [BAGD], 'to be (near)' [LN (85.13)], 'to come (down to)' [CEV], 'to come (upon)' [Lns; KJV].
  b. δόξα (LN 14.49) (BAGD 1.a. p. 203): 'glory' [AB, Arn, BECNT, Lns, NTC, WBC; all versions except CEV], 'brightness' [BAGD, LN], 'radiance' [BAGD, LN], 'splendor' [BAGD], 'the brightness (of the Lord's) glory' [CEV]. At the same time the angel appeared, God manifested his presence with a heavenly brightness that flashed around them [NTC]. The glory of the Lord was a dazzling display of the splendor that is associated with his presence and it illuminated the area around the shepherds [WBC]. It was the bright Shekinah glory that indicated the majestic presence of God [Alf, BECNT, BNTC], and this glory accompanied God's angels when they appeared to people [Alf, BNTC]. It

82   LUKE 2:9

is a luminous manifestation of God's power that indicated God's presence [NICNT].
   c. aorist act. indic. of περιλάμπω (LN 14.44) (BAGD p. 648): 'to shine around' [BAGD, BECNT, LN, Lns, NTC, WBC; HCSB, KJV, NASB, NCV, NET, NIV, NRSV, REB], 'to shine over' [TEV], 'to shine about' [AB, Arn], 'to flash around' [CEV], 'to fill the area with light' [GW], 'the radiance surrounded' [NLT].
   d. aorist pass. indic. of φοβέω (LN 25.252) (BAGD 1.a. p. 862): 'to be afraid' [BAGD, BECNT, LN], 'to fear' [Lns]. The phrase 'to be afraid with a great fear' is translated 'to be very much afraid' [BAGD], 'to become greatly afraid' [Arn], 'to be sore afraid' [KJV], 'to be terrified' [GW, HCSB, NIV, NRSV, REB], 'to be absolutely terrified' [NET], 'to be frightened' [CEV], 'to be very frightened' [NCV], 'to be terribly frightened' [NTC; NASB, NLT, TEV], 'to be deeply frightened' [WBC], 'to be struck with great fear' [AB].
QUESTION—How did the angel appear to them?
   The angel suddenly appeared [BECNT, ICC, Lns, My, NTC, TH; GW, NASB, REB], but they did not see the angel as he was in the process of coming [NTC]. The idea of suddenness is not part of the meaning of the verb, but it comes from the context [BECNT, ICC, My]. Although many have understood this to mean that the angel was suspended in the air, the phrase 'went back into heaven' (1:15) may imply that he and all the other angels stood on the ground [TG].

2:10 And the angel said to-them, Do not be-afraid, for behold I-announce-good-news^a to/for-you of-great joy^b which will-be^c to-all the people,
LEXICON—a. pres. mid. indic. of εὐαγγελίζω (LN 33.215) (BAGD 1. p. 317): 'to announce good news'. See translations of this word at 1:10. This word also occurs at 2:10; 3:18; 4:18, 43; 7:22; 8:1; 9:6; 16:16; 20:1.
   b. χαρά (LN 25.124) (BAGD 2.a. p. 875): 'joy' [AB, Arn, BAGD, BECNT, NTC, WBC; all versions except CEV, GW], 'cause of joy, reason for gladness' [LN]. This noun is also translated as a verb phrase: 'to make happy' [CEV], 'to fill with joy' [GW]. This refers to an event that will cause joy [BAGD, LN].
   c. fut. mid. (deponent = act.) indic. of εἰμί (LN 13.104) (BAGD I.4. p. 223): 'to be' [LN, Lns, WBC; KJV, NASB, NCV, NIV], 'to happen' [LN]. The phrase 'of great joy which will be to all the people' is translated 'that brings great joy to all people' [NET], 'which will bring great joy to all the people' [TEV], 'of great joy, that is for all the people' [BECNT; HCSB], 'of great joy, which is intended for all people' [Arn], 'a cause for great joy among all the people' [AB], 'of great joy for everyone/all the people/the whole nation' [NLT, NRSV, REB], 'which will make everyone happy' [CEV], 'a message that will fill everyone with joy' [GW]. The word ἥτις 'which' means 'which is of a kind that' [WBC].

QUESTION—What relationship is indicated by the dative case of ὑμῖν 'you' following the verb 'I announce good news'?
    1. It indicates the indirect object of the verb [AB, Arn, BECNT, BNTC, Lns, NTC, TH, WBC; HCSB, KJV, NASB, NCV, NET, NIV, NLT, NRSV]: I announce good news *to you*, or, I bring *you* good news.
    2. It is translated to indicate those who benefit from the good news [CEV, GW, REB, TEV]: I announce good news *for you*.

2:11 **because/that for-you a-savior was-born today who is Messiah (the) Lord in (the) city of-David.**

TEXT—Instead of Χριστὸς κύριος 'Messiah (the) Lord', some manuscripts read Χριστὸς κυρίου 'Messiah of the Lord', and a few manuscripts read Χριστὸς Ἰησοῦς 'Messiah Jesus'. GNT reads Χριστὸς κύριος 'Messiah (the) Lord' with an A decision, indicating that the text is certain.

QUESTION—Does the relationship indicated by ὅτι mean 'because' or 'that'?
    1. It indicates the reason for great joy [BECNT, NTC, WBC; KJV, NASB]: great joy will be to all the people *because* a savior was born today. It not only explains why the message is the reason for great joy, but also why it is good news [BECNT].
    2. It indicates the content of the good news [AB, Arn, BNTC, Lns, NIGTC, TH; NET, NRSV; probably CEV, GW, HCSB, NCV, NIV, NLT, REB, TEV which begin a new sentence without expressing a relationship]: I bring you the good news…*that* a savior was born today. It indicates the content of the good news, but at the same time the contents indicate the reason for great joy [NIGTC].

QUESTION—What relationship is indicated by the dative case of ὑμῖν 'you' in the phrase 'for you a savior was born'?
    It is the dative of advantage [BECNT, NIGTC, TH; CEV, HCSB, NASB]: a savior was born *for you* today. The birth of the savior will benefit the shepherds and everyone else who hears of it [NIGTC]. It is translated '*your* Savior was born today' [GW, NCV, NET, TEV]. The dative is also translated '*to* you' [AB, Arn, NTC, WBC; NIV, NRSV, REB], '*unto* you' [KJV]. The Savior has been born for *you shepherds*, so that what is for all people (2:10) is also for these shepherds [BECNT]. Or, 'you' includes all the people mentioned in 2:11 [AB]. This is addressed to the shepherds, but the shepherds represent all the people who are concerned [NIGTC, TH].

QUESTION—What is meant by describing the savior with the two connected names 'Messiah Lord'?
    'Lord' is in apposition to 'Messiah' and this is translated 'Christ and Lord' [NIGTC, TNTC], 'Christ the Lord' [AB, Arn, BECNT, NIBC, NIC, NTC, WBC; CEV, GW, KJV, NASB, NCV, NET, NIV, TEV], 'the Messiah, the Lord' [AB; HCSB, NLT, NRSV, REB]. Jesus is both the Messiah and the Lord [NIGTC]. 'Lord' means ruler and this word would finally be used by Christians as a proper name for Jesus [Su]. This combination is used by Luke in Acts 2:36 where he says that God made Jesus both Messiah and Lord at

the resurrection [AB, Lns]. Jesus' full authority will not be fully realized until the resurrection (Acts 2:36) [NAC]. They are separate titles, not personal names, and 'Lord' does not represent the Hebrew *Yahweh*, but *Adonai* as in Micah 5:2 '*Yahweh* said to my *Adon*' [Lns]. Or, others take it to represent *Yahweh* [Alf, TNTC].

2:12 **And this (will be) the sign^a for-you, you-will-find an-infant (who) has-been-swaddled^b and lying in a-manger.**

LEXICON—a. σημεῖον (LN 33.477) (BAGD 1. p. 747): 'sign' [AB, Arn, BAGD, BECNT, LN, Lns, WBC; HCSB, KJV, NASB, NET, NIV, NRSV, REB]. The phrase 'this will be the sign' is translated 'this is how you will recognize him' [GW, NLT], 'this is how you will know him' [NCV], 'you will know who he is because…' [CEV], 'this is what will prove it to you' [TEV]. The word 'sign' refers to some event that is regarded to be of some special meaning [LN]. The circumstances served as a sign because it was unusual to find a baby lying in a manger [BECNT, Lns, NAC, NTC, Su]. The sign served to identify the child [Gdt, NAC, Su; CEV, GW, NCV, NLT]. Or, the sign served to prove the truth of what has been said about the birth of the child [Arn, ICC, TH]. Or, it was meant to serve in both ways [NIGTC].
  b. perf. pass. participle of σπαργανόω (LN 49.6): 'to be swaddled'. See this word at 2:7.

2:13 **And suddenly there-was with the angel a-multitude^a of-(the)-heavenly army^b praising God and saying,**

LEXICON—a. πλῆθος (LN 11.1) (BAGD 2.b.α. p. 668): 'multitude' [BAGD, LN, NTC, WBC; HCSB, KJV, NASB, NET, NRSV], 'vast multitude' [Arn], 'throng' [BAGD], 'great company' [NIV, REB], 'crowd' [BAGD, LN], 'host' [Lns], 'vast host' [NLT]. This noun is also translated as an adjective: 'large (army)' [GW], 'great (army)' [TEV], 'very large (group)' [NCV], 'many other (angels)' [CEV].
  b. στρατιά (LN 12.30) (BAGD 1. p. 770): 'army' [BAGD, Lns; NLT, TEV], 'host' [Arn, NTC, WBC; HCSB, KJV, NASB, NET, NIV, NRSV, REB]. The phrase στρατιὰ οὐράνιος 'heavenly army' is an idiom for a large group or throng of angels [LN] and is translated 'the armies of heaven' [NLT], 'the angels of heaven' [LN]. The phrase 'a multitude of the heavenly army' is translated 'a great army of heaven's angels' [TEV], 'a large army of angels' [GW], 'a very large group of angels from heaven' [NCV], 'many other angels came down from heaven' [CEV]. This is an army of angels [LN, Lns, NTC; CEV, GW, NCV, NLT, TEV]. The word 'army' is appropriate since angels are mighty spirits [Lns], and in the OT angels are presented as heavenly warriors [TG]. Or, the noun 'army' does not focus on its military aspect and 'heavenly army' may be translated as 'those from heaven' or 'inhabitants of heaven' [TH].

QUESTION—How are the two verbs related in the phrase 'praising God and saying'?

The word 'saying' introduces the words of their praise [TH]. The angels must have said the words of 2:14 in unison and those words show an artistic or poetic parallelism: glory–peace, God–people, and heaven–earth. 'Saying' may include speaking, shouting, singing, or chanting [NTC]. Versions usually stay with the Greek text: 'praising God and saying'. However one version specifies the manner of praising: 'praising God by saying' [GW]. Another version combines the two verbs into one: 'praising God' [NLT]. Three translations take 'saying' to mean singing: 'singing praise to God' [REB, TEV], 'praising God and singing' [AB]. According to tradition they sang their words [AB, Alf, BNTC, Crd, EGT, Gdt, NIGTC, Su; REB, TEV]. Most commentaries point out that the text does not specify the form in which the following words were uttered. The words of Mary and Zechariah in chapter 1 were also poetic and they did not sing their messages [Lns, Su]. It cannot be determined whether or not they sang the words of 2:14, but it appears that they shouted it to show their adoration [NTC]. Some refer to 2:14 as a song [Arn, NIGTC].

QUESTION—How is the multitude related to the army in the genitive construction 'a multitude of the heavenly army'?

1. This multitude was composed of a heavenly army [Lns; CEV, GW, NCV, NLT]: a multitude consisting of the heavenly army. The genitive is one of content [TH]. The army of angels in heaven is so vast that it is able to send out this multitude, 'a heavenly army host', composed of thousands of angels [Lns].
2. This was a multitude of angels who were a portion of the heavenly army [BECNT, ICC]: a multitude from the heavenly army. The genitive is partitive [BECNT, ICC], and indicates that this multitude is a select group that came from the entire army that serves God in heaven [BECNT]. Visible was a multitude which formed a part of the army, but the whole army of heaven was praising God [ICC].

2:14 Glory[a] in (the) highest[b] to-God and on earth peace[c] among[d] people of-goodwill/favor.[e]

TEXT—Instead of the genitive εὐδοκίας 'of goodwill', some manuscripts read the nominative εὐδοκία 'goodwill'. GNT reads the genitive εὐδοκίας 'of goodwill' with an A decision, indicating that the text is certain. The nominative form is followed by Gdt, Lns, and KJV.

LEXICON—a. δόξα (LN 33.357, 87.4) (BAGD 3. p. 204): 'glory' [AB, Arn, BECNT, Lns, NTC, WBC; all versions except CEV, NCV], 'honor' [BAGD, LN (87.4)], 'praise' [LN (33.357)]. This noun is also translated as a verb: 'to give glory' [NCV], 'to praise' [CEV]. It means to give honor to God [NET].

b. ὕψιστος (LN 1.13) (BAGD 1. p. 850): '(the) highest' [Arn, BAGD, NTC; KJV, NASB, NET, NIV], 'highest places' [Lns], '(the) world above'

[LN], 'heaven' [CEV, NCV], 'highest heaven' [AB, WBC; GW, HCSB, NLT, NRSV, REB, TEV], '(the) heavenly places' [BECNT]. The 'highest part' is a synonym for heaven [BECNT, TG, WBC].

c. εἰρήνη (LN 25.248) (BAGD 3. p. 227): 'peace' [AB, Arn, BAGD, BECNT, LN, Lns, NTC, WBC; all versions], 'freedom from worry' [LN].

d. ἐν (LN 83.9) (BAGD 4.a. p. 261): 'among' [Arn, BAGD, BECNT, LN, NTC, WBC; NASB, NCV, NET, NRSV], 'with' [LN], 'to' [CEV, GW, HCSB, NIV, NLT, REB, TEV], 'toward' [KJV], 'for' [AB], 'on' [Lns]. Peace is *in their midst* so that all of them enjoy this peace, not just some among them [Arn].

e. εὐδοκία (LN 25.88) (BAGD 1 or 2 p. 319): 'goodwill' [BAGD (1); GW, KJV], 'favor' [BAGD (2); NIV], 'good pleasure' [BAGD (2), BECNT, Lns, NTC], 'what pleases' [LN]. This noun is also translated as a verb with God as the subject: 'to be pleased' [BAGD (2); NASB, NET, TEV], 'to be well pleased'. [Arn], 'to favor' [AB, BAGD (2), WBC; HCSB, NLT, NRSV], 'to delight in' [REB]; or with people as the subject: 'to please (God)' [CEV, NCV].

QUESTION—Are there two or three poetic lines to what the angels say?

1. There are two lines [AB, Arn, BECNT, ICC, NAC, NIGTC, NTC, Su, TG, TH, TNTC, WBC; all versions except KJV]: Glory in (the) highest to God. / And peace on earth among people of goodwill/favor. There is a correspondence between three parts of each line: glory–peace, highest (heaven)–earth, and God–people [Gdt, ICC, NICNT].

2. There are three lines [Gdt, Lns; KJV]: Glory in (the) highest to God. / And peace on earth. / Good will/favor toward people. This interpretation is the result of following the text having the nominative form of 'peace' rather than the text having the genitive form. Three poetical lines stress the three nouns 'glory', 'peace', and 'goodwill' [Lns].

QUESTION—Does 'in the highest' connect directly with glory, praise, or God?

1. It connects with *praise* and 'in the highest' indicates where the praise is given [AB, BECNT, BNTC, Gdt, Lns, My, NTC, Su, TH]: let those in the highest heaven praise God. This best satisfies the parallelism with 'on earth' in the next clause [TH]. God is praised by the angels in heaven [My, Su]. The angels want all creation to praise God [NTC]. Another view is that the angels urge all people to praise God and this praise will reach heaven to glorify God [Gdt].

2. It is connected with *glory* and 'in the highest' indicates the location of God's glory [WBC]: 'there is glory for God in highest heaven'. This shows that heaven is impressed by the glory God has achieved [WBC].

3. It is connected with *God* and 'in the highest' indicates the location of God [NIGTC, TG]. The sentence is taken to refer to the glorious light that manifests God's majesty, just as God's glory was manifest with the appearance of the angels in 2:9 [NIGTC]: majestic glory belongs to God in heaven where he dwells. Or, it refers to praise [TG]: 'may God, who lives in the highest heaven, be praised'.

LUKE 2:14

QUESTION—What is meant by εἰρήνη 'peace'?
1. It is peace between God and people [BECNT, Gdt, Lns, TNTC]. It is the harmonious relationship between God and people that is provided by Jesus [BECNT]. People must accept this peace to enter into a new relationship with God, but whether this happens or not, Jesus is the one who provides this peace [Lns].
2. It is both peace with God and a peace of heart [Arn, NTC]. It is first being reconciled to God, and then having assurance that one has been reconciled [NTC].
3. It is a peace reflecting the meaning of the Hebrew word *shalom* [AB, BNTC, NAC, NICNT, NIGTC, TG, TH, WBC]. It is connected with the messianic salvation and concerns the whole social order, referring to well being, prosperity, security, and harmony [WBC]. It refers to all the blessings resulting from the coming of the Messiah [NIGTC]. It is the kind of peace referred to in 1:79 [TG, TH]. This is a synonym for salvation [NAC].

QUESTION—Who are the subjects and objects of 'goodwill' or 'favor' and how is this related to the people in the genitive construction ἀνθρώποις εὐδοκίας 'people of goodwill/favor'?
1. It means people who are the recipients of God's goodwill or favor [AB, Alf, BECNT, BNTC, Crd, EGT, Gdt, ICC, Lns, MGC, NAC, NIBC, NIC, NICNT, NIGTC, NTC, Su, TG, TH, TNTC, WBC; GW, HCSB, NIV, NLT, NRSV]: peace among those whom God favors. The angels are praising God, not men, and the people are those whom God has graciously chosen [NTC].
1.1 This specifies a portion from among all people [Alf, BECNT, EGT, NIGTC, WBC]. It implies that God has elected them and has extended his favor [Alf, BECNT, NIGTC, WBC]. Peace is not universal, but is extended only to those who will respond to Jesus' coming [BECNT]. The genitive form limits these people to those who are favored by God and this does not assert that God favors all [EGT].
1.2 This is applicable to all people [Lns, NICNT, TH]. As in 2:10, God wills that all be saved even though some will reject it [Lns]. It does not indicate a restriction, but emphasizes that God is the one who establishes peace [TH]. God favors the whole world with his mercy [NICNT].
2. It means people who please God [Arn, My; CEV, NASB, NCV, NET, REB, TEV]: peace among those with whom God is pleased. This indicates that only those who please God are to be objects of his favor [NET].

2:15 **And it-happened when the angels departed from them to heaven, the shepherds were-saying to one-another, Let-us-go up-to Bethlehem now and let-us-see this thing that has-happened which the Lord made-known to-us.**
2:16 **And they-went hastening and they-found both Mary and Joseph and the baby lying in the manger.**

QUESTION—In 2:15, what is the significance of the imperfect tense of ἐλάλουν 'they were saying'?

It marks repetition [BECNT, ICC, NTC, Rb, TH]: they *kept saying*. Or, it is inceptive [BNTC, Rb, WBC; NASB]: they *began saying*. Most translate this as an aorist [AB, Lns; all versions except NASB]: they *said*. The phrase 'to one another' indicates that the shepherds discussed the message they had heard and as a result of this discussion resolved to go to Bethlehem [BECNT].

QUESTION—In 2:15, what is the referent of 'this thing that has happened'?

The 'thing' is the angel's announcement, and by referring to that announcement as the thing 'which the Lord has made known to us' the shepherds indicate that the angel had been the messenger of the Lord, the ultimate source of the message [NAC, TH] and it means 'what God caused the angels to tell us' [TH]. 'Thing' refers to the thing about which the angel spoke [ICC], that the baby had been born that day [TG].

QUESTION—In 2:16, what relationship is indicated by the use of the aorist participle σπεύσαντες 'hastening'?

The participle is coincident with the aorist verb 'they went', meaning 'they went hastening' [Lns]. It qualifies the action of the main verb, meaning they went with haste or went quickly [TH], showing their eagerness to see the sign [WBC]. The focus is on their obedience rather than the speed [NAC]. It is equivalent to an adverb, 'hurriedly they went out' [BECNT]. It is translated 'they hurried off' [CEV, NET, NIV, REB, TEV], 'they went quickly' [GW, NCV], 'they came in a hurry' [NASB], 'they ran' [NLT]. One wonders what happened to the flock of sheep, but we can assume that the shepherds found a solution [NTC].

QUESTION—What was involved in finding the baby?

The use of 'found' implies a search had been made [ICC, Lns, My, NIGTC, Rb, TG, TH].

QUESTION—What is meant by the statement 'they found both Mary and Joseph and the baby lying in the manger'?

1. It is expressed as one group of three persons [BECNT, EGT, Gdt, Lns, NIGTC; GW, NCV, NIV]: they found Mary, Joseph, and the baby, who was lying in the manger. 'They found Mary and Joseph with the baby, who was lying in a manger' [GW]. All members of the family are seen together [BECNT].

2. It is expressed as two groups [AB, BNTC, NIGTC, NTC, TG, TH, WBC; HCSB, KJV, NASB, NET, NRSV, REB, TEV]: they found Mary and Joseph, and (they found/saw) the baby lying in the manger. This view is supported by the fact that 'lying in the manger' refers only to the baby

[NTC, TG, TH]. The sign concerned the baby and by mentioning the parents, it shows that the child was not abandoned or left alone [WBC].
3. It is expressed as one group of two persons followed by a separate clause [CEV, NLT]: they found Mary and Joseph; and the baby was lying in the manger.

2:17 **And having-seen (him/them/this) they-made-known**[a] **concerning the word (which) told them about this child.** **2:18** **And all the (ones who) heard were-amazed**[b] **about the (things) spoken to them by the shepherds.**
LEXICON—a. aorist act. indic. of γνωρίζω (LN 28.26) (BAGD 1. p. 163): 'to make known' [AB, BAGD, BECNT, LN, Lns, NTC, WBC; NASB, NRSV], 'to tell' [CEV, NCV, NLT, TEV], 'to relate' [NET, REB], 'to report' [HCSB], 'to speak of' [Arn], 'to repeat' [GW], 'to spread the word' [NIV], 'to make known abroad' [KJV].
b. aorist act. indic. of θαυμάζω (LN 25.213) (BAGD 1.a.α. p. 352): 'to be amazed'. See translations of this word at 1:21. This word also occurs at 1:63; 2:18; 4:22; 7:9; 11:14, 38; 20:26; 24:12, 41.
QUESTION—In 2:17, what is the object of the verb 'having seen'?
1. The object is the baby [BNTC, TG; CEV, GW, NCV, NIV, REB, TEV]: when they saw the baby.
2. The object is Mary, Joseph, and the baby [TH; HCSB]: when they saw them.
3. The object is 'this' [AB, Arn, BECNT, EGT, NTC, WBC; KJV, NASB, NRSV]: when they saw this. They saw the very situation the angels had described [Arn].
QUESTION—What is the indirect object of 'they made known'?
1. The indirect object is 'Mary and Joseph' [CEV, TEV]: they made known to Mary and Joseph.
2. The indirect object is people in general [AB, ICC, Lns, My, NTC, Rb, WBC; KJV, NIV]: they made known to everyone. That it means more than just Mary and Joseph is seen in 2:18, 'all who heard what the shepherds told them' [BECNT, NTC, TH]. This is translated 'they made known abroad' [KJV], 'they spread the word' [NIV]. It included everyone in the house as well [My, WBC]. They told Mary and Joseph and many other people in town [AB, ICC, NTC].
QUESTION—Who were the people who were amazed?
1. They were the ones to whom the shepherds made known the word [Arn, NTC, Su, WBC; CEV]: all who heard what the shepherds told them were amazed. This may refer to the people in town as the shepherds searched for the baby and the people at the inn [Su].
2. It may include subsequent hearers [ICC, TH; GW, NIV]: all who heard about what the shepherds had said were amazed.

2:19 But Mary was-keeping[a] all these things pondering[b] (them) in her heart. **2:20** And the shepherds returned glorifying[c] and praising[d] God for all that they-heard and saw just-as was-spoken to them.

LEXICON—a. imperf. act. indic. of συντηρέω (LN **29.1**) (BAGD 3. p. 792): 'to keep' [Arn; KJV], 'to keep in mind' [**LN**], 'to keep thinking about' [LN; CEV], 'to remember' [LN; TEV], 'to store up' [WBC], 'to treasure up' [BAGD, NTC; HCSB, NET, NIV, NRSV, REB], 'to treasure' [AB; GW, NASB, NCV], 'to quietly treasure' [NLT], 'to guard closely' [Lns], 'to ponder' [BECNT]. The imperfect tense indicates that this continued for a long time [ICC, Lns, Rb, Su, TH]. She guarded these things in her heart since they were so sacred and miraculous to her [Lns]. The verb refers to a continuing contemplation of the events that had taken place [BECNT]. What Mary treasured was the arrival of the shepherds and the things that they told her [AB], what the angel had told Joseph, what the angel had told her, her experiences in Bethlehem [NTC], and the miraculous conceptions of John and Jesus [NAC].

b. pres. act. participle of συμβάλλω (LN **30.7**) (BAGD 1.a.β. p. 777): 'to ponder' [Arn, BAGD, Lns; KJV, NASB, NIV, NRSV], 'to ponder over' [AB; REB], 'to consider' [BAGD], 'to think deeply about' [**LN**; TEV], 'to meditate on' [HCSB], 'to always think about' [GW], 'to continue to think about' [NCV], 'to often think about' [NLT], 'to mull over' [NTC], 'to reflect on' [LN], 'to ponder what something might mean' [NET], 'to wonder what something means' [CEV], 'to try to penetrate the significance of something' [WBC], 'to try to put things together' [BECNT]. This word describes the preceding verb more fully [BECNT]. It means to mull things over so as to discern how they come together as a meaningful whole [BECNT, NIGTC]. It means to think about all the things that had happened, comparing them, and letting one thing explain or add to another [Lns]. It indicates that Mary did not fully understand all the implications of what had happened [NAC]. This verb is circumstantial to the main verb 'keeping' and indicates that she was trying to hit on the right meaning of all these things [AB].

c. pres. act. participle of δοξάζω (LN **33.357**) (BAGD 1. p. 204): 'to glorify' [AB, Arn, BECNT, LN, Lns, NTC, WBC; all versions except CEV, NCV, TEV], 'to praise' [BAGD, LN; NCV], 'to honor, to magnify' [BAGD], 'to say wonderful things about (God)' [CEV]. It means to speak favorably of someone [LN]. The phrase 'glorifying and praising' is translated 'singing praises to' [TEV]. It means to verbally give honor to God for what he has done [BECNT].

d. pres. act. participle of αἰνέω (LN **33.354**) (BAGD p. 23): 'to praise' [AB, Arn, BAGD, BECNT, LN, Lns, NTC, WBC; all versions except NCV, TEV], 'to thank' [NCV]. See c. above for TEV. It means to speak about the excellence of someone [LN].

LUKE 2:19–20

QUESTION—In 2:19, what relationship is indicated by δέ 'but'?

It indicates contrast [AB, Arn, BECNT, Crd, EGT, Gdt, ICC, Lns, NTC, TH, TNTC; CEV, HCSB, KJV, NASB, NCV, NET, NIV, NLT, NRSV, REB]. Most seem to understand the contrast to be with all who heard (2:18) [BECNT, EGT, Gdt, ICC, TH]. The people were astonished, but Mary was not [ICC]. Or, all were amazed, but Mary was both amazed and also kept these things in her heart [Arn]. The amazement of the people was a passing emotion (aorist tense), but the pondering of Mary was a continuing habit (imperfect tense) [EGT]. Or, the contrast is with the shepherds [Crd, ICC, TNTC]: the shepherds made known the event that had taken place, but Mary silently reflected on them.

QUESTION—What is the distinction between 'glorifying' and 'praising'?

The combination 'glory and praise' is common in the OT [BECNT]. All of the versions except TEV keep both words in their translations. LN assigns both words to the general domain of 'praise' and separate them into separate sub-domains with slight differences of meaning: 'glorifying' means 'to speak of something as being unusually fine and deserving honor' (LN 33.357) while 'praising' means 'to speak of the excellence of a person' (LN 33.354). 'Glorifying' is the stronger of the two words [TH]. 'Praising' is the more definite word [ICC]. While 'glorifying' is connected with the greatness of what they heard and saw, 'praising' is connected with the goodness shown by what had occurred [Gdt].

QUESTION—What are the objects of 'heard' and 'saw'?

The shepherds had heard what the angels said [BECNT, Gdt, Lns, WBC]. They had seen the sign of the baby in the manger [Gdt, WBC]. Or, it refers to seeing everything that they had experienced in Bethlehem [BECNT, Lns].

QUESTION—Where did the shepherds return to?

The shepherds went back to their flocks [Lns, Su, TH]. The returned to their work of shepherding their sheep [MGC]. Or, they returned home [BECNT].

DISCOURSE UNIT: 2:21–40 [AB, NAC, NIGTC, TNTC]. The topic is the baby Jesus [TNTC], the presentation of Jesus in the temple [NIGTC; NIV], the circumcision and the prophets Simeon and Anna [NAC], the circumcision and manifestation of Jesus [AB].

DISCOURSE UNIT: 2:21–39 [NICNT, Su]. The topic is the presentation of Jesus in the temple [NICNT], the circumcision, naming, and dedication of Jesus as the Firstborn [Su].

DISCOURSE UNIT: 2:21–38 [NASB]. The topic is the presentation of Jesus in the temple.

DISCOURSE UNIT: 2:21–24 [NICNT; GW, HCSB, NLT]. The topic is the presentation of Jesus [NLT], the circumcision and presentation of Jesus [NICNT; HCSB], Jesus' parents obey Moses' teaching [GW].

DISCOURSE UNIT: 2:21 [NRSV, TEV]. The topic is the naming of Jesus. This verse is both a conclusion to the account of Jesus' birth and a transition between that and the account of the purification [BECNT].

2:21 **And when eight days were-completed (for) him to-be-circumcised his name was called Jesus, the (name) called by the angel before he was-conceived in the womb.**

TEXT—Instead of αὐτόν 'him' before 'to be circumcised', some manuscripts read τὸ παιδίον 'the child'. GNT does not mention this variant. Τὸ παιδίον 'the child' is read by KJV.

QUESTION—What is the significance of the eight days and the events of the circumcision and naming?

This is similar to 1:59 where it tells about the eight days before the circumcision and naming of John. The Jewish law required that a male baby should be circumcised on the eighth day after birth [Arn, BECNT, Gdt, NTC, TH]. It is translated 'after eight days had passed, it was time to circumcise the child; and he was called Jesus' [NRSV; similarly AB; NIV], 'a week later, when the time came for the baby to be circumcised, he was named Jesus' [TEV]. Not only was it the time for circumcision, it is implied that the ceremony actually took place [NTC, TH], and some show this in their translations: 'at the end of eight days, when he was circumcised, he was named Jesus' [NET; similarly NLT], 'eight days after his birth, the child was circumcised and named Jesus' [GW], 'when the baby was eight days old, he was circumcised and was named Jesus' [NCV]. The naming of the baby was part of the circumcision ceremony [Rb]. The emphasis of this verse is on naming the baby with the name given by the angel [BECNT, NAC, NIGTC, NTC, TH, TNTC].

DISCOURSE UNIT: 2:22–40 [BECNT, WBC; NET]. The topic is the presentation of Jesus in the temple and the meetings with Simeon and Anna [NET], the recognition of Jesus by Simeon and Anna [WBC], the witness of the man and the woman at the temple [BECNT].

DISCOURSE UNIT: 2:22–38 [NRSV, TEV]. The topic is the presentation of Jesus in the temple.

DISCOURSE UNIT: 2:22–24 [NCV]. The topic is the presentation of Jesus in the temple.

2:22 **And when the days were-completed for-their purification[a] according-to the law of-Moses, they-brought him to Jerusalem to-present[b] (him) to-the Lord,**

LEXICON—a. καθαρισμός (LN 53.28) (BAGD 1. p. 387): 'purification' [AB, BAGD, BECNT, LN, Lns, NTC, WBC; HCSB, KJV, NASB, NET, NIV, NRSV, REB], 'purification offering' [NLT], 'the ceremony of purification' [TEV], 'cleansing' [Arn], not explicit [CEV]. This noun is also translated as a verb phrase: 'to make clean' [GW], 'to be made pure'

[NCV]. This is a cleansing from ritual contamination or impurity [LN]. It means to restore ritual cleanness [TH].
- b. aorist act. infin. of παρίστημι (LN 57.81) (BAGD 1.b.α. p. 627): 'to present' [AB, Arn, BAGD, BECNT, LN, Lns, NTC, WBC; all versions]. It has the sense of dedication [EGT].

QUESTION—What days had to be completed in regard to purification?

According to Leviticus 12:2–8, the mother of a male child was considered to be unclean for forty days and could not enter the temple courts until the end of that time [AB, BECNT]. The time of her purification was completed on the fortieth day and then she was restored to full participation with the temple worshippers by means of offerings [AB, Lns, NTC]. This clause means 'when the time for their purification had come' [TH].

QUESTION—Since the law concerned only the purification of the mother, why does it say '*their* purification'?

1. 'Their' refers to Mary and Joseph [AB, Arn, BAGD (p. 387), BECNT, Gdt, ICC, Lns, My, NTC, Su, TH, TNTC, WBC; NCV, NET, TEV].
   1.1 This does not mean that Joseph had to be purified [Lns, NTC, WBC]. 'Their' is used loosely of the purification being a family matter so that it was time for their Jewish purification ritual [WBC]. Joseph was head of the family, so he had to provide the sacrifice that Mary presented and he was responsible for seeing that the ceremony was carried out [Arn, Lns, NTC].
   1.2 This means that Joseph also had to be purified [AB, BECNT, Gdt, ICC, TNTC; NET]. Since Mary was ceremonially unclean, Joseph would have contact with her defilement and would also need to be cleansed [Gdt, ICC, TNTC]. Joseph might have helped with the birth and his contact with blood would have made him unclean and in need of purification before participating in the presentation of Jesus [BECNT].
2. 'Their' refers to Mary and Jesus [Alf, Crd, NIC]. A woman was ceremonially unclean for forty days after the birth of her son and her son was also considered to be unclean [NIC].
3. 'Their' combines the purification of Mary with the presentation of Jesus [MGC, NIGTC]. Only Mary was unclean from giving birth, so it is likely the presentation of the child is included in 'their' [NIGTC].

QUESTION—What was involved in presenting Jesus to the Lord?

Presenting a son to the Lord recognized that God claimed the male child for his own [TG]. The presentation was distinct from Mary's purification and it is the main focus of the sentence [ICC, Lns, NAC, NICNT]. The trip to Jerusalem for the purification provided the occasion for taking Jesus there for presenting him before the Lord at the temple [AB, WBC].

2:23 **just-as it-has-been-written in (the) law of-(the)-Lord, Every male[a] opening (the) womb will-be-called[b] consecrated[c] to-the Lord,**

LEXICON—a. ἄρσην (LN 79.102, **10.45**) (BAGD p. 110): 'male' [AB, Arn, BAGD, BECNT, LN, Lns, NTC, WBC; KJV, NASB]. The phrase ἄρσην διανοίγων μήτραν 'male that opens the womb' is an idiom closely related in meaning to πρωτότοκος 'firstborn' and means the first male offspring of a female: 'firstborn son, firstborn male' [LN (10.45)]. The phrase is translated 'firstborn male' [**LN**; HCSB, NCV, NET, NIV, NRSV, REB, TEV], 'firstborn boy' [GW], 'firstborn baby boy' [CEV], 'if a woman's first child is a boy' [NLT]. In the OT text, 'male' refers to both human and animal males. One commentary advises making this clear by choosing a word that applies to both, or even specifying 'every first-born baby boy and every first-born male of your domestic animals' [TG]. However, another points out that only the category of humans is important here [TH], and this is reflected in the above translations of CEV, GW, and NLT.

b. fut. pass. indic. of καλέω (LN 33.131) (BAGD 1.a.δ. p. 399): 'to be called' [Arn, BAGD, BECNT, LN, Lns, NTC, WBC; KJV, NASB], 'to be designated as' [NRSV], 'to be deemed' [REB], 'to be considered' [AB], 'to be set apart as' [GW], not explicit [CEV, HCSB, NCV, NET, NIV, NLT, TEV]. The passive form approaches the meaning 'to be' [BAGD].

c. ἅγιος (LN 53.46) (BAGD 1.b.α. p.9): 'consecrated' [BAGD, LN], 'holy' [Arn, BAGD, BECNT, Lns, NTC, WBC; GW, KJV, NASB, NRSV], 'sacred' [AB]. This noun is also translated as a verb phrase: 'to be given (to)' [NCV], 'to be set apart (to)' [NET], 'to be consecrated (to)' [NIV], 'to be dedicated (to)' [HCSB, NLT, TEV], 'to belong (to)' [CEV, REB]. It refers to being dedicated or consecrated to the Lord's service [LN]. It means to be the property of the Lord [TH], to be dedicated to the Lord [AB, TH], to be separated to the Lord [Lns], or to be set apart for the Lord's service [TG].

QUESTION—What is the comparison being made by καθώς 'just as'?

The consecration of the firstborn son is according to the law in Exodus 13:2, 12–13 [AB, Arn, BNTC, EGT, NICNT, NIGTC, Su, TG, TNTC, WBC], where the Lord said, "Sanctify to Me every firstborn, the first offspring of every womb among the sons of Israel, both of man and beast; it belongs to Me....You shall devote to the Lord the first offspring of every womb, and the first offspring of every beast that you own; the males belong to the Lord. But every first offspring of a donkey you shall redeem with a lamb, but if you do not redeem it, then you shall break its neck; and every firstborn of man among your sons you shall redeem" [NASB]. A firstborn son had to be presented to the Lord to serve the Lord as a priest, but since the priesthood had been limited to the tribe of Levi, the firstborn sons had to be redeemed from priestly service by a payment of five shekels to someone of a priestly family [Arn, Lns]. The firstborn sons had to be redeemed by a payment of five shekels to someone in the priestly family when the child was a month old [AB]. Some commentators imply that this payment of the redemption price was included in the presentation [BNTC, EGT, Gdt, ICC, Lns, NICNT, NTC, TNTC]. In spite of 2:27 where it says that Jesus was brought to do what the law required of him, other commentators do not connect the redemption payment with the presentation in the temple which occurred forty days after the time of Jesus' birth. It was not necessary to bring a child to the temple to pay the redemption prices, so presenting Jesus at the temple was an act beyond what the law required [AB, Arn, BECNT]. Since Jesus was in the temple and no ransom price is mentioned, it appears that he was not being redeemed here but consecrated to God's service [NIGTC]. The main point of this reference is Jesus' consecration rather than his redemption [NAC]. One commentary regards the presentation to be guided by the example of Samuel being given to the Lord (1 Sam. 1:11, 21–28) and it was not especially related to the reference of being redeemed from priestly service in Exodus 13 [NICNT].

2:24 **and to-offer a-sacrifice according-to the (thing) said in the law of-(the)-Lord, a-pair of-doves[a] or two young pigeons.[b]**
LEXICON—a. τρυγών (LN **4.44**) (BAGD p. 828): 'dove' [**LN**; CEV, NCV, NET, NIV, TEV], 'turtledove' [AB, Arn, BAGD, BECNT, Lns, NTC, WBC; HCSB, KJV, NASB, NLT, NRSV, REB], 'mourning dove' [GW], 'pigeon' [LN]. A 'pair' of doves means two doves and does not imply that they must be a combination of male and female [TG].

b. περιστερά (LN **4.44**) (BAGD p. 651): 'pigeon' [AB, Arn, BAGD, BECNT, **LN**, NTC, WBC; all versions], 'dove' [BAGD, LN, Lns].

QUESTION—What relationship is indicated by καί 'and'?
This refers back to Mary's purification in 2:22 [AB, Arn, Gdt, ICC, Lns, MGC, NIGTC, TG, TH, WBC]. Many translations enclose 2:23 in parentheses so that two purposes are given for the trip [AB, NTC, TH, WBC; HCSB, KJV, NASB, NCV, NET, NIV, NRSV, REB]: they brought Jesus to Jerusalem to present him to the Lord and to offer Mary's purification sacrifice.

QUESTION—Why does the quotation about the required sacrifice from Leviticus 12:1–8 not mention offering a lamb and only one dove or pigeon?
When the time was up, a mother was required to bring a one-year old lamb to the priest for a burnt offering and a young pigeon or turtledove for a sin-offering. If she was too poor to bring a lamb, she was allowed to bring two turtledoves or two pigeons [AB, BECNT]. One dove was to serve as a burnt offering instead of a lamb, and the other was a sin offering [Lns]. Since this verse does not mention the sacrifice of a lamb, it implies that Mary and Joseph were so poor that they could only sacrifice the birds [NAC, Su, WBC]. Since Joseph had an income as a carpenter, apparently a lamb was offered only by those who were fairly wealthy [BECNT, ICC], or perhaps Joseph had spent his money on his traveling expenses and living in Bethlehem for over forty days [NTC].

QUESTION—What is the difference between 'doves' and 'pigeons'?
There does not seem to be a significant difference between the two words in NT Greek and both words are included in the same semantic domain [LN]. A turtledove is a small type of pigeon [AB, TH]. Turtledoves are migratory

birds and not always available, but pigeons were always plentiful [ICC, NTC]. To be the right size to serve as sacrifices, pigeons had to be young, but the smaller turtledoves needed to be full grown [TH].

DISCOURSE UNIT: 2:25–35 [NICNT; CEV, GW, NCV, NLT]. The topic is the manifestation of Jesus to Simeon [NICNT], Simeon sees Jesus [NCV], Simeon praises the Lord [CEV], the prophecy of Simeon [GW, NLT].

2:25 And behold a-man was in Jerusalem whose name (was) Simeon and this man (was) righteous[a] and devout[b] waiting-for[c] (the) consolation[d] of-Israel, and (the) Holy Spirit was upon[e] him.

LEXICON—a. δίκαιος (LN 88.12) (BAGD 1.b. p. 195): 'righteous'. See translations of this word at 1:6. This word also occurs at 1:17; 5:32; 14:14; 15:7; 18:9; 20:20; 23:47, 50.
- b. εὐλαβής (LN **53.8**) (BAGD p.322): 'devout' [AB, BAGD, BECNT, Lns, NTC, WBC; all versions except CEV, NCV, TEV], 'pious' [Arn, **LN**], 'godly' [NCV], 'God-fearing' [TEV], 'reverent' [LN]. This noun is also translated as a verb phrase: 'he loved God' [CEV]. He was faithful in his religious duties [ICC, TNTC, WBC]. This word is practically synonymous with the preceding word 'righteous' [TH].
- c. pres. mid. or pass. (deponent = act.) participle of προσδέχομαι (LN 85.60) (BAGD 2.b. p. 712): 'to wait for' [BAGD, LN, NTC; CEV, GW, KJV, NCV, NIV, TEV], 'to wait expectantly for' [WBC], 'to look for' [NASB, NET], 'to look forward to' [HCSB, NRSV], 'to watch and wait for' [REB], 'to await' [BECNT, LN], 'to expect' [Arn, BAGD, Lns], 'to eagerly expect' [NLT], 'to live in expectation' [AB]. See this word at 2:38.
- d. παράκλησις (LN 25.150) (BAGD 3. p. 618): 'consolation' [AB, Arn, BAGD, BECNT, LN, NTC, WBC; HCSB, KJV, NASB, NIV, NRSV], 'Consolation' [Lns], 'the one who would comfort' [GW], 'encouragement' [LN], 'restoration' [NET, REB]. This noun is also translated as a verb: 'to save' [CEV], 'to rescue' [NLT], 'to be saved' [TEV]. The phrase 'the consolation of Israel' is translated 'the time when God would take away (Israel's) sorrow' [NCV].
- e. ἐπί with an accusative object (LN 90.57) (BAGD III.1.b.γ. p. 289): 'upon' [Arn, BAGD, BECNT, Lns, NTC, WBC; KJV, NASB, NIV, REB], 'on' [LN; HCSB, NET], 'in' [NCV], 'with' [AB; GW, TEV]. The phrase 'was upon him' is translated 'rested on him' [NRSV], 'came to him' [CEV], 'he was filled with' [NLT]. It marks the experiencer of an action [LN].

QUESTION—What was 'the consolation of Israel'?
This term is influenced by references in Isaiah, such as 40:1, 49:13, 51:3, 57:18, 61:2, where they speak of the comforting of God's people [BECNT, EGT, ICC, NIGTC, TH, WBC]. It concerns the consolation that would result from the coming of the Messiah to establish the messianic age [Arn, BECNT, BNTC, Lns, NAC, NIGTC, WBC]. 'The consolation of Israel' was considered by Simeon to be the appearance of the Messiah [NICNT, TNTC].

Rabbis referred to the Messiah as the Comforter [EGT]. The coming of the Messiah would bring consolation after all the sufferings endured by Israel [My]. It refers to God's promise to rescue Israel from it enemies [TG; NET]. Simeon was waiting to experience the salvation that would come through the Messiah [ICC, NAC, Su]. This describes the Jewish hope that God would restore theocracy to Israel [AB, ICC].

QUESTION—What is meant by the Holy Spirit being *upon* Simeon?

It was a rare blessing before Pentecost and meant that the Holy Spirit constantly rested upon him so as to constantly influence him [NTC, TNTC]. This means that God's Spirit was resting on him, and it is different from the Spirit coming upon someone [TH]. This refers to an enduring state [NTC, TH, TNTC, WBC]. This continuous presence of the Spirit is different from the descriptions of Elizabeth (1:41) and Zechariah (1:67) where they were filled with the Spirit for the purpose of prophesying [WBC]. Because God's Spirit was with him, he received the following revelation [Arn, Lns], and was able to make the following prophecy about the child [AB]. Or, this does not refer to an abiding presence of the Spirit, but means that the Spirit came upon him to enable him to prophesy [ICC, NIVS; NET].

2:26 And it-had been-revealed to-him by the Holy Spirit (that he would) not see[a] death before[b] he-might-see the Messiah of-the Lord.

LEXICON—a. aorist act. infin. of ὁράω (LN 90.79) (BAGD 5. p. 221): 'to see' [AB, Arn, BAGD, BECNT, Lns, NTC, WBC; HCSB, KJV, NASB, NRSV, REB], 'to experience' [BAGD, LN], 'to undergo' [LN]. The phrase 'to see death' is translated 'to die' [CEV, GW, NCV, NET, NIV, NLT, TEV]. It is an OT expression, meaning 'to experience death' [AB, TH] or simply 'to die' [NAC, TH]. This figurative use of 'see' in 'see death' makes a play on words with the literal phrase 'see the Messiah' [TH].

b. πρίν (LN 67.17) (BAGD 1.a. p. 701): 'before' [Arn, BAGD, BECNT, LN, Lns, NTC, WBC; HCSB, KJV, NASB, NCV, NET, NIV, NRSV, TEV], 'until' [AB; CEV, GW, NLT, REB].

QUESTION—How is 'Messiah' related to 'Lord' in the genitive construction 'the Messiah of the Lord'?

It means the Messiah whom the Lord would send [Gdt, My, TG; GW], gives [Gdt], promised [TG; NCV, TEV], or chose [TG]. One version equates the two words: 'Christ the Lord' [CEV]. It is an OT expression that referred to a king who had been anointed by or on behalf of the Lord [TH].

2:27 And he-came by[a] the Spirit into the temple. And when the parents brought-in the child Jesus (for) them to-do what was-customary (in) the law concerning him **2:28** then he received him in (his) arms and praised God and said,

LEXICON—a. ἐν with a dative object (LN 90.6) (BAGD I.5.d. p. 260): 'by' [LN; KJV], 'in' [BECNT, Lns, WBC; NASB], 'through' [Arn]. The phrase 'by the Spirit' means moved by the Spirit [Arn; GW, NIV], directed by the Spirit [NET], prompted by the Spirit [BECNT], guided by the Spirit [AB, NAC, NICNT, NIGTC, NTC, TH; HCSB, NRSV, REB], led by the Spirit [NCV, NLT, TEV], under the influence of the Spirit [BAGD, ICC], told by the Spirit [CEV]. The Holy Spirit motivated him to come to the temple at just the right time [AB, Lns, NICNT, NTC].

QUESTION—What was the customary thing to do concerning Jesus?

The purpose of the visit was to present Jesus to the Lord as explained in 2:22. Since the presentation was not required by the OT Law, many take this to be a redemption payment that was required by the Law [BNTC, EGT, Gdt, ICC, Lns, NICNT, NTC, TNTC]. This refers to what the Law said should be done for a new baby [CEV]. This refers to the ritual that was commanded by the Law [TG].

QUESTION—What place is indicated by the noun 'temple'?

The term can designate the temple area in general or its outer courts. Here it would be either the court of the women or the court of the Gentiles where Mary was allowed to go [AB, BECNT; NET]. It probably was the court of the women [ICC].

QUESTION—What is the function of καί 'then' at the beginning of 2:28?

It introduces the apodosis of the preceding subordinate clause [Alf, EGT, Gdt, NIGTC, TH]: when they brought in the child Jesus..., then he received him in his arms. The word can either be translated 'then' [GW, KJV, NASB], or omitted [CEV, NIV, NLT, NRSV, REB, TEV].

QUESTION—How are the verbs related in the phrase 'and praised God and said'?

1. They refer to one event [AB, NIGTC, NTC, Su, TH; CEV, GW, NCV, NET, NIV, NLT, NRSV, TEV]: and praised God by saying. This phrase is translated 'and praised God by saying' [GW], 'and praised God, saying' [NIV, NLT, NRSV], 'and praised God' [CEV], 'and thanked God' [NCV], 'and gave thanks to God' [NCV, NET, TEV], 'and blessed God, saying' [AB; NET].

2. They refer to two events [Lns, TNTC, WBC; probably KJV, NASB]: 'and praised God, and also said'. Since the words in 2:29–32 are not strictly a blessing, it is to be understood that he spoke a blessing something like what Simeon had said in 1:64 before he spoke the words of 2:29 [WBC].

2:29 Master, now you-dismiss[a] your servant in peace[b] according-to your word. **2:30** Because my eyes saw the salvation of-you, **2:31** which you-prepared before (the) face[c] of-all the people,

LEXICON—a. pres. act. indic. of ἀπολύω (LN 15.43) (BAGD 2.b. p. 96): 'to dismiss' [BAGD, LN], The phrase 'now you dismiss your servant in peace' is translated as a statement: 'now you are dismissing your servant in peace' [NRSV], 'you now dismiss your servant in peace' [NIV], 'now you are releasing your servant in peace' [Lns, NTC; REB], 'now you are releasing your servant from duty in peace' [WBC], 'now you are releasing your bond-servant to depart in peace' [NASB], 'now you are allowing

your servant to leave in peace' [GW], 'now I can die in peace' [CEV, NLT]. This is translated as an imperative or a request: 'now release your servant in peace' [BECNT], 'now let your servant depart in peace' [KJV], 'now permit your servant to depart in peace' [NET], 'now you may let your servant go in peace' [TEV], 'now dismiss your slave in peace' [Arn], 'now you may dismiss your servant in peace' [AB], 'you can dismiss your slave in peace' [HCSB], 'now you can let me, your servant, die in peace' [NCV].
- b. εἰρήνη (LN 25.248) (BAGD 3. p. 227): 'peace' [Arn, BAGD, LN, Lns, NTC; all versions]. It is a state of mind [TH] and refers to being free from anxiety and inner turmoil [LN]. It means to be perfectly contented [Lns], or to be in bliss [My]. It is the satisfaction of having his expectations fulfilled [Gdt, TH], or experiencing the comfort of knowing that God's work has come to fulfillment [BECNT, TH]. However, some take this to be speaking of death as a peaceful sleep [Crd, EGT].
- c. πρόσωπον (LN **83.34**) (BAGD 1.c.δ. p. 721): 'face' [BAGD, LN, Lns; KJV]. The phrase κατὰ πρόσωπον 'before the face' is an idiom meaning 'in the presence of' [BAGD, **LN**; HCSB, NASB, NET, NRSV, TEV], 'in the sight of' [NTC; NIV], 'in full view of' [REB], 'before' [NCV] not explicit [Arn; CEV, GW, NLT].

QUESTION—What is meant by 'dismiss'?
1. It is used as a euphemism for dying [Arn, BAGD, NAC, NIGTC, NTC, TG, TNTC; CEV, NLT]: now you are letting your servant die in peace. This indicates that there is nothing more that he must live to see before he dies [NIGTC]. The promise in 2:26 was in reference to his death [NTC]. This does not imply that Simeon would immediately die [TG].
2. It means release from his duties [AB, Alf, BECNT, Gdt, ICC, My, TH, WBC]: Master, now you can release your servant. The slave is being released from his duty as a watchman, since what he was to watch for has now happened [AB, ICC, WBC]. The figure is that of a master releasing his servant from his service on earth and expresses his readiness to die [BECNT]. The release will come in death [AB, ICC, TH].
3. It means to give freedom to a slave [Lns]: now you are releasing your slave from slavery. It does not refer to death. Holding the fulfillment of the messianic promise in his arms, he feels he is like a slave who has been set free by his master [Lns].

QUESTION—What is the significance of the present tense in 'now dismiss'?
1. The present tense indicates that God is now in the process of dismissing Simeon [BECNT, Lns, MGC, NAC, NIGTC, NTC, WBC; GW, NASB, NIV, NRSV, REB]: now you are dismissing your servant in peace. By seeing the Messiah, God was beginning to fulfill 2:26 and Simeon was in the process of experiencing his dismissal [NAC]. The present tense indicates that he was ready to die [BECNT].
2. This is translated as asking God to let him die [AB, BECNT; HCSB, KJV, NCV, NET, TEV]: now let your servant die in peace. Simeon has been

acting as a watchman for a long time and now the release from his task will take the form of death [AB].
3. This is the use of the present tense to signify a future occurrence [EGT]: now you will dismiss your servant in peace.

QUESTION—What was according to God's word?

This refers to what the Holy Spirit promised him in 2:26, that he would not see death before he had seen the Messiah [BECNT, ICC, NAC, NIGTC, NTC, TH]. Or, he is referring to the promises in the OT [Lns].

QUESTION—What is meant by the genitive construction 'the salvation of you' and how can it be seen?

The possessive pronoun 'your' refers to the one who initiates the saving act [TH]. This refers back to 'the Messiah of the Lord' (2:26) [TH]. In seeing Jesus, Simeon has seen God's salvation [BECNT, TG] since Jesus personifies God's salvation [BECNT]. It means that he has seen the baby through whom God would bring salvation [Arn, TNTC]. It refers to the child as the means of the salvation God offers to the world [Gdt, NIGTC]. Referring to the birth of this child, he saw what God had done to save the world [Lns]. Simeon had seen the Savior who would bring about the salvation of Israel [NAC]. 'I have seen what you have done to save your people' [CEV]. 'I have seen the Savior you have given' [NLT].

2:32 a-light for revelation[a] (to the) Gentiles and glory[b] of-your people Israel.

LEXICON—a. ἀποκάλυψις (LN 28.38) (BAGD 1. p. 92): 'revelation' [BAGD, LN, Lns, NTC; HCSB, NASB, NET, NIV, NRSV, REB], not explicit [CEV, NASB]. This noun is also translated as a verb: 'to reveal' [GW, NLT, TEV], 'to be revealed' [Arn], 'to lighten' [KJV].
   b. δόξα (LN 87.4): 'glory' [Arn, Lns, NTC; all versions except CEV, NCV], 'honor' [LN; CEV, NCV], 'respect, status' [LN].

QUESTION—In what way is salvation a light for revelation to the Gentiles?

Salvation is a light that reveals the true knowledge of God, holiness, and love to the Gentiles who dwelled in darkness [NTC]. The child will bring the light of divine revelation to the heathen who are enveloped in the darkness of ignorance [Gdt]. The light reveals to the Gentiles their terrible condition and shows them God's grace to deliver them from sin and death [Lns]. The darkness of the Gentile world is lightened to reveal the true God to them [TH]. The light shows them God's will [BECNT; TEV].

QUESTION—Which words are in coordinate construction?

1. 'Light' and 'glory' are coordinate, both being in apposition to 'salvation' in 2:30 [Alf, Crd, EGT, Gdt, ICC, Lns, NAC, NTC, Su, TG, TH, WBC; HCSB, KJV, NASB, NCV, NLT]: my eyes have seen your salvation, a salvation which is light for revelation to the Gentiles and which is the glory of Israel. The saving act of God in the birth of Jesus as an Israelite resulted in a glory that no other nation has ever had [Lns]. The child will deliver Israel from its reproach so that it may receive the glory that was

promised to it [Gdt]. He will bring honor to the people of Israel since God chose the nation of Israel to bring forth the Christ in regard to his human nature [NTC]. Parallel with light, this describes the glory of God, his visible presence with Israel [TG].
2. 'Revelation' and 'glory' are coordinate, both in apposition to 'light' [AB, BECNT; GW, NET, NIV, NRSV, REB, TEV]: my eyes have seen your salvation which is a light for all people, a light for revelation to the Gentiles and a light for glory to Israel.

2:33 And the father of-him and the mother were being-amazed[a] at the (things) being-spoken about him. **2:34** And Simeon blessed[b] them and said to Mary his mother, Behold this (one) is-destined[c] for (the) fall[d] and rising[e] of-many in Israel and for a-sign (that) will-be-opposed[f]

TEXT—In 2:33, instead of ὁ πατὴρ αὐτοῦ καὶ ἡ μήτηρ 'the father of him and the mother', some manuscripts read Ἰωσὴφ καὶ ἡ μήτηρ αὐτοῦ 'Joseph and the mother of him'. GNT reads ὁ πατὴρ αὐτοῦ καὶ ἡ μήτηρ 'the father of him and the mother' with a B decision, indicating that the text is almost certain. Ἰωσὴφ καὶ ἡ μήτηρ αὐτοῦ 'Joseph and the mother of him' is read by KJV.

LEXICON—a. pres. act. participle of θαυμάζω (LN 25.213) (BAGD 1.a.α. p. 352): 'to be amazed'. See translations of this word at 1:21. This word also occurs at 1:63; 2:18; 4:22; 7:9; 8:25; 11:14, 38; 20:26; 24:12, 41.
b. aorist act. indic. of εὐλογέω (LN 33.470) (BAGD 2.a. p. 322): 'to bless' [AB, Arn, BAGD, BECNT, LN, Lns, NTC, WBC; all versions]. It means to ask God to bless them [LN, TG], to ask that God will bestow his favor on them [LN].
c. pres. mid./pass. (deponent=pres.) indic. of κεῖμαι (LN **13.73**) (BAGD 2.a. p. 426): 'to be destined' [BAGD, NTC; HCSB, NET, NIV, NRSV, REB], 'to be appointed' [BAGD; NASB], 'to be set' [BAGD, BECNT, LN, Lns; KJV], 'to be placed as' [WBC], 'to be placed for' [Arn], 'to be chosen by God' [TEV], 'to be marked' [AB], 'to exist' [LN], not explicit [NLT]. The phrase 'he is destined for' is translated 'he is destined to be the cause of' [NET], 'he is destined to cause' [NTC; NIV], 'he is the reason that' [GW], 'he will cause' [CEV], 'God has chosen this child to cause' [NCV], 'he exists for (the fall and rise of man)' [LN]. The use of the passive implies that this is God's plan [Arn, Gdt, Lns; NCV, TEV].
d. πτῶσις (LN **87.75**) (BAGD p. 728): 'fall, falling' [AB, Arn, BAGD, BECNT, **LN**, Lns, NTC, WBC; HCSB, KJV, NASB, NCV, NET, NIV, NRSV], 'destruction' [TEV]. This noun is also translated as a verb: 'to fall' [CEV, REB], 'to be condemned' [GW], 'to be their undoing' [NLT]. The word refers to a radical change to a lower status [LN].
e. ἀνάστασις (LN **13.60, 87.39**) (BAGD 1. p. 60): 'rise, rising' [AB, Arn, BAGD, BECNT, **LN** (13.60), Lns, NTC, WBC; HCSB, KJV, NASB, NCV, NET, NIV, NRSV], 'rising up' [**LN** (87.39)], 'salvation' [TEV]. This noun is also translated as a verb: 'to stand' [CEV, REB], 'to be

saved' [GW], 'to be the greatest joy' [NLT]. It can either refer to a change for the better [LN (13.60)] or to a change to a higher status [LN (87.39)].

f. pres. pass. participle of ἀντιλέγω (LN 33.455) (BAGD 2. p. 75): 'to be opposed' [BAGD, LN, WBC; HCSB, NASB, NRSV], 'to speak in opposition to' [LN], 'to be rejected' [AB; NET, NLT, REB], 'to be spoken against' [Arn, Lns, NTC; KJV, NIV]. This passive verb is also translated actively: 'to reject' [CEV, GW], 'to not accept' [NCV], 'to speak against' [TEV]. This verb is also translated as a noun: 'contradiction' [BECNT]. This refers to speaking against someone [LN].

QUESTION—Why were they amazed at this prophesy after having heard the prophesies from Gabriel, Elizabeth, and the shepherds?

They were amazed at Simeon's prophesy because it had gone beyond the angel's outline [Arn, Rb]. For the first time, they learned from this stranger the effect Jesus would have on the Gentiles [NIGTC].

QUESTION—Who are the 'them' that Simeon blessed?

1. Simeon blessed Joseph and Mary [BECNT, Gdt, Lns, MGC, My, NIC, NICNT, NIGTC, NTC, Su, TG, TNTC, WBC]: the father and mother were amazed…and Simeon blessed them. The blessing is not recorded, but it must have pertained to having such a child under their care [Lns]. It was probably a priestly blessing like when Eli blessed the parents of Samuel (1 Samuel 2:20) [WBC]. The blessing must have been for the parents in view of what lies ahead for them [NIGTC].
2. Simeon blessed Joseph, Mary, and Jesus [Arn, TH].

QUESTION—What happened after Simeon blessed them?

After speaking the blessing, he prophesied directly to Mary [Arn, TH]. Perhaps he did not include Joseph because the virgin birth particularly concerned Mary [Gdt, NAC, NIGTC], or because the prophecy took into account that Joseph would die before the crucifixion and not experience the same sorrow that Mary would [Lns, NAC, NIGTC].

QUESTION—Who are the 'many in Israel'?

1. The 'many' comprise two groups, many will fall and many others will rise [Arn, BECNT, BNTC, Crd, Gdt, ICC, Lns, My, NAC, NIBC, NIC, NIVS, Rb, Su, TG, TH, WBC; CEV, GW, NET, NLT]. Unbelievers will fall and believers will rise in response to their faith [BECNT]. 'Many' is to be understood as 'all' [NAC].
2. The 'many' refers to one group that will first fall and then rise [Alf, Crd, MGC, NIGTC]. This group is in contrast with those who oppose the sign [NIGTC]. If this interpretation is taken, it means that people must not depend upon their spiritual achievements, but that they will fall to a lowly place and then they will rise and enter into salvation [TNTC].

QUESTION—What is meant by the fall and rising of many in Israel?

The image of falling is taken from Isaiah where he spoke of setting up a stone of stumbling (Isa. 8:14–15) [Alf, BECNT, BNTC, Gdt, NICNT, WBC], while rising is the natural opposite and does not fit in the picture of building stones [WBC]. Falling refers to perishing [Lns], being destroyed

[TEV], being judged or condemned [NAC, Su; GW, NET], or being excluded from the kingdom [NTC]. Rising refers to being saved [Lns, NAC, Su; GW, TEV], being blessed [NET], or being welcomed into the kingdom [NTC].

QUESTION—In what way will Jesus be a sign that will be opposed?

The sign is Jesus himself [Arn, ICC, NIGTC, NTC, TG, TH, WBC]. He is a sign that God's plan of redemption will be carried out [Arn]. He is a sign that points to his Father's love for sinners [NIVS]. He is a sign through whom God signals his salvation and proof of its reality [NIGTC]. The sign refers to Jesus' person and message as he confronts people with God's demands [TG]. He will be a warning sign [TG, TH; CEV]. He is a sign of salvation [NIGTC, WBC], but to the people who oppose him, he is a sign of judgment [WBC]. People oppose him by refusing his message and speaking against it [TG]. They will not regard Jesus to be a real sign from God [NIGTC].

2:35 —and a-sword will-pierce your own soul also—so-that[a] (the) thoughts from many hearts will-be-revealed.

LEXICON—a. ὅπως (LN 89.59) (BAGD 2.a.β. p. 577): 'so that' [AB, BECNT, LN; NCV, NIV, NRSV], 'in order that' [Arn, BAGD], 'in order to' [LN, Lns], 'to the end that' [NASB], 'that' [NTC, WBC; HCSB, KJV], 'as a result' [NET], 'thus' [NLT], 'this will show' [CEV], 'and so' [REB, TEV], not explicit [GW].

QUESTION—How is the clause 'and a sword will pierce your own soul also' related to its context?

1. Since the following clause is directly related to the previous verse by ὅπως 'so that', this clause is treated as a parenthesis [BECNT, Crd, EGT, MGC, NIGTC, Su, TG; KJV], or it is separated by dashes [AB, NTC, WBC; HCSB, NASB], or it is reordered so that it comes last in the verse [GW, NCV, NET, NIV, NRSV, TEV]. The phrase occurs here in order to highlight the comparison of the fate of Mary with the fate of the sign in 2:34 [WBC].

2. This clause is an addition to the preceding clause, and the following 'so that' clause gives the purpose or result of the unit 2:34–35a [Alf, Arn, BNTC, Gdt, ICC, Lns, My, TH; CEV]: many will oppose him and you will suffer, so that the thoughts from many hearts will be revealed. The opposition against her son will cause Mary's grief [Gdt, ICC].

QUESTION—What is meant by the metaphor of a sword piercing Mary's soul?

This concerns pain and suffering and means 'pain will pierce your heart like a sword pierces a body' [TG]. It is translated 'and you, Mary, will suffer as though you had been stabbed by a dagger' [CEV], 'pain will pierce your heart like a sword' [TG]. Non-metaphorically it means 'you will experience anguish' [TH].

1. This refers to Mary's extreme grief when opposition against her son culminates in Jesus' death on the cross [Arn, EGT, Gdt, ICC, Lns, My, NIGTC, NTC, TH, TNTC, WBC; TEV].

2. This refers to the difficulty that Mary will have in understanding that obedience to God's word will transcend even family ties [AB, BECNT, NAC, NICNT]. This passage focuses on the division Jesus brings and the metaphor refers to the extreme emotional pain Mary will have as she sees Jesus create his own family of disciples and have his own priorities [BECNT]. This refers to Mary's difficulty in accepting her son's mission [NAC, NICNT].
3. Mary is a figure of Israel and the crucifixion will divide the nation and cause division [Alf, BNTC]. This refers to the many Israelites, including Mary, who struggle through repentance to faith in the Savior, so that the sword of the pangs of sorrow for sin will pierce the heart so that those who receive Jesus and those who reject him may be revealed [Alf].

QUESTION—What relationship is indicated by ὅπως 'so that'?
1. It indicates the purpose for which God destined Jesus [AB, BECNT, EGT, Gdt, ICC, Lns, NAC, NIC, NICNT, NIGTC, NTC, WBC; NASB, NCV]: this one is destined for the fall and rising of many and to be a sign that people will oppose *in order that* their secret thoughts will be apparent. The hatred against Jesus that will also cause Mary's grief will bring out the hidden hostile thoughts of the people who oppose him [Gdt].
2. It indicates the result of many people opposing the sign [TG, TH; NET, REB, TEV]: this one is destined to be a sign that people will oppose, *with the result that* their secret thoughts will be apparent [TG]. It is the expected result [TH].
3. It indicates the result of all that precedes [CEV]: 'but all this will show what people are really thinking' [CEV].

QUESTION—How will the thoughts of their hearts be revealed?

By accepting or rejecting Christ, it will be clear as to what everyone's inner position really is [AB, Alf, Arn, EGT, ICC, Lns, My]. Opposition to the sign will show the true state of the hearts of many [WBC]. Opposition will reveal the hostile thoughts of many [BECNT]. By revealing the Messiah, God forced people to react, either for or against him [AB, ICC]. Their opposition will bring out the hostile thoughts toward God that were covered by outward forms of religious piety [Gdt].

DISCOURSE UNIT: 2:36–40 [GW, NLT]. The topic is the prophecy of Anna.

DISCOURSE UNIT: 2:36–39 [NICNT]. The topic is the manifestation of Jesus to Anna.

DISCOURSE UNIT: 2:36–38 [CEV, HCSB, NCV]. The topic is Anna's testimony [HCSB], Anna sees Jesus [NCV], Anna speaks about the child Jesus [CEV].

2:36 And there-was a-prophetess[a] Anna, a-daughter of-Phanuel, from (the) tribe of-Asher. This (woman) was-advanced in many days (= was very old), having-lived with (her) husband seven years from her virginity[b] **2:37** and

LUKE 2:36–37   105

she (was) a-widow until eighty-four years, who did- not -depart (from) the temple serving^c with-fastings and prayers night and day.

LEXICON—a. προφῆτις (LN **53.80**) (BAGD p. 724): 'prophetess' [AB, Arn, BAGD, BECNT, **LN**, Lns, NTC, WBC; HCSB, KJV, NASB, NCV, NET, NIV, REB], 'prophet' [CEV, GW, NLT, NRSV, TEV]. This refers to a woman who proclaims inspired utterances on behalf of God [LN]. She had the gift of prophecy and was known for that gift [ICC, Lns].

b. παρθενία (LN **23.64**) (BAGD p. 626): 'virginity' [BAGD, LN, WBC; KJV], 'maidenhood' [Lns]. The phrase 'from her virginity' is translated 'since she was a virgin' or 'since the time of her marriage' [**LN**], 'after her virginity' [Arn], 'after her marriage' [AB, NTC; HCSB, NASB, NIV, NRSV], 'after she was first married' [REB]. The phrase 'having lived with her husband seven years from her virginity' is translated 'having lived with a man seven years from her youth' [BECNT], 'she had been married for seven years' [CEV, NCV, NET], 'her husband had died seven years after they were married' [GW], 'her husband had died when they had been married only seven years' [NLT], 'she had been married for only seven years' [TEV]. This informs us that this marriage had been her first [TH].

c. pres. act. participle of λατρεύω (LN 53.14) (BAGD p. 467): 'to serve' [Arn, BAGD; CEV, NASB], 'to serve God' [HCSB, KJV], 'to give service' [BECNT], 'to worship' [AB, LN, Lns, NTC, WBC; GW, NCV, NET, NIV, NLT, NRSV, REB, TEV]. It refers to carrying out religious duties [BAGD], to performing religious rites as a part of worship [LN]. See this word at 1:74 and 4:8.

QUESTION—In 2:37, what does 'until eighty-four years' refer to in regard to Anna?

1. This refers to her age [Crd, My, NTC, TH, WBC; CEV, KJV, NASB, NIV, NLT, NRSV, REB, TEV]: and she was a widow of eighty-four years of age.

2. This refers to the time she had been a widow [AB, BECNT, ICC, Lns, MGC, NIGTC; GW, HCSB, NCV, NET]: and she had been a widow for eighty-four years. Since widowhood is the subject of the sentence, this refers to the time of her widowhood and she would then be around 105 years of age [BECNT].

QUESTION—Is the statement that 'she did not depart from the temple, worshipping God night and day' to be taken literally?

The wording allows one to understand either that she arrived at the temple in the morning and spent the day there, or that she remained there at night also, spreading a pallet somewhere in the temple court [Gdt]. This is hyperbole [ICC, NIGTC, NTC, TG, TH] and means that she went to the temple regularly [NTC], constantly [ICC, TNTC], often [TG], frequently [TH], or as much as circumstances allowed [Arn]. She never missed a service and spent most of her time there between services [Arn, ICC]. She was in the temple daily, fasting and praying all day, but she would not have a place to stay there all of the time [BECNT]. This does not mean that she slept in the temple [AB, Lns, NAC, TG, WBC]. Or, this means she lived inside the temple precincts [Crd].

2:38 And at-that same hour having-approached she-was-praising God and she-was-speaking about him to-all the-ones waiting-for[a] (the) redemption[b] of-Jerusalem.

TEXT—Instead of θεῷ 'God', some manuscripts read κυρίῳ 'Lord'. GNT does not mention this variant. Κυρίῳ 'Lord' is read by KJV.

TEXT—Instead of Ἰερουσαλήμ 'Jerusalem' (an indeclinable form used here as a genitive, 'of Jerusalem'), some manuscripts read ἐν Ἰερουσαλήμ 'in Jerusalem', a few other manuscripts read ἐν Ἰσραήλ 'in Israel', and a few others read τῷ Ἰσραήλ 'for Israel'. GNT reads Ἰερουσαλήμ 'of Jerusalem' with an A decision, indicating that the text is certain. Ἐν Ἰερουσαλήμ 'in Jerusalem' is read by KJV.

LEXICON—a. pres. mid./pass. (deponent = act) participle of προσδέχομαι (LN 85.60) (BAGD 2.b. p. 712): 'to wait for'. See this word at 2:25.

b. λύτρωσις (LN 37.128) (BAGD 1. p. 483): 'redemption'. See this word at 1:18, 68.

QUESTION—What relationship is indicated by the use of the participle 'having approached'?

The participle indicates an action previous to the main verb 'she was praising' [TH]: she approached and then praised God. She had come up and stood nearby the group of Jesus, his parents, and Simeon and heard what Simeon said about the baby [Lns, Rb]. Having heard Simeon, she now came close and joined the family group [NTC].

QUESTION—Who is the 'him' of whom she spoke, and when did she do this?

She spoke about the child, Jesus [all commentaries]. This is made explicit in most versions [CEV, GW, HCSB, NCV, NET, NIV, NLT, NRSV, REB, TEV].

1. This took place at that time [Alf, My, Su]. This tells what happened at that very hour and those who were waiting for the redemption were also present in the temple [My]. She spoke to all those present: Jesus' family, Simeon, and others nearby [Su].
2. This took place at that time and it also went on after Jesus left the temple [AB, EGT, Gdt, Lns, NTC, TH]. The imperfect verb 'she was speaking' does not mean that she spoke only on this occasion, but means that she spread the news abroad [AB, TH]. It means that she was habitually speaking about Jesus since those who were waiting for the redemption were not all present when she met Joseph and Mary [ICC, Lns]. This became a habit with her [NTC].
3. This refers to what she did after Jesus and his parents left the temple [ICC]. The ones who were waiting for the redemption of Jerusalem were not present when she came up and met Joseph and Mary and the baby [ICC].

QUESTION—What was the redemption of Jerusalem?
Jesus was the one who fulfilled the hope of the pious people of Israel [BECNT]. Jerusalem was the capital of the nation of Israel and 'redemption of Jerusalem' is equivalent to the 'consolation of Israel' in 2:25 [AB, BECNT, BNTC, Lns, MGC, NAC, NTC, TG]. It is not clear whether the people were waiting for a political or spiritual redemption, or both [Rb]. It was a redemption to be accomplished by the Messiah [Su, TNTC, WBC]. This means deliverance from sin through the Savior [NTC]. It refers to the one who would pay the ransom to release Israel from spiritual bondage [Lns].

DISCOURSE UNIT: 2:39–40 [CEV, HCSB, NASB, NCV, NRSV, TEV]. The topic is the return to Nazareth [CEV, NASB, NRSV, TEV], the family's return to Nazareth [HCSB], Joseph and Mary return home [NCV].

2:39 **And when they-completed everything according-to the law of-(the) Lord, they-returned to Galilee to their city Nazareth.**
QUESTION—Who are the 'they' who completed everything and what did they complete?
This refers to Mary and Joseph [AB, Arn, NIBC; NIV, TEV]. They completed the ceremonies of circumcision and the naming of Jesus and then went to the temple to present him there and to take care of their own purification [Lns, MGC, Su].
QUESTION—How soon did they return to Nazareth?
This does not imply that they immediately traveled to Nazareth after completing their religious duties [NTC]. This is a summary which omits the events of Matthew 2 and merely leads to the information that Jesus grew up in Nazareth and not in Bethlehem where he was born [Lns]. Joseph probably found employment in Bethlehem, so they returned to Nazareth to get their belongings and then came back to Bethlehem before the wise men arrived [Arn].

DISCOURSE UNIT: 2:40–52 [NICNT, Su]. The topic is the growth of Jesus, Son of God [NICNT], the childhood years of Jesus [Su].

2:40 **And the child was-growing and being-strengthened being-filled with-wisdom, and (the) favor[a] of-God was upon him.**
TEXT—Following ἐκραταιοῦτο 'was being strengthened', some manuscripts add πνεύματι 'in spirit'. GNT does not mention this variant. Πνεύματι 'in spirit' is read by KJV.
LEXICON—a. χάρις (LN 88.66) (BAGD 2.a. p. 877): 'favor' [AB, BAGD, BECNT, NTC; GW, NET], 'special favor' [NLT], 'grace' [Arn, BAGD, LN, Lns, WBC; HCSB, KJV, NASB, NIV] 'gracious care' [BAGD], 'kindness' [LN], 'goodness' [NCV]. This noun is also translated as a verb with God as the subject: 'to bless' [CEV]. See this word at 1:30.

QUESTION–In what respect was Jesus strengthened?

1. This refers to his physical development [Arn, EGT, ICC, MGC, NIC, NTC, Rb, Su, TG; probably all versions except KJV, since they translate with the adjective 'strong']: the child grew in size and strength. Jesus needed to develop his physical strength in order to work as a carpenter and later to accomplish his earthly ministry [NTC]. The following phrase 'being filled with wisdom' refers to his spiritual growth [ICC, NTC] and also his intellectual and moral growth [ICC].
2. This refers to his spiritual development [Alf, BECNT, Gdt, Lns, NAC, TH; KJV]: the child grew physically and developed spiritually. He was strengthened in respect to his mental and moral growth [TH], his mental and spiritual growth [Lns], or his spiritual, intellectual, and religious development [Gdt]. 'Being filled with wisdom' is to be connected to his being strengthened as a closely related concept and means that wisdom (his perception of the will and rule of God) increasingly became the dominating power of his life [TH]. 'Being filled with wisdom' was the main feature of his mental and spiritual increase of strength [Gdt]. Wisdom refers to his perception of the will of God [BECNT]. This should be taken in the same way as the similar description in 1:80 where it says John became strong in spirit [Lns, NAC, TH]. 'In spirit' must be understood here to prevent the participial phrase 'being filled with wisdom' from restricting the strengthening only to intellectual strength [Lns].

QUESTION—In what respect was the favor of God upon him?

It means either that God kept on blessing Jesus or that God was pleased with him [TG], or both [EGT]. 'Grace' is to be taken in the broader sense of God's favor, not in the narrower sense of God's undeserved favor to sinners [Lns]. This is similar to God's favor being on Mary in 1:28 and 30 [AB, BECNT]. God guided Jesus day by day [NTC]. Jesus' growth in wisdom resulted from God's favor and grace [TH].

DISCOURSE UNIT: 2:41–52 [AB, BECNT, NAC, NIGTC, TNTC, WBC; CEV, GW, NASB, NCV, NET, NIV, NLT, NRSV, TEV]. The topic is Jesus as a boy [NCV], the visit to Jerusalem [NASB], Jesus in the temple [NAC, TNTC; NET], the boy Jesus in the temple [CEV, NIV, NRSV, TEV], the Passover visit of Jesus to the temple [NIGTC], Jesus in the house of his Father [WBC], Jesus speaks with the teachers [NLT], finding Jesus in the temple [AB], Mary and Joseph find Jesus with the teachers in the temple courtyard [GW], Jesus' revelation of his self–understanding [BECNT].

DISCOURSE UNIT: 2:41–50 [HCSB]. The topic is Jesus in his Father's house.

2:41 And his parents were-traveling every year to Jerusalem for-the feast of-the Passover. 2:42 And when he-became twelve years (old), going-up with-them according-to the custom of-the feast 2:43 and having-fulfilled

the days, when they were-returning the boy Jesus remained in Jerusalem, and his parents did- not -know.

TEXT—In 2:43, instead of οἱ γονεῖς αὐτοῦ 'his parents', some manuscripts read Ἰωσὴφ καὶ ἡ μήτηρ αὐτοῦ 'Joseph and his mother'. GNT does not mention this variant. Ἰωσὴφ καὶ ἡ μήτηρ αὐτοῦ 'Joseph and his mother' is read by KJV.

QUESTION—In 2:42, what was according to the custom of the feast?

Passover, along with Pentecost and Tabernacles, was an annual festival that Jewish men were expected or required to observe in Jerusalem [AB, BECNT, ICC, Lns, NAC, NIGTC, NTC, Rb, TG, TNTC, WBC], and by this time in history women also accompanied their husbands [NIGTC]. Here the parents again made their annual pilgrimage [Lns]. Perhaps this refers to the custom of going up to the feast in a caravan [Gdt].

QUESTION—Had Jesus accompanied his parents to Jerusalem before he was twelve?

When a Jewish boy was considered to have attained maturity he acquired the responsibility of keeping God's commandments, including attending the Passover. Some think that the age of maturity was reached at the age of twelve [Alf, EGT, Gdt, ICC, Lns, My, Rb, Su, TG, TH], and others think it was reached at the age of thirteen [AB, BECNT, BNTC, MGC, NAC, NIBC, NIC, NIGTC, NTC, TNTC, WBC]. If the age of maturity was at thirteen, the reason for taking Jesus to the Passover at the age of twelve could be that it was a custom of pious Jews to take their sons at an earlier age in order to get them accustomed to their obligations [AB, NIC, TNTC]. The text does not indicate whether or not Jesus had gone to Jerusalem with his parents since his presentation [Alf, BECNT, TNTC]. For some, the mention of Jesus' age implies that he had not gone to Jerusalem with his parents since his presentation [EGT, ICC, NTC]. Another view is that it is natural to assume that Jesus had accompanied his parents from year to year [WBC].

QUESTION—How could Mary and Joseph not know that Jesus stayed behind in Jerusalem?

The verb 'they were returning' covers the first day of the trip home for Mary and Joseph [TH]. It might have been a custom at that time that the women and small children traveled in the front part of the caravan and young men followed at the end and perhaps Joseph thought Jesus was with Mary and Mary thought Jesus was with Joseph [ICC, NTC, TNTC]. They thought that Jesus was with some of the other people in the group [Arn; CEV, GW, NLT], probably with relatives [BECNT, NIGTC], or with other boys [Lns, NAC, Su]. At any rate, hundreds were returning to Galilee and they were strung out along the road [Lns].

2:44 But supposing him to-be in the caravan[a] they went a-day's journey and they-were-looking-for him among relatives and acquaintances, **2:45** and not having-found (him) they-returned to Jerusalem looking-for him.

LEXICON—a. συνοδία (LN **15.150**) (BAGD p. 791): 'caravan' [BECNT, Lns; NASB], 'company' [NTC; KJV, NIV], 'party' [REB], 'traveling party' [AB, WBC; HCSB], 'group' [NCV, TEV], 'group of travelers' [BAGD, LN; NET, NRSV], 'others who were traveling with them' [GW], 'the group of those traveling with them' [**LN**], 'their traveling companions' [Arn], 'the other travelers' [NLT], not explicit [CEV]. The people from one village or several neighboring villages would form a caravan so they could travel together on the trip to and from Jerusalem [ICC]. They traveled together for security and company [Alf].

QUESTION—When did Mary and Joseph begin looking for Jesus?

Although a few of the commentators think that the imperfect tense 'they were looking for him' implies that they spent the day looking for Jesus as they traveled [Gdt, TH, TNTC, WBC], most think that they had traveled the whole day before they started looking for him [Alf, Arn, BECNT, EGT, Lns, NIGTC, NTC, Su; all versions except KJV].

QUESTION—In 2:45, when 'they returned to Jerusalem looking for him', where did they look for Jesus?

1. They were looking for Jesus on the way back to Jerusalem [Alf, Gdt, ICC, Lns, NTC, TH]: they returned to Jerusalem, looking for him as they went along. The present participle 'looking for' is simultaneous with the returning [TH], so they began looking as soon as they started back [ICC]. They searched all along the road [Gdt, Lns] and getting to Jerusalem, they went to where they had lodged [Lns].
2. They looked for him in Jerusalem [Arn, BECNT; CEV]: they returned to Jerusalem and started looking for him there. When they arrived in Jerusalem they began the process (present participle) of searching for Jesus [BECNT].
3. This indicates that their purpose for going to Jerusalem was to look for Jesus and it does not specify whether they looked for him on the way or only when they arrived in Jerusalem [EGT, WBC; GW, HCSB, NCV, NET, NIV, NLT, NRSV, REB]: they returned to Jerusalem in order to look for him. The present participle expresses the purpose of the journey and not where the search took place [EGT].

2:46 And it-happened after three days they-found him in the temple sitting in (the) midst of-the teachers and listening to-them and questioning them. **2:47** And all the-ones listening to-him were-astounded[a] at his intelligence[b] and answers.

LEXICON—a. imperf. mid. indic. of ἐξίστημι (LN 25.220) (BAGD 2.b. p. 276): 'to be astounded' [HCSB], 'to be amazed' [BAGD, BECNT, Lns; NASB, NCV, NIV, NLT, NRSV, REB, TEV], 'to be astonished' [BAGD, NTC, WBC; KJV, NET], 'to be greatly astonished' [LN], 'to be surprised'

[CEV], 'to be stunned' [GW], 'to be struck' [AB]. See this word at 8:56; 24:22.
b. σύνεσις (LN32.26) (BAGD 1. p. 788): 'intelligence' [BAGD, LN; REB], 'insight' [LN, NTC], 'understanding' [BECNT, Lns, WBC; GW, HCSB, KJV, NASB, NCV, NET, NIV, NLT, NRSV], 'comprehension' [AB], 'how much he knew' [CEV]. This noun is also translated as an adjective: 'intelligent (answers)' [TEV]. This describes his insight in understanding the heart of an issue [BECNT].

QUESTION—What days were covered in the phrase 'after three days'?
1. The three days began with their departure for Nazareth [AB, Arn, BECNT, Crd, EGT, Gdt, ICC, Lns, MGC, NAC, NIC, NIGTC, NIVS, NTC, Rb, TG, TH]. The first day they started the trip to Nazareth and that night found that he wasn't in the caravan; the second day they traveled back to Jerusalem; the third day they found in him at the temple [Arn, Crd, ICC, NAC, NIGTC, NTC]. 'After the third day' means 'on the third day' [NIGTC]. It was measured from the time they had last seen Jesus [EGT].
2. The three days began on the day they began to search in Jerusalem [Alf, My]. The day they returned to Jerusalem was the first day and they found him two days later [My].

QUESTION—Where in the temple did they find Jesus in the midst of the teachers and who were the teachers?
Various ideas are given as to where within the Temple enclosure this would have taken place. It was in a room of the temple buildings where scribes met for teaching [Crd], or in one of the covered porches around the inside walls of the enclosure [NTC, Su], or on a terrace [ICC, Rb]. It must have been somewhere where Mary could go, such as a hall or portico in the outer courts [AB]. The teachers involved would be scribes, who were the teachers of the law [AB, Su, TG], or they would be rabbis [ICC, Lns, Rb]. There was a group of teachers in the gathering [Alf, Crd, NIGTC]. Perhaps one rabbi had begun teaching and then other rabbis and listeners gathered about him [Lns].

QUESTION—How was Jesus' intelligence revealed?
Jesus' intelligence was manifested by both his questions and his answers [Gdt, NAC, NIGTC, NTC, Su, TG, TH]. His intelligence was manifested in his answers [AB, EGT, Gdt, Lns, My; TEV]. The instruction would concern the Torah and its application to Jewish life [AB]. Usually instruction from the scribes included the pupils asking questions, as well as answering them [AB, Alf, Gdt, ICC, NTC]. 'His intelligence and answers' is an example of hendiadys, meaning 'his intelligent answers' [AB, MGC, NIGTC; TEV]. In the context of interaction with the scribes, the word ἀποκρίσεσιν 'answers' does not need to mean anything more than 'observations' [WBC].

2:48

And having-seen him they-were-astonished,[a] and his mother said to him, Son, why did-you-do thus to-us? Behold, your father and-I being-anxious[b] were-looking-for you.

LEXICON—a. aorist pass. indic. of ἐκπλήσσομαι (ἐκπλήσσω) (LN 25.219) (BAGD 2. p. 244): 'to be astonished' [HCSB, NASB, NCV, NIV, NRSV, REB, TEV], 'to be astounded' [NTC], 'to be greatly astounded' [LN], 'to be amazed' [Arn, BAGD, BECNT, WBC; CEV, KJV], 'to be shocked' [GW], 'to be struck with a shock' [Lns], 'to be startled' [AB], 'to be overwhelmed' [NET], 'to not know what to think' [NLT]. It is a response of fright, wonder, or perhaps here of joy [BAGD, NIGTC]. The verb 'astonish' expresses a stronger feeling than the 'amazement' of the listeners in 2:47 [Lns, TH]. See this word at 4:32; 9:43.

b. pres. pass. participle of ὀδυνάομαι, ὀδυνάω (LN **25.236**) (BAGD 2. p. 555): 'to be anxious' [BAGD], 'to be terribly worried' [AB, **LN**; TEV], 'to be very worried' [CEV, NCV], 'to be worried sick' [GW], 'to be distressed' [Lns], 'to be very much distressed' [LN], 'to be frantic' [NLT], 'to be in agony' [WBC], 'to be with great pain' [BECNT], 'to be sorrowing' [KJV]. This verb is also translated as an adverbial phrase modifying 'were looking for': 'anxiously' [NTC; HCSB, NASB, NET, NIV, REB], 'in great anxiety' [NRSV], 'with grief' [Arn]. This describes their worry and apprehension of what might have happened to Jesus [TH].

QUESTION—Who were astonished and why?

There is a change of subject from the previous verse so that the subject is not 'all the ones listening to him', but Jesus' parents [AB, EGT, ICC, NIGTC, TH; NET]. This astonishment has a different cause than the amazement of the people in 2:47 and indicates both amazement and relief [WBC]. Their joy in finding him was overcome by the fact that he had done something that caused them such agony [AB]. They were astonished to find him there speaking with the teachers [Arn, ICC, Lns, My, NIGTC, Su], without a thought of his parents [ICC]. Perhaps he had never spoken up in a synagogue before [Lns]. They may have been astonished at Jesus' present boldness when previously he had been quiet and reserved [EGT]. The cause of their astonishment is uncertain, it could be from seeing the manifestation of Jesus' wisdom [NAC].

QUESTION—When did Mary speak to Jesus?

Probably this did not happen as soon as they saw him in the midst of the crowd. Perhaps Jesus saw them, got up, and walked away with his parents [Lns]. Most think that Mary and Joseph were present for some of the conversation between Jesus and the teachers.

QUESTION—What did Mary mean by her question?

Mary wanted to know why Jesus had caused his parents so much trouble and worry by not starting back to Nazareth with the group [Arn, TG]. Mary could not comprehend why Jesus had done this [AB], and the question might have been asked without an implied reproach [Alf]. The question includes surprise, reproach, and anguish [NTC]. It has a tone of reproach [AB, Crd,

Gdt, ICC, Lns, MGC, TH, TNTC]. It expresses a mild complaint against what she perceived to be his insensitivity [BECNT]. The question implies that Jesus had not acted as an obedient or responsible child [AB]. It accuses him of betraying his position as their son [WBC].

2:49 **And he-said to them, Why (is it) that you-were-looking-for me? Did-you- not -know that it-is-necessary (for) me to-be in the (places/things) of-my Father?** **2:50** **And they-did- not -understand the word which he-spoke to-them.**

QUESTION—What is implied in Jesus' question, 'Why is it that you were looking for me'?

The question expressed Jesus' surprise that they did not know where to find him [Arn, Gdt, ICC, Lns, Rb, Su, TG, TH, TNTC, WBC; NET]. This merely expresses his surprise without a hint of reproach [Alf, ICC, Lns, NAC, WBC]. Instead of looking all over for him, they should have expected him to be in the temple [Arn, TH]. Some think that the question implied a gentle reproach [AB, Gdt, ICC, NIGTC, TG; CEV]: 'Why did you have to look for me? Didn't you know…?' [CEV]. They should have realized at once that they would find him in the temple [Gdt]. A child should be in his father's house, and Jesus' Father is God [ICC]. The second question 'Did you not know…?' expects an affirmative reply [BECNT, ICC, NIGTC, Su]. It implies that they knew it or ought to have known it [ICC].

QUESTION—Where was it necessary for Jesus to be?

1. The plural article τοῖς 'the (places/things)' should be taken as masculine and then it refers to 'the places of my Father', that is, the temple buildings, or the house of his Father [AB, Arn, BECNT, Crd, EGT, Gdt, ICC, MGC, My, NAC, NICNT, NIGTC, NTC, Rb, TG, TH, TNTC, WBC; all versions except KJV]: it is necessary for me to be in the house of my Father. There are parallel expressions using 'the house of God' in 6:4 and 'my house' in 19:46 [NAC]. This interpretation is best since the point is *where* they could find him [ICC, NICNT, NIGTC, NTC, WBC]: 'Why were you looking all over for me. Didn't you know I would be in my Father's house?' Jesus was not surprised that they were looking for him, but that they did not know where to find him [ICC]. Rather than focusing on *where*, it can be taken to focus on *why* [NAC]: 'Why were you looking for me? Didn't you know I must be in my Father's house?' Jesus must be in God's house because God's presence resides there in a special way and instruction about God is given there [BECNT].
2. The plural article τοῖς 'the (places/things)' should be taken as neuter and then it refers to 'the things of my Father' [Alf, BNTC, Lns, NIC; KJV]: it is necessary for me to be in the things/affairs of my Father. This means that he must be about his Father's business [Lns; KJV]. His Father's business is the richer interpretation and it also includes the place since it would be conducted in the temple [Lns]. His Father's matters would include learning the word of God [Alf].

QUESTION—Who didn't understand what?

The word 'they' refers to Mary and Joseph [AB, Arn, NTC, WBC]. They didn't understand what he meant [Arn, MGC; CEV, GW, NCV, NLT, REB]. They did not understand the full implications and intent of what Jesus had said [TH]. They did not understand the nature of Jesus' mission to reveal his Father's will or his full identity [BECNT]. They didn't know all that his Messiahship involved [ICC, TNTC, WBC]. They did not grasp Jesus' reference to God as his Father [Alf, Rb], and the implications of his sonship to the divine Father [NIGTC]. Jesus had never spoken about himself in this way and they couldn't understand [Lns].

DISCOURSE UNIT: 2:51–52 [HCSB]. The topic is being in favor with God and with people.

2:51 And he-went-down with them and he-came to Nazareth and he-was-being subject-to[a] them. And his mother was-treasuring[b] all the matters in her heart.

LEXICON—a. pres. pass. participle of ὑποτάσσω (LN 37.31) (BAGD 1.b.β. p. 848): 'to be subject to' [Arn, BAGD, LN; KJV], 'to be in subjection to' [Lns; NASB], 'to be submissive to' [BECNT], 'to be obedient to' [AB, WBC; GW, HCSB, NCV, NET, NIV, NLT, NRSV, TEV], 'to be under someone's authority' [REB], 'to obey' [CEV], 'to render obedience to' [NTC].

b. διατηρέω (BAGD p. 189): 'to treasure' [BAGD; GW, NASB, NIV, NRSV, TEV], 'to treasure up' [NTC; REB], 'to keep on thinking about' [CEV], 'to cherish' [AB], 'to keep' [Arn, BECNT; HCSB, KJV, NET], 'to keep in one's mind' [NCV], 'to carefully keep' [Lns], 'to store' [NLT], 'to store up' [WBC].

QUESTION—What are all the matters Mary treasured in her heart?

Similar to the clause 'Mary was keeping all these things pondering (them) in her heart' in 2:19, this refers to all that had happened [BECNT, Crd]. More than what happened at the temple is referred to [BECNT]. Although she did not fully understand, she remembered [EGT, TNTC].

2:52 And Jesus was-increasing in wisdom and stature/age[a] and in-favor[b] with God and people.

LEXICON—a. ἡλικία (LN 81.4, 67.156) (BAGD 1.b., 2. p. 345): 'stature' [Arn, BAGD (2.), BECNT, LN (81.4), Lns, NTC, WBC; HCSB, KJV, NASB, NET, NIV], 'height' [NLT], 'body' [TEV], 'age' [AB, BAGD (1.b.), LN (67.156)], 'years' [NRSV], 'maturity' [GW]. This noun is also translated as a verb: 'to grow' [REB], 'to become strong' [CEV]; and as an adverb modifying 'to grow': 'physically' [NCV].

b. χάρις (LN 25.89) (BAGD 2.b. p. 877): 'favor' [AB, BAGD, LN, Lns, NTC, WBC; all versions except CEV, NCV, NLT], 'grace' [Arn, BECNT], 'good will' [BAGD, LN]. The phrase 'he was increasing in favor with God and people' is translated 'God was pleased with him and so were the people' [CEV], 'people liked him and he pleased God' [NCV], 'he was loved by God and by all who knew him' [NLT]. Jesus increasingly experienced God's loving kindness [NTC]. See this word at 1:30 and 2:40.

QUESTION—Does ἡλικία refer to Jesus' stature or age?
1. It refers to his stature [BECNT, BNTC, Crd, EGT, Gdt, ICC, Lns, My, NIC, NTC, Rb, TH, WBC; HCSB, KJV, NASB, NCV, NET, NIV, TEV]: Jesus increased in wisdom and in stature. This refers to his physical growth [BECNT, ICC, NTC; NCV]. The information that he increased in age is not relevant after speaking of growth in wisdom [TH].
2. It refers to his age or maturity [AB, Alf, MGC, NICNT, NIGTC; GW, NRSV, REB]: Jesus increased in wisdom and in years/maturity. This refers to the maturity that accompanies aging [NIGTC]. That he grew in stature does not need to be stated [AB].
3. It refers to his strength [CEV]: Jesus became wise and he grew strong.

DISCOURSE UNIT: 3:1–4:15 [NAC]. The topic is the preparation for Jesus' ministry.

DISCOURSE UNIT: 3:1–4:13 [AB, BECNT, NICNT, NIGTC, Su, WBC]. The topic is the preparation for Jesus' ministry [AB, BECNT, NICNT, Su, WBC], John the Baptist and Jesus [NIGTC].

DISCOURSE UNIT: 3:1–20 [BECNT, NAC, NICNT, NIGTC, TNTC; CEV, GW, HCSB, NASB, NCV, NET, NIV, NLT, NRSV, REB, TEV] The topic is John the Baptist [NAC], the ministry of John the Baptist [NICNT, TNTC; NET], the preaching of John the Baptist [NIGTC; CEV, NASB, NCV, NRSV, TEV], the role and ministry of John the Baptizer [Su], John the Baptist: the one who goes before [BECNT], John the Baptist prepares the way [GW, NIV, NLT], the Messiah's herald [HCSB], John the Baptist and Jesus [REB].

DISCOURSE UNIT: 3:1–6 [AB, NAC, NIGTC, WBC]. The topic is the person of John the Baptist [AB, NAC, WBC], the beginning of John's ministry [NIGTC].

3:1 Now in the fifteenth year of-the reign of-Tiberius Caesar,[a] (while) Pontius Pilate was-governor of-Judea, and Herod was-tetrarch[b] of-Galilee, and his brother Philip was-tetrarch of-(the)-country of-Iturea and Trachonitis, and Lyssania was-tetrarch of-Abilene,

LEXICON—a. Καῖσαρ (LN 37.74, 93.208) (BAGD p. 396): 'Caesar' [AB, Arn, BECNT, LN (93.208), Lns, NTC, WBC; HCSB, KJV, NASB, NCV, NET, NIV], 'Emperor' [LN (37.74); CEV, GW, NRSV, TEV], 'the emperor' [REB], 'the Roman emperor' [NLT]. 'Caesar' was originally a proper name of Caesar Augustus, but later it was used as a title with the meaning Emperor, as 'Emperor Tiberius' in 3:1 [BAGD]. See this word at 2:1.

b. pres. act. participle of τετρααρχέω (LN 37.79) (BAGD p. 814): 'to be tetrarch' [AB, Arn, BAGD, BECNT, LN, Lns, NTC, WBC; KJV, NASB, NET, NIV, REB], 'to be governor' [HCSB], 'to be ruler' [CEV, NCV, NLT, NRSV, TEV], 'to rule' [GW]. The title was first used of a governor who ruled a fourth part of a territory, but later the title was used of a governor of any division of territory or merely a ruler of a minor domain [AB, ICC, NIGTC]. It became a title for a petty prince [AB, WBC]. However, some see four divisions covered here when Judea is counted as one of them [ICC, Lns]. This rank was equivalent to a governor over a region [NET].

QUESTION—Which Herod is referred to here?

This was Herod Antipas, the younger son of Herod the Great who had ruled at the time Jesus was born [AB, Arn, BECNT, ICC, Lns, MGC, NAC, NIBC, NIC, NIGTC, NTC, Su, TNTC; NET]. He is the Herod of the Gospels, except for the references to Herod I (Herod the Great) in Matt. 2:1–9 and Luke 1:5 [NTC].

QUESTION—Where are the countries mentioned along with Judea and Galilee?

Iturea was not as clearly defined as Galilee but was northeast of Galilee [Su]. It is the territory along the Lebanon and Anti-Lebanon ranges [NIGTC]. Trachonitis was about 35 miles east of Galilee [NIGTC] and south of Damascus [Lns, WBC]. Both were northeast of the Jordan River and bordered on Syria [AB]. Iturea and Trachonitis were only two of the various small areas ruled by Philip [AB], and the designation 'of the country of Iturea and Trachonitis' seems to indicate that more than these two are included [ICC]. The location of Abilene is uncertain, but it probably was north of the other regions that are mentioned [TNTC], being the territory west of Damascus [AB, Su, WBC] at the southern end of the Anti-Lebanon range [AB], the area around the city of Abila [MGC, NIGTC].

3:2 **at-the-time-of (the) high-priesthood of Annas and Caiaphas, (the) word of-God came to John the son of-Zechariah in the desert.**[a]

LEXICON—a. ἔρημος (LN 1.86) (BAGD 2. p. 309): 'desert'. See translations of this word at 1:80.

QUESTION—How could both Annas and Caiaphas be the high priest?

The term 'high priesthood' is in the singular form and although two names are given, there was only one high priest at the time and that was Caiaphas [AB, Arn, BECNT, EGT, NAC, NIC, NICNT, NIGTC, NTC]. Annas was a retired high priest and as such, he kept his title [AB, Arn, Gdt, NAC, NIGTC], and still had great influence [Arn, EGT, Lns, NAC, NIC, NICNT, NIGTC, TNTC]. Annas was the father-in-law of Caiaphas [Alf, MGC, NIGTC, WBC]. Since the Roman authorities appointed and changed high priests, a group of Jews refused to acknowledge that Annas was deposed and this could well be translated 'in the time of the high priest Annas, and of Caiaphas' [WBC]. In practice, both Annas and Caiaphas shared the authority of high priest [BECNT, NTC], with Annas exercising his power behind the scenes [BECNT, MGC]. Either they discharged the duties of high priest between them or in different senses each of them was regarded as high priest [ICC].

QUESTION—What is the significance of the word of God *coming* to John?

It means that God spoke to John [Lns; CEV, GW]. This was a call from God to be a prophet [AB, BECNT, BNTC, Crd, EGT, ICC, NIGTC, NIVS, NTC, Su, TNTC, WBC], and to begin the ministry predicted of him [BECNT]. What God said to John can be deduced from the result that follows [Lns]. God's message must have ordered John to awaken the people to the need of repentance and to introduce them to the Messiah [NTC]. Here ῥῆμα 'word' means a particular utterance [ICC, Lns] and is distinct from λόγος 'word' which refers to the Gospel message as a whole [ICC]. It points to the content of the message [Lns].

QUESTION—What is the significance of the call coming to John in the desert?

Although this indicates the geographical place of the call, it implies that John was the promised prophet of Isaiah 40:3, the voice calling in the desert [NAC, NIGTC]. Its exact location is unknown [NIGTC]. This connects this portion with 1:80 where John was in the desert until the time of his manifestation to Israel [Gdt, ICC, NTC, TH].

3:3 And he-came to all the surrounding-region of-the Jordan preaching[a] a-baptism of-repentance[b] for[c] (the) forgiveness of-sins,

LEXICON—a. pres. act. participle of κηρύσσω (LN33.256) (BAGD 2.b.β. p. 431): 'to preach' [AB, BAGD, BECNT, LN, Lns, WBC; HCSB, KJV, NASB, NCV, NET, NIV, NLT, TEV], 'to proclaim' [Arn, BAGD, NTC; NRSV, REB], 'to tell people' [CEV, GW]. It means to proclaim a religious message [BAGD], to announce religious truths and principles and urge the listeners to accept them and comply with them [LN]. It is an authoritative proclamation [TH]. 'To preach baptism' means to preach about the necessity and value of baptism [ICC], to proclaim the significance of baptism and the need to submit to it [NIGTC]. See this word at 4:18, 19, 44; 8:1, 39; 9:2; 12:3; 24:47.

b. μετάνοια (LN 41.52) (BAGD p. 512): 'repentance' [AB, Arn, BAGD, BECNT, LN, Lns, WBC; GW, HCSB, KJV, NASB, NET, NIV, NRSV, REB], 'a change of mind' [BAGD], 'changed hearts and lives' [NCV], 'a turning about' [BAGD], 'conversion' [BAGD, NTC]. This noun is also translated as a verb phrase: 'to turn away from sin' [TEV], 'to turn back to God' [CEV], 'to turn from sin and turn to God' [NLT]. It refers to changing one's way of life so that there is a complete change of thought and attitude with regard to sin and righteousness [LN]. It includes remorse over shortcomings and errors [BAGD]. It means a change of mind [ICC, Su], with a corresponding change of conduct [Su]. It is a turning away from evil [WBC]. It is a change of heart so that one turns from sin to God's cleansing and forgiveness [Lns]. The word connotes conversion or reform of life in its religious sense [AB]. It includes sorrow for sin and a resolve to break with the evil past, and also fruit-bearing [NTC]. See this word at 3:8; 5:32; 15:7; 24:47.

c. εἰς (LN 89.57) (BAGD 4.f. p. 229): 'for' [AB, Arn, BAGD, BECNT, Lns, WBC; all versions except CEV, NLT, TEV], 'in order to' [BAGD, LN], 'for the purpose of' [LN], 'so that' [BAGD], 'to' [NLT], 'with a view to' [NTC], 'then' [CEV], 'and' [TEV].

QUESTION—How are the event words 'baptism' (people should be baptized by John the Baptizer) and 'repentance' (people should repent of their sinful lives) related in the genitive construction 'a baptism of repentance'?

Baptism is qualified or defined by 'repentance' [AB, ICC, Lns, NAC, NICNT, NIGTC, Su, TH, TNTC]. It was a 'repentance-baptism' and only a repentant person was qualified for this baptism [ICC, Lns, NICNT]. John was telling people to express their repentance by being baptized [NIGTC, TH]. Baptism follows repentance and it is a sign or symbol of repentance [ICC, TNTC]. It reminds the people who are baptized of their new obligations [ICC]. Baptism is the external symbol of the inward change [ICC, NIC, NIGTC]. The act of baptism in itself does not primarily signify repentance, rather it is a symbol of being cleansed from sin as God's response to their repentance [WBC]. The requirement for baptism was repentance and one's conversion was powerfully stimulated by undergoing baptism, which is both an outward sign of God's cleansing grace and forgiving love and a sign of an inward grace applied to the heart and life [NTC].

1. Some translations bring out the fact that baptism symbolizes repentance [NLT, REB]. This is translated 'people should be baptized to show that they had turned from their sins and turned to God' [NLT], 'a baptism in token of repentance' [REB].
2. Some translations express this as two acts, with repentance coming before baptism [NTC; CEV, TEV]. This is translated: 'turn back to God and be baptized' [CEV], 'turn away from your sins and be baptized' [TEV].

QUESTION—What relationship is indicated by εἰς 'for' in the phrase 'for the forgiveness of sins'?

1. It indicates the purpose of the baptism of repentance [AB, BAGD, BECNT, BNTC, Gdt, ICC, Lns, My, NAC, NIGTC, NTC, Su, TH; NLT; probably all versions except CEV, TEV, since they translate as 'for']: a baptism of repentance *in order to* be forgiven of one's sins. Forgiveness is the desired result of John's baptism of repentance [NAC].
2. It indicates the result of the baptism of repentance [Lns, NIC, NIGTC; CEV, TEV]: repent and be baptized *and then* your sins will be forgiven. Every such baptism granted forgiveness to the person baptized [Lns]. This is translated 'Turn away from you sins and be baptized, and God will forgive your sins' [TEV], 'Turn back to God and be baptized! Then your sins will be forgiven' [CEV].

QUESTION—Is baptism the requirement for forgiveness?

'For the forgiveness of sins' depends grammatically on the whole phrase 'baptism of repentance' [Gdt]. The rite of baptism did not automatically bring forgiveness and it is not to be isolated from repentance since forgiveness is intimately associated with repentance [NAC]. Forgiveness is possible only to those who repent, so John told the people to express their repentance in baptism [NIGTC]. Forgiveness is the purpose of repentance [Su].

QUESTION—Is this forgiveness of sins the equivalent of New Testament salvation?

John was preparing the people for the Messiah, but John's baptism was not the same as Jesus' baptism with the Holy Spirit (3:16). John's baptism pointed forward to the cleansing that comes to those who put their faith in the Messiah [BECNT]. Repentance and forgiveness are key parts of salvation and in John's ministry they have the quality of readying the people for Jesus' arrival, and therefore whoever is prepared by John's baptism will be ready to welcome the Messiah [WBC]. John's baptism was administered according to what had been revealed at that time and it made them followers of the coming Messiah, while Christian baptism is administered on the level of Jesus' completed work and it makes them followers of the Messiah who has come [Lns].

3:4 as it-has-been-written in (the) book of-(the) words of-Isaiah the prophet, A-voice[a] shouting[b] in the desert, Prepare the road[c] of-(the)-Lord, make straight his paths.[d]

TEXT—Following προφήτου 'prophet', some manuscripts add λέγοντος 'saying'. GNT does not mention this variant. Λέγοντος 'saying' is read by KJV.

LEXICON—a. φωνή (LN 33.103) (BAGD 2.e. p. 871): 'voice' [Arn, BAGD, BECNT, LN; all versions except CEV, NLT, TEV], 'a voice of one' [Lns, NTC], 'a voice from someone' [AB, WBC], 'someone' [CEV, TEV]. Using the metonymy 'voice' directs the focus to the contents of the utterance and not to the person [Gdt, ICC, Lns].

b. pres. act. participle of βοάω (LN 33.81) (BAGD 2. 144): 'to shout' [BAGD, LN, Lns; CEV, NLT, TEV], 'to call out' [WBC; NCV], 'to call' [NIV], 'to cry out' [AB, BAGD, LN; GW, HCSB, NET, NRSV], 'to cry' [Arn, BECNT, NTC; KJV, NASB, REB].

c. ὁδός (LN 1.99) (BAGD 1.a. p. 554): 'road' [BAGD, LN; CEV, TEV], 'way' [AB, Arn, BAGD, BECNT, LN, Lns, NTC, WBC; all versions except CEV, NLT, TEV], 'pathway' [NLT], 'highway' [BAGD, LN]. This word is a general term for a thoroughfare, either within a population center or between two such centers [LN]. See this word at 1:76.

d. τρίβος (LN 1.100) (BAGD p. 826): 'path' [AB, Arn, BAGD, BECNT, LN, Lns, NTC, WBC; all versions except NCV, NLT], 'beaten path'

LUKE 3:4

[BAGD, LN], 'road' [NCV, NLT]. This word refers to a well-worn path or thoroughfare [LN].

QUESTION—What relationship is indicated by ὡς 'as'?

This indicates a comparison and shows that John's ministry is a fulfillment of the prophetic message of Isaiah [AB, BECNT, Gdt, NAC, NIC, NIGTC]. This serves to connect John's ministry to announcing the promised salvation and has no direct reference to the baptism he administered [TH]. The ὡς 'as' suggests a deliberate fulfillment of the prophecy rather than only following a general pattern [NIGTC]. In John 1:23 John applied the passage in Isaiah 40:3 to himself when he denied that he was the Messiah.

QUESTION—What is the reference for this quotation from the book of Isaiah?

The quotation is from Isaiah 40:3–5. Matthew and Mark only quote from Isaiah 40:3. Luke extended the quotation so as to include the idea he brings up in 3:6 concerning universalism and salvation [WBC]. In the Hebrew text for Isaiah 40:3, the phrase 'in the desert' modifies the following verb 'prepare': A voice shouting, 'In the desert prepare the road of the Lord'. However, in the Greek text of the Septuagint and of Luke, the phrase 'in the desert' could be taken either with the preceding verb 'shouting' or with the following verb 'prepare' [Gdt, ICC]. All commentators and versions of the Greek text interpret the phrase to modify the preceding verb: A voice shouting in the desert, 'Prepare the road of the Lord'. This arrangement is described as being more natural [ICC]. Of course both the shouting and the preparing of those who heard took place in the desert [Lns]. The Hebrew text for Isaiah 40:5 has 'and the glory of the Lord shall be revealed, and all flesh shall see it together'. The Septuagint text translates the second clause 'and all flesh shall see the salvation of God', and only this second clause is selected by Luke in his quote. Since the glory of the Lord is that of Christ and glory is revealed in the work of salvation, there is no essential difference in any of the texts [NTC]. God's glory is seen in his salvation [BECNT].

QUESTION—How is 'Lord' related to the road in the genitive construction 'the road of the Lord' and who is the Lord?

The road is to be made ready for the Lord to travel over [WBC; CEV, GW, NCV, NET, NIV, REB, TEV], or for the Lord's coming [NLT]. The preparation is for the Lord to come to Israel [WBC]. The road over which the Lord is coming must be made ready [TH]. By using 'his paths' instead of the Septuagint's 'the paths of our God', the distinction between God and the Messiah is blurred [BNTC].

1. 'The Lord' refers to God's coming as in the OT text [BECNT]. In 1:17, John is prophesied to go ahead of the Lord their God [BECNT, ICC, NAC, NICNT, Rb, WBC; CEV, GW, NASB, NCV, NET, NIV, NLT, TEV]. The one who repents awaits God's salvation (3:6) which is revealed in the Spirit baptism that is brought by Christ, and in the following verses judgment is also brought by God [BECNT].
2. 'The Lord' refers to Christ's coming [Arn, NAC]. 'Lord' refers to the Christ, who is called Lord in 2:11 [NAC].

3:5 Every valley will-be-filled-in and every mountain and hill will-be-leveled-off, and the crooked (paths) will-be (made) into straight (roads) and the rough (roads) into smooth roads.

QUESTION—What is to be supplied with the adjectives 'crooked' and 'rough'?

For 'crooked', translations supply 'roads' [Arn; NCV, NIV, TEV], 'paths' [CEV, REB], 'ways' [GW], or 'places' [BECNT, Lns, WBC]. For 'rough', translations supply 'roads' [CEV, GW, NASB, NCV], 'paths' [TEV], 'ways' [AB, WBC; KJV, NET, NIV, NRSV, REB], or 'places' [BECNT].

QUESTION—What is the metaphor involved in this quotation?

The *image* is that of physical work on the roads, preparing the roads to make them fit for a king or someone of high rank to travel over when he arrives to that part of his realm [TNTC, WBC]. The work is done on already existing roads [TH] and makes it easier to travel over them [NAC, NIGTC]. They were to tear down the high places and use the soil to fill in the low places so as to make the roads straight and smooth [TNTC]. The *topic* is that of the internal moral and spiritual preparation of the people for the coming of the Lord [ICC]. Repentance is primarily in focus [BECNT, ICC, NIGTC]. The *point of comparison* is preparation, a term that can apply to both roads and people. As kings send couriers ahead of them to tell the people of their lands to prepare roads for their coming, so the Messiah sends his herald to tell his people to prepare their hearts for his coming [ICC]. The extensive figurative language should be retained in a translation if possible [TG].

3:6 And all people[a] will-see the salvation of-God.

LEXICON—a. σάρξ (LN 9.11) (BAGD 3. p. 743): 'person' [BAGD, LN; GW, NCV, NLT], 'human being' [AB, LN], 'humanity' [NET], 'man' [BECNT], 'mankind' [NIV, REB], 'flesh' [Arn, BAGD, Lns, NTC, WBC; KJV, NASB, NRSV]. The phrase 'all people' is translated 'everyone' [CEV, HCSB], 'the whole human race' [TEV]. It includes both Jews and Gentiles [MGC, NIBC]. The word 'flesh' is used figuratively here to indicate 'people' or 'human beings' [LN].

QUESTION—How is God related to the word 'salvation' in the genitive construction 'the salvation of God'?

People will see the salvation that God gives [GW], sends [NLT], or has prepared [Arn]. It is the saving power of God [CEV], or the saving gift of God [Lns]. They will see the salvation of God in the sense that they will know about it [NCV]. It means that they will see how God will save them or they will see the Savior that God will send them [TG]. The phrase is equivalent to the Messiah [BNTC]. The Messianic salvation will appear in and with the coming of the Messiah [My]. What Simeon had seen in 2:30 would be seen by everyone [NIGTC].

DISCOURSE UNIT: 3:7–20 [NAC]. The topic is the mission of John the Baptist.

DISCOURSE UNIT: 3:7–18 [AB, NICNT, WBC]. The topic is the preaching of John [AB, WBC], John proclaims the Good News [NICNT].

DISCOURSE UNIT: 3:7–14 [BECNT]. The topic is the preaching of John the Baptist.

DISCOURSE UNIT: 3:7–9 [NIGTC]. The topic is the preaching of John.

3:7 So[a] he-was-saying to-the crowds coming-out to-be-baptized by him, Children of-vipers,[b] who warned[c] you to-flee from the coming wrath?[d]

LEXICON—a. οὖν (LN 91.3) (BAGD 2.a. p. 593): 'so' [BAGD, LN; NASB, NET], 'then' [KJV], 'now' [BECNT], 'therefore' [Lns, NTC], 'accordingly' [AB], 'and' [Arn], 'here is a sample of John's preaching' [NLT], 'then' [HCSB], not explicit [WBC; CEV, GW, NCV, NIV, NRSV, REB, TEV].

    b. ἔχιδνα (LN 88.123) (BAGD p. 331): 'viper' [AB, Arn, BAGD, LN, Lns, NTC, WBC; HCSB, KJV, NASB, NET, NIV, NRSV, REB], 'snake' [BECNT, LN; CEV, NCV, NLT, TEV], 'poisonous snake' [GW]. The phrase 'children of vipers' is translated 'offspring of vipers' [Arn, Lns, NTC, WBC; NET], 'brood of vipers' [AB; HCSB, NASB, NIV, NRSV], 'vipers' brood' [REB], 'brood of snakes' [NLT], 'generation of vipers' [KJV], 'you bunch of snakes' [CEV], 'you snakes' [TEV]. 'Viper' is used figuratively for an evil person [LN]. A viper was a desert snake [NTC], small and poisonous [AB, Lns, TH, WBC]. 'Viper' can refer to any of over twenty varieties of poisonous snakes in Israel [NAC].

    c. aorist act. indic. of ὑποδείκνυμι (LN 28.47) (BAGD 2. p. 844): 'to warn' [AB, BAGD, Lns, NTC, WBC; all versions except GW, TEV], 'to make known' [LN], 'to show' [BAGD, LN], 'to show how' [GW], 'to instruct' [Arn], 'to demonstrate' [LN], 'to tell' [BECNT; TEV].

    d. ὀργή (LN 38.10) (BAGD 2.b. p. 579): 'wrath' [AB, Arn, BAGD, BECNT, Lns, NTC, WBC; HCSB, KJV, NASB, NET, NIV, NRSV, REB], 'anger' [BAGD], 'God's anger' [GW], 'judgment' [BAGD; CEV, NLT], 'punishment' [LN; TEV], 'God's punishment' [NCV]. This refers to God's punishment based on his anger against someone [LN]. It is God's reaction to evil [BAGD, Lns]. The coming wrath alludes to the day of the Lord when he judges all people [AB, BECNT, BNTC, NAC, NICNT, TG]. See this word at 21:23.

QUESTION—What relationship is indicated by οὖν 'so'?
    1. It indicates the resumption of the narrative after the interruption of 3:4–6 [BAGD (2.a. p. 593), TH].
    2. It indicates the result of the quote from Isaiah [AB, ICC, Lns]. Since John was a voice shouting in the wilderness, he therefore preached in the following manner [AB, Lns].

QUESTION—What is meant by the metaphor 'children of vipers'?
    This is reproachful language [TH], and insulting [TG]. This harsh language was intended to awaken the listeners to the realities of their state [NIGTC].

1. The *image* is vipers [BECNT, Lns, NTC]. The *topic* is the crowd. Matthew 3:7 says that he spoke to the Pharisees and Sadducees. Speaking to the crowd, he probably looked at those two groups as he spoke [BECNT]. Probably John was speaking to the crowd, but focused on the Pharisees and Sadducees [BECNT, Lns]. Some think that calling them *the children* of vipers is significant [Gdt, ICC, Lns, NICNT, NIGTC, Su]. The multitudes remind John of a family of snakes wriggling along ahead of a fire [Su]. The multitudes are compared to successive broods of vipers coming forth alive from their parent viper [Gdt]. Attacking their trust in descent, this indicates another parentage than that of Abraham [Gdt, ICC, NICNT, NIGTC]. They have taken up the sins of their fathers who had preceded them [Lns]. The relationship between the snake and the devil might be intended [NICNT, NTC], but the plural form 'vipers' prevents one from pressing the point too far [NIGTC]. The *point of comparison* is being destructive [AB, BECNT, NIGTC], evil [NICNT, NIGTC, WBC], wicked [Gdt, TG], deceptive [Lns, NTC], cunning [TH], clever [TG], crafty [Gdt], hypocritical, treacherous [Lns], hostile to life [NICNT], and repulsive [AB].
2. Some include the question 'who warned you to flee from the coming wrath' as part of the metaphor so that the *image* is that of vipers fleeing from fire [BECNT, NIC, NIGTC, Su; NET]. The *topic* is the crowd fleeing from the coming wrath. The *point of comparison* is the act of trying to escape from danger. Just as vipers escape from a brush fire, so the Jews are trying to escape from the coming judgment [NIC, NIGTC; NET].

QUESTION—What is the intent of John's question 'Who warned you to flee from the coming wrath'?
1. It is rhetorical and implies that it was not John who told them that it was possible to escape [Lns, NAC, NIGTC, NTC, TH; TEV]: *who deluded you* into thinking that it is possible to evade the coming wrath? This is translated 'Who told you that you could escape from the punishment God is about to send?' [TEV]. The implied answer is 'I certainly have not' [NAC, NIGTC], it is the devil [Lns]. The point is that no one can escape by insincere outward forms [Lns, NIGTC, TH]. However, there is a real way of escape still open [Lns].
2. It is rhetorical and implies that they need to think about John's message [BECNT]: *Who is it that* warned you to flee from the wrath to come? This is a rebuke to grab their attention and cause them to consider what John's baptism was all about [BECNT].

3:8 Therefore[a] produce fruits[b] worthy[c] of-repentance[d] and do- not -begin to-say within yourselves, We-have Abraham (for our) father. Because I-say to-you that God is-able from these stones to-raise-up[e] children to-Abraham.
LEXICON—a. οὖν (LN 89.50): 'therefore' [Arn, BECNT, LN, Lns, NTC; HCSB, KJV, NASB, NET], 'so, consequently' [LN], 'then' [WBC],

'come now' [AB], not explicit [CEV, GW, NCV, NIV, NLT, NRSV, REB, TEV].
- b. καρπός (LN 3.33, 13.86) (BAGD 2.a. p. 405): 'fruit' [AB, Arn, BAGD, BECNT, LN (3.33), Lns, NTC, WBC; HCSB, KJV, NASB, NET, NIV, NRSV, REB]. The phrase 'produce fruits worthy of' is translated 'do something to show that you really have' [CEV], 'do the things that show you really have' [NCV], 'do those things that will show that' [TEV], 'do those things that prove that' [GW], 'prove by the way you live that' [NLT]. The phrase ποιέω καρπόν 'to make/produce fruit' is an idiom and means to produce results [LN (13.86)]. It is best to preserve the metaphor of bearing fruit so as to tie this in with the trees bearing fruit in 3:9 [TH]. Fruits are the deeds resulting from some inner moral force [NAC, TH]. The plural form 'fruits' is used to cover the different examples given in 3:10–14 [AB, MGC, NAC, WBC]. The plural form suggest repetitiveness of the action [BECNT].
- c. ἄξιος (LN 65.17) (BAGD 1.b. p. 78): 'worthy (of)' [Arn, BAGD, BECNT, LN, Lns, WBC; KJV, NRSV], 'in keeping (with)' [BAGD, NTC; NASB, NIV], 'consistent (with)' [HCSB], 'really' [CEV, NCV, NLT], 'that prove' [GW, NET], 'that will show' [TEV], 'prove (your repentance by)' [REB]. The phrase 'fruits worthy of repentance' is translated 'the fruit of worthy repentance' [AB]. The deeds are worthy of repentance when they harmonize with repentance so that inner repentance can be judged to be present by visible deeds [Lns].
- d. μετάνοια (LN 41.52) (BAGD p. 512): 'repentance'. See translations of this word at 3:3. This word also occurs at 5:32; 15:7; 24:47.
- e. aorist act. infin. of ἐγείρω (LN **13.83**) (BAGD 1.a.ε. p. 214): 'to raise up' [AB, Arn, BAGD, BECNT, **LN**, Lns, NTC, WBC; GW, HCSB, KJV, NASB, NET, NIV, NRSV], 'to bring into being' [BAGD], 'to turn into' [CEV], 'to change into' [NLT], 'to make' [NCV, REB, TEV]. It means to cause something to come into existence [LN].

QUESTION—What relationship is indicated by οὖν 'therefore'?

It indicates the consequence of an implied step [ICC, My, NIGTC, TH, WBC]: *since you want to escape the coming wrath,* you must *therefore* produce fruits worthy of repentance.

QUESTION—How does the conjunction καί 'and' connect 'and do not begin to say within yourselves, We-have Abraham for our father' with the preceding clause 'therefore produce fruits worthy of repentance'?

After commanding a positive response, John adds a warning against a response that should not enter their minds [BECNT, NICNT]. This is added to prevent the awakening of their need for repentance from being excused by the fact that they are descendants of Abraham [Gdt]. Another view is that the second part does not fit smoothly and interrupts the idea of fruit bearing with 3:9 which deals with trees that bear fruit. Probably the rest of 3:8 is a separate utterance of John that has been added here [NIGTC].

QUESTION—The Jews were actually descendants of Abraham, so why shouldn't they say that they have Abraham as their father?

To say that they 'have Abraham as their father' implies that they thought Abraham's merits applied also to them [NIGTC, TH, TNTC]. They relied on their descent from Abraham for their eternal security [NTC]. They thought that they inherited God's blessings through Abraham, so that being Abraham's descendant would bring them salvation [AB, Lns, WBC], and they had no need for repentance [Lns]. They needed to be warned against thinking that they would escape God's punishment of sinners just because they were Jews [Arn, TG]. God did not have to depend on Jews who were physically descended from Abraham since he could raise up a new Israel from even the stones. It is implied that God would not be unfaithful to his promises to Abraham, but that he has other ways of extending those promises to human beings [AB].

QUESTION—What is the argument introduced by γάρ 'because' in the last clause?

This clause gives the reason why the Jews should not depend on a false hope of being saved by being descendants of Abraham [Lns].

QUESTION—What is meant by raising up children from the stones?

1. The stones would be changed into children [Arn, BECNT, Lns, NICNT, NTC, Su, TG, TH, WBC]. God could provide all the descendants that Abraham needed [TG]. God could turn the stones on the ground into better children of Abraham than they were [Su]. God is able to fill the places left vacant by unrepentant, false children of Abraham by turning the stones lying about in the desert into spiritual children of Abraham [Lns]. Stones were chosen for the example because they were a feature of the desert landscape and because these lifeless and useless objects illustrated the range of options God had in replacing the unrepentant Jews [WBC]. Stones do not become children of God, but God creates children from them [BECNT]. This is said in sarcasm [Su]. This illustration may suggest that God can raise up spiritual children from the Gentiles [AB, BECNT, Gdt, Lns, NICNT, NTC].
2. The stones would produce children [NIGTC]. Rather than meaning that the stones would be changed into living people, he meant that the stones could bring forth living people as their children [NIGTC].

3:9 And even[a] already[b] the ax is-laid[c] at the root of-the trees. Therefore every tree not producing good fruit is-cut-down and is-thrown into (the) fire.

LEXICON—a. The phrase δὲ καί 'and even' is translated 'even' [NET, NLT, NRSV], 'indeed' [AB, WBC; NASB], 'and also' [KJV], 'but even' [Arn], 'and' [BECNT, NTC], 'moreover' [Lns], not explicit [CEV, GW, HCSB, NCV, NIV, REB, TEV].

b. ἤδη (LN 67.20) (BAGD p. 344): 'already' [AB, BAGD, BECNT, LN, Lns, NTC, WBC; NASB, NIV, REB], 'now' [Arn, BAGD; GW, HCSB, KJV, NCV, NLT, NRSV, TEV], not explicit [CEV, TEV].

c. pres. mid/pass. (deponent = act.) indic. of κεῖμαι (LN 85.3) (BAGD p. 426): 'to be laid' [AB, Arn, BAGD, LN, NTC; KJV, NASB, NET, NRSV, REB], 'to be placed (against)' [WBC], 'to lie' [Lns], 'to be laid and aimed' [BECNT], 'to be, to rest on' [LN]. It means to be in place [LN]. The phrase 'the ax is laid at the root of the trees' is translated 'the ax is at the root of the trees' [NIV], 'the ax is ready to cut the trees down at their roots' [CEV, TEV], 'the ax is ready to cut the roots of the tree' [GW], 'the ax is ready to strike the root of the trees' [HCSB], 'the ax is ready to cut down the trees' [NCV], 'the ax of God's judgment is poised, ready to sever your root' [NLT].

QUESTION—How does δὲ καί 'and even' connect this verse with the previous one?

It indicates an addition to what John said in 3:8 [NIGTC]. The δέ 'and' means 'moreover' and indicates that this verse is something else and the καί with the meaning 'also' adds this verse to 3:8 and here the figure of producing fruit is now expanded [Lns]. This combination indicates emphasis [ICC]. It is a special emphasis to 'already' so as to highlight the urgency of John's call [TH].

QUESTION—How can one ax be laid at one root of many trees?

There is a difficulty in that both 'ax' and 'root' are singular and 'trees' is plural. Since there is a single ax lying at the root of many trees, the figure is strained [Lns, WBC], but this is necessary because one judgment will strike many individuals [Lns]. The ax is ready to cut down one tree after another [NTC]. Or, since the plural form 'trees' is in the text, this describes an orchard of trees with an invisible ax laid at the root of every tree [Gdt]. Some translate so that the ax is ready to cut the roots (plural) of the trees (plural) [CEV, GW, TEV].

QUESTION—What is meant by the metaphor of an ax already poised at the roots of a tree to chop down the trees that do not bear good fruit?

This builds on the mention of fruit in 3:8 [Gdt, ICC, TH] and connects with the following sentence where trees not producing good fruit are chopped down. The *image* is of an ax already laid in position at the root of a tree to chop down all the trees that do not bear fruit. That the ax is lying at the root indicates that the ax is directed towards the roots [ICC, TH], or placed at the root [Lns, Rb]. Various pictures are possible. One is that the woodsman is estimating the swing of his ax by first touching the ax to the place where he will begin his strokes to chop down the tree [TH]. Another is that the woodsman has the ax aimed at the roots and when he swings, the tree will be cut down [BECNT]. The ax is poised to strike [NIGTC]. Another omits the woodsman and has the ax lying at the roots, waiting to be used [AB, Lns]. The 'root' refers to the lowest part of the trunk above ground [WBC], that is, the base of the tree [TH]. The implied *topic* is that God is ready to judge those who do not show the results of repentance. The felling of trees is a prophetic symbol of judgment [BECNT, Lns, TG, TH, WBC]. The good fruits are the fruits worthy of repentance mentioned in 3:8 [Gdt, NIGTC, TH, TNTC]. The *point of similarity* is the fact of judgment [Gdt, NAC, NICNT, Su, WBC], the inevitableness of judgment [ICC], and the immanence of judgment [BECNT, ICC, NIC, NICNT, NIGTC, NTC]. The initial position of the adverb ἤδη 'already' stresses the nearness of the coming judgment [BECNT].

QUESTION—What is meant by the cut-down trees being thrown into the fire?
1. Throwing the cut-down trees into the fire is a metaphor of judgment [BECNT, Lns, NIVS, NTC, TH; NET]. The fire is a symbol of God's wrath outpoured on the wicked [NTC]. Fire symbolizes hell [TG].
2. Throwing the cut-down trees into the fire is just part of completing the picture of disposing bad trees [AB, NIGTC, WBC]. Here, fire merely refers to burning dead wood and has a different connotation from that of the fire in 3:17 [AB].

DISCOURSE UNIT: 3:10–14 [NIGTC]. The topic is John's ethical teaching.

3:10 **And the crowds were-questioning him saying, Then what should-we-do? 3:11 And answering he-was-saying to-them, The (one who) has two shirts[a] let-him-share[b] with-the-(one) not having (a shirt), and the (one who) has food let-him-do likewise.**

LEXICON—a. χιτών (LN 6.176) (BAGD p. 882): 'shirt' [BAGD, NTC; GW, HCSB, NCV, REB, TEV], 'undergarment' [BECNT], 'tunic' [AB, Arn, BAGD, LN, Lns, WBC; NASB, NET, NIV], 'coat' [LN; CEV, KJV, NLT, NRSV]. It was a garment worn under the outer cloak [EGT, LN, NAC, NIGTC, TH, TNTC], the garment next to the skin [BAGD, TG, TH, WBC]. This was a short undershirt that was worn underneath a longer outer garment or tunic and although both were usually worn, the inner garment was not necessary [BECNT, ICC]. It was a tunic worn by both sexes next to the skin [NTC]. The garment had short sleeves and was knee length [TG]. In cold weather a person might wear two shirts [ICC, Lns, NTC, TNTC, WBC]. This command may mean that the person is to give up one of the shirts he is wearing, or he might give one of the spare shirts he has in his wardrobe [NIGTC, WBC]. This refers to another shirt he possessed and does not imply that it is one of two shirts he is wearing at the same time [EGT, ICC, TG, TH, WBC]. See this word at 6:29; 9:3.
b. aorist act. impera. of μεταδίδωμι (LN **57.96**) (BAGD p. 511): 'to share' [AB, Arn, BAGD, **LN**, Lns, NTC, WBC; GW, HCSB, NASB, NCV, NET, NIV, NRSV, REB], 'to give' [BAGD, BECNT, LN], 'to give one' [CEV, NLT, TEV], 'to impart' [KJV]. To give someone a share of two coats is to give him one shirt [ICC]. It is implied that the one with whom it is shared has none [WBC].

QUESTION—What is the force of the imperfect tense in the clause ἐπηρώτων αὐτὸν οἱ ὄχλοι 'the crowds *were questioning* him'?
1. The imperfect tense indicates repetition [Arn, BECNT, EGT, Gdt, ICC, NTC, Rb, TH; HCSB, NASB, NET]: the crowds were questioning him. They asked this question continually [ICC], or frequently [Gdt]. The question would be asked frequently due to the repeated exhortation to repentance [EGT].
2. The imperfect tense does not indicate repetition here [AB, BNTC, Crd, Lns; CEV, GW, KJV, NCV, NET, NIV, NLT, NRSV, REB, TEV]: the crowds questioned him. The imperfect form does not differ here from the aorist εἶπαν 'they said' regarding the soldiers in 3:12 [Crd, Lns]. The imperfect is merely descriptive here [Lns]. It is used in a vivid style in conjunction with the following aorist verbs [NET].

QUESTION—What is the intent of the crowds' question 'What should we do'?
They wanted to know what the fruits of true repentance involved [BECNT, Gdt, Lns, NAC, NICNT, NIGTC, WBC]: what are the fruits that we should produce in order to show true repentance? This was their response to John's message [NAC, TH], and it did not imply that they wanted to know how they could be saved by their works [NAC]. The people assumed that they must do something in order to escape being punished by God [NIC, TG], and the severe punishment John had just described made them want to escape it [Gdt, ICC]. This is not a rhetorical question expressing a despair of ever escaping judgment, but it indicates that they wanted to know how they could bear fruit that God considered good [TH]. The people asked themselves as much as they asked John [Lns].

QUESTION—How did these instructions show repentance?
These are concrete examples of the fruits of repentance in a reformed life [AB, EGT, Lns, NAC, WBC]. The answers are meant to be characteristic of the type of answers he gave [EGT]. These examples indicate an unselfish approach to life [BECNT]. The answers to the first question may be suited to the poverty of the crowd [WBC]. The three answers show the practical meaning of repentance in terms of love and justice [Alf, WBC]. Basic to all three answers is the principle that they should show genuine love [Lns, NTC, Su], something that is impossible apart from God [NTC].

3:12 And also tax-collectors came to-be-baptized and they-said to him, Teacher, what should-we-do? **3:13** And he-said to them, Collect nothing more than the (amount) you have-been-ordered.[a]

LEXICON—a. perf. pass. participle of διατάσσω (LN 33.325) (BAGD p. 189): 'to be ordered' [BAGD, LN; GW, NASB, NCV], 'to be appointed' [BECNT, WBC; KJV], 'to be prescribed' [Lns; NRSV], 'to be fixed' [Arn], 'to be authorized' [AB; HCSB], 'to be required' [NTC], 'to be required (to collect)' [NET, NIV]. The whole sentence is translated 'exact no more than the assessment' [REB], 'don't collect more than is legal' [TEV], 'don't make people pay more than they owe' [CEV], 'make sure you collect no more taxes than the Roman government requires you to' [NLT]. They were to charge only what were the legitimate tolls and commissions [AB], and not charge more than they had been ordered to collect [TG]. Tax collectors had instructions on how much to collect [NICNT].

QUESTION—Who were tax collectors and when did they come?
Chief tax collectors purchased the right from the Roman government to collect indirect taxes such as customs or tolls on merchandise that passed through the region [AB, NIGTC, NTC, WBC]. They would have to collect not only the tax demanded by Rome, but also a surcharge to meet their expenses and profits [AB, BECNT]. The chief tax collector employed agents who were the tax collectors who actually carried out the work [AB, BECNT, NIGTC, NTC] and he received a commission on what they collected [WBC]. Probably the tax collectors who were on the lower rung of the profession were addressed here [NICNT, NTC, TH, TNTC]. 'Toll collector' is likely the more exact term for such men [AB, BECNT, NAC, NICNT], since they collected indirect taxes such as tolls, tariffs, and customs [AB]. Toll collectors were stationed at commercial centers to collect tolls, customs, and tariffs [NAC]. They collected taxes on the goods and produce taken in or out of town [TG]. The taxes involved both the sale of goods and their movements [WBC]. The tax system made it possible to abuse it in many ways and as a result the collectors were hated and despised by their fellow countrymen [NAC, NICNT, NIGTC]. They charged as much as the traffic would bear [NTC]. Some think that the tax collectors were also present in the crowds [NICNT, NIGTC; REB]. Others think that they came as a group at another time [WBC].

3:14 And also soldiers were-asking him saying, Also us what should-we-do? And he-said to-them, Extort-money[a] (from) no-one nor bring-false-charges-against[b] (anyone) and be-satisfied with your wages.

LEXICON—a. aorist act. subj. of διασείω (LN 57.245) (BAGD p. 188): 'to extort money' [LN], 'to extort' [NIV, NLT], 'to practice extortion' [AB, WBC], 'to extort money by threats' [NRSV], 'to extort money by violence' [BAGD, NTC], 'to take money by violence' [NET], 'to take money by force' [**LN**; HCSB, NASB, TEV], 'to force people to give money' [NCV], 'to use threats to get money' [GW], 'to intimidate' [Lns], 'to rob by violence' [BECNT], 'to do violence' [KJV], 'to treat with violence' [Arn], 'to bully' [REB]. The phrase 'extort money from no one nor bring false charges against anyone' is translated 'don't force people to pay money to make you leave them alone' [CEV].

b. aorist act. subj. of συκοφαντέω (LN **33.434**) (BAGD 1. or 2. p. 776): 'to bring false charges against someone' [**LN**], 'to accuse falsely' [Arn, BAGD (1.), NTC; KJV, NASB, NIV, TEV], 'to lie about someone' [NCV], 'to use blackmail to get money' [GW], '(to take money) by false accusation' [HCSB, NET], '(to extort money by) false accusation'

[NRSV], 'to accuse people of things you know they didn't do' [NLT], 'to practice unlawful exaction' [WBC], 'to practice blackmail' [AB], 'to blackmail' [REB], 'to rob by fraudulent extortion' [BECNT], 'to extort' [BAGD (2.)]. See a. above for CEV.

QUESTION—Who were the soldiers?

A few think that these were soldiers of the Roman occupation army [Su, TG], or perhaps Jewish members of the Roman army [Su]. Most think that they were not Roman soldiers, but the soldiers employed by Herod Antipas to serve in Peraea [AB, Arn, NIBC, NIGTC], or perhaps soldiers used in Judea for police duties [NIGTC]. They were probably Jewish soldiers acting as police who supported and protected tax collectors [BECNT, Gdt, ICC, NIC, TNTC, WBC], and they would be associated with the same corrupt practices of the tax collectors [WBC]. That they are of this last group is supported by taking καί to mean 'also' in their question '*Also* us, what should we do?' [BECNT]. Another view is that the καί means 'even' and implies that the soldiers were not Jews [TH], or that their work was out of keeping with Jewish piety [NIGTC]. No matter who the soldiers were, John spoke to them as though they were Gentiles [NICNT].

QUESTION—What is the difference between extorting money and bringing false charges?

Both verbs involve extortion and often occur together as synonyms [WBC]. Some explain the differences. The verb διασείω 'to extort money' is explained as being practically a synonym with the next verb, but can be more violent than the second [BECNT, WBC]. This verb refers to terrifying people by shaking them and it is possible to extend the idea to extorting money [AB, BECNT, Lns, NIGTC]. It means to rob someone by violence [BECNT, TH]. The verb συκοφαντέω 'to bring false charges' refers to extortion [BECNT]. It means to extort money by fraud or false representation [BECNT], by violence [NIGTC], or by intimidation [EGT, NIGTC]. It means to rob someone by blackmail [TH], or to rob by false accusation [Crd, NIGTC]. They used blackmail by threatening to use a false accusation in order to extort money [Lns]. Another view is that it means to obtain money by acting as informers against the rich [Alf, EGT]

QUESTION—What is the significance of adding the command to be satisfied with their wages?

This refers to another sin common to soldiers [Lns, NAC]. The first two prohibitions concerned ways of obtaining money to supplement the basic wages of the soldiers and now comes an exhortation to be content with their wages, which would cause them to be less tempted to do what was prohibited [BECNT].

DISCOURSE UNIT: 3:15–18 [BECNT]. The topic is the promise made by John the Baptist.

DISCOURSE UNIT: 3:15–17 [NIGTC]. The topic is the coming of the stronger one.

3:15 And (while) the people were-expecting[a] and all were-wondering in their hearts concerning John, whether-perhaps he might-be the Messiah,

LEXICON—a. pres. act. participle of προσδοκάω (LN 30.55) (BAGD 3. p. 712): 'to expect' [BAGD, LN; NLT], 'to wait expectantly' [HCSB, NIV], 'to be in expectation' [KJV], 'to be in expectancy' [Arn, WBC], 'to be in a state of expectation' [NASB], 'to be in constant expectation' [Lns], 'to be filled with expectation' [NRSV], 'to be on the tiptoe of expectation' [NTC], 'to be expectant' [BECNT], 'to anticipate' [LN], 'to be filled with anticipation' [NET], 'to look for' [BAGD], 'to hope for' [NCV], 'to be excited' [CEV], 'to be all agog' [REB], 'to be piqued with curiosity' [AB]. This is also translated as a phrase: 'hopes were rising' [GW], 'hopes began to arise' [TEV].

QUESTION—What were the people being expectant about?

Since the participle does not have an object, it should be taken in an absolute sense and mean that because of John's message the people who heard him were in a state of expectation [TH]. The people were expecting something marvelous to happen [TG]. They thought the end-times were drawing near [BECNT]. The people were looking for the coming of the Messiah [Arn, Lns, NIGTC, NTC, TNTC; NET, NLT]. This implies that John had already proclaimed the coming of the Messiah [Lns]. The subject of the coming of the Messiah has already been mentioned in 1:76–79, 2:25, 26, and 38 [NTC]. As shown by the following text, they were waiting for John's explanation about himself [Alf, My]. They were waiting expectantly for the outcome of John's preaching, especially wondering if John would be involved in the Messianic judgment [ICC, WBC].

3:16 John answered everyone saying, I baptize you with-water. But the (one) greater-than[a] I is-coming, of-whom I-am not worthy[b] to-untie the strap of-his sandals; he will-baptize you with[c] (the) Holy Spirit and with-fire;

LEXICON—a. ἰσχυρός (LN 87.44) (BAGD 1.a. p. 383): 'great' [LN], 'powerful' [BAGD, LN], 'strong, mighty' [BAGD]. The comparative form used here is translated 'greater than' [Arn; NCV, NLT, TEV], 'more powerful than' [AB; CEV, GW, HCSB, NET, NIV, NRSV], 'mightier than' [NTC, WBC; KJV, NASB, REB], 'stronger than' [BECNT, Lns]. The word means that the coming one has more authority or power than John has or is more important than John [TG]. The implication is 'If you think I am great, he who will be here presently is infinitely greater' [Lns]. The Messiah is superior to John in terms of his status and especially in his mode of baptism [NICNT]. The stronger one is stronger in view of his superior baptismal powers [NIGTC].

b. ἱκανός (LN 75.2) (BAGD 2. p. 374): 'worthy' [Arn, BAGD, BECNT, WBC; GW, HCSB, KJV, NET, NIV, NLT, NRSV, REB], 'qualified' [BAGD, LN], 'adequate' [LN], 'to be good enough' [CEV, NCV, TEV], 'to be fit' [AB, Lns, NTC; NASB]. The metaphor emphasizes John's lowly rank in contrast to Jesus' more powerful one [AB]. Only the lowest slave had the duty of removing the master's sandals to clean them, so if John is not fit for such a duty, then how great must the Messiah be! [Lns]. A Hebrew slave would find the action too demeaning for him to do for his master, but even such a lowly act done for the coming one would be a privilege beyond the reach of John [BECNT, NAC, TNTC, WBC]. A slave would unfasten his master's sandals when he returned home and bring them when his master went out [Gdt, ICC]. See this word at 7:6.

c. ἐν with a dative object (LN 90.10) (BAGD p. 59): 'with' [AB, Arn, BAGD, LN (90.10), NTC, WBC; all versions], 'with regard to' [LN (89.5)], 'in connection with' [Lns].

QUESTION—What is meant by Jesus baptizing people *with the Holy Spirit*?

'Baptize' is used metaphorically and ἐν means 'with' [AB, BAGD, BECNT, Gdt, Lns, NIVS, NTC, TNTC, WBC; all versions]: he will baptize you with the Holy Spirit and fire. The preposition ἐν indicates the element in which baptism takes place [ICC], and makes 'he will baptize you *with* the Holy Spirit and fire' figurative language (probably all which translate the preposition 'with'). The metaphor of baptizing with means that he will impart the Spirit in a generous measure [TNTC]. It means that he will cause the Spirit and the Spirit's gifts to come upon his followers and this is described in other verses which say that the Spirit will be poured out on them, and fall upon them [NTC]. This happened at Pentecost [NIVS]. This refers to sending the Holy Spirit with the outpouring of the Spirit at Pentecost being the final great mark of the Messiah [Lns].

QUESTION—What is meant by Jesus baptizing people *with fire*?

1. 'Baptism with the Holy Spirit and fire' is one concept and fire signifies the purification of the believer [Gdt, ICC, Lns, MGC, WBC; NET]: he will baptize you (who repent) with the Holy Spirit and purifying fire. Baptism is always regarded as a cleansing, so fire signifies purification [Lns]. In this baptism, the Spirit will cleanse and purge the person [NET]. The initial fulfillment of this promise is described in Acts 2 at Pentecost [NET].
2. 'Baptism with the Holy Spirit and fire' are two distinct baptisms and fire refers to the punishment of the unbelievers [Arn, EGT, NAC, NIBC, NIVS, Rb, Su, TG, TH, TNTC]: he will baptize you who repent with the Holy Spirit and will baptize you who do not repent with fire. The following verse connects fire with judgment, and fire is also used throughout Luke as a metaphor for judgment (9:54; 12:49; 17:29), so in terms of the following verse, the 'wheat' will receive the Spirit but the 'chaff' will endure the judgment of burning [NAC].
3. Fire has two different applications [NIC, NTC]: he will baptize you (who repent) with the Holy Spirit and purifying fire, and he will baptize you (who do not repent) with the fire of judgment. In the case of his followers, he will baptize with the Holy Spirit by causing the Spirit to come upon

believers and will baptize them with purifying fire; in the case of the godless, he will baptize them with the fire of final judgment [NTC].
4. 'Baptism with the Holy Spirit and fire' is one baptism that has two consequences [BECNT, NTC, WBC]: he will baptize you (who repent) with the Holy Spirit and his fire (of purification) and he will baptize you (who do not repent) with the Holy Spirit and his fire (of judgment). Baptism with both Spirit and fire results in purification for the repentant and destruction for the godless [WBC]. The Spirit purges people and divides them according to their decision in regard to this baptism [BECNT]. The Spirit is spoken of in regard to an eschatological purging in which the penitent are purified with fire and the godless are destroyed with fire [WBC].

3:17 of-whom the winnowing-fork[a] (is) in his hand to-clean-out[b] his threshing-floor[c] and to-gather the wheat into his barn, but he-will-burn-up the chaff with-an-unquenchable[d] fire.

TEXT—Instead of διακαθᾶραι...καὶ συναγαγεῖν 'to clean out...and to gather', some manuscripts read καὶ διακαθαριεῖ...καὶ συνάξει 'and he will clean out...and he will gather'. GNT does not deal with this variant. Καὶ διακαθαριεῖ...καὶ συνάξει 'and he will clean out...and he will gather' is read by KJV.

LEXICON—a. πτύον (LN 6.6) (BAGD p. 727): 'winnowing fork' [BECNT, WBC; NASB, NET, NIV, NLT, NRSV], 'threshing fork' [CEV], 'winnowing shovel' [BAGD, LN, Lns, NTC; GW, HCSB, REB, TEV], 'winnowing fan' [AB, Arn], 'fan' [KJV], not explicit [NCV]. This was a fork-like shovel [AB, BAGD, BECNT, LN, NAC] made of wood [BECNT], and it was used to throw threshed grain into the air so that the wind would blow the chaff away from the grain [BAGD, LN]. The instrument was a large wooden shovel [Lns] with two or more prongs [NTC].

b. aorist act. infin. of διακαθαίρω (LN **79.51**) (BAGD p. 183): 'to clean out' [BAGD, LN; NET], 'to clean off' [LN], 'to clean up' [AB; GW, NLT], 'to thoroughly clean' [**LN**, Lns], 'to clean' [Arn; NCV], 'to clear' [BECNT, WBC; HCSB, NIV, NRSV, REB], 'to thoroughly clear' [NTC; NASB], 'to thoroughly purge' [KJV], 'to thresh out' [TEV], 'to separate' [CEV].

c ἅλων (LN 79.5, 3.43) (BAGD 2. p. 41): 'threshing floor' [AB, Arn, BECNT, LN, Lns, NTC, WBC; GW, HCSB, NASB, NET, NIV, NRSV, REB], 'floor' [KJV], 'threshing area' [NLT]. The word itself refers to a surface of hard ground or stone where grain was threshed out [LN (79.5)]. Although most take ἅλων 'threshing floor' to refer literally to the floor itself [AB, BECNT, BNTC, Gdt, ICC, Lns, NICNT, NTC, Su, TNTC, WBC; all versions except CEV, NCV, TEV], some understand the 'threshing floor' to be a metonymy that refers to the threshed grain still lying on the threshing floor [TH; CEV, NCV, TEV] and the phrase διακαθᾶραι τὴν ἅλωνα αὐτοῦ 'to clean up his threshing floor' is translated 'to thresh out completely all of the grain' [LN (79.5)], 'to clean his threshed grain' [LN (3.43)], 'to cleanse (winnow) what has been threshed' [BAGD], 'to thresh out all the grain' [TEV], 'to clean the grain' [NCV], 'to separate the wheat from the husks' [CEV].

    d. ἄσβεστος (LN 14.71) (BAGD 1. p. 114): 'unquenchable' [Arn, BECNT, LN, Lns, NTC; KJV, NASB, NIV, NRSV], 'inextinguishable' [BAGD, WBC; NET], 'never-ending' [NLT], '(a fire) that never goes out' [CEV, HCSB, TEV], '(a fire) that will never go out' [AB], '(a fire) that cannot be put out' [NCV], '(a fire) that can never be put out' [GW, REB].

QUESTION—What is the background of this verse, all of which is the image of an extended metaphor except for the actor and the word 'unquenchable'?

The floor surface could be a flat rock or a prepared area of about thirty to fifty feet in diameter that had been cleared of stones, wetted down, and packed hard [NTC]. A farmer would clean the threshing floor by removing all of the straw and chaff with a winnowing shovel so as to leave in the center of the floor a heap of only the grain [Lns]. The threshing floor was a level area on a hill where it could catch the breeze. Then the grain would be beaten or trampled so that when it was thrown up with a winnowing shovel, the wind would blow away the chaff to the side [Su]. The light, useless chaff would be blown away while the heavier, usable grain would fall directly down to the threshing floor [BECNT]. Winnowing makes it possible to gather up separately the grain and the chaff [WBC]. The chaff would be gathered to burn in the cooking ovens [NAC].

QUESTION—What is the topic and point of similarity of this metaphor?

The *topic* is the separation of the godly (those who repent and accept the coming one) from all the rest of mankind and the disposal of the separated parts [Lns]. The *point of similarity* is the act of sorting or separating one class from another [AB, BECNT, NICNT, WBC], sorting according to worth [AB], separating the good from the worthless [TG], separation and disposal [Lns], or judgment [Lns, NIGTC, NTC, TG, TH, TNTC]. He will judge all people by separating the good people from the bad people and he will keep the good people safe in heaven and will cause the bad people to be destroyed in hell [TG]. Jesus is ready to divide people so that those who draw near to him will be spared and those who refuse him will have to endure eternal judgment [BECNT]. The Coming One will take God's children into his presence in the new heaven and earth, but he will cast the wicked into the unquenchable fire of hell where their punishment is unending [NTC].

DISCOURSE UNIT: 3:18–20 [NIGTC]. The topic is John's imprisonment.

3:18 And therefore (with) many other/different exhortations he-was-announcing-good-news[a] to-the people.

LEXICON—a. aorist mid. infin. of εὐαγγελίζω (LN 33.215) (BAGD 1. p. 317): 'to announce good news'. See translations of this word at 1:19. This word also occurs at 2:10; 4:18, 43; 7:22; 8:1; 9:6; 16:16; 20:1.

QUESTION—Since the word ἕτερος can mean 'other' or 'different', what is meant by 'many other/different exhortations'?
1. The word ἕτερος has the meaning 'other' [Arn, BECNT, NIGTC, TH; GW, HCSB, KJV, NASB, NCV, NET, NIV, NRSV, REB]: with many *other* exhortations. The word had lost the sense of different and was used as a synonym for ἄλλος 'other' [NIGTC]. It means that he preached many such things [NLT]. He preached about much more than what is presented here [BECNT]. This refers to many other exhortations in addition to those already reported [Arn].
2. The word ἕτερος has the meaning 'different' [EGT, ICC, My, NTC, Rb, WBC; CEV, TEV]: with many *different* exhortations. It means different in kind [ICC, My, Rb], and this indicates that not all of John's preaching was like what has just been indicated [ICC]. He preached many things different from these warnings of judgment and the following verb 'announcing good news' points to a more evangelistic content [EGT]. John exhorted the people in respect to many and different matters [NTC].

DISCOURSE UNIT: 3:19–20 [AB, BECNT, NICNT, WBC]. The topic is the imprisonment of John the Baptist. Luke's account is not chronological here, but logical. For about a year the ministries of John and Jesus were concurrent, but at this point nothing has been said about Jesus' ministry. Luke simply wants to bring the account of John's ministry as a free man to a close in order to focus on Jesus' ministry [NTC]. John has been the primary actor since the word of God came to him (3:2), but now Luke removes him from the stage before introducing Jesus [NICNT]. This explains the sudden end to John's ministry and also provides the background for the account in 7:18 where John is in prison when he sent two disciples to Jesus [Gdt].

3:19 And Herod the tetrarch,[a] **being-reproved by him about Herodias the wife of his brother and about all (the) evil which Herod did, 3:20 he-added**[b] **this also on-top-of everything (else) and he-locked-up John in prison.**
TEXT—In 3:19, following γυναικός 'wife' some manuscripts add Φιλίππου 'of Philip'. GNT does not deal with this variant. Φιλίππου 'of Philip' is read by KJV.
LEXICON—a. τετραάρχης (LN 37.78) (BAGD p. 181): 'tetrarch' [AB, Arn, BAGD, BECNT, LN, Lns, NTC, WBC; HCSB, KJV, NASB, NET, NIV, REB], 'governor of a region' [LN], 'governor' [NCV, TEV], 'ruler' [CEV, GW, NRSV], 'ruler of Galilee' [NLT]. This was Herod Antipas who was mentioned in 3:1 [Lns]. See also the verb form of this word τετραρχέω 'to be tetrarch' in 3:1.
b. aorist act. indic. of προστίθημι (LN **59.72**) (BAGD 1. p. 719): 'to add' [BAGD, LN]. The phrase προσέθηκεν καὶ τοῦτο ἐπὶ πᾶσιν 'he added this also on top of everything' is translated 'added also this on top of all' [Lns], 'also added this to them all' [NTC, WBC; NASB, NET, NIV], 'added also this to all of them' [Arn], 'added this to everything else' [HCSB], 'added to them all' [NRSV], 'added this above all' [BECNT],

'added yet this above all' [KJV], 'added one more evil to all the others' [GW], 'adding this sin to his many others' [NLT], 'crowned them all' [AB; REB], 'did something even worse' [NCV], 'did an even worse thing' [TEV], 'finally this was the worst thing he had done' [CEV]. Some state or translate that he did one more evil deed in the sequence of evil deeds he had done [WBC; NASB, NET, NIV, NLT, NRSV], while others indicate that this was the crowning instance of all the evil he had done [AB, BECNT, EGT, Gdt, Lns, NAC, NIGTC, TG, TH; CEV, KJV, NCV, REB, TEV]. His greatest sin was to reject and persecute God's messenger [NAC]. Up to this point at least, this was the climax of his sins [NIGTC]. Luke does not mention the beheading of John, either assuming this deed was already known or shrinking from writing about such a gruesome deed [EGT].

QUESTION—What was the reason for reproving Herod about Herodias, his brother's wife?

Luke doesn't say what it was, but it is implied that it was something sinful that needed to be reproved [Lns]. This vague reference to John's rebuke perhaps assumes that the story behind it was of common knowledge [NICNT]. The sin that John rebuked is recorded in Matthew 14:3–5 and Mark 6:17–20. It was that both Herod Antipas and Herodias had left their previous marriages to marry each other and that Herodias' previous marriage had been to Herod's half-brother Philip [BECNT]. Herod's half-brother was not the same Philip mentioned in 3:1, but was the Philip of Mark 6:1 who lived in Rome [TG]. The rebuke would have been based on Leviticus 18:16 where it commands that a man should not have intercourse with his brother's wife and Leviticus 20:21 where it states that marriage to a brother's wife is a sin [AB, BECNT, WBC]. The present tense of the participle 'being reproved' indicates that John reproved Herod more than once [Lns, NICNT, NTC, TH]. John used to reprove Herod for all the wicked things he did, but this reproof concerning Herodias was what caused Herod to imprison John [TH].

DISCOURSE UNIT: 3:21–4:15 [NAC]. The topic is Jesus.

DISCOURSE UNIT: 3:21–4:13 [BECNT, NICNT, TNTC]. The topic is the introduction of Jesus, Son of God [NICNT], Jesus, the one who comes after [BECNT], the beginning of Jesus' ministry [TNTC].

DISCOURSE UNIT: 3:21–38 [NAC; NIV, REB]. The topic is the person of Jesus [NAC], the baptism and genealogy of Jesus [NIV], the ancestry of the Messiah [REB].

DISCOURSE UNIT: 3:21–23a [GW]. The topic is the baptism of Jesus.

DISCOURSE UNIT: 3:21–22 [AB, BECNT, NICNT, NIGTC, Su, TNTC, WBC; CEV, HCSB, NASB, NCV, NET, NLT, NRSV, TEV]. The topic is the baptism of Jesus [AB, BECNT, NIGTC, Su, TNTC; CEV, HCSB, NASB, NLT,

NRSV, TEV], Jesus is baptized by John [NCV], Jesus' baptism and the heavenly endorsement [NET], the anointing of Jesus [NICNT], Jesus endowed with the Spirit and affirmed as Son [WBC]. These two verses consist of a single sentence in Greek. Unlike the parallel passages in Matthew and Mark, the baptism takes a subordinate place in this section and the emphasis is on the unique events that accompanied the baptism [BECNT, EGT, Lns, NICNT, NIGTC, TNTC, WBC]. The sentence centers on the three infinitive clauses 'the heaven was opened', 'the Holy Spirit descended' and 'a voice came', actions that occurred while Jesus was praying after his baptism [NICNT].

3:21 **And it-happened when all the people had-been-baptized also Jesus had-been-baptized and (as) he-was-praying heaven was-opened**[a]

LEXICON—a. aorist pass. infin. of ἀνοίγω (LN 79.110) (BAGD 1.b. p. 71): 'to be opened' [Arn, BAGD, LN, Lns, NTC; KJV, NASB, NIV, NRSV, TEV]. This passive form is also translated actively with the sky or heaven as the subject: 'to open' [AB, BECNT, WBC; GW, HCSB, NCV, NET, NLT, REB], 'to open up' [CEV].

QUESTION—Who were all the people who were baptized before Jesus was baptized?

It does not mean all of the people of Israel, rather it means all the people whom John baptized, and this summarizes the climax of John's work although chronologically there was an overlap between the ministries of John and Jesus [NIGTC]. It refers to the crowds mentioned in 3:7 [MGC]. 'All the people' is not to be taken literally, but refers to a great number of those present [Arn, TH]. 'All the people' is hyperbolic [BECNT, My] as shown by 7:30 where it states that not all had been baptized [BECNT]. The hyperbole is used to emphasize the large number who responded, not the total number of individuals [BECNT]. The phrase stresses the universal reaction of the people and at this point the distinction between the people and their leaders has not been introduced [AB]. There is a difference of opinion as to whether or not these people were present when Jesus was baptized. Some think all the people referred to were present when John baptized Jesus [MGC, My; probably CEV, NLT, REB]. Others think that probably Jesus waited until he could be alone with John [Gdt, ICC, NIC]. It was not until *after* every one had been baptized [ICC]. We are not to think that Jesus patiently stood by until all the others were baptized and then he presented himself for baptism. It simply means that at the height of John's ministry of baptizing many people, Jesus was also baptized [NTC].

QUESTION—Since Jesus had nothing to repent of, why did he submit to John's baptism?

Luke does not tell us why Jesus submitted to a baptism of repentance, but the fact that God said he was well pleased with his beloved Son indicates that Jesus was not in need of repentance [NAC]. Submitting to baptism showed Jesus' endorsement of John's ministry and message [BECNT, MGC]. It indicated that Jesus identified himself with the people and endorsed the need of people to repent [BECNT]. It provided the opportunity for the Spirit's descent to identify Jesus as the Coming One who would bring the greater baptism [NIGTC]. Jesus accepted John's baptism as a mark of his initial association with him and as preparation for his own ministry [AB]. Jesus' participation in John's ministry of preparing the people showed his identification with John's imperatives and expectations [WBC]. It was the way Jesus publicly assumed the task of taking upon himself the sin of the world [NTC]. By accepting baptism, Jesus entered into his Messianic office, placing himself alongside the sinful ones for whom baptism was ordained and signifying that he was now ready to take upon himself the burden of their sins [NTC]. Jesus was identifying himself with the sinners he had come to save [Su, TNTC].

QUESTION—What is meant by heaven being opened?

The Greek word οὐρανὸν 'heaven' refers to the sky, so the picture is that of a portion of the sky opening like a curtain drawing open and through that opening the Holy Spirit came as from heaven itself [Su]. It was like a door of a temple or palace being opened [TH]. It seemed as though heaven was rent asunder [NTC]. The heavenly glory became visible for a short time so that John and all the others who were present saw its radiance until the heavens closed [Lns]. Another view is that only Jesus saw this place of eternal light [Gdt].

3:22 and the Holy Spirit descended upon him in-bodily form[a] like a-dove, and a-voice came out-of heaven, You are my Son the beloved (one), with you I-am-well-pleased.

TEXT—Following γενέσθαι 'came', some manuscripts add λέγουσαν 'saying'. GNT does not deal with this variant. Λέγουσαν 'saying' is read by KJV.

TEXT—Instead of Σὺ εἶ ὁ υἱός μου 'You are my Son', some manuscripts read Υἱός μου εἶ σύ 'My Son are you', and some manuscripts read Οὗτός ἐστιν ὁ υἱός μου, 'This is my Son'. GNT reads Σὺ εἶ ὁ υἱός μου, 'You are my Son', with a B decision, indicating that the text is almost certain.

TEXT—Instead of ὁ ἀγαπητός, ἐν σοὶ εὐδόκησα 'the beloved, with you I am well pleased', some manuscripts read ὁ ἀγαπητός, ἐν ᾧ εὐδόκησα 'the beloved, in whom I am well pleased', and some manuscripts read ἐγὼ σήμερον γεγέννηκά σε 'I today have begotten you'. GNT reads ὁ ἀγαπητός, ἐν σοὶ εὐδόκησα 'the beloved, with you I am well pleased', with a B decision, indicating that the text is almost certain.

LEXICON—a. εἶδος (LN 58.14) (BAGD 1. p. 221): 'form' [AB, Arn, BAGD, BECNT, LN, Lns, NTC, WBC; all versions except KJV], 'shape' [KJV], 'appearance' [BAGD, LN]. The phrase σωματικῷ εἴδει ὡς περιστερὰν 'in bodily form like a dove' [AB, BECNT; NASB, NET, NIV, NRSV, REB, TEV; similarly Arn, NTC] is also translated 'with bodily form as a dove' [Lns], 'in a bodily shape like a dove' [KJV], 'in a physical appearance like a dove' [HCSB], 'in the form of a dove' [CEV, GW, NCV, NLT], 'with a bodily form like that of a dove' [WBC].

QUESTION—What was the appearance of the Holy Spirit when he descended?
1. The Holy Spirit assumed a bodily form like a dove and his dove-like form was seen to come down [Arn, ICC, Lns, NIGTC, NTC, Su, TG, TH, WBC]. There is no need to think of a visible form different than that of a dove since the Spirit can reveal himself in any form, whether like a dove or tongues of fire [ICC]. What was seen was a bodily form resembling a dove which was descending on Jesus [NTC]. The Spirit gently descended upon the head of Jesus like a dove would descend so that his visible form looked like a dove [NIGTC]. The words 'bodily' and 'form' indicate the Spirit's appearance and 'like' identifies approximation, not of identification [WBC]. The Spirit is by nature invisible, but he had no difficulty in appearing to people in the form of a dove [Lns]. The dove was a symbol of purity and also peace [Arn].
2. The Holy Spirit assumed a bodily form that is not described and in that form was seen to descend in the same way that a dove would come down [BECNT, Gdt, NAC; NET]. This is a simile and does not mean the Spirit actually took the form of a dove when he descended on Jesus [NAC]. What was visible was something that could be compared to a dove, but it was not a dove. The comparison was mainly in the manner of the Spirit's descent which was like the way a dove gracefully floats through the air [BECNT]. A light, like a vibrating luminous ray, came down on Jesus' head like the fluttering of the wings of a dove [Gdt].

QUESTION—How is the phrase 'the beloved (one)' connected with 'You are my Son'?
1. 'Beloved' is in an attributive position, either 'you are my beloved Son' [AB, Arn, NIGTC, WBC; CEV, HCSB, KJV, NASB, NET, NLT, REB, TEV], or 'you are my Son whom I love' [GW, NCV, NIV].
2. 'Beloved' is in apposition to 'Son' [BECNT, ICC, Lns, NTC, TH; NRSV]: 'you are my Son, the beloved one'. The repetition of the articles '*the* son of me, *the* beloved one' presents two facts about Jesus [ICC].

QUESTION—What is the significance of the aorist tense of the verb εὐδόκησα 'I was pleased'?
This aorist is best translated as present tense [Arn, BECNT, ICC, NTC, TH; all versions]: I am well pleased. It is a timeless aorist [ICC, NTC]. Or, the aorist refers to that past event when the Father chose him for his redemptive work and this means 'I was well pleased in choosing you' [Lns]. Or, the aorist is inceptive, meaning 'in you I have come to delight' [WBC], 'in you I have taken delight' [AB].

DISCOURSE UNIT: 3:23–38 [AB, BECNT, NICNT, NIGTC, Su, TNTC, WBC; CEV, HCSB, NASB, NCV, NET, NLT, NRSV, TEV]. The topic is the genealogy of Jesus [AB, BECNT, NICNT, NIGTC, Su, TNTC, WBC; HCSB, NASB, NET], the ancestors of Jesus [CEV, NRSV, TEV], the record of Jesus' ancestors [NLT], the family history of Jesus [NCV]. In Greek this unit is only one sentence. The list of ancestors given here greatly differs from the genealogy list given in Matthew 1:1–17. Here it begins with Jesus and works backwards to Adam (and God) while in Matthew it begins with Abraham and works forward to Joseph and then Jesus. The two lists between David and Jesus are in almost total disagreement. See more about this in the answer to the question in 3:23, Who was Heli's descendant?

DISCOURSE UNIT: 3:23b–38 [GW]. The topic is the ancestors of Jesus.

3:23 **And beginning, Jesus himself was about thirty years (of age), being (the) son, as it-was-supposed,**[a] **of Joseph the (one) of-Heli,**

LEXICON—a. imperf. pass. indic. of νομίζω (LN 31.29) (BAGD 2. p. 541): 'to be supposed' [BECNT, LN, Lns, NTC; KJV, NASB, NET], 'to be thought' [Arn, BAGD, LN; HCSB, NIV, NRSV], 'to be reckoned' [WBC], 'to be known as' [NLT]. This passive is also translated actively: '(everyone) thought' [CEV], '(people) thought' [GW, NCV, REB, TEV]; or as a prepositional phrase: 'in the minds of the people' [AB].

QUESTION—How is the participle ἀρχόμενος 'beginning' related to this sentence?

It refers to the beginning of Jesus' ministry [AB, Alf, Arn, BECNT, ICC, NIC, NIGTC, Su, TG, TH; HCSB], and the participle indicates the temporal circumstance [CEV]: *when* he began his ministry, Jesus was about thirty years old. The participle is translated 'when beginning' [Lns], 'when he made a beginning' [WBC], 'when he/Jesus began his ministry' [NTC; GW, NASB, NCV, NET, NIV, NLT], 'when he/Jesus began his work' [NRSV, REB, TEV], 'when Jesus began to preach' [CEV], 'as he began his ministry' [AB; HCSB]. It was the beginning of his Messianic office [BNTC, Gdt, Lns, My], which began with his baptism and it was announced by the voice from heaven [My]. The commission by God marked the beginning of Jesus' actions as the Son of God empowered by the Spirit [WBC]. One version relates the participle to Jesus' age: 'Jesus himself began to be about thirty years of age' [KJV].

QUESTION—What is the reason for adding 'as it was supposed' to the statement that Jesus was the son of Joseph?

1. This refers to what uninformed people supposed Jesus' place in Joseph's family to be [Lns, NAC, NICNT, TH; probably all versions]. In this way it is indicated that Joseph was not the physical father of Jesus [EGT, NIGTC]. By the use of 'supposed', Luke signals that the characters in the story will view Jesus as an ordinary human being, but the readers share with Luke the correct view about Jesus [NICNT].
2. This refers to the reckoning of Jesus' legal standing, giving Jesus the legal status of son and heir in the Joseph's family and thus a place in the list of ancestors of Joseph [WBC].

QUESTION—What kinship term is to be supplied in the list of ancestors beginning with τοῦ 'Ηλί 'the (one) of-Heli' and running through to τοῦ θεοῦ 'the (one) of God' in 3:38?

Each name in the list merely has the article with the genitive noun. The word 'son' is supplied by most translations [AB, BECNT, Lns, NTC, TG, WBC; all versions except CEV, which merely lists the names]: 'the son of Heli…the son of God. In both Matthew's and Luke's lists there are gaps in the genealogies and in several cases 'son' would not refer to the immediate male descendant but must mean 'grandson' or 'great-grandson' [NTC]. The use of 'son' is different in reference to God in 3:38 [Lns].

QUESTION—Who was Heli's descendant?

1. Heli was the father of Mary and the grandfather of Jesus [Arn, Gdt, Lns, NIC, NIVS, NTC, Rb]: Jesus (supposedly the son of Joseph) was the son (= descendant) of Heli, Mary's father. After explaining that Jesus was not the real son of Joseph, Luke goes on to the first male link of the genealogical chain and the text has the sense 'being a son (as was supposed of Joseph but really) of Heli' [Gdt]. The word υἱός 'son' in this case would be used in two senses, *son* as was supposed of Joseph, and *grandson* through Mary of Heli [Rb]. Any reader would already know of the virgin birth and would understand that 'being a son of Heli' could only mean being Heli's son through Mary and it would be unreasonable for Luke to attach a genealogy of Joseph after saying that Jesus was only supposed to be Joseph's son. In the case of Matthew's list, Joseph's genealogy is given as 'the husband of Mary of whom was born Jesus' [Lns].

2. Heli was the father of Joseph [AB, Alf, BECNT, BNTC, Crd, EGT, ICC, MGC, My, NIGTC; NCV, NET, NLT, NRSV, REB, TEV]: Jesus was (supposedly) the son of Joseph, who was the son of Heli. According to Jewish law, Jesus was the heir of Joseph and so it is Joseph's descent that is important [ICC]. While Matthew gave the legal line of descent from David by stating who was heir to the throne in each case, Luke lists the actual descendants of David in the family to which Joseph belonged [NIGTC]. Many commentators say that in spite of many different complicated suggestions of how to reconcile Luke's list with Matthew's, it is not clear how they are to be reconciled [AB, Alf, ICC, My, NIGTC].

3:24–38 the (son) of-Matthat, the (son) of-Levi…the (son) of-Adam, the (son) of-God.

TEXT—In 3:26, instead of 'Ιωσήχ 'Josech', some manuscripts read 'Ιωσήφ 'Joseph'. GNT does not deal with this variant. 'Ιωσήφ 'Joseph' is read by KJV.

TEXT—In 3:26, instead of 'Ιωδά 'Joda', some manuscripts read 'Ιούδα 'Judah'. GNT does not deal with this variant. 'Ιούδα 'Judah' is read by KJV.

TEXT—In 3:29, instead of 'Ιησοῦ 'Joshua', some manuscripts read 'Ιωσή 'Jose'. GNT does not deal with this variant. 'Ιωσή 'Jose' is read by KJV.

142 LUKE 3:24-38

TEXT—In 3:32, instead of Σαλά 'Sala', some manuscripts read Σαλμών 'Salmon'. GNT reads Σαλά 'Sala' with a B decision, indicating that the text is almost certain. Σαλμών 'Salmon' is read by KJV and NIV.

TEXT—In 3:33, instead of τοῦ 'Αμιναδάβ τοῦ 'Αδμὶν τοῦ 'Αρνί 'of Amminadab of Admin of Arni', some manuscripts read τοῦ 'Αδάμ τοῦ 'Αδμὶν τοῦ 'Αρνί 'of Adam of Admin of Arni', one important manuscript reads τοῦ 'Αδμὶν τοῦ 'Αρνί 'of Admin of Arni', some manuscripts read τοῦ 'Αμιναδάβ τοῦ 'Αδμὶν τοῦ 'Αράμ 'of Amminadab of Admin of Aram', some manuscripts read τοῦ 'Αμιναδάβ τοῦ 'Αράμ τοῦ 'Ιωράμ 'of Amminadab of Aram of Joram', some manuscripts read τοῦ 'Αμιναδάβ τοῦ 'Αράμ τοῦ 'Αδμὶ τοῦ 'Αρνί 'of Amminadab of Aram of Admi of Arni', and some manuscripts read τοῦ 'Αμιναδάβ τοῦ 'Αράμ 'of Amminadab of Aram'. GNT reads τοῦ 'Αμιναδάβ τοῦ 'Αδμὶν τοῦ 'Αρνί 'of Amminadab of Admin of Arni' with a C decision, indicating that the Committee had difficulty making the decision. Τοῦ 'Αμιναδάβ τοῦ 'Αράμ 'of Amminadab of Aram' is read by KJV.

QUESTION—In what way was Adam the son of God?

Here, 'son' cannot mean the same in both 'son of Adam' and 'son of God' [NTC]. 'Son of God' refers to Adam's creation by God [Lns]. Adam can be called the son of God because he was created by God's hand [BECNT, NAC, NIGTC], and made in God's image [BECNT]. This affirms the divine origin of the human race [ICC, NICNT].

DISCOURSE UNIT: 4:1–15 [NAC]. The topic is the prelude to Jesus' mission.

DISCOURSE UNIT: 4:1–13 [AB, BECNT, NICNT, NIGTC, Su, TNTC, WBC; CEV, GW, HCSB, NASB, NCV, NET, NIV, NLT, NRSV, REB, TEV]. The topic is the temptation of Jesus [AB, NIGTC, Su, TNTC, WBC; HCSB, NASB, NET, NIV, NLT, NRSV, REB, TEV], the testing of Jesus [NICNT], Jesus and the devil [CEV], Jesus is tempted by the devil [GW, NCV], Messianic preparation: resisting Satan [BECNT]. The order of the last two temptations (the view from a high place and then the pinnacle of the temple) is different from Matthew's order (the pinnacle of the temple and then the view from a mountain). There are various explanations. Matthew gives a chronological report while Luke rearranged his material here, as in other places, perhaps so as to end with the temple scene [BECNT, Crd, Lns, MGC, NIGTC, NTC, WBC]. Matthew presented the historical order of the temptations, with the command for Satan to leave following the third temptation which was on the mountain. Luke left out the command to depart in order to reorder the locations so that the climax would be at the Temple [Lns]. Luke has a theological motive in changing the order of Matthew so that Jerusalem would be seen as the climatic location of conflict in Jesus' life [BECNT]. The order of each fits into their theological interests, Matthew preferring the mountain pattern while Luke concentrated on Jerusalem [NAC]. Luke's order follows a geographic sequence with the first two temptations occurring in the wilderness and the third in Jerusalem. Matthew's order follows a logical sequence from the lowest level of temptation concerning hunger, to the highest level of temptation concerning the supreme authority in Jesus' life, God or Satan [Su].

4:1 And Jesus full of-(the)-Holy Spirit returned/departed[a] from the Jordan and was-being-led[b] by the Spirit in the desert[c]

LEXICON—a. aorist act. indic. of ὑποστρέφω (LN 15.88) (BAGD p. 847): 'to return' [Arn, BAGD, LN, NTC; all versions except GW, NLT], 'to turn back' [Lns], 'to depart' [AB, WBC], 'to leave' [GW, NLT], 'to withdraw' [BECNT].

    b. imperf. pass. indic. of ἄγω (LN 36.1) (BAGD 3. p. 14): 'to be led' [BAGD, BECNT, LN, Lns, NTC; all versions except CEV, NASB, NCV], 'to be led around' [NASB], 'to be led about' [AB, Arn, WBC], 'to be guided, to be directed' [LN]. The passive voice is also translated actively with the Spirit as subject: 'to lead' [CEV, NCV]. The imperfect tense indicates that the Spirit continuously led Jesus about in the desert [Arn, EGT, ICC, Rb] from place to place [TH]. Translating the verb as 'to be led about' in the desert avoids a false implication that Jesus was not already in the desert when he was baptized by John [WBC]. Jesus was led *in* the desert, not *into* the desert, so that in his wanderings in the desert he was under the Spirit's influence and guidance [ICC]. Jesus was continuously under the guidance of the Spirit [TH]. This gives the picture of Jesus being on the offensive as he was led by the Spirit to confront the devil [Alf, NAC].

    c. ἔρημος (LN 1.86) (BAGD 2. p. 309): 'desert'. See translations of this word at 1:80. This would be the wilderness of Judea. Perhaps it was chosen to be a place for contact with God or because it was the place where wild animals and demons lived [AB, NAC]. Jesus needed to be alone while he considered the significance of God's words 'You are my Son, the beloved (one), with you I am well pleased' (3:22), and as he considered the nature of his messianic role [Su]. There he could contemplate his personal relationship with the Father and the task it imposed on him in reference to Israel and to the world [EGT].

QUESTION—Does the verb ὑπέστρεψεν mean that Jesus 'returned from' or 'departed from' the Jordan River?

    1. The verb means 'to return' [Arn, BAGD, Gdt, TH; all versions except GW, NLT]: Jesus returned from the Jordan. This is to be connected with 4:14 where it says that he returned to Galilee [Arn, TH]. Jesus left the place where he was baptized in order to return to Galilee, but on the way he stayed in the desert for forty days [Arn, Gdt, TH].

    2. The verb has the weaker sense 'to depart' [AB, BECNT, Lns, NICNT, NIGTC, WBC; GW, NLT]: Jesus departed from the Jordan. This does not mean that Jesus began his return trip and in 4:14 completed it, but that Jesus turned back from the Jordan and went into the desert [Lns]. Since Luke did not write that earlier Jesus came from Nazareth or Galilee, here

the verb means that he withdrew or turned aside from the Jordan River [AB, BECNT].

QUESTION—What is meant by Jesus being full of the Holy Spirit?

This is closely connected with the descent of the Holy Spirit at Jesus' baptism (3:22) [AB, EGT, Gdt, ICC, Rb]. The Holy Spirit descended on Jesus and then Jesus, under the Spirit's influence, went into the desert [ICC]. Being 'full of the Holy Spirit' means to be fully under the control of the Spirit [Su]. It means that the power of the Holy Spirit was with him [CEV]. Here, in contrast with 1:41 and 67 where Elizabeth and Zechariah were filled with the Spirit in order to prophesy, this describes a permanent condition [NIGTC, TH].

4:2 forty days being-tempted[a] by the devil.[b] And he-did- not -eat anything in those days and those (days) having-ended he-hungered.

TEXT—Before ἐπείνασεν 'he hungered', some manuscripts insert ὕστερον 'afterward'. GNT does not mention this variant. Ὕστερον 'afterward' is read by KJV.

LEXICON—a. pres. pass. participle of πειράζω (LN 88.308) (BAGD 2.d. p. 640): 'to be tempted' [AB, Arn, BAGD, BECNT, LN, Lns, NTC, WBC; GW, HCSB, KJV, NASB, NIV, NRSV, REB, TEV], 'to endure temptations' [NET], 'to be tested' [CEV]. The passive voice is also translated actively with the devil as subject: 'to tempt' [NCV, NLT]. The verb means 'to try, to test, to put to the proof' and derives its bad sense from the context [Lns]. Here it is used in the bad sense of trying to tempt Jesus to sin [Arn, BAGD, LN].

b. διάβολος (LN 12.34) (BAGD 2. p. 182): 'devil'. This word is literally 'the slanderer' [BAGD, LN], and was used as another title for Satan [LN]. See this word at 8:12.

QUESTION—What is the phrase 'forty days' to be connected with?

1. 'Forty days' is to be taken with 'was being led by the Spirit in the desert' [AB, Arn, EGT, Lns, NTC, Rb, TH, WBC; CEV, HCSB, NASB, REB]: he was being led by the Spirit in the desert for forty days, being tempted by the devil. With this interpretation, it is not necessary to understand 'being tempted by the devil' as describing a constant temptation throughout the forty days, rather the constant temptation could have occurred only at the close of that period [NTC]. Or, the phrase 'being tempted' indicates that the tempting occurred over forty days no matter how the phrase is connected [BECNT, ICC].

2. 'Forty days' is to be taken with 'being tempted by the devil' [Alf, BECNT, BNTC, NICNT; GW, KJV, NCV, NET, NIV, NLT, NRSV, TEV]: he was being led by the Spirit in the desert while being tempted for forty days by the devil.

LUKE 4:2

QUESTION—What is the significance of the use of the present participle πειραζόμενον 'being tempted'?
1. The present participle 'being tempted' indicates that the devil was tempting Jesus throughout the time the Spirit was leading him in the desert for forty days [AB, Alf, Arn, BECNT, BNTC, EGT, Gdt, Lns, My, NAC, NICNT, NIGTC, Rb, TG, TH; GW, KJV, NCV, NET, NIV, NLT, NRSV, REB, TEV]. The phrase 'being tempted' describes temptations which occurred before the three temptations described in the following verses [TH]. This covers the time described by Mark 'he was in the desert forty days, being tempted by Satan' (Mark 1:13) [AB, Lns]. The following three temptations marked the culmination of the forty days of temptation [Arn, NAC, NIGTC, NIVS; NET], and they did not occur during the general period of forty days [NIGTC]. Or, the three temptations could have occurred at any time during the forty days [TG].
2. Jesus was led by the Spirit for forty days in the desert and then at the end of this period the devil was tempting him [NTC; CEV]. The present participle 'being tempted' just describes the three temptations that closed the period since only those are described [NTC].

QUESTION—In what way could the devil tempt Jesus?

The form of those temptations is not stated, but probably Satan tried to shake Jesus' conviction that he was God's Son [Arn]. Perhaps the forty days were meant for communion with God and the devil attempted to destroy such communion [NIGTC]. This does not refer to testing Jesus' faith but an attempt to frustrate God's plan of salvation [AB]. Jesus' fidelity is proved by the testing provided by the devil's temptations [WBC]. The temptations were not mere psychological experiences but they are portrayed as a battle between real beings [BECNT]. The temptations did not occur in Jesus' own thoughts, rather they were brought to Jesus by the devil. We do not know in what way Jesus was tempted during these days [Lns].

QUESTION—How literal is the statement that Jesus did not eat anything?

This refers to total abstinence of food [EGT, Lns, NTC, Su]. Possibly the mental and spiritual strain was so great that for a time Jesus did not crave any food [ICC, Rb], and probably there was nothing to eat anyway [Rb]. It does not seem that this was a planned fast, but that the matters of the spirit so controlled Jesus' thoughts that he was not conscious of physical need [Arn, Gdt, Su]. The phrase is a popular way of referring to fasting and the nature of this fasting is not clear [BECNT]. It refers to fasting as a religious act [TG]. If this is the equivalent of Matthew's account where he termed this 'fasting' (Matt. 4:2), it need not involve more than abstaining from certain foods or from all food during certain parts of a day [NAC]. It could mean that Jesus ate only what was to be found in the desert [NET]. It is not known if Jesus took only drink or ate only what could be found in the desert, thus eating nothing substantial [BECNT].

LUKE 4:3

4:3 And the devil said to-him, If you-are (the) Son of-God, tell this stone that (it) become bread.[a]

LEXICON—a. ἄρτος (LN 5.8) (BAGD 1.a. p. 110): 'bread' [AB, Arn, Lns, WBC; all versions except GW, NLT, NRSV], 'loaf of bread' [BAGD, BECNT, LN; GW, NLT, NRSV]. It was a relatively small loaf of bread about the size and shape of a roll or bun [LN], but flat [Lns]. Being a round flat cake, the stones on the ground looked like cakes of bread [EGT, ICC, Rb, Su, TG, WBC].

QUESTION—What is implied by εἰ 'if' in the statement 'if you are the Son of God'?

The devil referred to the words Jesus had heard when he was baptized (3:22) [AB, BNTC, Crd, Gdt, NAC, TNTC, WBC].

1. It assumes the reality of the statement [BECNT, Gdt, MGC, NIBC, NICNT, NIGTC, NTC, Rb, Su, TG, WBC; NET]: *since* you are the Son of God. The devil means 'Since this is what the Father told you and what you believe, make use of your power and no longer be tortured by hunger' [NTC]. The devil did not doubt that Jesus was the Messiah [AB, NICNT]. Neither the devil nor Jesus doubted that Jesus had the power to transform a stone into bread [WBC]. The purpose of this statement was not to raise doubts that Jesus was the Son of God, but to provide a basis to tempt Jesus to use his power in such a way as to avoid suffering [Su].
2. It questions the fact that Jesus is the Son of God [Arn, ICC, Lns, NICNT, TH]: *if* you really are the Son of God. Although using a condition of reality, the 'if' questions the fact, since the devil demands proof [Arn, Lns]. The devil knew who Jesus was, but wanted to cause Jesus to doubt the fact [ICC, NICNT]. This is a challenge for Jesus to prove that he was really the Son of God and means 'if it is a fact that you are' or 'you say that you are' [TH].

QUESTION—What is the temptation in performing a miracle to turn a stone into bread?

The devil wanted to strike at Jesus' relationship as the Son of his Father God [NICNT]. The devil tempted Jesus to work a miracle in order to prove that God's declaration of his sonship was true, and if God did not allow the miracle, it would cause Jesus to doubt his relationship to God [ICC]. The act of turning a stone into bread would indicate that Jesus did not trust his Father because it was the Father's will that brought him to this state of hunger [Lns]. This was a temptation to distrust his Father's care and take matters into his own hands [AB, Arn, Crd, NAC, NICNT, NIGTC, NTC, WBC], rather than faithfully depending upon God [WBC] and being obedient to him [Crd, NIGTC]. It would indicate distrust in God's provision and protection [AB, NAC]. God had led Jesus into the desert and if Jesus satisfied his hunger with his own miraculous power, he would be rejecting his dependence on God, thinking he could take care of himself better than God would [BECNT]. The devil wanted Jesus to use his power to elevate his miserable condition to the dignity that his Sonship could demand, thus violating the earthly conditions to which he had submitted [Gdt].

4:4 **And Jesus answered him, It-is-written Not by bread^a alone will a-person^b live.**

TEXT—Before γέγραπται 'It is written' some manuscripts insert λέγων 'saying'. GNT does not mention this variant. 'Saying' is read by KJV.

TEXT—At the end of the verse some manuscripts add ἀλλ' ἐπὶ παντὶ ῥήματι θεοῦ 'but upon every word of God' and other manuscripts add ἀλλ' ἐπὶ παντὶ ῥήματι ἐκπορευομένῳ διὰ στόματος θεοῦ 'but upon every word preceding through (the) mouth of God'. GNT rejects these additions with a B decision, indicating that the text is almost certain. 'But upon every word of God' is included by KJV.

LEXICON—a. ἄρτος (LN 5.1, 5.8) (BAGD 1.a. p. 110): 'bread' [AB, Arn, BAGD, BECNT, LN (5.8), Lns, NTC, WBC; all versions except CEV], 'food' [LN (5.8); CEV]. This word can be used generically for any kind of food [LN (5.8)]. Although most translate this word as 'bread' to agree with 4:3, two take the quotation to be more generic and have the meaning 'food' [TG; CEV], so that the quotation would mean 'In order to have real life a person needs more than just food' [TG].

b. ἄνθρωπος (LN 9.1): 'person' [LN; GW, NCV], 'human being' [LN], 'one' [NRSV], 'man' [AB, Arn, BECNT, Lns, WBC; HCSB, KJV, NASB, NET, NIV, REB]. The singular form is also translated as plural: 'people' [NLT], 'human beings' [TEV]. The negative is applied to the subject: 'no one (can live)' [CEV]. The text includes an article (ὁ ἄνθρωπος 'the man') and this is a generic article, indicating that this saying applies to all people [ICC, Lns, TH; NET]. Women are not excluded from the statement [TG]. Jesus includes himself as a 'person' [TH]. This suggests that God can sustain any human being with or without food [ICC].

QUESTION—What is the OT passage that Jesus quoted?

The reference is Deuteronomy 8:3a in the Septuagint translation. Luke omitted the rest of the quotation as found in Matthew 'but on every word that comes from the mouth of God' (Matt. 4:4) to simplify the reply for Theophilus [Lns]. Luke omitted material to leave room for other topics [NTC]. The original point of the passage was to tell Israel to continue trusting God to be faithful to fulfill his promises and protection [BECNT].

QUESTION—What is the significance of Jesus' answer, 'Not by bread alone will a person live'?

This means that human life does not depend primarily on material food and it is more important to obey God's word even if obedience involves being hungry [NIGTC]. When the Israelites were hungry, God provided manna, so there was no need to leave off serving God in order to seek one's own welfare [WBC]. Just as Israel needed to trust God for their sustenance, so must God's Son [NAC]. God can sustain his own Son with or without food

[Arn, Gdt, ICC]. Trust in God is primary [Lns]. It expresses Jesus' confidence in his Father's care [NTC]. Jesus' purpose in life was to do God's will, not to provide for himself, and therefore he would trust God to provide for him in God's own way [BECNT].

4:5 And having-taken- him -up[a] he-showed him all the kingdoms of-the world in a-moment of-time.

TEXT—Following ἀναγαγὼν αὐτόν 'having taken him up' some manuscripts add ὁ διάβολος εἰς ὄρος ὑψηλόν 'the devil into a high mountain'. GNT does not mention this variant. Ὁ διάβολος εἰς ὄρος ὑψηλόν 'the devil into a high mountain' is read by KJV.

LEXICON—a. aorist act. participle of ἀνάγω (LN 15.176) (BAGD 1. p. 53): 'to take up' [AB, Arn, BECNT, WBC; HCSB, KJV, NLT, TEV], 'to take' [GW, NCV], 'to bring up' [BAGD, LN], 'to lead up' [BAGD, LN, Lns; CEV, NASB, NET, NIV, NRSV], 'to lead up to a high place' [NTC], 'to lead' [REB].

QUESTION—Where did the devil take Jesus and how did he take him there?

It could be some high place or merely high up in the air [TG]. Matthew includes the information that the devil took Jesus to a very high mountain (Matthew 4:8). The location is supplied in some translations: 'a high place' [NTC; CEV, GW, NET, NIV], 'a height' [REB], 'a high mountain' [KJV]. Perhaps Luke omitted reference to a mountain since the mountain would have to be used metaphorically since he viewed all the kingdoms of the world in a moment of time [AB, NIGTC].

1. This describes a visionary experience [AB, BECNT, BNTC, Crd, ICC, NIBC, NICNT, NIGTC, NTC, Rb, Su, TNTC]. We are not to think that the devil transferred Jesus bodily from the desert to a high mountain [ICC]. The devil could present all the kingdoms of the world to Jesus' mind in a moment of time while he was physically in the desert [ICC]. If it was a vision, we may be sure that what Jesus saw in the vision was as real to his mind as if there had been no vision at all [NTC].
2. Some think that Jesus was actually taken to a high mountain from where the devil used his power to present a view of the realms he ruled [Arn, Lns, MGC, Su, TH]. We are not to understand that the devil could project thoughts and feelings into Jesus' mind and make him think that he was some place he actually wasn't. The devil could only reach Jesus from the outside by his words [Lns]. As Jesus looked out from the mountaintop, the devil used his power to flash out a view of the kingdoms of the world that Jesus could see with his eyes [Arn, Lns]. From this high mountain Jesus' mind envisioned all the kingdoms at his feet [MGC, Su].

4:6 And the devil said to-him, To-you I-will-give all this authority/ territory[a] and their splendor,[b] because to-me it-has-been-given[c] and to-whomever I-desire I-give it.

LEXICON—a. ἐξουσία (LN 37.36) (BAGD 4.b. p. 278): 'authority' [AB, Arn, BECNT, Lns, WBC; HCSB, NIV, NLT, NRSV], 'jurisdiction' [LN],

'power' [CEV, GW, KJV, NCV, TEV], 'dominion' [REB], 'domain' [BAGD, NTC; NASB], 'realm' [NET]. In Luke 4:6 it is possible to translate this word as 'territory', 'land', or even 'people' [LN]. It refers to the domain over which the power is exercised [BAGD].
- b. δόξα (LN 79.18) (BAGD 2. p. 204): 'splendor' [BAGD, LN, NTC; HCSB, NIV], 'glory' [AB, Arn, BECNT, LN, Lns, WBC; all versions except HCSB, NIV, TEV], 'wealth' [TEV]. This would be the glory that would be accredited to the one who rules the kingdoms [NIGTC].
- c. perf. pass. indic. of παραδίδωμι (LN **57.77**) (BAGD 1.a. p. 614): 'to be given' [Arn; CEV, GW, NCV, NIV], 'to be handed over' [BAGD, **LN**, NTC; NASB, TEV], 'to be given over' [BAGD, LN, WBC; HCSB, NRSV], 'to be made over to' [AB], 'to be delivered' [BAGD, BECNT, Lns; KJV], 'to be entrusted' [BAGD], 'to be put in one's hands' [REB], 'to be relinquished' [NET]. This clause is translated 'they are mine to give to anyone I please' [NLT].

QUESTION—Is the focus on the authority Jesus would have or on the territories Jesus would possess?
1. The devil offered Jesus authority over those kingdoms [AB, BECNT, Lns, MGC, NIGTC, TG, WBC; CEV, GW, HCSB, KJV, NCV, NIV, NLT, NRSV, TEV]: I will give you authority over all these kingdoms. Along with the authority would be the power to control them [Lns].
2. The devil offered Jesus the realms of all those kingdoms [BAGD, NICNT, NTC, TH; NASB, NET]: I will give you all these kingdoms. 'This' refers to the regions ruled by a king, so this refers to the domains in which the power is exercised [TH].

QUESTION Does the 'splendor' of the kingdoms pertain to the kingdoms themselves or to the one who rules them?
1. 'Splendor' describes the kingdoms [AB, Arn, BECNT, Lns, NIGTC, NTC, TG]. Glory is used to describe the fame and wealth of the nations [TG]. 'Authority' is used as a metonymy to denote all the kingdoms Satan had authority over [Arn]. It refers to the kingdoms' magnificence and greatness [Lns]. The devil pointed out the goods to the perspective buyer by referring to the splendor and value of the kingdoms [BECNT, NIGTC].
2. 'Splendor' describes what will come to the ruler of the kingdoms [NAC, NIGTC].

QUESTION—What is meant by the devil's words 'to me it has been given'?
The passive form implies that the devil claims God gave him this authority [AB, Lns, My, NAC, Rb, TG].
1. The statement is in some sense true [AB, Arn, Gdt, MGC, NAC, NICNT, Rb]. In God's permissive will, the devil has temporary rule of the kingdoms of the world [NAC]. In John 12:31, 14:30, and 16:11 Jesus calls Satan the ruler of this world [Gdt, Rb]. Jesus does not here deny this claim and, perhaps because of mankind's sin and God's permission, Satan has this authority [Rb]. The people of the world are actually ruled by the devil

and this authority has been allowed by God [NICNT]. Perhaps God had given Satan this authority when he was the archangel [Gdt].
2. The statement is a false claim [BECNT, ICC, Lns, My, NIGTC, NTC]. The claim is a mixture of truth and error since the devil does have great authority here on earth and may even believe he has such authority. However, the claim is exaggerated as seen when Jesus cast out demons [BECNT]. Passages such as Luke 6:12 and 1 John 5:19 merely prove that Satan exercises a very powerful influence for evil over wicked people and demons. However, many passages prove that he is not the ultimate owner or ruler of the nations and Jesus knew that Satan was lying. For this to be a temptation, we might assume that an offer to obtain the kingdom without suffering on the cross would bring about a bitter struggle in Jesus' mind like the struggle that would occur in Gethsemane [NTC].

4:7 Therefore if you bow-down-and-worship[a] before me, everything will-be yours.

LEXICON—a. aorist act. subj. of προσκυνέω (LN 53.56) (BAGD 3. p. 717): 'to bow down and worship' [BECNT, LN; NLT], 'to bow down' [AB], 'to prostrate oneself in worship' [LN], 'to worship' [LN, NTC, WBC; CEV, GW, HCSB, KJV, NASB, NCV, NET, NIV, NRSV, TEV], 'to do obeisance to' [Arn, BAGD], 'to do homage' [REB], 'to do an act of worship' [Lns]. This act is an indication of entire submission and intense adoration, so it would be an admission of Satan's authority [ICC]. This would give the devil the respect and honor due to God alone [BECNT].

QUESTION—What is the temptation in this offer?

The temptation is to accept the offer of worldwide dominion, thus switching Jesus' allegiance from the Father to the devil [AB, WBC]. Jesus would give to the devil what belongs to God alone [NIGTC]. The devil's offer was for the Messiah to receive his throne in one short act instead of enduring the long and bitter suffering that God had planned for him [ICC, Lns, MGC, NAC, NIVS]. The temptation was to seize power on his own, apart from God [BECNT].

4:8 And answering Jesus said to-him, It-is-written You-shall-bow-down-and-worship (the) Lord your God and him only you-shall-serve.[a]

TEXT—Instead of γέγραπται 'It is written', some manuscripts read Ὕπαγε ὀπίσω μου, Σατανᾶ· γέγραπται γάρ 'Go behind me, Satan; for it is written'. GNT does not mention this variant. Ὕπαγε ὀπίσω μου, Σατανᾶ· γέγραπται γάρ 'Go behind me, Satan; for it is written' is read by KJV.

LEXICON—a. fut. act. indic. of λατρεύω (LN 53.14) (BAGD p. 467): 'to serve' [Arn, BAGD, BECNT, Lns, NTC, WBC; all versions except REB], 'to worship' [BAGD, LN; REB], 'to adore' [AB]. 'To bow down and worship' may indicate a greater reverence for God than does the more general term 'serve', but both words are close synonyms in this verse [TH]. See this word at 1:74 and 2:37.

QUESTION—What is the OT passage where this is written?
The passage is Deuteronomy 6:13 [AB, Arn, BECNT, Gdt, ICC, Lns, MGC, NAC, NICNT, NTC, Su, TG, WBC]. Luke gives a summary of that verse [BECNT]. The wording is slightly different than the Hebrew or Septuagint text, but the sense is in harmony with both [NTC]. Instead of 'you shall bow down and worship', which conforms to the devil's words in the preceding verse, the passage in Deuteronomy has 'you shall fear' [Lns, NAC, NIGTC]. However, the Hebrew word for 'fear' denotes the reverent fear expressed by the Greek word here [Lns]. The word 'only' is added to the Hebrew text by both Luke and Matthew and this brings out the intent of the Hebrew [NIGTC]. This word summarizes the intent of the command to give honor only to God [BECNT, NTC]. Some manuscripts of the Septuagint translation of the Hebrew text do contain the word 'only' [AB, WBC]. The word 'only' occurs in 1 Samuel 7:3 where it says 'serve him only' [NTC].

QUESTION—Does Jesus mean that the passage is specifically addressed to the devil when it says 'you'?
The command in Deuteronomy 6:13 is addressed to Israel. If a translation implies that this was written in the OT as a command directed to the devil, it would be better to translate 'The scripture says that a person should worship the Lord his God and serve only him' [TG].

QUESTION—What is Jesus' intention in quoting this Scripture?
There can be no question of Jesus offering worship to the devil even for such a great reward [NIGTC]. Besides rejecting the idea of worshipping Satan, Jesus is rejecting the idea of ruling at Satan's side, but this does not rule out the possibility of an earthly rule for Jesus later [BECNT]. Some think that Jesus rejected the principle of an earthly political rule [ICC].

4:9 And he-took^a him to Jerusalem and set (him) upon the pinnacle^b of-the temple and he-said to-him, If you-are (the) Son of-God, throw^c yourself down from-here.

LEXICON—a. aorist act. indic. of ἄγω (LN 15.165) (BAGD 3. p. 14): 'to take' [AB; CEV, GW, HCSB, NLT, NRSV, REB, TEV], 'to bring' [LN, Lns, WBC; KJV, NET], 'to lead' [Arn, BAGD, BECNT, LN, NTC; NASB, NCV, NIV]. The devil did not force Jesus to go against his will [TG].
  b. πτερύγιον (LN 7.53) (BAGD p. 727): 'pinnacle' [AB, Arn, BAGD, BECNT, LN, NTC, WBC; HCSB, KJV, NASB, NRSV], 'parapet' [REB], 'summit' [BAGD, LN], 'top' [CEV], 'highest part' [GW], 'highest point' [NET, NIV, NLT, TEV], 'a high place' [NCV], 'wing' [Lns]. It is the highest point of the building [BAGD, LN, NAC].
  c. aorist act. impera. of βάλλω (LN 15.215) (BAGD 1.b. p. 131): 'to throw' [AB, Arn, BAGD, LN, Lns, NTC; HCSB, NASB, NET, NIV, NRSV, REB, TEV], 'to cast' [BECNT, WBC; KJV]. The phrase 'throw yourself down from here' is translated 'jump from here' [GW], 'jump down' [NCV], 'jump off' [CEV, NLT].

QUESTION—How did the devil take Jesus to the temple in Jerusalem?
  1. Those who think that the previous temptation describes a visionary experience think that this too took place in Jesus' thoughts [BECNT, BNTC, NIBC, NICNT]. This is a private affair without an audience [BECNT].
  2. This was a physical transfer [Lns, NTC, TG]. The suggestion to throw himself down only makes sense if it is taken literally. This was a physical transfer using the devil's motive power to which Jesus submitted himself [Lns]. It does not mean that the devil carried Jesus there [TG].

QUESTION—Where was the pinnacle of the Temple?
'Pinnacle' describes some prominent part of the temple, but since the word for 'temple' includes the whole complex of precincts, porticos, courts, and buildings, its location cannot specifically be determined [AB, BECNT, ICC, NAC, NIGTC, NTC, TG, TH, WBC]. Probably it was not the sanctuary itself since that would have been referred to by the noun ναός [Gdt, ICC]. Suggested locations are the top of the Royal Porch where it looked down upon an abyss, the top of Solomon's Porch, or the roof of the sanctuary [ICC]. It would have been one of the towers that overlooked the courtyard or else the Kidron Valley [WBC]. Probably it was part of the outer wall that encircled the Temple area, most likely the Royal Porch on the southern wall where there was a deep ravine on the outside [Lns, NTC; NET]. No matter where it was located, it was a very high place [BECNT, TG, TH], and if Jesus jumped off he would need miraculous protection to avoid being killed [BECNT].

QUESTION—What is implied by εἰ 'if' in the statement 'if you are the Son of God'?
This is worded in the same way the first temptation began. See the answers given to this question in 4:3.

4:10 Because it-has-been-written, He-will-give-orders to-his angels concerning you to-protect[a] you, **4:11** also, They-will-lift-up[b] you upon (their) hands, lest you-strike[c] your foot against a-stone.

LEXICON—a. aorist act. infin. of διαφυλάσσω (LN **21.21**) (BAGD p. 191): 'to protect' [AB, BAGD, BECNT, **LN**, WBC; HCSB, NET, NRSV], 'to keep safe' [**LN**], 'to guard' [Arn, BAGD, LN, NTC; NASB], 'to thoroughly guard' [Lns], 'to protect and guard' [NLT], 'to guard carefully' [NIV], 'to take care of' [CEV], 'to take good care of' [TEV], 'to watch over' [GW, NCV], 'to keep' [KJV], 'to be in charge of' [REB]. In the Septuagint the verb pertains to God's care over his people, but here it pertains to protection from danger [TH].

b. fut. act. indic. of αἴρω (LN 15.203) (BAGD 2. p. 24): 'to lift up' [BAGD, BECNT, LN; NET, NIV], 'to bear' [Arn], 'to bear up' [AB, Lns, NTC; KJV, NASB, NRSV], 'to carry' [GW], 'to catch' [CEV, NCV], 'to hold' [NLT], 'to hold up' [TEV], 'to raise up' [WBC], 'to support' [HCSB, REB]. It means to lift up and carry away or carry along [BAGD, LN]. The

picture is of the angels bearing him up so that he would float slowly down to the ground without being injured [Su]. The angels would catch Jesus under his arms and let him float down to the rocks below as lightly as a feather [Lns].
   c. aorist act. subj. of προσκόπτω (LN 19.5) (BAGD 1.a. p. 716): 'to strike' [AB, BAGD, BECNT, LN, Lns, NTC, WBC; HCSB, NASB, NET, NIV, REB], 'to hit' [GW, NCV], 'to dash' [Arn; KJV, NRSV], 'to hurt' [CEV, TEV]. One version brings out the fact that he would land on his feet by translating 'so that not even your feet will be hurt on the stones' [TEV]. Assuming that he would land feet first, the feet would be the first to strike the stones, but actually the whole body would be hurt [TG].

QUESTION—What relationship is indicated by γάρ 'because'?

It indicates the reason for an implicit statement [BECNT, NTC]: Throw yourself down from here. *No harm will happen to you because* it is written, He will give orders to his angels to protect you. The implicit statement is 'no harm will happen to you' [NTC], or 'you need not worry' [BECNT].

QUESTION—What is the OT passage where this is written?

The devil quoted from the Septuagint translation of Psalm 91:11–12. The word 'you (singular)' in the OT passage was directed to people in general, not specifically to the Messiah [TH], but the devil refers this to Jesus [TG]. The stones in the quotation do not specifically refer to the temple's pavement or to rocks at the bottom of the valley next to the wall, rather they are the stones on the ground that one stumbles against [ICC]. He used this passage to imply that God would command his angels to come and hold Jesus as he fell to the ground from the pinnacle so that he would not hurt himself on the stones when he landed [TG].

   1. The OT passage says 'to protect you *in all your ways*' and the devil misapplied the passage by leaving out the crucial phrase 'in all your ways' [AB, ICC, NTC, WBC]. The devil used the quotation to mean that God would protect a righteous person no matter what he does, including jumping off the pinnacle [NTC]. Jumping from a height is not going 'in one's ways', rather it is going out of them [ICC]. Besides, the devil leaves out the OT truths that God does not condone trifling with God's providence by rashly rushing into unwarranted danger [NTC].

   2. The devil only abbreviated the verses and did not misapply them [BECNT, Gdt, Lns, NAC, NICNT, NIGTC]. The devil only invented an act to match the verses [Lns]. The Scripture was concerned with any believer, but how much more it would be true of the Messiah [Gdt, NAC].

QUESTION—What temptation was involved when the devil told Jesus to throw himself off the pinnacle of the temple?

   1. The temptation was to make a miraculous demonstration of Jesus' power in the sight of the people so that they might see that he was a messenger from God [AB, ICC, Su]. If Jesus had landed unharmed among the crowds on the ground, they would have regarded him as the Messiah from heaven and accepted him at the very start of his ministry [ICC]. The devil

tried to tempt Jesus to take the easy way of being accepted as Messiah and thus avoid the way of suffering [Su]. This seems to be the point of mentioning the temple, but it probably also includes challenging God with a test of Jesus' own choosing [ICC].

2. The temptation was to prove the truth of God's word by putting it to the test [Arn, BECNT, BNTC, Lns, NAC, NICNT, NIGTC, NTC, TNTC, WBC]. Jesus was to confirm his position as Son of God by trusting God to miraculously protect him [BECNT, WBC]. There is no mention of any spectators standing below who would see the miracle [NAC, NIGTC, WBC]. The devil wanted Jesus to doubt God's faithfulness [NICNT]. Proving the truth of God's promise is something that a righteous man who has faith in God does not need to do, but following the devil's suggestion would have shown a lack of faith [NIGTC]. If Jesus proved the truth of the passage by this act, he would no longer be living by faith [BNTC]. If Jesus were to put his life into danger by jumping, it would appear that he had a heroic faith in God and this would be a supreme proof that he truly was God's Son. But it would only amount to tempting and challenging God with a presumption as to what God must do to keep his promises [Lns].

4:12 And answering Jesus said to-him, It-has-been-said, You-shall- not -put-to-the-test[a] the Lord your God.

LEXICON—a. fut. act. indic. of ἐκπειράζω (LN **27.46**) (BAGD p. 243): 'to put to the test' [AB, BAGD, **LN**, NTC, WBC; NASB, NET, NIV, NRSV, REB, TEV], 'to test' [BECNT, LN; HCSB, NCV, NLT], 'to try to test' [CEV], 'to test out' [Lns], 'to tempt' [Arn, BAGD; GW, KJV]. This refers to challenging God to do something that you know is not his will [TH].

QUESTION—What is the OT passage where this is written and what is its import?

The quotation is from Deuteronomy 6:16. The Hebrew text has the plural form 'you', but Luke used the singular form in agreement with the Septuagint [ICC, NIGTC]. In the OT, 'you' and 'your' are directed to Israel, not the devil, and here Jesus applied the passage to his own situation [Gdt, NIGTC, TG]. Jesus did not answer the devil's use of the quotation from Psalm 91:11–12 by correcting the quotation. Rather he accepted the devil's application and showed that the devil was really setting one Scripture against another [Lns]. Jesus characterized the devil's suggestion as tempting God [Gdt]. This is an implied rebuke against the devil, since in tempting Jesus he was actually putting God to the test [AB, Gdt]. Jesus' quotation denied the suitability of the passage quoted by the devil [NICNT].

QUESTION—What is meant by putting the Lord to the test?

From the background of Exodus 17:7, it seems to be a lack of trust and an attempt to try out God regarding his promise [Lns]. This was a test to see if God would keep his word [Su]. This describes what Jesus would be doing if he exposed himself to danger in order to see if his Father would help him or not [NTC]. If Jesus were presumptuous enough to jump down, it would be an artificially created test and would amount to unbelief since the premise of the test is that maybe God would not protect his Son [BECNT].

4:13 And having-completed every temptation the devil went-away from him until a-time.^a

    a. καιρός (LN 67.1) (BAGD 1. p. 394): 'time' [BAGD, LN], 'occasion' [LN]. The phrase ἄχρι καιροῦ 'until a time' is translated 'until another time' [BAGD; GW], 'for a time' [BECNT; HCSB], 'for a while' [AB, BAGD; CEV, TEV], 'for a season' [KJV], 'until some point in the future' [Arn], 'until an opportune time' [NTC, WBC; NASB, NIV, NRSV], 'until a more opportune time' [NET], 'until a suitable season' [Lns], 'until the next opportunity came' [NLT], 'to wait until a better time' [NCV], 'biding his time' [REB]. This implies that Satan intended to attack Jesus again when an opportunity seemed likely to succeed [Lns].

QUESTION—What is meant by the devil completing every temptation?

It means that the devil had finished every temptation of which he was capable at that time [Lns, TG]. Luke took the three temptations to be the end of a string of temptations in the desert [Arn, BECNT]. This does not refer to all the temptations Jesus endured, but to *every kind* of temptation: to temptations regarding his person, the nature of his ministry, and his use of God's aid [Gdt]. This means that the devil had fully tried every kind of temptation [EGT, ICC, NAC, NICNT, NIGTC, TH]. The different kinds of temptations occurred during the forty days and the three ending temptations were illustrations of what the devil tried [ICC, NAC].

QUESTION—What is meant by the devil going away 'until a time'?

    1. He went away until another time [AB, Arn, BAGD, BECNT, BNTC, Su, TH; CEV, GW, HCSB, KJV, TEV]: the devil went away for a while. The devil challenged Jesus all through his ministry [BECNT, NIGTC, Su] and his activity intensified in chapter 22 [BECNT].

    2. He went away until an opportune time arrived [Gdt, ICC, Lns, My, NAC, NIGTC, NTC, Rb, TNTC, WBC; NASB, NCV, NET, NIV, NRSV, REB]: the devil went away until there was an opportune time. This refers to an evaluation made by the devil, a time when he thought he would have a better chance of success to approach Jesus [My]. Satan expected he would have another opportunity to attack Jesus at the arrival of another special occasion such as the one just concluded [Gdt]. The devil left Jesus until a new opportunity came [TNTC]. From time to time the devil returned to attack Jesus when a good opportunity appeared [Rb]. This does not indicate that he would wait a long time, but that he would again attack Jesus and his cause at the earliest opportunity [NTC]. Satan would seek a suitable time to try to turn Jesus from his course, but instead of doing so personally, he would work through others, such as Peter (Mark 8:33), the multitudes (John 6:15), and others [Lns]. Temptations occurred throughout Jesus' ministry, but the opportune time refers to the passion period

156 LUKE 4:13

[NAC, WBC] when the devil directly confronted Jesus [NAC]. The opportune time came when Satan entered into Judas (22:3) [ICC].

DISCOURSE UNIT: 4:14–9:50 [AB, BECNT, NICNT, NIGTC, Su, TNTC]. The topic is Jesus' ministry in Galilee.

DISCOURSE UNIT: 4:14–6:19 [REB]. The topic is Jesus in Galilee.

DISCOURSE UNIT: 4:14–5:16 [AB]. The topic is the beginning of the ministry in Nazareth and Capernaum.

DISCOURSE UNIT: 4:14–5:11 [NIGTC]. The topic is the Good News of the kingdom.

DISCOURSE UNIT: 4:14–44 [BECNT, NICNT, WBC]. The topic is Jesus' proclamation of the Good News in Jewish synagogues [NICNT, WBC], an overview of Jesus' ministry [BECNT].

DISCOURSE UNIT: 4:14–37 [NASB]. The topic is Jesus' public ministry.

DISCOURSE UNIT: 4:14–30 [Su, TNTC; GW, NCV, NIV, NLT]. The topic is the sermons at Nazareth [TNTC], Jesus teaches the people [NCV], Jesus rejected at Nazareth [Su; GW, NIV, NLT].

DISCOURSE UNIT: 4:14–15 [AB, BECNT, NICNT, NIGTC, WBC; CEV, HCSB, NET, NRSV, TEV]. The topic is Jesus' return to Galilee [NICNT, WBC], Jesus begins his work [CEV], Jesus begins his work in Galilee [NET, NRSV, TEV], ministry in Galilee [HCSB], a summary of the beginning of Jesus' ministry [AB], a summary of Jesus' Galilean ministry [BECNT, NIGTC].

4:14 And Jesus returned to Galilee in the power[a] of-the Spirit. And a-report went-out through all the surrounding-region[b] about him. **4:15** And he was-teaching in their synagogues, being-praised by all.

LEXICON—a. δύναμις (LN 76.1) (BAGD 1. p. 207): 'power' [AB, Arn, BAGD, BECNT, LN, Lns, NTC, WBC; all versions], 'might, strength, force' [BAGD]. The phrase ἐν τῇ δυνάμει τοῦ πνεύματος 'in the power of the Spirit' is translated 'with the power of the Spirit' [CEV], 'by the power of the Spirit' [BECNT], 'the power of the Spirit was with him' [GW, TEV], 'filled with the power of the Holy Spirit' [NRSV; similarly NLT], 'armed with the power of the Spirit' [AB; REB].

b. περίχωρος (LN 1.80) (BAGD p. 553): 'surrounding region' [LN, NTC], 'surrounding country' [Arn; GW, NLT, NRSV], 'surrounding countryside' [NET], 'neighboring countryside' [AB], 'neighboring land' [Lns], 'surrounding district' [NASB], 'the region around' [BAGD], 'the region round about' [KJV], 'region' [BECNT], 'area' [NCV], 'territory' [TEV], 'countryside' [WBC; NIV, REB], 'neighborhood' [BAGD], 'vicinity' [HCSB]. The phrase 'through all the surrounding region' is translated 'everywhere' [CEV]. It refers to the area within Galilee around Capernaum (4:23) [NIGTC]. The region covered the whole of Galilee

[WBC]. It refers to all the land adjoining Galilee [Lns]. It is Galilee and the regions surrounding it [TH].

QUESTION—What is meant by Jesus returning ἐν τῇ δυνάμει τοῦ πνεύματος 'in the power of the Spirit'?

The Holy Spirit had descended on Jesus at the baptism (3:2) and filled him (4:1). Then Jesus was 'led in (ἐν) the Spirit' to the desert (4:1) and now 'in (ἐν) the power of the Spirit' Jesus was led to return to Galilee [AB]. 'In the power of the Spirit' is not here talking about works of power, rather it refers to the Spirit's guidance about returning to Galilee [BECNT; NET]. However, others take 'power' to imply mighty works (4:36; 5:17; 9:1) [Alf, WBC]. It was Jesus' power to do mighty works since it is implied that his power was seen and reported [Gdt, NIGTC, WBC]. It was the power he had received at his baptism and displayed in his preaching and performing miracles [Gdt]. It was the Spirit's power which guided him to go to Galilee and guided him in his teaching of the Scriptures [AB]. This does not refer to being led by the Spirit, but to endowing Jesus' human nature with power for all that he did in word and deed [Lns]. The primary reference is to Jesus' authority to teach [NIGTC]. This means that everything Jesus did was as one who was filled with the Holy Spirit [NTC, TNTC]. He received power from the Spirit for his ministry [NICNT].

QUESTION—What was there to report about Jesus at this stage of his ministry?

Up to this point nothing has been written about him doing anything, so it appears that people could see that he was filled with the Holy Spirit [TNTC]. Jesus was famous when he returned, so this implies a ministry that is not described here [EGT]. It implies that Jesus had been preaching and perhaps that he had performed some miracles [ICC]. It assumes the ministry that is reported in the Gospel of John [Rb]. It would be a report of his miracles in Capernaum and possibly of his teachings at the feast in Jerusalem [Alf]. The people's interest was in what Jesus taught in the synagogues (4:15) [BECNT].

DISCOURSE UNIT: 4:16–9:50 [NAC]. The topic is Jesus' ministry in Galilee.

DISCOURSE UNIT: 4:16–5:16 [NAC]. The topic is the beginning of Jesus' ministry.

DISCOURSE UNIT: 4:16–30 [AB, BECNT, NAC, NICNT, NIGTC, WBC; CEV, HCSB, NET, NRSV, TEV]. The topic is Jesus' sermon in Nazareth [NAC], Good News in Nazareth [NICNT], an example of Jesus' preaching [BECNT], Jesus teaches at Nazareth [AB, NIGTC, WBC], Jesus is rejected at Nazareth [HCSB, NET, NRSV, TEV], the people of Nazareth turn against Jesus [CEV].

4:16 And he-came to Nazareth where he-had-been brought-up, and he-entered according-to his custom on the day of-the Sabbath into the synagogue and stood-up to-read. **4:17** And (the) scroll[a] of-the prophet

Isaiah was-given to-him and having-unrolled the scroll he-found[b] the place where it-had-been written,

TEXT—In 4:17, instead of ἀναπτύξας 'having unrolled', some manuscripts read ἀνοίξας 'having opened'. GNT reads ἀναπτύξας 'having unrolled' with a B decision, indicating that the text is almost certain. Ἀνοίξας 'having opened' is followed by Lns, CEV, GW, KJV, NASB, RSV, NEB (although some versions that read 'having opened' may do so because they refer to a 'book' rather than a 'scroll', not because they accept this textual variant).

LEXICON—a. βιβλίον (LN **6.64**) (BAGD 1. p. 141): 'scroll' [AB, BAGD, LN, NTC, WBC; HCSB, NET, NIV, NLT, NRSV, REB], 'roll' [Lns], 'book' [Arn, BAGD, BECNT, **LN**; CEV, GW, KJV, NASB, NCV, TEV]. It was a parchment scroll of the whole text of Isaiah [WBC]. Although translating this as a 'book', some refer to it as a scroll [Arn, BECNT]. The word can mean a book or a scroll, but with the verb ἀναπτύσσω 'having unrolled', it is clearly a scroll [NAC, TH].

b. aorist act. indic. of εὑρίσκω (LN27.27) (BAGD 1.b. p. 325): 'to find' [AB, Arn, BAGD, BECNT, LN, Lns, NTC, WBC; all versions except CEV, NLT], 'to come upon' [BAGD, LN], not explicit [CEV, NLT]. It means to go to the location of the passage either by searching for it or by unexpectedly discovering it [LN].

QUESTION—What was Jesus' custom?
1. It had been his custom from the time he was a youth to attend the synagogue on the Sabbath [Arn, Gdt, ICC, My, NICNT, Rb]. The phrase 'and stood up to read' is not stated as part of his custom [ICC].
2. It was his custom in his public ministry to go to the synagogue on Sabbath [Alf, EGT, Lns, NICNT, NIGTC, NTC, WBC]. Wherever Jesus happened to be, he attended the synagogue [NTC]. This does not refer to an earlier custom in Nazareth or even to his custom of attending a synagogue, rather it refers to his practice of using synagogues for teaching [NIGTC, WBC]. It is already mentioned in 4:15 that Jesus was teaching in the synagogues before he arrived at Nazareth [Lns]. The phrase 'and stood up to read' is also related to his custom [NICNT].

QUESTION—How did Jesus find the place in Isaiah?
1. 'Found' implies that he searched for the passage he wanted [AB, Arn, BECNT, ICC, Lns, NAC, NIGTC, NTC, Rb, TH]. Jesus selected the passage to read from [NTC] and found the place he was looking for [Arn, TH]. He kept unrolling the scroll until he found the passage he wanted to read [Rb].
2. 'Found' implies that he came upon the passage without searching for it [Alf, Gdt, My]. Jesus let himself be guided by God and read from the place to which the roll opened [Gdt].

LUKE 4:18

4.18 (The) Spirit of-(the)-Lord (is) upon[a] me on-account-of[b] which he-anointed[c] me to-announce-good-news[d] to-(the)-poor,

LEXICON—a. ἐπί (LN 83.46): 'upon, on' [LN]. The phrase 'is upon me' [AB, Arn, BECNT, NTC, WBC; KJV, NASB, NLT, NRSV, REB, TEV] is also translated 'is on me' [HCSB, NET, NIV], 'has come to me' [CEV], 'is with me' [GW], '(the Lord has put his Spirit) in me' [NCV]. This signifies that the Spirit would inspire him to prophesy [TH]. This is to be connected with 3:22 'the Holy Spirit descended upon him' [NAC, WBC]. Jesus is described in 4:1 as being full of the Spirit [TG].

b. ἕνεκεν (LN 89.31) (BAGD p. 226): 'on account of' [BAGD, LN]. The phrase οὗ εἵνεκεν 'on account of which' is translated 'because' [Arn, BECNT, NTC, WBC; all versions except GW, NLT], 'for' [NLT], 'since' [Lns], not explicit [AB; GW]. The coming of the Spirit upon Jesus indicates a special anointing for the special work of doing God's business on behalf of people as described in this quote [BECNT].

c. aorist act. indic. of χρίω (LN **37.107**) (BAGD 1. p. 887): 'to anoint' [AB, Arn, BAGD, BECNT, LN, Lns, NTC, WBC; GW, HCSB, KJV, NASB, NET, NIV, NRSV, REB], 'to appoint' [**LN**; NCV, NLT], 'to assign' [LN], 'to choose' [CEV, TEV]. Here the verb is the figurative use of 'to anoint' and means 'to appoint' [LN]. The OT action of anointing was to pour olive oil on a person's head and this was a sign that he was chosen to be a priest or a king [TG]. In Isaiah, the anointing was to appoint a prophet [AB, ICC, NIGTC, WBC], or a priest [ICC]. Here the anointing was not literal and it occurred at Jesus' baptism [AB, BECNT, Gdt, ICC] when the Spirit descended from heaven upon Jesus [TG, TH] and the Father spoke to him [Rb, TNTC]. Jesus was anointed with the Spirit as prophets and priests were anointed with oil [ICC]. For Jesus it was both a prophetic anointing and a messianic one [NAC]. The verb refers to a ceremonial anointing and therefore the recipient is the Christ (the anointed one) who was set apart and equipped for the mighty work described in the quote [Lns].

d. aorist mid. infin. of εὐαγγελίζω (LN 33.215) (BAGD 1. p. 317): 'to announce good news'. See translations of this word at 1:19. This word also occurs at 2:10; 3:18; 4:43; 7:22; 8:1; 9:6; 16:16; 20:1.

QUESTION—What is the source of this quotation?

It is Isaiah 61:1–2. In this passage, Isaiah wrote the words spoken by 'the servant of the Lord' [ICC, Lns], the coming Messiah [NTC, TNTC], or perhaps it is Isaiah's description of his own mission [NIGTC] in terms of his servant role [BECNT]. The identification of the speaker in Isaiah is not important, what is important is that the functions of the OT person are fulfilled in Jesus [NIGTC, WBC]. It is quoted quite freely from the Septuagint translation of the Hebrew text [ICC, NIGTC]. The phrase 'to send forth the ones having been oppressed in freedom' has been added from the Septuagint translation of Isaiah 58:6 [Arn, BECNT, ICC, NAC, NIGTC, NTC, WBC]. This insertion may be due to Luke summarizing the material that Jesus used in the synagogue since a normal reading of the scroll would not mix the passages [BECNT]. On the other hand, it may be considered a comment by Jesus on the preceding passage about the blind receiving their sight [NTC]. Probably Luke was not copying the passage that Jesus read line by line, but reported the words Jesus preached as his text [Lns]. Still another explanation is that Luke added this description of the suffering servant to help his readers better understand Jesus' mission [NAC]. The final phrase of the passage in the Septuagint 'and a day of vengeance' is omitted since Jesus did not wish to speak of this at the time [Lns], perhaps so as to focus on God's grace [NIGTC], or because the current time of Jesus' application was primarily a time of release and not of judgment [AB, BECNT, NAC, WBC].

QUESTION—What relationship is indicated by οὗ εἵνεκεν 'on account of which'?

1. This indicates the reason for the Spirit being upon him [AB, Alf, Arn, BECNT, BNTC, Gdt, ICC, Lns, My, NTC, TH, WBC; all versions except GW]: the Spirit of the Lord is upon me *because* he anointed me. 'Anointed' is used figuratively for the descent of the Spirit upon Jesus in 3:22 and the purpose of the anointing is to bring about what is described in this passage from Isaiah [TH]. This agrees with the text in the OT [NTC].

2. This indicates the result the Spirit being upon him [TG]: the Spirit of the Lord is upon me and *therefore* he anointed me.

QUESTION—Who is the subject of the statement 'he anointed me'?

The subject is made explicit in the OT text, it is the Lord, Yahweh [Arn, Lns].

QUESTION—What is the significance of making the poor the recipients of the good news?

The reference to the poor is a generalization and it does not exclude others [BECNT], yet the description applies especially to the poor in that they characterize those who are most in need of God's help, and who are most eager to hear his word [BECNT, NIGTC]. They are the people who have little to expect from their circumstances and so are most dependent upon God [TH]. This describes the whole of Jesus' ministry and it is expanded upon by the remainder of the quote [WBC]. This refers to economic poverty, but probably includes spiritual poverty as well in which the poor realize their sinfulness before God [MGC]. Poor is more than a condition, it also refers to an attitude of the soul toward God, the poor in spirit [Lns]. This is to be taken figuratively and the poor are those who lack righteousness [Arn].

QUESTION—Which verb is connected to the phrase 'to announce good news to the poor'?

1. A stop is put *after* this phrase so that it is connected to the preceding verb 'he anointed' [Arn, BECNT, BNTC, Lns, NTC, TH; all versions except REB]: he anointed me to announce good news to the poor. A new sentence begins with 'He has sent me', on which the following three following infinitives depend [TH]. The rest of 4:18–19a is an exposition

LUKE 4:18

of announcing the good news [Lns]. The following four clauses are divided as follows.

1.1 The following four clauses state what he was sent for and there are three divisions based on the three infinitive verbs [Arn, BECNT, Lns, NTC; GW, HCSB, NASB, NCV, NET, NIV, NLT, NRSV, TEV]. He has sent me (1) *to proclaim* to the captives release, and to the blind recovery of sight, (2) *to send* into freedom the ones who are oppressed, (3) *to proclaim* the year of the Lord's favor.

1.2 The following four clauses state what he was sent for and there are four divisions based on the three infinitive verbs and a supplied infinitive [CEV]. He has sent me (1) *to proclaim* to the captives release, (2) (*to give*) the blind recovery of sight, (3) *to send* into freedom the ones who are oppressed, (4) *to proclaim* the year of the Lord's favor.

1.3 The following four clauses state what he will proclaim and they have four divisions based on the number of clauses [NLT]. He has sent me to proclaim (1) that captives will be released, (2) that the blind will see, (3) that the downtrodden will be freed from their oppressors, (4) and that the time of the Lord's favor has come.

2. A stop is put *before* this phrase so that the phrase is connected to the following verb 'he has sent' [AB, MGC, NAC, NIGTC, WBC; REB]: 'The Spirit of the Lord is upon me, on account of which he anointed me. He has sent me to announce good news to the poor'. The following infinitive clauses detail the significance of announcing the good news [NIGTC]. This punctuation agrees with the text of OT [AB, NIGTC]. This make four division based on the verbs: he sent me (1) *to announce* good news to the poor, (2) *to proclaim* to the captives release, and to the blind recovery of sight, (3) *to send* into freedom the ones who are oppressed, (4) *to proclaim* the year of the Lord's favor.

he-has-sent me to-proclaim[a] to-(the)-captives release,[b] and to-(the)-blind recovery-of-sight,[c] to-send[d] into freedom (the ones who) are-oppressed, 4:19 to-proclaim (the) acceptable[e] year of-(the)-Lord.

TEXT—Following ἀπέσταλκέν με 'he has sent me', some manuscripts add the phrase ἰάσασθαι τοὺς συντετριμμένους τὴν καρδίαν 'to heal the crushed in heart'. GNT rejects this phrase with an A decision, indicating that the text is certain. This phrase is read by KJV.

LEXICON—a. aorist act. infin. of κηρύσσω (LN 33.256) (BAGD 2.b.β. p. 431): 'to proclaim' [AB, Arn, BECNT, NTC, WBC; HCSB, NASB, NET, NIV, NLT, NRSV, REB, TEV], 'to announce' [CEV, GW], 'to herald' [Lns], 'to tell' [NCV], 'to preach' [KJV]. See this word at 3:3; 4:44; 8:1, 39; 9:2; 12:3; 24:47.

b. ἄφεσις (LN **37.132**) (BAGD 1. p. 125): 'release' [AB, BAGD, Lns, NTC; NASB, NET, NRSV, REB], 'liberty' [**LN**, WBC; TEV], 'liberation' [Arn], 'freedom' [CEV, HCSB, NIV], 'deliverance' [KJV]. The clause 'to proclaim to the captives release' is translated 'to announce forgiveness to the prisoners of sin' [GW], 'to tell the captives they are free' [NCV], 'to proclaim that captives will be released' [NLT].

c. ἀνάβλεψις (LN 24.42) (BAGD p. 51): 'recovery of sight' [BAGD, NTC, WBC; HCSB, KJV, NASB, NIV, NRSV, REB, TEV], 'restoring of sight' [GW], 'gaining of sight' [LN], 'regaining of sight' [NET], 'return of sight' [Lns]. The clause 'and to the blind recovery of sight' is translated 'and (to proclaim) sight for the blind' [AB], 'and (to proclaim) sight to blind people' [Arn], 'to give sight to the blind' [CEV], 'and to tell the blind that they can see again' [NCV], '(to proclaim) that the blind will see' [NLT]. This noun refers to being able to see either again or for the first time [LN].

d. aorist act. infin. of ἀποστέλλω (LN 15.66) (BAGD 1.d. p. 99): 'to send' [LN], 'to send out' [BAGD]. The phrase 'to send into freedom the ones who are oppressed' is translated 'to send the oppressed away in liberty' [WBC], 'to send away such as have been broken in release' [Lns], 'to set free the oppressed' [Arn, NTC; HCSB, TEV], 'to set free those who are oppressed' [NASB, NET], 'to let the oppressed go free' [NRSV], 'to let the broken victims go free' [REB], 'to free everyone who suffers' [CEV], 'to forgive those who have been shattered by sin' [GW], 'to set at liberty them that are bruised' [KJV], 'to release the oppressed' [NIV], 'God sent me to free those who have been treated unfairly' [NCV], 'to send the downtrodden away relieved' [AB], '(to proclaim) that the downtrodden will be freed from their oppressors' [NLT]. The verb means to send away into freedom, that is, 'to free' [NTC].

e. δεκτός (LN 34.54): 'acceptable' [BAGD, LN], 'favorable' [BAGD]. The clause 'to proclaim the acceptable year of the Lord' is translated 'to proclaim an acceptable year of the Lord' [Arn], 'to proclaim the year acceptable to the Lord' [WBC], 'to herald a year acceptable to the Lord' [Lns], 'to preach the acceptable year of the Lord' [KJV], 'to proclaim the favorable year of the Lord' [NASB], 'to proclaim/announce the year of the Lord's favor' [NTC; GW, HCSB, NET, NIV, NRSV, REB], 'to proclaim the Lord's year of favor' [AB], 'to proclaim that the time of the Lord's favor has come' [NLT], 'to announce the time when the Lord will show his kindness' [NCV], 'to say, This is the year the Lord has chosen' [CEV], 'announce that the time has come when the Lord will save his people' [TEV].

QUESTION—What is meant by 'to proclaim to the captives release'?

The OT reference (Isa. 61:1) refers to the captive Jews in exile, but here the picture is being released from spiritual captivity to sin [BECNT, NTC]. The release of prisoners is a feature of the year of Jubilee when debts were dismissed and slaves were set free, but probably this also has a spiritual meaning of being released from the debt of sin [MGC]. The captives are prisoners of Satan [Arn, Lns, NTC]. Freedom refers to the forgiveness of sins [NAC].

QUESTION—What is meant by 'to proclaim to the blind recovery of sight'?
The OT reference is Isaiah 61:1. This refers to miracles of healing the physically blind [BECNT, NAC]. Also there are overtones of the spiritually blind [BECNT, NAC]. They are people who cannot find their way to heaven [Arn]. Jesus will give the sight of faith to those who have been brought to realize their spiritual blindness [Lns].

QUESTION—What is meant by 'to set free the oppressed'?
The OT reference is probably Isaiah 58:6 [BECNT]. This pictures Jesus' healing miracles that were to be seen in messianic terms [BECNT]. These are people who are crushed by the weight of their sins [Arn, Lns]. Their oppression consisted of enduring Satan's dark dungeon [NTC].

QUESTION—What is the phrase 'the acceptable year of the Lord' based upon?
The OT reference is a return to Isaiah 61:2. Underlying the figure is the Hebrew year of Jubilee (Lev. 25) [Alf, Arn, BECNT, Gdt, Lns, MGC, My, NICNT, NIGTC, NIVS, NTC, Rb, WBC; NET]. Every fifty years a trumpet was blown and liberty throughout the land was proclaimed. This was symbolic of the coming messianic age which was now beginning with Jesus [Lns, NIGTC, NTC, Rb]. It refers to the era of salvation [MGC, TNTC]. It pictures the beginning of God's new age, but it does not mean that Jesus would call people to fulfill the legal requirements of the Jubilee, it is a prophetic usage of the passage to picture total forgiveness and salvation through Jesus [BECNT]. It is a metaphor for salvation so that the time for forgiveness of debts refers to God's readiness to forgive sin totally [NET]. In Isaiah this refers to a period when Zion receives God's favor and deliverance and it is now applied to the period inaugurated by Jesus and his new way of salvation [AB]. This phrase is almost a synonym for the good news of God's kingdom as shown by 4:43 [NAC].

QUESTION—Does δεκτός refer to 'favor' or 'acceptance' in this context?
1. It means favor [AB, Arn, Gdt, ICC, NICNT, NIGTC, NTC, TG, TH; HCSB, NCV, NIV, NLT, NRSV, REB, TEV]: the year in which the Lord bestows his favor. It means a season upon which God looks with satisfaction and favor, and this refers to a season when God will bless people in general with the appearance of the Messiah who will accomplish their redemption [Arn].
2. It means acceptance [BECNT, BNTC, Lns, Rb, Su, WBC; KJV]: the year that is acceptable to the Lord. It is the time that is acceptable and pleasing to the Lord because it begins the new age to be ushered in by the Messiah [Lns]. The word refers to God's will and purpose, specifically his will to save [WBC].

4:20 And having-rolled-up the scroll (and) having-given-(it)-back to-the attendant[a] he-sat-down. And the eyes of-all in the synagogue were-focused on-him. **4:21** And he-began[b] to-say to them, Today this Scripture has-been-fulfilled[c] in your ears.

LEXICON—ὑπηρέτης (LN 35.20) (BAGD p. 842): 'attendant' [AB, Arn, BAGD, BECNT, Lns, NTC, WBC; all versions except CEV, KJV, NCV], 'assistant' [BAGD; NCV], 'servant' [LN], 'man in charge' [CEV], 'minister' [KJV]. This word is used of any kind of attendant or servant [ICC]. Here, the attendant was one of the subordinate officers of the synagogue [AB]. He would have been the one who had given Jesus the scroll to begin with and who would now put it away in its case [Rb].
- b. aorist mid. indic. of ἄρχομαι (LN 68.1) (BAGD 2.a.β. p. 113): 'to begin' [AB, Arn, BECNT, LN, Lns; HCSB, KJV, NASB, NCV, NET, NIV, NRSV, REB], 'to start out' [NTC], 'to set about' [WBC], not explicit [CEV, GW, NLT, TEV].
- c. perf. pass. indic. of πληρόω (LN 13.106) (BAGD 4.a. p. 671): 'to be fulfilled' [AB, Arn, BAGD, BECNT, LN, Lns, NTC, WBC; HCSB, KJV, NASB, NET, NIV, NRSV], 'to come true' [CEV, GW, NCV, NLT, REB, TEV]. The perfect tense indicates an existing state of fulfillment, but with 'today' it functions like a present tense, meaning 'this Scripture is being fulfilled today' [BECNT]. The predictions were then being realized [AB, Lns]. With the coming of Jesus, the messianic age was realized [NAC]. The inauguration of the epoch of salvation occurred as Jesus began his ministry [NICNT]. See this word at 1:20.

QUESTION—In 4:21, what is the significance of ἤρξατο 'he began' to say?
1. It indicates a turn in the narrative and does not have the primary sense of 'to begin' [BAGD, Gdt, TH; probably CEV, GW, NLT, TEV which do not translate the word]: and he said to them. This merely means that his activity has taken a new turn and the verb is almost superfluous [BAGD]. Here it indicates a turning point in the narrative and might be translated 'thereupon he said' [TH]. It does not point to the first thing he said, but indicates the solemnity of the occasion [Gdt].
2. It is a significant part of the verse and has the primary sense of 'to begin' [AB, Alf, Arn, BECNT, EGT, Gdt, ICC, Lns, My, NTC, TNTC, WBC]: and he began to say to them. The message that impressed the crowd with his gracious words was more than the sentence recorded here [BECNT]. It means that he began his message [NTC, TNTC], he began to speak to them [AB]. This introduces the initial words that he spoke [Gdt, My]. 'He began' indicates the point of beginning and 'to say' indicates the message that followed [Lns]. Or, this sentence summarizes the content of the message [Alf, ICC, NAC, WBC].

4:22 And everyone was-witnessing[a] in-favor-of/against-him and they-were-amazed[b] at the words of graciousness/grace[c] coming-out from his mouth and they-were-saying, Is not this (one) Joseph's son?

LEXICON—a. imperf. act. indic. of μαρτυρέω (LN **33.263**, 33.262) (BAGD 1.c. p. 493): 'to witness' [LN (33.262)], 'to bear witness' [WBC], 'to bear (him) witness' [KJV], 'to testify about' [BECNT], 'to give testimony' [Arn, Lns], 'to speak well of' [BAGD, **LN** (33.263), NTC; GW, HCSB, NASB, NCV, NET, NIV, NLT, NRSV], 'to approve of' [BAGD], 'to talk about' [CEV], 'to acknowledge' [AB]. The phrase 'everyone was witnessing in favor of him' is translated 'they were well impressed' [**LN**; TEV], 'there was general approval' [REB].

b. imperf. act. indic. of θαυμάζω (LN 25.213) (BAGD 1.a.β. p. 352): 'to be amazed' [BAGD, BECNT, LN, NTC; CEV, GW, HCSB, NCV, NET, NIV, NLT, NRSV], 'to be astonished' [REB], 'to marvel' [Arn, Lns, WBC; TEV], 'to wonder' [LN; KJV, NASB], 'to be surprised' [AB]. The people were impressed, not surprised [WBC]. Whether this is a favorable or unfavorable reaction depends on the context [BAGD, LN]. See this word at 1:21, 63; 2:18, 33; 7:9; 8:25; 11:14, 38; 20:26; 24:12, 41.

c. χάρις (LN 88.66) (BAGD 1., 2. p. 877): 'graciousness' [BAGD (1.), LN], 'attractiveness' [BAGD], 'grace' [BAGD (2.), LN; NCV]. The phrase 'words of graciousness' is translated 'the gracious words' [AB, BECNT; GW, HCSB, KJV, NASB, NET, NIV, NLT, NRSV], 'the eloquent words' [TEV], 'the wonderful things' [CEV], 'the words of grace' [Arn, Lns, NTC, WBC; NCV], 'the words of such grace' [REB].

QUESTION—Since the case of αὐτῷ 'him' can be taken either as a dative of advantage (they were witnessing *in favor of* him) or a dative of disadvantage (they were witnessing *against* him) and 'to be amazed' can be a favorable or unfavorable reaction, were the people in favor of Jesus or against him at this point?

Since the crowd was angry and hostile by 4:28, the problem is whether (1) the people had an initial favorable response to Jesus and then swiftly became hostile when they considered that he was only Joseph's son, or (2) the people were hostile from the start. All the commentaries which come to a decision favor an initial favorable reaction towards Jesus [Alf, Arn, BAGD, BNTC, EGT, Gdt, LN (33.263), MGC, NAC, NICNT, NTC, Su, TG, TH, TNTC; GW, HCSB, NASB, NCV, NET, NIV, NLT, NRSV, REB, TEV]. Some focus on the component of witnessing [AB, Alf, Arn, BECNT, BNTC, Gdt, ICC, Lns, NAC, NIC, TH, TNTC; KJV]. The people witnessed to the truth of his claims [Alf, BNTC, NAC]. They witnessed to the truth of what people had been saying about Jesus' power as a teacher [Arn, Gdt, ICC, TNTC]. They testified to his ability [NIC]. They told others that Jesus' words were true, that he was right [TH]. Others focus on the component of speaking well about Jesus [BAGD, Crd, LN (33.263), NTC; GW, HCSB, NASB, NCV, NET, NIV, NLT, NRSV]. They were impressed by Jesus' wisdom and the miracles he performed [NTC].

QUESTION—What amazed the crowd?
Most commentators seem to take the verb in its positive sense as expressing the crowd's admiration. They were amazed at the gracious words with which he spoke [NAC, Su], and his rhetorical skill [BECNT]. Jesus' words showed his conviction, freshness, authority, and graciousness [NTC]. However, several commentaries think that the word describes only their amazement, not their admiration [EGT, Gdt, ICC].

QUESTION—What is meant by 'the words of graciousness/grace'?
1. This is a description of the way Jesus presented his message [AB, Arn, BECNT, Crd, ICC, Lns, NICNT, NTC, Rb, Su, TG, TH, TNTC]: they were amazed at his gracious words. Jesus' words were persuasive and eloquent [TG]. Jesus spoke with winning words [ICC]. He spoke in an attractive way [TNTC].
2. This refers to the power behind the words [Alf, NIGTC, WBC]: they were amazed at the words endued with the power of God's grace. God's influence was shown in the words which produced such an impact [WBC]. The people considered Jesus' words to be filled with God's grace as he presented the message of salvation [NIGTC].
3. This refers to the content of his message [BNTC, EGT, Gdt, NAC, NIGTC]: they were amazed at his words about grace. The word 'grace' is an objective genitive which indicates that the words were about God's grace [NAC]. Jesus' words described God's works of grace [Gdt]. It was God's grace by which the prophesies were fulfilled [EGT].

QUESTION—What is implied by their question, 'Is this not Joseph's son'?
1. This is a rhetorical question expressing their surprise [AB, MGC, NICNT, TNTC]. It signifies the crowd's pleasant surprise and admiration [AB]. This is a positive statement, indicating that the people were glad that such a man as Jesus was one of them. It wasn't until Jesus continued to teach that they turned against him [NICNT]. They were astonished that a man from their hometown could speak like that [Su, TNTC]. It was afterwards, when they understood what his message meant that they changed from wonder to fury [Su].
2. This is a rhetorical question expressing their perplexity and doubt [BECNT]. They wondered how this neighbor of theirs could say that he was the fulfillment of this passage [BECNT].
3. This is a rhetorical question expressing their rejection [Alf, Arn, Crd, EGT, Gdt, ICC, Lns, NICNT, NIGTC, NTC, Rb, Su, WBC]. In connection with the following verses, this is a negative statement [NAC]. This signals the crowd's turn to unbelief since they cannot believe Jesus is the Messiah in spite of his attractive words [EGT, Lns]. They looked down on someone they were so familiar with and wondered why he thought he was so great [NTC]. Their initial reaction turned to criticism [Gdt]. They were jealous of him [Alf]. It indicates their rejection of Jesus' claims [WBC].

4. This is a rhetorical question expressing several reactions [TH]. It indicates that they were astonished that Joseph's son had become such a fine speaker and at the same time it shows their indignation that he would presume to speak as a prophet [TH].

4:23 And he-said to them, Doubtless[a] you-will-tell me this proverb,[b] Physician, heal yourself. Whatever we-heard was-done in Capernaum do also here in your hometown.

LEXICON—a. πάντως (LN 71.16) (BAGD 1. p. 609): 'doubtless' [BAGD, LN, Lns; NRSV], 'no doubt' [LN, WBC; HCSB, NASB, NET, REB], 'undoubtedly' [NTC], 'surely' [BECNT; KJV, NIV], 'certainly' [CEV], 'of a truth' [Arn], 'probably' [AB, BAGD; GW, NLT]. This adverb is also translated as a verb phrase: 'I know that' [NCV], 'I am sure that' [TEV]. This is a word used to make a strong affirmation [ICC, TH]. Jesus is sure that the proverb expresses the people's feeling towards him [TH]. This indicates that Jesus knew the thoughts of his audience, a characteristic of a Spirit-endowed prophet [NICNT].

b. παραβολή (LN 33.15) (BAGD 2. p. 612): 'proverb' [AB, Arn, BAGD, BECNT, Lns, NTC, WBC; all versions except CEV, KJV, NCV], 'parable' [LN; KJV], 'saying' [CEV], 'old saying' [NCV]. The word 'parable' covers a wide range of meanings and here it refers to a well-known proverbial saying [Arn, EGT, Gdt, NAC, NIGTC, NTC, TH, TNTC].

QUESTION—What would be the point of telling Jesus 'Physician, heal yourself'?

1. The explanation of the proverb is stated in the next sentence, 'Whatever we heard was done in Capernaum do also in your hometown' [Alf, Arn, Crd, EGT, Lns, My, NICNT, NIGTC, NTC, Rb, Su, TG, TH, TNTC]. Jesus explained in the second sentence the way the proverb applied to them [Lns]. The explanation of the proverb does not exactly match the figure [EGT, TNTC]. Doing what he had done in Capernaum is not exactly the same thing as a physician healing himself, but the general idea is that every sensible benefactor begins in his immediate surroundings [EGT]. The point is not that Jesus should heal himself, but perhaps the idea is that he would benefit himself in respect to saving his reputation by working miracles in his hometown [TNTC]. Since the 'physician' is an inhabitant of Nazareth, 'yourself' must be expanded to 'your hometown' [Alf, NIGTC, NTC]. The proverb's explanation is that a person must not benefit others while refusing to benefit his own relations [NICNT]. A common man who says he is the prophet of messianic salvation, cannot boast like that until he proves his claim by doing in his hometown what he did in Capernaum [TH]. The point of the proverb is that a man who claims to be able to heal people should be able to prove his claim by healing himself. Therefore Jesus should be able to prove his claim to be the one Isaiah spoke about by doing in his hometown the miracles he had done in

Capernaum [TG]. Since Jesus came to them with a high claim about himself, they wanted him to demonstrate that it is true by performing miracles [Arn].

2. The following sentence is separate from the proverb [BECNT, Gdt, ICC, NICNT, WBC]. There is no neat parallelism in trying to make a comparison 'as a Physician should first heal himself, so should you heal your neighbors'. The explanation is not found in the following sentence because the words of the proverb 'physician' and 'yourself' should be interpreted of the same person and not one of a person and the other of his neighbor. The intent of the proverb is that before bettering the condition of others, Jesus should better his own condition by making it more secure and giving evidence that he really was the fulfillment of Isaiah's prophecy [ICC]. The parable is spoken in irony and means 'you pretend to save humanity from its misery, but first begin by saving yourself from your miseries'. Then the next sentence suggests the means by which Jesus can escape the people's contempt [Gdt]. The proverb is a demand for Jesus to prove his claims and then the people requested that they receive the same treatment as Capernaum [BECNT]. Although in the form of a request, it is an insulting retort and has the force of 'Who do you think you are to offer us what you do not have for yourself?' The next sentence is a cynical request for Jesus to perform miracles in Nazareth in order to dispel their impression that he was only Joseph's son [WBC].

QUESTION—What had Jesus done in Capernaum?

The people probably referred to unrecorded miracles done by Jesus during the short time he spent in Capernaum (John 2:12) after his miracle in Cana [Arn, ICC, TNTC]. In Luke 4:14 it implies that Jesus did mighty deeds as he went about teaching in the synagogues [NIGTC].

4:24 **And he-said, Truly**[a] **I-say to-you that no prophet is acceptable**[b] **in his hometown.**

LEXICON—a. ἀμήν (LN 72.6) (BAGD 2. p. 45): 'truly' [BAGD, BECNT, LN; NASB, NRSV, REB], 'verily' [KJV], 'of a truth' [Arn], 'amen' [BAGD, Lns, WBC]. The phrase 'truly I say to you' is translated 'I tell you the truth' [NCV, NET, NIV], 'I assure you' [HCSB], 'I solemnly assure you' [NTC], 'you can be sure' [CEV], 'I can guarantee this truth' [GW], 'the truth is' [NLT], 'I tell you this' [TEV], 'believe me' [AB]. The word ἀμήν is the only Semitic word used by Luke [AB] who transliterated it into Greek [Lns] and it is transliterated into English as 'amen'. Always used with 'I say', it begins a solemn declaration [BAGD, EGT, Lns, TH]. 'Truly I tell you' has the same sense of 'I tell you in truth' in the next verse [AB]. Here it means 'It is surely proved once more by you people of Nazareth among whom I grew up' [Lns].

b. δεκτός (LN **34.54**) (BAGD p. 174): 'acceptable' [Arn, BAGD, BECNT, **LN**, Lns, WBC; NET], 'welcome' [BAGD, LN; NASB]. The phrase 'is acceptable' is translated 'is accepted' [AB, NTC; GW, HCSB, KJV,

NCV, NIV, NLT, NRSV], 'is recognized' [REB], 'are welcomed' [TEV], 'are liked' [CEV]. There is a word play with 4:19, 'the *acceptable* year of the Lord' had arrived, yet Jesus was not being *accepted* by his people [BECNT, BNTC, NICNT].

QUESTION—What is the application of the statement 'no prophet is acceptable in his hometown'?

In using this proverb, Jesus identified himself as a prophet [AB, BECNT, NAC, WBC], and he used the proverb to indicate that he was receiving the standard fate of prophets [Arn, ICC, WBC]. It is implied that Jesus would not answer their demand to prove himself by miracles [ICC]. Jesus was not able to carry out his ministry in his hometown because the people there resisted him [NICNT]. When Jesus saw the audience's unbelief, he described the situation with a proverb which succinctly states a general rule, meaning 'wherever a prophet may be honored, he is certainly not honored in his hometown' [NTC]. He rebuked the audience's desire for signs by observing that like OT prophets he was not accepted in his own country [BECNT]. Most commentaries refer to this as a proverb, but one thinks that it probably was not considered to be a proverb at the time Jesus stated it [TH].

4:25 And I-tell you in truth, there-were many widows in Israel in the days of-Elijah, when the sky was-shut[a] for three years and six months, when a-great famine occurred over all the land, **4:26** and Elijah was-sent to none of-them but-instead[b] to Zarephath of-Sidon, to a-woman a-widow. **4:27** And many lepers[c] were in Israel during (the time of) Elisha the prophet, and not-one of-them was-cleansed[d] but-instead Naaman the Syrian.

LEXICON—a. aorist pass. indic. of κλείω (LN 79.112) (BAGD 2. p. 434): 'to be shut' [Arn, BAGD, LN, NTC; NIV], 'to be shut up' [Lns, WBC; HCSB, KJV, NASB, NET, NRSV], 'to be closed' [BECNT, LN], 'to be stopped up' [AB]. The phrase 'the sky was shut' is translated 'the skies never opened' [REB], 'there was no rain' [CEV, NLT, TEV], 'it did not rain' [NCV]. 'The sky was shut up' is a metaphor for 'no rain fell' [TH]. The passive voice indicates that God is the one who caused this [AB, NAC, NIGTC].

b. εἰ μή (LN 89.131): 'except that, but, however, instead, not only' [LN]. The expression εἰ μή shows contrast by designating an exception [LN]. It is translated 'but rather' [AB], 'but' [Arn, NTC; HCSB, NIV, REB], 'instead' [NLT], 'except' [BECNT, LN, Lns; GW, NRSV], 'save' [KJV], 'only' [WBC; CEV, NCV], 'but only' [NASB, NET, TEV]. The expression could indicate an exception (to none of them except to one of them) but here it indicates a contrast (to none of them, but to someone else) [Crd, NIGTC]. The use of 'except' views widows in general, not being limited to only Israelite widows [Gdt].

c. λεπρός (LN 23.162) (BAGD p. 472): 'leper' [BAGD, LN], 'one having a dreaded skin disease' [LN]. See a description of λέπρα 'leprosy' at 5:12.

d. aorist act. indic. of καθαρίζω (LN 23.131) (BAGD 1.b.α. p. 387): 'to be cleansed' [Arn; KJV, NASB, NET, NIV, NRSV], 'to be healed' [CEV, HCSB, NCV, NLT, REB, TEV], 'to be cured' [GW], 'to be healed and made ritually pure or acceptable' [LN]. It means to heal a person of a disease that has caused ceremonial uncleanness [LN]. See this word at 5:12; 7:22; 17:14.

QUESTION—Where is the account of the famine found?

This is related in 1 Kings 17. The time of three and a half years of famine here and in James 5:17 follows Jewish tradition [ICC]. In 1 Kings 18:1 it says that the rain came in the third year. However the famine probably lasted longer [ICC, Rb]. The passage in 1 Kings 17:1 says 'these years' and implies several years, while 18:1 does not say 'in the third year of the drought' but refers to the third year of Elijah's coming to Sarepta [Lns].

QUESTION—What was the purpose of telling about Elijah being sent to a Gentile widow instead of an Israelite widow, and about Elisha healing a Gentile leper?

After using a proverb to indicate that he was being treated like the other prophets (4:24), Jesus went on to OT examples that show his principles of action were like the prophets who performed miracles to benefit outsiders although many of their own people would have been glad to receive such blessings [ICC]. The stories of the two greatest OT prophets show that God did not direct them to act according to the proverb 'Physician heal yourself' [Alf]. Instead of speaking more about a prophet being without honor in his own country, Jesus told what a prophet may do in response to being rejected. The application is that Jesus' fellow Jews may miss God's blessing while the Gentiles will receive it [BECNT]. Since Jesus had performed miracles elsewhere, they thought that he certainly ought to distinguish his hometown by performing miracles there as well. But Jesus used OT examples to show that this logic had no basis [Lns]. Jesus refuted the mistaken idea that his hometown Nazareth had a special claim on him and showed that God's grace was not limited to one town or even to the people of Israel [NTC]. In a situation parallel to the ministries of OT prophets, the people's unbelief resulted in forfeiting the benefits that could have been theirs [WBC]. Jesus implied that he would leave Nazareth and minister to those outside his hometown [NIGTC], even to foreigners [Arn].

4:28 And hearing these-things all in the synagogue were-filled[a] with-anger.
4:29 And having-arisen they-dragged-out[b] him outside the city and they-took[c] him up-to (the) cliff[d] of-the hill upon which their city had-been-built in-order to-throw-down him.

LEXICON—a. aorist pass. indic. of πίμπλαμαι, πίμπλημι (LN 78.46) (BAGD 1.a.β. p. 658): 'to be filled' [Arn, BAGD, BECNT, LN, Lns, NTC, WBC; KJV, NASB, NET, NRSV, TEV]. Some drop the metaphor of being filled in the phrase 'to be filled with anger' and translate 'to be furious' [NIV, NLT], 'to become furious' [AB; GW], 'to become very angry' [NCV], 'to become so angry' [CEV], 'to be enraged' [HCSB], 'to be roused to fury' [REB]. 'To be filled' with something means that one is completely involved in that state [LN]. The ingressive aspect of the verb is suggested by the aorist tense [AB, TH; CEV, GW, NCV, REB].

b. aorist act. indic. of ἐκβάλλω (LN 15.220) (BAGD 1. p. 237): 'to drag out' [TEV], 'to throw out' [BAGD, LN, Lns; CEV], 'to cast out' [AB, Arn, BECNT], 'to expel' [BAGD], 'to drive out' [BAGD, NTC; HCSB, NASB, NIV, NRSV, REB], 'to force out' [GW, NCV, NET], 'to thrust out' [KJV], 'to hustle out' [WBC], 'to mob someone' [NLT]. 'Expel' suggests that they held him by the arms and walked along with him to the hill [TG].

c. aorist act. indic. of ἄγω (LN 15.165) (BAGD p. 3): 'to take' [AB, WBC; NCV, NIV, NLT, REB, TEV], 'to bring' [BAGD, LN, Lns; HCSB, NET], 'to drag' [CEV], 'to lead' [Arn, BAGD, BECNT, LN; GW, KJV, NASB, NRSV], 'to push' [NTC].

d. ὀφρῦς (LN **1.49**) (BAGD p. 600): 'cliff' [**LN**, WBC; GW], 'edge' [AB, BAGD; HCSB, NCV, NLT], 'brow' [Arn, BAGD, BECNT, Lns, NTC; KJV, NASB, NET, NIV, NRSV, REB], 'top' [TEV]. The phrase 'the cliff of the hill' is translated 'the edge of the cliff' [CEV]. The brow of a hill is not necessarily the top of a hill [TH].

QUESTION—What made the crowd furious?

Jesus had implied that they were worse than Phoenician widows and Syrian lepers [BECNT, NTC]. Jesus implied that he would have had better results among people other than his own townspeople who were like those who persecuted the prophets of old [AB]. Jesus' illustrations implied that the people were less worthy of God's blessings than the heathen [Arn, EGT, ICC]. They recognized that Jesus had as much as accused them of rejecting God's prophet and counted them as outsiders to what God was doing [WBC]. Since Jesus rejected them, they would reject him [Gdt]. They regarded Jesus' words to be blasphemous [Arn].

QUESTION—Why did they plan to throw Jesus down from the cliff?

Evidently they planned to cast Jesus off of some elevation and then throw or drop stones on him to carry out his execution by stoning [Su, WBC]. This was a mob action, not a formal execution [NIGTC]. Perhaps they thought that throwing Jesus to his death would clear them of being technically guilty of murder [Lns].

4:30 But having-gone-through[a] through their midst he was-going-on-his-way.[b]

LEXICON—a. aorist act. participle of διέρχομαι (LN 15.21) (BAGD 1.b.α. p. 194): 'to go through' [BAGD], 'to travel through' [LN]. The verb 'to go through' with the preposition 'through' is translated 'to go through' [Lns], 'to go out through' [BECNT], 'to pass through' [Arn, WBC; KJV, NASB, NET, NRSV], 'to pass right through' [HCSB], 'to slip through' [AB; CEV], 'to slip away through' [NLT], 'to walk through' [NCV,

TEV], 'to walk right through' [NTC; GW, NIV], 'to walk straight through' [REB].
  b. imperf. mid/pass. (deponent = act.) indic. of πορεύομαι (LN 15.10, 15.34): 'to go on one's way' [AB, BECNT, Lns, NTC, WBC; HCSB, KJV, NASB, NCV, NET, NIV, NRSV, TEV], 'to go' [LN (15.10)], 'to go on' [Arn], 'to go away' [LN (15.34); CEV, GW, REB], 'to leave' [NLT]. This refers to going towards a goal, and here he was on his way to Capernaum [ICC, My]. His way would eventually lead him to Jerusalem and his destiny [AB, BECNT, NAC]. It does not suggest he had a place in mind and merely means 'he went on his way' [TH]. The imperfect tense indicates that he simply walked on and on. There is no reference to the disciples who were present [Lns].

QUESTION—How did Jesus go through the midst of the angry people?
  1. There was no miracle involved [AB, Arn, EGT, Gdt, NTC, TG, TH, TNTC]. The participle 'going' assumes that Jesus had freed himself and then as the people watched, he went through their midst without them daring to touch him again [TH]. Jesus just walked through the midst of the people and they did not attempt to stop him [TG]. Jesus had such majesty that the people were overawed [Arn, EGT, Gdt, NTC, TNTC].
  2. A miracle was involved [Alf, Crd, ICC, Lns, My]. The implied restraint of the people was miraculous [Alf, Crd, Lns, My]. It was a miracle brought about by the will of Jesus [ICC, My]. The majesty of Jesus did not deter the mob from dragging him to the cliff, so it took a miracle for him to be able to calmly walk through their midst unmolested [Lns].

DISCOURSE UNIT: 4:31–44 [BECNT, NAC, NICNT, NIGTC, Su; CEV, NET]. The topic is Jesus' work at Capernaum [NIGTC], ministry in Capernaum [NET], examples of Jesus' ministry [BECNT], Jesus' healings in Capernaum [NAC], Good News in Capernaum [NICNT], acceptance at Capernaum [Su].

DISCOURSE UNIT: 4:31–41 [TNTC]. The topic is a healing by Jesus.

DISCOURSE UNIT: 4:31–37 [AB, TNTC, WBC; CEV, GW, HCSB, NCV, NIV, NLT, NRSV, TEV]. The topic is preaching in Capernaum [WBC], teaching and a cure in the Capernaum synagogue [AB], the man with an unclean spirit [TNTC; NRSV], a man with an evil spirit [CEV, TEV], Jesus casts out a demon [NLT], Jesus drives out an evil spirit [NIV], driving out an unclean spirit [HCSB], Jesus forces an evil spirit out of a man [GW, NCV].

4:31 And he-went-down to Capernaum a-city of-Galilee. And he-was-teaching them on the Sabbaths/Sabbath. 4:32 And they-were-astonished[a] at his teaching, because his word was with authority.[b]

LEXICON—a. aorist pass. indic. of ἐκπλήσσομαι, ἐκπλήσσω (LN 25.219) (BAGD 2. p. 244): 'to be astonished' [BECNT, NTC; HCSB, KJV], 'to be astounded' [WBC; NRSV], 'to be greatly astounded' [LN], 'to be amazed' [Arn, BAGD; GW, NASB, NCV, NET, NIV, NLT, REB, TEV], 'to be so in astonishment' [Lns], 'to be struck' [AB]. The passive form is

also translated actively with Jesus' teaching as the subject: 'to amaze' [CEV]. See this word at 2:48; 9:43.
  b. ἐξουσία (LN 37.41) (BAGD 2. or 3. p. 278): 'authority' [AB, Arn, BAGD (3.), BECNT, Lns, NTC, WBC; all versions except CEV, KJV, REB], 'a note of authority' [REB], 'power' [BAGD (2.); CEV, KJV]. Here the word may refer to the ability to do something [BAGD (2.)] or to the authoritative manner of teaching [BAGD (3.), LN]. See this word at 4:36.

QUESTION—What is meant by the plural noun σάββασιν 'Sabbaths' in the sentence 'He was teaching them on the Sabbaths'?
  1. This refers to teaching on several Sabbath days [AB, Gdt, MGC, My, Su; KJV, NLT]. The imperfect 'he was teaching' stresses a habitual activity on the Sabbaths [AB].
  2. This refers to teaching on the particular Sabbath day of the healing [Arn, BECNT, BNTC, ICC, Lns, NAC, NIGTC, NTC, TH, WBC; probably all versions except KJV, NLT, since they translate with the singular form]. The plural form σάββασιν 'Sabbaths' is often singular in meaning [Arn, BECNT, ICC, Lns]. In the parallel passage in Mark 'Sabbath' is in the singular and so we can assume that the word here is intended to be taken as a singular [BECNT, Lns, NIGTC, TH]. Luke refers to a particular Sabbath and therefore 4:31–32 introduces the setting for the following event [BECNT, TH]. The imperfect 'he was teaching' indicates that he was engaged in teaching on this Sabbath [AB, Lns]. .

QUESTION—In what way were Jesus' words spoken with authority?
  Unlike the scribes who taught from traditions, Jesus taught directly and independently and in fact spoke from God [BECNT]. Rooted in the power of the Spirit (4:14) [AB, MGC, NICNT, NIGTC] he taught authoritatively and this brought about conviction in his hearers [AB]. His teaching gave evidence to the fact that he had a God-given commission to exercise authority [ICC]. He spoke as though he had the right to command [TG]. His words were positive and definite [Arn]. Although all other commentaries refer this to the manner in which he taught, one takes this to refer to his power to heal [NAC].

4:33 **And in the synagogue there-was a-man having**[a] **a-spirit of-an-unclean**[b] **demon**[c] **and he-cried-out with-a-loud voice,**

TEXT—Following φωνῇ μεγάλῃ 'with a loud voice', some manuscripts add λέγων 'saying'. GNT does not mention this variant. Λέγων 'saying' is added by KJV as the first word in 4:34.

LEXICON—a. pres. act. participle of ἔχω (LN 90.65) (BAGD I.2.e.α. p. 78): 'to have' [Arn, BAGD, BECNT, LN, Lns; KJV, NET, NRSV], 'to have within/in' [NCV, TEV], 'to experience' [LN]. This active verb is also translated as passive: 'to be possessed by' [GW, NASB, NIV, NLT, REB], 'to be under the influence of' [AB], '(to be) with;' [WBC; CEV,

HCSB]. It means that the man was possessed by, or under the control of, the demon [TG].
- b. ἀκάθαρτος (LN 53.39) (BAGD 2. p. 29): 'unclean' [AB, Arn, BAGD, BECNT, Lns, NTC, WBC; HCSB, KJV, NASB, NET, NRSV, REB], 'ritually unclean' [LN], 'impure, vicious' [BAGD], 'evil' [CEV, GW, NCV, NIV, TEV], not explicit [NLT]. See this word at 4:36, 8:29.
- c. δαιμόνιον (LN 12.37) (BAGD p. 39): 'demon' [Arn, BAGD, LN, Lns, NTC, WBC; GW, NASB, NET, NIV, NLT, NRSV, REB, TEV], 'devil' [KJV], 'evil spirit' [BAGD, LN]. The phrase 'a spirit of an unclean demon' is translated 'an unclean demonic spirit' [BECNT; HCSB], 'an evil spirit' [CEV, NCV], 'an unclean spirit' [AB].

QUESTION—How is 'unclean demon' related to 'spirit' in the genitive construction 'a spirit of an unclean demon'?

The genitive 'of an unclean demon' is in apposition to 'spirit' and clarifies the kind of spirit [Arn, Lns, NAC, NTC, TH, WBC; GW]: a spirit, namely an unclean demon. The reverse apposition is also translated by modifying 'spirit' with 'unclean' [NIV, REB]: a demon, namely an unclean spirit. Another way to take the genitive is that it indicates the quality of the spirit [Alf, BECNT]: an unclean and demonic spirit. Some evidently consider the phrase to be cumbersome and reduce it: 'an evil spirit' [CEV, NCV], 'an unclean spirit' [AB], 'a demon' [NLT]. This 'spirit of an unclean demon' is referred to as 'the demon' in 4:35, and as 'unclean spirit' in 4:36 [TG]. Also Luke writes of 'demons' in 4:41, 'unclean spirits' in 6:18, 'evil spirits' in 7:21, 'demon possession' in 8:36, and 'a spirit' in 9:39. Here in 4:33 Luke seems to define his vocabulary concerning demon possession for Greek readers [NICNT, NIGTC].

QUESTION—What is meant by the adjective 'unclean'?
1. It refers to the man's personal habits [Alf, BNTC]: a demon who caused the man to be filthy. It refers to the man's filthy personal presentation [Alf]. The man was filthy in appearance and in speech [BNTC].
2. It refers to being ceremonially unclean [TG]: a demon who caused the man to be ceremonially unclean. The demon is unclean in that when it possessed the man it caused bodily disorders or actions that made the person ritually unclean and unable to partake in public worship [TG].
3. It refers to the moral character of the demon as being evil [BAGD, BECNT, NIGTC, TH; CEV, GW, NCV, NIV, TEV]: a demon, who was an evil demon. The ceremonial meaning 'unclean' had faded and the moral sense is predominant 'impure, vicious, unclean' [BAGD]. It describes the spirit's character as being evil since no personal habits are described [BECNT]. This stresses the fact that the demon was evil and prepares for a contrast with 'the Holy One' in 4:34 [NIGTC, TH].

4:34 **Ah/let-(us)-alone! What (is this) to-us and to-you, Jesus of-Nazareth? You-came to-destroy^a us? I-know who you are, the holy (one) of-God.**
LEXICON—a. aorist act. infin. of ἀπόλλυμι (LN 20.31) (BAGD 1.a.α. p. 95): 'to destroy' [Arn, BAGD, BECNT, LN, Lns, NTC, WBC; all versions except CEV], 'to ruin' [BAGD, LN], 'to get rid of' [CEV], 'to put an end to' [AB]. This destruction refers to being sent to await judgment in the abyss that is mentioned in 8:31 [Gdt, NTC]. This does not mean to annihilate the demons, but to drive them out of the people they possessed so that they no longer controlled humans and as a result their work would be destroyed [Lns].

QUESTION—Is the initial word ἔα an interjection 'ah!' or an imperative 'let us alone!'?

1. It is an interjection [AB, Arn, BECNT, Crd, EGT, ICC, LN (88.191), Lns, MGC, My, NIGTC, NTC, Rb, TG, TH; CEV, GW, NET, NIV, TEV; probably NCV, REB which do not translate the word]: 'Ah! What is this to us and to you'? This is a particle indicating surprise [AB, BAGD, BECNT, Crd, LN, NIGTC, NTC, Rb], alarm [Arn], displeasure [AB, BAGD, BECNT, MGC, NIGTC], dismay [ICC, TH], indignation [Crd, LN, Lns, Rb], anger [ICC, LN], hostility [NTC, TG], or disgust [Arn, NTC]. It is translated 'Ah!' [BECNT; TEV], 'Ha!' [AB, Lns, NTC; NET, NIV], 'Hey!' [CEV], 'Oh, no!' [GW], not explicit [NCV, REB].
2. It is the imperative of ἐάω 'to leave alone' [BNTC, Gdt, NICNT, WBC; HCSB, KJV, NASB, NLT, NRSV]: 'Let us alone! What is this to us and to you?'. It is also translated 'Go away!' [NLT], 'Let me be!' [WBC].

QUESTION—What is the import of the rhetorical question τί ἡμῖν καὶ σοί 'What (is this) to us and to you?

The question expresses a rebuke, 'Don't meddle with us' [Arn, NIGTC, TG]. This is an idiom with the meaning 'we have nothing to do with one another' or 'Why bother us!' [BECNT; NET]. Here it indicates hostility and means 'Leave us alone' [NET]. It is translated 'What do you want with us?' [CEV, GW, NCV, NIV, REB, TEV], 'What have we to do with you?' [Lns; KJV], 'What have you to do with us?' [BECNT, NICNT; NRSV], 'What business do we have with each other?' [NASB], 'What common interest is there between us?' [WBC], 'Why are you bothering us?' [NTC; NLT]. This outburst was provoked by Jesus' teaching [WBC].

QUESTION—Who are the referents of the plural forms 'what is this to *us* and to you' and 'did you come to destroy *us*')?

One commentary says that the man was speaking on behalf of all other men who were possessed by demons [Su]. All other commentaries think the real speaker is the demon. The demon was using the man's organs of speech so that the man was not the originator of the words [Lns]. The man was not possessed by more than one demon [AB, Arn, Gdt, ICC, Lns, NICNT, NTC, Su, TG]. The demon realized that what was going to happen to him would also happen to his fellow demons elsewhere [Arn, NTC]. The demon was speaking as a representative of all the other demons who had obtained

176 LUKE 4:34

possession of other human beings [AB, Gdt, ICC, NTC, TG]. The demon wanted to get rid of Jesus for all others of his kind [Lns]. When Jesus attacked this one demon, he had initiated an ongoing ministry of casting out evil spirits and bringing about an end to Satan's rule [NICNT]. Or, it is possible that the demon used 'us' to refers to both itself and the man if it thought that in order for Jesus to get at the it, Jesus might have to destroy the man as well [BECNT].

QUESTION—Is the sentence 'you came to destroy us' a question or a statement?

1. It is a question [AB, BECNT, BNTC, NTC, TG, TH; all versions]: did you come to destroy us? The question voices the demon's fear that Jesus would destroy demons [TG]. The demon asked if Jesus, the holy one from God, had come from heaven not only to seek and save the lost but also to destroy the demons [NTC]. It is a rhetorical question since that was the very thing Jesus came to do [BNTC].
2. It is a statement of fact [Arn, Lns, WBC]: you came to destroy us. The demon supernaturally knew who Jesus was and therefore knew his intentions [WBC]. In anger the demon said this in order to blame Jesus [Lns]. The demon spoke this in despair and terror [Arn].

QUESTION—How is God related to the holy one in the genitive construction 'the holy one of God'?

It is a possessive genitive, the Holy One who belongs to God [TH]. It means that the Holy One is closely associated with God [AB, WBC]. The Holy One has been anointed by God and is God's servant [BECNT]. God set Jesus apart, selected him, and consecrated him [Arn]. He is consecrated to God [NIGTC, TNTC]. The Holy One is a messenger sent by God [TG; TEV]. The Holy One comes from God and is dedicated to him [TH]. It could mean either consecrated by God or consecrated to God [ICC].

4:35 **And Jesus rebuked/commanded**[a] **him saying, Be-silent and come-out from him. And having-thrown him (down) in the midst (of them) the demon came-out from him without having-harmed him.**

LEXICON—a. aorist act. indic. of ἐπιτιμάω (LN, 33.419, 33.331) (BAGD 1. p. 303): 'to rebuke' [Arn, BAGD, BECNT, LN (33.419), Lns, NTC, WBC; HCSB, KJV, NASB, NET, NRSV, REB], 'to reprove' [BAGD], 'to sternly speak to' [NIV], 'to cut someone short' [NLT], 'to command' [LN (33.331); NCV], 'to order' [CEV, GW, TEV], 'to charge' [AB]. Since 'rebuke' signifies strong disapproval, the situation here calls for a command, perhaps with the implication of a threat [NET].

QUESTION—Does ἐπετίμησεν mean that Jesus *rebuked* the demon or *commanded* the demon?

1. It means that Jesus rebuked the demon [Arn, BECNT, ICC, Lns, NAC, NTC, TH, TNTC, WBC; HCSB, KJV, NASB, NET, NIV, NRSV, REB]: Jesus rebuked him, saying, 'Be silent and come out from him'. Jesus rebuked the demon for possessing the man [TNTC]. The devil was

rebuked for using the man as his mouth-piece [ICC]. Jesus rebuked him with a terse command [NTC]. This is an effective rebuke, an activity of power and not only criticism [NAC, WBC]. Jesus checked him, brought him to a stop [TH].
2. It means that Jesus commanded the demon [AB, TG; CEV, GW, NCV, TEV]: Jesus commanded him, saying 'Be silent and come out from him'. When referring to demons this is a technical use of the verb to indicate a commanding word to bring evil spirits into submission [AB].

QUESTION—Why did Jesus command the demon to be silent?

Jesus did not want to have the testimony about his person come from an evil demon [Lns, NTC]. He preferred to have his works testify for him, not such an inglorious person. Perhaps he was responding to the whole content of the demon's words [BECNT]. Because of political misconceptions associated with the title of Messiah, Jesus did not want to be publicly proclaimed as the Messiah [NAC]. First of all, the command for silence was to end the demon's defensive attitude in all that it had said. In addition, it was to prevent an agent of evil from giving a testimony about Jesus since this might give the impression that Jesus was working in league with the demon [NICNT].

QUESTION—What is meant by the description of the demon 'throwing the man down in their midst'?

The man fell down in the middle of the people [BECNT, Lns, NTC, TH; NASB], or in the middle of the synagogue [NIGTC, WBC; GW], or in front of everyone [AB; CEV, NCV, NIV, NLT, NRSV, REB, TEV], and this action gave the impression that someone had thrown him down [TH]. This indicates that the demon had caused the man to have convulsions [BECNT, ICC, Lns, NIGTC, NTC, Su] as stated in the parallel passage in Mark 1:26. This resulted from the malice of the demon who wanted to make the healing as painful as possible [Gdt, ICC]. In a gesture of defeat, the demon handed the man over to Jesus by 'projecting' the man into the middle [WBC]. When the demon threw the man down before the people, it indicated that the demon acquiesced to what it had been commanded by delivering the man over to Jesus [NICNT].

4:36 And amazement[a] came upon everyone and they-were-talking to one-another saying, What (is) this word/matter[b]? Because with authority[c] and power he-commands the unclean[d] spirits and they-come-out. **4:37** And a-report was-going-out about him into every place of-the-surrounding-region.

LEXICON—a. θάμβος (LN 25.208) (BAGD p. 350): 'amazement' [AB, BECNT, Lns, NTC; NASB, REB], 'astonishment' [Arn, BAGD, LN, WBC], 'fear' [BAGD], 'alarm' [LN]. The phrase 'astonishment came upon' is translated 'to be amazed' [CEV, KJV, NCV, NET, NIV, NLT, NRSV, TEV], 'to be stunned' [GW], 'to be struck with amazement' [HCSB]. It is amazement akin to terror [ICC]. It means 'to wonder' and perhaps fear is mingled with it [WBC]. See this word at 5:9.

b. λόγος (LN 33.98) (BAGD 1.a.β. p. 477): 'word' [BECNT, LN, Lns, WBC; KJV], 'words' [AB; NLT, REB, TEV], 'command' [BAGD; GW], 'message' [LN, NTC; HCSB, NASB], 'teaching' [Arn; CEV, NIV], 'utterance' [NRSV], 'this' [NCV], 'happening' [NET]. This word means 'speaking' and can take many different forms according to the context [BAGD].

c. ἐξουσία (LN 37.41) (BAGD 2., 3. p. 278): 'authority'. See this word at 4:32.

d. ἀκάθαρτος (LN 12.39, 53.39) (BAGD 2. p. 29): 'unclean'. The phrase πνεῦμα ἀκάθαρτον 'unclean spirit' refers to an evil spirit which is ritually unclean and which causes persons to be ritually unclean [LN (12.39)]. See this phrase at 4:33, 8:29.

QUESTION—Were the people referring to what was said or what was done in their question 'What is this λόγος'?

1. It refers to what Jesus had said [AB, Arn, Crd, Gdt, ICC, Lns, My, NICNT, NTC, Su, TG, TH, WBC; all versions except NCV, NET]: what is this word? This refers to Jesus' command to the demon in the preceding verse [AB, My, TG, TH, WBC]. It refers to the kind of speech that commands [My]. It refers to Jesus' teachings [Arn, Lns]. It refers to his preaching in general [Gdt]. This does not mean that the people did not understand what Jesus had said to the demon, and it could be represented by an exclamation, 'What powerful words he speaks!' [TG].

2. It refers to what had happened [NAC; NET]: what is this matter? The Greek word λόγος has a wide range of meanings and here it seems to refer to this *matter* and the question is 'What's happening here?' [NET].

QUESTION—What relationship is indicated by ὅτι 'because'?

1. It indicates reason [ICC, My, NIGTC, NTC, TH, WBC; KJV, NASB, NET, NRSV]. It is the reason for asking the previous question: '*we ask this question* because...' [My, NIGTC]. It is the reason for being amazed: '*we have reason to be amazed* because...' [NTC].

2. It requests an explanation [Lns]: in view of the authority and power with which he issues orders, what is this doctrine that we have heard?

QUESTION—Why is there a change from the singular form 'the *demon* came-out' to the plural form 'he commands the unclean *spirits* and they come out'?

There was only one demon in the man, but when the people spoke about it they generalized from that one case and used present tenses of the verb as for any general statement [Lns, WBC]. The present tense of the verbs indicates that Jesus did this habitually [TNTC].

QUESTION—What is the difference between commanding with 'authority' and with 'power'?

Authority refers to Jesus' right to command and power refers to his capacity to have his commands obeyed [TG]. Authority refers to what cannot be contradicted, while power refers to what cannot be resisted [ICC, TH]. Jesus taught with authority (4:32) and this was backed by the power he had to force out demons [Gdt]. Jesus had power to order the evil spirits [CEV]. This refers to Jesus' powerful authoritative word with which he commanded the demon [WBC]. Jesus possessed power because of his divine authority and his power was expressed as he exercised that authority [NIGTC].

DISCOURSE UNIT: 4:38–44 [CEV, NASB, NCV, NIV]. The topic is the healing of many people by Jesus.

DISCOURSE UNIT: 4:38–41 [GW, HCSB, NLT, NRSV, TEV]. The topic is the healing of many people by Jesus [NLT, TEV], healings at Capernaum [HCSB], healings at Simon's house [NRSV], Jesus cures Simon's mother–in–law and many others [GW].

DISCOURSE UNIT: 4:38–39 [AB, TNTC, WBC]. The topic is the healing of Simon's mother–in–law.

4:38 **And having-left^a from the synagogue he-entered into Simon's house. And Simon's mother-in-law was suffering-with a-high fever and they-asked him on-behalf-of^b her.**

LEXICON—a. aorist act. participle of ἀνίσταμαι (LN **15.36**, 17.6) (BAGD 2.a. p. 70): 'to leave' [AB, **LN** (15.36), NTC; all versions except KJV, NASB], 'to set off' [WBC], 'to stand up' [BAGD, LN (17.6)], 'to get up and leave' [NASB], 'to arise and leave' [Arn], 'to arise (out of)' [KJV], 'to arise (from)' [Lns], 'to rise up (from)' [BECNT]. The verb means to move away from some location and it may imply getting up and leaving [LN (15.56)]. The same verb is used in the next verse to refer to the woman getting up from her bed after being cured of a fever and all versions translate that as the action of arising. In this verse, the use of the verb 'having arisen' implies a finite verb following it, such as 'he went out' [AB, TH]. When there is no context of sitting, it means no more than preparation for leaving and here it refers to leaving the synagogue [ICC]. The verb 'having arisen' does not literally mean that Jesus arose from a seat, rather it is used to reinforce an implied verb 'he left' [TG]. When used in connection with 'from the synagogue' it assumes the meaning 'to go away' or 'to leave' [TH].

b. περί (LN 89.6, 90.36): 'on behalf of, for the sake of' [LN (90.36)], 'concerning' [LN (89.6), Lns], 'in relation to, with regard to' [LN (89.6)], 'for' [KJV], 'about' [AB, BECNT; HCSB, NRSV]. The clause 'they asked him on behalf of her' is translated 'they made a request to him on her behalf' [WBC], 'they spoke to Jesus about her' [TEV], 'they asked him to help her' [Arn, NTC; GW, NASB, NCV, NET, NIV, REB], 'Please heal her, everyone begged' [NLT], 'he was told that (…was sick)' [CEV].

QUESTION—What did 'they' ask in behalf of Simon's mother-in-law and who were they?

Implicit is the request that Jesus heal the woman [NAC, WBC]. Many translations specifically state that they asked Jesus to help her [NTC; GW, NASB, NCV, NET, NIV, REB], or to heal her [NLT]. In this passage it is natural to assume that the people who asked Jesus were the members of the woman's household [AB, Su, TH], including Simon Peter [My]. It could be her friends who were there to take care of her [TG]. It would have been Simon and Andrew, whose house it was [NTC]. In the parallel passage in Mark, it could be understood to refer to the four disciples [AB].

4:39 **And having-stood over[a] her, he-rebuked[b] the fever and it-left her. And at-once having-arisen she-was-serving them.**

LEXICON—a. ἐπάνω (LN 83.49) (BAGD 2.a. p. 283): 'over, above' [BAGD, LN]. The phrase 'to stand over' [AB, Arn, Lns, NTC, WBC; HCSB, KJV, NASB, NET, NRSV, REB] is also translated 'to stand above' [BECNT], 'to bend over' [GW, NIV], 'to go over to' [CEV], 'to come to her side' [NCV], 'to stand at her bedside' [NLT, TEV]. The aorist tense of the verb 'having stood' is ingressive and indicates that Jesus went to the woman and came to stand over her [TH]. This probably means that Jesus stood at her head [BAGD] and possibly means that he was bending over her [BAGD, My, NICNT]. He is standing over her since she is lying on a pallet [NIGTC, WBC]. Mark says that Jesus took her by the hand to lift her up.

b. aorist act. indic. of ἐπιτιμάω (LN 33.419) (BAGD 1. p. 303): 'to rebuke' [Arn, BAGD, BECNT, LN, Lns, NTC, WBC; HCSB, KJV, NASB, NIV, NLT, NRSV, REB], 'to command' [AB; NET], 'to command to leave' [NCV], 'to order to go away' [CEV], 'to order to leave' [GW, TEV]. See this word applied to a demon at 4:35.

QUESTION—What is meant by 'rebuking' the fever?

This is the same verb used of rebuking or commanding the demons in 4:35 and the verb stresses the fact that both miracles were brought about by the words Jesus spoke [NIGTC]. Jesus rebuked the fever as though it were a demon and the fever left as a demon leaves, so, although this is not demon possession, the sickness appears to be the result of a demonic force [BNTC, WBC]. Or, although the same verb was used in both events, this does not imply that a demon was responsible for the woman's fever [ICC, NAC, NICNT, NIGTC, NTC]. This verb may have been used as a personification of the fever [Arn, BECNT, Crd, My, NIGTC; NET]. The fever is treated as though it was a hostile person [My], as though it was a demon [Arn]. Jesus rebuked the fever just as he rebuked the inanimate wind and the waves in other miracles [Lns].

QUESTION—Why and how did the healed woman serve them?

The woman was so completely cured that she immediately resumed her household duties [ICC, NAC, NICNT, Su, TNTC, WBC]. This comment indicates that her healing was complete and there was no weakness left as usually happens when a fever subsides [BECNT, Lns]. Probably the healed woman was the mistress of the house and had the responsibility of serving the guests who had come to the house for a meal. Possibly Simon was a widower and his mother-in-law lived with him [TG]. If Peter's wife was still alive, her mother would have been assisting her [NTC]. The verb suggests that the woman helped with the evening meal to which Jesus and his disciples had been invited [Lns] and she served food and drink to the guests [TG]. She prepared and served them a meal [WBC; CEV, GW, NLT]. The reference to 'them' who were served is a matter of conjecture. Probably it refers to Simon, Jesus, and whatever disciples were with Jesus [ICC, TG]. Mark 1:29 lists James and John as also being there with Jesus at the home of Simon and Andrew [Arn].

DISCOURSE UNIT: 4:40–41 [AB, TNTC, WBC]. The topic is the healing of many at sundown.

4:40 **And (while) the sun was-setting all who had ailing (ones) with-various diseases brought them to him. And laying (his) hands (on) each-one of-them he was-healing them.**
QUESTION—How did Jesus lay his hands on people and what was the significance of this act?

Jesus probably laid his hands on their heads [TH], or on the afflicted part of the body [TG]. Although other healings did not depend upon Jesus laying his hands on the person, the act seemed to signify the transmission of spiritual and physical wholeness [TH]. It was a gesture of healing [AB]. It indicated that Jesus was acting in their behalf [Arn]. This was a symbolic, not magical, act and indicated the flow of divine power from Jesus to the person being healed [NIGTC]. This act was not necessary for healing, but Jesus often accompanied healing with this act, possibly to aid the faith of those needing to be healed [ICC]. No power flowed out of Jesus and the touch of his hand was merely symbolical of bestowing a blessing [BECNT, ICC, Lns]. It was a gesture of tenderness [BECNT, EGT, Gdt].

4:41 **And also demons were-coming-out from many shouting and saying, You are the Son of-God. But rebuking (them) he-was- not -allowing them to-speak, because they-knew him to-be the Messiah.**
TEXT—Following σὺ εἶ 'you are', some manuscripts add ὁ Χριστός 'the Christ'. GNT does not mention this variant. Ὁ Χριστός 'the Christ' is read by KJV.
QUESTION—What is the significance of καί 'also' in the phrase 'and also demons were coming out from many'?

Now we learn that demon-possessed people were also brought to Jesus and the demons were cast out of them by Jesus [ICC]. The demoniacs were not covered by the designation 'ailing ones' with various diseases in 4:40 [BECNT, Lns, NAC, TH; NET]. Another interpretation is that the term 'ailing ones' in 4:40 includes the demoniacs and not only were the sick healed but also demons were cast out [Gdt, WBC].

182 LUKE 4:41

QUESTION—What relationship is indicated by ὅτι 'because' in the final clause?

It indicates the reason for not allowing them to speak [all commentaries and versions]: Jesus did not allow them to speak *because* they knew he was the Messiah and would proclaim this to the people unless he stopped them. Jesus did not want them to tell who he was because this was not the time or the manner for this fact to be made public. The correct knowledge of Jesus as the Messiah could only be gained in connection with the cross [NIBC, WBC]. Jesus did not want to be proclaimed as the Messiah by demons who opposed him [BECNT, ICC, NICNT, NIGTC], since people must come to this knowledge in a more positive way [NIGTC]. He wanted to forestall any nationalistic messianic movement that would be based on wrong political expectations [BECNT, ICC, MGC, NIGTC, NTC]. It was not Jesus' purpose to have a movement get started to make him king since such a movement would bring about a premature crisis with his enemies [NTC]. Probably the shouts of the demons were not due to their desire to proclaim the nature of Jesus to the people, but an involuntary exclamation of dismay [ICC], a despairing cry [EGT], or involuntary homage [Gdt]. Or they were confessing the superior might of Jesus who had defeated them [NIGTC].

DISCOURSE UNIT: 4:42–44 [AB, TNTC, WBC; GW, HCSB, NLT, NRSV, TEV]. The topic is the departure from Capernaum for a wider ministry [AB, WBC], a preaching tour [TNTC], preaching in Galilee [HCSB], Jesus continues to preach [NLT], Jesus preaches in the synagogues [NRSV, TEV], spreading the Good News [GW].

4:42 **And day having-come, having-gone-forth he-went to a-lonely^a place. And the crowds were-seeking him and they-came to him and they-were-hindering^b him (so as) not to-depart from them. 4:43 But he-said to them, It-is-necessary (for) me to-announce-good-news^c (about) the kingdom of-God also to-the other cities, because for this I-was-sent.^d**

TEXT—In 4:43, instead of the aorist passive ἀπεστάλην 'I was sent', some manuscripts read the perfect passive ἀπέσταλμαι 'I am sent'. GNT does not mention this variant. The perfect passive ἀπέσταλμαι 'I am sent' is read by KJV.

LEXICON—a. ἔρημος (LN 1.86) (BAGD 1.a. p. 309): 'lonely' [LN], 'desolate, uninhabited' [BAGD]. The phrase 'a lonely place' [Arn, Lns, NTC; NCV, TEV] is also translated 'a secluded place' [NASB], 'a solitary place' [NIV], 'a deserted place' [BECNT; HCSB, NET, NRSV], 'a wilderness place' [WBC], 'a desert place' [KJV], 'a deserted spot' [AB], 'a remote spot' [REB], 'a place where he could be alone' [CEV, GW], 'the wilderness' [NLT]. See the substantive use of this word at 5:16.

b. imperfect act. indic. of κατέχω (LN **37.17**) (BAGD 1.a.α. p. 422): 'to hinder' [BAGD], 'to prevent from going away' [BAGD], 'to keep from leaving' [**LN**]. The phrase 'to hinder him so as not to depart' is translated 'to stay him that he should not depart' [KJV], 'to try to stop him from

leaving' [LN; CEV], 'to try to keep him from leaving' [NTC, WBC; GW, HCSB, NCV, NET, NIV, TEV], 'to try to keep him from going away' [Lns; NASB], 'to endeavor to hold him so he would not get away from them' [Arn], 'to beg him not to leave' [NLT], 'to press him not to leave' [REB], 'to want to prevent him from leaving' [NRSV], 'would have kept him from leaving' [BECNT], 'would not permit him to move on' [AB]. The imperfect tense is conative, they *tried* to keep him from leaving [Arn, ICC, LN, Lns, NIGTC, NTC, Rb, TH, WBC; CEV, GW, NASB, NCV, NIV, TEV] and indicates that they were unable to keep him from leaving [TG]. The inhabitants of Capernaum wanted Jesus to stay in their town [TG], in order to keep him for themselves [NTC, WBC].
   c. aorist mid. infin. of εὐαγγελίζω (LN 33.215) (BAGD 2.a.α. p. 317): 'to announce good news'. See translations of this word at 1:19. This word also occurs at 2:10; 3:18; 4:18; 7:22; 8:1; 9:6; 16:16; 20:1.
   d. aorist pass. indic. of ἀποστέλλω (LN 15.66) (BAGD 1.b.γ. p. 98): 'to be sent' [AB, Arn, BAGD, BECNT, LN, Lns, NTC, WBC; all versions]. The passive implies that Jesus was sent by God [AB, BNTC, EGT, ICC, NAC, TG, TH].
QUESTION—Where was the lonely place and why did Jesus go there?
   This would be a lonely place outside the city and Mark says that he went there to pray [BECNT, Lns, NTC]. It was a place where no people were living and people seldom came there [TH]. By not adding the information about praying, perhaps Luke is indicating that this was a departure from Capernaum and not just a temporary departure for morning prayer [WBC].
QUESTION—What is meant by announcing good news about the Kingdom of God?
   The kingdom is the topic of his message and it concerns the total program about the kingdom's nearness and also the manifestation of its rule in the millennium [BECNT]. The kingdom of God was what he was establishing through his ministry [WBC]. It is the kingdom that belongs to God and that he rules [Lns]. Luke speaks about entering and seeking the kingdom of God in the present, but it is not only at hand but also belongs to the future. In essence it is spiritual, but it includes the material realm. It is God's rule recognized by his people and operates for their salvation, their constitution as a church, and for a redeemed universe [NTC]. He preached that God would soon establish his rule over the world [TG]. God was already active in bringing salvation to people through the ministry of Jesus and thus bringing people into the sphere of his rule, a rule he will consummate in the future [NIGTC]. Jesus preached about its coming and nearness and he summoned people to surrender to God's rule [TH].

4:44 And he-was preaching[a] in the synagogues of-Judea.
TEXT—Instead of Ἰουδαίας 'Judea', some manuscripts read Γαλιλαίας 'Galilee'. GNT does not mention this variant. Γαλιλαίας 'Galilee' is read by KJV.

LEXICON—a. aorist act. infin. of κηρύσσω (LN 33.256) (BAGD 2.b.β. p. 431): 'preach'. See translations of this word at 3:3. This word also occurs at 3:3; 4:18, 19, 44; 8:1, 39; 9:2; 12:3; 24:47.

QUESTION—Since the parallel passages in Mark 1:39 and Matthew 4:23–25 say that Jesus went throughout all Galilee, what is meant by 'he was preaching in the synagogues of Judea'?

'Judea' has the broader sense of Palestine so that it would include a preaching tour in Galilee as indicated in the parallel passages [AB, Arn, BECNT, BNTC, Lns, NIGTC, NTC, TH, WBC]. Jesus preached to all Jews, those in Galilee and in Judea [BECNT, Lns, NIGTC]. His preaching tour probably was through a portion of Galilee [NTC].

DISCOURSE UNIT: 5:1–6:16 [BECNT, WBC]. The topic is the gathering of disciples [BECNT], making a response to Jesus [WBC].

DISCOURSE UNIT: 5:1–6:11 [NICNT]. The topic is about missions and controversy.

DISCOURSE UNIT: 5:1–26 [TNTC]. The topic is Jesus' miracles.

DISCOURSE UNIT: 5:1–11 [AB, BECNT, NAC, NICNT, TNTC, WBC; CEV, GW, HCSB, NASB, NCV, NIV, NLT, NRSV, TEV]. The topic is the first disciples [HCSB, NASB, NCV, NLT], Jesus calls the first disciples [NAC, NICNT; GW, NET, NIV, NRSV, TEV], Jesus chooses his first disciples [CEV], a call to four fishermen [Su], fishing associates for Jesus [WBC], the miraculous catch of fish [TNTC], the miraculous catch and Peter [BECNT], the role of Simon and the catch of fish [AB].

5:1 And it-happened while the crowd was-pressing-upon him and listening to-the word of-God he was standing beside the lake of-Gennesaret **5:2** and he-saw two boats standing[a] beside the lake. And having-gone-away from them the fishermen were-washing the nets. **5:3** And getting into one of-the boats, which was Simon's, he-asked him to-put-out[b] a-little from the land, and having-sat-down he-was-teaching the crowds from the boat.

LEXICON—a. perf. act. participle of ἵσταμαι (LN 85.8): 'to stand' [Lns], 'to be' [LN]. The phrase 'to be standing beside' [Lns] is also translated 'standing by' [WBC; KJV], 'standing at the edge of' [Arn], 'by' [BECNT; NET], 'at the shore' [NCV, NRSV], 'at the edge of' [HCSB], 'lying at the water's edge' [REB], 'at the water's edge' [NIV, NLT], 'on the shore' [GW], 'pulled up on the beach' [TEV], 'lying at the edge' [NTC; NASB], 'left near the shore' [CEV], 'moored there' [AB]. The verb ἵσταμαι is used of Jesus in 5:1 'he was *standing* beside the lake' and the two boats in 5:2 'he saw two boats *standing* beside the lake.' The verb refers to being in a location, with the focus on the location, not on the act of standing upright [LN].

b. aorist act. infin. of ἐπανάγω (LN 54.5) (BAGD 1. p. 282): 'to put out' [BAGD, BECNT, Lns; HCSB, NASB, NIV, NRSV, REB], 'to put off'

[AB, WBC], 'to push off' [GW, NCV, TEV], 'to push out' [Lns; NET, NLT], 'to draw away' [Arn], 'to row out' [CEV], 'to thrust out' [KJV], 'to put out to open water, to go away from the shore' [LN].

QUESTION—How is 'God' related to 'the word' in the genitive construction 'the word of God'?

It was either a message from God or a message about God [TG, TNTC]. It means the word coming from God rather than the word about God [AB, BECNT, MGC, NAC]. It was a message based on revelation from God [BECNT]. Jesus was transmitting the word God speaks or the message God sends [TH].

QUESTION—What lake was the Lake of Gennesaret?

Gennesaret was the Greek name for the district west of the lake and the name of that district was extended to the lake [AB]. This verse is the only place where the lake is called Gennesaret, elsewhere it is always called the Lake of Galilee [TNTC]. Some versions translate it according to its better known name, the Lake of Galilee [GW, NCV, NLT].

QUESTION—Where were the boats?

1. The boats were pulled up out of the water onto the shore [Gdt, Lns, Su, TG, TH; GW, TEV]. The verb is a general word and means about the same as 'being' and here the boats were on the shore as Jesus himself was [TH]. The boats were pulled onto the shore so that they would not drift away [Gdt, Su, TG; TEV]. 'Standing beside the lake' means that the boats had been hauled up on the shore [Lns].
2. The boats were in the shallow water next to the shore [AB, Arn, EGT, NIGTC, Su]. They were moored at the shore [NIGTC], in the shallow water [Su]. They were close to land so that Jesus could step into one from the shore [EGT].

5:4 And when he-stopped speaking, he-said to Simon, You(singular)-put-out[a] into the deep (water) and you(plural)-let-down[b] your nets for a-catch. **5:5** And answering Simon said, Master,[c] having-labored throughout (the) whole night we-caught nothing. But on-account-of your word I-will-let-down the nets.

LEXICON—a. aorist act. impera. of ἐπανάγω (LN 54.5) (BAGD 1. p. 282): 'to put out'. See this word at 5:3.

b. aorist act. impera. of χαλάω (LN 15.111) (BAGD p. 874): 'to let down' [AB, Arn, BAGD, BECNT, LN, NTC, WBC; all versions except GW, NCV, NET], 'to lower' [LN, Lns; GW, NET], 'to put in the water' [NCV]. From the command to 'let down' rather than 'throw out' it appears that δίκτυον, a general term for 'net', is a dragnet, not a casting net [AB, TG, TH]. One commentary translated the verb as 'to let down' but speaks of casting the nets [BECNT].

c. ἐπιστάτης (LN 87.50) (BAGD p. 300): 'master' [Arn, BAGD, Lns; all versions except GW], 'teacher' [GW]. This title was used to address a person of high status, particularly in regard to his role of leadership [LN].

This recognizes Jesus' authority [BECNT, NTC, WBC]. It implies authority of any kind, not just that of a teacher [ICC]. The emphasis is on a respectful and intimate relationship [TH]. It replaces the titles of rabbi and teacher that are used in the other Gospels [BECNT, Lns, NIGTC, NTC] and seems to be an equivalent term [NIGTC]. Luke is the only writer to use this term. See this word at 8:24, 45; 9:33, 49; 17:13.

QUESTION—Why is there a change from singular to plural in Jesus' orders to put out and let down?

Jesus gave the command to put out into the deep to Simon, who was the captain of the boat [Crd, EGT, Gdt, My, NIGTC, Rb, WBC], or the steersman of the boat [Alf, BECNT]. Most understand the nets to be heavy dragnets. Letting down the heavy dragnets required more than one person, so the command was to the fishermen collectively [Crd, EGT, Gdt, ICC, My, NIGTC, NTC, Rb, TH], and the plural 'nets' required several men to do this [Lns]. When Peter replied, 'I will let down the nets', he was speaking as the one in command [ICC, Lns, My] and it could be translated 'I'll have the nets lowered' [NTC].

5:6 And having-done this they-enclosed a-great multitude of-fish, and their nets were-being-torn. 5:7 And they-signaled for-the partners in the other boat (to) come (and) to-help them. And they-came and they-filled both boats so-as to-be-sinking them.

QUESTION—Did the nets tear?

The imperfect tense 'were being torn' means that the nets were at the breaking point and threatened to break, but didn't [EGT, NICNT, NIGTC, TG, TH]. The nets were about to break but did not actually break since the men were able to fill two boats with fish [AB]. The tearing had begun [Arn, ICC, Lns, My, NTC, Rb], but the assistance from the other boat prevented further damage [ICC, My]. The nets did not tear enough for the fish to escape, but little cords must have been snapping here and there [NTC].

5:8 And having-seen (this), Simon Peter fell-down-at/on^a the knees of/before-Jesus saying, Depart^b from me, because I-am a-sinful man, Lord.

LEXICON—a. aorist act. indic. of προσπίπτω (LN 17.22) (BAGD 1. p. 718): 'to fall down before' [BAGD, LN], 'to prostrate oneself before' [LN]. This refers to the knees of Jesus and the phrase 'to fall down at the knees of Jesus' [Arn, Lns, WBC; KJV, NET, NRSV] is also translated 'to fall at Jesus' knees' [BECNT, NTC; HCSB, NIV, REB], 'to fall at Jesus' feet' [BAGD; NASB]. Instead of referring to Jesus' knees, this refers to the knees of Simon and the phrase 'to fall to his knees before Jesus' [NLT, TEV] is also translated 'to drop to his knees before Jesus' [AB], 'to kneel down in front of Jesus' [CEV], 'to kneel in front of Jesus' [GW], 'to bow down before Jesus' [NCV]. See this word at 8:28, 47.

b. aorist act. impera. of ἐξέρχομαι (LN 15.40) (BAGD 1.a.α. p. 274): 'to depart from' [LN], 'to go away' [BAGD]. The phrase 'depart from me' [Arn, WBC; KJV] is also translated 'leave me' [BAGD; GW, NLT], 'go and leave me' [AB; REB], 'go away from me' [NTC; HCSB, NASB, NCV, NET, NIV, NRSV, TEV], 'go away' [BECNT], 'go out from me' [Lns], 'don't come near me' [CEV].

QUESTION—What is the significance of referring to Simon as 'Simon Peter'?

The use of his full name perhaps indicates the developing importance of this disciple [BECNT]. The first time Jesus met Simon, he gave him the name Peter, meaning 'rock' in Greek (John 1:42). The name 'Peter' occurs here in Luke for the first time and assumes that the readers were already acquainted with it [Su]. Except for this verse, Luke uses only 'Simon' up to 6:14 and after that he uses only 'Peter' unless he quotes from others who used 'Simon' [TNTC].

QUESTION—Since Ἰησοῦ 'Jesus' can be taken to be in either the genitive or dative case, what is meant by 'Simon Peter fell down at/on the knees of/before Jesus'?

1. The word Ἰησοῦ 'Jesus' is to be taken as a genitive, indicating that the knees belonged to Jesus [Arn, BECNT, Lns, NIGTC, NTC, TG, TH, WBC; HCSB, KJV, NASB, NET, NIV, NRSV, REB]: Simon Peter fell down at Jesus' knees. This describes Simon as kneeling down and bowing until his head was level with Jesus' knees [TG, TH]. Simon fell down at Jesus' knees because Jesus would have been sitting down in the boat [Lns]. It indicates that Simon recognized Jesus' authority and the act displayed Simon's humility before such a superior being [BECNT, NIGTC].

2. The word Ἰησοῦ 'Jesus' is to be taken as a dative, indicating that the knees belonged to Simon Peter [AB, BNTC, LN, TNTC; CEV, GW, NLT, TEV]: Simon Peter fell down on his knees before Jesus. Although taking the word 'Jesus' to be in the genitive case, two commentaries translate in a way that supports this interpretation: 'dropped to his knees before Jesus' [AB], 'fell on his knees before Jesus' which is the equivalent of saying 'he knelt down before Jesus' as a sign of worship [LN (17.22)].

QUESTION—What did Simon mean when he requested Jesus to depart?

Peter felt that he was unworthy of having Jesus in his boat and requested Jesus to get out of the boat when they reached land [Lns]. His request expressed his sense of unworthiness [Arn, BECNT, Lns, NAC, NIVS, NTC] in contrast with Christ's greatness and holiness [NTC]. It was Simon's reaction to the display of Jesus' power in the miraculous catch of fish [AB]. Simon wanted Jesus to depart from his boat [Alf, My]. He was saying 'go out of my boat and depart from me' [Gdt]. Simon told Jesus not only to get out of the boat, but to leave the vicinity [AB, ICC]. However, Simon did not expect Jesus to immediately get out of the boat and step into the water [Lns, NAC, NTC].

QUESTION—What relationship is indicated by ὅτι 'because' in the clause 'because I am a sinful man'?

It indicates the grounds for Simon's request that Jesus depart [ICC, Lns, My, NTC, Su, TG, TH]. Simon felt unworthy to be in Jesus' presence [Lns, NTC,

Su, TG]. Simon could not bear the presence of one who had such supernatural power [TH]. He was terrified because, being a sinner in the presence of such holy and divine power, he might have some misfortune fall upon him [My]. Christ's holiness was so intense that Simon could not tolerate it, not because it was a peril, but because he regarded Christ's presence as a reproach and condemnation [ICC]. Simon knelt because he realized that he was a sinful man, thinking not only of his personal acts of sin, but of his sinful character before God and God's representative [BECNT]. Simon was a sinner in the general sense as being in the class of people who did not carefully observe the Law and could not bear being in the presence of one who had such supernatural power [TH].

QUESTION—What did Simon mean by calling Jesus 'Lord'?

1. 'Lord' did not indicate divinity [AB, NICNT, NIGTC, TH; NET]. In its unemphatic final position, 'Lord' is used in polite address [AB]. This had a deeper meaning than ἐπιστάτης 'master' in 5:5 [BECNT, NICNT, NIGTC, TH], being more respectful [TH; NET]. Simon used this title in recognition of Jesus' authority and the fact that God was working through such a one. If the disciples already considered Jesus divine, they would not be discussing who Jesus was in 8:25 [BECNT]. Simon recognized that Jesus was an agent of God in his role as a teacher and prophet [NICNT].

2. 'Lord' indicated divinity [Lns, NTC, TG, WBC]. By referring to his sinfulness, Simon used 'Lord' in the sense of divine Lord, just as did all the Apostles and later the church [Lns]. Simon had become aware that Jesus was superhuman, that he was God and worthy of worship [NTC]. As Luke usually refers to Jesus in his narration, he uses the title 'Lord' in the sense of 1:43 and 2:11 and this does not clearly indicate the disciples' developing awareness of who Jesus actually was [WBC]. Luke used the distinctive title that believers applied to Jesus [TG].

5:9 Because amazement[a] seized[b] him and all the (ones) with him on-account-of the catch of-fish which they-took,

LEXICON—a. θάμβος (LN 25.208) (BAGD p. 350): 'amazement'. See this word at 4:36. This indicates wonderment combined with fear [NIGTC], because they realized that the catch of fish had no rational explanation [NIGTC].

b. aorist act. indic. of περιέχω (LN 90.69) (BAGD 1.b. p. 647): 'to seize' [BAGD, LN]. It means to experience some emotion in an overwhelming manner [LN]. The phrase 'amazement seized him' is translated 'amazement had seized him' [Arn; NASB], 'amazement had taken hold of him' [WBC], 'amazement had gripped him' [AB, NTC], 'astonishment enveloped him' [Lns], 'was amazed' [GW, HCSB, NCV, NRSV, REB, TEV], 'was astonished' [BECNT, LN; KJV, NET, NIV], 'was completely surprised' [CEV], 'was awestruck' [NLT].

QUESTION—What relationship is indicated by γάρ 'because'?
It indicates the reason for Simon's exclamation in 5:8 [BECNT, ICC, Lns, Su, TNTC; NET]: *he said this because* he was amazed. Simon was the one who spoke in the previous verse, but the others had a response similar to his [NET].

QUESTION—Who were the ones with Simon?
These were the men in the same boat with Simon [Crd, TG, TH]. They are to be distinguished from Simon's partners in the second boat [Crd, TH]. 'All the ones with him' refers to more than one, one of whom was probably Andrew [BECNT, TG].

5:10 and likewise also James and John, (the) sons of-Zebedee, who were partners[a] with-Simon. And Jesus said to Simon, Do- not -be-afraid. From now (on) you-will-be catching[b] people.

LEXICON—a. κοινωνός (LN **34.6**): 'partner' [BECNT, LN, NTC, WBC; all versions except NET], 'business partner' [NET], 'associate' [Arn, Lns], 'companion' [AB]. James and John were partners in business with Simon [BECNT, Lns; NET], perhaps owning and operating the other boat [Lns]. In 5:7 the technical term μέτοχος is used for partner [AB] or business partner [NICNT], and here the more generic term κοινωνός 'companion' is used [AB, NICNT]. These two terms are virtually synonymous [TH].

b. pres. act. participle of ζωγρέω (LN 18.8) (BAGD p. 340): 'to catch' [AB, BAGD, LN, NTC, WBC; all versions except CEV, NCV, NLT], 'to bring in' [CEV], 'to fish for' [NCV, NLT], 'to be fishers of' [BECNT]. The verb contains the two morphemes ζωός 'alive' and αγρεύω 'to catch', but only a few make explicit the aspect of catching people alive in their translations: 'to capture alive' [BAGD, LN], 'to catch alive' [Arn, Lns]. However, many comment about it [AB, BECNT, ICC, Lns, NICNT, NIGTC, NTC, TNTC, WBC]. Fish are caught and killed, while people are 'caught' alive and the gospel saves from death [Lns]. Jesus' disciples will no longer be catching dead fish but will catch people to give them liberty [NICNT]. They will be catching for life, not for death [TNTC]. The focus is on catching people in the sense of gathering and rescuing them and being 'caught alive' pictures their entrance into a new life [BECNT]. On the other hand, the verb should be taken in the common sense of catching both fish and men [Alf]. 'To catch men' is figurative language and means to win men for God's kingdom [BAGD]. 'You will be catching people' is a prophecy that has the effect of a command [NIGTC, TG]. The future 'will be' assures a measure of success and the continuity is stressed to indicate that this will be an ongoing work [BECNT, NTC]. The tense is continuous to indicate a habitual practice [Gdt, ICC, TNTC]. Catching people will be his occupation [TH].

QUESTION—What relationship is indicated by ὁμοίως 'likewise'?

Simon's partners were amazed also [AB, BECNT, NTC, WBC; CEV, HCSB, KJV, NASB, NCV, NET, NIV, NLT, NRSV, REB, TEV]: and *so were* James and John amazed. They all shared the same amazement [AB].

QUESTION—What is meant by catching people?

Since this is addressed to fishermen, 'catching people' is the same metaphor as making the fishermen 'fishers of people' in Matthew 4:19 and Mark 1:17 [AB, Lns, NTC, TG, WBC; NET], but the words are more definite here [NTC]. Simon is going to quit his work of catching fish and start catching people and he will do this by causing people to become Jesus' disciples [TG]. This metaphor refers to gathering people for salvation [WBC]. The picture is of net fishing [NET]. They were to catch people in the gospel net in order to rescue them from death and to impart life [NTC]. The verb includes the idea of catching something alive and refers to catching men alive in contrast to catching fish which were killed [Lns, NTC]. The point of similarity is 'gathering in' and this mean that he will gather in human beings for God's kingdom [AB]. This might be expressed, 'Just as you have worked to bring in fish, from now on you will work to bring people to me' [TG].

5:11 And having-brought the boats on the land (and) having-left everything they-followed[a] him.

LEXICON—a. aorist act. indic. of ἀκολουθέω (LN 36.31) (BAGD 3. p. 31): 'to follow' [Arn, BAGD, BECNT, LN, NTC, WBC; all versions except CEV], 'to go with' [CEV], 'to be a disciple of' [LN]. It refers to following someone as a disciple [BAGD]. This is translated 'they became his disciples' [NIGTC]. It refers to being with Jesus and this will prepare them for their apostolic mission [WBC]. Not just the apostles were called to follow Jesus, rather every Christian is to follow him [NAC]. See this word at 5:27; 9:57; 18:43.

QUESTION—Who left everything to follow Jesus?

Jesus' command was addressed to Simon, but his companions realized that it included them also [EGT, ICC, NAC, NIGTC, Su]. Luke was focusing on Simon and did not clearly indicate who were involved when he used the plural 'they'. From his Markan source we know that Luke was thinking of Simon, James, and John [WBC], but nothing is said about Andrew in any of the accounts [Lns]. They abandoned: all of their possessions [TH], their boats [BECNT, Lns, NICNT, Su], their homes [Lns], their business [ICC, Lns, Rb], their father Zebedee [Lns, Su], their families [Lns], and their hired servants [Su]. They even abandoned the large catch of fish [ICC, Lns, NICNT], although Zebedee and the hired help would have attended to the sale of the fish [Lns]. To leave everything means that they gave up everything [TH] as they entered into a permanent commitment to follow Jesus [Su].

DISCOURSE UNIT: 5:12–6:11 [NIGTC]. The topic is the beginning of controversy with the Pharisees.

LUKE 5:12

DISCOURSE UNIT: 5:12–26 [BECNT; NASB]. The topic is the two miracles of authority [BECNT], the leper and the paralytic [NASB].

DISCOURSE UNIT: 5:12–16 [AB, BECNT, NAC, NICNT, NIGTC, Su, TNTC, WBC; CEV, GW, HCSB, NCV, NET, NIV, NLT, NRSV, TEV]. The topic is the man with leprosy [NIV], Jesus heals a man [CEV, TEV], Jesus heals a sick man [NCV], cleansing a leper [HCSB], Jesus cleanses a leper [NRSV], Jesus heals a leper [AB, BECNT, NAC, NICNT, NIGTC, Su, TNTC, WBC; NET, NLT], Jesus cures a man with a skin disease [GW].

5:12 And it-happened while he was in one of-the cities, behold (there was) a-man full of-leprosy.[a] And (when) he-saw Jesus, having-fallen[b] on (his) face he-begged him saying, Lord,[c] if you-are-willing, you-are-able to-cleanse[d] me.

LEXICON—a. λέπρα (LN 23.161) (BAGD p. 471): 'leprosy' [BAGD, LN], 'a dread skin disease' [LN]. The phrase 'to be full of leprosy' [Arn, BECNT, Lns, NTC, WBC; KJV] is also translated 'to be covered with leprosy' [AB; NASB, NET, NIV, NRSV, REB], 'to be covered with a skin disease' [NCV], 'to be covered with a serious skin disease' [GW], 'to have leprosy' [CEV], 'to suffer from a dreaded skin disease' [TEV], 'who had a serious skin disease all over him' [HCSB], 'with an advanced case of leprosy' [NLT]. In this verse it means to be all covered with leprosy [BAGD]. The leprosy was in an advanced stage [Arn, Gdt, ICC, NTC, TNTC]. The man's face and hands would have been covered with ulcers and sores [ICC]. This word refers to a dreaded condition of the skin and includes what is now regarded as leprosy and also certain other types of infectious skin diseases. A person having this disease was regarded as being ceremonially unclean and was therefore excluded from normal relations with other people [LN]. The word 'leprosy' is a broader term than Hansen's Disease and covers a whole series of contagious skin diseases. This disease resulted in the rotting of flesh and loss of hair, fingers, eyes, and other parts of the body [Su]. The description for identifying a leper in Leviticus 13–14 shows that it includes more conditions than the disease called leprosy today has [AB, BECNT, NIGTC]. The word does not mean Hanson's disease, but it covers many kinds of skin diseases, some regarded to be highly contagious and incurable, and it is not possible to know exactly what disease is meant here [NIGTC].

b. aorist act. participle of πίπτω (LN 17.21) (BAGD 1.b.α. p. 659): 'to fall down' [BAGD], 'to prostrate oneself before' [LN]. The phrase 'to fall on one's face' [Arn, BECNT, Lns, NTC, WBC; KJV, NASB] is also translated 'to fall with one's face to the ground' [NIV], 'to fall to the ground, face down in the dust' [NLT], 'to fall facedown' [HCSB], 'to throw oneself down' [TEV], 'to throw oneself to the ground' [REB], 'to bow before' [NCV], 'to bow down with one's face to the ground' [AB; NET, NRSV], 'to kneel down to the ground in front of' [CEV]. The action

indicated reverence and did not necessarily have a religious connotation [AB]. The leper dropped to his knees (Mark 1:40) and then lowered his face to the ground [Lns]. It would have been normal to bow to any superior in that culture [BECNT].
  c. κύριος (LN 12.9, 87.53): 'Lord' [Arn, BECNT, LN (12.9), Lns, NTC, WBC; all versions except GW, REB, TEV], 'sir' [AB, LN (87.53); GW, REB, TEV].
  d. aorist act. infin. of καθαρίζω (LN 23.137) (BAGD 1.b.α. p. 387): 'to cleanse' [Arn, BAGD, Lns, NTC], 'to make clean' [AB, BECNT, WBC; all versions except CEV, NCV, NLT], 'to make well' [CEV, NLT], 'to heal' [NCV], 'to heal and make ritually clean or acceptable' [LN]. See this word at 4:27; 7:22; 17:44.

QUESTION—What did the leper mean by addressing Jesus as 'Lord'?
  This term was generally used a title of respect like the English word 'sir' [AB, Su, TG; GW, REB, TEV]. However, he must have meant more than a polite 'sir' since he was convinced that Jesus could heal him [BECNT, Lns, NTC, WBC]. He was addressing Jesus with the belief that Jesus had special power from God [NIGTC], or that he was the Messiah [Arn, Su]. 'Lord' was probably not used in recognition of Jesus' deity since even Jesus' disciples did not recognize it at this stage [BECNT, NIGTC, NTC]. The leper probably used 'Lord' as a title of respect, but for Luke and those who read the account, the full significance of the address would have been understood [NAC].

QUESTION—Why did the leper use the conditional clause 'if you will'?
  The leper had heard that Jesus was healing people. Although the leper believed that Jesus had the power to heal him, he was not sure that he would [BECNT, EGT, Lns, NICNT, NTC, TG, TNTC, WBC]. He indicated his submission to Jesus' will [Su]. He submitted himself to Jesus' will, but was hopeful that he too may be one who received healing [Arn, Lns, NTC]. This sentence was a polite request for healing [NIGTC]. Or, this shows he doubted that Jesus would heal him [ICC].

5:13 **And having-stretched-out (his) hand he-touched him saying, I-am-willing, be-cleansed. And immediately the leprosy left[a] from him.**
LEXICON—a. aorist act. indic. of ἀπέρχομαι (LN 13.93) (BAGD 1.b. p. 84): 'to leave' [AB, Arn, BAGD, LN, NTC, WBC; HCSB, NASB, NET, NIV, NRSV, REB, TEV], 'to depart' [KJV], 'to go away' [Lns; GW], 'to go out' [BECNT], 'to disappear' [CEV, NCV, NLT], 'to cease to exist' [LN]. The body that had parts eaten away and covered with raw sores was instantly restored to wholeness [Lns].

QUESTION—What is the significance of Jesus stretching out his hand and touching the leper?
  The Jewish ceremonial laws forbid touching a leper and anyone who did so became ceremonially defiled and was separated from others [Su]. A spoken word would have healed the man, but the gentle touch confirmed Jesus' care

for the man [BECNT]. Jesus touched the leper to indicate his sympathy [EGT], compassion [TNTC], pity, and love for him [ICC, Su]. Reaching out to touch the leper was proof of Jesus' will to cleanse him [BECNT, EGT]. Some think that Jesus added his touch to aid the leper's faith [ICC], but one disputes this, saying that the leper had already shown his faith by coming to Jesus and the healing did not depend on increasing the leper's faith [Lns].

5:14 **And he gave-orders to-him to-tell no-one, But, (he said), having-departed show^a yourself to-the priest and make-an-offering for your cleansing as Moses commanded, for a-proof^b to-them.**

LEXICON—a. aorist act. impera. of δείκνυμι (LN 28.47) (BAGD 1.a. p. 172): 'to show' [AB, Arn, BAGD, BECNT, LN, Lns, NTC, WBC; all versions except NLT, TEV]. The phrase 'show yourself to the priest' is translated 'go straight to the priest and let him examine you' [NLT, TEV]. The purpose of showing himself to a priest was to have the priest examine him in order to confirm that he no longer had leprosy [TH].

b. μαρτύριον (LN 33.262) (BAGD 1.a. p. 493): 'proof' [AB, BAGD], 'testimony' [BAGD, BECNT, NTC, WBC; HCSB, KJV, NASB, NET, NIV, NRSV], 'witness' [Arn, LN, Lns]. The phrase 'for a proof to them' is translated 'as proof to people that you are clean' [GW], 'so everyone will have proof of your healing' [NLT], 'to prove to everyone that you are cured' [TEV], 'and everyone will know that you have been healed' [CEV], 'that will certify the cure' [REB], 'this will show the people what I have done' [NCV].

QUESTION—Why would Jesus tell the healed leper not to tell anyone?

This instruction was given in order to comply with the OT law that a priestly investigation was required prior to a public claim of cleansing from leprosy [BECNT, ICC, NICNT, NIGTC, Su, WBC]. Jesus did not want the priests to know that he had cured the leper until after the leper had already been pronounced clean at the temple, a process that required a week [Lns]. There was no time to lose in getting to the priest [NIGTC, TG]. Perhaps this command was also given in order to avoid a display of uncontrollable excitement among the people concerning the miracle [BECNT, Gdt, NAC, NIGTC, NTC, Su, TNTC]. Jesus did not want crowds coming just for healing without regard to his message [NAC].

QUESTION—What was the purpose of showing himself to the priest?

The OT law in Leviticus 14 required that a claim of being cleansed could not be made until investigated by a priest who would make it official [WBC]. The offering of a sacrifice would have to be done at the Temple in Jerusalem [TG]. 'The priest' refers to the priest on duty in the Temple when the man arrives [AB, Arn, ICC, TG]. The former leper could not be restored to full social and religious fellowship with people until he passed the inspection of a priest and then brought the offerings that the law required [NTC].

QUESTION—What was the offering that Moses commanded?
    The offering is specified in Leviticus 14:1–8. The offering consisted of two birds; one bird was killed and the other bird was dipped in the blood and then released. After the rest of the blood was sprinkled over the healed person, the priest would pronounce the man cured and clean in regard to his associating with people [NTC]. A week after offering the two birds, which symbolized physical cleansing, there was a ceremony in which two lambs were offered (Leviticus 14:9–32), which symbolized spiritual cleansing so that the man was clean in regard to the temple [Lns].

QUESTION—Who are referred to by the pronoun 'them' and what is meant by 'a proof to them'?

1. 'Them' refers to people in general [Arn, Crd, ICC, NIGTC, Rb, TH, TNTC, WBC; CEV, GW, NCV, NLT, TEV]: show yourself to the priest and make an offering, for a proof *to the people*. The priestly ritual authenticated the cleansing to the people [WBC]. It is a proof that the leper had been physically healed [TNTC; CEV, NLT, TEV] or ceremonially cleansed [GW]. People knew that the man had been a leper and they would be hesitant to accept him, but if a priest pronounced him cured, and accepted his offerings, they would be convinced that he had truly been healed [TNTC]. It is a proof to all, the priests and people, that Jesus did not disregard the law [Arn, ICC]. It was to be evidence of God's messianic act in Jesus [NIGTC].

2. 'Them' refers to the priests [BECNT, Gdt, Lns, MGC, NICNT, NTC]: show yourself to the priest and make an offering, for a proof to the priests. The antecedent is 'the priest' who represents the priests in Jerusalem [Gdt, Lns]. Upon hearing that it was Jesus who had healed the leper, the priests would recognize the power possessed by Jesus and also know that he did not disobey the law [NTC]. When the priests finally learned the story of the man, they would have a testimony of the Messiah's power and reverence for the law of Moses [Lns]. The testimony is not that Jesus obeyed the law, but that God's power was expressed through Jesus and that this testified to the presence of messianic times [BECNT]. The priests would have evidence that Jesus followed the ceremonial laws and that he was the Messiah [NICNT].

5:15 **But the news about him was-spreading^a (even) more, and great crowds were-assembling to-listen and to-be-healed from their sicknesses. 5:16 But he was withdrawing^b in the lonely-places^c and was-praying.**

LEXICON—a. imperf. mid./pass. (deponent = act.) indic. of διέρχομαι (LN 15.21) (BAGD 3. p. 194): 'to spread' [BAGD, Lns, NTC, WBC; all versions except KJV, NRSV], 'to spread abroad' [AB; NRSV], 'to go out more and more' [Arn], 'to travel around through' [LN], 'to go abroad' [BECNT; KJV]. In regard to a report, this is a figurative use of 'to go about from place to place' [BAGD]. The news spread through the public grapevine [BECNT].

LUKE 5:15–16

b. pres. act. participle of ὑποχωρέω (LN **15.53**) (BAGD 1. p. 848): 'to withdraw' [BAGD, BECNT, LN; KJV, NRSV], 'to frequently withdraw' [NET], 'to often withdraw' [HCSB, NIV, NLT], 'to withdraw from time to time' [REB], 'to regularly withdraw' [Arn], 'to go away' [**LN**, NTC; GW, TEV], 'to often slip away' [NASB, NCV], 'to often retire' [AB], 'to often go' [CEV], 'to go off to' [NTC], 'to keep going quietly' [Lns]. The imperfect tense is iterative, meaning that from time to time Jesus would slip away for prayer [AB, Lns, NTC, TG, TH, WBC; CEV, HCSB, NASB, NCV, NET, NIV, NLT, REB]. Jesus habitually withdrew for prayer [AB, BECNT, NAC, NICNT]. Whenever Jesus had opportunity, he would slip away quietly and secretly from the crowds [Lns]. Or, the imperfect tense refers to duration and means that he retired to the desert places and stayed there in order to pray [NIGTC]. See this word at 9:10.

c. ἔρημος (LN 1.86): 'lonely places' [Arn, LN, Lns, NTC; NIV, TEV], 'desert' [LN], 'desert places' [NRSV], 'deserted places' [AB; HCSB], 'remote places' [REB], 'wilderness' [BECNT, LN; KJV, NASB, NET, NLT], 'wilderness spots' [NTC], 'some place where he could be alone' [CEV], 'places where he could be alone' [GW], '(to be) alone' [NCV]. This refers to any place where there were no people, a place where Jesus could be alone [Su]. See the adjectival use of this word at 4:42.

QUESTION—In 5:15, what is being compared with the news spreading 'even more'?

In spite of Jesus' instructions to the leper to tell no one, the news spread even more than ever [ICC, NTC, TH], more than before [ICC], more and more [TG], or ever wider [BECNT]. Luke omits Mark's statement that the leper disobeyed Jesus' command and concentrates on the effects of the disobedience [AB, Alf, Gdt, ICC, Lns, NIGTC]. The healed man took the lead in spreading the news about Jesus' miracle [NTC], but he was not alone in being responsible for spreading that news [Lns].

QUESTION—What was the news about?

It was the news about Jesus that was spreading even more [AB, BECNT, EGT, Lns, NIGTC, NTC, Rb, WBC; CEV, GW, NASB, NCV, NLT, NRSV, TEV]. The news was about Jesus healing the leper [Su]. The imperfect tense means that Jesus' fame kept going out [Rb].

DISCOURSE UNIT: 5:17–6:11 [AB, NAC]. The topic is the beginning of controversy.

DISCOURSE UNIT: 5:17–26 [AB, BECNT, NAC, NICNT, NIGTC, Su, TNTC, WBC; CEV, GW, HCSB, NCV, NET, NIV, NRSV, TEV]. The topic is the healing of a paralytic [AB, BECNT, Su, TNTC], Jesus heals a crippled man [CEV], Jesus heals a paralytic [NIV, NRSV], Jesus heals a paralyzed man [NCV, TEV], the Son of Man forgives and heals [HCSB], healing and forgiving a paralytic [NET], the forgiveness of a paralyzed man [WBC], Jesus forgives sins [GW], Jesus' authority to forgive sins [NIGTC], conflict over Jesus' forgiveness of sins [NAC, NICNT].

5:17 And it-happened on one of-the days he was teaching, and Pharisees and teachers-of-the-law were-sitting-down who had come from every village[a] of-Galilee and Judea and Jerusalem. And (the) Lord's power was for[b] him to-heal.

TEXT—Instead of οἳ ἦσαν ἐληλυθότες 'who had come', some manuscripts read οἳ ἦσαν συνεληλυθότες 'who had come together', and others read ἦσαν δὲ συνεληλυθότες 'and they had come together'. GNT reads οἳ ἦσαν ἐληλυθότες 'who had come' with a B decision, indicating that the text is almost certain.

TEXT—Instead of εἰς τὸ ἰᾶσθαι αὐτόν 'for him to heal' some manuscripts read εἰς τὸ ἰᾶσθαι αὐτούς 'to heal them'. GNT reads εἰς τὸ ἰᾶσθαι αὐτόν 'for him to heal' with an A decision, indicating that the text is certain. Ἐἰς τὸ ἰᾶσθαι αὐτούς 'to heal them' is read by KJV.

LEXICON—a. κώμηα (LN 1.92) (BAGD 1. p. 461): 'village' [AB, Arn, BAGD, BECNT, LN, Lns, NTC, WBC; all versions except KJV, NCV, TEV], 'town' [KJV, NCV, TEV]. It to be contrasted with πόλις 'city' and means a relatively unimportant population center [LN].

b. εἰς (LN 90.59): 'for' [LN]. The phrase ἦν εἰς 'was for' is translated 'was present for (him to heal)' [NASB, NIV], 'was there for (him to heal)' [Lns, WBC], 'was in' [HCSB], 'was with' [AB, BECNT, NTC; NET, NLT, NRSV, REB, TEV]. This is also translated as a verb phrase 'Jesus had (the power)' [GW], 'God had given' [CEV], 'the Lord was giving Jesus' [NCV].

QUESTION—What is the distinction between Pharisees and teachers of the law?

Most of the teachers of the law were Pharisees [Lns, NAC, Rb, WBC], but most of the Pharisees were not teachers of the law [Lns, Rb]. The teachers of the law probably were a specific group within the Pharisees [AB, BECNT]. Although all translations indicate that Pharisees and teachers of the law were there, one commentary states that since most teachers of the law were Pharisees, the statement is a hendiadys where one noun modifies the other: Pharisaic teachers of the law were there [NIGTC].

QUESTION—Does 'every village' go only with Galilee or also with Judea?

1. 'Village' goes only with Galilee [Arn, NTC; NIV, REB]: from every village in Galilee and (from the province of) Judea and (from the city of) Jerusalem. 'Every village' is not to be repeated before 'Jerusalem' and there is not reason to repeat it before 'Judea' [Arn].
2. 'Village' goes with both Galilee and Judea [AB; all versions except NIV, REB]: 'from every village in both Galilee and Judea and from Jerusalem.

QUESTION—How literal is the statement that these people came from *every* village in Galilee and Judea and Jerusalem?

This is not to be taken literally [Alf, TG, WBC], rather it is a way to emphatically describe Jesus' popularity [TG]. The statement uses hyperbole [ICC, My, NTC, TH]: they came from many villages in Galilee and Judea as well as from the city of Jerusalem. Of course not every village of Galilee had scribes and Pharisees [Arn].

QUESTION—What is meant by saying that the Lord's power was for him to heal?

Here 'Lord' refers to God [Alf, ICC, Lns, NIGTC, NTC, TG, TH, TNTC], as indicated by the absence of the article with 'Lord' [Alf, ICC, NIGTC]. God's power was present for Jesus to heal with that power [ICC, WBC]. Jesus had power from the Lord to heal the people [Rb]. The preposition εἰς 'for' indicates result, not purpose [Lns, TH]: there was power from God so that Jesus could use it to heal people. God's power enabled Jesus to heal [NTC]. This does not imply that it was an intermittent power; rather this explains what it meant for Jesus to have become the repository of God's power through the descent of the Spirit [WBC]. It is translated 'the power of the Lord was present for him to heal the sick' [NIV], 'the power of the Lord was present for him to perform healing' [NASB], 'the Lord's healing power was strongly with Jesus' [NLT], 'the Lord was giving Jesus the power to heal people' [NCV], 'God had given Jesus the power to heal the sick' [CEV]. This sentence prepares the readers for the miracle that is to follow [NAC].

5:18 And behold men (came) carrying on a-pallet[a] a-man who had-been paralyzed[b] and they-were-trying to-carry- him -in and to-place him before him.

TEXT—Following θεῖναι 'to place', some manuscripts omit αὐτόν 'him'. GNT does not deal with this variant in its apparatus but brackets αὐτόν 'him' in the text, indicating that the Committee had doubts about including it. 'Him' is italicized in KJV, indicating that αὐτόν 'him' is omitted in the Greek text that KJV follows.

LEXICON—a. κλίνη (LN 6.106) (BAGD p. 436): 'pallet' [BAGD], 'stretcher' [AB, BAGD, LN; GW, HCSB, NET], 'mat' [CEV, NCV, NIV], 'sleeping mat' [NLT], 'bed' [Arn, BAGD, BECNT, LN, Lns, NTC, WBC; KJV, NASB, NRSV, REB, TEV], 'couch, cot' [LN]. This is a rather generic word for anything used for reclining or lying on [LN]. The pallet would be a poor man's bed that perhaps was a thin straw-filled mattress or a mat [NTC]. It was something easy to carry a man on and could have been a sleeping mat [TG]. It was a stretcher [AB, BECNT; GW, NET], or a stretcher-like couch [Arn]. The diminutive form κλινίδιον 'little pallet' is used in the next verse. Some take the two words to describe the same thing [AB, Lns, NTC, TH; NET], and the diminutive was used to explain why it could have been lowered through the hole in the roof [Lns]. Others think that the second word describes only a part of the first [ICC]. The κλινίδιον 'little pallet' is something the healed man could pick up and carry off to his house (5:24).

b. perf. pass. participle of παραλύομαι (LN 23.170): 'to be paralyzed' [AB, Arn, BECNT, LN, Lns, NTC, WBC; all versions except CEV, KJV, NIV], 'to be crippled' [CEV], 'to be lame' [LN], 'to be taken with palsy' [KJV].

The phrase 'a man who had been paralyzed' is translated 'a paralytic' [NIV]. It means to suffer from the paralysis of one or more limbs [LN]. The passive voice indicates a permanent condition [TH]. The disease is generally the result of the muscles being unable to function, perhaps because of an injury to the brain or spinal cord [NTC]. The man was crippled [BECNT]. He could not walk because one side of his body was helpless [Lns].

5:19 **And not having-found a-way they-might-carry him because-of the crowd, having-gone-up onto the roof they-lowered him with the pallet through the tiles[a] into the midst in-front-of Jesus.**

LEXICON—a. κέραμος (LN **6.224**) (BAGD 2. p. 429): 'tile' [AB, Arn, BECNT, LN, Lns, NTC, WBC; CEV, GW, KJV, NASB, NIV, NLT, NRSV, TEV], 'roof tile' [BAGD, **LN**; HCSB, NET], 'tiling' [REB], 'ceiling' [NCV]. It was a thin slab of baked clay [LN].

QUESTION—What was involved in lowering the man on a pallet through the tiles?

They would have gone up onto a flat roof [Crd, Lns, My, NTC, Rb, TG, TH, TNTC; NET]. Since they lowered the man through the tiles, they had to use ropes attached to the four corners of the pallet [NTC, Rb]. House roofs were usually made by placing wooden rafters across the top of stone or mud walls. Then the beams were covered with a layer of reeds and thorns topped with a layer of clay [AB, BECNT, NTC]. The reference to tiles is a problem to some commentators, and some speculate that Luke has changed the clay and thatch roof that must be dug through to a tile roof in order to make it more intelligible to readers such as Theophilus who knew only of the Greek type of tile roof [AB, BNTC, NAC, WBC]. But κέραμος 'tile' can also refer to clay and it could mean that lumps of clay were removed, although it is possible that tile roofs were also used on the houses of that time [BECNT; NET]. Tile roofs had come into use by this time [NIGTC, NTC, TNTC].

5:20 **And having-seen their faith he-said, Man,[a] your sins have-been-forgiven you.**

TEXT—Following εἶπεν 'he said', some manuscripts add αὐτῷ 'to him'. GNT does not mention this variant. Αὐτῷ 'to him' is read by KJV.

LEXICON—a. ἄνθρωπος (LN 9.24) (BAGD 1.a.γ. p. 68): 'man' [Arn, BAGD, BECNT, LN, Lns, NTC, WBC; KJV], 'friend' [BAGD; HCSB, NASB, NCV, NET, NIV, NRSV], 'my friend' [CEV, TEV], 'son' [NLT], 'sir' [GW]. 'Man' was a friendly term used for someone who was not personally known [TG]. Because of unfavorable connotations in English of the vocative 'Man', some translations change it to an indirect object: 'he said *to the man*, Your sins have been forgiven' [AB; REB]. The parallel passages in Matthew and Mark have τέκνον 'child, son' and perhaps Luke thought his readers would not understand it to be a term of affection or would take it to refer to a boy rather than to a man [BECNT].

QUESTION—What is meant by 'their faith'?

The pronoun 'their' refers to the faith of the paralytic and the people who brought him [AB, Arn, Gdt, ICC, Lns, NAC, NTC, Rb, TG, TNTC; NET]. Two commentaries mention only the faith of the men who brought the man [BECNT, Su]. Their faith was visible by the way they were so persistent in placing the paralytic before Jesus that they removed the tiles from the roof [Lns, NAC, NIGTC]. They had faith that Jesus could do something for the needs of the man [AB, BECNT, NTC; NET]. They were confident that Jesus had the power to heal [NIBC, TH]. Their faith was in Jesus as one who came from God and who could heal [NAC]. The friends had faith that Jesus had power to heal, but the paralytic's faith also involved his burden of sin [Lns].

QUESTION—What is meant by the perfect passive verb 'your sins have been forgiven'?

The perfect tense emphasizes entering into a state of being forgiven [BECNT, Lns, NAC, NIGTC, NTC]. We are not to assume that the man's paralysis was the result of a sinful life [Lns, NTC, Su]. The sins referred to are not some specific sins but the general disorder of creation [BECNT]. The man probably believed that his paralysis was due to his own sin [ICC, NIGTC], and Jesus dealt with the sin which caused the illness before curing him [NIGTC].

1. The passive voice implies that God does the forgiving [AB, BECNT, NICNT, Su, TG, TH, WBC]: God has forgiven your sins. This implication was picked up by the theologians in the audience [BECNT]. Luke did not specify the agent of the passive verb in order to provide the basis for the following discussion with the Pharisees. Jesus never said 'I forgive your sins' and in 5:24 he speaks of the authority he derived from God to forgive sins [TH]. The statement asserted that God had authorized Jesus to announce forgiveness on his behalf [NICNT]. The Pharisees and teachers understood the passive statement to be a declaration pronounced by Jesus [AB, BECNT]. If the passive form must be changed to active, a possible translation is 'I declare to you, God has forgiven your sins' [TH].

2. The passive voice implies that Jesus does the forgiving [Lns, MGC, NAC, NIGTC, NTC]: I have forgiven your sins. The following verses show that Jesus' words were understood to be a claim of equality with God [NAC]. Jesus is the agent since the following verses rest on the fact that Jesus forgives the man's sins. The evidence of Jesus' divinity is that, as God, Jesus forgives the man's sins and proves it with the miracle [Lns]. In his own right Jesus canceled the paralytic's debt of sin [NTC]. The perfect tense indicates the abiding force of the forgiveness [NIGTC].

5:21 **And the scribes[a] and the Pharisees began to-reason[b] saying, Who is this who is-speaking blasphemies?[c] Who is-able to-forgive sins except God alone? 5:22 But Jesus having-known their thoughts, answering said to them, Why are-you-reasoning in your hearts?**

LEXICON—a. γραμματεύς (LN 53.94): 'scribe' [AB, Arn, BECNT, Lns, NTC, WBC; GW, HCSB, KJV, NASB, NRSV, REB], 'one who is expert in the Law' [LN], 'expert' [CEV], 'expert in the law' [NET], 'teacher of the law' [NIV, TEV], 'teacher of religious law' [NLT]. 'Jewish teacher of the law' [NCV]. The νομοδιδάσκαλοι 'teachers of the law' in 5:17, are now identified as scribes [AB, BECNT, ICC, Lns, Su, TNTC] and the nouns here and in 5:17 are translated the same [NIV, NLT]. Originally the term referred to men whose profession was to copy the Scripture, but by this time such men were professional interpreters of the Scriptures [Su]. Scribes served as legal counselors [BECNT].

b. pres. mid./pass. (deponent = act.) infin. of διαλογίζομαι (LN 30.10, 33.158) (BAGD 1. p. 186): 'to reason' [BAGD, LN (30.10), Lns, NTC; HCSB, KJV, NASB], 'to consider' [BAGD, LN (30.10)], 'to question' [NRSV], 'to question (by thinking)' [BECNT], 'to raise questions' [Arn], 'to ponder' [AB, WBC], 'to think' [GW], 'to think to oneself' [NCV, NET, NIV], 'to say to themselves' [TEV], 'to discuss, to converse' [LN (33.158)], 'to argue' [CEV], 'to say to each other' [NLT], 'to ask among themselves' [REB].

c. βλασφημία (LN 33.401) (BAGD 2.b. p. 143): 'blasphemy' [Arn, BAGD, BECNT, LN, Lns, NTC, WBC; HCSB, KJV, NASB, NET, NIV, NLT, NRSV, TEV], 'blasphemous talk' [REB]. It is speaking against God [BAGD], or injuring the reputation of God [LN]. This word is translated as a verb phrase: 'to speak so blasphemously' [AB], 'to dishonor God' [GW], 'Jesus must think he is God!' [CEV], 'this man who is speaking as if he were God' [NCV].

QUESTION—As the scribes and Pharisees began to reason, did they speak the question out loud?

1. They spoke these words aloud to one another [Gdt, My, Su, TH, WBC; CEV, NLT, REB]. They expressed their thoughts to one another [My]. Perhaps Luke did not include 'in their hearts' from Mark's account in order to allow the idea of verbal interchange [WBC]. From the crowd's excitement and words, Jesus understood what they were saying [Su].
2. They thought the words to themselves [AB, Arn, BECNT, NIGTC, NTC, TG; GW, NCV, NET, NIV, TEV]. The word 'saying' does not always imply speech and here it refers to unspoken thoughts since Mark 2:6 indicates that they were thinking these words to themselves [NIGTC, TG]. They were reasoning in their hearts as indicated in the next verse [NTC]. In the next verse the statement that he knew their thoughts means that being God, he divinely penetrated their thoughts [NTC]. That Jesus fully knew (ἐπιγνούς) their hearts indicates more than natural perception

[BECNT, NIGTC, TNTC]. However, there is no need to posit Jesus' divine wisdom since he could see the crowd's reaction [AB].

QUESTION—In 5:21, does the question 'Who is this?' indicate that they didn't know who Jesus was?

They were not asking for information since they already thought that they knew who Jesus was. They used the question to rebuke Jesus for speaking as he did [TG] and in effect they stated 'Who does this man think he is?' [TG; NLT]. The question expressed their contempt and indignation [TH]. The pronoun οὗτος 'this' is used in a depreciating manner, much like 'this fellow' [AB, Lns], and it shows their contempt [ICC].

QUESTION—Why would the scribes and Pharisees say that Jesus was speaking blasphemies?

Their line of reasoning was that only God can forgive sin and for a man to claim to forgive sins is blasphemy; therefore this man Jesus is blaspheming [Lns, Su]. Blasphemy refers to impious talk concerning God [TH]. Jesus was speaking as if he thought himself to be God [CEV, NCV]. They assumed that Jesus' words did not merely indicate that he knew that God had forgiven the man's sins, but that the words were a claim to pardon the man's sins on his own authority [ICC]. By claiming the power to forgive sins, Jesus was guilty of attacking the majesty of God and implying that he was on a par with God [AB, BECNT]. They were right that only God could forgive sin and since they did not accept the implication that Jesus was God, they said that Jesus blasphemed by sinfully claiming the attributes and prerogatives of God [NTC, WBC]. Some think that the plural form 'blasphemies' has no special implication [TH] and it is translated in the singular [NIV, NLT, TEV]. Others account for the plural as being the scribes' deduction that if Jesus spoke this blasphemy, he would speak more [Lns]. Many translate it in the plural [BECNT, Lns, NTC, WBC; KJV, NASB, NET, NRSV].

QUESTION—What is the function of the question 'Who is able to forgive sins except God alone?'

It is a rhetorical question and makes the statement that God alone has the right to forgive sin [BECNT, TG]. It is translated as a statement: 'Only God can forgive sins' [CEV, NCV], 'God is the only one who can forgive sins' [TEV], 'No man can forgive sins, God alone can' [TH]. Sin is an offense against God and only the offended person can forgive the offender [NIGTC]. Their belief that only God can forgive sin is correct, but there are OT examples of God using a human agent to communicate his forgiveness [BECNT, ICC, NIGTC].

QUESTION—In 5:22, what is the function of the question, 'Why are you reasoning in your hearts?'

It is a rhetorical question reprimanding them for thinking such things [NTC]. They were falsely accusing him [NTC]. The question is directed to their consciences [Lns].

5:23 **Which is easier, to-say, Your sins have-been-forgiven you, or to-say, Get-up and walk?**

QUESTION—Which of the two statements in the rhetorical question is presumed to be easier to say?

1. It is easier to say 'Your sins have been forgiven you' [AB, Alf, Arn, BECNT, Gdt, ICC, MGC, NIBC, NICNT, TG, TH]: it is easier to say 'Your sins have been forgiven you', than to say 'Get up and walk'. Most who take this interpretation focus on the verb 'to say'. 'Your sins have been forgiven you' is easier *to say* since there is nothing concrete that would prove that it didn't happen. But to say 'Get up and walk' is much harder since a visible miracle would have to happen if Jesus actually had such power to heal [AB, Arn, TG]. It is easier to claim the power to forgive sins than to claim the power to heal since only the latter can be subjected to a test. So Jesus will prove his right to forgive sins by doing the harder act of healing [Alf]. Neither act is easy, but it is easier to convict a man of imposture who falsely claims to heal than one who falsely claims authority to pardon sin [Gdt]. It is easier to say something that cannot be visually substantiated, so from the opponent's point of view it is easier for Jesus to claim to forgive sins since there is nothing concrete to disprove his authority to do so. But it is impossible to falsely claim to be able to heal the man since there would be visible proof that it didn't happen [BECNT]. It is a question of whether or not Jesus had authority to do either and if he has authority to heal the man, it will show that he has authority to forgive sin [Arn, TG].
2. It is easier to say 'Get up and walk' [NAC, TNTC]: it is easier to say 'Get up and walk', than to say 'Your sins have been forgiven you'. The question is addressed to theologians who recognized that only God could forgive sin (5:21) and who knew of OT healings and the many healings already done by Jesus (5:15). Since only God can forgive sin and many people were known to have performed healings, it was easier for a man to heal than to do the impossible act of forgiving sin [NAC]. Probably Jesus meant that it was harder to pronounce forgiveness than to pronounce a word of healing since he was doing more than the healers of that time could do [TNTC].
3. Jesus implied that both are equally impossible for a man and possible only for God [Lns, NIGTC, NIVS, NTC, Su, WBC; NET]. The focus is not on 'to say' since both alternatives are pronouncements that equally require the authority of God, making it impossible to give any answer [Lns]. There isn't a clear answer since both alternatives needed to have divine authority to accomplish their effects. [WBC]. To forgive sins is impossible for man since it is God's prerogative alone and to heal is impossible for a man since it can be done only by God's power [NIGTC].

5:24 **But in-order-that**[a] **you-may-know that the Son of-Man**[b] **has authority**[c] **on earth to-forgive sins,—he-said to (the one) having-been-paralyzed, To-you I-say, Get-up and having-picked-up your pallet go to your house.**

LEXICON—a. ἵνα (LN 89.59): 'in order that' [Arn, BECNT, LN, Lns, NTC]. 'so that' [LN; NASB, NET, NRSV], 'so' [HCSB], 'that' [KJV, NIV, REB], 'to let (you know)' [AB]. Instead of being followed by a main clause, the dependent clause 'but in order that you may know that...' is left unfinished when Jesus turned to address the paralytic. This clause is also translated as an independent clause: 'but now you will see that...' [CEV], 'I want you to know that...' [GW], 'know that...' [WBC], 'but I will prove to you that...' [NCV, TEV], 'I will prove that...' [NLT].

   b. υἱὸς τοῦ ἀνθρώπου 'Son of Man'. This title for Christ occurs at 5:24; 6:5, 22; 7:34; 9:22, 26, 44; 11:30; 12:8, 40; 17:22, 24, 26; 18:8, 31; 19:10; 21:27, 36; 22:22, 48, 69; 24:7. See the discussions of this title at 5:24, 6:5, and 9:22.

   c. ἐξουσία (LN 37.35) (BAGD 3. p. 278): 'authority' [AB, Arn, BAGD, BECNT, LN, Lns, NTC, WBC; all versions except CEV, KJV, REB], 'the right' [CEV, REB], 'power' [KJV]. The focus is not on power concerning what he can or cannot do, but on what authority he has or does not have. He is God's agent, authorized to grant forgiveness of sin [Su]. This is an authority based on the fact that he was a spokesman for God [AB].

QUESTION—How would they know that Jesus had authority to forgive sins when Jesus healed the man?

  1. The situation was that they thought that it was easier to claim authority to forgive sins than to heal a person. By proving he could do the harder, Jesus would prove he could do the (apparently) easier [TH]. Although both were equally easy for Jesus, by doing what the Pharisees would consider harder, he would prove his authority to do the easier [AB]. It is a question of whether or not Jesus had authority, and by commanding the man to walk would show that he had authority to forgive sins [TG].
  2. The situation was that they thought that it was easier to heal a person than to claim authority to forgive sins. If God granted Jesus authority to perform miracles of healing as he had been doing, then God supported Jesus' claim that he could forgive sins [NAC]. If Jesus can do one, he can do the other [TNTC].
  3. The situation was that they thought that either act was beyond human ability. Since miraculous healing can only be done by God's power, it follows that the person who heals is also authorized to forgive sins [NIGTC]. By granting Jesus power to heal the man, God himself supported Jesus' claim to forgive sin [NAC]. The act of healing can be observed and it proves the reality of the act of forgiveness which is invisible [Lns]. Both forgiveness and healing require omnipotent power, and since Jesus' opponents required a miracle to prove that he had authority in the spiritual realm, he would show them the miracle of a physical healing [NTC]. The import of the Jesus' question is 'You are

scandalized at this act of mine which is not subject to public verification. What will you make of this other which is plain for all the world to see?' [WBC].

QUESTION—Who is the Son of Man?

Jesus was undoubtedly referring to himself [BECNT, Lns, NAC, NIGTC]. It was his self-designation to indicate that he was not the nationalistic Messiah Jews expected [NTC]. Jesus derived this cryptic title for himself from the reference to the Son of Man in Daniel 7:13 [Arn, BECNT, Lns, MGC, NAC, NIBC, NIGTC, TG, WBC]. In the Daniel reference, the phrase 'the Son of Man' simply refers to a human figure in contrast to the four beasts, but this person rides on the clouds and brings vindication to the saints [BECNT]. It is applied to a person of heavenly origin who had a human figure and who was given rule over the earth [NIGTC]. The title does not emphasize Jesus' humanity, rather it emphasizes his honor and power [TG]. The Jews had not deduced from the Daniel passage that the Son of Man was a title for the Messiah [Lns]. Since the title is not explained, Luke shows that the title was known to his readers [NAC]. This title had become a messianic title [TH]. Or, probably the people did not recognize the origin of this term and Jesus used it instead of a more explicit term because his time had not yet come [Arn].

5:25 And at-once having-arisen in-front-of them, having–picked-up (that) on which he-was-lying, he-departed to his house praising[a] God. **5:26** And astonishment[b] seized everyone and they-were-praising God and they-were-filled-with-fear[c] saying, We-saw remarkable-things[d] today.

LEXICON—a. pres. act. participle of δοξάζω (LN 33.357) (BAGD 1. p. 204): 'to praise' [Arn, BAGD, LN; GW, NCV, NIV, NLT, REB, TEV], 'to glorify' [AB, BAGD, BECNT, LN, Lns, NTC, WBC; HCSB, KJV, NASB, NET, NRSV], 'to give thanks to' [CEV]. This is the same word for 'praising' in the next verse. The man attributed his healing to God [Su] and was thanking God for it [TG]. People glorify God by recognizing some of his glorious attributes and acknowledging that those attributes belong to him [Lns]. See this word at 7:16; 13:13.

b. ἔκστασις (LN **25.217**) (BAGD 1. p. 245): 'astonishment' [BAGD, LN], 'amazement' [LN], 'terror' [BAGD]. The phrase 'astonishment seized everyone' is translated 'astonishment seized them all' [Arn, BECNT, Lns; NET, NRSV], 'were all very much astonished' [**LN**], 'astonishment gripped them all' [AB, WBC], 'they were all struck with astonishment' [NASB], 'everyone was astounded' [HCSB], 'everyone was amazed' [CEV, GW, NIV], 'they were all amazed' [KJV], 'all the people were fully amazed' [NCV], 'they were all completely amazed' [TEV], 'amazement gripped everyone' [NTC], 'everyone was gripped with great wonder' [NLT], 'they were all lost in amazement' [REB]. This describes the crowd's reaction to the supernatural authority of Jesus [NIGTC].

c. φόβος (LN 25.251) (BAGD 1.a.α. p. 863): 'fear' [BAGD, LN, Lns, WBC; KJV, NASB, TEV], 'awe' [Arn, BECNT, NTC; GW, HCSB, NET, NIV, NRSV], 'deep awe' [AB], 'much respect' [NCV]. The phrase 'they were filled with fear' is translated 'what they saw surprised them' [CEV], 'everyone was gripped with awe' [NLT].

d. παράδοξος (LN **31.44, 58.56**) (BAGD p. 615): 'remarkable' [**L N** (58.56)], 'wonderful' [BAGD], 'incredible' [LN (31.44)]. This adjective is translated as a noun phrase: 'remarkable things' [AB; NASB, NIV], 'incredible things' [Lns, NTC; HCSB, NET], 'amazing things' [NCV, NLT], 'marvelous things' [TEV], 'wonderful things' [BECNT], 'strange things' [Arn, WBC; KJV, NRSV], 'a great miracle' [CEV], 'things we can hardly believe' [GW], 'the things are beyond belief' [REB].

QUESTION—In 5:26, who were praising God?

They were those who were watching. At Matthew 9:8 it says that this was the crowd [Lns]. A few think that this included the Pharisees and scribes [Arn, BNTC, NICNT, Su], although it was a transitory emotion for them [Arn]. However, others think that the Pharisees and the scribes are not included among those who praised God [Lns, My, NTC, WBC] since they remained hostile and became more hardened as seen later on in the book [NTC].

DISCOURSE UNIT: 5:27–39 [NICNT, WBC; NASB]. The topic is the call of Levi (Matthew) [NASB], table practices or table talk [NICNT], the new and the old [WBC].

DISCOURSE UNIT: 5:27–32 [AB, BECNT, NAC, NIGTC, Su, TNTC; CEV, GW, HCSB, NCV, NET, NIV, NLT, NRSV, TEV]. The topic is the calling of Levi [Su, TNTC; NIV], Jesus calls Levi [NRSV, TEV], Jesus calls Levi (Matthew) [NLT], Jesus chooses Levi [CEV], Jesus chooses Levi (Matthew) to be a disciple [GW], Levi follows Jesus [NCV], the call of Levi and the banquet [AB], the calling of Levi and eating with sinners [HCSB, NET], the call of Levi and a complaint [BECNT], a conflict over Jesus' association with tax collectors and sinners [NAC], Jesus' attitude to sinners [NIGTC].

5:27 And after these (things) he-went-out and saw a-tax-collector named Levi sitting in the tax-office,[a] and he-said to-him, Follow[b] me.

LEXICON—a. τελώνιον (LN 57.183) (BAGD p. 812): 'tax office' [BAGD, BECNT, LN, Lns; GW, HCSB], 'tax booth' [NASB, NET, NIV, NRSV], 'tax collection booth' [NLT], 'tax collector's booth' [NTC; NCV], 'revenue office' [BAGD, LN], 'the place for paying taxes' [CEV], 'custom house' [REB], 'custom booth' [Arn], 'tollhouse' [AB, WBC], 'the receipt of custom' [KJV], '(his) office' [TEV]. It was a simple structure, a toll booth or customs shed [TG]. The tax office was likely a bench at a table which held balances for weighing merchandise. Tax offices were located on main roads at the edges of towns where farmers, merchants, and caravans passed [Su]. Levi would probably be sitting in or

near the entrance of the tax booth [NTC], or in front of it since Jesus was able to see him [Gdt, ICC, TNTC].
   b. pres. act. impera. of ἀκολουθέω (LN 36.31) (BAGD 3. p. 31): 'to follow' [AB, BAGD, BECNT, LN, Lns, NTC, WBC; all versions except CEV, NLT], 'to be (my) follower' [Arn], 'to be a disciple of' [LN; NLT], 'to come with' [CEV]. This was a command to become a disciple [AB, NAC, TG]. It was a general call to be a disciple [WBC]. Although not all disciples were called to literally accompany Jesus in his travels, here the literal sense is intended in this call [NIGTC]. This imperfect tense is ingressive: 'he *began* following' [Lns; NASB]. See this word at 5:11; 9:57; 18:43.

QUESTION—What did Jesus go out of?

Probably he went outside the house mentioned in 5:19 [AB, My, Su, TNTC]. More likely, he went out of the city [Gdt, ICC, TH, TNTC; NLT] since the tax office would have been outside the city [Gdt, NTC] and Mark 2:13 says that he went out beside the lake [TH].

QUESTION—Who was Levi?

Levi is the same person as Matthew [AB, Arn, Gdt, ICC, Lns, NIGTC, NTC, Rb, Su, TG, TNTC]. The parallel account in Matthew 9:9 calls him Matthew and the list of apostles in Matthew 10:3 includes the name 'Matthew the tax collector', so we can be sure that this Levi was one of the apostles [AB, Arn, BECNT]. Levi was his Aramaic name and he was also called Matthew, an added Hebrew name [Lns]. Some think that Jesus named Levi Matthew, meaning gift of God [Gdt], while others believe that Levi also had the name Matthew all along [NTC]. He was a Jew who collected taxes on behalf of the Roman authorities [Su, TG], a profession despised by the rest of the Jews, especially since the tax collectors usually charged more than necessary for their own profit [Su]. He was probably a subordinate to a tax-farmer and was involved in the actual collection of the tolls [ICC, NAC, NIGTC]. He was not a chief tax collector as was Zacchaeus, but was a lower-level collector who sat at a booth to collect a levy from the people who traveled from city to city [BECNT].

QUESTION—What taxes would Levi collect?

The taxes would probably be toll or customs duties [Arn, EGT, ICC, Lns, MGC, NIGTC, NTC, TG, TH, TNTC, WBC]. Levi would have been collecting customs taxes for the goods that arrived into Herod Antipas' kingdom [ICC, NIGTC]. He was a custom's officer who collected taxes on goods moving in and out on the caravan route and the boat route [EGT, Lns]. A prominent commercial route going to Damascus passed by the Lake of Galilee at or near Capernaum [ICC]. The taxes collected would go to Herod Antipas [ICC, TNTC], without passing through the hands of the Roman authorities [Gdt].

5:28 And having-left-behind everything (and) having-arisen he-was-following him.

TEXT—Instead of the imperfect tense ἠκολούθει 'he was following', some manuscripts read the aorist tense ἠκολούθησεν 'he followed'. GNT does not mention this variant. 'He followed' is read by KJV and also other versions that would probably not make the distinction between the two tenses of the verb here.

QUESTION—What was the actual sequence of the verbs 'left behind', 'arising', and 'followed'?
1. Levi left everything, got up, and followed Jesus [Arn, BECNT, BNTC, My, NTC; HCSB, KJV, NASB, REB]. He began with a mental resolution to leave his past occupation to follow Jesus [Arn].
2. Levi got up, followed Jesus, and so left everything [TH; NET]. Leaving everything behind was realized by following Jesus [TH].
3. Levi got up, left everything, and followed Jesus [AB, ICC, Lns; GW, NCV, NIV, NLT, NRSV, TEV]. Although nothing is said about it, Levi must have had personal contact with Jesus before this call to follow him [Lns].
4. Levi left everything and followed Jesus [CEV].

QUESTION—How could Levi simply leave everything behind?

It must refer to leaving everything in the tax office, such as accounts, money, and other records [Lns]. We need not think of him being alone in the tax office since there might have been other clerks in the office and perhaps a superior tax officer. The point is that he gave up his position as tax collector at once, and it would have been in an orderly way [Lns]. He immediately got up and followed Jesus, leaving his business behind [NTC]. It is probable that Levi did not immediately walk away from his office, but there must have been a formal settling of his business before he started traveling with Jesus [NIGTC]. The focus is not on the things he left behind, but the attitude with which he started out to follow Jesus [Alf]. Leaving everything indicates that he left one occupation for another [AB]. The aorist participle 'having left behind' describes a decisive break with his old life and is not to be taken literally since it can be assumed that there was still some formal settling of his business that had to be done [NIGTC]. The phrase καταλιπὼν πάντα 'having left behind everything' is synonymous with the phrase ἀφέντες πάντα 'having left everything' concerning the fishermen in 5:11 [TH].

5:29 And Levi arranged a-great banquet for-him in his house, and there-was a-great crowd of-tax-collectors and others who were reclining[a] with them.

LEXICON—a. pres. mid./pass. (deponent = act.) participle of κατάκειμαι (LN 23.21) (BAGD 3. p. 411): 'to recline' [BAGD, LN], 'to recline at the table' [BECNT, Lns, NTC, WBC; NASB], 'to sit down' [KJV], 'to sit at the table' [NET, NRSV], 'to be at table' [LN], 'to sit down to the meal' [Arn], 'to eat' [LN; GW, NCV, NIV], not explicit [AB; CEV, HCSB,

NLT, REB, TEV]. It was customary at festivals for the participants to recline on rugs or cushions [TG], or mattresses or couches around low tables, each person resting on his left elbow [NTC]. They would recline on broad couches, each of which could accommodate several persons who would lay on their left sides and take food with their right hands [Lns].

QUESTION—Who were the 'others' in the great crowd of tax collectors and others?

Luke indicates the type of the 'others' as 'sinners' in 5:30 [AB, BECNT, EGT, Lns, NIGTC, NTC, Su]. In Mark 2:15 it says that many tax collectors and sinners were eating with Jesus and his disciples. However, the disciples have not yet been introduced into the story, so the 'others' would include the disciples as well as the 'sinners' [WBC]. Both groups are mentioned as participating in the feast in the following verse.

QUESTION—Who is the referent to 'them' in the last phrase 'who were with them reclining'?
1. 'Them' refers to Jesus and Levi [Lns, NIGTC, TH, WBC]. These two were the only ones named so far [TH].
2. 'Them' refers to Jesus and his disciples [Rb].
3. 'Them' refers to Jesus, his disciples, and Levi [NTC].

5:30 **And the Pharisees and their scribes were-complaining[a] to/against[b] his disciples saying, Why are-you(plural)-eating and drinking with the tax-collectors and sinners[c]?**

TEXT—Instead of οἱ Φαρισαῖοι καὶ οἱ γραμματεῖς αὐτῶν 'the Pharisees and their scribes', some manuscripts transpose the word order to οἱ γραμματεῖς αὐτῶν καὶ οἱ Φαρισαῖοι 'their scribes and the Pharisees'. GNT does not mention this variant. Οἱ γραμματεῖς αὐτῶν καὶ οἱ Φαρισαῖοι 'their scribes and the Pharisees' is read by KJV.

LEXICON—a. imperf. act. indic. of γογγύζω (LN 33.382) (BAGD 1. p. 164): 'to complain' [LN; GW, HCSB, NCV, NET, NLT, NRSV, REB, TEV], 'to complain bitterly' [NLT], 'to grumble' [AB, BAGD, BECNT, LN, Lns, NTC, WBC; CEV, NASB], 'to murmur' [Arn; KJV].

b. πρός (LN 90.33, 90.58): 'to' [AB, Arn, BECNT, LN (90.58), WBC; all versions except KJV, NASB], 'against' [LN (90.33), NTC; KJV], 'at' [Lns; NASB].

c. ἁμαρτωλός (LN 88.295) (BAGD 2. p. 44): 'sinner' [AB, Arn, BAGD, BECNT, LN, Lns, NTC, WBC; all versions except CEV, NLT, TEV], 'other sinners' [CEV], 'outcast' [LN], 'other outcasts' [TEV], 'irreligious, unobservant people' [BAGD]. The phrase 'the tax collectors and sinners' is translated '(with) such scum' [NLT]. This term was applied to people who did not observe the Law in detail [BAGD, LN], and therefore were treated as social outcasts [LN]. See this word at 15:1.

QUESTION—Where did this conversation with the Pharisees take place?

The Pharisees and their scribes would not have attended the banquet given for tax collectors and sinners. Perhaps they entered the house during the meal [ICC]. They would not have been invited, so this conversation took place after the banquet [BECNT, NIGTC]. It was probably when the guests were departing the banquet that the Pharisees approached the disciples [Lns, NIVS, NTC].

QUESTION—What is the function of the question asked by the Pharisees?

It expressed their disapproval of the disciples and, by implication, of Jesus [BECNT, TH]. It expressed their criticism and disgust since it seemed unthinkable for a good Jew to eat with such despised people as tax collectors and sinners [Arn, NTC, TNTC]. Eating with such people who were sure to be ceremonially unclean would show that such people were accepted as friends [BECNT, TNTC], and it would make Pharisees ceremonially impure [NTC].

QUESTION—What is meant by 'their scribes'?

This indicates that the scribes belonged to the Pharisees party as distinguished from scribes who were Sadducees [Arn, BNTC, Crd, ICC, Lns, NIGTC, NTC, Rb, TG, TH, TNTC, WBC]. Both of the main religious parties included scribes as members who would interpret the law for them [Su]. The phrase 'the Pharisees and their scribes' identifies these critics to be the same people who argued with Jesus in 5:17–26 [Gdt, WBC].

QUESTION—Why did the Pharisees call the guests 'sinners'?

'Sinners' refers to people who were open sinners known to everybody to be such [Lns]. The term 'sinners' would include tax collectors and the phrase means 'tax collectors and *other* sinners' [NIGTC, TG; CEV]. The word was a specialized term Pharisees used for Jews whom they despised because of their refusal to obey all of the religious rules, and especially those rules that prohibited eating certain foods and associating with the Gentiles [TG]. They did not follow the Pharisee's interpretation of the Mosaic law in regard to ceremonial details or moral precepts [NAC]. They were unsavory people who were not accepted in respectable society [WBC]. Some translate the word 'sinners' by enclosing it in quote marks to show that it is being used with a specialized meaning [NIV] or by using another term: 'other outcasts' [TEV], 'such scum' [NLT].

5:31 **And answering Jesus said to-them, The (ones who) are-healthy have no need of-a-physician but the (ones who) are ill.** **5:32** **I-have- not -come to-call (the) righteous[a] but sinners to repentance.[b]**

LEXICON—a. δίκαιος (LN 88.12) (BAGD 1.b. p. 195): 'righteous'. See translations of this word at 1:6. This word also occurs at 1:17; 2:25; 14:14; 15:7; 18:9; 20:20; 23:47, 50.

b. μετάνοια (LN 41.52) (BAGD p. 512): 'repentance'. The phrase 'to call to repentance' [Arn, Lns, WBC; HCSB, KJV, NASB, NET, NIV, NRSV, REB] is also translated 'to call to repent' [TEV], 'to call to conversion' [NTC], 'to invite to repentance' [BECNT], 'to call to turn from their sins' [NLT], 'to invite to turn to God' [CEV], 'to invite to change their hearts and lives' [NCV], 'to invite to reform' [AB], 'to call to change the way they think and act' [GW]. Jesus called people to conversion, not just sorrow for sin, but complete transformation, a change of heart, mind, and conduct [NTC]. This word also occurs at 3:3, 8; 15:7; 24:47.

QUESTION—How is it that Jesus answered the question addressed to his disciples?

We don't know if the disciples attempted a reply. Jesus must have seen that his disciples were being questioned and went over to give an answer [Lns]. Jesus replied on behalf of the disciples [NIGTC], but he ignored the criticism against his disciples and answered for himself since he was responsible for having anything to do with the tax collectors and sinners [ICC].

QUESTION—What was the point of answering with the parabolic or proverbial saying 'The healthy have no need of a physician, but the ones having illness'?

It indicated how absurd the Pharisees' position was. In effect, they were saying that the physician should only associate with healthy people for fear of catching an infection. Jesus is seeking the 'ill' who sense their position before God, but the 'healthy' Pharisees do not want to be treated for something they do not recognize to be a disease [BECNT]. The Pharisees would consider themselves to be the healthy and the tax collectors and sinners to be the sick, and it is the business of the healer to heal the sick [Lns, NTC].

QUESTION—What is the function of the statement 'I have not come to call the righteous to repentance, but to call sinners to repentance?

The figurative language of the proverb is now changed to a literal statement [Lns]. Jesus further explained the previous statement [BECNT, NIGTC]. Or, the proverb didn't need an explanation and here he gave an application to it [Su]. There are correspondences between the Physician and Jesus, between healthy people and righteous people, and between ill people and sinners [BECNT, Lns, NAC]. He implies that as a religious teacher, he should associate with those who need his teachings and not with people who did not need them [TG].

QUESTION—Did Jesus think that the Pharisees were the righteous people who did not need a physician?

Jesus took the Pharisees at their estimation of themselves [Lns]. Jesus did not endorse the Pharisees' view of themselves [BECNT]. The form of the argument is 'Let us grant that you are righteous and do not need me and my message, If this is true, leave me to bring my message of repentance to those who do need it' [Su]. The Pharisees saw themselves as righteous and hence did not need to repent [NIGTC, Su, TNTC] and so they must admit that Jesus' conduct was justified [TNTC]. The question of whether the Pharisees were actually righteous is not raised since the stress is on the call to sinners to repent [NAC, NIGTC]. It is obvious that truly righteous people have no need to be called to repentance, but the question comes up as to who are righteous [ICC]. The Pharisees were not actually righteous and Jesus used the term ironically [TNTC]. This is brought out in a translation: 'people who think they don't have any flaws' [GW].

DISCOURSE UNIT: 5:33–6:11 [BECNT]. The topic is three controversies in the rise of opposition.

DISCOURSE UNIT: 5:33–39 [AB, BECNT, NAC, NIGTC, Su, TNTC; CEV, GW, HCSB, NCV, NET, NIV, NLT, NRSV, TEV]. The topic is Jesus' answer to a question [NCV], the question about fasting [AB, BECNT; GW, HCSB, NRSV, TEV], Jesus is questioned about fasting [NIV], a discussion about fasting [NLT], teaching about fasting [Su, TNTC], people ask about going without eating [CEV], Jesus' attitude to fasting [NIGTC], a conflict over the disciples not fasting [NAC], the superiority of the new [NET].

5:33 And they-said to him, The disciples of-John fast often and make[a] prayers, also the (ones) of-the Pharisees (do) likewise, but your (disciples) eat and drink.

TEXT—Before Οἱ μαθηταὶ Ἰωάννου 'the disciples of John', some manuscripts add διὰ τί 'on account of what' (= 'why'). GNT omits this addition with a B decision, indicating that the text is almost certain. Διὰ τί 'why' is read by KJV.

LEXICON—a. pres. mid. indic. of ποιέω (LN 90.45) (BAGD II.1. p. 683): 'to make' [BAGD, LN], 'to practice' [LN]. The phrase 'to make prayers' [KJV] is also translated 'to pray' [CEV, NCV, NET, NIV, NLT, NRSV], 'to say prayers' [AB, NTC; GW, HCSB], 'to offer prayers' [BECNT, WBC; NASB, TEV], 'to offer up prayers' [Arn], 'to be given to the practice of prayer' [REB], 'to make petitions for oneself' [Lns]. Perhaps John taught his disciples certain prayer forms [AB]. The phrase 'make prayers' may refer to set prayers offered at specific times [TNTC].

QUESTION—Who are the 'they' who spoke to Jesus?
1. 'They' refers to the Pharisees and their scribes [AB, Arn, Crd, EGT, Gdt, ICC, MGC, Su, TH; NLT]. It refers to the same people who are the subject of 5:30 [Arn, EGT, Gdt, ICC, Su, TH]. This narrative is a continuation of the previous dialogue between Jesus and the Pharisees and their scribes [Su]. It was particularly the scribes who continued the conversation with Jesus [Gdt].
2. 'They' refers to the disciples of John the Baptist [Lns, NICNT, NTC, Rb]. The referent is not explicit because the parties are not named, but from the parallel account in Matthew 9:14 we learn that it was John's disciples who spoke to Jesus and this happened just as they came from Levi's feast [Lns]. Probably there is no close connection in time with the preceding narrative, and while it might be translated 'some people', they can be identified as the disciples belonging to John [NTC].
3. 'They' refers to both the Pharisees and the disciples of John [Rb, TNTC].
4. 'They' is meant to be indefinite [BECNT, NICNT, NIGTC, TG; CEV, TEV]: 'some people'. The context would supply the Pharisees and their scribes, but the statement refers to the disciples of the Pharisees in the third person and this narrative should not be linked too closely with the preceding one. In Mark 2:18 the subject is indeterminate and it probably

should be taken that way here [NIGTC]. It is likely a separate incident [TG]. The indefinite form indicates that this issue was a community concern [BECNT].

QUESTION—What is the import of what they said to Jesus?

1. It functions as an expression of criticism [AB, Crd, EGT, Gdt, ICC, NIGTC, Rb, Su, WBC; NLT]. The speakers were opponents who found fault with Jesus and their words were meant as a reproof [AB].
2. It functions as a question for information [BECNT, Lns, NTC, TNTC, WBC]. Those who think that the speakers were John's disciples consider this to be a request for enlightenment and information [Lns, NTC]. Since Jesus' ethical standards were no lower than those of John and the Pharisees, the speakers wondered why Jesus' disciples were not as strict in these observances [WBC].

QUESTION—What was their practice of fasting often and offering prayers?

Fasting involved abstaining either partly or completely from food for a time as a religious practice [TH]. Fasting was a familiar practice [NIGTC]. It was highly regarded by the Jewish community and it prepared them for all kinds of activities. It was often accompanied by confession and intercession. People fasted to focus their attention on God. [BECNT]. Fasting was usually accompanied with prayer [Lns, NIGTC]. In addition to the few set times for national fasting, there were a variety of other times when people fasted as a sign of their religious zeal [NIGTC]. The Pharisees had a practice of fasting twice a week (18:12) [BECNT, ICC, Lns, NICNT, NIGTC, NTC], although such fasting was voluntary [ICC]. John's disciples probably followed John's ascetic practices [NIGTC], or John simply allowed his disciple to continue with their previous practices [Lns]. Although Jesus explained why his disciples did not follow the practice of fasting, he did not say the same about prayer [TNTC]. Although the prayers of John's disciples often were accompanied by fasting, the prayers of Jesus' disciples were accompanied by the life-style of celebration [WBC]. The illustrations Jesus used imply that fasting was a means of expressing sorrow and gloom, and it was not appropriate with the joy of being with the bridegroom [AB, NAC]. Jesus regarded fasting as an expression of grief rather than a required religious duty [TG].

QUESTION—Who were the οἱ τῶν Φαρισαίων 'the ones of the Pharisees'?

Following 'the disciples of John' in the preceding clause, this means 'the disciples of the Pharisees' [AB, Lns, NICNT, NIGTC, NTC, TG, TH, WBC; all versions except CEV, KJV], or 'the followers of the Pharisees' [BECNT; CEV]. Since not all Pharisees were teachers who gathered disciples around them, speaking of their disciples can be explained as being assimilated in form from the preceding phrase 'the disciples of John' [NICNT, NIGTC] so that the phrase refers to people who had accepted the ideals of the Pharisees [NIGTC] and the phrase can be simply translated as 'the Pharisees' [NCV]. Perhaps the phrase means the disciples of scribes [NTC] or teachers [TH] who belonged to the Pharisee party. Scribes as such did not belong to a particular party, so these scribes referred to themselves as being the ones of the Pharisee party [Gdt].

5:34 **And Jesus said to them, You-cannot make^a the sons^b of-the wedding-hall fast while the bridegroom is with them (can you)?**

TEXT—Some manuscripts omit Ἰησοῦς 'Jesus'. GNT does not mention this variant. Ἰησοῦς 'Jesus' is omitted by KJV.

LEXICON—a. aorist act. infin. of ποιέω (LN 90.45) (BAGD II.1.b.θ. p. 681): 'to make' [AB, Arn, BAGD, LN, Lns, NTC, WBC; HCSB, KJV, NASB, NET, NIV, NRSV, REB, TEV], 'to cause' [BAGD], 'to force' [GW], not explicit [NLT]. The phrase 'you can not make (them)' is translated 'are (they) able (to fast while the groom is with them)?' [BECNT]. Fasting is not to be a mechanical arrangement set for fixed days, since fasting is determined by the conditions [Lns]. Rather than the idea of forcing them to fast, the meaning is closer to *expecting* them to fast [TH].

b. υἱός (LN 11.7) (BAGD 1.c.δ. p. 834): 'son' [BAGD, Lns]. It indicates one who shares in something or has a close relationship to it [BAGD]. The phrase οἱ υἱοὶ τοῦ νυμφῶνος 'the sons of the wedding hall' is an idiom for guests at a wedding or, more specifically, friends of the bridegroom participating in wedding festivities [LN]. The phrase is translated 'the wedding guests' [LN; GW, HCSB, NET, NLT, NRSV], 'the guests at a wedding party' [TEV], 'the guests of the bridegroom' [NIV], 'the friends of the bridegroom' [LN; CEV, NCV; similarly REB], 'the attendants of the bridegroom' [NASB; similarly AB, BECNT, NTC], 'the wedding attendants' [WBC], 'the sons of the bridechamber' [Arn], 'the children of the bridechamber' [KJV]. The phrase was a Semitism in which 'son' indicates a close relationship of the guests to the groom [AB, ICC, WBC], an allusion to the intimate relationship Jesus had with his disciples [BECNT]. They were the groom's attendants [AB, Arn, BECNT, TH, WBC; NASB]. They were close friends in charge of the wedding arrangements [Lns, NTC]. Or, they were just the guests in general at the wedding [GW, NET, NLT, NRSV, TEV].

QUESTION—What is the function of Jesus' question?

The question with the interrogative particle μή expects a negative reply 'No' [BECNT, Lns, NAC, NTC, TG, TH]. It is a rhetorical question used to make a strong statement [TG]. It would be absurd to think of the disciples fasting while Jesus was with them [NTC]. Jesus used the question to illustrate the disciples' current situation in which their happiness forbids fasting [BECNT]. It is just as foolish to expect Jesus' disciples to fast as it is to expect the bridegroom's attendants to fast [NIGTC]. Jesus reproached them for trying to compel people to fast [NIGTC].

5:35 But days will-come, and/namely when the bridegroom is-taken-away[a] from them, then they-will-fast in those days.

LEXICON—a. aorist pass. subj. of ἀπαίρω (LN 15.177) (BAGD p.79): 'to be taken away' [AB, Arn, BAGD, BECNT, LN, NTC; all versions except CEV], 'to be taken' [Lns, WBC; CEV], 'to be led away' [LN]. This refers to a departure but does not denote a violent death [AB]. It may imply violence [TH]. Violence is implied since only such an end can explain why a period of fasting would occur after the wedding [NIGTC]. It means a violent removal by force and can describe killing someone [TG]. It describes the violent death Jesus would endure [NTC]. This refers to the act of taking away Jesus by means of a violent death and the agents involved are hidden [Lns].

QUESTION—How is the clause λεύσονται δὲ ἡμέραι 'but days will come' related to the following clause καὶ ὅταν ἀπαρθῇ 'and/namely when the bridegroom is taken away'?

1. The second clause begins a new sentence linked with the following 'then' clause [BNTC, EGT, ICC, Lns, TH, WBC; NASB, NET]: But (those) days will come. And when the bridegroom is taken away from them, then they will fast.
2. The second clause is linked to the first [AB, BECNT, NTC; all versions except NASB, NET]: But the days will come when the bridegroom is taken away from them. Then they will fast.

QUESTION—How does the bridegroom being taken away fit into the picture of a wedding?

Since the figurative language of comparing Jesus to the bridegroom is still kept, most commentaries treat this verse as a tragedy occurring in the wedding hall as the bridegroom is removed from the scene of his wedding [BECNT, Lns, TG, WBC]. The bridegroom is murdered and the wedding guests fast in deep gloom [Lns]. However, this is an unnatural removal of the bridegroom since normally the wedding guests are the ones who depart, so this points to the crisis period of Jesus' passion before the renewal of their joy when the resurrection occurred [WBC]. The verse begins 'but days will come' which suggests an event not connected to the wedding festival and which points to a different kind of period when fasting will be appropriate, the time when the 'groom' is taken away from the disciples [BECNT]. Most commentaries take this to be a prophetic reference to Jesus' death at the end of his ministry [Arn, BECNT, Gdt, ICC, Lns, MGC, NAC, NICNT, NIGTC, NTC, WBC; NET]. It is the application of the figurative language about the present condition of Jesus and his disciples (5:34) to the future taking away of Jesus by a violent death [Lns]. Here the fasting is caused by their sadness [WBC], grief [NIGTC], and mourning [NTC]. Those days refer to the sorrowful days beginning with the arrest and crucifixion, and ending with the resurrection [NAC, NIGTC, NTC, WBC]. Today the proper attitude is being glad again, not sad [NTC] because of Jesus' continual spiritual presence with the church [NIGTC]. Perhaps those days also refer to other days of persecution of the church [Lns]. It alludes to the physical absence of Jesus, perhaps until the totality of deliverance occurs at his future return [BECNT]. Fasting seems to have been an exception in the early church and was limited to special occasions in Acts, which had nothing to do with mourning [NAC].

5:36 And also he-was-telling a-parable[a] to them, No-one having-torn[b] a-patch[c] from a-new garment[d] puts (it) on an-old garment. Otherwise, not-only the new (he) will-tear[e] but the patch from the new will- not -match[f] the old.

TEXT—Some manuscripts omit σχίσας 'having torn'. GNT does not mention this variant. This word is omitted in KJV.

TEXT—Instead of the future tense συμφωνήσει 'will not match', some manuscripts read the present tense συμφωνεῖ 'does not match'. GNT does not mention this variant. The present tense συμφωνεῖ 'does not match' is read by KJV.

LEXICON—a. παραβολή (LN 33.15) (BAGD 2. p. 612): 'parable' [AB, Arn, BAGD, BECNT, LN, Lns, NTC, WBC; HCSB, KJV, NASB, NET, NIV, NRSV, REB, TEV], 'illustration' [BAGD; GW, NLT], 'story' [NCV], 'saying' [CEV]. It is a short narrative that has a symbolic meaning [LN]. It is a story based on everyday situations that is used to teach spiritual truths [TG]. This word is used in the sense of metaphor [BECNT, NAC]. Here it is more of an illustration than a parable [TH]. See this word at 6:39; 13:6, 14:7.

b. aorist act. participle of σχίζω (LN 19.27) (BAGD 1.a. p. 797): 'to tear' [Arn, BAGD, LN, Lns, NTC, WBC; all versions except CEV, KJV, NCV], 'to divide, to separate, to tear apart' [BAGD], 'to take' [NCV], 'to cut' [AB], not explicit [KJV]. The phrase 'having torn a patch' is translated 'having a piece of torn cloth' [BECNT], 'uses a new piece of cloth to patch' [CEV].

c. ἐπίβλημα (LN 6.157) (BAGD p. 290): 'patch' [AB, Arn, BAGD, LN, Lns, WBC; HCSB, NET, NIV]. This is a piece of cloth that is sewed onto clothing to repair a hole or a tear [LN]. In order to avoid the idea that it is a patch already on the new garment, many translate so as to indicate that it is a piece of material from a new garment that will serve as a patch for an old garment: 'a piece of cloth' [BECNT; CEV, GW, NASB, NLT], 'a piece' [NTC; KJV, NRSV, REB, TEV], 'cloth' [NCV].

d. ἱμάτιον (LN 6.162) (BAGD 1. p. 376): 'garment' [AB, Arn, BAGD, BECNT, NTC, WBC; HCSB, KJV, NASB, NET, NIV, NLT, NRSV, REB], 'clothing' [LN], 'clothes' [CEV], 'apparel' [LN], 'coat' [GW, NCV, TEV], 'robe' [Lns].

e. fut. act. indic. of σχίζω (LN 19.27) (BAGD 1.a. p. 797): 'to tear'. This is the same word as b. above.

f. fut. act. indic. of συμφωνέω (LN **64.10**) (BAGD 1.a. p. 780): 'to match' [AB, BAGD, BECNT, **LN**, Lns, NTC, WBC; all versions except CEV, KJV, NCV], 'to be like' [LN], 'to be the same as' [NCV], 'to agree with'

[Arn; KJV]. It will not fit properly [NIGTC]. The patch will not look or feel like the old garment [TG]. This does not refer to color but to the difference in the material; one is strong and new while the other is old and fragile [Lns]. The phrase 'otherwise, not only the new he will tear but the patch from the new will not match the old' is translated like the situation in Matthew and Mark: 'the patch would shrink and make the hole even bigger' [CEV].

QUESTION—Why are details different from the parallel passages in Matthew 9:16 and Mark 2:21?

In both Matthew and Mark the patch is from unshrunken material and it pulls away from the old material to make a worse tear. As Jesus taught from place to place, he probably varied his parables [NTC, Su, TNTC]. In all versions, the patch that was intended to solve the problem created an even bigger problem [NTC]. To the bad effect on the old garment presented in the other Gospels, Luke adds the bad effect on the new [Lns]. Instead of concentrating attention on the old garment, here attention is directed to the new garment that would be sacrificed without satisfactory results in the old [AB]. However, the CEV uses virtually the same wording as in Matthew so that there is no noticeable difference.

QUESTION—What is the point of the parable?

There is irony in the absurd picture of ruining a new garment in an attempt to patch an old garment [BECNT]. The point is the incompatibility of the two pieces of cloth and the application is that the old and new ways cannot be combined [NIGTC]. Attempting to graft the new upon the old spoils both systems in that the new system loses its completeness and the old loses it consistency [Alf]. The lesson is that we should not try to mix the new with the old. Instead, accept the new teaching of Jesus and in the joy resulting from his teaching there is no room for legalistic fasting [NTC]. To take only part of Jesus' teaching spoils the whole system and even a part of his teaching is incompatible with the old life of Judaism [NIGTC]. The material torn from the new garment probably represents exemption from fasting. To take away that exemption from Christ's disciples would spoil the new system in which they were being trained, and to provide that exemption for the disciples of John and the Pharisees would spoil the system in which they had been taught [ICC, TH]. The asceticism of the Pharisees and the holy joy of Jesus' disciples are incompatible [Arn]. Jesus has generalized beyond the subject of fasting [BECNT, Gdt, WBC] and explains that it is not right to attempt to contain the new affairs he has inaugurated within the constraints of the old [WBC]. The ways of Jesus and the traditions of the religious hierarchy cannot be mixed without damaging the new since the two approaches do not really go together [BECNT]. No one should take away the joy that Jesus' disciples experienced by requiring them to conform to the old Jewish practices because the new and the old do not fit one another [Su].

5:37 And no-one puts new[a] wine into old[b] wineskins.[c] But if (he acts otherwise), the new wine will-burst[d] the wineskins and it will-be-spilled and the wineskins will-be-destroyed. **5:38** Rather new wine must-be-put into new[e] wineskins.

TEXT—In 5:38, instead of βλητέον 'must be put', some manuscripts read βλητέον καὶ ἀμφότεροι συντηροῦνται 'must be put, and both are preserved', and other manuscripts read βάλλουσιν καὶ ἀμφότεροι τηροῦνται 'they put, and both are preserved'. GNT reads βλητέον 'must be put' with a B decision, indicating that the text is almost certain. Βλητέον καὶ ἀμφότεροι συντηροῦνται 'must be put, and both are preserved' is read by KJV.

LEXICON—a. νέος (LN 6.198) (BAGD 1.a.α. p. 536): 'new' [AB, Arn, BAGD, BECNT, LN, Lns, NTC, WBC; all versions], 'fresh' [BAGD]. The phrase οἶνος νέος 'new wine' is a set phrase referring to newly pressed grape juice which is unfermented or is in the initial stages of fermentation [LN]. It refers to wine that is still fermenting [BAGD]. It is wine that is beginning to ferment and has not stopped fermenting [TG]. Νέος means new in reference to time, in contrast with 'aged' [Arn, ICC].

   b. παλαιός (LN 58.75): 'old' [AB, Arn, BECNT, LN, Lns, NTC, WBC; all versions except TEV], 'used' [TEV].

   c. ἀσκός (LN 6.132) (BAGD p. 116): 'wineskin' [AB, BAGD, BECNT, LN, Lns, NTC, WBC; all versions except KJV, NCV], 'leather bag' [NCV], 'bottle' [KJV], 'skins' [Arn]. It is a leather bag and in the NT it is used only for holding wine [LN]. The wineskin was usually made from the dehaired skin of a goat [AB, BECNT, Gdt, ICC, NAC, NTC, Pnt, TG] or of a sheep [BECNT, NTC, Pnt]. The flesh and bones were extracted from the skin without ripping it and the neck of the animal became the neck of the container [ICC]. The skin was tanned, the hair was cut short, and turned inside out. Then the neck became the mouth of the container and the other openings at the feet and tail were sewn shut [NTC].

   d. fur. act. indic. of ῥήγνυμι (LN **19.31**) (BAGD 1. p. 735): 'to burst' [AB, BAGD, **LN**, Lns, NTC, WBC; all versions except CEV, NCV], 'to swell and burst' [CEV], 'to tear' [BECNT, LN], 'to rip' [LN], 'to break' [Arn; NCV].

   e. καινός (LN 58.71) (BAGD 1. p. 394): 'new' [Arn, BAGD, BECNT, LN, WBC; CEV, KJV, NCV, NET, NIV, NLT], 'fresh' [AB, Lns, NTC; GW, HCSB, NASB, NRSV, REB, TEV]. Καινός means new in reference to quality, and contrasts with 'worn out' [Arn, ICC].

QUESTION—What relationship is indicated by the initial conjunction καί 'and'?

This second parable reinforces the first parable [NTC] and completes the thought of trying to combine all of the new with the old [Lns]. It carries on and develops the teaching of the first. While the patch made from the new garment represents only part of the new system, the wine represents the whole of it. The new garment and the old garment were only marred, while

LUKE 5:37–38

all of the new wine was lost and the old wineskins were destroyed. In this illustration the right method is indicated [ICC].

QUESTION—Why would new wine burst an old wineskin?

When a wineskin is fresh, it stretches to some extent under the pressure of fermenting wine, but when it is old, it is stiff and brittle and the pressure of the expansion of fermentation would cause it to burst or split [BECNT, Lns, Pnt, WBC]. During the original fermentation of new wine in a wineskin, the wineskin had stretched as far as possible. Then when the wineskin is filled with new wine again, it would not be able to stretch any more when fermentation took place [Su]. It would be too much for the weakened and aged fibers of the old skin [AB].

QUESTION—What are the contrasts and correspondences set up in the previous verse, this verse, and the next?

In 5:36 there is a contrast between the new (καινός, unused) garment and the old (παλαιός, used, worn out, threadbare) garment. In 5:37 there is a contrast between 'new' (νέος, fresh, beginning to ferment) wine and 'old' (παλαιός, used, dried out, stretched, rotten) wineskins. In 5:37–38 there is a contrast between 'new' (καινός, unused, strong, and elastic) wineskins and 'old' (παλαιός, used, dried out, stretched, rotten) wineskins. In 5:38 there is a correspondence between 'new' (νέος, fresh, beginning to ferment) wine and 'new' (καινός, unused, strong, and elastic) wineskins. In 5:39 there is a contrast between 'new' (νέος, fresh, beginning to ferment) wine and 'old' (παλαιός, matured, mellow) wine. The neat literary contrasts and correspondences between 'new' and 'old' can be attempted by using generic words for new and old, but this is not allowed by the vocabularies of some languages [TH]. The generic words 'old' and 'new' are not kept by some English translations that translate 'old and 'new' wineskins as 'old' and 'fresh' wineskins [AB, ICC, Lns, NTC; GW, NASB, NRSV, REB] or 'used' and 'fresh' wineskins [TEV].

QUESTION—What is the point of this parable?

The new ways of the gospel cannot be contained within Judaism without destroying both [BECNT, NIGTC, Pnt]. The fact that Jesus' new teaching will not survive by forcing it to conform to the old ways is summarized in 5:38 by a positive illustration indicating that the new ways require a new form, spirit, and approach [BECNT]. Like new wine and old wineskins are incompatible [NAC, NICNT, NIGTC], so is the gospel incompatible with Judaism and trying to confine the gospel within Judaism would only destroy both. The conclusion is that the radically new gospel must be allowed to express itself in its own way [NIGTC]. The old forms of the Jewish religion were inadequate for the new way of life that Jesus offered, and trying to force conformity would cause the loss of significance for both [Su]. There is a need for compatibility and Jesus' new system of salvation must have its own forms of piety that are suited to it [AB]. New contents require new forms [TH]. The old Pharisaic ways are to be left behind and only the new ways of life that fit the new teachings are to be taken [Lns]. The parable does not deny the continuity of Jesus' teaching with Judaism but illustrates the need for the new to be allowed to have its own integrity and not be constrained within the limitations of the old [WBC]. Or, both parables illustrate the fact that things that are not suited for each other should not be joined together and both teach that the observance of fasting which expresses sadness was not them fitting for Jesus' disciples at that time [Arn].

5:39 **And no-one having-drunk (the) old**[a] **desires (the) new.**[b] **Because he-says, The old is good.**[c]

TEXT—Some manuscripts omit καί 'and' at the beginning of this verse. GNT includes this word with a C decision, indicating that the Committee had difficulty making the decision. Καί 'and' is omitted by KJV.

TEXT—Following παλαιόν 'old', some manuscripts add εὐθέως 'immediately'. GNT does not mention this variant. Εὐθέως 'immediately' is read by Gdt, KJV.

TEXT—Instead of χρηστός 'good', some manuscripts read χρηστότερος 'better'. GNT reads χρηστός 'good' with an A decision, indicating that the text is certain. Χρηστότερος 'better' is read by KJV and others whose translations may be stylistic and not based on the reading χρηστότερος 'better' [CEV, GW, NCV, NIV, NLT, TEV].

TEXT—Some manuscripts omit this verse. GNT includes this verse with an A decision, indicating that the text is certain.

LEXICON—a. παλαιός (LN 58.75) (BAGD 1. p. 605): 'old' [BAGD, BECNT, LN, Lns, WBC]. This adjective is also translated 'old wine' [AB, Arn, NTC; all versions]. Old wine refers to matured and mellow wine [TH].

b. νέος (LN 6.198) (BAGD 1.a.α. p. 536): 'new' [BAGD, BECNT, LN, Lns, NTC, WBC; HCSB, KJV, NASB, REB]. This adjective is also translated 'new wine' [AB, Arn; CEV, GW, NCV, NRSV, TEV], 'the new' [NET, NIV], 'the fresh and the new' [NLT].

c. χρηστός (LN **65.25**) (BAGD 1.a.α. p. 886): 'good' [AB, BAGD, BECNT, NTC, WBC; NRSV, REB], 'good enough' [Lns; NASB, NET], 'pleasant' [Arn], 'better' [**LN**; CEV, GW, HCSB, KJV, NCV, NIV, NLT, TEV]. It refers to being superior for a particular use [LN]. Luke sometimes used the positive degree 'good' in the sense of a comparative, so this could be translated 'better' [AB] since a comparison is implicit [TG]. Or, the positive sense 'good' is sufficient because there does not need to be a comparison when one is satisfied with the old and makes no attempt to try the new [Crd, NIGTC, TNTC]. The new has not been tasted, so the old wine is 'good enough' and no new wine is desired [Alf]. The judgment that the wine is good is from the viewpoint of those who are content with the old and won't even try the new [NIGTC].

QUESTON—How is this verse connected with the previous two verses?

Its close link to the preceding parable is evident by leaving the implied word 'wine' to be understood from the context of the previous verse [WBC]. This illustration makes a comparison with wine because of the wine in the previous one [Lns]. This parable is not found in Matthew or Mark. Although it continues an illustration concerning wine and wineskins, most treat this as a third parable [AB, BECNT, Gdt, ICC, Lns]. The thought was already present in a form of Jewish and Greek proverbs [AB, BECNT, NIGTC].

QUESTION—Why wouldn't the person desire the new?

He is accustomed to the old and has no desire for something different [Arn, MGC, NICNT]. The prejudiced person knows that the taste of the old is pleasant and suits him, so that is enough and he won't change [ICC, TH].

QUESTION—What is the point of this parable?

1. This parable is an admission that the old ways are more satisfactory to those who are accustomed to them and new ways are less attractive [Arn, EGT, ICC, MGC, NICNT, NIVS, TH]. This parable indicates that it is natural for those who have been brought up under the old forms to be unwilling to abandon them for something that is new and untried [ICC, TH]. Some people are set in their ways and will reject the new way Jesus brings [ICC]. The Pharisees disliked the teaching of Jesus because the old religion had become so dear to them that they wanted to cling to it [Arn]. This reveals Jesus' understanding of the difficulty the disciples of John and the Pharisees had in accepting his new way of life. In treating John's disciples with consideration, Jesus made this 'genial apology for conservatism in religion' [EGT].

2. This parable is a rebuke to those who insist on remaining in the inflexible traditionalism of the Pharisees [AB, BECNT, Blm, Lns, NAC, NIGTC, NTC]. Taking this proverb as a factual statement, it seems to excuse the Pharisees for rejecting Jesus' teaching. However, it was said in irony [AB, Blm, NAC, NIGTC], and indicates that they are wrong and should accept the new [AB]. This is a rebuke to those who reject the new way and it indicates that it is likely that many Jews will reject the new message because they do not sense the need for it [BECNT]. The other parables were concerned with the value of the new and so here this must be an ironical condemnation of those who cling to the past and will not accept the present realization of God's kingdom [NAC]. Jesus did not excuse such people for clinging to practices such as fasting, but pointed out that their difficulty was the fact that they just did not want to change. He did so as a gentle call for them to abandon the old for the new [Lns]. This comment on the ultraconservatism of the Pharisees warns that their rejection of the new life-imparting teachings of Jesus will be their downfall [NTC].

3. This parable holds out hope for the eventual acceptance of the new [Gdt; KJV]. The use of εὐθέως 'immediately' is vital to this parable and in saying that the person does not '*immediately* desire the new' the parable points out that change from the law comes slowly. It is difficult to leave a lifelong system to adopt a different way of life and Jesus understood that such people must be given time to familiarize themselves with it [Gdt].

4. This parable affirms that the old is best [NICNT]. It was conventional wisdom and common experience that recognized that old wine was good. So Jesus regarded his ways as showing God's old purposes coming to fruition while the Pharisees' criticisms are rejected as being new and inconsistent with God's program [NICNT].

DISCOURSE UNIT: 6:1–11 [AB, NAC, NICNT, TNTC; NIV]. The topic is about the Sabbath [NICNT], debates about the Sabbath [AB], the conflict over Jesus' attitude toward the Sabbath [NAC], the right use of the Sabbath [TNTC], the Lord of the Sabbath [NIV].

DISCOURSE UNIT: 6:1–5 [BECNT, NIGTC, Su, TNTC, WBC; CEV, GW, HCSB, NASB, NCV, NET, NLT, NRSV, TEV]. The topic is a question about the Sabbath [CEV, NRSV, TEV], a discussion about the Sabbath [NLT], a question about plucking grain on the Sabbath [BECNT], plucking corn on the Sabbath [NIGTC], teaching about Sabbath observance [Su], provision for the Sabbath by the Son of Man [WBC], Lord of the Sabbath [TNTC; HCSB, NET], Jesus is the Lord of the Sabbath [NASB, NCV], Jesus has authority over the day of worship [GW].

6:1 **And it-happened on a-Sabbath (that) he is-passing[a] through grain-fields,[b] and his disciples were-picking and eating the heads[c] (of grain), rubbing[d] (them) in (their) hands.**

TEXT—Following σαββάτῳ 'Sabbath', some manuscripts add δευτεροπρώτῳ 'the second after the first'. GNT rejects this addition with a C decision, indicating that the Committee had difficulty making the decision. Δευτεροπρώτῳ 'the second (Sabbath) after the first' is read by Gdt and KJV.

LEXICON—a. pres. mid./pass. (deponent = act.) infin. of διαπορεύομαι (LN 15.22) (BAGD p. 187): 'to pass through' [Arn, LN, NTC; HCSB, NASB], 'to go through' [BAGD, BECNT, Lns, WBC; KJV, NET, NIV, NRSV, REB], 'to walk through' [AB, BAGD; CEV, GW, NCV, NLT, TEV].

b. σπόριμα (LN 43.7) (BAGD p. 763): 'grain field' [Arn, BAGD, LN, WBC; GW, HCSB, NASB, NET, NIV, NLT, NRSV], 'field of grain' [AB, BECNT], 'field of standing grain' [NTC], 'wheat field' [CEV, TEV], 'corn field' [KJV, REB], 'the grain' [Lns].

c. στάχυς (LN 3.40) (BAGD 1. p. 765): 'head of grain' [BAGD, BECNT, WBC; GW, HCSB, NASB, NCV, NIV, NRSV], 'head of wheat' [LN; NLT, TEV], 'wheat' [CEV], 'grain' [NET], 'ear' [AB, Arn, Lns], 'ear of corn' [KJV, REB]. This refers to the spiky cluster in which the wheat seeds grow [LN]. Although it seems to say that they ate the heads of wheat, the participial clause about rubbing the heads in their hands indicates that only the grain was eaten [WBC]. They would have to rub the heads in their hands to separate the wheat grains from the husks before eating the wheat kernels [Su].

d. pres. act. participle of ψώχω (LN **19.50**) (BAGD p. 894): 'to rub' [AB, Arn, BAGD, BECNT, **LN**, Lns, NTC, WBC; HCSB, KJV, NASB, NCV, NIV, NRSV, REB, TEV], 'to rub off the husks' [NET], 'to rub the husks off' [CEV], 'to remove the husks' [GW]. The wheat has chaff and 'beards' of stiff projections coming out of the end of each kernel, so it was necessary to remove all of this by rubbing the grains between their hands [LN]. This action would follow picking the heads and it would precede eating the wheat kernels, so some translate the actual sequence [AB; all versions except KJV]. As the group of disciples were eating while walking along, both rubbing the heads and eating the grain would be going on at the same time [TH].

QUESTION—Who was passing through the grain fields?

'He' refers to Jesus [AB]. The following clause makes it clear that Jesus was accompanied by his disciples and instead of 'he is passing through grain fields', some have 'Jesus and his disciples were passing through grain fields' [TH; CEV].

6:2 **And some of-the Pharisees said, Why are-you(plural)-doing what is-not -permitted**[a] **on-the Sabbath?**

TEXT—Following εἶπαν 'said', some manuscripts add αὐτοῖς 'to them'. GNT does not mention this variant. Αὐτοῖς 'to them' is read by KJV.

TEXT—Following ἔξεστιν 'is permitted', some manuscripts add ποιεῖν 'to do'. GNT does not mention this variant. Ποιεῖν 'to do' is read by KJV.

LEXICON—a. pres. act. indic. of ἔξεστι (LN 71.32) (BAGD 1. p. 275): 'to be permitted' [BAGD], 'must, ought to' [LN]. The phrase 'what is not permitted' [NTC] is also translated 'something which is not permitted' [Arn], 'what is not lawful' [Lns, WBC; HCSB, KJV, NASB, NCV, NRSV], 'what is unlawful' [NIV], 'what is not allowed' [BECNT], 'what is forbidden' [REB], 'what is prohibited' [AB], 'what is against the law' [NET, NLT], 'what our Law says you cannot do' [TEV], 'something that is not right to do' [GW], 'you're not supposed to do that' [CEV]. See this word at 6:9; 14:3.

QUESTION—How did the Pharisees come into the situation?

Without any explanation given, it is just assumed that the Pharisees were there [TH]. They had suddenly arrived [NTC]. By referring to 'some of the Pharisees', it indicates not all of the Pharisees mentioned in 5:17 were there and perhaps they were not even part of the same group [Lns]. They were observing the actions of the disciples [Su]. It could be that gossip about the disciples reached the Pharisees and this exchange occurred later [NIGTC].

QUESTION—What is the import of the question, 'Why are you (plural) doing what is not permitted?' and who is being addressed?

This question implies criticism [AB], and showed the indignation and disapproval of the Pharisees [TH]. It is a rhetorical question intended as a rebuke [TG]. It was a warning [BECNT]. The question was asked with the assumption that there was no satisfactory answer possible [Lns].

1. It is addressed to Jesus and his disciples [AB, BECNT, MGC, NAC]. In the parallel passage in Mark 2:24, the Pharisees spoke to Jesus and asked why the disciples were doing what is not permissible. Here Jesus is included in the criticism [AB]. They are treated as a group since Jesus is really the target [BECNT].
2. The question is addressed to the disciples [Crd, ICC, Lns, NICNT, NIGTC, TG, TH, WBC; NET]. As in 5:30, the criticism was addressed to the disciples and Jesus took the responsibility for their behavior [WBC]. Jesus defended the disciples by answering the Pharisees [NICNT, NIGTC].
3. It is addressed to Jesus [GW]: Why are your disciples doing what is not permitted on the Sabbath?

QUESTION—Why wasn't it permitted to eat the grain from the fields on the Sabbath?

They were not stealing, since Deuteronomy 23:25 gives permission to pick grain from a neighbor's field with one's hands, only forbidding the use of a sickle [NICNT, Su]. The problem was that they were doing this on the Sabbath [NAC, NICNT, TNTC, WBC]. Exodus 34:21 forbids labor on the Sabbath, even during harvest time, and the Pharisees had made rules to ensure that the commandment would not be disobeyed [AB]. Plucking the grain would be considered to be reaping [AB, Arn, BNTC, Lns, MGC, NICNT, NIGTC, NTC, TG, TNTC, WBC]. Rubbing the heads in their hands would be considered to be threshing [Arn, BAGD, BNTC, EGT, LN (19.50), NICNT, NTC, TG, TNTC, WBC]. According to their code of rules, the disciples could be accused of reaping, threshing, winnowing, and preparing food on a Sabbath [BECNT, BNTC, TNTC]. It is not that they were trespassing on someone's property. They would have been walking on a public path that went through a grain field [Su, TG]. It was either a path that went between two adjoining fields or a path that went through a single field [Lns]. They were cutting through the edge of a field [BECNT]. Probably Jesus did not agree with the interpretation the Pharisees made of the situation, but he did not go on to argue about the validity of their interpretation [NAC, WBC].

6:3 **And answering Jesus said to them, Have-you- not-even -read what David did when he was-hungry and the (ones) with him being (hungry)?**

QUESTION—What is the function of the question, 'Have you not even read what David did…?'

Of course the Pharisees had read this account in 1 Samuel 21:1–6. The question was asked in irony [AB, Gdt], and rebuke [BECNT, TH]. The irony is brought out by translating 'Have you *not even* read what David did…?' [AB, EGT, Gdt, Lns, NTC, Rb, TH, WBC; NASB]. It is a rhetorical question that means 'you know very well what David did…' [TG]. Although knowing the passage, they failed to see how it is connected with the rule about not working on the Sabbath [Lns]. The question suggests that the Pharisees had read the passage but had not understood the real meaning [NICNT]. They should take into account this fact as well as the command about the Sabbath [ICC]. It implies that what the disciples did is even justified by Scripture [AB]. Some translate the sentence as a statement: 'you surely have read...' [CEV].

6:4 How[a] he-entered into the house[b] of-God and having-taken the loaves of-the presentation[c] he-ate and he-gave to-the (ones) with him, which is- not -permissible to-eat except only the priests?

TEXT—Some manuscripts omit the first word, ὡς 'how'. GNT does not deal with this variant in the apparatus but brackets it in the text, indicating that the Committee had difficulty making the decision. Ὡς 'how' is omitted by NIV, but the omission in this and any other versions may be stylistic rather than implying the omission of ὡς 'how'.

TEXT—Following ἔδωκεν 'he gave', some manuscripts add καί 'also'. GNT rejects this addition with an A decision, indicating that the text is certain. Καί 'also' is added by KJV and NIV.

LEXICON—a. ὡς (LN 90.21) (BAGD IV.4. p. 899): 'how' [AB, Arn, BECNT, Lns, NTC, WBC; GW, HCSB, KJV, NASB, NET], 'that' [BAGD, LN], not explicit [CEV, NCV, NIV, NLT, NRSV, REB, TEV]. It marks the content of a discourse [LN] and is equivalent to ὅτι 'that' [BAGD].

b. οἶκος (LN 7.2) (BAGD 1.a.β. p. 560): 'house' [BAGD, LN], 'temple, sanctuary' [LN]. The phrase 'the house of God' [AB, Arn, BECNT, Lns, NTC, WBC; all versions except NCV] is also translated 'God's house' [NCV]. The meaning of 'house' is extended to include the temple as a result of referring to the temple as God's dwelling place [LN]. In the time of David, this refers to the Tabernacle, not the Temple which Solomon later built [TH]. David entered the courtyard of the sanctuary in Nob where he was free to go [Lns, NTC], the place where the Ark was kept [NTC].

c. πρόθεσις (LN 53.26) (BAGD 1. p. 706): 'presentation' [BAGD]. The phrase 'the loaves of the presentation' is translated 'the presentation loaves' [AB, WBC], 'the bread of the presence' [BECNT; GW, NRSV], 'the bread offered to God' [LN; TEV], 'the consecrated bread' [BAGD, LN, NTC; NASB, NIV], 'the holy bread' [NCV], 'the sacred bread' [HCSB, NET, REB], 'the sacred loaves of bread' [CEV], 'the showbread' [Lns; KJV], 'the loaves of showbread' [Arn], 'the special bread' [NLT]. The phrase is a Hebrew idiom that refers to bread that was set out as an offering in the presence of God in the Tabernacle and later in the Temple [LN]. These were the loaves of bread set out in God's presence. The loaves were set on a table every Sabbath and the loaves of the preceding week were eaten by the priests [AB, WBC]. There were twelve loaves set forth in two rows on a gold-covered table in the Holy Place of the Tabernacle (Leviticus 24:5–9). The loaves David ate were not then lying on the table but were some that had been replaced by new ones [Lns].

QUESTION—Where does the OT say that David gave the sacred bread to the ones with him?

David went to Nob by himself (1 Samuel 21:1). The ones with him were the young men he was to meet afterwards [ICC]. Although not stated in the passage, it is implied that David would not have asked for five loaves for only himself [BECNT, Gdt]. Jesus added this clause in order to make a parallel with his disciples and David's companions [Gdt].

QUESTION—What is the point of referring to what David did?

In eating food that was for only the priests, what David and his companions ate was illegal. This overriding of the law was done in view of human need [NIGTC]. This doesn't imply that David's need was so great that he was starving, it was enough that he was very hungry [Lns]. Jesus proved by David's own example that the ceremonial law was not intended to be absolute in its application [Lns]. David too looked like a law breaker when he acted according to what the law truly intended [WBC]. Jesus assumed that the Pharisees would agree that David did right in taking the bread, eating it, and giving some to others [Lns]. Jesus argued that if the Pharisees condemned Jesus' disciples about this, then they also condemned David and his men although the OT text did not question what David did and neither did the priest who gave him the bread [BECNT]. If David had the right to set aside a ceremonial law ordained by God when necessity demanded it, then God's anointed one had a right in a similar case of need to set aside an unwarranted, man-made Sabbath law [NTC].

6:5 And he-said to-them, The Son of-Man[a] is Lord of-the Sabbath.

TEXT—After αὐτοῖς 'to them', some manuscripts add ὅτι 'that'. GNT does not mention this variant. Ὅτι 'that' is read by KJV. If this word is interpreted by any version as introducing a direct quotation it would not be translated, and in any such case it would therefore not be possible to determine whether this word was accepted or not.

TEXT—Instead of κύριός ἐστιν τοῦ σαββάτου ὁ υἱὸς τοῦ ἀνθρώπου 'Lord is of the Sabbath the Son of Man', some manuscripts read κύριός ἐστιν ὁ υἱὸς τοῦ ἀνθρώπου καὶ τοῦ σαββάτου 'Lord is the Son of Man of the Sabbath also', and one ancient manuscript and one Old Latin manuscript place this clause, with the latter wording, following 6:10. GNT reads κύριός ἐστιν τοῦ σαββάτου ὁ υἱὸς τοῦ ἀνθρώπου 'Lord is of the Sabbath the Son of Man' with a B decision, indicating that the text is almost certain.

LEXICON—a. υἱὸς τοῦ ἀνθρώπου 'Son of Man'. This title for Christ occurs at 5:24; 6:5, 22; 7:34; 9:22, 26, 44; 11:30; 12:8, 40; 17:22, 24, 26; 18:8, 31; 19:10; 21:27, 36; 22:22, 48, 69; 24:7. See the discussions of this title at 5:24, 6:5, and 9:22.

QUESTION—How is this verse related to the preceding one?

1. This adds another justification [EGT, Gdt, Lns, Su, TNTC]: and besides that. This is a further and very different justification for what his disciples

have done [TNTC]. Jesus stated the principle that guided him when Sabbath observance and human need came into conflict [Su].
2. This indicates a conclusion to Jesus' answer [BECNT, NICNT, TH]: and therefore.

QUESTION—What did Jesus mean by calling himself the Son of Man?

Jesus had already referred to himself as the Son of Man in 5:24. He used the designation as a title for the Messiah: if David could override the law without blame, how much more could the greater Son of David do so? [TNTC]. The phrase is used as a title and it played a part in developing his role as Messiah [AB, NAC]. As the God-man, Jesus is man, yet more than man, the incarnate Son, the Messiah [Lns]. Or, the messianic use of the title is unlikely this early in Jesus' ministry, and here it means that he is the representative man in the way a king is a representative figure [BECNT]. The title is a mysterious term of authority and dignity and means 'the Man' or 'the man, divinely raised up and given authority, with whom the destiny of humankind (Israel) is bound up' and here it means neither simply 'I' nor yet the exalted messianic Son of Man [WBC].

QUESTION—What is meant by 'Lord of the Sabbath'?

'Lord' means the master of the Sabbath, and Jesus is saying that if David was exempt from the law, so much more would the Son of Man be exempt [TH]. Jesus had authority to evaluate and to interpret tradition and law in regard to the Sabbath [BECNT, NICNT]. As Lord, he was over all the laws and institution and he was there to honor and fulfill all that they meant [Lns]. He is Lord of the Sabbath because of his authority as the Son of Man in preaching the kingdom. If in certain cases David could dispense with regulations set down in Scripture, then so could the Son of Man [AB]. As the sovereign Lord, Jesus had the authority to lay down the principles that govern the Sabbath [NTC]. He had the authority to give the divine intention for the Sabbath [WBC]. As the Son of Man he ruled over the Sabbath and properly interpreted it [NAC]. He had the power to cancel the literal rules of observing the Sabbath in order to permit what was in accordance with the spirit of the rules [ICC]. In effect, Jesus claimed authority equal to God with respect to interpreting the law [NIGTC]. The Son of Man, who had interpretive authority over the Sabbath, had permitted the disciples to pluck and eat the wheat on the Sabbath and therefore they had not violated that day [NICNT]. Jesus had the responsibility of determining the proper use of the Sabbath in regard to God's original purpose for it [Su].

DISCOURSE UNIT: 6:6–11 [BECNT, NIGTC, Su, TNTC, WBC; CEV, GW, HCSB, NCV, NET, NLT, NRSV, TEV]. The topic is the man with a paralyzed hand [HCSB, TEV], the man with a withered hand [NRSV], the man with a crippled hand [CEV], healing a withered hand [NET], Jesus heals a man's hand [NCV], Jesus heals on the Sabbath [GW, NLT], healing a man with a withered hand on the Sabbath [NIGTC, Su, TNTC], a question about healing on the Sabbath [BECNT], doing good on the Sabbath [WBC].

6:6 **And it-happened on another Sabbath (that) he entered into the synagogue and taught. And a-man was there also whose right hand was paralyzed.**[a]

TEXT—Following ἐγένετο δέ 'and it came to pass', some manuscripts add καί 'also'. GNT does not mention this variant. Καί 'also' is read by KJV.

LEXICON—a. ξηρός (LN 23.173) (BAGD 2. p. 548): 'paralyzed' [LN; GW, HCSB, TEV], 'withered' [Arn, BAGD, BECNT, LN, Lns, WBC; KJV, NASB, NET, NRSV, REB], 'shriveled' [NTC; NIV], 'stunted' [AB], 'deformed' [NLT], 'withered and paralyzed' [LN], 'crippled' [CEV, NCV]. In reference to a body part, this is a figurative extension of ξηρόςα 'dry, withered' (79.80) and pertains to a shrunken, withered, and hence immobile, part of the body [LN].

QUESTION—What was wrong with the man's hand?

In 6:10 Jesus tells him to stretch out his hand, so it is implied that his hand must have been paralyzed [MGC, NIBC, TH]. It was paralyzed [BECNT, NTC; NET] and shrunken [NET], perhaps due to muscular malfunction [NTC] or atrophy [Gdt, NIGTC, NTC, TNTC]. It was atrophied in growth [AB]. The hand was withered with the muscles and nerves dried up, perhaps due to some injury that had gradually produced this state [Lns]. Or, it was stiff due to lack of use, not shrunken in size [TG]. Pointing out that it was the right hand that most people use for work makes the condition even worse [AB, EGT, Lns, NAC, NICNT, NIGTC, WBC].

6:7 **And the scribes and the Pharisees were-watching him (to see) if he-heals on the Sabbath, in-order-that they-might-find (a reason) to-accuse**[a] **him.**

TEXT—Instead of the infinitive κατηγορεῖν 'to accuse', some manuscripts read the noun κατηγορίαν '(an) accusation'. GNT does not mention this variant. Κατηγορίαν '(an) accusation' is read by NTC; KJV, and NRSV.

LEXICON—a. pres. act. infin. of κατηγορέω (LN 33.427) (BAGD 1.a. p. 423): 'to accuse' [LN], 'to bring charges' [BAGD, LN]. The phrase 'they might find (a reason) to accuse him' [NASB, NET] is also translated 'they might accuse him' [BECNT], 'they could accuse him' [NCV], 'they could find a charge against him' [HCSB], 'they may find how to be accusing him' [Lns], 'they might find out how to make an accusation against him' [WBC], 'they might find an accusation against him' [KJV, NRSV], 'they might find something of which they could accuse him' [Arn], 'they could find a charge to bring against him' [REB], 'they might find a charge against Jesus' [NTC], 'to find some legal charge to bring against him' [NLT], 'they might be able to file a charge against him' [AB], 'to find a way to accuse him of doing something wrong' [GW], 'wanted a reason to accuse Jesus of doing wrong' [TEV], 'they wanted to accuse Jesus of doing something wrong' [CEV], 'were looking for a reason to accuse Jesus' [NIV]. It refers to a legal action in court [NAC, WBC]. See this word at 23:2.

QUESTION—Who were the scribes and the Pharisees watching?
    They were watching Jesus, not the man who is the subject of the preceding sentence [MGC, NICNT, TH; NET]. The imperfect tense 'were watching' implies that they continued to watch Jesus all the time he was teaching [Lns]. They wanted to trap Jesus [WBC]. They did not doubt that Jesus had the ability to heal [NAC] and from Jesus' past actions they were sure that he would heal someone when asked [TG]. They were watching him in hope of seeing him heal someone on the Sabbath so they could bring charges against him [NICNT, TNTC].

QUESTION—What would be a reason for accusing Jesus?
    The Pharisees had a law that on a Sabbath medical help was only allowed in the case of a mortal illness [Arn, MGC, NIGTC; NET]. It was against the law to practice medicine, healing, or surgery other than circumcision on the Sabbath [Su]. In this incident, the man's life was not in danger and healing could be put off for another day [BECNT, NICNT, NTC].

6:8 But he knew their thoughts, and said to-the man having the paralyzed hand, Rise and stand in the midst. And having-arisen he stood.
QUESTION—Where did Jesus tell the man to stand?
1. He was to come to stand before Jesus [Arn, BECNT, ICC, NTC, Rb, TG, TH, TNTC; probably HCSB, NASB, NET, NLT, NRSV, REB, TEV]: rise and *come* take your stand *here* with me in the midst of the people. He was to come into the midst and stand there [ICC]. He was to come stand in the midst of the group surrounding Jesus [TH], in the front [TEV], where everyone could see [NLT]. He was to stand in a place where there could be no doubt about what was happening [TNTC].
2. He was to stand there where he was [Lns; probably CEV, GW, NCV, NIV]: rise and stand *there* in the midst of the people. The purpose of standing was for everyone to see him [CEV]. He was to stand in the center of the synagogue [GW], in front of everyone [NIV]. Since all the people, including Jesus, would be sitting cross-legged on the floor, the man was told to stand where he was so all could see him. However he was not told to approach Jesus since the healing was to be accomplished by a word, not by a touch [Lns].

6:9 And Jesus said to them, I-ask you whether it-is-permitted[a] on-the Sabbath to-do-good[b] or to-do-evil,[c] to-save[d] life or destroy[e] (it)?
TEXT—Instead of ἐπερωτῶ 'I ask', some manuscripts read ἐπερωττήσω 'I will ask'. GNT does not mention this variant. Ἐπερωττήσω 'I will ask' is read by KJV.
TEXT—Instead of εἰ ἔξεστιν 'whether it is permitted' some manuscripts read τί ἔξεστιν 'what is permitted'. GNT does not mention this variant. Τί ἔξεστιν 'what is permitted' is read by KJV.
LEXICON—a. pres. act. indic. of ἔξεστι (LN 71.32) (BAGD 1. p. 275): 'to be permitted'. See this word at 6:2.

b. aorist act. infin. of ἀγαθοποιέω (LN 88.3) (BAGD 1. p. 2): 'to do good' [Arn, BAGD, BECNT, LN, NTC, WBC; all versions except CEV, NLT, TEV], 'to do good to people' [AB], 'to perform good deeds' [LN], 'to do good deeds' [CEV, NLT], 'to do a good deed' [Lns], 'to help' [TEV]. This has the sense of helping people [TH].

c. aorist act. infin. of κακοποιέω (LN 20.12 or 88.112) (BAGD 1. or 2. p. 397): 'to do evil' [Arn, LN, WBC; GW, HCSB, KJV, NCV, NET, NIV, REB], 'to do evil deeds' [CEV], 'to do wrong' [BAGD (1.), LN (88.112)], 'to do a base deed' [Lns], 'to harm' [BAGD (2.), LN (20.12); TEV], 'to do harm' [AB, BECNT, NTC; NASB, NLT, NRSV], 'to injure' [BAGD (2.), LN (20.12)], 'to hurt' [LN (20.12)].

d. aorist act. infin. of σῴζω (LN 21.18, 21.27, 23.136) (BAGD 1.a. p. 798): 'to save' [AB, BAGD, BECNT, LN (21.27), Lns, NTC, WBC; all versions except GW], 'to save from death' [BAGD], 'to rescue' [LN (21.18)], 'to preserve' [Arn], 'to heal' [LN (23.136)], 'to give health' [GW]. This does not refer to salvation, but to deliverance in a general sense, and here specifically to a restoration that would give the man full use of his arm [BECNT].

e. aorist act. infin. of ἀπόλλυμι (LN 20.31) (BAGD p. 22): 'to destroy' [Arn, BAGD, BECNT, LN, Lns, NTC, WBC; all versions], 'to do away with' [AB].

QUESTION—Did Jesus want them to answer the question he asked?

In the form of the rhetorical question there could be only an affirmative answer, which would remove the objection that the Pharisees had [NIGTC]. It had the effect of asking, 'Why delay a healing when good can be done now?' [BECNT]. The question was asked in irony as though it was a grave problem that was hard to answer and it was intended to correct the ideas they had about the Sabbath [Lns].

QUESTION—What is meant by doing evil?

1. It characterizes the moral quality of the deed as being evil [BECNT, ICC, Lns, NAC, NICNT, NIGTC, TG, WBC; CEV, GW, KJV, NCV, NET, NIV, REB]: to do what is good or to do what is evil. By refusing to do good, one is doing evil [ICC, Lns, NAC, NIGTC]. The general term 'evil' is the opposite of 'good' [WBC].

2. It describes the effect of the deed on its recipient [AB, BECNT, NIGTC, NTC, TH; NASB, NLT, NRSV, TEV]: to help people or to harm them. If Jesus failed to do good and heal the man, it would be harming the man who would have to continue to suffer [NIGTC].

QUESTION—What is meant by saving a life or destroying it?

This explains what the previous pair, 'to do good or to do evil' refer to [TH]. This is a specific set of alternatives that interprets the previous general set [WBC]. To 'save life' means to save a person (ψυχή) and refers to saving someone from death, not damnation [NIGTC]. Saving a life or a limb represented doing good on a Sabbath [BECNT, Su]. To save or to destroy a life carries the question to its extreme limits, and being the ultimate action with all the lesser applications of the same nature included [Lns]. By adding 'to destroy life', Jesus referred to what the objectors were doing since they were breaking the Sabbath by plotting to destroy him on this day (6:7) [ICC, Lns, NTC, Rb]. In both pairs, the first items of the pairs (good, saving a life) characterize what Jesus was doing and the second items (doing harm, destroying) characterize what the Pharisees were doing [BECNT].

6:10 And having-looked-around (at) all of-them he-said to-him, Stretch-out your hand. And he-did and his hand was-restored.[a]

TEXT—Following αὐτούς 'them', some manuscripts add ἐν ὀργῇ 'with wrath'. GNT rejects this addition with an A decision, indicating that the text is certain.

TEXT—Instead of αὐτῷ 'to him' some manuscripts evidently read τῷ ἀνθρώπῳ 'to the man', although GNT does not mention this variant. Τῷ ἀνθρώπῳ 'to the man' is read by KJV.

LEXICON—a. aorist pass. indic. of ἀποκαθίστημι (LN 13.65) (BAGD 1. p. 92): 'to be restored' [AB, Arn, BAGD, BECNT, LN, NTC, WBC; HCSB, NASB, NET, NRSV, REB], 'to be completely restored' [Lns; NIV], 'to be restored whole' [KJV], 'to become normal again' [GW, NLT], 'to be healed' [NCV], 'to become well again' [TEV], 'to become completely well' [CEV]. His hand was restored to its former state [Rb], implying that his hand had once been sound [TG, TH]. The passive verb implies that Jesus was the agent [Lns].

QUESTION—Why did Jesus look around at the Pharisees and scribes?

By looking at each one in turn [TH], Jesus was challenging them [NIGTC]. This gave them an opportunity to answer him, although none did so [EGT, Lns, TNTC]. The only possible answer would have ridiculed their entire philosophy of life, so they remained silent [NTC].

6:11 But they were-filled with-fury[a] and they-were-discussing with one-another what they-might-do to-Jesus.

LEXICON—a. ἄνοια (LN **88.183**) (BAGD p. 70): 'fury' [BAGD; NRSV], 'rage' [Arn; HCSB, NASB, TEV], 'extreme fury, great rage' [LN], 'mindless rage' [BECNT; NET], 'senseless rage' [NTC], 'madness' [Lns, WBC; KJV]. The phrase 'to be filled with fury' is translated 'to be extremely furious' [**LN**], 'to be furious' [CEV, GW, NIV], 'to be wild with rage' [NLT], 'to be very angry' [NCV], 'to be beside oneself with fury' [AB], 'to totally fail to understand' [REB]. 'Fury' is more than anger, and refers to losing all sense and reason [Lns]. It is violent anger, unreasoning fury [TG]. It is insane fury [TH], or senseless wrath [NIGTC]. Being unable to answer with the only satisfactory answer possible made them angry and the miracle made matters even worse [NTC]. They held that God did not hear sinners or Sabbath violators, yet Jesus had healed the man with only a word, a fact that made it difficult to even say that he labored on a Sabbath [BECNT]. They were angry that Jesus had defied them and had gotten away with it [Su].

QUESTION—What did they consider doing to Jesus?
Perhaps they had decided to kill Jesus and sought the best way of doing it [Rb]. Both Matthew and Mark explicitly say that they wanted to kill Jesus, so their discussion was about what they could do to kill him [Gdt, Lns, NTC]. They wondered what they should do if they did anything [ICC]. They were not sure what to do, but they were sure that something had to be done [BECNT, NIGTC] against this person who had challenged their approach to religion [BECNT]. Luke has mollified the plan to kill Jesus that the other Gospels made explicit [AB] and leaves it vague [NIGTC], and only implied [TH]. Or, here in Luke it is not actually stated that they wanted to kill Jesus [Gdt, Su] and the discussion was about how to discredit him in the eyes of the people who were accepting him [Su].

DISCOURSE UNIT: 6:12–49 [AB, NAC, NICNT, NIGTC]. The topic is Jesus' instructions to his disciples [NICNT, NIGTC], teaching the disciples with the sermon on the plain [NAC], the preaching of Jesus [AB].

DISCOURSE UNIT: 6:12–26 [NIV]. The topic is blessings and woes.

DISCOURSE UNIT: 6:12–19 [NASB]. The topic is choosing the twelve.

DISCOURSE UNIT: 6:12–16 [AB, BECNT, NAC, NICNT, NIGTC, Su, TNTC, WBC; CEV, GW, HCSB, NCV, NET, NIV, NLT, NRSV, TEV]. The topic is the twelve apostles [HCSB, NIV], Jesus chooses his Apostles [NCV], Jesus chooses the twelve disciples [AB, BECNT, NAC, TNTC, WBC; CEV, NLT, NRSV, TEV], Jesus appoints twelve apostles [GW], the calling of the Twelve [NICNT, NIGTC, Su], the naming of the twelve apostles [NET].

6:12 And it-happened in these days he went-out[a] to the mountain to-pray, and he-was spending-the-night in prayer to-God. **6:13** And when day came, he-summoned his disciples, and having-chosen twelve from them, whom also[b] he-named apostles,

LEXICON—a. aorist act. infin. of ἐξέρχομαι (LN 15.40): 'to go out (to)' [AB, Arn, BECNT, Lns, NTC, WBC; HCSB, KJV, NET, NIV, NRSV, REB], 'to go out of, to depart out of' [LN], 'to go off (to)' [CEV, NASB, NCV], 'to go up (a hill)' [TEV], 'to go' [GW, NLT]. He went out of Capernaum [Alf, EGT]. Most commentaries do not focus on the point of departure but on the destination.

b. καί (LN 89.93): 'also' [AB, Arn, BECNT, LN, Lns, NTC; HCSB, KJV, NASB, NET, NIV, NRSV], 'and' [LN; GW, REB], not explicit [WBC; CEV, NCV, TEV]. This conjunction indicates the naming to be a separate act from choosing them [ICC, TH] and does not indicate whether it happened at the same time or later [TH]. Naming them as apostles probably happened afterwards [AB, BECNT, Crd, ICC, TH]. Or, it happened at the same time [Lns]. Some translate it as being the same act: 'and chose twelve of them to be his apostles' [CEV], 'and chose twelve of them to be apostles' [NLT].

QUESTION—Which days are referred to by 'these days'?

It is a general reference and does not necessarily refer to the preceding event [TH, TNTC]. This indefinite reference probably refers to the days shortly after the preceding events [EGT, NTC]. Probably this vague reference shows that Luke did not exactly know where to introduce this incident in this period of Jesus' ministry [Alf].

QUESTION—Where is the end of the sentence in 6:13?

The syntax is difficult because after the participial clause 'and having chosen' there is no main verb until 'he stood' in 6:17. Only one commentary translates this as a sentence that continues on into 6:17 [Lns]. This can be considered an anacoluthon (lacking a grammatical connection) in which there is an abrupt change so that there is a second construction inconsistent with the first [NIGTC, TH]. The syntactic difficulty is solved by making the participle 'having chosen' the main verb [AB, BECNT, NTC, WBC; all versions]: and he chose twelve from them, whom also he named apostles. Some end the sentence with 6:13 and provide verbs to make a new sentence of 6:14–16 [CEV, GW, NLT]. Some use a colon to include the list of names in the sentence and end the sentence at the end of the list in 6:16 [AB, Arn, BECNT, NTC, WBC; HCSB, NASB, NCV, NET, NIV, NRSV, REB, TEV]. A semicolon is used by KJV.

QUESTION—What was involved in naming twelve of his disciples 'apostles'?

At this time they received the title 'apostle' to distinguish them from the rest of the disciples [Alf, Gdt]. The word 'apostle' means someone who is commissioned for a certain task [TH]. It means someone sent or commissioned [Lns, NTC], and it is the equivalent of being an ambassador [Arn, Lns], a commissioned messenger [Arn, BECNT], or an authorized representative [NICNT]. The word is sometimes used in a wide sense to include men such as Barnabas, Epaphroditus, Apollos, Silvanus, and Timothy, but it is regularly used of the Twelve for their distinctive office that was shared later by only Paul [Lns, NTC]. Mark described their function as being a group selected out of the wider body of disciples that Jesus wanted to accompany him and later go out to preach and have authority over demons (Mark 3:14–15) [NIGTC]. Although the term 'apostle' refers to men who are sent out, they were to be more than messengers since they would both speak and act with an authority derived from Jesus. They would be sent out with Jesus' authority [TG]. They would be constantly with Jesus and, after being taught by him, would be sent out by him, appointed with authority over life and doctrine [NTC].

6:14 Simon whom also he-named Peter, and Andrew his brother, and James and John and Philip and Bartholomew **6:15** and Matthew and Thomas and James (the son of) Alphaeus, and Simon the (one) being-called a-zealot,[a] **6:16** and Judas (the son/brother of) James, and Judas Iscariot, who became a-traitor.[b]

LEXICON—a. ζηλωτής (LN **11.88**) (BAGD 2. p. 338): 'Zealot' [Arn, BAGD, BECNT, **LN**, Lns, NTC; all versions except CEV, KJV, TEV], 'Zelotes' [KJV], 'zealot' [AB, WBC], 'nationalist' [LN], 'enthusiast, fanatic' [BAGD], 'the Patriot' [TEV], 'the Eager One' [CEV].

b. προδότης (LN **37.113**) (BAGD p. 704): 'traitor' [AB, BAGD, BECNT, Lns, NTC, WBC; all versions except CEV, NCV, NLT], 'betrayer' [Arn, BAGD, **LN**]. The phrase 'who became a traitor' is translated 'who later betrayed Jesus' [CEV, NLT], 'who later turned Jesus over to his enemies' [NCV]. This is written looking back from when Luke wrote this account [Lns].

QUESTION—Was Simon named Peter at this time?

This does not mean that Jesus named him Peter at this time [Arn, ICC, Lns]. He had been referred to as Simon Peter in 5:8, but it is here that we learn that Jesus had given him his new name [NICNT]. The time when Jesus named him Peter is described in John 1:42 [NTC]. Up to this point, he has been referred to as Simon, but from now on Luke calls him Peter except at 22:31 and 24:34 [BECNT, NIGTC] where Luke followed his sources [NIGTC].

QUESTION—Why was Simon called a zealot?

1. Simon was called a Zealot to describe his affiliation with a nationalistic party [AB, BECNT, Crd, Gdt, Lns, NAC, NIGTC, NTC, Su, TG, TH; NET, TEV]. He was a nationalistic Israelite before becoming a follower of Jesus [BECNT]. He was a former member of this patriotic and rebellious Jewish party [Lns]. He either had been or was at the present time a member of this nationalistic party that would even resort to force to get rid of Roman authority [TG]. The Zealots were a radical group who violently resisted Rome [TNTC]. The label Zealot was used for a resistance movement that emerged shortly before the first revolt against Rome in A.D. 66–70. Simon may have been a zealot in the individual sense before then, or he could have later been called a Zealot because of being associated with the Zealots when they emerged as a party [AB]. It could indicate that he was a follower of a nationalist group which later developed into a unified party of Zealots [NAC, NIGTC]. Or, it probably indicated that he belonged a group that practiced zeal for the Law [TH].
2. Simon is called a zealot to describe his attribute of zeal [WBC; CEV]. He was called a zealot because Jews admired such a characteristic exemplified by the zeal displayed by Phineas and Elijah in Numbers 25:11 and 1 Kings 18:40; 19:10 [WBC].

QUESTION—Does 'Judas, the (one) of James' mean that he was the son or brother of James and who was he?
    1. Judas was the son of James [AB, BNTC, Crd, Gdt, ICC, Lns, MGC, My, NAC, NICNT, NIGTC, NTC, Su, TNTC, WBC; all versions except KJV]. He is probably the same person as Thaddaeus in Mark's list of apostles at Mark 3:18 [BECNT, Gdt, ICC, NAC, NIGTC, NTC, TNTC].
    2. Judas was the brother of James [Alf; KJV].
QUESTION—What is meant by the designation Judas Iscariot
    1. Iscariot indicates a region in Judea [AB, Arn, BECNT, Gdt, ICC, Lns, MGC, NAC, NICNT, NTC, TH, TNTC; NET]: Judas, the man from Kerioth. It was probably the family name [BECNT]. The location was the village Kerioth-Hezron, about twelve miles south of Hebron in Judea [AB].
    2. Iscariot comes from an Aramaic term meaning 'false one' and indicates his character [NIGTC]: Judas, the false one. This name relates to his betrayal of Jesus [NIGTC].

DISCOURSE UNIT: 6:17–49 [BECNT, NICNT, Su, TNTC, WBC; NET]. The topic is Jesus' teaching [BECNT], a sermon for disciples [WBC], the sermon on the plain [Su, TNTC; NET], the status and practices of Jesus' community [NICNT].

DISCOURSE UNIT: 6:17–26 [NCV]. The topic is Jesus' teachings and healings.

DISCOURSE UNIT: 6:17–19 [AB, BECNT, NAC, NICNT, NIGTC, TNTC, WBC; CEV, GW, HCSB, NLT]. The topic is the setting of Jesus' teaching [BECNT], crowds follow Jesus [NLT], a crowd gathers [AB, NICNT, NIGTC, TNTC], ministry to the crowds [NAC], disciples and people come to hear and be healed [WBC], many people are cured [GW], Jesus teaches and heals [HCSB, NRSV, TEV], Jesus teaches, preaches, and heals [CEV].

6:17 And having-come-down with them he-stood[a] on a-level place,[b] and (there was) a-great crowd of-his disciples and a-great multitude of-people from all Judea and Jerusalem and the coastal-region of-Tyre and Sidon,
  TEXT—Some manuscripts omit πολύς 'great (crowd)', although GNT does not mention this variant. Πολύς 'great' is omitted by KJV.
  LEXICON—a. aorist act. indic. of ἵσταμαι (LN 17.1) (BAGD II.1.a. p. 382): 'to stand' [BECNT, LN, Lns; all versions except CEV, REB], 'to stand still' [BAGD], 'to stop' [AB, BAGD, NTC, WBC; REB], 'to station oneself' [Arn], not explicit [CEV]. This indicates that he stopped or remained standing and did not descend farther down the mountain [NTC]. The verb is not intended to indicate Jesus' posture as he began to teach [AB, ICC]. The fact that Jesus stood to heal people does not conflict with the fact that he sat down to teach them in Matthew 5:1 [BECNT, NIGTC].
    b. πεδινός (LN **79.85**) (BAGD p. 638): 'level' [BAGD, LN], 'flat' [BAGD]. The phrase 'a level place' [Arn, **LN**, NTC; GW, HCSB, NASB,

NET, NIV, NRSV, TEV] is also translated 'a level spot' [AB, WBC], 'level ground' [NCV], 'some level ground' [REB], 'a level plain' [Lns], 'the plain' [KJV], 'a plateau' [BECNT], 'some flat, level ground' [CEV], 'a large, level area' [NLT]. The level place contrasts with steep and uneven places and also with high and elevated places [BAGD].

QUESTION—Who accompanied Jesus when he came down?

Jesus came down from the mountain with the twelve apostles [BECNT, EGT, Lns, MGC, NTC, Su, TH; TEV]. Jesus had called all of the disciples to the mountain, but after he had chosen twelve of them, the rest must have gone back down, leaving Jesus and the twelve to confer privately [Lns]. Or, the group of disciples from whom Jesus had chosen the twelve are also included in the group that came down with Jesus [AB, Gdt].

QUESTION—Where was the level place?

It was some plain near the mountain [AB, Alf, EGT, ICC, My, TG, TH]. Perhaps it was on the mountainside since it is not the usual word for a plain [EGT, TNTC]. It suggests a level place lower down the hill [Arn, EGT, Gdt]. It was a plateau [NIVS]. The plateau could be located high up on the mountain face or at the end of relatively low incline [BECNT, NAC]. The parallel account of the Sermon on the Mount in Matthew says that Jesus went up on the mountainside to teach the people. This is not a different sermon from the one described in Matthew [Arn, BECNT, Gdt, Lns, NAC, NIGTC, NIVS, NTC, Rb; NET]. The level place may have been part of the mountain [NTC]. Jesus had gone up the mountain and now he has come down only far enough to reach a level place so the people could hear him [Lns]. Perhaps Matthew's statement was just a summary statement that did not mention what Luke has explained here about Jesus stopping his descent at the level place where he probably found a slight elevation on the mountainside from which to address the crowds [Rb].

QUESTION—Where did the people come from?

From Matthew 4:25 we see that the designation Judea is used of all Israel, including Galilee, Idumaea, and Transjordan. Jerusalem was in Judea but it receives special mention since it was the capital city [NIGTC]. Judea is all of Jewish Palestine [Arn, BECNT, Crd, NAC, WBC]. Another view is that since Jesus was still in Galilee the reference to the more distant areas shows that people were coming from far away also [AB], and mentioning Galilee would be superfluous [EGT]. Tyre and Sidon were outside of Judea and were important cities in Syria (Lebanon today) on the coast of the Mediterranean Sea [AB].

6:18 who came to-hear him and to-be-healed from their diseases. And the (ones who) are troubled[a] by unclean spirits were-being–cured.

TEXT—There is disagreement about where verse 18 begins. It begins with 'who came to hear him' [AB, GNT, NTC, WBC; all versions except KJV, NET, REB]. Or, it begins further along with 'And the ones who are troubled by unclean spirits' [BECNT, Lns; KJV, NET, REB].

TEXT—Before ἐθεραπεύοντο 'were being cured', some manuscripts add καί 'and', although GNT does not mention this variant. Καί 'and' is read by KJV.

LEXICON—a. pres. pass. participle of ἐνοχλέομαι (LN **22.17**) (BAGD p. 267): 'to be troubled' [BAGD], 'to suffer' [**LN**], 'to be afflicted' [LN]. The phrase 'to be troubled by' [AB, Arn, NTC, WBC; CEV, NCV, NIV, TEV] is also translated 'to be troubled with' [NASB, NRSV, REB], 'to be tormented by' [GW, HCSB], 'to suffer from' [NET], 'to be oppressed with' [BECNT], 'to be vexed with' [KJV], not explicit [NLT]. This makes a distinction between those who were obviously sick and those who were demon possessed [BECNT, Lns, NTC]. The demon-possessed were a special category of those who had come to be cured [TH]. 'To be troubled' was sometimes used to indicate an unrest caused by demons, but it could also simply mean 'to be sick' [NICNT].

6:19 And all the crowd were-seeking to-touch him, because power was-going-out[a] from him and it/he-was-healing everyone.

LEXICON—a. imperf. mid./pass. (deponent = act.) of ἐξέρχομαι (LN 15.40) (BAGD p. 63): 'to go out' [Arn, BAGD, LN, NTC; CEV, KJV, NLT, REB, TEV], 'to go forth' [AB, WBC], 'to come (from)' [GW, NASB, NCV, NIV], 'to come forth (from)' [BECNT], 'to come out (from)' [HCSB, NET, NRSV]. The imperfect is iterative and this means that people were being cured one after another [TH]. This verb seems to imply healing by physical contact with Jesus [Su]. The spiritual power in Jesus became effective when he spoke to the sick, or touched them, or when they touched him [TH]. It was a power to heal from God [AB].

QUESTION—What is the implied subject of the verb 'was healing'?

1. The subject is the power [Arn, BECNT, Gdt, Lns, NTC, WBC; all versions except NLT, which does not specify a subject]: power was going out from him and it was healing everyone. Taking 'power' to be the subject makes a better transition to the next verse which specifies Jesus as its subject [WBC]. Jesus sensed at times that healing power proceeded from him (8:46, Mark 3:30) [NTC]. The many who touched Jesus did not claim his personal attention as they were being healed since power kept going out (imperfect tense) to cure them as it also did for the woman who touched him in 8:43 [Lns]. Since the healing power came from Jesus, it is clear that Jesus accomplished the healing [NTC].
2. The subject is Jesus [AB, EGT, TH]: power was going out from him and he was healing everyone. 'To heal' and 'to cure' always occur with a personal subject elsewhere [TH].

DISCOURSE UNIT: 6:20–49 [AB, BECNT, NIGTC; REB]. The topic is Jesus' message with an offer and a call to love [BECNT], the sermon on the plain [AB, NIGTC], Jesus' sermon to the disciples [REB]. This sermon of twenty-nine verses is the same sermon that Matthew reports in one hundred and eleven verses at Matt. 5–7 [AB, Alf, Crd, EGT, Lns, NIC, NTC, Rb, Su, TNTC].

Many of the teachings in Matthew are in other places in Luke and some things in Luke are not in Matthew, so apparently each selected some of the parts of the sermon, omitted others, and used some of the same material for different purposes [Su]. Matthew reported things from the sermon that pertained to Jewish Christians and Luke left out much of that when he selected what he would write to Theophilus, a Gentile [Lns]. Or, Luke took the whole of the sermon from a document that reported a similar but different sermon than the one Matthew reported [ICC].

DISCOURSE UNIT: 6:20–45 [NASB]. The topic is the beatitudes.

DISCOURSE UNIT: 6:20–26 [BECNT, NAC, NICNT, NIGTC, WBC; CEV, GW, NRSV, TEV]. The topic is Jesus teaching his disciples [GW], blessings/ beatitudes and woes [BECNT, NAC, NICNT, WBC; NRSV], happiness and sorrow [TEV], blessings and troubles [CEV], two kinds of men [NIGTC].

DISCOURSE UNIT: 6:20–23 [TNTC; HCSB, NLT]. The topic is the beatitudes.

6:20 And **having-raised**[a] his eyes to his disciples he was-saying, **Blessed**[b] (are/are-you) the **poor**,[c] because yours **is**[d] the kingdom of-God.

LEXICON—a. aorist act. participle of ἐπαίρω (LN 15.105) (BAGD 1. p. 281): 'to raise' [LN], 'to lift up' [Arn, BAGD, BECNT, Lns, NTC, WBC; KJV]. The phrase 'to raise his eyes to' is translated 'to look up at' [HCSB, NET, NRSV, TEV], 'to look at' [CEV, GW, NCV, NIV], 'to turn to' [NLT, REB], 'to turn his gaze toward' [NASB], 'to fix his eyes on' [AB]. Jesus looked the audience full in the face [Rb], and took note of them [NIGTC]. The action indicates that it was a solemn occasion [EGT, My].

b. μακάριος (LN 25.119) (BAGD 1.b. p. 486): 'blessed' [AB, Arn, BAGD, BECNT, Lns, NTC; GW, HCSB, KJV, NASB, NET, NIV, NRSV, REB], 'fortunate' [BAGD, WBC], 'happy' [BAGD, LN; NCV, TEV]. This noun is also translated as a verb phrase: 'God blesses' [NLT], 'God will bless' [CEV]. It implies enjoying favorable circumstances [LN]. It is used in the sense of being a 'privileged recipient of divine favor' [BAGD]. See this word at 1:45; 7:23; 10:23; 11:27; 12:37, 43; 14:14; 23:29.

c. πτωχός (LN 57.53) (BAGD 1.a. p. 728): 'poor' [BAGD, LN], 'destitute' [LN], '(you) poor' [Arn, BECNT, NTC, WBC; KJV, TEV], '(you who are) poor' [AB; HCSB, NASB, NET, NIV, NLT, NRSV], '(you people who are) poor' [CEV, NCV], '(you who are) in need' [REB], '(those who are) poor' [GW], '(the) beggarly' [Lns]. The word describes someone who is so destitute that he has to beg [NIGTC].

d. pres. act. indic. of εἰμί (LN 13.1): 'to be' [LN]. The phrase 'yours is the kingdom of God' [Arn, BECNT, Lns, NTC, WBC; KJV, NASB, NIV, NRSV] is also translated 'the kingdom of God is yours' [AB; HCSB, REB, TEV], 'his kingdom belongs to you' [CEV], 'the kingdom of God belongs to you' [NCV, NET], 'the Kingdom of God is given to you' [NLT], 'the kingdom of God is theirs' [GW].

238   LUKE 6:20

QUESTION—By saying that Jesus raised his eyes to his disciples, does this mean that he was speaking only to his disciples?

Jesus primarily addressed his disciples [AB, Alf, Arn, BNTC, ICC, Lns, My, NAC, NIGTC, NTC, TH, TNTC, WBC]. The beatitudes would not be true if addressed to those who were not disciples since it is only to faithful disciples that poverty, hunger, sorrow, and unpopularity would be a blessing [ICC]. Jesus spoke first of all to his disciples, but it was in the presence of the crowd of people, and from 7:1 we see that what he said was intended for them all [My]. Jesus addressed the disciples, but he also intended that the rest of the crowd would hear it so as to draw them into becoming disciples [Lns, WBC]. Jesus' teaching was especially meant for his disciples and their needs. However the crowd also listened and the words in 6:24–26 seem to be especially addressed to the whole crowd [NIGTC]. The sermon as a whole was intended for the whole crowd, who were included in those who were listening (6:27). The beatitudes were suited for the disciples with an implied warning to others. The woes were pronounced on the wicked and the parable of the builders was a warning to those who were not disciples [NTC]. The sermon was about blessings and woes, so it was directed to the whole crowd as Jesus fulfilled the prophecy of sifting and causing division (2:34 and 3:17) [NICNT].

QUESTION—What is meant by the word μακάριος 'blessed'?

It is a word of congratulation [Arn, Su]. It means to be fortunate [Arn, Lns, NIGTC, TG, WBC]. To be blessed means to have received a sense of inner happiness at good fortune [BECNT]. It refers to the religious joy of a person who shares in salvation [NIGTC]. The sayings seem paradoxical by saying the opposite of what is commonly accepted as being blessed, and they have to be understood by taking into account the second part of each saying [Su]. The second part states in what way the blessedness consists [Lns]. The poor in this world are blessed because their share in the kingdom of God will guarantee them abundance, joy, and a reward in heaven [AB]. Using the word 'happy' appears to focus on feelings, but the focus really is on their status and situation, so 'favored' is a better translation [NAC].

QUESTION—Since the parallel passage in Matthew 5:3 is 'blessed (are) the poor in spirit', what is the meaning of 'poor' here?

Luke's first beatitude 'blessed are the poor' corresponds with Matthew's first beatitude 'blessed are the poor in spirit' and the question is whether Jesus says that poverty itself is a blessing or if Luke implies the same thing that Matthew made explicit, the poverty of spirit [Rb]. The decision as to whether this exactly corresponds with Matthew's meanings affects the following two beatitudes also.

  1. It refers to their material poverty [AB, EGT, ICC, My, Su, WBC]. We should not apply 'in spirit' because actual poverty is meant here, not even the idea that poverty makes people 'poor in spirit'. Poverty for disciples is a blessing because it keeps them depending on God. Furthermore, some of the disciples had made themselves poor to follow Jesus [ICC]. 'Poor' is

the antithesis of the literally rich in 6:24, and these are the poor who have a hard life that includes hunger and weeping (6:21), and in this context they are also followers of Jesus. Matthew has narrowed the beatitude to 'poor in spirit', but he has not falsified it since the literally poor would be free of the state of mind that causes the rich to think that the goal of having riches is simply to enjoy the good things of life [WBC]. Most of Jesus' first followers were socially and economically downtrodden [AB, EGT, Su], but were they to consider their treasure in the kingdom of God, they would realize their true wealth [Su].

2. It refers to the spiritual poverty of those who are materially poor [Arn, BECNT, Crd, Gdt, NICNT, NIGTC, NTC, TNTC]. Their poverty in regard to earthly goods is not necessarily a blessing, but when their poverty had made them aware of their spiritual poverty and their riches in God, they are blessed [NTC]. How the poor and the rich relate to God is crucial, and the poor disciple's dependence on God is fundamental [BECNT]. In the OT, the poor and needy person asks God for help and receives it. As a result, the 'poor' came to be a designation for pious and humiliated people [NIGTC]. Jesus' disciples were poor, but they relied on God and Jesus because they had nothing of their own on which they could rely and Matthew has brought out the meaning by calling them poor in spirit [BECNT, NIGTC, TNTC].

3. It is a metaphor for spiritual need [Alf, Lns, NAC]. Although Luke did not include the words 'in spirit', he has in mind the same poverty that Matthew specified as being 'the poor in spirit' and this refers to a spiritual condition of the soul. Neither wealth nor a lack of wealth determines inclusion in the kingdom [Lns]. Although the term fits those who are the believing poor, it refers to all those who have humbled themselves before God [NAC].

QUESTION—In this beatitude there is no verb in the first clause, 'blessed the poor' (as well as in the first clauses of the following two beatitudes), so should the supplied verb be in the second person or third person form?

Both Luke 6:20 and Matthew 5:3 begin with the same three words Μακάριοι οἱ πτωχοί 'blessed the poor'. However, in the following clause Luke uses a second person pronoun, 'because *yours* is the kingdom of God', while Matthew uses a third person pronoun, 'because *theirs* is the kingdom of heaven'.

1. It should be in the second person [AB, Arn, BECNT, NTC, Rb, TH, WBC; all versions except GW]: blessed *are you* the poor. The pronoun 'you' in the second clause justifies the translation 'you poor' [Rb]. In the beatitudes and woes that follow, explicit verbs and objects indicate that Jesus is addressing 'you (plural)'.

2. It should be in the third person [BNTC, Lns; GW]. The third person in the first clause makes the statement broad and general, while the second person in the second clause makes an application of the disciples [Lns]. Some create uniformity of address by changing the second person in the

second clause to third person to match the first clause [GW]. The corresponding beatitudes in Matthew have the second clause in the third person.

QUESTION—In what sense 'is' the kingdom of God theirs?

The present tense 'is' means that they belong to the kingdom and enjoy the blessings of those whom God rules [Arn, TG]. While the other beatitudes are in the future tense, this beatitude is in the present tense. The present tense can be taken to be timeless and practically equivalent to the future tense [NIGTC] so that possession of the kingdom is primarily future [WBC]. They will possess all the blessings brought about by the eschatological rule of God [WBC]. Probably the present tense indicates that there is a sense in which the poor are experiencing the kingdom already, even though the rewards of the kingdom are primarily in the future. Since the kingdom already belongs to the poor, they are assured that they will receive all the future blessings that come with it [NIGTC]. The present tense indicates that they are entitled to the kingdom of God [TH]. The blessings resulting from having God as King over their lives belong to the poor now [NTC]. They enter the kingdom now [TNTC]. The kingdom is in them as a present possession, consisting of grace, pardon, adoption, and sanctification, while the glory is not yet revealed [Lns]. Unlike the promises of the other beatitudes, this is a statement of fact. However the kingdom is not yet theirs in all the fullness promised in the other beatitudes [ICC]. God's spiritual reign in the hearts of those who worship him is a blessing that surpasses the misery of the poor [Su]. The kingdom and its present and prospective blessings are ample compensation for them [EGT]. The kingdom guarantees them abundance, joy, and a reward in heaven [AB].

6:21 Blessed (are/are-you) the (ones) hungering now, because you-will-eat-your-fill.[a]

LEXICON—a. fut. pass. indic. of χορτάζομαι (LN 25.82): 'to eat one's fill' [LN], 'to have one's fill' [AB], 'to have plenty to eat' [CEV], 'to be filled' [Lns; HCSB, KJV, NRSV, TEV], 'to be satisfied' [Arn, BECNT, LN, WBC; GW, NASB, NCV, NET, NIV, NLT, REB], 'to be fully satisfied' [NTC]. The verb has a figurative extension of being satisfied or content with one's state [LN]. The passive voice implies that God is the one who causes this [AB, BECNT, NAC, NIGTC, TG], that is, 'God will give you all you need' [TG], 'God will satisfy you' [NAC].

QUESTION—Since the corresponding passage in Matthew 5:6 is 'blessed (are) the (ones) hungering and thirsting for righteousness', what is the meaning of 'hungering' and 'eating one's fill' here?

1. It refers to physical hunger [AB, ICC, NAC, WBC]. Hunger and weeping are characteristic of poverty and this refers to a lack of food [WBC]. While the hunger refers to actual want in this life, the compensating blessing is spiritual [ICC] and refers to the eschatological banquet of the

OT [AB, NAC]. Satisfying hunger is not restricted to the eschatological banquet [WBC].
2. While referring to physical hunger, it includes the desire for righteousness [BECNT, Gdt, NIGTC]. These are the pious poor referred to in the preceding beatitude [BECNT]. Being hungry physically leads to a spiritual hunger of realizing the need for God's grace and then finding satisfaction in him [Gdt]. The reference to physical hunger is primary, but hunger can be extended to any kind of want and so includes the frequent OT reference to a desire for spiritual satisfaction [NIGTC]. Luke has given the original wording and Matthew has accurately brought out its intended force so that here hunger has both socioeconomic and religious overtones [BECNT]. Rather than a promise for physical filling, the promise is the spiritual satisfaction of being received by God as one of his children [BECNT]. Probably the image of eating their fill refers to the messianic banquet where they will fellowship with God at his table [BECNT, NIGTC].
3. It is a metaphor for having an intense desire for righteousness [Arn, Lns, NTC, Su, TNTC]. The spiritual hunger expressed in Matthew is implied here [NTC, TNTC], a hunger for mercy and forgiveness, peace of mind and heart, purity and holiness, and fellowship with God [NTC]. The spiritual meaning found in Matthew is likely since a future promise of abundant food does not provide relief for present physical hunger [Su]. Luke has abbreviated Matthew's account. Hunger and thirst are frequently used for strong spiritual desires and needs and this refers to daily crying to God for forgiveness. The future tense of the promise is an immediate future so that the moment one hungers, he is filled as God forgives his sin [Lns].

Blessed (are/are-you) the (ones) weeping now, because you-will-laugh.[a]
LEXICON—a. fut. act. indic. of γελάω (LN **25.135**) (BAGD p. 153): 'to laugh' [AB, Arn, BAGD, BECNT, **LN**, Lns, NTC, WBC; all versions]. See this word at 6:25.
QUESTION—What is the cause of their weeping?
Those who weep are 'those who mourn' in Matthew 5:4 [ICC, NAC, NTC]. No restrictions should be placed on this expression of mourning and sorrow, but perhaps the primary cause is their sorrow for the condition of the world and possibly their repentance for sin [NIGTC, NTC]. Weeping is a response to rejection, ridicule, and loss [NICNT]. It refers to sorrow over one's sorrowful state or to having sympathy for others in that state [Su]. Primarily, it is for the suffering in the world where God's people are scorned and persecuted [BECNT]. It concerns the sorrow suffered by those who were faithful to Jesus [WBC]. It is a characteristic of those who are sensitive to evil and who weep over the world's suffering brought on by its rebellion against God [TNTC]. Weeping is a figurative indication of crying to God because of the distress of recognizing the power of sin and one's helpless-

ness to escape this power [Lns]. They weep because of their weaknesses, imperfections, and shortcomings [Arn]. Probably the weeping is caused by the oppression and persecution that the following beatitude describes [AB, NAC].

QUESTION—What is the cause of their laughter?

They will laugh with joy [NIGTC; NCV, NET, NLT]. They will laugh because the sorrow is removed [BECNT, NIGTC]. It is caused by the joy brought into their lives by the kingdom of God [AB]. They will rejoice over being accepted by God and the future tense refers to their welcome at God's table [BECNT]. The future tense is the immediate response of God so that whenever there is godly weeping God immediately fills us with happiness by comforting us with his forgiveness and by his promises of future deliverance from all evil in his future kingdom [Lns]. Their joy is caused by turning themselves over to God who will pardon, strengthen, deliver, and reassure them [NTC].

6:22 **Blessed are-you when people hate you and when they-ostracize**[a] **you and they-reproach**[b] **(you) and they-throw-out**[c] **your name as evil because of-the Son of-Man.**[d]

LEXICON—a. aorist act. subj. of ἀφορίζω (LN **34.36**) (BAGD 1. p. 127): 'to ostracize' [NASB, REB], 'to exclude' [BAGD, BECNT, LN, NTC, WBC; HCSB, NET, NIV, NRSV], 'to exclude from their company' [**LN**], 'to separate from their company' [KJV], 'to set someone apart' [Arn], 'to avoid' [GW], 'to reject' [TEV], 'to not have anything to do with' [CEV], 'to shut out' [NCV], 'to outlaw someone' [AB], 'to excommunicate' [BAGD, Lns], 'to get rid of, to separate' [LN]. This active voice is also translated as passive: 'to be excluded' [NLT].

b. aorist act. subj. of ὀνειδίζω (LN 33.422) (BAGD 1. p. 570): 'to reproach' [Arn, BAGD, LN; KJV], 'to reprimand' [LN], 'to denounce' [AB], 'to revile' [BAGD, BECNT, Lns, WBC; NRSV], 'to insult' [all versions except KJV, NLT, NRSV], 'to heap insults on' [BAGD, NTC]. This active voice is also translated as passive: 'to be mocked' [NLT]. It refers to personal insults [NIGTC]. It probably refers to face-to-face insults [NIGTC]. It means to use abusive language about them [TH], or saying slanderous and wicked things about them [Lns].

c. aorist act. subj. of ἐκβάλλω (LN **33.396**) (BAGD 1. p. 237): 'to throw out' [BAGD, LN], 'to cast out' [Arn, BECNT, Lns, WBC; KJV]. The phrase ἐκβάλλω τὸ ὄνομα 'to throw out the name' is an idiom meaning to insult or slander someone [LN]. The phrase 'throw out your name as evil' is translated 'scorn your name as evil' [NASB], 'reject your name as evil' [AB; NET, NIV], 'slander your very name' [REB], 'slander your name as evil' [HCSB], 'spurn your name as evil' [NTC], 'say that you are evil' [NCV, TEV], 'say cruel things about you' [CEV], 'slander you' [**LN**; GW], 'defame you' [NRSV], 'you who are cursed' [NLT]. They will throw one's name contemptuously away and reject it as an evil thing [ICC].

d. υἱὸς τοῦ ἀνθρώπου 'Son of Man'. This title for Christ occurs at 5:24; 6:5, 22; 7:34; 9:22, 26, 44; 11:30; 12:8, 40; 17:22, 24, 26; 18:8, 31; 19:10; 21:27, 36; 22:22, 48, 69; 24:7. See the discussions of this title at 5:24, 6:5, and 9:22.

QUESTION—How is this beatitude different from the preceding ones?

Rather than treating a state (blessed are you who *are* poor, hungry, weeping), it treats a conditional event (blessed are you *when* you are mistreated). The preceding three beatitudes immediately proceeded to the reason why they were blessed, while this beatitude proceeds to an exhortation to rejoice followed by two reason clauses. This beatitude is unique in that it indicates the reason for being afflicted (because of the Son of Man). As an expanded form at the end of the list of beatitudes it serves as a climax and summary of the total thrust of the set [WBC]. This last beatitude shows that all of them have a spiritual base and not just a socioeconomic one [BECNT].

QUESTION—What happened when someone was ostracized?

1. This refers to social ostracism [BECNT, NIGTC, Su, WBC]. It is separation in the sense of excluding a person from one's company [NIGTC], including exclusion from worshipping with others [Su]. People might refuse to do business with them or eat with them [BECNT]. This is not dealing with formal excommunication, although the persecution of the Christians did lead to that [BECNT, WBC].
2. This refers to excommunication from the synagogue as well as social ostracism [AB, Alf, Arn, BNTC, Gdt, ICC, Lns, MGC, My, NAC, NTC, Rb, TH]. Jewish Christians would be excluded from the synagogues [AB]. Exclusion from the synagogue would also include exclusion from social intercourse [Alf, ICC, My, Rb].

QUESTION—What is meant by throwing out someone's name?

1. This refers to their individual names [BECNT, BNTC, Gdt, My, NTC, TG, TH, WBC]. They would not mention a person's name because they regarded it as a bad thing [TH]. They would not even mention a disciple's name because it represented an evil person [My]. They would say evil things about an individual, or use his name in a curse or as a curse [BNTC]. They would indicate their scorn for a person by refusing to mention his name, or they would say his name with disgust, or slander him [NTC], or remove his name from the synagogue membership roll [Gdt, NTC]. They would condemn them as being evil [TG]. The word 'name' refers to a person's reputation, but it does not mean 'Christian' since that would make the following reason clause redundant [WBC].
2. 'Your name' is their collective name as Christians [AB, Alf, Arn, Crd, ICC, Lns, MGC, Rb; CEV]. It is the name by which they are known as Jesus' disciples, that is, Christians [ICC]. It was their common name as Nazarenes or Christians, a name held to be pernicious and one that no man should be permitted to bear [Lns].

244 LUKE 6:22

QUESTION—What relationship is indicated by ἕνεκεν 'because of' in the phrase 'because of the Son of Man'?

This indicates the reason for their being the objects of such hatred and contempt [ICC, TG]. This shows that the beatitudes are addressed to believers [NAC]. The persecution must be undeserved and be endured for the sake of Christ [ICC, WBC], not because of one's own evil conduct [ICC, NTC]. They would be persecuted because they were followers of the Son of Man [Su, TG; CEV, NCV], because they were loyal to him [TH], because they were committed to him [GW], because they were identified with him [NLT], or because of their connection with him and their faith in him [NTC]. It would be because they believe in Jesus as the Son of Man, confess him, preach his message, and live as his disciples [Lns].

6:23 **Rejoice in that day and jump-for-joy,ᵃ because beholdᵇyour rewardᶜ (is) great in heaven. Because in-the-same-wayᵈ their ancestors were-doing to-the prophets.**

LEXICON—a. aorist act. impera. of σκιρτάω (LN **15.243, 25.134**) (BAGD p. 755): 'to jump for joy' [**LN** (15.243); CEV], 'to leap' [BAGD], 'to leap for joy' [BECNT, LN (15.243), NTC, WBC; HCSB, KJV, NASB, NIV, NLT, NRSV], 'to leap with joy' [AB], 'to leap in exultation' [Arn], 'to dance for joy' [**LN** (25.134); REB, TEV], 'to gambol' [Lns], 'to be extremely happy' [LN (25.134)], 'to be very happy' [GW], 'to be full of joy' [NCV]. It indicates that they cannot contain themselves because of the blessing that has come to them [Lns]. It is because of a tremendous joy [TH].

b. ἰδού (LN 91.13) (BAGD 1.b.ε. p. 371): 'behold' [Arn, BAGD, BECNT, WBC; KJV, NASB], 'lo' [Lns], 'look' [BAGD, LN], 'pay attention' [LN], 'take note' [HCSB], 'surely' [NRSV], 'indeed' [NTC], not explicit [AB; CEV, GW, NCV, NET, NIV, NLT, REB, TEV]. This particle is used to emphasize the importance of what is being said [BAGD, TH]. It emphasizes the clause as a whole [TH]. It is an exclamation in response to this astounding reason [Lns].

c. μισθός (LN 38.14) (BAGD 2.a. p. 523): 'reward' [AB, Arn, BAGD, BECNT, LN, Lns, NTC, WBC; all versions], 'recompense' [BAGD, LN]. 'Reward' was used in a religious sense as a reward for moral or ethical conduct and here for being despised as Jesus' disciples [AB]. This is not pay earned by works or suffering, but something that is unearned and bestowed by God's generous grace and refers to the greater glory that will be theirs in heaven [Lns]. It refers to God's vindication of his faithful servants [NIGTC]. The reward is in heaven at the time of trial and it will be reserved there until the day it is given to them, so this means 'God is ready in heaven to reward you greatly' [TH]. The accompanying words 'in heaven' indicate that God gives the reward and that it is safe there [TG]. See this word at 6:35.

d. κατὰ τὰ αὐτά (LN 64.16): The phrase κατὰ τὰ αὐτά 'in the same way' [Arn, LN, WBC; NASB] is also translated 'in just the same way' [AB, NTC], 'the same things' [NCV, NET], 'the very same things' [TEV], 'according to the same things' [Lns], 'that is how' [NIV, REB], 'that is what' [NRSV], 'these same things' [CEV], 'also that way' [NLT], 'that's the way…(treated)' [GW], 'this is the way' [HCSB], 'so' [BECNT], 'in the like manner' [KJV]. See this phrase at 6:26, 17:30.

QUESTION—What relationship is indicated by γάρ 'because' in the clause 'because your reward is great in heaven'?

It is the reason why they should rejoice and jump for joy [BECNT, Lns, NAC, NIGTC, Su, TG]: rejoice *because* your reward is great in heaven. What they gain in heaven is so much more important than what they suffered on earth [Lns, Su]. Heaven is a metaphor for God's presence [NAC]. God would reward them and that reward will be safe [TG].

QUESTION—What relationship is indicated by γάρ 'because' in the last clause 'because according to the same things their ancestors were doing to the prophets'?

1. It is another reason for saying that they were blessed in 6:22 [TH]: you are blessed *because* you share the prophet's fate. The people who persecuted the prophets were ancestors of the present persecutors in a moral sense, not necessarily in a physical sense [TH].
2. It is a second reason for rejoicing while being persecuted [BECNT, Lns, NAC, NTC, Su, TNTC]: rejoice *because* your reward is great in heaven and *because* your suffering parallels that of the prophets. Persecution like the prophets assures them they are really are God's servants [NAC]. It was a blessing to be classed with the prophets [Su]. Their suffering proves that they are successors of the prophets and as prophets they will receive a prophet's reward [NTC].
3. It is an additional explanation of why the disciples will be hated and persecuted [TG, TNTC]: you can be sure that you will be persecuted *because* the same thing happened to the prophets. This is evidence that the disciples were being faithful [TG]. Jesus' disciples can expect the same kind of persecution [TNTC].
4. This proves that they are God's servants [Gdt, NIGTC]: the fact that you are persecuted proves that you are God's servants *because* this is how God's prophets were treated. The idea of persecution for the sake of the Messiah was contrary to Jewish expectation, so Jesus justifies it by showing that it will raise them to the rank of God's prophets who endured persecution and also received a reward from God [Gdt].
5. This explains why they will be rewarded in heaven [ICC]: when you are persecuted like the prophets in this world, you will share in the prophets' rewards in heaven.

DISCOURSE UNIT: 6:24–26 [TNTC; HCSB, NLT]. The topic is the pronouncement of woes [TNTC], woe to the self-satisfied [HCSB], the sorrows foretold [NLT].

6:24 **But woe[a] to-you the rich (ones), because you-are-receiving-in-full[b] your comfort.[c]**

LEXICON—a. οὐαί (LN **22.9**) (BAGD 1.a. p. 591): 'woe' [AB, Arn, BAGD, BECNT, Lns, NTC, WBC; HCSB, KJV, NASB, NET, NIV, NRSV], 'alas (for you)' [BAGD; REB], 'disaster, horror' [LN]. The phrase οὐαὶ ὑμῖν 'woe to you' is translated 'how disastrous it will be for you' [**LN**], 'how horrible it will be for those' [GW], 'how terrible it will be for you' [NCV], 'how terrible for you' [TEV], 'what sorrows await you' [NLT], 'you are in for trouble' [CEV]. It is an exclamation denoting pain [BAGD, BECNT], pity [BECNT], or displeasure [BAGD]. The woes refer to the fact they will experience God's wrath rather than his blessing [NAC, TH]. See this word at 10:13; 11:42; 17:1; 21:23; 22:22.

b. pres. act. indic. of ἀπέχω (LN **90.67**) (BAGD 1. p. 84): 'to receive in full' [NASB], 'to have received in full' [Lns], 'to already have received in full' [NTC], 'to have received' [Arn, BECNT, WBC; HCSB, KJV, NRSV], 'to have already received' [NET, NIV], 'to already have' [AB; CEV], 'to have had' [GW, NCV, REB, TEV], 'to have (your) only (happiness) now' [NLT], 'to experience all one deserves' [LN], 'to experience all (the comfort) one is going to get' [**LN**], 'to receive a sum in full' [BAGD]. It is a commercial term [BAGD]. They can write a receipt saying 'received payment in full' [NTC]. This term was used in receipts to signify that they had received full payment of a debt and had no further claims on the debtor [BECNT, Lns, NIGTC, TNTC]. It means to receive comfort to the full so that there is nothing more to receive [ICC].

c. παράκλησις (LN 25.150) (BAGD 3. p. 618): 'comfort' [BAGD; GW, HCSB, NASB, NET, NIV], 'consolation' [AB, Arn, BAGD, BECNT, Lns, NTC, WBC; KJV, NRSV], 'encouragement' [LN], 'an easy life' [CEV, NCV, TEV], 'happiness' [NLT], 'time of happiness' [REB]. The word represents the thing or condition that brings someone satisfaction, happiness, and fulfillment [TG].

QUESTION—What is meant by saying 'Woe to you'?

1. This is an expression of compassion or pity [BECNT, NIGTC, TNTC]: alas for you. Instead of expressing a threat, it reveals compassion and regret [TNTC]. It expresses pity for those who will be judged by God [NIGTC]. This expression of pity was intended to warn them of danger and the nearness of judgment [BECNT].

2. This is a declaration of judgment [AB, BNTC, LN (22.6), Lns, NTC, TH; CEV, GW, NCV, NLT, TEV]: 'how disastrous it will be for you' [LN]. In the beatitudes the disciples were told how blessed they would be and here the wicked are told how cursed they would be [NTC]. The woes are virtually opposite to the beatitudes although 'blessed' is an adjective and

LUKE 6:24   247

'woe' is an interjection [AB]. Instead of expressing pity, it is a curse and judgment that expresses displeasure [TH]. This is an expression of the Lord's judgment [Lns]. Jesus is not pronouncing a curse on them but speaking of the future to which he has clear insight [BNTC]. This serves as a warning and threat [AB, NTC].

QUESTION—Who were the rich people Jesus addressed as 'you'?

The use of 'you' formally corresponds to the 'you' who are blessed in the preceding beatitudes [TH, TNTC]. The rich are the opposite of the poor in 6:20 [Lns, TG]. Jesus was not addressing the disciples since they were not rich [Crd, TNTC], and it is not until 6:27 that the disciples are directly addressed again [Crd]. This is a generalization since some disciples were rich [BECNT, Gdt, ICC]. This addresses the rich who trusted in their wealth [NTC]. Jesus was dealing with the historical condition at that time in which the rich and powerful people as a class were already opposed to Jesus' teaching and thus excluded themselves from the kingdom of God [Gdt]. The rich thought that they had all that they needed without the kingdom of God. This is a spiritual condition and some may be poor in money but still be trusting in themselves or in something they value while not trusting in God [Lns]. Therefore the rich are not excluded for merely being rich, but for the attitude the rich often displayed [BECNT]. The rich people here are not addressed just because of their economic status, but because of the accompanying arrogance, haughtiness, and dishonesty [NAC].

1. This is a case of apostrophe where an imaginary audience is addressed since the rich people were not present in the crowd [Crd, ICC, TH, WBC]. Even if the rich were not present, the woes served as a warning to those who heard them and to others who would hear about this teaching [ICC].

2. The rich people were among those who were listening to Jesus [AB, Gdt, My, NIGTC, TG]. They were not disciples [My, TG, TNTC]. They were people in the crowd who were in spiritual danger [NIGTC].

QUESTION—What is the comfort they have received?

Their comfort was obtained from their social and economic status [AB]. Their consolation consisted in thinking they had everything they wanted and needed nothing else [AB, Lns, Su]. They were contented with the good life they were able to provide for themselves [WBC]. The comfort they already have received consisted of the possessions they have acquired and that is their full payment, with nothing to come to them from God in the future [BECNT]. Whatever happiness or prosperity they now have will be all they will ever have [TG].

6:25 Woe to you, the (ones who) are-well-fed[a] now, because you-will-hunger.

LEXICON—a. perf. pass. participle of ἐμπίπλημι (LN 23.17) (BAGD 1. p. 256): 'to be well fed' [CEV, GW, NASB, NIV, REB], 'to be full' [HCSB, KJV, NCV, NRSV, TEV], 'to be filled' [Arn, BAGD], 'to have plenty to eat' [BAGD], 'to be well satisfied with food' [NET], 'to be satisfied with food, to be filled with food' [LN], 'to be satisfied and prosperous' [NLT].

QUESTION—What is meant by being well fed?

They are the people who are sated with food [NIGTC]. Some extend the idea of being sated with food to being sated with all the good things of life [ICC, Lns, TH, TNTC]. They have achieved earthly success and have reached their goals in life [Arn]. They have all that they want [TH, TNTC]. It means much the same as 'you who are rich', but emphasizes the state of the persons who think that their material possessions are all-sufficient and there is no need of God [TNTC].

QUESTION—What is meant by the threat of hunger?

The time will come when they will be hungry [TH]. Many take hunger to refer mainly to a spiritual condition [ICC, Lns, Su, TNTC]. They will not have the spiritual food of God's kingdom [ICC]. They may be satisfied throughout their lives, but in the kingdom of God these people are paupers [TNTC]. They will come to the realization that they are empty and nothing will bring them satisfaction [Su]. Everything that satisfies them now will be a disappointment in the end [Lns].

Woe (to you), the (ones who) are-laughing[a] now, because you will mourn[b] and weep.

LEXICON—a. pres. act. participle of γελάω (LN 25.135): 'to laugh'. See this word at 6:21.

b. fut. act. indic. of πενθέω (LN 25.42) (BAGD 1. p. 642): 'to mourn' [AB, Arn, BAGD, BECNT, Lns, NTC, WBC; all versions except CEV, NCV], 'to be sad' [BAGD, LN; NCV], 'to grieve' [BAGD, LN], 'to cry' [CEV]. This means to experience grief as the result of the depressing circumstances of one's condition [LN]. It refers to a person's inner state that causes him to weep [WBC]. The verbs 'mourn' and 'weep' occur together as a conventional pair [WBC], and together indicate intense grief [BECNT, TH].

QUESTION—Who are the ones who are laughing?

This does not refer to wholesome laughter [BECNT, MGC, Su, TNTC], rather it is a shallow merriment [TNTC]. They laugh because they are happy with their present lot in life [WBC]. Their laughter reflects their feeling of self-sufficiency and satisfaction with their material possessions [Su]. Their carefree laughter expresses their contentment with their present successes [AB] and prosperity [ICC]. They are delighted in all the pleasures of the world they have desired [Lns]. They revel in silly laughter while they reject God and never mourn over their sins [NTC]. They laugh because they are self-satisfied and there is an evil sense included as they look down on the needs of others [NIGTC, WBC].

QUESTION—Why will they mourn and weep?

Their success will turn to failure [AB]. Their loss of prosperity will cause them to grieve, but even worse will be the loss of spiritual joy in the hereafter [ICC]. In eternity their mourning will never cease [NTC]. They will come to realize that their present lifestyle has resulted only in a sense of emptiness and futility [Su]. They will weep over the lack of blessing in the eternal future [BECNT].

6:26 **Woe (to you) when all people speak well[a] of-you, because in-the-same-way[b] their ancestors were-doing to-the false-prophets.[c]**

LEXICON—a. καλῶς (LN 65.23) (BAGD 3. p. 401): 'well' [AB, Arn, BAGD, BECNT, LN, NTC, WBC; HCSB, KJV, NASB, NET, NIV, NRSV, REB, TEV], 'fair' [Lns], 'good things' [CEV, NCV], 'nice things' [GW]. The phrase 'to speak well of' is translated 'to praise' [NLT].

b. κατὰ τὰ αὐτά (LN 64.16): The phrase κατὰ τὰ αὐτά 'in the same way' [LN, WBC; NASB] is also translated 'in just the same way' [AB, NTC], 'in the same manner' [Arn], 'according to the same things' [Lns], 'the same things' [NCV, NET], 'the very same things' [TEV], 'that is how' [NIV, REB], 'that is what' [CEV, NRSV], 'that's the way' [GW], 'this is the way' [HCSB], 'so' [BECNT; KJV], 'also' [NLT]. The phrase 'because in the same way their ancestors were doing' is identical with the phrase in the last clause of 6:23.

c. ψευδοπροφήτης (LN 53.81) (BAGD p. 892): 'false prophet' [AB, Arn, BAGD, BECNT, LN, NTC, WBC; all versions except CEV], 'prophet who tells lies' [CEV]. This means someone who falsely claims to be a prophet and as a result proclaims what is false [BAGD, LN]. It refers to prophets who wrongly interpreted God's will [TH].

QUESTION—What is wrong with people speaking well of the disciples?

Popularity scarcely happens without a sacrifice of principle [TNTC], and may indicate failure to take the hard way involved in being a disciple [Su]. False prophets and wealthy people gained general approval by doing nothing to unsettle the status quo [NICNT, WBC]. The wealthy are admired and praised by those who hope to win their favor, but such praise is not an indication of merit [ICC]. People do not speak well of those who take a stand for the truth [NTC]. This warns the disciples and the crowd against seeking acceptance for one's message at the expense of truthfulness and if they do, they will be acting like the false prophets who set a bad precedent in the history of Israel [BECNT].

DISCOURSE UNIT: 6:27–38 [BECNT, NICNT, WBC]. The topic is on giving and receiving [NICNT], an exhortation to love and be merciful [BECNT], the call to the love of enemies and nonjudgmental generosity [WBC].

DISCOURSE UNIT: 6:27–36 [NAC, NIGTC, TNTC; CEV, GW, HCSB, NCV, NIV, NLT, NRSV, TEV]. The topic is love [TNTC], love for enemies [NAC; CEV, GW, NCV, NIV, NLT, NRSV, TEV], love your enemies [HCSB], love and mercy [NIGTC].

6:27 But to-you the (ones who) are-listening I-say, Love your enemies, do good[a] to-the (ones who) hate you, **6:28** bless[b] the (ones who) curse[c] you, pray for the (ones who) mistreat/threaten[d] you.

LEXICON—a. καλῶς (LN 65.23) (BAGD 3. p. 401): 'good' [BAGD, LN]. The phrase 'to do good to' [AB, Arn, BECNT, NTC, WBC; all versions except CEV, GW] is also translated 'to be good to' [CEV], 'to be kind to' [GW], 'to do well to' [Lns].
- b. pres. act. impera. of εὐλογέω (LN 33.470) (BAGD 2.a. p. 322): 'to bless' [AB, Arn, BAGD, BECNT, LN, Lns, NTC, WBC; all versions except CEV, NLT], 'to ask God to bless' [CEV], 'to pray for the happiness of' [NLT]. It means to ask God to bestow his favor on someone [LN, TG], to ask God's favor on another person [BECNT].
- c. pres. mid./pass. participle of καταράομαι (LN 33.471) (BAGD p. 417): 'to curse' [AB, Arn, BAGD, BECNT, LN, Lns, NTC, WBC; all versions]. To curse someone is to express a desire that the person will experience evil and suffering [TG]. It is asking God to harm or judge someone [BECNT]. It expresses a desire that God will strike someone with damnation [Lns].
- d. pres. act. participle of ἐπηρεάζω (LN **88.129**) (BAGD p. 285): 'to mistreat' [AB, BAGD, **LN**, NTC; HCSB, NASB, NET, NIV, TEV], 'to abuse' [Arn, BAGD, BECNT; NRSV], 'to be cruel to' [CEV, NCV], 'to hurt' [NLT], 'to treat spitefully' [REB], 'to despitefully use' [Lns; KJV], 'to threaten' [BAGD, WBC], 'to insult' [GW]. 'Mistreat' carries with it the implication of threats and abuse [LN].

QUESTION—Who were the ones who were listening to what Jesus was saying?
Jesus was addressing all the people who had gathered to listen, both the disciples and the crowd mentioned in 6:17–18, but since Jesus made a contrast between the people that he was exhorting to do as he says and 'sinners' (6:32–34), he was speaking to his disciples in particular [TG]. The transitional ἀλλά ὑμῖν 'but to you' indicates that Jesus was contrasting his faithful disciples with those upon whom he announced the 'woes' in 6:24–26 [BECNT, EGT, ICC, My, NAC, NIGTC, TH, WBC]. The audience was the disciples [TH]. Of course all who were there were listening. Jesus referred to those who were listening with a desire to heed what he says, that is, who were true disciples [Lns, My, NICNT].

QUESTION—How is it possible to love one's enemies?
Love is not an emotional affection here, but the desire to do good to other persons, even to enemies who hate and curse you [NIGTC]. It is not a sentiment, it is to actively and whole-heartedly pursue the good of enemies [WBC]. Disciples may not be able to like an enemy, but by God's help they can love their enemies by desiring to find out what is wrong with them and to seek to remove the wrong thing [Lns]. To love people is to recognize their value as persons and to desire what is best for them [Su]. Love is expressed by kind deeds, words of blessing, and prayer [Arn]. Love is the major topic of this section [BECNT, Lns, TNTC], and the command to love is the more

LUKE 6:27-28 251

general command in this section [NIGTC]. The following three commands specify the kind of love that Jesus commands [AB, BECNT, Gdt, Lns, NAC, NICNT].

QUESTION—What is meant by ἐπηρεάζω 'mistreat'?
1. It refers to physical ill-treatment [AB, BECNT, ICC, **LN**, Lns; HCSB, KJV, NASB, NET, NIV, NLT, NRSV, REB, TEV]: those who physically abuse you. It refers to the harsh treatment that comes with persecution [BECNT, ICC]. Since this is the climax of evil acts against disciples, it cannot mean speaking insults since it would then be less than the preceding cursings [Lns].
2. It refers to verbal abuse [EGT, NIGTC, TH, WBC; GW]: who insult or threaten you. This is synonymous with 'reproach' in 6:22 [TH].

QUESTION—Who were the people who were their enemies and who hated, cursed, and mistreated them?

The listeners would probably first think of the Romans who suppressed them and then of the Gentiles in general. But even among the Jews there were enemies because of religious, social, and economic conditions [Su]. In the context of 6:22, 'when people hate you and when they ostracize you and they reproach you and they throw out your name as evil because of the Son of Man', the reference is to people who hate the disciples because they are followers of Jesus [NAC, TH]. This refers to the enemies of Christians as a group [AB]. Persecutors are especially in mind, although it includes much more [NIGTC].

6:29 **To the (one) hitting[a] you (singular) on the cheek, offer[b] also the other, and from the (one) taking-away[c] your coat,[d] also do- not -withhold[e] the shirt.[f]**

LEXICON—a. pres. act. participle of τύπτω (LN 19.1) (BAGD 1. p. 830): 'to hit' [LN; HCSB, NASB, REB, TEV], 'to strike' [AB, Arn, BAGD, BECNT, LN, Lns, NTC, WBC; GW, NET, NIV, NRSV], 'to slap' [CEV, NCV, NLT], 'to smite' [KJV]. This describes a blow made with the hand or fist [NIGTC]. It probably is an insulting blow from someone who slaps a disciple for his allegiance to Jesus [AB, NAC], or a deliberate insult [TG]. This is an insulting slap made with the back of the hand [BECNT]. It probably indicates public rejection, perhaps accompanying expulsion from the synagogue [BECNT; NET]. Or, instead of a contemptuous slap, it appears to be a violent blow with the fist to the side of the jaw [Gdt, ICC, TNTC].

b. pres. act. impera. of παρέχω (LN 90.91) (BAGD 1.a. p. 626): 'to offer' [AB, Arn, BAGD, BECNT, NTC, WBC; GW, HCSB, KJV, NASB, NCV, NET, NRSV, REB], 'to turn' [NIV, NLT], 'to present' [BAGD, Lns], 'to give' [LN], 'to let (him) hit' [TEV], 'to not stop from slapping' [CEV].

c pres. act. participle of αἴρω (LN 15.203) (BAGD 4. p. 24): 'to take away' [BAGD, BECNT, LN, Lns, NTC; HCSB, KJV, NASB, NET, NRSV,

REB], 'to take' [AB, Arn, WBC; CEV, GW, NCV, NIV, TEV], 'to demand' [NLT].

d. ἱμάτιον (LN 6.172) (BAGD 2. p. 376): 'coat' [BECNT, LN; all versions except KJV, NIV], 'cloak' [AB, BAGD, LN, WBC; KJV, NIV], 'robe' [BAGD, Lns], 'mantle' [Arn], 'outer garment' [NTC]. This refers to all types of outer garments [AB, LN]. It was a long outer garment [Lns], a flowing garment which reached the feet [TG].

e. aorist act. subj. of κωλύω (LN 13.146) (BAGD 3. p. 461): 'to withhold' [BAGD, BECNT, Lns, NTC; NASB, NET, NRSV], 'to hold back' [HCSB], 'to try to keep back' [CEV], 'to stop from taking' [GW, NCV, NIV], 'to forbid to take' [KJV], 'to refuse' [Arn, BAGD, WBC], 'to deny' [BAGD], 'to hinder' [AB, LN]. The phrase 'do not withhold' is translated 'offer' [NLT], 'let him have' [REB, TEV]. Negating an action is a figure of speech in which the opposite action is urged, so 'do not withhold' means 'offer' the shirt as well [WBC].

f. χιτών (LN 6.176) (BAGD p. 882): 'shirt' [BAGD, LN; all versions except KJV, NET, NIV], 'tunic' [AB, Arn, Lns, WBC; NET, NIV], 'coat' [KJV], 'undershirt' [BECNT], 'undergarment' [NTC]. This refers to a garment that is worn underneath the outer garment [LN; NET]. It was a garment worn next to the skin [AB, Lns]. It was a long garment or tunic worn next to the skin and was longer than a shirt [NET]. This inner garment had short sleeves and reached to the knees [TG]. See this word at 3:11; 9:3.

QUESTION—Why does Jesus change from addressing his audience with second person plural forms of the pronouns and verbs (6:27–28 and 6:30b–36) to the second person singular form here in 6:29–30a?

It is an intentional change in order to address every person as an individual and it does not mean that Jesus has picked out one person in the audience to address [TG]. It personalizes the illustrations by making a direct appeal [BECNT]. The singular form is due to the specific nature of the illustrations and the use of plural forms would be clumsy [NAC]. The singular form is more appropriate for commands that relate to particular situations [NIGTC]. Or, it shows that Luke has combined passages from his sources [Crd, WBC].

QUESTION—What is the reason for offering the other cheek?

It would be an unusual and dramatic way to show that a follower of Christ did not live by the principle of getting even [Su]. It shows that a disciple bears an insult in a spirit of love and is ready to take more abuse [AB]. The spirit of hatred and yearning for revenge is condemned and turning the cheek shows in both attitude and deed that a disciple is filled with a spirit of love [NTC]. A literal offering of the other cheek is not always the best way to obey this command since this concerns an attitude of not seeking revenge and a readiness to accept another injury if need be [TNTC]. A disciple will yield in love, and if there is occasion to resist, it must be done in love [Gdt]. With persecution in mind, this means to continue ministering at the risk of further persecution [BECNT].

QUESTION—Why would someone take away a coat?

This is an action of a robber or thief [Arn, BECNT, Crd, EGT, Gdt, ICC, NAC, NIGTC, Su, TG]. It refers to a violent action in which the outer and more valuable garment is taken first [Crd, Gdt, ICC, NIGTC]. Reversing the sequence from Matthew 5:40, which describes a lawsuit in which first the shirt is taken, this seems to refer to highway robbery in which the robber first takes the outer coat [BAGD]. A robber tries to take away a coat and is offered the shirt as well [NIGTC]. Another view is a situation in which someone stole a coat after it had been removed and put aside to keep it from interfering with work and the owner then calls out to the thief that he will give him his shirt as well [Su].

QUESTION—What is the reason for giving the shirt as well?

This would dramatize the fact that the disciple lived a giving life, not a grasping one [Su]. Love knows no limits to its self-denial [Gdt]. The disciple is to try to keep contact with persons who are hostile to Jesus' way of life [NET]. Both commands in this verse are dramatic illustrations of the disciple's attitude to remain totally open to the actions of such people [WBC]. The point is that one should not seek revenge in regard to hostile religious opponents but remain vulnerable to repeated attacks [BECNT].

6:30 To-everyone asking[a] you (singular), give. And from the (one) taking-away[b] your (plural) things, do not demand-back.[c]

TEXT—Following παντί 'to everyone' some manuscripts add δέ 'but/and'. GNT does not mention this variant.

LEXICON—a. pres. act. participle of αἰτέω (LN 33.163) (BAGD p. 25): 'to ask' [Arn, BAGD, BECNT, Lns, NTC, WBC; CEV, HCSB, KJV, NASB, NCV, NET, NIV, REB], 'to ask for (something)' [BAGD, LN; GW, NLT, TEV], 'to beg' [AB; NRSV].

b. pres. act. participle of αἴρω (LN 15.203) (BAGD 4. p. 24): 'to take away'. See this word at 6:29.

c. pres. act. impera. of ἀπαιτέω (LN **33.165**) (BAGD 1. p. 80): 'to demand something back' [BAGD, BECNT; NASB, NIV, REB], 'to ask for something back' [BAGD, **LN**, Lns, WBC; HCSB, NCV, NET, TEV], 'to ask to return' [CEV], 'to ask again' [KJV, NRSV], 'to ask back' [Arn], 'to insist on getting something back' [GW], 'to try to get back' [NLT], 'to strive to get something back' [AB], 'to exact reimbursement' [NTC]. The verb means that a person asks for the return of something, such as a loan or stolen property, that he has the right to get back [TH]. The present tenses in this verse indicate continual action so that giving and not demanding back are to be habitual [ICC, Lns, TNTC, WBC]. A person must always be prepared to respond as Jesus commanded [BECNT].

QUESTION—What is being asked?

The object of the asking is not indicated and the cause for asking is intended to be of the widest application [AB, TH]. The context of 6:34–35 suggests that this includes loaning, but it must also include giving to the poor who have legitimate requests concerning their needs [BECNT]. Probably a person asks due to poverty [NTC], and 'asking' refers to begging [AB, Su, TH; NET, NRSV]. A very different view is that this is not about responding to the request of a beggar but to the request of someone who has the upper hand and who might go on to take it if refused [WBC].

QUESTION—Is the command to give to everyone meant to be taken literally?

The spirit of the command is stressed by some. Someone's need should not be met with selfish reserve [AB]. Generosity is a concrete expression of love [BECNT]. This is not to be taken literally [Su, TNTC] and the radical command is hyperbolical in order to shock the listeners out of their own way of thinking [BECNT]. We are to give to everyone what we can and which is in accord with love for that person [Arn]. It is an overstatement for effect and we find an exception in 2 Thessalonians 3:6–13 [NIC]. Jesus would not direct us to indiscriminate giving that would encourage shiftlessness and other evils, so here he is speaking about always being ready to help without expecting a return [Lns]. We ought to be willing to give whatever may be lawfully given and the wish to keep what we have is not to be a motive for refusing [ICC]. This was not intended to be followed literally, but the spirit that is commanded is to give out of love even if it means to be deprived of everything. In a given case, the decision of whether or not to give must be based on the motive of love [TNTC].

QUESTION—What is meant by someone taking away something which we are not to demand back?

The verb itself does not imply that force is used [ICC]. However, the context implies that force is used in taking it away [AB, BECNT, Lns, NAC, NIGTC, NTC, WBC]. The verb 'to take away' is the same word used in 6:29 where it means to wrongfully take away by force [Lns, NAC, NIGTC, NTC]. The verb is used here with the sense of theft, whether by stealth or force [AB]. This is not addressing the fact that there are times when a person should stand up for his rights. This passage focuses on the principle that our personal attitude should never be one of taking revenge and sometimes it is better to let a thief keep stolen goods [NTC]. The commands are not to be taken completely literally, rather the spirit being commended is that of giving freely, even to people who have no claim upon us [NIGTC]. It is better to suffer the loss of goods than to let wrong emotions possess one's soul [Lns].

6:31 And[a] just-as you-want that people do[b] to-you do to-them similarly.[c]

TEXT—Before ποιεῖτε 'do' in the last clause, some manuscripts insert καὶ ὑμεῖς 'you also'. GNT rejects this addition with a B decision, indicating that the text is almost certain. Καὶ ὑμεῖς 'you also' is read by KJV.

LEXICON—a. καί (LN 89.12): 'and' [AB, Arn, LN, Lns, NTC; KJV], not explicit [BECNT, WBC; all versions except KJV].
b. pres. act. subj. of ποιέω (LN 41.7) (BAGD I.2.a.β. p. 682): 'to do' [BAGD, LN], 'to do (to you)' [Arn, BECNT, Lns, NTC; KJV, NCV,

NIV, NRSV], 'to do (for you)' [GW, HCSB, NLT, TEV], 'to treat' [AB, WBC; CEV, NASB, NET, REB]. It means 'to behave towards' [TH]. This verb concerns behaving or acting in a particular way with respect to someone [LN].

c. ὁμοίως (LN64.1) (BAGD p. 568): 'similarly' [BAGD, LN], 'likewise' [BAGD, LN, Lns; KJV], 'so' [BECNT, NTC], 'in the same way' [BAGD, WBC], 'the same' [HCSB], 'in like manner' [Arn]. The combination καθώς 'just as' and ὁμοίως 'similarly' indicates a strong comparison [TH]. Most translations place the command clause in front of the comparison clause and leave out this word [AB; all versions except KJV]: do to them just as you want that people do to you.

QUESTION—How does the conjunction καί 'and' relate this command to the preceding ones?

This is the climax of the commands in 6:27–31 [Su]. It is a general principle that covers the others and can be translated 'in short' or 'in a word' [Gdt, ICC]. It indicates a summary of what it means to love one's enemies [NAC, TNTC]. This indicates the principle behind what has been described in the preceding applications [Gdt]. It introduces a rule that applies to all relationships [NTC, TH], and can be translated 'and further' [TH]. It appears to indicate a general heading for the hypothetical cases which follow [EGT]. This goes beyond the idea that you abstain from acts that you would not like done to you [TNTC]. This positive form means this is how you are to treat others regardless of the way they treat you [NIGTC, TNTC, WBC]. Since Matthew puts this command in a later place in the sermon (at Matt. 7:12), probably Luke has moved this command from its original position in the sermon so that it is not directly connected to the preceding verses [AB, Alf, EGT, WBC]. Others think that Luke has it in its original place [Gdt, NIGTC]. Or, since this is in a somewhat different form than the saying in Matthew, it is quite possible that two distinct sayings occurred in two places in the sermon [BECNT].

6:32 And if you-love the (ones who) love you, what-kind-of[a] credit[b] is (that) to-you? Because even the sinners[c] love the (ones who) love them. 6:33 Because even if you-do-good to-the (ones who) do-good to-you, what credit is (that) to-you? Even the sinners do the same.

TEXT—In 6:33, some manuscripts omit the beginning γάρ 'because'. GNT does not deal with this variant in the apparatus but brackets γάρ 'for' in its text, indicating that the Committee had difficulty making the decision. Γάρ 'because' is omitted by all versions. The omission by KJV is because it is omitted in the Textus Receptus; the omission by other versions may be either a textual or stylistic decision, since γάρ 'because' makes a difficult rendering.

TEXT—In 6:33, following καί 'even' in the last clause of this verse, some manuscripts add γάρ 'because'. GNT does not deal with this variant. Γάρ 'because' is read by KJV, NASB.

LEXICON—a. ποῖος (LN 58.30) (BAGD 1.a.β. p. 684): 'what kind of' [BAGD, LN], 'what sort of' [LN]. See the whole clause in b. below.
  b. χάρις (LN 25.89, 33.350) (BAGD 1.b. p. 877): 'credit' [BAGD], 'favor' [BAGD, LN (25.89)], 'good will' [LN (25.89)], 'thanks' [LN (33.350)]. The word comes close to meaning 'reward' in this passage [BAGD]. The clause 'what credit is that to you?' in 6:32 and in 6:33 is translated 'what credit is that to you?' [BECNT, NTC; HCSB, NASB, NET, NIV, NRSV], 'what credit is it to you?' [WBC], 'what credit is there in that?' [AB], 'do you deserve any thanks for that?' [GW], 'what thank have ye?' [KJV], 'what thanks are there for you?' [Lns], 'what praise should you get?' [NCV], 'what credit is that to you?...what credit is there in that?' [REB], 'what have you gained in God's sight?...what have you really gained?' [Arn], 'will God praise you for that?...will God be pleased with you for that?' [CEV], 'do you think you deserve credit...is that so wonderful?' [NLT], 'why should you receive a blessing?' [TEV].
  c. ἁμαρτωλός (LN 88.295): 'sinner' [AB, Arn, BECNT, LN, Lns, NTC, WBC; all versions]. The parallel passages in Matthew 5:46–47 use the words 'tax collectors' and 'Gentiles' and Luke has probably used the broader connotation of 'sinners' to cover them all [AB]. They are common and open sinners, people who had no regard for God's laws [NTC]. They were outsiders to the community because of their behavior [NICNT]. Or, sinners are all those who do not follow God's way [Su, TG], who are not religious [TG], or who act in a normal human way without consciously trying to obey God's rules [TG]. It refers to people in general [BECNT]. Although sinners may love with intelligence and purpose, they do so with selfish motives to get full returns [Lns].
QUESTION—In the last clause of 6:32, what relationship is indicated by γάρ 'because'?
  This explains why it is of no credit to them [MGC, WBC]: there is no credit to you *because* even sinners do that. Even sinners exhibit such a conditional kind of love [MGC]. This conjunction is not explicit in many translations [AB, NTC; CEV, GW, NCV, NIV, NLT, REB, TEV].
QUESTION—At the beginning of 6:33, what relationship is indicated by γάρ 'because'?
  The conjunction 'because' is unnecessary and probably was added in error [NIGTC]. It is not translated in any of the versions. Even if καὶ γάρ 'and because' is accepted as the text, it is best translated as a single καί 'and' [TH].
QUESTION—What is meant by the rhetorical question 'What kind of credit is that to you?'
  This rhetorical question implies a negative answer, 'no kind at all' [Lns, TG, TH]. Some focus on the credit one deserves [BECNT, Lns, TH; NASB, NET, NIV, NLT, NRSV, REB]: you haven't done anything for which you deserve credit. Others focus on a response of praise [CEV, NCV], thanks [Crd, ICC, Lns, WBC; KJV], or blessing and favor [EGT; TEV]. The credit

or praise may come from God [ICC, Lns, MGC], or from people [TH]. God will not give that person any recognition for that [Lns]. God's favorable response is virtually synonymous with a reward from him and the word 'reward' is used in 6:35 [BECNT]. Most understand this to mean the same as the parallel passage in Matthew 5:46. τίνα μισθὸν ἔχετε; 'what reward do you have?' [AB, BECNT, Crd, EGT, ICC, NIGTC]. It refers to God's recompense for this act [My]. The reward is God's recompense of beneficence to express his thanks [Crd]. This conduct is not wrong, but it brings no reward or gracious thanks from God [NIGTC].

6:34 And if you-lend[a] (to those) from whom you-expect[b] to-receive,[c] what-kind-of credit is (that) to-you? Even sinners lend to-sinners in-order-that they-may-get-back[d] the same.

TEXT—Before ἁμαρτωλοί 'sinners', some manuscripts add γάρ 'because'. GNT does not deal mention this variant. Γάρ 'because' is read by KJV.
LEXICON—a. aorist act. subj. of δανείζω (LN **57.209**) (BAGD 1. p. 170): 'to lend' [AB, Arn, BAGD, BECNT, **LN**, Lns, NTC, WBC; HCSB, KJV, NASB, NET, NIV, NRSV, REB, TEV], 'to lend money' [CEV, NLT], 'to lend things' [NCV], 'to lend anything' [GW].
  b. pres. act. indic. of ἐλπίζω (LN **30.54**) (BAGD 2. p. 252): 'to expect' [BAGD, **LN**, NTC; GW, HCSB, NASB, NIV, REB], 'to hope' [AB, BAGD, BECNT, LN, Lns, WBC; KJV, NCV, NET, NRSV, TEV], 'to think' [CEV], not explicit [Arn; NLT].
  c. aorist act. infin. of λαμβάνω (LN 57.125): 'to receive' [BECNT, LN, Lns, WBC; HCSB, KJV, NASB, NRSV], 'to get something' [AB], 'to get something back' [GW, NCV], 'to get it back' [TEV], 'to be repaid' [NET, REB], 'to receive payment' [Arn], 'to expect repayment' [NIV]. The phrase 'to those from whom you expect to receive' is translated 'to someone you think will pay you back' [CEV], 'only to those who can repay you' [NLT].
  d. aorist act. subj. of ἀπολαμβάνω (LN **57.136**) (BAGD 2. p. 94): 'to get back' [BAGD, **LN**], 'to receive back, to be paid back' [LN]. The phrase ἀπολάβωσιν τὰ ἴσα 'to get back the same' is translated 'to receive the same' [BECNT], 'to get back the same amount' [NCV, TEV], 'to get back as much again' [AB], 'to receive the same amount back' [Arn; NASB], 'they may duly receive the same' [Lns], 'to get it all back' [CEV], 'to be repaid in full' [NTC; HCSB, NET, NIV, REB], 'to get back what they lend' [GW], 'to receive as much again' [KJV, NRSV], 'for a full return' [NLT], 'to receive in turn the same favor' [WBC].
QUESTION—What is being lent?
  1. It is money [BAGD, ICC, Lns, NIGTC, NTC, Su, WBC; CEV, NASB, NET, NLT, TEV]: if you lend money.
  2. It can be anything [BECNT, TH; GW, NCV]: if you lend something. It may refer to money, food, etc. with the understanding that an equivalent sum or quantity be returned [TH].

258 LUKE 6:34

QUESTION—What is it that the lender expects to receive and the sinner expects to get back 'the same'?
>   1. They expect to receive back the equivalent amount of money that was lent [NIGTC, TH; CEV, GW, KJV], or the same quantity of things that were lent [TH]. They expect to get back the same sum [TH]. Charging interest to other Jews is forbidden in the OT, so this must refer to lending money out of kindness [BECNT, WBC].
>   2. They expect to receive back the interest as well as the amount lent [ICC, Lns, Rb, Su]. They will be repaid in full [ICC]. This refers to a business transaction [Lns].
>   3. They expect the person who borrowed from them will lend to them in the future [BECNT, Gdt, NAC, NICNT, NIGTC, NTC, WBC]. They expect similar treatment when it is their turn to borrow [WBC].

6:35 **But love your enemies and do-good and lend expecting-back/despairing[a] nothing. And your reward[b] will-be great, and you will-be children of-(the)-Most-High,[c]**

LEXICON—a. pres. act. participle of ἀπελπίζω (LN **30.54**) (BAGD p. 84): 'to expect in return' [BAGD, LN], 'to despair' [BAGD]. The phrase 'expecting nothing' is translated 'expecting nothing in return' [BECNT, **LN**, WBC; HCSB, NASB, NRSV], 'expecting nothing back' [NET; similarly TEV], 'without expecting to get anything back' [NTC; GW, NIV], 'without expecting to be paid back' [CEV], 'without expecting any return' [REB], 'without hoping to get anything back' [NCV], 'without the hope of receiving payment' [Arn], 'hoping for nothing in due return' [Lns], 'hoping for nothing again' [KJV], 'looking for nothing in return' [AB], 'don't be concerned that they might not repay' [NLT].
>   b. μισθός (LN 38.14) (BAGD 2.a. p. 523): 'reward'. See this word and phrase at 6:23.
>   c. ὕψιστος (LN 12.4) (BAGD 2.b.α. p. 850): 'the Most High'. The phrase 'children of the Most High' is translated 'children of the Most High God' [GW, NCV, TEV], 'sons of the Most High' [AB, BECNT, NTC, WBC; HCSB, NASB, NET, NIV, REB], 'sons of the Highest' [Arn, Lns], 'children of the Highest' [KJV], 'children of the Most High' [NLT, NRSV], 'true children of God in heaven' [CEV]. The phrase 'son of' is a Semitic idiom meaning 'a disciple of' or 'one having the same nature as' [BNTC]. To be a child of someone means to share his character by nature [NICNT]. The phrase means to have the same nature as God [BNTC, TG, TH] and the same attitude [TG]. Moral likeness proves one's parentage [ICC]. See this word at 1:32, 35, 76; 8:28.

QUESTION—What relationship is indicated by πλήν 'but' at the beginning of this verse?

This indicates a contrast with the hypothetical cases described in 6:32–34 [EGT, ICC, NIGTC, TG, TH, WBC]. What they are now commanded to do is in contrast with what sinners do [TG]. This is an adversative conjunction, 'on the contrary', and after the wrong attitude of selfish love shown by sinners, there is a return to the original command given in 6:27, 'Love your enemies, do good to the ones hating you' [Lns]. This is a positive conclusion to the passage [NIGTC, WBC].

QUESTION—To whom are they to do good and to lend?

Following the command 'love your enemies', these two commands also have as their objects 'your enemies' [NTC; GW, NCV, NIV, NLT]: love your enemies, do good to them, and lend to them. The similar passage in 6:27, 'love your enemies, do good to the ones hating you' and the preceding command to love their enemies indicate that these three closely connected commands here have as their object 'your enemies' [NTC]. However, enemies would not be borrowing from them, so the objects of the last two commands are to be left unspecified and not limited to 'your enemies' [Lns].

QUESTION—Does ἀπελπίζοντες mean 'expecting' or 'despairing'?

1. It means 'expecting' [AB, Alf, Arn, BAGD, BECNT, BNTC, Crd, EGT, Gdt, Lns, NICNT, NIGTC, NTC, Su, TG, TH, WBC; all versions except NLT]: lend, expecting nothing back. The normal meaning of the verb is 'despair' but this does not fit this context, which requires that this be taken to mean 'to expect nothing in return' from the one who asks to borrow something [BAGD, BECNT, Gdt, TH]. It means that they should not expect to get anything back [Crd, NTC, TH; CEV, GW, NIV]. They must lend without expecting to be repaid [TG]. They must lend without expecting any favor in return [BECNT]. They must lend without looking for a return [Lns]. This forbids lending with a view to gain interest [NIGTC].

2. It means 'despairing' [ICC, My, Rb, TNTC; NLT]: lend, despairing of nothing or no one. 'Despair' is the usual meaning of the verb [ICC, TNTC]. This means never despairing over not getting the money back, so it implies they must help in even hopeless cases [Rb]. They must not 'be concerned that they might not repay' [NLT]. It can be taken as 'despairing of nothing' (never despairing) [ICC, TNTC], and mean never doubting that God will requite you or else never despairing about your money. It could be taken as 'despairing of no one' [ICC, TNTC] and mean never doubting that the debtor will pay [ICC].

QUESTION—What relationship is indicated by καί 'and' which begins the second sentence, 'and your reward will be great'?

This indicates the result of obeying the three commands in the preceding sentence [NTC]: love, do good, and lend in those ways *and then* this will happen. This conjunction is translated 'then' to show that it the result [AB, NTC; CEV, GW, HCSB, NCV, NET, NIV, NLT, TEV]. The three commands are equivalent to conditions for receiving the reward [NIGTC]. Although he did not urge his disciples to obey for the sake of a reward, he states that a reward is there [TNTC].

QUESTION—What relationship is indicated by καί 'and' in the clause 'and you will be children of the Most High'?
1. This clause describes the reward [NTC, TH; REB]: your reward will be great: you will be sons of the Most High.
2. This clause refers to something different from the reward [AB, BECNT, Lns, NAC, NICNT, NIGTC, Su, WBC]: your reward will be great, *and also* you will show yourselves to be sons of the Most High. Love for enemies shows that the disciples have a nobility like that of God [WBC]. The second result is that they will display the character that belongs to God's children [Su], showing that they are 'true' children of God [CEV]. When they love their enemies, they are imitating their Father and show that they are faithful to him [BECNT]. They will show that they are God's children by their imitation of God's character [NIGTC]. Love is the mark of sonship [AB]. Love does not make us sons of God but it proves that we are his sons [Lns]. The verb ἔσεσθε 'you will be' does not mean that they will then become sons of God, but that they will show themselves to be sons of God [NAC, NICNT]. Instead of being a reward, it indicates the reason why they must obey the three commands [NICNT]. The reward is being recognized as a faithful child of God and receiving God's blessing for this [BECNT]. The reward is not payment for obeying, but the evidence of God's approval [WBC]. The reward is the sense of well-being in having done what is right [Su]. The reward is connected with communion with God and opportunities for further service [TNTC]. The reward includes inner satisfaction in helping others and all the blessings of salvation throughout eternity [NTC].

because[a] he is kind[b] to the ungrateful[c] and wicked[d] (people).
LEXICON—a. ὅτι (LN 89.33): 'because' [LN, Lns, NTC; NCV, NET, NIV, REB], 'for' [AB, Arn, BECNT, WBC; HCSB, KJV, NASB, NLT, NRSV, TEV], 'after all' [GW], not explicit [CEV].
b. χρηστός (LN 88.68) (BAGD 1.b.β. p. 886): 'kind' [AB, Arn, BAGD, BECNT, LN, Lns, NTC, WBC; all versions except CEV, HCSB, TEV], 'good' [CEV, TEV], 'gracious' [HCSB].
c. ἀχάριστος (LN **25.101**, **33.353**) (BAGD p. 128): 'ungrateful' [AB, Arn, BAGD, BECNT, **LN**, NTC, WBC; HCSB, NASB, NCV, NET, NIV, NRSV, REB, TEV], 'unthankful' [LN, Lns; CEV, GW, KJV, NLT]. They are ungrateful in that they do not thank God for the blessings he gives them [NTC].
d. πονηρός (LN 88.110) (BAGD 2.a. p. 147): 'wicked' [AB, BAGD, LN, Lns, NTC; NIV, NLT, NRSV, REB, TEV], 'evil' [Arn, BAGD, LN, WBC; GW, HCSB, KJV, NASB, NET], 'sinful' [BAGD], 'full of sin' [NCV], 'cruel' [CEV], 'selfish' [BECNT].

QUESTION—What relationship is indicated by ὅτι 'because'?
It indicates the reason why obeying the commands pertaining to love for others will show that they are the sons of the Most High [Lns, TH]. The

commands are based upon God's character [NAC], and their moral likeness to God will prove their parentage [ICC]. It indicates that the reason for the commands at the beginning of the verse is that God is also gracious to the wicked and ungrateful, and those who treats such people in a similar manner reflect their relationship to their Father [BECNT].

6:36 Be compassionate[a] just-as also your Father is compassionate.

TEXT—Following γίνεσθε 'be' some manuscripts evidently add οὖν 'therefore', although GNT does not mention this variant. Οὖν 'therefore' is read by KJV.

LEXICON—a. οἰκτίρμων (LN **88.81**) (BAGD p. 561): 'compassionate' [BAGD, LN, Lns, WBC; NLT, REB], 'merciful' [AB, Arn, BAGD, BECNT, **LN**; GW, HCSB, KJV, NASB, NET, NIV, NRSV, TEV]. The phrase 'be compassionate' is translated 'show mercy' [NCV], 'have pity' [CEV]. When this noun relates to 6:27–35, it refers to doing merciful deeds, and when it relates to the following verses, it refers to kindness and forbearance in judgment [TH].

QUESTION—How is this verse related to the preceding verses?

1. This verse is included in the same paragraph as the preceding verses [AB, NAC, NTC, TG, TNTC; all versions except KJV]. This is to be connected with what precedes since being like God is the theme in 6:35–36, but not in 6:37–38 [WBC]. What was described in 6:27–31 and implied in 6:32–34 is now summarized in this verse [NAC, NTC]. This restates the last clause of the previous verse and at the same time it is a transition to what follows since the topic of judging others is an example of imitating God's mercy [AB, MGC].
2. This verse begins a new paragraph containing the following verses [BECNT, Lns, TH, WBC]. This is an introduction to what follows [TH]. This command and the following commands and promises follow from the fact that they are children of God and will have this outstanding attribute of the Father [Lns]. The command to love suggests another trait of the Father to be imitated, that of mercy [BECNT, WBC], and mercy is implied in the following two verses [WBC].

DISCOURSE UNIT: 6:37–42 [NAC, TNTC; CEV, GW, HCSB, NCV, NIV, NLT, NRSV, TEV]. The topic is judging others [NAC, TNTC; CEV, NIV, NRSV, TEV], stop judging [GW], do not judge [HCSB], don't condemn others [NLT], look at yourselves [NCV].

6:37 And do- not -judge,[a] and by-no-means you-will-be-judged. Do- not -condemn,[b] and by-no-means you-will-be-condemned. Forgive,[c] and you-will-be-forgiven.

LEXICON—a. pres. act. impera. of κρίνω (LN 56.30) (BAGD 6.a. p. 452): 'to judge' [AB, Arn, BAGD, BECNT, Lns, WBC; all versions], 'to pass judgment on someone' [BAGD, NTC], 'to judge as guilty, to condemn' [LN].

b. pres. act. impera. of καταδικάζω (LN 56.31) (BAGD p. 410): 'to condemn' [AB, Arn, BAGD, BECNT, LN, Lns, NTC, WBC; all versions except CEV, NCV, NLT], 'to render a verdict of guilt' [LN], 'to find or pronounce guilty' [BAGD], 'to be hard on someone' [CEV], 'to criticize' [NLT], 'to accuse of being guilty' [NCV].

c. pres. act. impera. of ἀπολύω (LN 40.8) (BAGD 1. p. 96): 'to forgive' [AB, Arn, BECNT, LN, NTC, WBC; all versions except NASB, REB], 'to pardon' [BAGD, LN; NASB, REB], 'to acquit' [Lns].

QUESTION—Who is the implied performer of the passives 'you will not be judged', 'you will not be condemned', and 'you will be forgiven'?

1. The performer is God [AB, Arn, EGT, Gdt, Lns, NAC, NIGTC, TG, TH, WBC; CEV, NET, TEV]: and God will not judge you. This refers to the final judgment [Lns, TG]. This does not mean that they will escape being judged by God, but that on the day of judgment they will be treated mercifully [NAC, NIGTC].

2. The performers include both others and God [NTC, TNTC]: and no one will judge you. The fault-finder will himself be criticized and condemned by people and especially by God [NTC].

QUESTION—In what way are we not to judge?

These commands develop from the previous verse and relate to attitudes that fail to show mercy to the guilty [NIGTC]. The command not to judge does not refer to using discernment [NIGTC, NIVS], forming an opinion about someone [NTC, Rb, Su, TG], making moral judgments on the conduct of others [BECNT, Gdt, Su], making ethical evaluations [BECNT], voicing an adverse or unfavorable opinion [NTC], taking disciplinary action in the church [Lns, NAC, NTC], or making judicial decisions by a constituted judge [AB, BECNT, NAC, TNTC]. In fact, the NT says that we are to judge in certain circumstances: 'judge with right judgment' (John 7:24), 'is it not those who are inside that you are to judge' (1 Corinthians 5:12), 'test the spirits to see whether they are from God' (1 John 4:1) [Lns]. To determine the good or bad nature of the tree (6:43–45) one must judge its fruit [Su]. The judging prohibited here refers to usurping the place of God in judging and condemning others [NIGTC]. It is appointing oneself as a judge over people whom one has no right to judge [Arn]. It is being censorious [BECNT, ICC, NIGTC, NTC]. It is to criticize and find fault [AB, NAC, TNTC]. It is hypocritical faultfinding [Lns, NTC]. It refers to a disparaging criticism that points out the vices or moral inferiority of others [Su]. When someone sets himself up as a judge of the moral worth of others, judgment is usually done in an unkind spirit [Gdt]. This command forbids the self-righteous, self-exalting, and hypocritical judging of those who set themselves up as judges of all other people [Lns]. While it does not forbid forming opinions, it prohibits forming them rashly and unfairly [Rb, TG].

QUESTION—How is the verb 'to judge' different from the verb 'to condemn'?

'Condemn' elucidates and explains the meaning of judging in this context [NAC, NIGTC, NTC]. The idea of condemning is the same as judging, but it is a stronger expression and is the next step after judging [Su]. To judge is neutral and refers to assuming the position and authority of a judge while condemning refers to the verdict [Lns].

QUESTION—What is meant by the verb ἀπολύω 'to forgive'?

This is not the usual word that speaks of forgiving sins, but a word meaning 'to pardon' or 'to set free' [Su]. It implies holding nothing against a person and leaving the judging up to God [Lns]. It does not mean to pretend that some guilty person is innocent, but it means to forgive a guilty person [BECNT, NAC, NIGTC], such an action being amnesty, not acquittal [BECNT]. The reference is to personal insults and injuries, it does not mean to do away with the laws of society [NIGTC]. It means to release someone from his obligations in agreement with 'lend expecting nothing' [NICNT]. This refers to personal relationships and not to government actions, since the government is charged with creating a safe environment for its citizens [BECNT].

6:38 Give, and it-will-be-given to-you. A-good measure[a] having-been-pressed-down[b] (and) having-been-shaken-together[c] (and) overflowing[d] they-will-put into your lap.[e] Because by-what measure[f] you-measure it-will-be-measured-in-return[g] to-you.

TEXT—Before μέτρῳ 'measure' in the last clause, some manuscripts add αὐτῷ 'same'. GNT does not mention this variant. Αὐτῷ 'same' is read by KJV.

LEXICON—a. μέτρον (LN **81.1**) (BAGD 1.a. p. 515): 'measure' [BAGD, **LN**]. The phrase 'good measure' [AB, Arn, BECNT, NTC, WBC; HCSB, KJV, NASB, NET, NIV, NRSV, REB] is also translated 'a large quantity' [GW], 'a full measure' [TEV], 'an excellent measure' [Lns], 'a full amount in return' [CEV], 'you will be given much' [GW], 'your gift will return in full measure' [NLT]. It means a generous measure [WBC]. A good measure is a full measure in contrast with a bad measure that is only partly filled [NIGTC]. A μέτρον 'measure' is an instrument for measuring capacity [BAGD, TH].

b. perf. pass. participle of πιέζω (LN **19.49**) (BAGD p. 657): 'to be pressed down' [AB, Arn, BECNT, **LN**, Lns, NTC, WBC; GW, HCSB, KJV, NASB, NET, NIV, NLT, NRSV], 'to be pressed' [BAGD; REB], 'to be pressed together' [GW], 'to be packed down' [CEV]. The two phrases 'having been pressed down and having been shaken together' is translated 'a generous helping' [TEV]. The purpose for pressing down is to make it more compact so more can be added [LN]. The hand was used to press down the grain so that it filled all of the space available in the container [NAC, TH].

c. perf. pass. participle of σαλεύω (LN **16.7**) (BAGD 1. p. 740): 'to be shaken together' [AB, BAGD, BECNT, **LN**, Lns, NTC, WBC; CEV, GW, HCSB, KJV, NASB, NET, NIV, NRSV], 'to be shaken down' [GW, REB], 'to be shaken' [Arn], 'to be shaken together to make room for more' [NLT]. It means to rapidly move something back and forth [LN].

This describes a market scene where grain is poured into a container and then the container is shaken in order to level the grain so that still more can be poured into it [WBC; NET].

d. perf. pass. participle of ὑπερεκχύννομαι (LN 14.19) (BAGD p. 840): 'to overflow' [BAGD, LN], 'to run over' [AB, Arn, BECNT, LN, Lns, NTC, WBC; all versions except CEV, TEV], 'to spill over' [CEV], 'to pour out over' [LN], 'to be poured into your hands' [TEV]. The grain is continued to be poured into the container until it makes a rounded heap on top and then overflows the container [NAC].

e. κόλπος (LN 6.181) (BAGD 2. p. 442): 'lap' [BAGD, LN], 'the fold of a garment' [BAGD, LN]. The phrase 'they will put into your lap' is translated 'they will pour into your lap' [NASB], 'shall men give into your bosom,' [KJV], 'will they give into your bosom' [Lns], 'they will give you good measure in the fold of your garment' [**LN**], not explicit [NLT]. The third person plural form is also translated as a passive: 'will be put into your lap' [Arn, BECNT; NRSV], 'will be poured into your lap' [NTC, WBC; HCSB, NET, NIV, REB], 'it will spill into your lap' [NCV], 'will be poured into the lap of your garment' [AB], 'will be put into your pocket' [GW], 'and spilling over into your lap' [CEV], 'poured into your hands—all that you can hold' [TEV]. The word can refer to the fold of a garment that forms a type of pocket or container [BAGD, LN].

f. μέτρον (LN **81.1**) (BAGD 1.a. p. 515): 'measure' [BAGD, **LN**, Lns, NTC, WBC; KJV]. The phrase 'the measure you measure' [Arn] is also translated 'the measure you give' [BECNT; NRSV], 'the measure you use' [AB; HCSB, NET, NIV, TEV], 'your standard of measurement' [NASB], 'whatever measure you use in giving' [NLT], 'whatever measure you deal out to others' [REB], 'the way you give to others' [GW], 'the way you treat others' [CEV], 'the standards you use for others' [GW]. This noun is a measurement unit, either of length or volume [LN]. Or, it refers to the measuring instrument [TH].

g. fut. pass. indic. of ἀντιμετρέω (LN **57.93**) (BAGD p. 75): 'to be measured in return' [BAGD, Lns, NTC; KJV, NASB], 'to be measured' [NIV], 'to be measured back' [HCSB], 'to be the measure you get back' [BECNT; NRSV], 'to be the measure by which return is made' [AB], 'to receive measure in return' [WBC], 'to be repaid, to be paid back' [LN], 'to receive' [NET], 'to be dealt in turn' [REB], 'to be used to measure what is given back' [NLT], 'with it things will be measured out to you' [Arn]. The intention of the figure is translated 'to be treated' [CEV], 'to be applied' [GW], 'God will give' [GW], 'to be the one God will use' [TEV]. This means to give a measured portion to someone in repayment [LN]. The original reference was to a grain contract which would specify that delivery of the grain and payment for it would be measured with the same instrument used by the purchaser [WBC].

LUKE 6:38

QUESTION—What is the purpose of these instructions about measuring?

This does not connect with the teaching about judging [BNTC]. A disposition of forgiving is naturally connected with a disposition of giving, that is, rending service to all, even the greatest sinners [Gdt]. Giving is a form of mercy [EGT]. This goes beyond cases of forgiving personal injury and pertains to the positive action of treating the needs of others with generosity [NAC, NIGTC]. There is now a transition from mercy in judging others to benevolence in general [ICC]. Not only are we to forgive a person from the obligations of recompense, we are to be generous to the other person [WBC]. This is to be understood as a command to freely give to the needs of others [NIGTC]. It is a call for generosity [BECNT]. The mercy commanded in judgment has a broader application in compassion in giving [Lns]. It refers to an unstinted merciful standard in judging and giving [AB].

QUESTION—Who is the implied performer of the third person singular passive 'it will be given to you'?

1. The performer is God [AB, Arn, BECNT, BNTC, Gdt, Lns, NICNT, NIGTC, TH, WBC; TEV]: give, and God will give to you. Taking the passive to refer to God is consistent with 6:36 and also the good measure in return points to more than human generosity [TH]. What God will give to us at the judgment day is the degree of glory he has reserved for individuals [Lns].
2. The performer is another person [Su, TNTC]: Give, and others will give to you. When we keep giving, people respond in kind [TNTC].

QUESTION—What is meant by the reference to one's lap?

The word κόλπος 'lap' is used to refer to the fold of a garment that forms a type of pocket or container [BAGD, LN (6.181)]. It is the fold that is made in an outer garment by pulling it out as it hung over the girdle and it was used as a kind of pocket, holding more than just the lap could [AB, Arn, BECNT, BNTC, Crd, EGT, Gdt, ICC, Lns, My, NAC, NIGTC, NTC, Rb, Su, TG, TH, WBC]. An alternative way of taking this is that the skirt of the garment is spread out over the lap to receive the large quantity [WBC]. It is the lap of the garment [AB]. The picture is that of measuring out grain by volume in abundance [BECNT, WBC]. After all that is possible is put into the measure and it is even overflowing, it is poured into the loose fold above the belt so that it can be carried away [Lns].

QUESTION—Who is the implied performer of the third person plural 'they will put into your lap'?

1. The performer is God [AB, Arn, BECNT, BNTC, EGT, Lns, NAC, NICNT, NIGTC, TG, TH, WBC; GW, TEV]: God will put into your lap. The plural 'they will put' is indefinite, but the sense cannot be different from the preceding passives referring to God [Lns]. The third person is circumlocution for 'God will pour' [NAC].
2. The performers are angels [Alf, My]: angels will put into your lap. These would be the angels who are ministers of God's purposes [Alf, My].

3. The performers are other people [Gdt, ICC, Su, TNTC]: people will put into your lap. The plural 'they' refers to the instruments of God's generosity, whoever they may be [Gdt]. This is the kind of generosity that people will return for the generosity shown to them [Su].

QUESTION—What relationship is indicated by γάρ 'because' in the final clause?

It gives the reason for acting generously by stating a general principle, the principle being that by our giving we determine the measure that will be used in giving back to us [Lns, NIGTC, NTC]. It has a verbal link to the preceding instructions about giving, but serves as a conclusion to the whole paragraph [WBC].

QUESTION—What is meant by the statement 'by what measure you measure, it will be measured in return to you'?

It means that if we freely forgive and are generous or if we withhold forgiveness and lack generosity we are to expect that God will respond in kind with strict justice [WBC]. God will be as generous to us as we are to others [TG]. Although this may seem to refer to strict retribution, here the emphasis is on God's generosity, which is not confined to a precisely equivalent gift [NIGTC]. What a person does sets the standard of God's reaction and the return is not to be equated with prosperity but with the blessings of forgiveness, intimate fellowship with God, new relationships with believers, and God's transforming power in life [BECNT]. Human generosity is rewarded with God's generosity, which is far greater as the previous sentence shows [NAC]. There is an implied command to give in abundance in the way God gives [TH].

DISCOURSE UNIT: 6:39–49 [BECNT, NICNT, NIGTC, WBC]. The topic is the measure of a disciple [NICNT], a parabolic call to righteousness, fruit, and wise building [BECNT], the inward character of disciples [NIGTC], the importance of what Jesus teaches and the need to act upon it [WBC].

6:39 And also he-told a-parable[a] to-them. A-blind-person isn't-able to-lead[b] a-blind-person, (is he)? Will- not both -fall into a-pit[c]?

LEXICON—a. παραβολή (LN 33.15) (BAGD 2. p. 612): 'parable' [Arn, BAGD, BECNT, LN, Lns, NTC, WBC; HCSB, KJV, NASB, NET, NIV, NRSV, REB, TEV], 'illustration' [GW, NLT], 'saying' [CEV], 'proverb' [AB], 'story' [NCV]. This is a proverb [Alf, NAC, NICNT, TH]. It is an illustration [Arn]. See this word at 5:36; 13:6; 14:7.

b. pres. act. infin. of ὁδηγέω (LN 15.182) (BAGD 1. p. 553): 'to lead' [AB, Arn, BAGD, LN, Lns, NTC, WBC; CEV, GW, KJV, NCV, NET, NIV, NLT, TEV], 'to guide' [BAGD, BECNT, LN; HCSB, NASB, NRSV, REB].

c. βόθυνος (LN 1.55) (BAGD p. 144): 'pit' [Arn, BAGD, BECNT, LN, Lns, NTC; GW, HCSB, NASB, NET, NIV, NRSV], 'ditch' [AB, BAGD, LN, WBC; CEV, KJV, NCV, NLT, REB, TEV], 'hole' [LN]. This may be a natural depression or one dug by people, presumably for agricultural purposes [LN]. The ground was very rocky, so rocks were dug up for various purposes such as surfacing roads and this left dangerous holes on the surface of the ground [Lns]. Or, the image is a strong one and here pit refers to a mammoth hole that stresses the resulting disaster [BECNT]. The pit could be an open well or an unfenced quarry [ICC].

QUESTION—What relationship is indicated by δέ 'and' at the beginning of the verse?

Along with the repetition of 'he told' this marks the second half of the discourse [ICC]. The 'also' means that he told them another parable along with 6:38 [NIGTC]. There is no connection with what precedes and this is an independent part of the discourse [My]. It marks a new section that is only loosely connected with what precedes it [TH]. This is a break in the discourse in which Jesus sought for an illustration to impress the people with the consequences of passing judgment on others when this is done in the manner of the Pharisees [Gdt]. This adds to the preceding instructions about love for enemies and nonjudgmental generosity by warning against being led by blind teachers who suggest another way [WBC]. The three parables warn the disciples to take Jesus' teaching seriously [BECNT].

QUESTION—Who was Jesus speaking to?

Jesus told the parable to his disciples [TH], or to the people in general [CEV].

QUESTION—What are the implied answers to the two rhetorical questions?

The first rhetorical question expects the answer 'No' and the second question expects the answer 'Yes' [BECNT, Lns, NAC, NIGTC, NTC, Rb, TG, TH]. Translated as statements instead of questions it is 'One blind man cannot lead another one; if he does, both will fall into a ditch' [TEV]. The questions are so simple that there is a touch of humor to them [Lns].

QUESTION—What is the application of the parable?

This has a different application than that of the same parable in Matthew 15:14 that was addressed to the Pharisees. Being a parable, it could be applied in various ways [BECNT, ICC, Lns, NIGTC, WBC].

1. This is a warning not to follow blind leaders [AB, BECNT, NICNT, NTC, TNTC, WBC]. This parable is addressed to those being led and directs them not to be led by blind leaders who do not recognize the fundamental importance of the teaching on love and not judging [WBC]. People should not follow blind guides such as the scribes and there is an implication that the apostles should replace such guides by being trained for their task [NTC]. In the context of the following parable, blind leaders must be referring to false teachers [AB]. The disciples need to choose their teacher carefully [BECNT]. It is a warning about choosing who we will follow and it is also a warning about the leadership the disciples will exercise; they must clearly see where they are going [TNTC].

2. This is a warning not to be a blind leader [Arn, EGT, ICC, My, NAC, NIGTC, TH]. It may be connected to the topic of judging others, in that before judging others we must judge ourselves or we will be like blind

leaders of the blind [ICC]. This is a warning not to be blind to one's own faults when teaching or correcting others [NAC]. It is connected with 6:37 and means that the disciples are blind and unable to lead or criticize others until they are enlightened by their teacher [NIGTC]. The disciples who are to be leaders must not be blind. Only when they are fully trained and have become like their teacher can they give leadership [TH]. The person who does not know the divine truth is not able to lead others to Messianic salvation [My].

6:40 A-pupil[a] is not above[b] the teacher. But everyone having-been-fully-trained[c] will-be like his teacher.

LEXICON—a. μαθητή (LN **27.16**) (BAGD 1. p. 485): 'pupil' [AB, Arn, BAGD, **LN**, NTC; NASB, REB, TEV], 'student' [CEV, GW, NCV, NIV, NLT], 'learner' [BAGD], 'disciple' [BECNT, LN, Lns, WBC; HCSB, KJV, NET, NRSV].

    b. ὑπέρ (LN 87.30) (BAGD 2. p. 839): 'above' [Arn, BAGD, LN, Lns, WBC; HCSB, KJV, NASB, NIV, NRSV], '(ranks) above' [REB], 'superior to' [AB, BAGD, LN], 'better than' [CEV, GW, NCV], 'greater than' [BECNT; NET, NLT, TEV], 'to outrank' [NTC]. It has the sense of excelling or surpassing [BAGD]. It means 'more important' [TG, TH], 'wiser than' [TG].

    c. perf. pass. participle of καταρτίζω (LN **75.5**) (BAGD 1.b. p. 417): 'to be fully trained' [Arn, BAGD, NTC; CEV, HCSB, NASB, NCV, NET, NIV, REB], 'to be well trained' [GW], 'to be fully qualified' [NRSV], 'to be thoroughly qualified' [**LN**], 'to be fully prepared' [WBC], 'to be fully equipped' [BECNT], 'to complete their training' [TEV], 'to be fully schooled' [AB], 'to work hard' [NLT], 'to be perfected' [Lns], 'to be perfect' [KJV]. The perfect tense indicates the state at which the pupil has arrived, 'after having received the teacher's spirit and principles' [Lns]. It assumes that the training is more than just imparting information, it teaches the pupil to be the kind of person the teacher already is [WBC].

QUESTION—What relationship is indicated by δέ 'but' beginning the second sentence and in what sense will the pupil be like his teacher?

This can be translated 'moreover' since it adds a slightly different point to the parable [Lns]. This assures them that although they can never surpass him, they can become like him [ICC, NTC]. This generalizes to refer to all students and says that they can become like their teacher [Arn]. Or, this sentence just repeats the force of the preceding sentence, that a pupil does not go beyond his teacher, but he simply repeats what he has been taught [NIGTC]. After being prepared by his teacher, the pupil will be equal to the teacher, although never surpassing him [Arn, ICC, My]. This refers to the position of leadership and means being equal in authority or capability [TH]. He will be as important as this teacher [TG]. It does not mean that he will have the same degree of knowledge or wisdom, but he will reflect his teacher's image before people [NTC], or he will partake of his character and spirit [Lns].

QUESTION—What is the application of the parable?

The disciples should not follow a blind teacher [Gdt, TNTC, WBC]. The disciples should not accept inadequate teachers because they will be constrained by the teacher's limitations. If they chose a teacher that does not teach them to love their enemies and to avoid judging, they will be left in their blindness [WBC]. This warns them not to follow the Pharisees [Gdt]. The disciples should pick the right teacher [BECNT]. The disciples were not greater than Jesus, so they must train themselves to be like him [NAC, TNTC]. Teachers must beware of being blind and uninstructed [ICC].

6:41 And why do-you-see the speck[a] in the eye of-your brother,[b] but not notice[c] the beam[d] in your own eye?

LEXICON—a. κάρφος (LN 3.66) (BAGD p. 405): 'speck' [AB, BAGD, BECNT, LN, NTC, WBC; CEV, HCSB, NASB, NET, NLT, NRSV, REB, TEV], 'chip' [BAGD], 'splinter' [Arn], 'piece of sawdust' [GW], 'speck of sawdust' [NIV], 'sliver' [Lns], 'little piece of dust' [NCV], 'mote' [KJV]. It is a small piece of something such as wood [BAGD, BECNT, LN, NTC, TH], or straw [BAGD, BECNT, Gdt, LN, Lns, NTC, TH], or chaff [BAGD, BECNT, LN, TH]. It is anything that is small and dry [ICC].

b. ἀδελφός (3 times) (LN 11.89) (BAGD 4. p. 16): 'brother' [AB, Arn, BAGD, BECNT, LN, Lns, NTC, WBC; HCSB, KJV, NASB, NET, NIV, REB, TEV], 'neighbor' [LN; NRSV], 'friend' [CEV, NCV, NLT], 'another believer' [GW]. This is a person who is a fellow member of one's own group [TH]. This means one's fellowman, and is not restricted to a brother in a religious group [Su].

c. pres. act. indic. of κατανοέω (LN 24.51, **30.43**) (BAGD 1. p. 415): 'to notice' [BAGD, BECNT, LN (24.51), WBC; CEV, GW, HCSB, NASB, NCV, NRSV], 'to see' [AB; NET], 'to observe' [NTC], 'to discover' [LN (24.51)], 'to perceive' [Lns; KJV], 'to pay attention to' [NIV, TEV], 'to be aware of' [Arn], 'to be concerned about' [**LN (30.43)**], 'with never a thought for' [REB], not explicit [NLT]. 'To notice' and 'to see' are synonyms [TH].

d. δοκός (LN 7.78) (BAGD p. 203): 'beam' [AB, Arn, LN, Lns, NTC, WBC; KJV], 'beam of wood' [BAGD; NET], 'wooden beam' [GW], 'plank' [BECNT; NIV, REB], 'log' [CEV, HCSB, NASB, NLT, NRSV, TEV], 'big piece of wood' [NCV]. It is the large main beam that supports the other beams of the roof or floor of a house [ICC]. It is a building's main beam [BECNT], rafter, or joist [NTC].

QUESTION—What is the function of this rhetorical question?

The question expresses astonishment and indignation [TH]. The question implies that it is either impossible to do so, or at least it doesn't make sense [TH]. The contrast between a speck and a beam could hardly be greater and the use of hyperbole carries the emotive force of the question [BECNT]. The response is 'What nerve!' [BECNT]. Translated as a statement it would begin 'you should not…' [TG]. Both parts are governed by 'why?', but the second part has the emphasis [TH].

QUESTION—What is the metaphor involved?

In the *image*, the mote represents a defect of secondary importance [Gdt], a slight imperfection [TNTC], a minor personal fault [BECNT]. The beam represents a major personal problem that is worthy of correction [BECNT]. It is to be totally wrong in moral and spiritual perception [Lns]. The reference to the insignificant speck and the huge beam is intended to be grotesque [AB, WBC], ludicrous [Gdt], ridiculous [Su], and humorous [TNTC]. This is hyperbole [BECNT, NAC, Su].

6:42 **How are-you-able to-say to-your brother, Brother,^a let (me) remove the speck in your eye, (while) you-yourself (are) not seeing (the) beam in your eye? Hypocrite,^b first remove the beam from your eye, and then you-will-see-clearly^c to-remove the speck in the eye of-your brother.**

TEXT—Instead of πῶς 'how' some manuscripts read ἢ πῶς 'or how' and other manuscripts read ὡς δέ 'but/and how'. GNT does not mention this variant. Ἢ πῶς 'or how' is read by KJV, NASB.

LEXICON—a. ἀδελφός vocative (LN 11.89) (BAGD 4. p. 16): 'brother' [AB, Arn, BAGD, BECNT, LN, Lns, NTC, WBC; HCSB, KJV, NASB, NET, NIV, REB, TEV], 'neighbor' [LN], 'friend' [CEV, GW, NCV, NLT, NRSV].

    b. ὑποκριτής (LN 88.228) (BAGD p. 845): 'hypocrite'. [AB, Arn, BAGD, BECNT, LN, Lns, NTC, WBC; all versions except CEV], 'show-off' [CEV]. See this word at 12:56; 13:15.

    c. fut. act. indic. of διαβλέπω (LN 24.35) (BAGD 2. p. 181): 'to see clearly' [Arn, BAGD, BECNT, LN, Lns, NTC, WBC; all versions except CEV, NLT], 'to be able to see how to' [CEV], 'to see well enough to deal with' [NLT], 'to have the sight' [AB].

QUESTION—Why is the fault-finder called a hypocrite?

He is pretending to be so pained by the presence of a small evil that he feels he must remove it [ICC]. He is pretending not to see his own major fault [TH]. He professes to be pious and righteous, but his real character is the opposite [NIGTC]. This is a person who pretends that he is offended with another's sin while failing to deal with his own sin [BECNT]. He is unable to see his own imperfections but nevertheless tries to correct the imperfections he sees in others [NAC]. This refers to the inconsistency of a person who professes to be pious and righteous in matters in which he censures others, but in other aspects of his life his real impious character is revealed [NIGTC].

QUESTION—Do these instructions forbid correcting the faults of others?

This is not a command that they should never deal with other people's problems [AB, BECNT, Gdt, ICC, Lns, My, NICNT, NTC, Su]. This does not forbid the disciples from forming moral judgments about the conduct of people, but any attempts to correct others require a similar examination of self before doing so [AB]. Both self-discipline and mutual discipline are encouraged here [NTC]. Jesus is teaching the need of a rigid self-examination before judging others [TNTC]. Following the reference to a blind leader, this means that the disciples must correct themselves before correcting others [ICC, My]. This is connected with the previous command about not judging others [Su]. Or, this forbids judging others since we can never make ourselves perfect [NIGTC].

DISCOURSE UNIT: 6:43–49 [NAC]. The topic is the two foundations.

DISCOURSE UNIT: 6:43–45 [TNTC; CEV, GW, HCSB, NCV, NIV, NLT, NRSV, TEV]. The topic is a tree and its fruit [TNTC; CEV, HCSB, NIV, NLT, NRSV, TEV], two kinds of fruit [NCV], evil people [GW].

6:43 Because[a] there-is no good tree producing bad fruit, nor on-the-other-hand[b] a-bad tree producing good fruit.
LEXICON—a. γάρ (LN 91.1): 'for' [BECNT, Lns, NTC; KJV, NASB, NET], not explicit [AB, Arn, WBC; all versions except KJV, NASB, NET]. It marks a new sentence and it is often best to leave it untranslated or use 'and' or the conjunctive adverb 'then' [LN].
  b. πάλιν (LN 89.129) (BAGD 4. p. 607): 'on the other hand' [BAGD, LN, NTC; HCSB, NASB], 'again' [AB, BECNT, Lns, WBC; NET, NRSV], 'nor again' [Arn], 'yet' [REB], not explicit [CEV, GW, KJV, NCV, NIV, NLT, TEV].
QUESTION—What relationship is indicated by the opening γάρ 'because'?
  1. It indicates reason [AB, Arn, BECNT, Lns, NTC; KJV, NASB, NET]: first remove the beam from your own eye, because it is a serious defect showing that you are not bearing good fruit. It explains why self-correction is important [BECNT]. The disciples should correct themselves and be careful of whom they follow because their choices also reflect the nature of the tree and its fruit [NET]. A person cannot bring others to good conduct through criticism alone since his deeds must precede his corrections and reveal that he is really good [AB]. It means that they are to remove the beam of self-righteousness, because it is a serious defect that shows that they are spiritually sick [NTC].
  2. It merely indicates a continuation [NIGTC, TH, WBC; probably CEV, GW, NCV, NIV, NLT, NRSV, REB, TEV which do not translate the conjunction].
QUESTION—In this metaphor, what does 'fruit' represent?
  It refers to the ways a person expresses himself, including his life [BECNT], conduct [NICNT], moral attitude [My, NTC], deeds [AB, NIGTC, NTC, TNTC], and words [NIGTC]. The following statement, 'from the abundance of the heart his mouth speaks' (6:45) indicates that it includes his speech and

teaching [BECNT, NICNT, NIGTC, NTC]. Or, instead of speech, teaching, and moral conduct, it refers to the results of his labor in others [Gdt].

QUESTION—What is being contrasted between good trees and bad trees?

1. The contrast is between useful species of trees and useless species [BECNT, ICC, Lns, NIGTC, TNTC]. In the context of the following statement that each tree will be known by its own fruit (6:44), it must be referring to the kinds of trees, even though the similar passage in Matthew 12:33, 'make the tree good and the fruit will be good or make the tree bad and the fruit will be rotten', may be referring to unhealthy trees [NIGTC]. Both varieties of trees may look good merely as trees, but the fruit they produce will show what they really are worth [Lns]. The nature of the tree produces the fruit that corresponds to its nature [Su].

2. The contrast is between the quality of trees of the same species [AB, Gdt, NTC, Su, TG, TH, WBC; GW, TEV]. The contrast is between: good and rotten trees [AB; GW], healthy and sickly trees [NTC], healthy and poor trees [TEV], healthy and infected trees [Gdt], cultivated and native trees [Su], or trees that are growing well and those that are not growing well [TG].

6:44 Because[a] each tree is-known by its own fruit. Because[b] they-do- not - gather figs from thorn-plants[c] nor do-they-pick grapes from a-thorn-bush.[d]

LEXICON—a. γάρ (LN 89.23): 'because' [LN], 'for' [AB, Arn, BECNT, LN, Lns, NTC, WBC; HCSB, KJV, NASB, NET, NRSV], not explicit [CEV, GW, NCV, NIV, NLT, REB, TEV].

b. γάρ (LN 89.23): 'because' [LN], 'for' [Arn, BECNT, LN, Lns, WBC; KJV, NASB, NET], not explicit [AB, NTC; CEV, GW, HCSB, NCV, NIV, NRSV, REB, TEV].

c. ἄκανθα (LN 3.17) (BAGD p. 29): 'thorn plant' [BAGD, LN], 'thorny plant' [GW], 'thorn bush' [AB, Arn, Lns, NTC, WBC; CEV, HCSB, NCV, NIV, NLT, TEV], 'thistle, brier' [LN], 'thorns' [BECNT; KJV, NASB, NET, NRSV], 'brambles' [REB]. See this word at 8:7.

d. βάτος (LN 3.16) (BAGD p. 137): 'thorn bush' [BAGD, LN; CEV, GW], 'briar bush' [NASB], 'briers' [NIV], 'bramble bush' [Lns, NTC; HCSB, KJV, NLT, NRSV, TEV], 'brambles' [AB, Arn, BECNT, WBC; NET], 'thistles' [REB], 'bush' [LN; NCV].

QUESTION—What relationship is indicated by the opening γάρ 'because'?

This verse indicates the grounds for the statement made in 6:43 [BECNT, NIGTC]. It is the principle underlying the statements in 6:43 [TH]. It explains 6:43 by stating that the nature of the tree is shown by its fruit [BECNT]. It means that the principle stated in 6:43 is so true that everyone unhesitatingly knows the nature of a tree from its fruit [Gdt]. The emphasis on fruit is essential since there is no other way to determine the quality and nature of a tree [Lns].

QUESTION—What relationship is indicated by γάρ 'because' in the last sentence?

The general principle stated in the first sentence is illustrated with these two examples [TH] that show that you will produce what you are and not something different [BECNT, Lns]. The ridiculous illustrations make an obvious truth even more obvious [Lns].

QUESTION—What is the distinction between ἄκανθα 'thorn plants' and βάτος 'thorn bush'?

The ἄκανθα is any kind of thorny plant such as a thorn plant, thistle, or brier [LN (3.17)], while βάτος is any type of thorn bush or shrub [LN (3.16)]. The 'thorn plants' are any thorny plant, but the word especially refers to the cammock plant, while the 'thorn bush' probably refers to the 'bramble'. Probably proverbial combinations of the words 'grapes and figs' formed a pair and so would the proverbial combination of 'thorn plants and thorn bush' [NIGTC]. Identifying the various words for thorny shrubs is a hopeless task [ICC]. The two words are synonyms [TH]. The two words for thorny plants are combined in 'thorn bushes': 'You cannot pick figs or grapes from thorn bushes' [CEV].

6:45 The good man from the good treasure/treasure-house[a] of the heart[b] brings-out[c] the good,[d] and the evil (man) from the evil[e] brings-out the evil.[f] Beecause from (the) abundance[g] of-(the) heart his mouth[h] speaks.

LEXICON—a. θησαυρός (LN 7.32) (BAGD 1.b. p. 361): 'treasure' [Arn, BECNT, Lns, NTC, WBC; KJV, NASB, NET, NRSV, TEV], 'the store (of good)' [AB; REB], 'treasure room' [LN], 'storeroom' [LN; HCSB], 'treasury' [BAGD], not explicit [CEV, GW, NLT]. This noun is also translated as a verb: 'to store' [NCV], 'to be stored up' [NIV].

b. καρδία (LN 26.3): 'heart, inner self, mind' [LN]. The phrase 'the good treasure of the heart' [WBC; NRSV] is also translated 'the good treasure of his heart' [Arn, BECNT, Lns; KJV, NASB, NET], 'the good treasure stored in his heart' [NTC], 'the treasure of good things in his heart' [TEV], 'the good they stored in their hearts' [NCV], 'the good stored up in his heart' [NIV], 'the store of good in his heart' [AB], 'the store of good within themselves' [REB], '(the good) that is in them' [GW], 'the good storeroom of his heart' [HCSB], 'the good in their hearts' [CEV], 'a good heart' [NLT]. The heart refers to the inner being from which come attitudes and values [NAC].

c. pres. act. indic. of προφέρω (LN **13.85**) (BAGD p. 722): 'to bring out' [BAGD; NCV, NIV, TEV], 'to bring forth' [AB, **LN**, Lns, WBC; KJV, NASB], 'to produce' [Arn, BAGD, BECNT, LN, NTC; HCSB, NET, NLT, NRSV, REB], 'to cause to exist' [**LN**], 'to do' [CEV, GW].

d. ἀγαθός (LN 88.1): 'good' [LN]. The phrase τὸ ἀγαθόν 'the good' [Lns; GW] is also translated 'good things' [CEV, NCV, NIV], 'good deeds' [NLT], 'good' [AB, BECNT, WBC; HCSB, NET, NRSV, REB, TEV], 'what is good' [NTC; NASB], 'that which is good' [Arn; KJV].

e. πονηρός (LN 88.110) (BAGD 1.b. p. 690): 'evil, wicked' [BAGD, LN]. The phrase τοῦ πονηροῦ 'the evil' is translated 'the evil treasure' [Arn; NASB, NRSV], 'his evil treasure' [NET], 'his treasure of bad things' [TEV], 'the evil in their hearts' [CEV], 'the wickedness that is in him' [AB], 'the wicked treasure in his heart' [Lns], 'the evil treasure of his heart' [BECNT; KJV], 'his evil storehouse' [NTC], 'the evil within them' [REB], 'the evil they stored in their hearts' [NCV], 'the evil storeroom' [HCSB], 'an evil heart' [NLT], 'evil' [WBC], 'the evil that is in them' [GW].
f. πονηρός (LN 88.110) (BAGD 1.b. p. 690): 'evil'. The phrase τὸ πονηρόν 'the evil' [GW] is also translated 'the wicked' [Lns], 'evil things' [NCV], 'evil deeds' [NLT], 'that which is evil' [Arn; KJV], 'what is evil' [NTC; NASB], 'evil' [BECNT, WBC; HCSB, NET, NRSV, REB], 'wickedness' [AB], 'bad things' [CEV], 'bad' [TEV].
g. περίσσευμα (LN 59.53) (BAGD 1. p. 650): 'abundance' [BAGD, LN]. The phrase περισσεύματος καρδίας 'the abundance of the heart' [AB, BECNT, NTC, WBC; KJV, NRSV] is also translated 'the heart-abundance' [Lns], 'that which fills his heart' [NASB], 'what fills his heart' [NET], 'what his heart is full of' [TEV], 'things of which his heart is full' [Arn], 'the overflow of the heart' [HCSB], 'the overflowing of the heart' [REB], 'what is in your heart' [CEV], 'whatever is in your heart' [NLT], 'the things that are in their hearts' [NCV], 'from inside them' [GW]. This is derived from the verb περισσεύω 'to abound' and the noun means that which exists in abundance [LN]. It means what the heart is full of [BAGD]. It refers to that which fills and overflows the heart [TH]. The mouth reveals the thoughts of the mind [AB].
h. στόμα (LN 8.19): 'mouth' [LN]. The phrase λαλεῖ στόμα αὐτοῦ 'his mouth speaks' [Arn, BECNT, Lns, NTC; HCSB, NASB, NET] is also translated 'the mouth speaks' [AB, WBC; NRSV, TEV], 'what you say' [NLT], 'the words that the mouth utters' [REB], 'your words' [CEV], 'to say' [GW], 'to speak' [NCV].

QUESTION—How is this verse connected to the preceding one?

This applies to people what is said about trees and fruit [AB, BECNT, My, NAC, NIGTC, NTC, Su, TH]. Similar to a good tree, a good man produces good and similar to a bad tree, an evil man produces evil [Su]. The figure of trees and fruit is applied to people, but the figure is slightly changed by making the heart a storehouse [AB]. This verse gives a general principle to all that has preceded [Gdt].

QUESTION—Why is there an article in the opening words ὁ ἀγαθὸς ἄνθρωπος 'the good man'?

The article is generic and means 'a good man' [NIGTC, TH]. This is brought out by translating it 'a good man' [KJV], 'a good person' [NLT, TEV], 'good people' [CEV, GW, NCV, REB].

QUESTION—Does θησαυρός refer to a treasure room or to the treasure that is kept in it?
    1. It means the treasure itself [AB, Arn, BECNT, BNTC, Lns, NTC, TH, TNTC, WBC; KJV, NASB, NCV, NET, NIV, NRSV, REB, TEV]: the good treasure which is stored in his heart. It refers to a treasure [BECNT, Lns, NTC, WBC; KJV, NASB, NET, NRSV, TEV]. 'Good' refers to the quality of what is kept and not the place where it is kept [TH]. A person's heart is a storehouse for the treasure [BECNT, NTC]. Instead of understanding the genitive construction to mean that the treasure is located in the heart, one commentary takes the heart to be the treasure [BNTC].
    2. It means the place where the treasure is kept [BAGD, LN, NIGTC; NLT]: the good treasure room which is the heart. It is a room for storing valuables [LN (7.23)], and here the heart is the treasury for heavenly possessions [BAGD]. It refers to the person's good treasury, namely his heart [NIGTC]. He 'produces good deeds from a good heart' [NLT].

QUESTION—What relationship is indicated by the opening γάρ 'because' of the last sentence?
    It states the general principle or grounds behind the preceding statements [BECNT, Gdt, TH, TNTC]. The thought of the preceding figure is now applied to speech in general [MGC, NIGTC, TG]. It is especially applied to teaching [BECNT]. What is in one's heart brings forth good or evil in word, deed, and influence, and from the words of the mouth for instance, you can tell whether the heart treasures what is good or what is evil [Lns]. What people are internally is even shown in their words [Su]. Or, the saying refers to words rather than deeds, and in this context it concerns what is spoken in making judgments and censures (6:37–42) [NIGTC].

DISCOURSE UNIT: 6:46–49 [TNTC; CEV, GW, HCSB, NASB, NCV, NIV, NLT, NRSV, TEV]. The topic is two kinds of people [NCV], two house builders [CEV, TEV], the wise and foolish builders [NIV], the two foundations [HCSB, NRSV], builders and foundations [NASB], building on a sound foundation [NLT], build on the rock [GW], foundations [TNTC].

6:46 And why do-you-call me Lord, Lord, and you- don't -do what I-say?
QUESTION—How is this verse connected to its context?
    This verse is a transition to a new section dealing with the problem of words and deeds [TH]. The spoken word coming from the good treasure of the heart is verified in joining the doing with what is said [My]. It is not connected with the preceding verse, but gives the real point to the tree illustrations [BNTC, NICNT]. This stresses the need to produce good fruit [NTC]. Or, this drops all of the preceding figures to make an application [Lns]. Instead of concluding the previous section, it introduces the epilogue to the whole preceding discourse [EGT]. The conclusion of the sermon is a call to respond in obedience [AB, BECNT, NIGTC], and thus be wise [BECNT].

QUESTION—Who was the question addressed to?

The question was addressed to those who claimed that their allegiance was to the Lord [NIGTC, NTC, WBC], but who settled for less than obedience to Jesus' call to love their enemies and not judge others [WBC]. Some of the people had shown themselves to be false disciples [TNTC]. It is addressed to the whole crowd, including the Apostles whose conduct was not always consistent with their profession [Arn, Su]. The question is addressed to all disciples since none are perfect [ICC] and some might be in danger of disobedience [Lns].

QUESTION—What is the significance of the repetition, 'Lord, Lord'?

The doubled form is an emphatic way to catch someone's attention [BECNT, TH]. It indicates urgency in claiming a relationship to Jesus that is expressed in the title [Lns]. Doubling the title is a sign of giving great honor to the Lord [NIGTC]. To call Jesus 'Lord' is more than calling him 'Sir' since there is a recognition of his authority to demand obedience [NIGTC]. Lord is a title of honor and respect and was used to address a religious or civil authority. Here it would be used in addressing Jesus as a respected teacher [BECNT, WBC], or as the patron to whom they owe allegiance [NICNT]. This respectful title was sometimes used as merely 'Sir', but here it must include the ideas of the divine Lord, the Messiah, and Savior [Lns]. Here Jesus claims to be the Messiah [Gdt]. The doubled address was common among the Jews and is found in the OT at Genesis 22:11, 46:2, Exodus 3:4, and 1 Samuel 3:10 [BECNT, NIGTC].

QUESTION—What is the function of the rhetorical question?

It means 'It has no sense that you…' [TH]. It is a rebuke meaning 'You should not call me Lord, Lord, unless you do what I tell you' [TG].

6:47 Everyone coming^a to me and hearing^b my words and doing them, I-will-show^c you whom he-is like.^d

LEXICON—a. pres. mid./pass. (deponent = act.) participle of ἔρχομαι (LN 15.81): 'to come' [AB, Arn, BECNT, LN, Lns, WBC; all versions]. The person comes to listen to Jesus or comes to be his follower [TG]. It is implied that obedience must accompany the coming [NIGTC].

  b. pres. act. participle of ἀκούω (LN 31.56) (BAGD 1.b.g. p. 32): 'to hear' [Arn, BAGD, BECNT, Lns, WBC; GW, HCSB, KJV, NASB, NCV, NIV, NRSV, REB], 'to listen to' [AB, LN, NTC; CEV, NET, NLT, TEV], 'to accept, to listen and respond, to pay attention and respond, to heed' [LN]. Everyone needed to listen carefully since the meaning would not be clear without Jesus' explanation [Lns].

  c. fur. act. indic. of ὑποδείκνυμι (LN 28.47) (BAGD 2. p. 844): 'to show' [AB, Arn, BECNT, LN, Lns, NTC, WBC; all versions except CEV], 'to demonstrate' [LN], 'to make known' [LN], not explicit [CEV].

  d. ὅμοιος (LN 64.1) (BAGD 1. p. 566): 'like, similar' [BAGD, LN], not explicit [CEV]. The phrase τίνι ἐστὶν ὅμοιος 'whom he is like' [Arn, Lns, NTC, WBC; KJV, NASB] is also translated 'what he is like'

[BECNT; GW, NCV, NET, NIV, NRSV, REB, TEV], 'what such a one is like' [AB], 'what someone is like' [HCSB], 'what it's like when' [NLT]. Although some translate with *'what* he is like', verse 6:48 indicates that the word τίνι is masculine and means 'whom he is like' [TH].

QUESTION—What is meant by 'my words'?

Jesus' words were the substance of what he said [Lns]. They were his teachings [TG]. It refers to his teachings in this sermon [Arn, Su].

6:48 He-is likened to-a-man building a-house who dug and went-down-deep[a] and laid[b] a-foundation on the rock.[c] And a-flood[d] having-come the river[e] struck-against[f] that house, and it-was- not -strong (enough) to-shake[g] it because it had-been-built well.

TEXT—Instead of διὰ τὸ καλῶς οἰκοδομῆσαι αὐτήν 'because it had been built well' in the final clause, some manuscripts read τεθεμελίωτο γὰρ ἐπὶ τὴν πέτραν 'because it was founded upon the rock' and a few other manuscripts omit this phrase. GNT does not mention a variant. Τεθεμελίωτο γὰρ ἐπὶ τὴν πέτραν 'because it was founded upon the rock' is read by KJV.

LEXICON—a. aorist act. indic. of βαθύνω (LN **81.11**) (BAGD p. 130): 'to go down deep' [Arn, BAGD, **LN**], 'to go deep' [Lns, WBC]. The two verbs 'he dug' and 'he went down deep' express one concept, 'to dig deep' [AB, BECNT, **LN**, NTC, TH; HCSB, KJV, NASB, NCV, REB, TEV], 'to dig deeply' [NRSV], 'to dig down deep' [CEV, NET, NIV], 'to dig down (to bedrock)' [GW], not explicit [NLT]. Instead of taking the two verbs to be one concept as most do, some take the verbs to mean that he dug and kept on going deeper [Alf, EGT, ICC, Lns, My, Rb, Su]. This emphasizes the care he took in digging out the foundations and going down deep [NIGTC]. He dug down to the rock and even into the rock [Gdt, Su].

b. aorist act. indic. of τίθημι (LN 85.32) (BAGD I.1.a.β. p. 816): 'to lay' [AB, Arn, BAGD, BECNT, NTL; all versions except CEV], 'to place' [BAGD, LN, Lns, WBC]. The phrase 'to lay a foundation' is translated 'to build a house' [CEV].

c. πέτρα (LN 2.21) (BAGD 1.a. p. 654): 'rock' [Arn, BAGD, BECNT, LN, NTC, WBC; HCSB, KJV, NASB, NCV, NIV, NRSV, REB, TEV], 'bedrock' [AB, LN; GW, NET], 'solid rock' [CEV], 'underlying rock' [NLT], 'rock mass' [Lns]. It does not mean stones or stony ground, but the underlying bedrock [TG]. The article in τὴν πέτραν 'the rock' is generic and this means 'on rock' [AB, BECNT, NTC, TH; CEV, NCV, NET, NIV, NRSV, REB, TEV].

d. πλήμμυρα (LN 14.33) (BAGD p. 669): 'flood' [AB, Arn, BAGD, BECNT, LN, Lns, NTC, WBC; CEV, GW, HCSB, KJV, NASB, NET, NIV, NRSV], 'floods' [NCV], 'high water' [BAGD, LN], 'stream' [Arn]. This refers to a river overflowing its banks [LN]. This noun is combined with river: 'when the river was in flood' [REB], 'the river flooded over' [TEV], 'when the floodwaters rise' [NLT].

278   LUKE 6:48

- e. ποταμός (LN 1.76) (BAGD 1. p. 694): 'river' [AB, BAGD, LN, Lns, WBC; CEV, HCSB, NET, NRSV, REB, TEV], 'stream' [BECNT, LN; KJV], 'water' [NCV], 'floodwaters' [GW, NLT], 'torrent' [NTC; NASB, NIV].
- f. aorist act. indic. of προσρήγνυμι (LN **19.6**) (BAGD 2. p. 718): 'to strike against' [**LN**], 'to strike' [NIV], 'to hit' [TEV], 'to burst upon' [BAGD, WBC; REB], 'to burst against' [AB, LN, NTC; NASB, NET, NRSV], 'to rush against' [CEV], 'to push against' [GW], 'to beat vehemently upon' [KJV], 'to break against' [BECNT, Lns; NLT], 'to crash against' [HCSB], 'to dash against' [Arn], 'to try to wash away' [NCV].
- g. aorist act. infin. of (LN 16.7) (BAGD 1. p. 740): 'to shake' [BAGD, BECNT, LN, Lns, NTC, WBC; HCSB, KJV, NASB, NCV, NET, NIV, NRSV, TEV], 'to shake loose' [AB], 'to cause to move to and fro' [BAGD], 'to shift' [REB], 'to move' [Arn]. The house is made the subject of the verb: 'it didn't even shake' [CEV], 'it stands firm' [NLT], 'the house couldn't be washed away' [GW]. It withstood the onrushing, swirling water of the flood [NTC].

QUESTION—What is meant by 'a flood having come'?
The participle 'having come' is inceptive and it means 'when a flood came' [TH]. The picture is that of a river overflowing its banks [TG, TH], or a flash flood with a swiftly flowing stream striking the house [NAC, Su]. This refers to a nearby river [NIGTC, WBC] that overflowed its banks in flood time [WBC].

QUESTION—What had been built well?
The house was built well [NTC, TH; CEV, NCV] because the foundation of the house had been built on rock [Lns, My; GW]. This does not describe the appearance of the house [Lns].

6:49 But the (one) having-heard and not having-done is like a-man having-built a-house on the ground[a] without a-foundation, which the river struck-against, and immediately it-collapsed[b] and the destruction[c] of-that house was great.[d]

LEXICON—a. γῇ (LN 2.14) (BAGD 2. p. 157): 'ground' [Arn, BAGD, BECNT, LN, NTC, WBC; GW, HCSB, NASB, NCV, NET, NIV, NRSV], 'soil' [LN; REB], 'earth' [Lns; KJV], 'surface' [AB], not explicit [TEV]. The phrase 'built on the ground without a foundation' is translated 'wasn't built on solid rock' [CEV], 'builds without a foundation' [NLT]. This means that the house was built on the surface [Su]. It implies that the man built the house without digging into the ground and laying a foundation [EGT, NTC, Su, TH].
- b. aorist act. indic. of συμπίπτω (LN **20.51**) (BAGD 1. p. 779): 'to collapse' [AB, Arn, BAGD, **LN**, NTC, WBC; GW, HCSB, NASB, NET, NIV, REB], 'to fall in' [BAGD, Lns], 'to fall' [BECNT; KJV, NCV, NRSV, TEV], 'to crumble' [NLT]. The phrase 'immediately it collapsed and the destruction was great' is translated 'it was smashed to pieces' [CEV]. The

house fell down in a heap [ICC]. The raging water undermined the walls and carried away the soil on which the house was built [NTC].
c. ῥῆγμα (LN **20.58**) (BAGD p. 735): 'destruction' [LN; HCSB, NIV], 'crash' [**LN**, NTC; REB, TEV], 'ruin' [BAGD, BECNT, Lns, WBC; KJV, NASB, NRSV], 'wreck' [AB, BAGD], 'collapse' [BAGD], 'a heap of ruins' [NLT], not explicit [CEV, GW]. This noun is also translated as a verb: 'to be destroyed' [GW, NCV, NET], 'to be ruined' [Arn]. Since the context points to the event of destruction, it refers to the crash or destruction of the house [LN], or its collapsing [TH].
d. μέγας (LN 78.2): 'great' [AB, BECNT, LN, Lns, WBC; HCSB, KJV, NASB, NRSV, REB], 'tremendous' [NTC], 'terrible' [TEV], 'complete' [NIV], 'completely (destroyed)' [NCV], 'utterly (destroyed)' [NET], 'utterly (ruined)' [Arn], not explicit [CEV, NLT]. This refers to the degree of destruction [LN]. Being in the final position of the sentence, makes this description emphatic [BECNT, ICC, TH].

QUESTION—What is the application of this parable?

It is as foolish to listen to Jesus' teachings without obeying them as to build a house without taking care how it is built [NIGTC]. The main feature of the parable is the preparation of a foundation [Su, WBC], and contrasts hearing and doing Jesus' teaching with hearing and not doing his teaching [BECNT, Lns]. It illustrates the importance of obeying the message they have heard [NICNT]. Those who heed Jesus' teaching are in a solid position to resist the trials of life, but those who do not heed run the risk of collapsing in the midst of trials [BECNT]. The flood and river describe not merely the many trials in this life, but also the supreme trial of death [Lns]. The testing of a crisis comes for everyone, including trials, temptations, bereavement, death, and especially the final judgment [NTC, TNTC]. The crisis in focus is God's judgment [NAC, NICNT, WBC]. Obeying Jesus' message shows the true nature of a person that will be relevant in the final judgment [BECNT, NIGTC]. This is a warning to not only hear Jesus' words, but to obey them in order to escape God's judgment [NAC].

DISCOURSE UNIT: 7:1–8:56 [REB]. The topic is miracles and parables.

DISCOURSE UNIT: 7:1–8:3 [AB, BECNT]. The topic is the first movements to faith and Christological questions [BECNT], the reception accorded to Jesus' ministry [AB].

DISCOURSE UNIT: 7:1–50 [NAC, NICNT, NIGTC, WBC]. The topic is who Jesus is [NAC], the compassionate ministry of Jesus [NICNT], the compassion of the Messiah [NIGTC], something greater than John is here [WBC].

DISCOURSE UNIT: 7:1–17 [NASB]. The topic is the healing of a centurion's servant by Jesus.

DISCOURSE UNIT: 7:1–10 [AB, BECNT, NAC, NICNT, NIGTC, Su, TNTC, WBC; CEV, GW, HCSB, NCV, NET, NIV, NLT, NRSV, TEV]. The topic is the healing of a slave [NICNT], Jesus heals the centurion's servant [AB, NAC, NIGTC, Su, TNTC; NET, NRSV], Jesus heals an army officer's servant [CEV], Jesus heals a Roman officer's servant [TEV], Jesus heals a soldier's servant [NCV], the faith of a centurion [BECNT; HCSB, NIV], a believing army officer [GW], the faith of the Roman officer [NLT], the authority of Jesus over life and death [WBC].

7:1 When he-finished all his words in the ears[a] of-the people, he-entered into Capernaum.

LEXICON—a. ἀκοή (LN 24.52) (BAGD 1.c. p. 31): 'ear' [BAGD, WBC], 'hearing' [Arn, LN, Lns, NTC; HCSB, NASB, NIV, NRSV], 'audience' [KJV]. The clause 'he finished all his words in the ears of the people' is translated 'his words filled the ears of the people' [BECNT], 'Jesus had finished teaching the people' [CEV], 'Jesus had finished teaching all this to the people' [NET], 'Jesus had finished all his words to the people' [AB], 'he had finished addressing the people' [REB], 'Jesus had finished saying all these things to the people' [TEV], 'Jesus had finished everything he wanted to say to the people' [GW], 'Jesus finished saying all these things to the people' [NCV], 'Jesus had finished saying all this' [NLT].

QUESTION—How is this verse related to its context?

In spite of the chapter number, this verse actually forms a conclusion to the sermon [ICC, Rb, WBC]. However, the chapter number is appropriate here [NTC] and all translations include this verse with the following account, making it appear to be an introduction to it, although two translations make the verse a paragraph by itself [NTC; NASB]. This verse forms a transition between the sermon and the incident with the centurion [BECNT, NICNT, NIGTC]. It refers to the completion of the sermon and tells of the geographical change for the events that follow [NICNT]. Jesus left the plain near Capernaum and went into the town [BECNT, Lns].

7:2 And a-slave[a] of-a-certain centurion[b] who was highly-regarded[c] by-him, having an-illness[d] was-about to-die.

LEXICON—a. δοῦλος (LN 87.76) (BAGD 1.a. p. 205): 'slave' [Arn, BAGD, BECNT, LN, Lns, WBC; GW, HCSB, NASB, NET, NLT, NRSV], 'servant' [AB, NTC; CEV, KJV, NCV, NIV, REB, TEV]. A slave was someone who was forced to work without pay [TG].

b. ἑκατοντάρχης (LN 55.16) (BAGD p. 237): 'centurion' [AB, Arn, BAGD, BECNT, LN, Lns, NTC, WBC; HCSB, KJV, NASB, NET, NIV, NRSV, REB], 'army officer' [CEV, NCV], 'Roman officer' [NLT, TEV], 'Roman army officer' [GW], 'captain' [LN]. He was a Roman military officer who commanded about a hundred soldiers [AB, LN, NICNT] and he was a Gentile (see 7:9) [AB, Arn, Gdt, NICNT, NIGTC, NTC, TNTC, WBC]. Centurions were of various nationalities and it is unknown which country this centurion was from [BECNT, NIGTC], but he probably was a Roman [Gdt, NTC, Su]. Roman troops were stationed in cities all through the country [TG]. The number of men under his command did not need to be exactly one hundred [NTC] and could vary from fifty to a hundred [Rb, TH]. The nearest equivalent to his rank is an army captain [NTC, TG, TNTC]. Or, he probably was an officer in the service of Herod Antipas [AB, Arn, Gdt, ICC, Lns, NIGTC, NIVS, NTC, TNTC, WBC] and would not be in charge of Roman troops stationed in Capernaum [AB, BECNT]. He could have been an officer of mercenary troops or could have been in police service or customs service [AB]. Occurring in the emphatic position at the beginning of the verse, the centurion is the main character in the account [BECNT, TH]. See this word at 23:47.

c. ἔντιμος (LN 87.6) (BAGD 2. p. 269): 'highly regarded' [NASB, NET], 'respected, honored' [LN], 'very important' [NCV], 'dear' [BECNT; KJV], 'very dear' [NTC; TEV], 'precious' [Lns, WBC], 'valued highly' [HCSB, NIV, NLT, NRSV, REB], 'prized highly' [AB], 'valuable' [Arn, BAGD; GW], 'precious' [BAGD]. The phrase 'was highly regarded by him' is translated 'the officer liked this servant very much' [CEV]. Rather than the slave being valuable [Arn, BAGD; GW], the meaning 'highly respected' fits the context better [BECNT, NIGTC, Su; NASB, NET]. He was held in high esteem by the centurion [Su]. The word points to the great affection and esteem the centurion had for his slave [EGT, Gdt, ICC, NICNT, NIGTC, NTC, Su, TG, TH, TNTC; KJV, NASB, NET, TEV].

d. κακῶς (LN 23.148) (BAGD 1. p. 398): 'badly'. The phrase κακῶς ἔχω, literally 'to have badly' or 'to fare badly', is an idiom meaning 'to be ill' [AB, Arn, BAGD, BECNT, LN, Lns, WBC; NRSV, REB], 'to be sick' [BAGD, LN, NTC; all versions except NRSV, REB]. From Matthew's account at 8:6 it appears that he was paralyzed and suffered greatly. Perhaps he had a paralysis with muscular spasms [NTC] or acute rheumatism [Gdt]. He was so sick that he was at the point of death and could not be taken to where Jesus was [NIGTC].

7:3 **And having-heard about Jesus he-sent elders[a] of-the Jews to him asking him that having-come he-might-cure/save[b] his slave.**

LEXICON—a. πρεσβύτερος (LN 53.77) (BAGD 2.a.α. p. 700): 'elder' [AB, Arn, BAGD, LN, Lns, NTC, WBC; HCSB, KJV, NASB, NET, NIV, NRSV, REB, TEV], 'civil elder' [BECNT], 'leader' [CEV, GW, NCV], 'respected leader' [NLT]. This person would be a member of the local council in the city [BAGD]. Elders (literally 'older men') were mature men who had been appointed to leadership in the synagogue [Su]. They were leaders of the community who were responsible for discipline in the synagogue [NIGTC]. They were respected religious leaders [TG]. Or, they probably were elders of the city government rather than leaders of the synagogue [AB, Alf, Arn, BECNT, EGT, Lns, My, NICNT, NIVS, WBC]. They were prominent social leaders [BECNT], community leaders in Capernaum [AB].

b. aorist act. subj. of διασῴζω (LN **23.136**, 21.19) (BAGD p. 189): 'to heal' [**LN** (23.136), NTC; CEV, KJV, NCV, NET, NIV, NLT, NRSV], 'to cure' [Arn, BECNT, LN (23.136)], 'to make well' [LN (23.136)], 'to save' [AB, LN (21.19), WBC], 'to save the life (of the servant)' [GW, HCSB, NASB, REB, TEV], 'to bring safe through' [Lns].

QUESTION—What had the centurion heard about Jesus?

He had heard that Jesus healed sick people [BECNT, EGT, NTC, Su, TH, TNTC] and worked miracles [AB]. He already knew that Jesus healed people, but here '*when* he heard' means 'when he heard that Jesus had returned to the city' [Lns, TG].

QUESTION—Since the subject of the verb ἐρωτῶν 'asking' is singular and a delegation of elders went to Jesus, who asked?

The parallel account in Matthew 8:5–13 merely says that the centurion came to Jesus and asked for help without mentioning the elders. Here we find that the centurion used intermediaries to make the request [NTC]. The singular subject indicates that the centurion's request was transmitted by the elders he sent [NAC, TH]. What the centurion does through agents he really does himself [BECNT, Lns]. Since the centurion was a Gentile, he made his request through the Jews with whom he had a previous association [NICNT]. He did not consider himself worthy to approach Jesus personally [NIGTC]. Either Luke had access to more material than Matthew did [BECNT], or Matthew abbreviated the account [BECNT, NAC].

QUESTION—Was the request to heal or to save the slave?

1. The request was to heal the slave of his sickness [BAGD, BECNT, LN, NIGTC; CEV, KJV, NCV, NET, NIV, NLT, NRSV].
2. The request was to save the life of the slave who was at the point of dying [TH; GW, HCSB, NASB, REB, TEV].
3. The request was to save the slave from the illness and from dying [AB, Lns].

7:4 And the (ones who) came to Jesus were-begging[a] him earnestly saying, He-is worthy[b] that you-will-grant[c] this for-him, **7:5** because he-loves our nation[d] and he built the synagogue for-us.

LEXICON—a. imperf. act. indic. of παρακαλέω (LN 33.168) (BAGD 3. p. 617): 'to beg' [CEV, GW, NCV, NLT, TEV], 'to request' [BAGD, LN], 'to implore' [BAGD; NASB], 'to appeal' [BAGD; NRSV], 'to make an appeal' [REB], 'to entreat' [BAGD], 'to beseech' [Lns; KJV], 'to plead' [Arn, LN, NTC; HCSB, NIV], 'to earnestly ask' [LN], 'to exhort' [BECNT], 'to urge' [AB, WBC; NET]. The imperfect tense means that they began to do this and kept on with it [Lns, NIGTC, Rb, TH].

b. ἄξιος (LN 65.1) (BAGD 2.a. p. 78): 'worthy' [BAGD, BECNT, LN, Lns, NTC, WBC; HCSB, KJV, NASB, NCV, NET, NRSV]. The phrase 'to be worthy' is translated 'to deserve' [AB, Arn; CEV, GW, NIV, NLT, REB, TEV].

c. fut. mid. indic. of παρέχω (LN **13.127**) (BAGD 2.b. p. 626): 'to grant' [AB, BAGD, BECNT, NTC, WBC; HCSB, NASB], 'to do' [Arn, **LN**, Lns; KJV, NET, NIV, NRSV], 'to cause to happen' [LN]. The phrase 'you will grant this' is translated '(he deserves) your help' [CEV, GW, NLT, TEV], '(he is worthy) of your help' [NCV], '(he deserves) this favor from you' [REB].

d. ἔθνος (LN 11.55): 'nation' [AB, Arn, BECNT, LN, Lns, NTC, WBC; CEV, HCSB, KJV, NASB, NET, NIV, REB], 'people' [LN; GW, NCV, NRSV, TEV], 'the Jews' [NLT]. This noun refers to the Jewish people as a whole, not to a nation as a political entity [NAC, TH], or to their race [TH]. He admired and respected the pure worship of the Jews and felt affection for the people who practiced it [ICC].

QUESTION—What did the elders beg Jesus to do?

The elders did more than present the centurion's request. They went on to plead that Jesus would grant what the centurion asked for [Lns]. After the elders presented the centurion's request they added their own encouragement to do it [Su], and lobbied on his behalf in order to persuade Jesus to come and help him [BECNT]. That they kept on begging Jesus does not indicate that Jesus was unwilling. They were eager to press the case and perhaps felt that Jesus would not think that it was proper to help a Gentile [NIGTC, Su].

QUESTION—In what way was the centurion worthy?

Compared with others whom Jesus helped, this man was worthy of Jesus' consideration [Lns]. He was worthy because of his public reputation [NIGTC]. The reason for saying that he was worthy is given in the following γάρ 'because' clause: because he loved their nation and had built the synagogue for them [BECNT, Su, TH, WBC].

QUESTION—How did the centurion build the Jewish synagogue?

The presence of the pronoun αὐτός 'he' is emphatic, 'he himself' [Lns, Su, TH; NET], and indicates that the centurion either had the synagogue built or donated the amount needed for its construction [NET]. The centurion paid for the building of the entire synagogue at his own expense [Alf, ICC, Lns, NTC, Rb, TG; GW]. It would have been unusual for a Gentile to build an entire synagogue, so perhaps it means that he was the main contributor to the building [NIGTC]. Perhaps he was responsible for the building of the synagogue at Roman expense [Su]. He was not the direct agent who built it, rather he arranged for other people to build it [TH].

QUESTION—When the elders said that the centurion built the synagogue 'for us', does 'us' include Jesus?

1. It is inclusive and includes Jesus along with the elders [TH]. Jesus' permanent base was now at Capernaum and so he belonged to the local synagogue there [TH].
2. It is exclusive and means the elders but not Jesus [TG]. The 'us' means 'us citizens of Capernaum', but Jesus' home town was Nazareth [TG].

7:6 And Jesus was-going with them. And he already[a] not being far from the house, the centurion sent friends saying to-him, Lord,[b] do- not -trouble[c] (yourself), because I-am not worthy[d] that you-should-enter under my roof.[e]

LEXICON—a. ἤδη (LN 67.20) (BAGD 1.a. p. 344): 'already' [BAGD, BECNT, LN, Lns], 'still' [AB], 'by this time' [BAGD], 'now' [Arn; KJV], 'just before' [NLT], not explicit [NTC, WBC; CEV, GW, HCSB, NASB, NCV, NET, NIV, NRSV, REB, TEV]. Occurring at the beginning of the sentence makes this adverb emphatic and means that Jesus had already reached a point where he was not far from the house [TH]. The phrase 'already not being far from the house' is a litotes indicating that he was already quite near the house [EGT, NIGTC, WBC]. Probably the centurion could see Jesus approaching [Gdt], or word of his coming reached the centurion that Jesus was near [Arn, Lns].

b. κύριος (LN 87.53, 12.9): 'Lord' [Arn, BECNT, LN (12.9), Lns, NTC, WBC; all versions except GW, REB, TEV], 'sir' [AB, LN (87.53); GW, REB, TEV]. This is a title of respect when addressing a man or it is a title for God or Christ [LN]. It was used as a title of respect [AB, Arn, BECNT, TG], and this would be equivalent to addressing Jesus as 'Rabbi' [BECNT, NIGTC]. Or, the centurion's great faith (7:9) indicates that he was addressing Jesus as his divine Lord [Lns].

c. pres. pass. impera. of σκύλλομαι/σκύλλω (LN **22.16**) (BAGD 3. p. 758): 'to trouble oneself' [AB, Arn, BAGD, BECNT, Lns, NTC; HCSB, KJV, NCV, NET, NIV, NLT, NRSV, TEV], 'to further trouble oneself' [NASB, REB], 'to be bothered' [**LN**], 'to be troubled' [LN]. The negative 'do not trouble yourself' is translated 'don't bother' [GW], 'don't go to any trouble for me' [CEV], 'do not go to any further trouble' [WBC]. The present imperative means to stop an action already begun, 'stop troubling yourself' [ICC, Lns]. It implies 'do not trouble yourself *any further*' [TH; NASB]. It means that Jesus should not take the time and effort of going any further on his way to the house because the centurion believed that Jesus could heal the servant without being present [BECNT, TG].

d. ἱκανός (LN 75.2) (BAGD 2. p. 374): 'worthy' [BAGD, BECNT, WBC; CEV, HCSB, KJV, NASB, NCV, NET, NRSV, REB], 'worthy of such an honor' [NLT], 'qualified' [BAGD, LN], 'fit' [Arn, NTC], 'adequate' [LN], 'sufficient' [Lns]. This adjective is translated as a verb phrase: 'to deserve' [AB; GW, NIV, TEV]. This word is synonymous with ἄξιος 'worthy' in 7:4 [TH]. See this word at 3:16.

e. στέγη (LN 7.50) (BAGD p. 765): 'roof' [BAGD, LN]. The phrase 'to enter under/beneath my roof' [Lns; KJV] is also translated 'to come under my roof' [AB, Arn, BECNT, NTC, WBC; HCSB, NASB, NET, NIV, NRSV, REB], 'to come into my house' [CEV, GW, NCV, TEV], 'to come to my home' [NLT].

QUESTION—Why did the centurion feel that he was not worthy?

He had a feeling of personal unworthiness [BECNT, Gdt, NAC, NIGTC, NTC, Su, TG, WBC]. Jesus was too important a person to enter his house

[TG]. He realized that Jesus healed through God's power as a prophet or as someone who had a special relation to God [BECNT]. He was insignificant in comparison with the exalted person of Jesus [NTC]. The centurion also knew that entering a Gentile's house would defile a Jew [AB, Arn, BECNT, ICC, Lns, Su], but this is not his main concern [BECNT]. The centurion felt that it that a Jew would feel it improper to enter a ceremonially unclean house of a Gentile [Lns] and thus felt that he did not deserve the visit from Jesus [AB].

QUESTION—Why did the centurion's friends use the first person singular 'I am not worthy'?

The centurion sent the message by means of his friends and they delivered it with the very words of the centurion [BECNT, NIGTC, WBC], repeating the message verbatim [AB].

7:7 That-is-why[a] I-did- not -consider- myself -worthy to-come to you. But say a-word and (let) my servant[b] be-healed.

TEXT—Instead of the imperative ἰαθήτω 'let be healed', some manuscripts read the future indicative ἰαθήσεται 'he will be healed'. GNT reads the imperative ἰαθήτω 'let be healed' with a B decision, indicating that the text is almost certain. The future indicative ἰαθήσεται 'he will be healed' is read by KJV.

LEXICON—a. διό (LN 89.47): 'that is why' [NTC; GW, HCSB, NCV, NET, NIV, REB], 'this is why' [AB], 'for that reason' [WBC], 'for which reason too' [Arn], 'for this reason' [LN; NASB], 'therefore' [LN; NRSV], 'wherefore' [Lns; KJV], not explicit [BECNT; CEV, NLT, TEV].

b. παῖς (LN **87.77**) (BAGD 2.a.γ. p. 604): 'servant' [AB, Arn, BAGD, BECNT, Lns, WBC; all versions], 'child' [BAGD], 'boy' [NTC], 'slave' [BAGD, **LN**]. This word for 'child, boy' is used of a slave, especially one who is a personal servant and for whom the master would have a kindly regard [LN]. This word is synonymous with the word δοῦλος 'slave' in 7:2 [TH]. The word παῖς 'boy' was an affectionate term for a slave [ICC, Rb].

QUESTION—What relationship is indicated by διό 'that is why'?

The reason why is the centurion's unworthiness which he just expressed in 7:6 [Alf, My, NIGTC]: I am unworthy, and that is why I do not consider myself worthy to even come to you. He is explaining why he sent friends to Jesus instead of personally going himself [Lns, WBC]. Since the centurion is not worthy to have Jesus come into his house, it follows that he is not worthy to meet Jesus outside it either [NIGTC].

QUESTION—What is the force of the imperative passive ἰαθήτω 'let be healed'?

This imperative is the word that the centurion wants Jesus to speak. The imperative in the third person 'let my servant be healed' is a difficult form to translate and may be translated (1) as a request, 'please heal my servant', or (2) as an expression of confidence using the future tense [TH]. The future

7:8 Because[a] I also am a-man being-placed[b] under[c] authority[d] having soldiers under[c] me, and I-say to-this (one), Go, and he-goes, and to-another, Come, and he-comes, and to-my slave, Do this, and he does (it).

LEXICON—a. γάρ (LN 89.23): 'because' [LN], 'for' [Arn, BECNT, LN, Lns, NTC, WBC; HCSB, KJV, NASB, NET, NIV, NRSV], 'I know because/for' [AB; NLT, REB], 'as you know' [GW], not explicit [CEV, NCV, TEV].

  b. pres. pass. participle of τάσσω (LN **13.13**) (BAGD 1.b. p. 806): 'to be placed' [Arn, BAGD, LN; HCSB, NASB, TEV], 'to be set' [BAGD, BECNT, Lns, NTC; KJV, NET, NRSV], 'to be caused to be' [LN], 'to be (under)' [AB, **LN**, WBC; NCV, NIV, NLT, REB], not explicit [CEV, GW].

  c. ὑπό with accusative object (LN 37.7) (BAGD 2.b. p. 843): 'under' [AB, Arn, BAGD, BECNT, LN, Lns, NTC, WBC; all versions except CEV, GW], 'under the control of' [LN]. The reciprocal idea is given by some: 'I have officers who give orders to me' [CEV], 'I'm in a chain of command' [GW].

  c. ἐξουσία (LN 37.35) (BAGD 4.a. p. 278): 'authority' [Arn, BAGD, BECNT, LN, Lns, NTC, WBC; KJV, NASB, NCV, NET, NIV, NRSV], 'the authority of superior officers' [NLT, TEV], 'orders' [AB; REB], '(chain of) command' [GW], '(my) command' [HCSB], not explicit [CEV].

QUESTION—What relationship is indicated by γάρ 'because' at the beginning of the verse?

This indicates the reason the centurion knew that Jesus could heal by simply uttering a command [AB, BECNT, Crd, ICC, Lns, NIGTC, Su, TG, TH; NLT, REB]: I know that you need only to give a command to heal my servant, *because* I know what the command of one in authority can do. He gives this explanation so as not to appear to be presumptuous in telling Jesus how he might proceed [Lns]. This verse justifies his request that Jesus give a command [TG].

QUESTION—What is the force of the centurion's argument in mentioning that he was also under authority?

  1. He compared himself being both under authority and having authority over others with Jesus being under authority and having authority over others [BECNT, Crd, NIGTC, TG, WBC]. Jesus is regarded as being under God's authority [NIGTC, TG]. Jesus serves God and has a sphere of authority [BECNT]. The argument is from the less to the greater [BECNT]. Because of Jesus' relationship to God, he has access to the comprehensive authority that is God's [WBC]. Under this interpretation,

he means that just as he was under authority and therefore could do things because of that authority, so Jesus, had greater power because he was under God's authority, and therefore could command the healing of the servant in God's name [NAC].

2. The argument is not based on Jesus being under authority [AB, Arn, Gdt, ICC, Lns, NAC, NTC, Su]. The centurion is referring to his intimate knowledge of authority in regard to his being under authority and also having authority over others [ICC]. Although he was down the chain of command, the centurion had people under him through whom he could act without going to the place personally, so Jesus, who had far greater authority, could easily make use of similar powers [Gdt]. The centurion was a mere human being, yet his word was obeyed, so how much more powerful is the word of God's great prophet [Arn]. Certainly Jesus who had independent authority could command whatever he wanted to be done [NTC]. The word 'also' must not be taken to mean that Jesus was also under authority. Rather it means 'I like other officers' [Lns]. The argument is from the less to the greater [AB, Lns]. Under this interpretation, he means that although he was under authority, he could still give orders, but Jesus has even more power since he is not under authority [NAC].

7:9 And having-heard these (things) Jesus was-amazed[a] (at) him and having-turned he said to-the crowd following him, I say to-you, not-even in Israel have-I-found such-great[b] faith. **7:10** And having returned to the house the (ones who) were-sent found the slave being-in-good-health.[c]

TEXT—In 7:10, before δοῦλον 'slave', some manuscripts add ἀσθενοῦντα 'being sick'. GNT rejects this addition with an A decision, indicating that the text is certain. Ἀσθενοῦντα 'being sick' is read by KJV.

LEXICON—a. aorist act. indic. of θαυμάζω (LN 25.213) (BAGD 1.b.β. p. 352): 'to be amazed'. See translations of this word at 1:21 and 4:22. Jesus was amazed that the centurion believed Jesus could cure the servant with just an oral command without actually seeing and touching him [Arn, TG]. Jesus was amazed that it was a Gentile and not a Jew who had such faith [Su]. Only two times is it said that Jesus was amazed, here at the centurion's faith and in Mark 6:6 at the lack of faith of the people in his home town [TNTC]. His amazement was due to his self-imposed limitations upon his omniscience in his state of humility [Arn]. Although almost all take the verb to refer to Jesus being amazed, one commentary thinks that nothing seems to take Jesus by surprise so that here the verb means that Jesus admired him [WBC]. This word also occurs at 1:63; 2:18, 33; 7:9; 8:25; 11:14, 38; 20:26; 24:12, 41.

b. τοσοῦτος (LN 59.18) (BAGD 1.a.b. p. 823): 'so great' [Arn, BAGD, LN, Lns; HCSB, KJV], 'such great' [NTC; NASB, NIV], 'greatest' [NCV], 'so much' [BAGD, LN], 'this much' [CEV], 'as great as this' [GW], 'like

this' [NLT, TEV], 'such as this' [AB], 'his kind of' [WBC], 'such' [BECNT; NET, NRSV, REB].
    c. pres. act. participle of ὑγιαίνω (LN 23.129) (BAGD 1. p. 832): 'to be well' [Arn, LN, Lns; CEV, NET, NIV, TEV], 'to be healthy' [BAGD, LN; GW], 'to be in good health' [AB, BAGD, NTC, WBC; HCSB, NASB, NCV, NRSV, REB], 'to be in sound health' [BECNT], 'to be whole' [KJV], 'to be completely healed' [NLT]. He was well again like any other person [Lns, TH]. Not only was he cured, he was in good health [ICC]. This verb focuses on the good health that the healing produced [BECNT].
QUESTION—When Jesus said, 'not even in Israel', what did he mean since the centurion was also living in Israel?
    This indicates that the centurion was a Gentile [ICC, Lns, TG]. The designation 'Israel' refers to the Jewish nation as a religious entity as well as a geographical entity [TH]. Israel refers to the Jews. The translation should not be understood to mean that Jesus was outside of the country of Israel [TG].
QUESTION—Had not Jesus found Jews with great faith?
    By saying 'such great faith' Jesus implies that he had found great faith among the Jews, although not as great as this centurion's faith [Arn, Lns, NTC, TNTC, WBC]. The centurion had shown faith greater than that of any Jew Jesus had met [TG]. None of the Jews had believed that Jesus could heal without being present [ICC]. This refers to faith in Jesus' authority and the power of his word over illness in spite of distance [BECNT, NICNT]. This refers to faith in the power of God that Jesus revealed in himself [NIGTC]. His faith centered in Jesus' word and in its power and also in the exalted person of Jesus [Lns]. Jesus' emphasis on faith probably meant more than faith that the slave would be healed and meant that the centurion trusted in Jesus and accepted him as Lord [TNTC]. Some take this statement to be a criticism against the Jews [AB, ICC], others think that no criticism is implied [WBC]. Jesus' approval of such faith challenged the crowd to trust in Jesus as the centurion had [BECNT].
QUESTION—What actions are implied before the words 'And having returned to the house' in 7:10?
    The parallel account in Matthew 8:13 provides information that the servant was healed at the moment Jesus replied to the messengers. The account does not indicate whether Jesus spoke a word that healed the servant or whether the healing was done without a word [Lns, TNTC]. It is assumed that Jesus did speak a word of healing and did not go to the centurion's house [TH].

DISCOURSE UNIT: 7:11–17 [BECNT, TNTC, WBC; CEV, GW, NCV, NRSV]. The topic is a widow's son [CEV], the widow of Nain's son [TNTC], Jesus raises a widow's son at Nain [NRSV], Jesus brings a widow's son back to life [GW], Jesus brings a man back to life [NCV], resuscitation of a widow's son and questions about Jesus [BECNT], God has visited his people [WBC].

7:11 And it-happened on the next[a] (time) he-proceeded to a-town[b] called Nain and his disciples and a-great crowd were-accompanying[c] him.

TEXT—Instead of ἐν τῷ ἑξῆς 'on the next' (the masculine article presumably implying the masculine noun χρόνῳ 'time'), some manuscripts read ἐν τῇ ἑξῆς 'on the next' and other manuscripts read τῇ ἑξῆς 'on the next' (the feminine article presumably implying the feminine noun ἡμέρᾳ 'day'). GNT reads ἐν τῷ ἑξῆς 'on the next' with a B decision, indicating that the text is almost certain. Ἐν τῇ ἑξῆς 'on the next' is read by KJV.

TEXT—Instead of οἱ μαθηταὶ αὐτοῦ 'the disciples of him', some manuscripts read οἱ μαθηταὶ αὐτοῦ ἱκανοί 'many disciples of him' and other manuscripts read οἱ μαθηταὶ ἱκανοί 'many disciples'. GNT reads οἱ μαθηταὶ αὐτοῦ 'the disciples of him' with a B decision, indicating that the text is almost certain. Οἱ μαθηταὶ αὐτοῦ ἱκανοί 'many disciples of him' is read by KJV.

LEXICON—a. ἑξῆς (LN **67.52**) (BAGD 2. p. 276): 'next' [BAGD]. The phrase ἐν τῷ ἑξῆς 'on the next' is an idiom referring to a point of time subsequent to another point of time [LN]. The phrase is translated 'later, next' [**LN**], 'afterwards' [BAGD; REB], 'the day after' [KJV], 'soon' [CEV], 'soon afterwards' [AB, NTC, WBC; all versions except CEV, KJV, REB], 'thereafter' [BECNT], 'the time soon after' [Lns], 'in the following time' [Arn].

b. πόλις (LN 1.88) (BAGD 1. p. 685): 'town' [AB, LN, NTC; CEV, HCSB, NCV, NET, NIV, NRSV, REB, TEV], 'village' [NLT], 'city' [Arn, BAGD, BECNT, LN, Lns, WBC; GW, KJV, NASB]. Although this noun can be used for 'city' in contrast with other nouns for village and town, it can simply refer to a population center without reference to its size [LN]. Nain was a small town about six miles southeast of Nazareth [NAC; NET] and about twenty miles southwest of Capernaum [BECNT], or twenty-five miles [NAC, WBC]. No remains of this town have been found [WBC]. Some think it was built on the same site as the present town of Nein [AB, BECNT, BNTC, NIGTC, NTC], which now only has about two hundred residents [BECNT].

c. imperf. mid./pass. (deponent = act.) indic. of συμπορεύομαι (LN **15.148**) (BAGD 1. p. 780): 'to accompany' [AB, LN; REB, TEV], 'to go with' [BAGD, BECNT, **LN**, Lns, WBC; GW, KJV, NET, NRSV], 'to go along with' [NTC; CEV, NASB, NIV], 'to travel with' [HCSB, NCV], 'to journey with' [Arn], 'to follow' [NLT].

QUESTION—When did this happen?

The masculine article implies a masculine noun χρόνῳ 'time' [AB, Crd, EGT, Gdt, ICC, Lns, NIGTC, NTC, Rb]: the next time. The link with the precious account is only a very general term [BECNT, NIGTC]. It does not indicate any specific day, only that this incident took place some time after the previous one [Arn]. It was soon after [Lns, NTC, TH, WBC; all versions except KJV, REB]. The variant reading with a feminine article implies a feminine noun ἡμέρᾳ 'day' [KJV]: the next day.

QUESTION—Where did the crowd accompanying Jesus come from?
As Jesus traveled from town to town, people joined the group accompanying Jesus and his disciples [TNTC]. This is the same crowd referred to in 7:9 [WBC]. At this point the disciples, who were not mentioned in 7:1–10, are specifically differentiated from the general crowd that accompanied Jesus [EGT, NICNT]. Or, the designation 'his disciples' refers to the twelve apostles [Gdt].

7:12 **And as he-approached the gate[a] of-the town, behold[b] (one) having-died was-being-carried-out (the) only son of-his mother and she was a-widow, and a-large crowd of-the town was with her.**
LEXICON—a. πύλη (LN 7.48) (BAGD 1. p. 729): 'gate' [AB, Arn, BAGD, BECNT, LN, NTC, WBC; all versions except GW], 'entrance' [GW], 'portal' [Lns]. The town was surrounded by a wall and the gate was a portal in the wall [Lns, TG]. Usually gates were built for defense, but the town was so small it probably was merely decorative [BECNT]. Since there has been no evidence of a wall in the remains of the town, this word must refer to the road entrance into the town [Su].
  b. ἰδού (LN 91.13): 'behold' [BECNT; KJV], 'lo' [Lns], 'look, listen, pay attention, come now, then' [LN], not explicit [AB, Arn, NTC, WBC; all versions except KJV]. This particle calls attention to the following statement and emphasizes it [LN, NTC]. The surprise caused by the meeting of the two groups is marked by this word [Lns] and shows that this encounter was something unexpected [Gdt].
QUESTION—Why was the corpse being carried out of the town?
The corpse was being carried out for burial [NAC, NIGTC, Su] in a funeral procession [Arn, TNTC; NET], since it was customary for burials to take place outside a Jewish town's walls [Alf, Arn, WBC]. The city was in the hills and there were many caves outside it that served as burial places [Su].

7:13 **And having-seen her the Lord had-compassion[a] upon her and said to-her, Do not cry.**
LEXICON—a. aorist pass. (deponent = act.) indic. of σπλαγχνίζομαι (LN 25.49) (BAGD p. 762): 'to have compassion on/for' [BECNT, LN, WBC; HCSB, KJV, NET, NRSV], 'to feel compassion for' [NASB], 'to be filled with compassion for' [Arn, Lns], 'to have pity' [AB, BAGD], 'to feel sorry for' [CEV, GW], 'to feel very sorry for' [NCV], 'to have one's heart go out to' [NTC; NIV, REB], 'to have one's heart overflow with compassion' [NLT], 'to have one's heart be filled with pity for' [TEV]. This is the motive for the miracle [AB, EGT]. See this word at 10:33, 15:20.
QUESTION—How did Luke use the designation ὁ κύριος 'the Lord' here?
This is the first time Luke himself refers to Jesus as 'Lord' and he also does this in 7:19; 10:1, 39, 41, etc. [NTC]. Luke was writing from his historical perspective of Jesus after the resurrection when believers universally referred to Jesus as 'Lord' or 'Lord Jesus' [Su]. This reflects the designation the early

church used to indicate the exaltation of Jesus by God to be Lord [BECNT, NIGTC, WBC], and Luke is thinking especially of Jesus' authority [BECNT, WBC]. Luke means the heavenly Christ who is Lord of the Church [EGT]. After the resurrection, 'Lord' came to designate Jesus as the divine Lord and Messiah-Ruler [Lns]. For Luke and his readers the Jesus of this account is the church's risen Lord [NAC].

7:14 And having-approached he-touched the bier,[a] and the (ones who) were-carrying (it) stood.[b] And he-said, Young-man,[c] I-say to-you, get-up.[d]
7:15 And the dead-man sat-up and he-began to-speak, and he-gave[e] him to-his mother.

LEXICON—a. σορός (LN **6.109**) (BAGD p. 759): 'bier' [BAGD, BECNT, **LN**, Lns, WBC; KJV, NET, NRSV, REB], 'coffin' [AB, Arn, BAGD; NASB, NCV, NIV, NLT, TEV], 'open coffin' [GW, HCSB], 'stretcher' [NTC], 'the stretcher on which the people were carrying the dead boy' [CEV]. This refers to a stretcher or even a plank that was used to carry a corpse to the place of burial [LN].
- b. aorist act. indic. of ἵσταμαι (LN 17.1) (BAGD II.a.α. p. 382): 'to stand' [LN], 'to stand still' [Arn, BAGD, BECNT; KJV, NET, NIV, NRSV], 'to stop' [AB, BAGD, Lns, WBC; CEV, GW, HCSB, NCV, NLT, TEV], 'to halt' [REB], 'to come to a halt' [NTC; NASB].
- c. νεανίσκος (LN 9.32) (BAGD 1. p. 534): 'young man' [AB, Arn, BAGD, BECNT, LN, Lns, NTC, WBC; all versions]. This is a designation for a male who is past puberty, but normally before marriage [LN]. It is a man between 24 and 40 years of age [TH]. It is refers to a man in his late teens or early twenties [TG].
- d. aorist pass. impera. of ἐγείρω (LN 23.94) (BAGD 2. p. 215): 'to get up' [AB, BAGD, NTC, WBC; CEV, HCSB, NCV, NET, NIV, NLT, REB, TEV], 'to arise' [Arn, BAGD, BECNT; KJV, NASB, NRSV], 'to rise up' [Lns], 'to rise to life, to be alive again' [LN], 'to come back to life' [GW]. This is used of those who are called back to life [BAGD]. Although the verb can mean to stand up or to wake up, it also refers to rising to life [LN]. The passive voice is often used with the force of the middle voice (that is, intransitive) [AB, WBC]. It means the same as the active imperative in 5:23, 24; 6:8; 8:54. The passive is also used of the dead being raised in 7:22; 9:7, 22; 20:37; 24:6, 34, but 'to be raised up' is too much at this stage of Jesus' ministry [AB]. Here the command 'arise' means to go from a lying position to a sitting position (not a standing position), or simply to come to life again [TH].
- e. aorist act. indic. of δίδωμι (LN 57.71): 'to give' [Arn, BECNT, LN, Lns, WBC; HCSB, NRSV], 'to give back' [AB, NTC; CEV, GW, NASB, NET, NIV, NLT, TEV], 'to deliver' [KJV], 'to restore' [REB].

QUESTION—Was the corpse being carried on a bier or in a coffin?
  1. The corpse was being carried on a bier [BECNT, Gdt, Lns, NAC, NICNT, NIGTC, NTC, Rb, TG, TH, TNTC, WBC; NET]. It would have been a

plank [BECNT, Gdt, NICNT; NET] so that the shroud-wrapped body would be visible to all [BECNT, Gdt, NICNT]. The corpse was laid on a wooden stretcher to be carried out for burial [TG]. The Jews did not use coffins because they did not bury the dead in the soil but placed them in chambers hewn in the rock [Lns]. The following verse makes a closed coffin impossible [NICNT].
2. The corpse was being carried in an open coffin [Alf, Arn, EGT, My, NIVS].

QUESTION—Why did Jesus touch the bier?
Jesus touched the bier in order to halt the funeral procession [Alf, Arn, EGT, Gdt, ICC, Lns, My, NICNT, NIGTC, NTC, Rb, TH, TNTC, WBC]. Without speaking, he indicated that the bearers were to stop and stand still [ICC].

QUESTION—Was the young man dead when he sat up?
Since a dead person does not sit up, it meant that the young man who was now alive sat up [TG]. The 'dead man' is translated 'the boy' [CEV], 'the son' [NCV], 'he that was dead' [KJV].

QUESTION—How did Jesus give the young man to the mother?
Jesus did not carry the young man over to the mother, but walked with him over to where the mother stood [TG]. Jesus said to the mother, 'Here is your child' [TH]. Luke's focus is on the widowed mother whom Jesus felt compassion for and to whom he now restores her son [NICNT, TNTC].

7:16 **And fear[a] seized all and they-were praising[b] God saying, A-great prophet was-raised-up[c] among us. And (saying), God visited[d] his people.**

LEXICON—a. φόβος (LN 25.25) (BAGD 1.a.α. p. 863): 'fear' [BAGD, LN]. The idiom 'fear seized all' [Arn, BECNT, WBC; NET, NRSV] is also translated 'fear took all' [Lns], 'fear took hold of them all' [NTC], 'fear gripped them all' [NASB], 'fear came over everyone' [HCSB], 'everyone was frightened' [CEV], 'everyone was struck with fear' [GW], 'they all were filled with fear' [TEV], 'there came a fear on all' [KJV], 'great fear swept the crowd' [NLT], 'all the people were amazed' [NCV], 'they were all filled with awe' [NIV], 'everyone was filled with awe' [REB], 'deep awe came over all of them' [AB]. Some think that instead of taking it to be a great fear produced by terror, this refers to 'deep awe' in response to seeing a miracle [AB, Arn, EGT, NAC, TNTC; NIV, REB]. Seeing a dead man raised to life would strike the people with such a fear that they would tremble [Lns]. See this word at 5:26.

b. imperf. act. indic. of δοξάζω (LN 33.357) (BAGD 1. p. 204): 'to praise'. See translations of this word at 5:25. The imperfect tense indicates that they began to praise God and continued to do so [Lns, Rb; NET]. This word also occurs at 5:25, 13:13.

c. aorist act. indic. of ἐγείρω (LN 13.83) (BAGD 2.e. p. 215): 'to be raised up' [AB, BECNT, LN, WBC], 'to be caused to exist, to be provided' [LN]. Most take the passive to be used intransitively: 'to appear' (passive intransitive) [BAGD, NTC; GW, NET, NIV, TEV], 'to come' [NCV], 'to

be' [CEV], 'to rise up' [Lns; KJV], 'to rise' [NLT, NRSV], 'to arise' [Arn; HCSB, NASB]. This means that he had been brought on the scene [AB], and had been sent by God [TG]. The passive implies that God raised up Jesus [BECNT, TH] by bringing him onto the historical scene [BECNT].
  d. aorist mid. (deponent = act.) indic. of ἐπισκέπτομαι (LN 34.50) (BAGD 3. p. 298): 'to visit'. See translations of this word at 1:68. In the OT this word is frequently used to mean that God has blessed the people. It means that God has shown his concern for them [NTC]. He has come to help them [Lns, NTC; NCV, NET, NIV], to look after them [NTC], and to save them [TEV]. God has used his power on their behalf [BECNT, Crd]. After many centuries without an appearance of a prophet, God had visited his people by sending the greatest prophet of all [ICC].
QUESTION—What did the people say when they praised God?
  After 'they were praising God saying', the two following clauses are introduced by the word ὅτι, which can be interpreted either as an untranslated marker that introduces direct speech or as a conjunction that means 'because'.
    1. In both clauses, the word ὅτι is a marker that introduces the contents of what the people said [AB, ICC, Lns, NIGTC, Su; all versions]: they were praising God saying, 'A great prophet was raised up among us' and 'God visited his people'. Luke gives two of the typical expressions of praise [Lns]. The words they used to praise God also function as the reasons they were praising him [AB, ICC, Lns, NIGTC, Su].
    2. In both clauses the word ὅτι functions as a conjunction meaning 'because' and these two reasons need something supplied, such as 'We praise God' [My, TH]: they were praising God saying, '(We praise God) because a great prophet was raised up among us and because God visited his people'. Strictly speaking, the two clauses indicating what the crowd said give the reasons why they praised God [TH].
QUESTION—Why did the people call Jesus a great prophet?
  OT prophets spoke for God and some also performed miracles. Jesus validated his ministry by doing both and so the people recognized him to be a prophet [Su]. The magnitude of the miracle of raising the young man from death convinced them that he was a prophet [WBC]. Jesus was a *great* prophet because he could do things that most prophets could not do [NIGTC]. The people recognized a parallel between Jesus and the OT prophets Elijah and Elisha based on raising someone from the dead [AB, BECNT]. Jesus had implicitly referred to himself as a prophet like Elijah and Elisha previously (4:24–27) [AB]. At this point it is unlikely that they were thinking of the coming prophet who was greater than Moses (Deut. 18:15) [BECNT, NIGTC], although it is possible [AB]. They thought he was a prophet sent in advance of the Messiah [Lns].

7:17 **And this report/word**[a] **about him went-out in all Judea and in-all the surrounding-countryside.**

LEXICON—a. λόγος (LN 33.211): 'report' [Arn, BECNT, LN; HCSB, NASB, NET, NLT], 'news' [LN; CEV, GW, NCV, NIV, TEV], 'story' [REB], 'account' [Lns], 'rumor' [KJV], 'word' [NRSV], 'talk' [AB, WBC]. Similar statements about the news spreading are at 4:37; 5:15.

QUESTION—Was the λόγος that went out about Jesus the words spoken by the people who praised God or the account of the miracle?

    1. The report concerned the praise mentioned in the previous verse [AB, Gdt, ICC, My]: this comment about him. This manner of speaking περί 'concerning' Jesus spread abroad [Gdt].

    2. The report was the account about raising the young man to life [Alf, Lns, NICNT, NIGTC, NTC, Rb, TH]: this report about what he had done. This refers to the entire account described by Luke [Lns].

QUESTION—What was the area designated as Judea?

    1. Judea is used to include Galilee and Perea [Arn, BECNT, Crd, ICC, Lns, My, NAC, NIGTC, NTC, TG, TNTC, WBC; TEV]. Most think that Luke meant that the report spread through Palestine, the land of the Jews including Galilee and the province of Judea. It reached John the Baptist who was then in the city of Machaerus in Perea on the east side of the Dead Sea [BECNT]. However one commentary restricts the area the report spread and thinks it is likely that Luke did not mean to include the province of Judea which was far to the south of Nain [TG]. This is translated 'went through all the country and the surrounding territory' [TEV].

    2. Judea refers to the province of Judea separate from Galilee [EGT, Gdt]. Although the report would have traveled in all directions, Luke is anticipating the next incident about John's question and therefore stresses the southward spread to where John was imprisoned [EGT]. Without mentioning Galilee, Luke stresses the fact that it passed beyond its natural limit of Galilee and went as far as the whole province of Judea [Gdt].

QUESTION—Where was the surrounding countryside?

It augments the force of the location of Judea and means the countryside around Judea [ICC, NIGTC] and does not mean the countryside around Nain [ICC]. Perhaps Luke was thinking of the report reaching John the Baptist at Machaerus which was outside Judea [EGT, Gdt, My, NIGTC, TH]. This addition prepares the reader for the next incident which begins with the report reaching the imprisoned John the Baptist [ICC].

DISCOURSE UNIT: 7:18–39 [NASB]. The topic is the deputation from John.

DISCOURSE UNIT: 7:18–35 [BECNT, NICNT; CEV, NCV, NET, NIV, NLT, NRSV]. The topic is John the Baptist [CEV], Jesus and John the Baptist [NICNT; NET, NIV, NLT], John asks a question [NCV], messengers from John the Baptist [NRSV], questions about Jesus and John the Baptist [BECNT].

DISCOURSE UNIT: 7:18–30 [HCSB]. The topic is the praise of John the Baptist.

DISCOURSE UNIT: 7:18–23 [AB, NAC, NIGTC, Su, TNTC, WBC; GW, TEV]. The topic is the messengers from John the Baptist [TEV], John sends two disciples [GW], Jesus reveals himself to John the Baptist [NAC], John the Baptist's questions [TNTC], Jesus' answer to John's questions [AB, NIGTC, Su], Are you the coming one? [WBC].

7:18 And John's disciples reported to-him about all these (things). And having-summoned a-certain two of-his disciples John **7:19** sent (them) to the Lord saying,[a] Are you the (one) coming[b] or should-we-be-looking[c] for-another? **7:20** And having-come to him the men said, John the Baptizer[d] sent us to you saying, Are you the (one) coming or should-we-be-looking for-another?

TEXT—In 7:19, instead of ἔπεμψεν πρὸς τὸν κύριον λέγων 'he sent to the Lord, saying', some manuscripts read λέγει·πορευθέντες εἴπατε αὐτῷ 'he says, Having gone say (i.e., 'go and say') to him'. GNT deals with this variant together with the following one which has a C decision; but GNT would doubtless reject this variant with an A decision, indicating that the text is certain.

TEXT—In 7:19, instead of κύριον 'Lord', some manuscripts read Ἰησοῦν 'Jesus' and a few manuscripts of versions read κύριον Ἰησοῦν 'Lord Jesus'. GNT reads κύριον 'Lord' with a C decision, indicating that the Committee had difficulty making the decision. 'Jesus' is read by KJV.

LEXICON—a. pres. act. participle of λέγω (LN 33.69) (BAGD I.8.c. p. 469): 'to say' [Arn, BAGD, BECNT, LN, Lns, WBC; KJV, NASB], 'to ask' [AB, NTC; all versions except KJV, NASB, REB], 'with this question' [REB].

b. pres. mid./pass. (deponent = act.) participle of ἔρχομαι (LN 15.81) (BAGD I.1.a. p. 311): 'to come' [BAGD, LN]. The phrase 'the one coming' is translated 'the one who is coming' [GW], 'the one who is to come' [HCSB, NET, NRSV, REB], 'the One who is to come' [AB, Arn; NCV], 'he that should come' [KJV], 'the one who was to come' [NIV], 'the one who comes' [BECNT], 'the One coming' [Lns], 'the Coming One' [NTC, WBC], 'the Expected One' [NASB], 'the one we should be looking for' [CEV], 'the Messiah we've been expecting' [NLT], 'the one John said was going to come' [TEV]. The present participle may be a timeless expression and have a future meaning [Lns, NIGTC]. Used as a substantive, it characterizes the person [Lns]. It refers to one whose coming is popularly accepted as a certainty [ICC, TH].

c. pres. act. subj. of προσδοκάω (LN 30.55) (BAGD 1. p. 712): 'to look for' [AB, BAGD, BECNT, NTC; CEV, HCSB, KJV, NASB, NET, NLT], 'to wait for' [BAGD, WBC; CEV, NCV, NRSV], 'to expect' [Arn, BAGD, LN, Lns; NIV, REB, TEV].

d. βαπτιστής (LN 53.42) (BAGD p. 132): 'the Baptizer' [BAGD, LN; GW], 'the Baptist' [AB, Arn, BAGD, BECNT, Lns, NTC, WBC; all versions except GW]. This is almost equivalent to 'he who baptizes' in Mark 1:4 [TH]. This title also occurs at 7:33; 9:19.

QUESTION—Where was John the Baptist and what things were reported to him?

In 3:20, Luke has already said that John the Baptist had been imprisoned by Herod, so restating this fact is unnecessary [Arn, BECNT, EGT, Gdt, NAC]. Although not mentioning it here, the fact that he was in prison explains why John could not have direct contact with Jesus and had to summon two of his disciples and send them with a question to ask Jesus [NIGTC]. John was in prison in the fortress of Machaerus east of the Dead Sea [AB, BECNT, Lns, NTC]. John's disciples could visit him from time to time and so they reported about 'these things', that is, the entire activities of Jesus found in 4:14 onward [Arn, Crd, Lns, NIVS], the activities of Jesus in general and especially the miracles just reported [NAC, NIGTC], Jesus' mighty works [WBC], the healing of the centurion's servant and the raising of the widow's son [EGT, ICC, My, Su, TG], Jesus' sermon on the plain, his teachings, and his miracles [AB, BECNT].

QUESTION—Why did John wonder who Jesus was?

John's expectations of what Jesus would do as the Messiah did not match the actual deeds of Jesus [BECNT, NICNT, WBC]. John had prophesied that the coming one would punish and destroy sinners (3:7, 9), but Jesus' gracious words and miracles of mercy did not harmonize with such prophecy [Gdt, NTC, TG]. John was puzzled how God's agent of salvation could be so opposed by God's people [NICNT]. John's question was whether Jesus was to be identified with 'the coming one' or if someone else was to fulfill that role [NIGTC]. If Jesus was not the Coming One, John had been wrong in his identification and his role of preparing the way still had not been fulfilled [Su]. John was sure that Jesus was the one coming after him, but John knew that the Messiah was to do works of grace and judgment, yet Jesus did nothing but grace without any judgment. So he wanted to know if there was still another one to come to do the judgment that John had prophesied or if there would be another coming of the first person [Lns]. Or, it was not John's faith that needed reassurance, but John asked the question in order to give Jesus the opportunity to strengthen the wavering faith of John's disciples [Arn].

QUESTION—What did John mean by 'the coming one'?

John was referring to the coming of the Messiah [AB, BECNT, Crd, Gdt, ICC, Lns, NAC, NICNT, NIGTC, Su, TH, TNTC; NLT]. It was common for the Jews to refer to the Messiah as the Coming One [Lns]. In 3:16 John had announced that a greater one than he was coming, and perhaps he was asking if Jesus really was that one [NAC, NIGTC, WBC; TEV]. Perhaps he meant the coming messenger of God, that is, Elijah returned to life [AB, BNTC], and this would be rejected by Jesus' answer [AB].

7:21 In that hour he-healed many of diseases[a] and afflictions[b] and evil spirits and he-granted[c] many blind (persons) to-see.

TEXT—Instead of ἐν ἐκείνῃ τῇ ὥρᾳ 'in that hour', some manuscripts read ἐν αὐτῇ δε τῇ ὥρᾳ 'and in the same hour'. GNT does not mention this variant. Ἐν αὐτῇ δε τῇ ὥρᾳ 'and in the same hour' is read by KJV.

LEXICON—a. νόσος (LN 23.155) (BAGD 1. p. 543): 'disease' [AB, Arn, BAGD, LN, Lns, NTC, WBC; GW, HCSB, NASB, NET, NIV, NLT, NRSV, REB], 'sickness' [LN; NCV, TEV], 'illness' [BAGD], 'infirmity' [KJV]. This noun is also translated as a verb: 'to be sick' [CEV]

b. μάστιξ (LN 23.153) (BAGD 2. p. 495): 'affliction' [Arn, WBC; NASB], 'disease' [BECNT, LN; NCV, NLT, TEV], 'sickness' [GW, NET, NIV, NTC], 'torment, suffering' [BAGD], 'plague' [AB, BECNT; HCSB, KJV, NRSV, REB], 'scourge' [Lns]. This noun is also translated as a verb: 'to be in pain' [CEV]

c. aorist mid. (deponent = act.) indic. of χαρίζομαι (LN 57.102) (BAGD 1. p. 876): 'to grant' [BAGD, LN, WBC; NET], 'to grant (sight)' [HCSB], 'to graciously grant' [Lns], 'to bestow generously' [LN], 'to graciously bestow (sight)' [NTC], 'to bestow (sight)' [BECNT; REB], 'to give (sight)' [Arn, LN; CEV, KJV, NASB, NCV, NIV, NRSV, TEV], 'to give back (sight)' [GW], 'to restore (sight)' [AB; NLT]. This means to give freely or graciously as a favor [BAGD], to bestow a blessing [Arn]. This verb is related to χάρις 'grace' and emphasizes the gracious exercise of Jesus' power [BECNT].

QUESTION—What hour is referred to?

It is not to be taken in the general sense 'at that time' but specifically 'at that very time' [TH]. John's disciples arrived at the very time Jesus was healing people [AB, Lns, NTC]. Perhaps John's disciples had to wait during the time of healing before they could present John's question [Lns]. This enabled them to be eyewitnesses of Jesus' mighty works [NAC, NIGTC, Su, WBC]. Or, this verse is a parenthetical comment giving the historical setting of Jesus' reply and it does not indicate that John's disciples were eyewitnesses to all of these miracles [BECNT].

QUESTION—What is the difference between diseases and afflictions?

The first term νόσος 'disease' refers to any unhealthy condition of the body or mind [NTC] and is a general term for illness [BECNT]. The second term μάστιξ 'affliction' emphasizes the painful nature of the diseases [BECNT, NTC], diseases that bring suffering [TH], severe illness [WBC], fearful and painful affliction [Lns]. The second term 'affliction' is stronger than the general word 'disease' and refers to the diseases that are accompanied with much suffering [TH]. Or, the two words mean the same [TG], or are nearly synonymous [TH]. The two words are translated as one phrase: 'various diseases' [NLT].

QUESTION—In what way were people healed of evil spirits?

Using the same verb 'healed' reveals that people at that time did not distinguish between diseases and demon-possession [AB]. Although healing includes casting out evil spirits here, it does not mean that no distinction is drawn between illness and exorcism [WBC]. The illnesses are distinguished from demon possession [BECNT, NIGTC]. There is a distinction because at 13:32 evil spirits are cast out and healings are performed [NAC]. By separately mentioning evil spirits, Luke has distinguished between those who are naturally sick and the demoniacs [Alf, My]. The evil spirits (used here and at 8:2; 11:26) are also called unclean spirits by Luke at 4:33, 36; 6:18; 9:42 without any difference in meaning [TH].

QUESTION—Why are the blind people given special mention?

This separate mention of healing the blind shows that Jesus was carrying out the role that he claimed when he read from Isaiah 61:1 in the synagogue at 4:18 [AB, NAC]. This separate clause and verb makes this event prominent [My, NTC]. The blind people represent the handicapped people [NTC].

7:22 And answering he-said to-them, Having-gone, report to-John what you-saw and heard; blind (persons) receive-sight, lame (persons) walk, lepers[a] are-cleansed[b] and deaf (persons) hear, dead (persons) are-raised, poor (people) have-the-good-news-announced (to them).[c]

TEXT—Instead of εἶπεν 'he said', some manuscripts read ὁ Ἰησοῦς εἶπεν 'Jesus said', although GNT does not mention this variant. The words ὁ Ἰησοῦς εἶπεν 'Jesus said' is read by KJV.

TEXT—Before τυφλοί 'blind', some manuscripts add ὅτι 'that'. GNT does not mention this variant. Ὅτι 'that' is read by KJV.

TEXT—Some manuscripts omit καί 'and' following καθαρίζονται 'are cleansed'. GNT does not mention this variant. It is omitted by KJV and NIV.

LEXICON—a. λεπρός (LN 23.162) (BAGD p. 472): 'leper' [BAGD, LN], 'one having a dreaded skin disease' [LN]. See a description of λέπρα 'leprosy' at 5:12.

b. pres. pass. indic. of καθαρίζω (LN 23.137) (BAGD 1.b.α. p. 387): 'to be cleansed'. See this word at 4:27; 5:12; 17:14.

c. pres. pass. indic. of εὐαγγελίζω (LN 33.215) (BAGD 1. p. 317): 'to announce good news'. See translations of this word at 1:19. This word also occurs at 2:10; 3:18: 4:18, 43; 8:1; 9:6; 16:16; 20:1.

QUESTION—Did Jesus answer the question from John?

Instead of answering with a simple 'Yes, I am the coming one', Jesus told them to tell John all they had seen and heard so he could draw his own conclusion from the compelling evidence [AB, EGT, NAC, Su]. All the things Jesus listed were mentioned in Isaiah 29:18–19, 35:5–6, and 61:1 as the things God would bring about in the future, and now the age of the Messiah had arrived [Su]. The things Jesus was doing reflected the OT prophecies concerning the messianic age, so the implicit answer was that Jesus was the coming one [Arn, TH]. The implied answer is that Jesus was the one to come, but not as the fiery reformer John expected [AB].

7:23 And blessed[a] is whoever does- not -take-offense[b] at me.

LEXICON—a. μακάριος (LN 25.119) (BAGD 1.b. p. 48:6): 'blessed'. See translations of this word at 1:45 and 6:20. This word also occurs at 10:23; 11:27; 12:37, 43; 14:14; 23:29.

    b. aorist pass. subj. of σκανδαλίζομαι (LN 25.180, 31.77) (BAGD 1.b. p. 752): 'to take offense' [BAGD, LN (15.180); NASB, NET, NRSV], 'to be offended' [BECNT; HCSB, KJV, NLT], 'to be shocked' [AB], 'to be scandalized' [WBC], 'to be repelled by' [NTC], 'to be caused to give up believing' [LN (31.77)], 'to reject' [CEV], 'to fall away' [NIV], 'to have doubts about' [TEV], 'to lose faith in' [GW], 'to stumble in one's faith' [NCV], 'to be made to stumble' [Arn], 'to find (Jesus) as an obstacle to faith' [REB], 'to be trapped' [Lns].

QUESTION—How does this beatitude apply in this context?

The beatitude is stated as a general one that includes anyone who hears this statement and responds [AB, Arn, BECNT, NIGTC]. In this context it focuses on John [AB, BECNT, ICC, NAC, NIGTC, TG]. Introduced by καί 'and', the beatitude is connected especially to the answer to John [AB, WBC]. The blessing has an implied warning or rebuke [Gdt, ICC, Lns, NAC, NIGTC, NTC, TG]. The negative form of the beatitude has the positive meaning that that the one who retains his faith is blessed and invites John to consider the significance of Jesus' ministry and attain a deeper faith in him [NIGTC]. Jesus did not want John to lose the joys that make up this blessedness [Lns]. It implies that John had found something to be offended about in Jesus and it also encourages him to overcome this temptation [ICC]. Because of Jesus' activities, John had doubted that Jesus was the Messiah [TG]. Instead of scolding John for wavering, Jesus tenderly reminds him that there is a special blessing for everyone who does not fall into such a trap [NTC].

QUESTION—What is involved in taking offense at Jesus?

When applied to John, it would perhaps refer to losing confidence in Jesus [NIGTC], and doubting Christ's divine character or even to rejecting him [Arn]. It involves misunderstanding the significance of what Jesus had been doing and not recognizing him for what he was [TH]. People who had preconceived ideas of what the Messiah was supposed to do would consider Jesus' words and deeds to be offensive [NAC, NIGTC].

DISCOURSE UNIT: 7:24–35 [GW]. The topic is Jesus' appraisal of John the Baptist [Su], Jesus speaks about John.

DISCOURSE UNIT: 7:24–30 [AB, BECNT, NAC, TNTC]. The topic is Jesus' view of John [AB, BECNT], Jesus' witness to John the Baptist as his forerunner [NAC], the greatness of John [TNTC].

DISCOURSE UNIT: 7:24–28 [NIGTC]. The topic is Jesus' witness about John.

7:24 And (after) John's messengers departed he-began to-speak about John to the crowds, What[a] did-you-go-out into the desert[b] to-see? A reed[c] being-shaken by (the) wind?

LEXICON—a. τί (LN 92.14): 'what' [AB, Arn, BECNT, LN, Lns, NTC, WBC; all versions except CEV, NLT], 'what kind of person' [CEV], 'who is this man' [NLT].
  b. ἔρημος (LN 1.86) (BAGD 2. p. 309): 'desert'. See this word at 1:80 and 3:1. When John was active, he was located in the wilderness where thousands went to hear him preach [Lns].
  c. κάλαμος (LN 3.19) (BAGD 1. p. 398): 'reed' [AB, Arn, BAGD, BECNT, LN, Lns, NTC, WBC; all versions except CEV, GW, TEV], 'tall grass' [CEV, GW], 'a blade of grass' [TEV].

QUESTION—What was the reason Jesus immediately spoke to the crowd about John after the messengers had left?

Those who heard what Jesus said to John's disciples might have taken the implied rebuke to mean that Jesus was repudiating John [TNTC]. Those in the crowd might be blaming John for lacking confidence [Su]. Jesus spoke about John to remove such thoughts and to state how highly he esteemed him [Lns]. Jesus waited until John's messengers had left because if they reported what Jesus would now say about him it might have cancelled the effect of the rebuke [ICC].

QUESTION—Is the reed to be taken figuratively or literally?
  1. The reed is to be taken as a reference to an actual reed in the desert [BECNT, NAC, NICNT, TH, WBC; NET; probably GW, HCSB, KJV, NASB, NCV, NIV, NRSV, REB, TEV which translate with 'what']: 'What did you go out into the desert to see? Just a reed being shaken in the wind? No you went out to see a man who was prophet'. Swaying reeds were common in the desert, but they were not the reason crowds went into the desert [BECNT, WBC]. The question is ironic and means that it takes more than the scenery to draw people to the desert, it takes a prophet to bring them [BECNT]. Such a trivial thing would not attract an audience [NAC, NICNT]. It means that they did not go out into the desert for nothing [TH].
  2. The reed is to be taken as a reference to John the Baptist [AB, Arn, Lns, NIGTC, NTC, TG, TNTC; CEV, NLT]: 'Did you go out to see a man who was like a reed being shaken in the wind? No he wasn't that kind of man'. This describes John as being weak [Arn; NLT], frail and fickle [AB], easily swayed [TNTC], wavering and easy-going [NIGTC], uncertain, vacillating, without strong convictions [Arn, TG], and yielding to popular opinion [Lns, TG].

7:25 But what did-you-go-out to-see? A-man dressed in soft[a] garments?[b] Behold[c] the (ones) with splendid[d] clothing[e] and living in-luxury[f] are in the palaces.

LEXICON—a. μαλακός (LN **79.100**) (BAGD 1. p. 488): 'soft' [Arn, BAGD, BECNT, NTC, WBC; HCSB, KJV, NASB, NRSV], 'luxurious' [**LN**], 'fine' [AB; CEV, GW, NCV, NIV], 'fancy' [NET, TEV], 'expensive' [NLT]. The phrase 'soft garments' is translated 'finery' [REB]. The word describes clothes made of fine material [NIGTC]. Ordinary clothing was made of coarse material and only those who were wealthy wore imported clothing made of silk and linen [WBC]. It is material that is soft to the touch [Lns], and makes a contrast with the rough texture of the cheap coat of camel's hair worn by John [Arn, Lns, NIGTC, TH]. However, Luke never describes John's clothes as Mark did, so an allusion to the specific type of clothing is probably not present [BECNT, NAC]. It probably refers to expensive clothing made of wool or soft linen [Arn, BECNT]. It refers to the rich clothing of the royal court [WBC].

b. ἱμάτιον (LN 6.162) (BAGD): 'garment' [Arn, BAGD, WBC], 'clothing' [BECNT, LN; NASB], 'apparel' [LN], 'clothes' [CEV, GW, NCV, NET, NIV, NLT, TEV], 'raiment' [KJV], 'garment' [NTC], 'robes' [AB; HCSB, NRSV], not explicit [REB]. It probably refers to outer clothing [TH].

c. ἰδού (LN 91.13): 'behold'. See this word at 7:12.

d. ἔνδοξος (LN **79.19**) (BAGD 2. p. 263): 'splendid' [BAGD, **LN**; GW], 'glorious' [BAGD, LN], 'gorgeous' [WBC], 'wonderful' [LN], 'beautiful' [NLT], 'grand' [REB], 'elegant' [AB], 'expensive' [CEV, NIV], 'costly' [Arn], 'fine' [NCV, NRSV], 'fancy' [NET], not explicit [TEV]. This adjective is also translated as an adverb: 'splendidly (clothed/dressed)' [HCSB, NASB], 'beautifully (clothed)' [BECNT], 'gorgeously (appareled)' [NTC; KJV]. Splendid clothing refers to the preceding term 'soft garments' [TH].

e. ἱματισμός (LN 6.162) (BAGD p. 379): 'clothing' [Arn, BAGD, LN, WBC; NRSV], 'apparel' [BAGD, LN], 'clothes' [CEV, GW, NCV, NET, NIV, NLT, REB], 'garment' [AB]. This noun is also translated as a verb: 'to be clothed' [BECNT; NASB], 'to be appareled' [NTC; KJV], 'to be dressed' [HCSB], 'to dress' [TEV]. The two nouns for clothing ἱμάτιον and ἱματισμός are translated the same as 'clothes' [CEV, GW, NCV, NET, NIV, NLT].

f. τρυφή (LN 88.253) (BAGD 2. p. 828): 'luxury' [AB, BAGD, BECNT, LN, NTC, WBC; all versions except KJV, NCV, NIV]. The phrase 'to live in luxury' is translated 'to indulge in luxury' [NIV], 'to have much wealth' [NCV], 'to live delicately' [KJV], 'luxurious clothing' [Arn]. To live in luxury is to spend money on unnecessary and expensive things [TG]. This word brings out the significance of the preceding descriptions of clothing [NIGTC].

QUESTION—What relationship is indicated by the beginning conjunction ἀλλά 'but'?
    1. It indicates an alternative question [Arn, BECNT, NTC, TH; KJV, NASB, NCV, NIV]: but if not that, then why did you go? The rhetorical question in 7:24 called for a negative answer [TG], so an alternative rhetorical question is posed [TH].
    2. It merely turns to a new point [Lns]: if not that, what was it that you wanted to see? There is no contrast indicated here [Lns].

7:26 But what did-you-go-out to-see? A prophet? Yes I-say to-you, and more-than[a] a-prophet. 7:27 This (one) is-he about whom it-has-been-written, Behold I-send my messenger before your face,[b] who will-prepare[c] your way before you.

LEXICON—a. περισσότερος (LN 78.31) (BAGD 2. p. 651): 'more than' [BAGD, BECNT, WBC; CEV, NASB, NCV, NET, NIV, NLT, NRSV], 'much more than' [KJV, TEV], 'far more than' [GW, HCSB, REB], 'even more than' [Arn, NTC], 'much greater' [LN], 'greater than' [AB], 'surpassing' [LN], 'far beyond' [Lns].
    b. πρόσωπον (LN 67.19) (BAGD 1.c.z. p. 721): 'face' [BAGD]. The idiom πρὸ προσώπου σου 'before your face' [Lns, NTC; KJV] is also translated 'before you' [Arn, BECNT; NLT], 'ahead of you' [AB, WBC; all versions except KJV, NLT].
    c. fut. act. indic. of κατασκευάζω (LN 77.7) (BAGD 1. p. 418): 'to prepare, to make ready' [BAGD, LN]. The phrase 'to prepare your way before you' [AB, Arn, BECNT, NTC, WBC; HCSB, KJV, NASB, NET, NIV, NLT, NRSV, REB] is also translated 'to prepare the way in front of you' [GW], 'to prepare the way for you' [NCV], 'to make ready your way in front of you' [Lns], 'to get things ready for you' [CEV], 'to open the way for you' [TEV].

QUESTION—In what way was John the Baptist more than a prophet?
    This is explained in the following two verses [AB, NAC, NIGTC, WBC]. John's mission was more important than that of a regular prophet [Su, TG]. This speaks of his position in God's plan as the bridge from one era to another [BECNT]. He himself was the subject of prophecy [Gdt, Lns, NAC, NTC] as being sent to prepare the way before the Messiah [BECNT, Crd, Lns, NTC, Su]. He was the messenger who heralded the arrival of the Messiah [Crd]. In addition to the reason that he was such a messenger, the second reason is that he was the greatest of all men [AB, NAC].

QUESTION—Who are the participants in the quotation from the OT?
    This is a quotation from Malachi 3:1, which says 'Behold, I will send my messenger, who will prepare the way before me'. The speaker is 'I, God' [Arn, Gdt, Lns, NIGTC, NTC, TG, WBC; CEV, TEV]. The messenger is unnamed by Malachi, but it refers to John [AB, Arn, NIGTC, NTC, Su, WBC; CEV]. In Malachi, it appears that the messenger prepares the way before the coming of God, but Jesus has this refer to 'you'. The quotation

from Malachi is influenced by the wording of Exodus 23:20 which says, 'I am sending a messenger/angel ahead of *you* to guard you along the way' [BECNT, NICNT, NIGTC, WBC]. The pronoun 'you' is addressed to the Messiah [AB, Arn, Gdt, Lns, NAC, NIGTC, NTC, Su, TG, WBC]. Yahweh was not speaking of himself, but of Jesus and therefore the form 'before you' [Gdt]. This is Christ's own interpretation of Malachi [Lns, NTC]: Yahweh will come to the people in the person of the Messiah [Lns]. In 1:76 where John is told he will go before the Lord to prepare his way, the 'Lord' is to be taken as referring to Jesus [NAC]. John was God's agent to the Jews for God's coming [BECNT, NICNT] in the person of the Messiah [BECNT].

7:28 **I-say to-you, no-one is greater[a] among (those) born of-women than John. But the (one) of-least-importance[b] in the kingdom of-God is greater (than) he.**

TEXT—Instead of μείζων ἐν γεννητοῖς γυναικῶν Ἰωάννου 'a greater among (the) ones born of women than John' some manuscripts read μείζων ἐν γεννητοῖς γυναικῶν προφήτης Ἰωάννου 'a greater prophet among (the) ones born of women than John', other manuscripts read μείζων ἐν γεννητοῖς γυναικῶν Ἰωάννου τοῦ βαπτιστοῦ 'a greater among (the) ones born of women than John the Baptist', and other manuscripts read μείζων ἐν γεννητοῖς γυναικῶν προφήτης Ἰωάννου τοῦ βαπτιστοῦ 'a greater prophet among (the) ones born of women than John the Baptist'. GNT reads μείζων ἐν γεννητοῖς γυναικῶν Ἰωάννου 'a greater among (the) ones born of women than John' with a B decision, indicating that the text is almost certain. Μείζων ἐν γεννητοῖς γυναικῶν προφήτης Ἰωάννου τοῦ βαπτιστοῦ 'a greater prophet among (the) ones born of women than John the Baptist' is read by KJV.

LEXICON—a. μέγας (LN 87.22, 87.28) (BAGD 2.b.α. p. 498): 'greater' [AB, Arn, BAGD, BECNT, LN, Lns, NTC, WBC; all versions], 'great, important' [LN (87.22)]. Although the form is comparative, the effect is superlative, he is the greatest of all men [Crd, NIGTC]. See this word at 1:15, 32; 9:46, 22:24.

b. μικρός (LN 87.58): 'least important' [CEV, GW, NCV], 'unimportant' [LN], 'least' [Arn, BECNT, NTC; HCSB, KJV, NASB, NET, NIV, NRSV, REB, TEV], 'less' [AB, Lns], 'littlest' [WBC], 'most insignificant' [NLT]. This concerns importance in matters of esteem, influence, and power [BAGD]. He is less than any who are among the more insignificant [ICC]. Although the form is comparative, the effect is superlative, he is the least one in the kingdom [Gdt, NAC, WBC].

QUESTION—In what way was John to be considered greater than all other men?

This is not speaking of his personal worth as though his inward life surpassed Abraham and Elijah, rather John was the greatest in connection with his position and work [Gdt, Lns, TNTC]. John was the one to announce the Messiah's coming [AB, NTC, Su]. Luke assumed that Jesus is excluded from this comparison since all his readers knew that Jesus was greater than John [Arn, NAC], and that Jesus belonged to another category [Arn].

QUESTION—In the last sentence, what relationship is indicated by δέ 'but'?

Rather than depreciating John, this is a contrast between human greatness and being a member of the kingdom of God [NAC]. Following the highest praise of John, this is a paradoxical statement [Lns]. This immediately qualifies the statement of praise for John [NIGTC]. This does not depreciate John, but explains and excuses the unsteadfastness of his faith [Gdt].

QUESTION—In what way are the least important greater than John?

1. This implies that John is not part of the kingdom of God [Arn, ICC, TNTC, WBC]. Although John is the culmination of the old order, he is not part of the new and superior order [TG]. John belonged to the time of promise, not to the time of fulfillment [TNTC]. This pertains to the spiritual privileges of grace and knowledge that are superior to John's position as one who served in the era of preparation [ICC]. In prison, John is not yet a participant in the new state of affairs begun by Jesus' ministry [WBC]. The humblest member of the kingdom of God has privileges John never had in the old dispensation of the Law and the Prophets [Arn].
2. The question of whether John is in the kingdom of God is not raised [BNTC, Lns, NAC, NIGTC, NTC, TG]. This does not exclude John from being in the kingdom of God [TG]. In 13:28 it is stated that Abraham, Isaac, Jacob, and all the prophets are in the kingdom of God, but here the question of whether John was in the kingdom is not raised. It simply makes the point that being in the kingdom of God is more important than being the greatest of prophets [NIGTC]. John would not live to see the consummation of Jesus' ministry which all believers would witness [Lns]. The least were more privileged by being in touch with Jesus, a privilege John could not have while being in prison [NTC]. John is in the kingdom but would not live to receive the new covenant benefits such as fellowship with Jesus and the indwelling of the Holy Spirit [BECNT]. The point of this statement is to emphasis the greatness of the coming era of fulfillment by pointing out that those who are reborn in God's kingdom are greater than the greatest person born by human generation [BECNT].

DISCOURSE UNIT: 7:29–35 [NIGTC, WBC]. The topic is the rejection of John and Jesus [NIGTC], John and Jesus and this generation and the children of wisdom [WBC].

7:29 **And having-heard (Jesus/John) all the people and the tax-collectors justified**[a] **God, (because/by) having-been-baptized (with) the baptism of-John.**

LEXICON—a. aorist act. indic. of δικαιόω (LN **36.22**) (BAGD 2. p. 197): 'to justify, vindicate, treat as just' [BAGD], 'to obey righteous commands' [LN]. The phrase 'to justify God' [Arn, BECNT, Lns, WBC; KJV] is also translated 'to obey God's righteous commands' [**LN**], 'to obey God's righteous demands' [BAGD], 'to acknowledge God's justice' [BAGD;

NASB, NET], 'to acknowledge the justice of God' [NRSV], 'to acknowledge God's way of righteousness' [HCSB], 'to acknowledge that God's way was right' [NIV], 'to acknowledge the goodness of God' [REB], 'to acknowledge God's claims on them' [AB], 'to obey God and do what was right' [CEV], 'to obey God's righteous demands' [TEV], 'to admit that God was right' [GW], 'to agree that God's teaching was good' [NCV], 'to agree that God's plan was right' [NLT], 'to vindicate God's righteous requirements' [NTC].

QUESTION—How are the two verses 7:29–30 connected with their context?

1. These verses are a comment by Luke [AB, Alf, BECNT, BNTC, Crd, EGT, My, NAC, NICNT, NIGTC, Su, TG, WBC; all versions except GW, KJV]. This is a parenthetical comment by Luke [Alf, BECNT, NIGTC; NCV, NET, NRSV]. This awkwardly placed parenthesis is a summary of the Jewish response to John [BECNT]. These two verses set the scene for Jesus' comment in 7:31–35 [NIGTC]. These verses are a bridge between what Jesus had said about John and the evaluation of the current generation in the following verses [BECNT]. Luke adds his comments to those of Jesus as they both endorse the importance of John in God's plan and Luke also provides a guide to the reader's interaction with the rest of the book [NICNT]. The third person references to the people, tax collectors, and Pharisees would be unnatural if Jesus was addressing them [BECNT].

   1.1 'Having heard' refers to hearing Jesus' comments about John [Alf, Crd, NAC, NICNT, NIGTC, Su, WBC]. This insertion by Luke comments on the effect of Jesus' preaching on the people [Alf]. Luke is explaining the way people reacted to the roles of John and of Jesus [Su]. The people had heard Jesus' reply to John's messengers in 7:18–23 and Jesus' comments about John's place in setting up the eschatological events of 7:24–28 [WBC].

   1.2 'Having heard' refers to those who had previously heard John's preaching [AB, BECNT, EGT, TG; TEV]. This can mean only listening to John and accepting his baptism [AB, BECNT], so this is a historical comment by Luke to summarize the reaction of all the people to Jesus' statements about John [AB]. It is an historical reflection by Luke telling how the popular judgment endorsed the estimate just rendered by Jesus [EGT]. It cannot refer to the crowd listening to Jesus, since Jesus would not be administering John's baptism [BECNT].

2. These two verses are a continuation of Jesus' speech [Arn, Gdt, ICC, Lns, My, NTC, Rb, TH, TNTC; GW]. It is improbable that a parenthetical comment would be inserted in the middle of Christ's words [ICC]. The phrase 'having heard' then refers to hearing John [Arn, NTC, TNTC; GW]. Jesus was describing the reactions of people to John's preaching [TH]. Jesus is contrasting the effect of John's preaching between the people and those of the hierarchy [ICC].

QUESTION—Who were πᾶς ὁ λαὸς 'all the people' in 7:29?

'All' is a hyperbole in ordinary speech and refers to the great mass of common people [Lns, NTC], the people in general [Arn]. They are the common people in contrast with the Pharisees and the teachers of the law [TG, TH]. Since 'having heard' is in the singular, the addition about the tax collectors appears to be added on as an after-thought [NIGTC, TH]. The addition 'and the tax collectors' selects them for special mention [Lns, NIGTC] and means 'even such great sinners as the tax collectors' [Lns]. 'All the people' would include the tax collectors, but the tax collectors were such a hated sub-group that they are emphasized [TNTC]. The added phrase 'and the tax collectors' means *including* the tax collectors [TG; GW, NCV, NLT, NRSV, REB], *even* the tax collectors [AB, Lns, NTC, TH; NET], *especially* the tax collectors [NIGTC; TEV].

QUESTION—In the genitive construction τὸ βάπτισμα Ἰωάννου 'the baptism of John', how is John connected with the baptism?

John performed the baptism [TG, TH; CEV, GW, NCV, NIV, TEV]. The people had obeyed God's righteous command and had been baptized by John [TG; TEV]. This phrase is not necessarily contrasted with Christian baptism [NIGTC]. It was a baptism of the type that John performed, the baptism that John administered with a view to repentance and preparation for the coming work of Jesus [TNTC].

QUESTION—In what way did they justify God?

They acknowledged that God was right [Arn, NAC, NIGTC], just [TG, TH], or righteous [AB, NTC], and that his requirements were righteous [NTC]. They responded to God's offer of forgiveness because they recognized that God's call for repentance was correct [BECNT]. They acknowledged that God's requirements preached by John were just and they showed that they believed this by repenting and being baptized [ICC, NTC]. By being baptized, they declared that God's will for them to be baptized by John was right [My]. By being baptized they rendered their verdict of approval on God's plan of salvation [AB, NICNT]. The act of being baptized declared that God was right and just [Lns]. They considered that God was just or righteous in making demands of them [TG]. They accepted God's ways as they were and did not try to constrain him into their own preferences [TNTC]. The verb 'justified' is used by Luke because of its occurrence in 7:35, but here the meaning is not much different than 'they glorified God' since there is nothing that calls for God to be acknowledged as being in the right [WBC].

QUESTION—What relationship is indicated by the use of the participles 'having been baptized' and 'not having been baptized' (7:30) with the opening clause 'having heard'?

1. When 'having heard' refers to hearing what Jesus just said, it indicates the reason they were disposed to justify God (7:29) or to set aside God's purposes (7:30) [Alf, Crd, NIGTC, Su, WBC; NCV, NET, NIV, NLT, NRSV, REB, TEV]: when they heard this, they justified God *because*

they had been baptized by John...others set aside God's purpose *because* they had not submitted to baptism. The people praised God that Jesus spoke so highly of John because they had already been baptized by John [NIGTC].
2. When 'having heard' refers to hearing John's preaching, it indicates the means by which they justified God (7:29) or set aside God's purpose (7:30) [AB, BECNT, BNTC, EGT, ICC, Lns, My, NTC, TG, TH, TNTC; CEV, GW]: when they heard John, they justified God *by* being baptized by John...others set aside God's purpose *by* not being baptized.

7:30 **But the Pharisees and the lawyers[a] rejected[b] the purpose of-God for themselves, (because/by) not having-been-baptized by him.**

LEXICON—a. νομικός (LN 33.338) (BAGD 2. p. 541): 'lawyer' [BAGD; KJV, NASB, NRSV, REB], 'legal expert' [BAGD], 'expert in the Law' [LN], 'expert in the law' [HCSB, NIV], 'expert on the Law' [NCV], 'expert in the Law of Moses' [CEV], 'expert in Moses' Teachings' [GW], 'expert in religious law' [NET, NLT], 'interpreter of the Law' [LN], 'teacher of the Law' [TEV], 'scribe' [Arn]. This describes the scribes as being learned in the Law [Arn]. See this word at 10:25; 11:45, 46, 52; 14:3.

b. aorist act. indic. of ἀθετέω (LN **76.24**) (BAGD 1.a. p. 21): 'to reject, to regard as invalid' [LN], 'to set aside, to declare as invalid' [BAGD]. The phrase 'to reject the purpose of God for themselves' is translated 'to reject the plan of God for themselves' [**LN**; HCSB], 'to reject God's plan for them' [GW, NLT], 'to reject for themselves the counsel of God' [BECNT], 'to nullify for themselves the counsel of God' [Lns], 'to set at naught God's plan so far as it concerned themselves' [WBC], 'to reject God's purpose for themselves' [NET, NIV, NRSV, REB, TEV], 'to reject God's purpose concerning them' [NTC], 'to reject the counsel of God against themselves' [KJV], 'to refuse to accept God's plan for themselves' [NCV], 'to refuse to obey God' [CEV], 'to thwart the plan of God for themselves' [Arn], 'to thwart God's design on their behalf' [AB].

QUESTION—Does the phrase οἱ Φαρισαῖοι καὶ νομικοί 'the Pharisees and the lawyers' indicate that the lawyers were not Pharisees?

The lawyers were usually Pharisees [BECNT]. The phrase is synonymous with the designation 'scribes' (see 5:17 and 5:21) [AB, BECNT, NIGTC, NTC]. See 5:17 where this question is discussed.

QUESTION—In the clause 'they rejected the purpose of God for themselves', how is the phrase εἰς αὐτούς 'for themselves' connected?
1. It modifies the phrase 'the purpose of God' [AB, Arn, EGT, ICC, NTC, TG, TH; GW, KJV]: they rejected the purpose God had for them. This refers to the relevance of God's plan concerning themselves [AB, ICC]. They did not do what God wanted them to do [TH]. God's plan was for their salvation, but people have the power to refuse to go along with God's plan [Arn].

2. It modifies the verb 'rejected' [BECNT, Crd, Gdt, Lns, My, NIGTC, Rb, Su, WBC]: as far as they were concerned, they rejected the purpose of God. God's purpose refers to John's preaching about repentance and baptizing, so when they would not be baptized it proved that they had rejected his purpose [BECNT]. John's general call to repentance and baptism was not regarded as applicable to themselves and so they treated God's plan with contempt [Su]. God's purpose was expressed in John's ministry and they made it ineffective as far as they were concerned [Lns]. By their disobedience in refusing to be prepared for the coming kingdom of God by being baptized, they annulled God's will [My].

DISCOURSE UNIT: 7:31–35 [AB, BECNT, TNTC; HCSB]. The topic is the reaction of the hearers [TNTC], an unresponsive generation [HCSB], Jesus experiences rejection [NAC], Jesus' view of this generation [AB, BECNT].

7:31 Therefore[a] to-what will-I-compare the people of-this generation[b] and to-what are-they like?

TEXT—Before τίνι 'to what' at the beginning of this verse, some manuscripts add εἶπεν δὲ ὁ κύριος 'and the Lord said', although GNT does not mention this variant, which is read by KJV. Probably not because of the text, some versions add a phrase to indicate that Jesus is again speaking: 'Jesus went on to say' [CEV], 'Jesus continued' [TEV], 'then Jesus said' [NCV], 'Jesus asked' [NLT].

LEXICON—a. οὖν (LN 89.50) (BAGD 1.c.γ. p. 593): 'therefore' [BAGD, LN, Lns, NTC] 'whereunto' [KJV], 'then' [AB, Arn, WBC; HCSB, NASB, NCV, NET, NIV, NRSV], 'now' [TEV], not explicit [BECNT; CEV, GW, NLT, REB].

b. γενεά (LN 11.4) (BAGD 2. p. 154): 'generation' [BAGD], 'contemporaries' [BAGD], 'those of the same generation, those of the same time' [LN]. The phrase 'the people of this generation' [AB, NTC, WBC; HCSB, NET, NIV, NRSV, REB] is also translated 'the men of this generation' [Arn, BECNT, Lns; KJV, NASB], 'the people of this time' [NCV], 'the people of this day' [TEV], 'the people who are living now' [GW], 'this generation' [NLT], 'you people' [CEV]. It refers to the contemporary generation of Jews [BAGD] and generalizes the current response to both John and Jesus [BECNT]. See this word at 1:48, 50; 9:41; 11:29, 50; 16:8; 17:25; 21:32.

QUESTION—What relationship is indicated by the initial οὖν 'therefore'?

1. When 7:29–30 are interpreted to be a comment by Luke, it indicates a conclusion of what Jesus said in 7:24–28 [NICNT]. Because of John's importance and the fact that his ministry prepared people for Jesus' coming, how are we to think of this generation? [NICNT].

2. When 7:29–30 are interpreted to be a part of Jesus' discourse, it indicates the conclusion of the statements in 29–30 [ICC]. This conjunction would not be very intelligible if 7:29–30 were omitted. Since the Jewish leaders

have rejected God's invitation delivered by John and the Jews followed them in refusing to follow Jesus, Jesus presented this question [ICC].
QUESTION—What is the purpose of this question?
It is a rhetorical question used to introduce the following question [TH]. Making it a double question strengthens the effect [TH], but both questions mean the same [TG]. It shows the difficulty of finding a comparison for such senseless conduct [Gdt]. It causes the hearers to search for a suitable comparison [Lns, WBC]. The two τίνι 'what' are neuter (not 'who'), so the questions are about the likeness to what the children did [Lns]. The question has the thought, 'The situation about which we are talking can be compared to the following analogy' [NAC], 'the people of this generation are to be likened to a situation in which….' [WBC].

7:32 They-are like children in (the) marketplace[a] sitting and calling to-one-another who say, We played-the-flute[b] for-you and you-did- not -dance, we-sang-a-funeral-song[c] and you-did- not -weep.
TEXT—Instead of ἃ λέγει 'who say', some manuscripts read καὶ λέγουσιν 'and saying' or 'and they say'. GNT does not mention this variant. Καὶ λέγουσιν 'and saying' is read by KJV.
TEXT—Instead of ἐθρηνήσαμεν καὶ οὐκ ἐκλαύσατε 'we wailed, and you did not weep', some manuscripts read ἐθρηνήσαμεν ὑμῖν καὶ οὐκ ἐκλαύσατε 'we wailed for you, and you did not weep', and other manuscripts omit this clause. GNT reads ἐθρηνήσαμεν καὶ οὐκ ἐκλαύσατεε 'we wailed, and you did not weep' with a B decision, indicating that the text is almost certain. Ἐθρηνήσαμεν ὑμῖν καὶ οὐκ ἐκλαύσατε 'we wailed for you, and you did not weep' is read by KJV.
LEXICON—a. ἀγορά (LN 57.207) (BAGD p. 12): 'marketplace' [AB, Arn, BAGD, LN, Lns, NTC, WBC; all versions except CEV, NLT], 'the market' [BECNT; CEV], 'public square' [NLT]. In the illustration, some think the market would not be in progress and therefore the marketplace would be a convenient open area for the children to play [Lns, NTC]. Another view is that the market was in progress and the children would be playing while their parents shopped [Su]. See this word at 11:43.
b. aorist act. indic. of αὐλέω (LN 6.87) (BAGD p. 121): 'to play the flute' [Arn, BAGD, BECNT, LN, NTC; CEV, HCSB, NASB, NET, NIV, NRSV], 'to play music' [GW, NCV], 'to play wedding songs' [NLT], 'to play wedding music' [TEV], 'to pipe' [AB, Lns, WBC; KJV, REB]. This would occur during a mock wedding [AB, Kst, Lns, NAC, NIGTC, NTC, Rb, Su, TG, TH, WBC; NLT], because it is in contrast with a funeral [TH]. It refers to a round dance at a wedding celebration [AB]. Perhaps the children imitated the flutes used in a wedding by blowing little whistles they had made or by merely whistling with their lips [Lns].
c. aorist act. indic. of θρηνέω (LN **33.115**) (BAGD 1.b. p. 363): 'to sing a funeral song' [**LN**; CEV, GW], 'to sing funeral songs' [TEV], 'to play funeral songs' [NLT], 'to sing a dirge' [BAGD, NTC; NASB, NIV], 'to

310   LUKE 7:32

chant a dirge' [LN], 'to sing a lament' [HCSB], 'to sing a sad song' [NCV], 'to wail' [AB, BECNT, Lns, WBC; NRSV], 'to lament' [REB], 'to mourn' [KJV], 'to wail in mourning' [NET], 'to shed tears' [Arn]. 'Singing a dirge' is better than 'mourning' in this context since its purpose is to incite a mournful response [Hlt]. This would occur during a mock funeral [AB, Hlt, ICC, Kst, NAC, NIGTC, NTC, Rb, Su, TG, TH, WBC]. Professional mourners at a funeral would express grief by wailing [Lns, WBC].

QUESTION—How are the children in the illustration compared to 'this generation'?

1. One group of children suggests both games and those children are to be compared with Jesus and John and their followers; a second group of children refuses to play and those children are to be compared with the Jews [AB, BNTC, Crd, Gdt, TNTC]: the people of this generation are like the case of children in (the) marketplace sitting and calling to one another. The children who play the flute represent Jesus with his promises of grace and his happy followers, while the children who sing a funeral song represent John with his call to repentance and his penitent followers [Gdt]. Since John and Jesus (not the people of this generation) become the children who invite the others, the sense of the introductory formula is 'the children of this generation are like the case of children…' [AB], 'the conduct of the present generation towards the messengers sent to it by God is like that which takes place amongst children who…' [Gdt].

2. One group of children suggests both games and those children are to be compared with the Jews; a second group of children refuses to play and those children are to be compared with Jesus and John and their followers [BECNT, ICC, Kst, Lns, My, NAC, NICNT, NIGTC]: the people of this generation are like children in (the) marketplace sitting and calling to one another. The current generation is compared with the seated children [BECNT, Lns] who represent the leaders who complain about Jesus and John because they do not do what the leaders want [BECNT]. The leaders cannot get their own way [Lns] with the result that the people of this generation reject John and Jesus as being deviants and not to be taken seriously [NICNT]. The complaint about not responding to the festive piping was directed towards John and the complaint about not responding to the mourning was directed towards Jesus [ICC]. Luke says that the children are talking with one another, some suggesting a game and others refusing, but he quotes only the reproaches of the seated group. The Jews tell the ascetic John to dance and the joyful Jesus to weep, but neither John nor Jesus can satisfy them [NIGTC]. Since only the taunts of one group are given, probably the use of 'to one another' is not to be pressed [Kst].

3. All of the children are to be compared with the Jews; Jesus and John are not intended to be compared with any of the children in the story; it is not important whether one group suggests both games or whether each group

makes its own suggestion [Arn, Hlt, NTC, Pnt, Su, TNTC]: the people of this generation are like children in the marketplace sitting and calling to one another. One group wanted to play wedding and the other group wanted to play funeral [Su]. The words 'calling to one another' means that the children call in a chaotic fashion to one another, not to others outside the group [Hlt]. Without identifying John and Jesus, the point is that the chief characteristic of the children of this generation, the Pharisees, is that they insist on having their own way and wanted their followers to do as they say [Pnt]. This is not an allegory where the participants are to be identified as John, Jesus, and the Pharisees. Jesus is here pointing to the general characteristics of children at play as being frivolous, irresponsible, inconsistent, and never satisfied, thus implying that his critics are acting childishly [NTC].

7:33 Because[a] **John the Baptist has-come not eating bread nor drinking wine, and you-say, He has a demon.**[b] **7:34** **The Son of-Man**[c] **has-come eating and drinking, and you-say, Behold a-man (who is) a-glutton and a-drunkard, a-friend of-tax-collectors and sinners.**

LEXICON—a. γάρ (LN 89.23): 'because' [LN], 'for' [AB, Arn, BECNT, Lns, NTC, WBC; HCSB, KJV, NASB, NET, NIV, NLT, NRSV, REB], not explicit [CEV, GW, NCV, TEV].

b. δαιμόνιον (LN 12.37) (BAGD 2. p. 169): 'demon' [BAGD, LN]. The phrase 'he has a demon' [BECNT, Lns, NTC, WBC; HCSB, NASB, NET, NIV, NRSV] is also translated 'he has a devil' [Arn; KJV], 'he has a demon in him' [CEV, NCV, TEV], 'there's a demon in him' [GW], 'he is possessed' [REB], 'he's demon possessed' [NLT], 'he is mad' [AB]. See this word at 4:33.

c. υἱὸς τοῦ ἀνθρώπου 'Son of Man'. This title for Christ occurs at 5:24; 6:5, 22; 7:34; 9:22, 26, 44; 11:30; 12:8, 40; 17:22, 24, 26; 18:8, 31; 19:10; 21:27, 36; 22:22, 48, 69; 24:7. See the discussions of this title at 5:24, 6:5, and 9:22.

QUESTION—What relationship is indicated by γάρ 'because' which begins 7:33?

In indicates the reason the parable of the children in the marketplace describes the present generation [Lns]. The parable in 7:32 is now given its application [BECNT, NIGTC, Su, TH].

QUESTION—What is meant by John not eating bread nor drinking wine?

In Mark 1:6, John is said to eat locusts and wild honey and in Luke 1:15 it is prophesied that he would never drink wine or strong drink. He did not eat the ordinary food of people in general [ICC]. This pertains to John's way of life, an ascetic life in the wilderness [BECNT, Su, TG, TH, TNTC]. The word ἄρτον 'bread' sometimes stands for 'food' and this is a hyperbole meaning either that he suffered hunger and thirst or that he fasted [TH]. It means he often fasted [NLT, TEV].

QUESTION—Why would people say that John had a demon?
They thought his way of life was associated with demon possession [NIGTC]. They thought that John was in the desert because of madness and the desert was the haunt of demons [Su]. John's nonconformity with their social mores was attributed to demons [AB]. They rationalized their rejection of John's message by saying he was unbalanced and possessed by a demon [BECNT]. A deranged behavior was considered to be a sign of being demon-possessed [ICC, Lns, NAC, WBC].

QUESTION—What is meant by Jesus eating and drinking?
In contrast with John, Jesus ate and drank like ordinary people [Arn, TNTC]. In connection with the previous verse, it is implied that Jesus ate bread and drank wine like other men [Lns, TG, TH]. It refers to a way of life and refers to Jesus' practice of entering into the social life in the towns and even attending banquets with sinners [Su]. He had no ascetic restraints such as John's [AB]. Jesus behaved as though there was always something to celebrate [WBC].

QUESTION—Why would people say that Jesus was a glutton and a drunkard?
By beginning with 'behold' they showed their contempt of Jesus [TH]. Just as they slandered John by saying that he was demon possessed, they slandered Jesus by saying that he was a winebibber who ate and drank to excess [Lns]. They were not criticizing the drinking of wine, but the excessive drinking of it [TH].

QUESTION—How is the added accusation 'a friend of tax collectors and sinners' connected to their accusation?
It was an added complaint about Jesus' dining companions [TNTC]. It was not an elaboration of the preceding phrase, 'a glutton and a drunkard' [TH]. It was the impression the critics had about Jesus' dealings with social groups [AB].

7:35 Yet/and[a] wisdom is-justified[b] by all her children.[c]

LEXICON—a. καί (LN 89.92, 91.12): 'yet' [LN (91.12), NTC; CEV, GW, HCSB, NASB], 'and yet' [REB], 'but' [KJV, NCV, NET, NIV, NLT], 'however' [TEV], 'nevertheless' [WBC; NRSV], 'and' [Arn, BECNT, LN (89.92), Lns], 'indeed' [AB].

b. aorist pass. indic. of δικαιόω (LN 88.16) (BAGD 2. p. 197): 'to be justified' [Arn, BAGD, BECNT, Lns, WBC; KJV], 'to be vindicated' [AB, BAGD, NTC; HCSB, NASB, NET, NRSV], 'to be shown to be right' [LN; CEV, NLT], 'to be shown to be true' [TEV], 'to be proved right' [GW, NIV, REB], 'to be proved to be right' [NCV]. The aorist tense is timeless [AB, Arn, NIGTC, WBC] and is translated in the present tense [all versions]. Or, the aorist tense refers to the past actions of John and Jesus [Lns].

c. τέκνον (LN58.26) (BAGD 2.f.b. p. 808): 'child' [BAGD, LN]. The phrase 'by all her children' [AB, NTC, WBC; HCSB, NASB, NET, NIV, NRSV] is also translated 'by her children' [Arn], 'of all her children'

LUKE 7:35

[KJV], 'by all who are her children' [REB], 'by its children' [BECNT], 'by what its followers do' [CEV], 'by all who accept it' [TEV], 'by the lives of those who follow it' [NLT], 'by what it does' [NCV], 'by all its results' [GW]. 'Child' is used figuratively of one who has the characteristics of wisdom [LN], of one who attaches himself to wisdom and lets himself be led by it [BAGD].

QUESTION—What relationship is indicated by καί, which can mean 'yet' or 'and'?

1. It indicates contrast [BECNT, Gdt, ICC, NIGTC, NTC, TH, WBC; all versions]: and yet. In spite of the Jew's rejection of John and Jesus, wisdom is shown to be right by her children [NIGTC]. In spite of the nation's rejection, there were some who believed that God's wisdom was doing what was right [ICC]. This is a weak contrast suggesting some form of acceptance in contrast with the rejection of the Jews [TH]. Those who accepted God's message are contrasted with the Pharisees and lawyers who rejected it [BECNT]. Although the saying does not belong to the parable, it is a counterpart to it [WBC].

2. It indicates a connective [AB, Arn, BECNT, Su]: and. This saying allegorizes the parable and recalls the vindication of God in 7:29 [AB]. This is a statement of a general truth [Arn].

QUESTION—What is meant by the saying 'wisdom is justified by her children'?

'Wisdom' is personified [AB, BAGD, BECNT, ICC, NAC, NICNT, Su, WBC]. Wisdom is depicted as a mother and what wisdom produces is referred to as her children. Wisdom is justified by the nature of the children she has produced [Su].

1. 'Wisdom' refers to God's wisdom [AB, BECNT, Hlt, ICC, Kst, Lns, NICNT, NIGTC, TG, TH, WBC], the rightness of God's plan [NIGTC]. In the light of 7:29, Wisdom is a way of speaking about God and his purposes [NICNT]. There is no link to the children in the parable and here the children are those whose lives are formed by the directives of God's wisdom. Those who justify Wisdom do so by recognizing God's plan in what was happening to John and Jesus and aligning themselves with it [WBC]. The children are all those who justified God by accepting God's message [BECNT]. The children are all who align themselves with God's purpose revealed in Jesus and his work [NICNT]. The children are John and Jesus [AB, Lns, NICNT] and all who accepted their teaching [AB], all those who align themselves with God's purpose [NICNT]. Or, it is improbable that John and Jesus are to be included with the children since the children are all those who have accepted the message of wisdom delivered by John and Jesus [NAC, NIGTC]. The results of a course of action determine whether the action followed divine wisdom or human folly. Jesus' contemporaries did not follow God's instructions and this would be proved by the results of their actions [TG]. Wisdom was justified when the men of this generation slandered John and Jesus who

were the representatives of the divine wisdom, so that their contradictory slander unknowingly pronounced this wisdom innocent of all blame [Lns].
2. 'Wisdom' refers to John's and Jesus' wisdom [BNTC, NTC]. Wisdom is vindicated by what it accomplishes in those who accept it for their guidance. John's wisdom was shown in his insistence on conversion and Jesus' wisdom was shown in offering the hope of salvation to all. The children are all those were guided by such wisdom [NTC]. Whether Christ was right or the Pharisees were right would be shown in the lives of the two groups of followers [Pnt].
3. 'Wisdom' is the quality possessed by those who are wise [Arn, EGT, Su]. Those who are wise make the right choice and what is chosen indicates the nature of that wisdom. The people who accepted John and Jesus justified their wisdom and it is implied that the Pharisees were foolish in rejecting John and Jesus [Su]. The children are those who are wise [EGT]. People who are wise will see that the unbelievers of this generation are wrong in that they do not humble themselves before God [Arn]. The people and tax collectors in 7:29 were wise and their choice of accepting both Jesus and John justified their wisdom [Su].

QUESTION—What relationship is indicated by ἀπό 'by' in the phrase 'by all her children'?

It indicates the source from which the acquittal is drawn [Lns]. Justification comes from them [ICC]. Wisdom is justified by what its followers do [CEV]. The claims of 'wisdom' are proved to be true by her children [NIGTC]. They prove that wisdom is right by their lives and perhaps by their acceptance of the messages of John and Jesus [TH].

DISCOURSE UNIT: 7:36–50 [AB, BECNT, NAC, NICNT, NIGTC, Su, TNTC, WBC; CEV, GW, HCSB, NCV, NET, NIV, NLT, NRSV, TEV]. The topic is the woman who washed Jesus' feet [NCV], Jesus forgives sin [NAC], Simon the Pharisee [CEV], Jesus at the home of Simon the Pharisee [TEV], Jesus, a Pharisee, and a woman [NICNT], a sinful woman forgiven [AB, BECNT; GW, NRSV], the woman who was a sinner [NIGTC], the Pharisee and the sinful woman [WBC], Jesus' anointing [NET], Jesus anointed by a sinful woman [Su, TNTC; NIV, NLT], much forgiveness, much love [HCSB].

7:36 And one of-the Pharisees was-asking him that he-eat with him, and having-entered into the house of-the Pharisee he-reclined-at-table.[a] **7:37** And behold a-woman who was a-sinner in the city, and having-learned that he-was-reclining-at-table in the house of-the Pharisee, having-brought an-alabaster-jar[b] of-perfume,[c]

LEXICON—a. aorist pass. indic. of κατακλίνομαι (LN **17.23**) (BAGD p. 411): 'to recline at table' [AB, BAGD, Lns, NTC, WBC], 'to recline at the table' [HCSB, NASB, NIV], 'to sit at the table' [NCV], 'to sit down at the table' [Arn], 'to be at table' [LN], 'to take one's place at the table' [NET, NRSV, REB], 'to recline' [BECNT, LN], 'to sit down to eat' [**LN**; NLT,

TEV], 'to eat' [LN], 'to get ready to eat' [CEV], 'to eat at the table' [GW], 'to sit down to meat' [KJV]. This would be a formal dinner where the guests would recline to eat [BECNT, NAC, Su]. Reclining at the table was a Roman custom [Su], and in Palestine this was done only at banquets [AB]. The guests reclined on couches, resting on their left elbows with their feet extended away from the table [Lns, NTC, TNTC].

b. ἀλάβαστρον (LN 6.131) (BAGD p. 34): 'alabaster jar' [LN, NTC, WBC; NCV, NIV, NRSV, TEV], 'alabaster flask' [AB, Arn, BAGD, BECNT, Lns; HCSB], 'alabaster vial' [NASB], 'bottle' [GW], 'a small flask' [REB]. 'an expensive bottle' [CEV], 'a beautiful jar' [NLT]. An alabaster jar had a rather long neck which would be broken off in order to use its contents [BAGD, LN, NTC, Su, TNTC]. It was a vial made of alabaster, a semitransparent white or yellow stone [AB, Lns].

c. μύρον (LN 6.205) (BAGD p. 530): 'perfume' [AB, BAGD, BECNT, LN, Lns, NTC, WBC; CEV, GW, NASB, NCV, NIV, NLT, TEV], 'perfumed oil' [LN; NET], 'fragrant oil' [HCSB], 'ointment' [Arn, BAGD; KJV, NRSV], 'oil of myrrh' [REB]. The perfume in the jar would be expensive and aromatic [BECNT]. The word for perfume covers a number of substances [NIGTC]. It was a valuable scented oil [Su, TNTC]. When the vial was opened, the costly perfume would evaporate rapidly, unlike an ointment or oil [Lns].

QUESTION—What is the significance of beginning 7:38 with ἰδού 'behold'?

After introducing the setting, here the real action begins [NICNT, NIGTC]. Special attention is directed towards this strange incident concerning the woman [NTC], who was a sinner [BECNT]. Her presence was unexpected [ICC] and the guests were astonished that this woman would enter [Lns]. At festive occasions the doors would be left open so that uninvited persons could enter and sit by the walls to hear the conversation [BECNT, Lns, NTC].

QUESTION—What is signified by calling the woman a sinner?

Although her sin is not specified, she probably was a prostitute [Alf, EGT, ICC, Kst, NICNT, NIGTC, NIVS, Su, TG, TH, TNTC, WBC]. The woman had a bad reputation in regard to adultery or fornication [Arn]. 'Sinner' does not have to mean more than that she had gone wrong at some time and her reputation was therefore damaged [Lns]. Some say that the verb ἦν 'she was' in the imperfect voice indicates that she was a sinner up to this very time [Alf]. However others think that she had apparently repented previously but was still known as a sinner [ICC, NTC]. 'She was' refers to her public character [ICC]. Probably she had previously heard and responded to Jesus' teaching [ICC]. She must have repented previously since when she heard about Jesus being at the house, she brought along the perfume [NTC]. If she hadn't already repented before she arrived, Jesus' words at the banquet informed her that God would be gracious to her [BECNT].

LUKE 7:36-37

QUESTION—What does 'in the city' modify?
1. 'In the city' locates where the woman sinned [NICNT, Rb, TH, WBC; GW, NIV, REB]: there was a woman who was a sinner in the city. She lived a sinful life in that city [GW]. She was publicly a sinner [WBC]. This means that she was known to be a sinner in the town [NICNT, Rb].
2. 'In the city' locates where the woman lived [AB, Alf, Arn, BECNT, Lns, NIGTC, NTC; CEV, HCSB, KJV, NASB, NCV, NET, NRSV, TEV]: there was a woman in the city who was a sinner. Since she was from the town, she was recognized and the townspeople knew of her reputation as a sinner [Lns].

QUESTION—There are two participles in 7:37 ('having learned', 'having brought'), and two more in 7:38 ('having stood' and 'weeping') before the main verb phrase in 7:38 ('she began to wet his feet'). How is the text divided in translations?
1. All of these participles and main verb are translated in one long sentence as in the Greek text [Arn, Lns, WBC; KJV, NASB, NIV, TEV]. The succession of participles lead up the main act of anointing Jesus' feet [Lns].
2. A sentence break is after the second participle [BECNT; NET, NRSV]: When a woman...learned...she brought.... As she stood...weeping, she began to wet his feet.
3. Sentence breaks are after the second participle and after the third participle [CEV]: When the woman learned...she brought.... Then she stood... She wept and began to wet his feet....
4. A sentence break is after the fourth participle [AB, NTC]: When the woman learned...she brought...and stood, weeping. She began to wet his feet....
5. Sentence breaks are after the second participle and after the fourth participle [NLT, REB]: A woman learned... and she brought.... Then she stood...weeping. She began to wet his feet....
6. Sentence breaks are after the first participle and after the third participle [GW]: A woman learned.... So she brought...and stood.... She wept and began to wet his feet....
7. Sentence breaks are after the first participle and after the fourth participle [HCSB, NCV]: A woman learned.... So she brought...and stood..., weeping. She began to wet his feet....

7:38 and having stood[a] behind (him) at his feet weeping, she-began to-wet[b] his feet with tears and she-was-wiping (them) with the hairs of her head and was-kissing his feet and was-anointing[c] (them) with-the perfume.
LEXICON—a. aorist act. participle of ἵσταμαι (LN 17.1) (BAGD II.1.b. p. 382): 'to stand' [AB, BAGD, BECNT, LN, WBC; all versions except GW, NLT, REB], 'to take one's stand' [Lns, NTC], 'to come up to' [BAGD], 'to take one's place' [REB], 'to station oneself' [Arn], 'to kneel' [GW, NLT].

b. pres. act. infin. of βρέχω (LN **79.79**) (BAGD 1. p. 147): 'to wet' [Arn, BAGD, BECNT, **LN**, Lns, WBC; NASB, NET, NIV, TEV], 'to make wet' [NTC], 'to wash' [CEV, GW, HCSB, KJV, NCV], 'to bathe' [AB; NRSV]. This verb is also translated as a phrase: 'her tears fell on his feet' [NLT], 'his feet were wet with her tears' [REB].
c. imperf. act. indic. of ἀλείφω (LN 47.14) (BAGD 1. p. 35): 'to anoint' [AB, Arn, BAGD, BECNT, LN, Lns, NTC, WBC; HCSB, KJV, NASB, NET, NRSV, REB], 'to pour on' [CEV, GW, NIV, TEV], 'to put on' [NLT], 'to rub' [NCV].

QUESTION—Where was the woman standing?
Those at the meal reclined on benches with their feet extended away from the table and the woman could easily approach to stand at Jesus' feet [AB, EGT, Gdt, ICC, Kst, Lns, My, NICNT, NIGTC, NTC, Rb, Su, TG, TH, TNTC, WBC]. Before kneeling to anoint Jesus' feet she may have stood there, fearing that he might not understand or permit her to carry out the anointing. When he did not object, she knelt and began to weep [Lns]. She hesitated and stood there overcome by emotion [NTC].

QUESTION—What was involved in wetting Jesus' feet with her tears?
The dinner guests would have removed their sandals before the meal [Arn, BECNT, Gdt, ICC, Lns, Su, TNTC]. Standing behind Jesus, she broke out weeping and her tears fell upon Jesus' feet and wetted them [NIGTC]. It was not her original plan to wet Jesus' feet with her tears, but she became overcome with her feelings and when she began to weep her tears fell on his feet and then she felt the need to dry them [Alf, EGT, ICC, NIGTC, TG, TH, TNTC, WBC]. The cause of her weeping may have been in repentance for her sins [AB, Gdt, Lns, NTC, Su, WBC], and perhaps for joy and gratitude at having been forgiven [AB, BECNT, NIGTC, TH, WBC], or because of the chance to honor Jesus [BECNT]. Perhaps the emotional stress of the situation caused her to weep [EGT]. Impulsively she wiped the tears away from his feet [Lns, NTC]. She was anxious to make up for wetting Jesus' feet so she let down her hair and bent down to wipe them [NIGTC]. She had no cloth to dry his feet, so she used her hair [Gdt]. Wiping away the tears with her hair showed her self-humiliation and abnegation [Lns].

QUESTION—Why did she kiss Jesus' feet?
The imperfect active verb indicates that she repeatedly kissed Jesus' feet [Bai, ICC, Pnt, Rb; GW, NCV, NLT, NRSV]. The imperfect tense of the verbs mean that while she wept, she kept on wiping Jesus' feet and kept on kissing them [NTC; NASB]. Or, the imperfect tenses describe the progression of the narrative from one act to another, each act taking some time so that only after she wiped away the tears did she kiss his feet and then anointed them [BECNT]. Kissing the feet was a sign of deep reverence [AB, BECNT, ICC, My, NIGTC, TH], and also an expression of gratitude [NIGTC, WBC]. This expresses her deep emotional devotion and in 7:47 her motive is described as love [BECNT].

QUESTION—Why did she anoint Jesus' feet with perfume?

Perhaps originally she wanted to present the costly alabaster jar of perfume to him [Kst], or planned to anoint his head with it [NIGTC, WBC], or had actually planned to anoint his feet [BECNT, ICC, Lns]. Normally, it was the head that was anointed [NIGTC, TNTC, WBC]. From 7:46 it is seen that she anointed Jesus' feet [NIGTC]. She broke the neck of the alabaster jar and poured the perfume on Jesus' feet [Lns, Su]. Although having intended to anoint his head, she anointed his feet to which she had ready access and had already made contact [WBC]. Perhaps she anointed the feet as a mark of humility since this would be the task of a slave [TNTC]. She felt that she was unworthy to do more than touch his feet [Lns].

7:39 And having-seen (this) the Pharisee who had-invited him said[a] within himself saying, If this (one) was a-prophet, he-would-have-known who and what-sort-of woman (she is) who is-touching him, that/because[b] she-is a-sinner.

TEXT—Instead of προφήτης '(a) prophet', some manuscripts read ὁ προφήτης 'the prophet'. GNT reads προφήτης '(a) prophet' with an A decision, indicating that the text is certain.

LEXICON—a. aorist act. indic. of λέγω (LN 31.5) (BAGD 5. p. 226): 'to say' [BAGD, LN]. The phrase λέγω ἐν ἑαυτῷ 'to say within oneself' [Arn, Lns; KJV] is also translated, 'to say to oneself' [BAGD, BECNT, LN, NTC, WBC; all versions except GW, KJV, NCV], 'to think to oneself' [AB, LN; NCV], 'to think' [GW].

b. ὅτι (LN 90.21, 89.33): 'that' [LN (90.21), Lns, NTC, WBC; NASB, NET, NIV, NRSV], 'because' [LN (89.33)], 'for' [Arn, BECNT; KJV], 'seeing that' [AB], not explicit [GW, HCSB, NCV, NLT, REB, TEV].

QUESTION—What is the implication of calling Jesus 'this one'?

This is spoken in a derogatory sense to show contempt [ICC, Lns, My, Rb, TH]. Simon was offended that Jesus tolerated the woman's behavior [NTC]. The Pharisee used 'if' as a contrary-to-fact condition, expressing his belief that it was untrue that Jesus was a prophet [BECNT, Lns, NAC, NIGTC, NTC, Su, TG, TH, WBC]. He believed that Jesus did not know who the woman was and therefore was not a true prophet [Alf, Lns, NIGTC, TG, TNTC]. He referred to the popular belief that Jesus was a prophet only to criticize it [WBC].

QUESTION—What is the distinction between knowing 'who' and 'what sort of person' the woman was?

These two terms refer to knowing who she was and the sort of life she led [ICC, NIGTC, TH]. 'Who' refers to her name and family, while 'what sort' refers to her character and conduct [Gdt]. However some think that both mean the same thing [TG]. 'Who' is defined by 'of what kind' and means 'who, namely of what kind' [Lns].

QUESTION—Does ὅτι mean 'that' or 'because' in the last clause?
1. It indicates the content of what he would have known [ICC, Lns, NIGTC, NTC, TH, WBC; CEV, NASB, NET, NIV, NRSV]: he would have known *that* she is a sinner.
2. It indicates the reason for something [AB, Arn, BECNT; KJV]: he would have known she was a bad woman, *because* she is a sinner.

DISCOURSE UNIT: 7:40–50 [NASB]. The topic is the parable of two debtors.

7:40 **And answering Jesus said to him, Simon, I-have something to-say to-you. And he says, Teacher, speak. 7:41 Two (persons) were debtors to-a-certain moneylender.**[a] **The one was-owing five-hundred denarii,**[b] **and the other fifty.**
LEXICON—a. δανιστής (LN 57.211) (BAGD p. 170): 'moneylender' [AB, Arn, BAGD, BECNT, LN, Lns, NTC; CEV, GW, NASB, NIV, REB, TEV], 'creditor' [BAGD, WBC; HCSB, KJV, NET, NRSV], 'banker' [NCV]. The phrase 'two persons were debtors to a certain moneylender' is translated 'a man loaned money to two people' [NLT].
b. δηνάριον (LN 6.75) (BAGD p. 179): 'denarius' [Arn, BAGD, BECNT, LN, Lns, NTC, WBC; HCSB, NASB, NIV, NRSV], 'silver coin' [CEV, GW, NET, TEV], 'silver piece' [REB], 'piece of silver' [AB; NLT], 'coin' [NCV], 'pence' [KJV]. This was a silver coin issued by the Roman government and it had the value of what a common laborer could earn in a day [BAGD, LN]. It was the daily wage of an agricultural laborer [NIGTC, TG]. It was a soldier's or laborer's daily wage and the contrast is between one-and-three-quarter year's wages and two month's wages, figuring a six-day workweek [BECNT]. The important fact is that one owed ten times the amount of the other [TG, TH].
QUESTION—How could Jesus answer if Simon had not spoken his thoughts out loud?
The question was expressed by Simon's expression and attitude [Alf, EGT, TG]. Jesus knew the questions in Simon's mind [Arn, Gdt, ICC, My, NICNT, NIGTC, NTC, Rb, Su, WBC]. Jesus was answering to the situation in which no question was spoken [Lns].

7:42 **Not having (anything) of-themselves to-pay,**[a] **he-cancelled-the debt**[b] **of-both. Therefore which of-them will-love**[c] **him more? 7:43 Answering Simon said, I-suppose**[d] **(the one) to-whom he-forgave the more. And he-said to-him, You judged correctly.**
TEXT—In 7:42, before πλεῖον 'more', some manuscripts add εἰπέ 'tell'. GNT does not mention this variant. Εἰπέ 'tell' is read by KJV.
LEXICON—a. aorist act. infin. of ἀποδίδωμι (LN 57.153) (BAGD 2. p. 90): 'to pay' [Arn, LN; KJV, NET, NRSV, REB], 'to pay back' [AB, BAGD; CEV, GW, HCSB, NIV, TEV], 'to pay off' [Lns], 'to repay' [BECNT; NASB, NLT], 'to give back' [WBC], 'to pay what they owed' [NCV], 'to pay back what is owed' [NTC]. The verb was often used to mean the

320   LUKE 7:42–43

repayment of debts [NIGTC]. The aorist tense points to the complete amount [Lns].

b. aorist mid. (deponent= act.) indic. of χαρίζομαι (LN **57.223**) (BAGD 1. p. 876): 'to cancel a debt' [BAGD, **LN**, WBC; NET, NIV, NRSV, REB, TEV], 'to freely forgive a debt' [BECNT], 'to graciously cancel a debt' [AB, NTC], 'to kindly forgive, canceling the debts' [NLT], 'to be kind enough to cancel the debts' [GW], 'to graciously grant the amount' [Lns], 'to made a present of the debt' [Arn], 'to forgive a debt' [LN], 'to graciously forgive' [HCSB, NASB], 'to frankly forgive' [KJV]. The phrase 'he cancelled the debt of both' is translated 'he said that they didn't have to pay him anything' [CEV], 'the banker told both of them they did not have to pay him' [NCV]. This refers to the debtors being forgiven by having their debts cancelled [Hlt]. The debtors' debt was cancelled, and the debtor's themselves were forgiven [Hlt]. This verb was a common business term for remitting a debt [AB, BECNT, WBC]. The verb is used of forgiving debts and also of forgiving sins [AB, WBC]. In 7:21 it means 'to bestow, to give as a favor', but here it means 'to remit, to cancel the debt' [TH].

c. fut. act. indic. of ἀγαπάω (LN 25.43) (BAGD 1.a.α. p. 4): 'to love' [AB, Arn, BAGD, BECNT, LN, Lns, NTC, WBC; all versions except CEV], 'to like' [CEV], 'to regard with affection' [LN], 'to be grateful' [BAGD]. The love is based on sincere appreciation and high regard [LN]. The debtors gratitude is suffused with genuine affection [Hlt].

d. pres. act. indic. of ὑπολαμβάνω (LN **31.29**) (BAGD 4. p. 845): 'to suppose' [AB, Arn, BAGD, BECNT, **LN**, WBC; all versions except NCV, REB], 'to think' [BAGD, LN; NCV, REB], 'to presume' [Lns], 'to take it' [NTC].

QUESTION—In the question at the end of 7:42, what relationship is indicated by οὖν 'therefore'?

It introduces the concluding question [TH]. The question asks what is to be inferred from the situation Jesus described [TH]. This is the point of the parable [ICC, Lns, Rb].

QUESTION—How could the parable of the two debtors determine which would love the creditor the most?

The verb ἀγαπάω is used here to express the reaction of each of the debtors after their debts have been cancelled by the creditor and therefore included the feeling of gratitude and this may be the primary meaning in this context. Love is the way in which gratitude is expressed [NIGTC]. There is no specific word for 'to show gratitude' or 'to thank' in Hebrew or Aramaic, so 'to love' was used to express gratitude and here it probably means to be grateful or thankful [NAC]. Since Jesus goes on to speak of the woman loving much, love is primary although the context also has the nuance of gratitude or grateful affection [Hlt, WBC]. The verb means 'love' and it is best to retain this meaning in translation [TG]. The verb refers to gratitude that expresses both appreciation and love and the principle is that the larger the debt that is forgiven, the larger is the gratitude and love [BECNT]. The degree of their gratitude would be proportionate to the benefits they received [TH].

QUESTION—Why did Simon use the verb ὑπολαμβάνω 'I suppose' when he gave the obvious answer?

He was probably hesitant to commit himself, thinking that Jesus had an ulterior motive in asking the question [WBC]. He was being cautious, wondering what the question might lead to [TH, WBC]. It was a grudging admission, knowing that Jesus could give surprising responses [BECNT]. Probably Simon realized that he was caught in a trap [MGC, NIGTC] and he reluctantly answered, anticipating the criticism of his own lack of gratitude to Jesus [NIGTC]. Perhaps he was thinking 'that is, if they feel as they ought' [Alf]. Some think he answered with a supercilious indifference [ICC, Rb].

7:44 **And having-turned toward the woman he-said to-Simon, Do-you-see this woman? I-entered into your house, you-did- not -give me water for (my) feet but with (her) tears she wet my feet and with her hairs she-wiped (them).**

TEXT—Instead of θριξὶν αὐτῆς 'her hairs', some manuscripts evidently read θριξὶν τῆς κεθαλῆς αὐτῆς 'hairs of her head' although GNT does not mention this variant. Θριξὶν τῆς κεθαλῆς αὐτῆς 'hairs of her head' is read by KJV.

QUESTION—What is the significance of Jesus turning towards the woman?

This is the first time Jesus looked at the woman and he asked Simon also to look at her [Rb]. Turning towards the woman while speaking to Simon reduces her from her role of central actor to that of an object lesson [NICNT]. This draws attention to the woman [Arn, TG], from whom Simon is to learn a lesson [BECNT, EGT, Lns]. This implies that the parable applies to the woman and to Simon [TH]. Although Jesus was speaking to Simon as he looked at the woman, it really was a speech in praise of her kindness, and the speech ended with Jesus directly addressing her [Bai]. Jesus directed Simon's attention to the woman who had done what Simon had failed to do, and what she had done exceeded what Simon could have been expected to do [Lns]. The comparisons between Simon and the woman were not so much a contrast of their deeds, but of the love shown by each of them [AB]. It is not likely that the woman consciously did what she did in order to make up for Simon's lack of affection [NAC].

QUESTION—Why would Simon be expected to provide water for Jesus' feet?

Simon was criticized for not ordering his servants to provide water [TH]. The guests' sandaled feet would be dusty from traveling to the feast, so it was courteous for the host to provide water to sponge off their feet before reclining on the couch [Pnt]. Simon was not expected to take the role of a servant, rather Jesus only spoke of providing water so that Jesus could have washed his own feet [Bai]. Had Simon provided the water, his servants would have washed Jesus' feet [NAC, Su]. It was a common courtesy [Arn, NIVS, Su], but Simon had treated Jesus as an inferior [Arn]. Or, although courtesy did not demand that water be provided, Simon had not performed any special acts of hospitality for Jesus [Alf, NAC, NIGTC, WBC]. It is debatable whether such an act was required of all hosts. If required, then Simon was discourteous, if not, the woman's actions were extraordinary and even more commendable [BECNT].

7:45 You did- not -give me a-kiss, but she from (the time) I-entered did-not -stop kissing my feet. 7:46 You-did- not -anoint my head with-oil, but with-perfume she anointed my feet.

TEXT—In 7:45, instead of εἰσῆλθον 'I entered', some manuscripts read εἰσῆλθεν 'she entered'. GNT reads εἰσῆλθον 'I entered' with an A decision, indicating that the text is certain.

QUESTION—Why would Simon be expected to give Jesus a kiss?

Kissing was a customary greeting, showing respect and friendship [BECNT, Lns, NAC, WBC]. Kissing was part of a ceremonial welcome given to guests [TH]. Kissing indicated respect and affection and this would be expected of the host [Arn, Pnt, TNTC], even if given hypocritically [Pnt]. Although a kiss was a form of greeting, it was not a required act of hospitality to a guest [NIGTC]. The kiss would have been on the cheek [ICC, Su, TG], or forehead [Su], or mouth [My]. If given with great respect, the kiss could be upon the hand [ICC]. Equals kissed each other on the cheek, inferiors kissed the hand of their teacher, master, or parent. Since Simon addressed Jesus as 'teacher' he should have kissed Jesus' hand [Bai]. For the woman, the kisses on Jesus' feet expressed her humility and appreciation [BECNT].

QUESTION—From the account in 7:37–38, how could it be that the woman had kissed Jesus' feet from the time Jesus had entered?

This was a spoken as a hyperbole [AB, BECNT, My, NIGTC, TH, WBC], to make his point [AB]. The hyperbole was suggested by the mention of the kiss that was appropriate at entering the feast [My] and cast her in the role of hostess [WBC], or it stresses the constancy of her action [BECNT]. Instead of taking it as a hyperbole, it is explained that the woman entered when Jesus did and she had approached Jesus' feet as soon as the guests were in place [Alf, Bai, Gdt, ICC].

QUESTION—Why would Simon be expected to anoint Jesus' head with oil?

Anointing the head of a guest with olive oil was an act of hospitality [Arn, Lns, Pnt, TH]. It was usual to anoint an honored guest [Gdt, TNTC], although it is questionable that this was always done [NIGTC]. The guest's face would be anointed as a sign of joy at being invited to the banquet [Pnt]. The guest would rub olive oil on his hair and face after coming in from the hot sun [TG]. It was not required, but it would be a special courtesy [BECNT, NAC, WBC]. Inexpensive olive oil would normally be used to anoint the head of a guest, but the woman had used expensive perfume to anoint Jesus' feet [BECNT].

7:47 For-this-reason[a] I-say to-you, Her sins (which are) many have-been-forgiven,[b] because[c] she-loved greatly.[d] But to-whom little is-forgiven, he/she-loves little.

LEXICON—a. The Greek phrase οὗ χάριν 'for this reason' [AB; NASB] is also translated 'for which reason' [BECNT], 'on the basis of this' [WBC], 'that is why' [GW], 'therefore' [NTC; HCSB, NET, NIV, NRSV], 'so' [CEV, REB], 'then' [TEV], 'wherefore' [Arn; KJV], 'thanks to which' [Lns], not explicit [NCV, NLT].

b. perf. pass. indic. of ἀφίημι (LN 40.8) (BAGD 2. p. 126): 'to be forgiven' [AB, Arn, BAGD, BECNT, LN, NTC, WBC; all versions], 'to be dismissed' [Lns]. See this word at 6:37.

c. ὅτι (LN 89.33): 'because' [Arn, BECNT, LN, Lns], 'for' [LN, NTC; KJV, NASB, NIV], 'that is why' [CEV, HCSB], 'seeing that' [AB, WBC], 'thus' [NET], 'so' [NCV, NLT], 'hence' [NRSV]. The phrase is also translated '(her great love) proves that' [GW, REB, TEV].

d. πολύς (LN **78.3**) (BAGD I.2.c.β. p. 689): 'greatly' [BAGD, LN], 'much' [Arn, BAGD, LN; HCSB], 'very much' [BAGD]. This word can be translated as an adverb or an adjective [LN]. The phrase 'she has loved greatly' [AB, WBC] is also translated 'she loved much' [BECNT, Lns, NTC; KJV, NASB, NET, NIV], 'she has shown great love' [CEV, NRSV], 'she has shown me much love' [NLT], 'she showed great love' [NCV], 'the great love she has shown' [**LN**; TEV], 'her great love' [GW, REB].

QUESTION—What relationship is indicated by οὗ χάριν 'for this reason' and how is the phrase 'I say to you' connected?

It indicates Jesus' conclusion to the preceding account [AB, Alf, Bai, BECNT, EGT, ICC, Lns, NAC, NIGTC, NTC, TH, WBC; GW]: on the basis of what she has done, I say to you that her sins have been forgiven. The phrase οὗ χάριν 'for this reason' is to be linked with 'I say to you' and this states how the forgiveness of her sins had become evident [Arn, ICC, Lns, WBC]. It is a summary of all that has preceded in 7:44–46 and introduces the reason for what Jesus then declares [AB]. The actions of the woman caused Jesus to respond and to make a point from the preceding parable [BECNT]. The woman's attitude revealed in her loving much was evidence that she had already experienced forgiveness [NAC].

QUESTION—What relationship is indicated by ὅτι 'because' in Jesus' statement 'because she loved much'?

1. It specifies the grounds for concluding that her sins are forgiven [AB, Alf, Arn, BECNT, Blm, EGT, Gdt, ICC, Lns, MGC, My, NAC, NIVS, NTC, Rb, Su, TG, TH, TNTC, WBC; GW, NET, REB, TEV]: I say to you that she has been forgiven since (it is clear that) she loved me greatly. It is implied '*and I say this to you* because she loved much' [ICC]. This clause

states why her forgiveness is known to exist, not the reason for her forgiveness, since love is the consequence of forgiveness [AB]. The woman's great love proves in a visible manner that she has been forgiven [Gdt, Lns, TH; GW, REB, TEV]. The point is that the expression of love results from the sense of having been forgiven [NTC]. The actions of the woman prove the presence of love in gratitude for being previously forgiven [BECNT]. The conjunction means 'as evidenced by the fact that' or 'thus we know' [NAC], 'for you see that' [Alf, Gdt]. Some keep the argument that love is the consequence of forgiveness and not the cause, but use a conjunction that indicates result [CEV, NCV, NET, NLT, NRSV]: she has been forgiven, so she has shown great love.

2. It indicates the reason her sins were forgiven [Crd]: she has been forgiven because she loved greatly. This is the easier reading and it is supported by Jesus' concluding statement of forgiveness in 7:48 [Crd].

QUESTION—Who forgave the woman's sins and when was she forgiven?

The passive voice implies that God has forgiven her sins [AB, Bai, NIGTC, TH, WBC]. The perfect voice of ἀφέωνται 'have been forgiven' indicates that her present state of forgiveness is the result of having been forgiven previously, not at this moment [Bai, BECNT, MGC, NICNT]. Perhaps this happened when the woman heard Jesus preaching in the synagogue just before this, or when he preached to the multitudes [NAC]. Jesus recognized that the woman's manifestation of love was a sign of her state of forgiveness [AB].

QUESTION—Whom did the woman love?

The woman's gratitude and love to God was focused on Jesus [WBC]. From Jesus the woman had come to know that even she could be forgiven and therefore she had such affection for him [EGT]. Love for Jesus means love for God [NTC].

QUESTION—What is the import of adding the phrase 'which are many' to describe her sins?

Some take it to refer to the fact that she had many sins [NIGTC, TNTC; all versions]: 'her sins, many as they are' [NIGTC]. It does not mean that Simon's sins were fewer, but this is added because the woman is pictured in the parable as the debtor who owed 500 denarii and also because she actually felt that she had many sins [Lns]. This shows that Jesus did know who the woman was, so Simon should recognize that he was a prophet [BECNT]. Another takes it to refer to Simon's estimate of her, 'the many sins which you think there are' (referring to 7:39) [ICC].

QUESTION—How can 'little is forgiven' be applied to Simon?

The Pharisee thought that he has committed only a little that needed forgiveness [Arn, EGT, ICC]. Simon was not aware of his many sins and had not repented of them with the result that he was forgiven of little and loved little [Bai]. This is a general principle that Simon and all loveless men should apply to themselves [Lns, NIGTC, TH]. Their total lack of love indicates they have no forgiveness [Lns]. It does not imply that Simon showed a little love for being forgiven. It ironically asks those who had little love for Jesus whether they have realized how great their sins were and their great need for forgiveness [NIGTC]. By his lack of love, Simon proved that he had not been forgiven and this inference has been softened by stating 'has been forgiven little' [NTC].

7:48 And he-said to-her, Your sins have-been-forgiven. 7:49 And the (ones who) were-reclining-with (him) began to-say to/among^a themselves, Who is this who even/also^b forgives^c sins?

LEXICON—a. ἐν (LN 31.5) (BAGD I.5.b. p. 259): 'to' [BAGD]. The phrase ἤρξαντο λέγειν ἐν ἑαυτοῖς 'began to say to themselves' [AB, WBC; NASB, TEV] is also translated 'began to ask themselves' [REB], 'began to say among themselves' [BECNT; HCSB, NCV, NET, NIV, NRSV], 'said among themselves' [NLT], 'began to say within themselves' [Lns, NTC; KJV], 'began to say in themselves' [Arn], 'started saying to one another' [CEV], 'thought' [GW].
  b. καί (LN 89.93): 'even' [AB, Arn, BECNT, LN, Lns, NTC, WBC; GW, HCSB, NASB, NCV, NET, NIV, NRSV, TEV], 'also' [KJV], not explicit [NLT, REB]. This adverb is also translated as a verb: 'dares to' [CEV].
  c. pres. act. indic. of ἀφίημι (LN 40.8) (BAGD 2. p. 126): 'to forgive'. See this word in the passive voice at 7:47.

QUESTION—What is the significance of the perfect tense used by Jesus when he said 'Your sins have been forgiven'?

Her sins had been forgiven before Jesus said this to her [Arn, Bai, BECNT, Gdt, ICC, Lns, My, NAC, NIGTC, NTC, TH, WBC]. God had forgiven her [Arn; NET]. Jesus' words were a confirmation of what had already happened in order to assure the woman of God's dealing with her through Jesus [NAC, NIGTC]. This was a confirmation of her forgiveness on the basis of Jesus' authority [WBC]. Jesus both confirms her assurance and publicly declares that she is forgiven [BECNT, EGT, ICC, NTC], in the face of the Pharisees rejection of her [BECNT]. The woman did not need to be assured, but she needed recognition of her new life and forgiveness among God's people [NICNT].

QUESTION—What is the significance of the present tense used by the guests when they said 'Who is this who forgives sins?'

The present tense shows that they considered Jesus to be actively declaring such forgiveness [BECNT]. They understood 'your sins have been forgiven' to mean that Jesus was then forgiving her [AB, NAC, Su]. They recognized that Jesus was exercising God's prerogative of forgiving sins and not merely telling of forgiveness by someone else [Lns].

QUESTION—Did each of the guests speak inwardly to himself or to other guests?

  1. They thought this [AB, Arn, BECNT, ICC, LN, Lns, NTC, TH, WBC; GW, KJV, NASB, TEV]: they began to think to themselves. The phrase λέγω ἐν ἑαυτῷ 'to say to oneself' is an idiom that means to think about

something without communicating the content to others, 'to think to oneself, to say to oneself' [LN (31.5)]. Even with the plural reference, this probably refers to internal perceptions [BECNT]. Jesus answered their thoughts [ICC].
2. They spoke to other guests [CEV; probably BECNT; NCV, NET, NIV, NLT, NRSV which translate with 'among']: they began to say to one another.

QUESTION—Why did the guests ask the question 'Who is this?'
They were puzzled about Jesus and probably offended [Bai]. The use of 'this' shows at least a slight contempt [ICC]. The question probably implies condemnation as in 5:21 [Rb, Su, TG]. In 5:21 the critics called Jesus' words blasphemy since only God could forgive sin [BECNT, Rb, Su]. The guests were probably mostly Pharisees who were provoked to resentment at Jesus' words [NTC]. This rhetorical question is a complaint about Jesus presuming to forgive sin [BECNT]. Or, two commentators think that the speakers were not hostile and asked in a reverential spirit [Alf, WBC], and these were fellow guests rather than the scribes and Pharisees of 5:21 [WBC].

QUESTION—In 7:49 does καί mean 'even' or 'also'?
1. It means 'even' [AB, Arn, BECNT, Gdt, ICC, Lns, WBC; GW, NASB, NCV, NET, NIV, NRSV, TEV]: who even forgives sins. He does this even besides all the other extraordinary things he has done [Gdt, Lns].
2. It means 'also' [Bai; KJV]: who also forgives sins. Along with all the other outrageous things he has done, he also forgives sins [Bai].

7:50 And he-said to the woman, Your faith has-saved[a] you. Go in peace.[b]

LEXICON—a. perf. act. indic. of σῴζω (LN 21.27) (BAGD 2.a.γ. p. 798): 'to save' [BAGD, LN]. The clause 'your faith has saved you' [Arn, BECNT, Lns, NTC, WBC; all versions except CEV, NCV] is also translated 'your faith has brought you salvation' [AB], 'because of your faith, you are now saved' [CEV], 'because you have believed, you are saved from your sins' [NCV]. This clause is identical to the ones in 8:48; 17:19; 18:42.
b. εἰρήνη (LN 22.42) (BAGD 2. p. 227): 'peace' [BAGD, LN], 'tranquility' [LN]. The clause 'Go in peace' [AB, Arn, BECNT, NTC; all versions except CEV] is also translated 'be going in peace' [Lns], 'may God give you peace' [CEV], 'go into peace' [WBC].

QUESTION—What was the object of the woman's faith?
The woman had expressed her faith by boldly coming to Simon's house, and by the sincerity of her weeping and demonstrating her devotion to him [Su]. The woman's faith was her trust in Jesus [NTC]. The woman believed in Jesus [Lns, Pnt, TH], and his readiness to save, pardon, and receive a repentant sinner [Lns]. Here faith was a confidence in God which caused her to respect and love Jesus whom she understood to be God's agent [AB]. She believed that God's help was to be found in Jesus [WBC].

QUESTION—What is meant by the parting words, 'Go in peace'?
This was a common dismissal formula as used also in 8:48 and Acts 16:36 [AB, ICC, NIGTC, WBC], but now it had a deeper significance [NIGTC, WBC]. This is a kindly dismissal and peace is her possession as she leaves [Lns]. Jesus told her to go with peace resting on her, that is, with the full measure of God's blessing [Arn]. Jesus wanted the woman to leave with a sense of God's blessing, knowing that God has seen her faith [BECNT]. 'Peace' is the Hebrew *shalom*, prosperity for body and soul [NTC]. A person has peace when his sins are forgiven, he possesses salvation, God is his friend, and as result of all this he has a feeling of peace in his heart [Lns]. Peace is a state of being without doubts, full of assurance and confidence [TG].

DISCOURSE UNIT: 8:1–9:20 [WBC]. The topic is the itinerant preaching with the Twelve and the women.

DISCOURSE UNIT: 8:1–56 [NICNT]. The topic is the proclamation of the Good News of the kingdom of God.

DISCOURSE UNIT: 8:1–21 [NAC, NIGTC]. The topic is Jesus' teachings in parables.

DISCOURSE UNIT: 8:1–15 [NIV]. The topic is the parable of the sower.

DISCOURSE UNIT: 8:1–3 [AB, BECNT, NAC, NICNT, NIGTC, Su, TNTC, WBC; CEV, GW, HCSB, NASB, NCV, NET, NLT, NRSV, TEV]. The topic is the parable of the soils [NAC], Good News of the kingdom of God [NICNT], the group with Jesus [NCV], the ministering women [BECNT; NASB], women who followed Jesus [AB; NLT], the women who accompanied Jesus [NRSV, TEV], women who helped Jesus [TNTC; CEV], women who supported Jesus [GW], many women support Christ's work [HCSB], traveling arrangements [NIGTC], itinerant preaching with the Twelve and the women [WBC], beginning a second tour of Galilee [Su], Jesus' ministry and the help of women [NET].

8:1 And it-happened in the next[a] he was-traveling-through every city and village preaching[b] and announcing-the-good-news[c] (of) the kingdom of-God and the twelve (were) with him,

LEXICON—a. καθεξῆς (LN 61.1, 67.52): 'next' [LN (61.1)]. The phrase ἐν ᾧ καθεξῆς 'in the next' is an idiom translated 'next, later' [LN (67.52)], 'soon after this' [CEV], 'soon afterwards' [AB, NTC; HCSB, NASB, NRSV], 'sometime afterward' [NET], 'some time later' [TEV], 'in the subsequent time' [Arn], 'after this' [GW, NCV, NIV, REB], 'afterward' [BECNT, Lns; KJV], 'not long afterward' [NLT], 'in what follows' [WBC]. This was soon after the last event in chapter 7 [NTC, Su, TH]. It is a vague expression of time [TG], and it was not necessarily *soon* afterwards [EGT; NET].

b. pres. act. participle of κηρύσσω (LN 33.256) (BAGD 2.b.β. p. 431): 'to preach'. See translations of this word at 3:3. This word also occurs at 4:18, 19, 44; 8:39; 9:2; 12:3; 24:47.
c. pres. mid. participle of εὐαγγελίζω (LN 33.215) (BAGD 2.a.β. p. 317): 'to announce good news'. See translations of this word at 1:19. This word also occurs at 2:10; 3:18: 4:18, 43; 7:22; 9:6; 16:16; 20:1.

QUESTION—Is there a significant difference in the two participles 'preaching' and 'announcing the good news'?

They are not two separate actions since the second participle indicates the content of the first [NIC; NET]. The second specifies the prevailing character of his preaching [Gdt]. The two participles joined by 'and' form a hendiadys meaning 'to preach the good news' [MGC, NIGTC; TEV], 'to proclaim the good news' [NIV, REB], 'to announce the Good News' [NLT], 'to spread the good news about' [GW]. The verbs supplement each other, with 'preaching' stressing his authority and 'announcing the good news' stressing the good tidings and they could be combined in translation 'proclaimed/preached everywhere the good news of' [TH], 'telling the good news about God's kingdom' [CEV]. Many translate with the two verbs joined with 'and' [AB, BECNT, Lns, NTC, WBC; KJV, NASB, NCV, NET, NRSV].

QUESTION—Who were the 'twelve' and what did they do?

The designation 'the Twelve' functions as a title to identify the apostles as a group [TH]. 'The Twelve' is translated 'the/his twelve apostles' [CEV, GW, NCV, NLT, TEV]. These were the twelve disciples he chose and named as Apostles in 6:13, and at Mark 3:14 it says that they were to accompany Jesus in preparation for their task [NIGTC, WBC]. The Twelve were witnesses of Jesus' ministry and also were being trained for their upcoming mission (9:1–11) [MGC]. This does not indicate that they preached in Jesus' presence, if at all [ICC, Lns].

QUESTION—What is meant by the kingdom of God?

See the discussion of this question at 4:43.

8:2 and some women who had-been healed from evil spirits and diseases, Mary the (one) called[a] Magdalene, from whom seven demons[b] had-gone-out,[c]

LEXICON—a. pres. pass. participle of καλέω (LN 33.129) (BAGD 1.a.γ. p. 399): 'to be called, to be named' [BAGD, LN]. The phrase 'Mary the one called Magdalene' is translated 'Mary called Magdalene' [AB, Arn, BECNT, Lns, NTC; HCSB, KJV, NCV, NET, NIV, NRSV], 'Mary who was called Magdalene' [NASB, TEV; similarly WBC], 'Mary, also called Magdalene' [GW], 'Mary, known as Mary of Magdala' [REB], 'Mary Magdalene' [CEV, NLT].
b. δαιμόνιον (LN 12.37): 'demon'. This means the same as 'evil spirit' in the previous clause [TG]. See this word at 4:33.

c. pluperf. act. indic. of ἐξέρχομαι (LN 15.40): 'to go out' [LN, Lns; KJV, NASB, NCV, NET, NRSV], 'to come out' [AB, WBC; HCSB, NIV, REB], 'to have departed' [Arn], 'to be driven out' [TEV], 'to be expelled' [BECNT, NTC]. The phrase 'from whom seven demons had gone out' [GW] is also translated 'who once had seven demons in her' [CEV], 'from whom he had cast out evil spirits' [NLT]. The intransitive 'had gone out' is equivalent to the passive 'had been driven out' [TH; TEV]. This refers to exorcism performed by Jesus [AB, Lns, TG].

QUESTION—What had these women been healed from and how many had been healed?

Possession by evil spirits is distinguished from diseases [BECNT, ICC, Lns, NICNT, NTC]. Perhaps only Mary had been freed from demons and the others had been cured of their diseases [ICC]. It is not grammatically certain that the 'many others' were also women who had been healed by Jesus or that the women who are named are included with the many who helped in providing for Jesus and the Twelve [WBC].

1. The three women mentioned by name and all the other women had been cured by Jesus [AB, Arn, BECNT, NIC, NICNT, NIGTC, WBC]. The 'some' women at the beginning of the verse becomes 'many others' at the end of the verse [AB]. Many had been healed and Luke has singled out three from among them for special mention [BECNT, NIGTC].
2. Only the three women mentioned by name were included in the reference to 'some women' [TH]. The 'some' who were cured refers to the three women who are mentioned by name while the 'many others' refers to the whole group of women so that this means 'Many women went with Jesus also. Some among them had been healed from evil spirits and diseases, namely, Mary, Joanna, and Susanna. All of them provided for them' [TH].

QUESTION—What was Mary's name?

She was Mary, who was called the one from Magdala, that is, Mary, who was called Mary of Magdala [Arn, TH; REB]. She apparently was from the town of Magdala [AB, BECNT, BNTC, Gdt, ICC, Lns, MGC, NAC, NIBC, NIGTC, NTC, Rb, Su, TG, TH, TNTC, WBC]. The location of the town is not certain [WBC]. Magdala was a town on the west side of Lake Galilee, about three miles from Tiberias [AB, MGC, NIGTC, NTC]. This name was used to distinguish her from other women who were named Mary [Gdt, ICC, Su, TH, TNTC].

QUESTION—What is significant about there having been seven demons or evil spirits driven out of Mary?

This indicates a simultaneous possession by seven different demons [My]. There is no reason to attach a symbolic meaning to the number seven here [ICC, TH]. That there were seven demons indicates the severity of the possession [AB, MGC, NAC, NIBC, NIC, WBC], the possession being of extraordinary malignity [ICC, TH], the worst possible state of demon possession [NIGTC]. She had suffered from seven different diseases [BNTC], or she had had seven attacks [Gdt]. It is not clear whether there were seven different maladies cured at the same time or on seven different occasions, or whether the number seven is used symbolically of the completeness or fullness of her possession before Jesus healed her [Su].

8:3 **and Joanna (the) wife of Chuza (the) steward^a of-Herod and Susanna, and many others, who were-providing for-them from the (possessions) belonging^b to-them.**

TEXT—Instead of αὐτοῖς 'for them', some manuscripts read αὐτῷ 'for him'. GNT reads αὐτοῖς 'for them' with a B decision, indicating that the text is almost certain. Αὐτῷ 'for him' is read by KJV.

LEXICON—a. ἐπίτροπος (LN 37.86) (BAGD 1. p. 303): 'steward' [AB, Arn, BAGD, BECNT, Lns, WBC; HCSB, KJV, NASB, NRSV, REB], 'foreman' [BAGD, LN], 'official' [CEV], 'officer in the court' [TEV], 'administrator' [GW], 'manager' [NCV], 'business manager' [NLT], 'household manager' [NET], 'manager of the household' [NTC; NIV]. The noun applies to someone in charge of supervising workers [LN], although the office may have been of a political nature and mean 'governor, procurator' [BAGD]. He was a high officer in Herod's court [BECNT, NIGTC]. He would have been the manager of Herod's household and estate [AB, ICC, Lns, NIBC, NTC], or his financial minister [Lns]. His duties probably were concerned with finances [TG].

b. pres. act. participle of ὑπάρχω (LN57.16) (BAGD 1. p. 838): 'to belong to' [LN]. The phrase τὰ ὑπάρχοντα 'the (things) belonging to' is translated 'possessions' [Arn, BAGD, LN; HCSB], 'what they owned' [CEV], 'financial (support)' [GW], 'money' [NCV], 'resources' [BECNT, NTC; NET, NLT, NRSV, REB, TEV], 'means' [AB, Lns, WBC; NASB, NIV], 'substance' [KJV].

QUESTION—How could the women provide for Jesus and his disciples from their possessions?

It is implied that the women were persons of substance and could provide financially for Jesus and the group traveling with him [ICC, Lns, MGC, NIGTC; GW, NCV]. The imperfect tense 'they were providing for them' indicates repetition, 'they kept providing for them' [Lns]. They provided for 'them', that is, for Jesus and his twelve disciples [AB, ICC, TH; CEV, GW, NCV, NLT, TEV]. Jesus and his apostles would have a common purse out of which all their expenses were paid and these women kept replenishing the purse [ICC, Lns, TNTC].

DISCOURSE UNIT: 8:4–21 [AB, BECNT, NIBC, NICNT]. The topic is the need for authentic hearing [NICNT], a call to faith [BECNT], the preached and accepted word of God [AB], the parable of the sower [NIBC].

DISCOURSE UNIT: 8:4–18 [GW]. The topic is a story about a farmer.

DISCOURSE UNIT: 8:4–15 [BECNT, NAC, Su, TNTC; NASB, NCV, NET, NLT]. The topic is the parable of the sower [Su, TNTC; NASB, NET], the parable of the soils [NAC], the story of the farmer scattering seed [NLT], a story about planting seed [NCV], the issue of response: seed parable [BECNT].

DISCOURSE UNIT: 8:4–8 [AB, NIGTC; CEV, HCSB, NRSV, TEV]. The topic is the parable of the sower [NIGTC; HCSB, NRSV, TEV], a story about a farmer [CEV], the parable of the sowed seed [AB].

DISCOURSE UNIT: 8:4–8a [WBC]. The topic is the potent seed and varied soil.

8:4 And (when) a-large crowd was-gathering and the (ones) in-every city were-coming[a] to him, he-spoke by-means-of a-parable,[b]
LEXICON—a. pres. mid. (deponent = act.) participle of ἐπιπορεύομαι (LN 15.83) (BAGD p. 298): 'to come to' [Arn, BECNT, LN, NTC, WBC; GW, KJV, NCV, NET, NIV, NRSV, TEV], 'to keep coming to' [**LN**], 'to make one's way to' [AB; REB], 'to go to' [BAGD], 'to journey to' [BAGD; NASB], 'to resort to' [Lns], 'to flock to' [HCSB], not explicit [CEV, NLT].
  b. παραβολή (LN 33.15) (BAGD 2. p. 612): 'parable' [AB, Arn, BAGD, BECNT, LN, Lns, NTC; HCSB, KJV, NASB, NET, NIV, NRSV, REB, TEV], 'story' [CEV, NCV, NLT], 'story used as an illustration' [GW]. The phrase 'he spoke by means of a parable' is translated 'he spoke parabolically' [WBC].
QUESTION—What is the significance of the present participles συνιόντος 'was gathering' and ἐπιπορευομένων 'were coming to'?
  The present participles indicate that the number of people was constantly and progressively increasing as the people flocked to hear Jesus [AB, ICC, NAC]. The present tense shows the progress of the people coming and the crowd gathering [BECNT]. It was because of the growing crowd that Jesus had to get into a boat in Mark 4:1 [ICC].
QUESTION—What relationship is indicated by the καί 'and' in the second clause 'and the ones in every city were making their way to him'?
  1. The καί explains [EGT, ICC, Lns, My, NIGTC, TH, WBC; CEV, NLT, REB, TEV]: a crowd was gathering, *that is,* those in every city were making their way to him. The conjunction explains that the crowd did not consist of only the local people and it also explains why the crowd was so large [Lns, NIGTC, WBC]. The second clause is an elaboration of the first to indicate that the gathering crowd consisted of people from every town [EGT, My, TH]. It is translated 'people kept coming to Jesus from one town after another; and when a great crowd gathered' [TEV], 'when a large crowd from several towns had gathered around Jesus' [CEV], 'people were now gathering in large numbers, and as they made their way to him' [REB].
  2. The καί indicates a coordinate relation [AB, BECNT, BNTC, NTC; GW, KJV, NASB, NCV, NET, NIV, NRSV]: a crowd was gathering *and* those in every city were making their way to him.

QUESTION—How many cities are meant by 'every city'?
Probably 'every city' refers to the towns in the vicinity that were referred to in 8:1 [AB, NAC, NIGTC, TH]. They came 'from ever so many places' [NTC].

8:5 The (one) sowing[a] went-out to-sow his seed. And while he sows some fell on/along[b] the path[c] and it-was-trampled-on,[d] and the birds[e] of-the sky ate it.

LEXICON—a. pres. act. participle of σπείρω (LN 43.6) (BAGD 1.a.α. p. 761): 'to sow' [BAGD, LN]. This verb means to scatter seed over tilled ground [LN]. The phrase 'the one sowing went out to sow' is translated 'the sower went out to sow his seed' [NTC, WBC; NASB], 'a sower went out to sow his seed' [Arn, BECNT; HCSB, KJV, NET, NRSV, REB], 'there went out the sower in order to sow his seed' [Lns], 'a farmer went out to sow his seed' [AB; NIV], 'a farmer went out to plant his seed' [NCV], 'a farmer went out to plant some seed' [NLT], 'a farmer went out to scatter seed in a field' [CEV], 'a farmer went to plant his seeds' [GW], 'once there was a man who went out to sow grain' [TEV]. The alliteration 'a sower sowed seed' would catch the attention of the listeners [MGC]. The definite article '*the* sower' is used generically of a class of such individuals [AB, ICC, Lns]. Being generic, the translation is often 'a sower' and he would have gone out from his house or settlement to his field [TH].

b. παρά (LN 83.25) (BAGD III.a.d. p. 611): 'on' [BAGD; NLT, NRSV], 'by' [BECNT, LN; KJV, NCV], 'by the side of' [NTC], 'at, alongside' [LN], 'beside' [LN; NASB], 'along' [AB, Arn, Lns, WBC; CEV, GW, HCSB, NET, NIV, REB, TEV].

c. ὁδός (LN 1.99) (BAGD 1.a. p. 554): 'path' [Lns, NTC, WBC; HCSB, NET, NIV, NRSV, TEV], 'footpath' [AB; NLT, REB], 'way' [BAGD, LN], 'road' [Arn, BAGD, BECNT, LN; CEV, GW, NASB, NCV], 'way side' [KJV].

d. aorist pass. indic. of καταπατέω (LN 19.52) (BAGD 1.a. p. 415): 'to be trampled on' [AB, BECNT, LN; HCSB, NET, NIV, NRSV, REB], 'to be trampled under foot' [BAGD, WBC], 'to be trampled' [GW], 'to be stepped on' [CEV, NLT, TEV], 'to be trodden under foot' [Arn, NTC], 'to be trodden down' [Lns; KJV]. The passive form is also translated actively: 'people walked on' [NCV]. The seeds would be crushed and would not be able to germinate [WBC].

e. πετεινόν (LN 4.41) (BAGD p. 654): 'bird' [BAGD]. The phrase πετεινὰ τοῦ οὐρανοῦ 'birds of the sky' is an idiom used to designate wild birds in contrast with domesticated birds such as chickens [Arn, LN]. In the idiom, the genitive 'of the sky' had lost its specific meaning and so the phrase can be simply translated 'birds' [TH]. The phrase 'birds of the sky' [AB; HCSB, NET] is also translated 'birds of the heaven' [Arn, BECNT, Lns, WBC], 'birds of the air' [NTC; NASB, NIV, NRSV], 'fowls of the air'

[KJV], 'wild birds' [LN], 'birds' [CEV, GW, NCV, NLT, REB, TEV]. See this phrase at 13:19.

QUESTION—What was involved in sowing seed?

The seeds of grain were scattered on the soil as the farmer walked through the field [TG]. The grain was wheat [NTC, Pnt, TG], or barley [NTC, TG]. The farmer had a bag of seed slung around his neck and as he walked he cast the seeds in strips across the field [Kst].

1. The soil was plowed after the seed was sown [AB, MGC, NAC, NIVS, Pnt, TNTC]. After clearing the field of old growth, the ground would look all the same and the farmer did not know what roots or rocks lay under the surface. Then a plow would scratch the seeds under the surface of the soil [Pnt].
2. The soil was plowed before the seed was sown to make it easier for the seeds to get started [WBC].

QUESTION—Why would some of the seeds be sown on a path?

The paths were made by people who walked through the fields after the last harvest, so the farmer scattered the seeds all over the surface [Su]. He could not avoid having some of the seed fall on and along the path he was walking on as he sowed the seed [NTC]. It was a narrow footpath through the field [TG]. The next verb 'trampled upon' shows that the seeds were on the road [TH], or on a path that divided the field from another field [Lns]. Since the seeds were trodden under foot, it must have been a regularly used path [TNTC]. The path would have been a hardened path used by travelers [BECNT]. The farmer felt his seed was very hardy and so was carefree in sowing his seed so that a little fell on an established footpath [WBC]. Perhaps the farmer was careless [BECNT].

QUESTION—Where did the seeds fall in relation to the path?

1. The seeds fell by the side of the path [BNTC, ICC, NICNT, NIGTC; KJV, NASB, NCV]: some seeds fell alongside the path. They fell along the path and not on it [NIGTC]. The seeds fell in the field by the side of the road, close enough to the road to be trampled on by those who walked by [ICC]. The seeds fell on the hardened edge of a path and people walked on these seeds because they were so close to the road [ICC, NIGTC].
2. The seeds fell upon the path [Arn, BECNT, Lns, NTC, Su, TG, TH, TNTC; NLT, NRSV]: some seeds fell upon the path. Some of the seeds would fall on the edge of the road and would be walked on by people or eaten by birds [BECNT]. As he sowed, he also walked on a path through the field and trampled some of the seed [NTC]. The context indicates that it was on the road, not alongside it [Arn].

8:6 **And another**[a] **(part of the seeds) fell upon the rock,**[b] **and having-come-up**[c] **it-dried-up because it has no moisture.**

LEXICON—a. ἕτερος neuter singular (LN 58.30): 'another' [LN]. This singular form is translated 'another part' [Lns], 'another lot' [WBC], 'other seed' [HCSB, NASB, NET, NLT], 'others' [GW], 'other seeds' [CEV], 'some'

[BECNT, NTC; KJV, NIV, NRSV, REB], 'some of it' [TEV], 'some seed' [NCV], 'some other seed' [AB, Arn]. This refers to the second portion of the seed [BECNT]. In 8:5, ὃ μὲν 'some' and ἕτερον 'another' here and also in 8:7 and 8 mean 'one portion' since the singular form occurring with each of the different fates of the seeds is neuter so that it means 'another part' and does not refer directly to the masculine noun 'seed' [EGT, Lns, NIGTC].

b. πέτρα (LN 2.21) (BAGD 1.a. p. 654): 'rock' [Arn, BAGD, BECNT, LN, Lns, NTC, WBC; HCSB, NCV, NET, NIV, NRSV, REB], 'a rock' [KJV], 'bedrock' [LN], 'rocky soil' [AB, BAGD; GW, NASB], 'rocky ground' [CEV, TEV], 'shallow soil with underlying rock' [NLT]. The article in τὴν πέτραν 'the rock' is generic [NTC, TH]. The following explanation shows that this refers to rock that was covered with a thin layer of soil [AB, Arn, BECNT, ICC, Lns, MGC, NAC, NIC, NIGTC, NTC, Pnt, Su, TG, TH, TNTC, WBC]. It was not rocky ground full of stones but ground with no depth of earth, possibly with rock appearing at intervals [ICC]. The rock was limestone [BECNT].

c. aorist pass. participle of φύω (LN 23.191) (BAGD p. 870): 'to come up' [Arn, BAGD, WBC; GW, NET, NIV, REB], 'to sprout' [AB; TEV], 'to grow' [BECNT], 'to start growing' [CEV], 'to begin to grow' [NCV, NLT], 'to spring up' [Lns, NTC; HCSB, KJV], 'to grow up' [BAGD, LN; NASB, NRSV]. This refers to the seed sprouting [Su, TH; TEV].

QUESTION—Why did the seeds have no moisture?

The sun would dry up the thin layer of soil [Gdt]. Matthew 13:6 and Mark 4:6 only speak of the plants withering because they had no roots, meaning they did not have a developed root system [BECNT, NIGTC]. At first the seeds would quickly sprout and grow, but eventually they would wither because the soil could not hold the moisture they needed [BECNT, MGC]. Since the plants could not develop a good root system because of the rock close to the surface, they would dry up and die [Gdt, NTC]. The plants did not have deep roots to draw water from the subsoil [NAC].

8:7 And another (part of the seeds) fell in middle[a] of-the-thorn-plants,[b] and the thorns having-grown-up-with[c] (it) choked[d] it.

LEXICON—a. μέσῳ (LN 83.9) (BAGD 2. p. 507): 'middle' [BAGD]. The phrase ἐν μέσῳ 'in middle' is translated 'in the middle of' [WBC], 'in the midst of' [Arn, Lns, NTC], 'amid' [AB], 'among' [BECNT, LN; all versions except CEV], 'where (thorn bushes grew up)' [CEV].

b. ἄκανθα (LN 3.17) (BAGD p. 29): 'thorn plant'. See this word at 6:44.

c. aorist pass. participle of συμφύομαι (LN 23.193) (BAGD p. 780): 'to grow up with' [BAGD, LN; GW, NASB, NCV, NIV, REB, TEV], 'to grow with' [BECNT; NRSV], 'to grow up together' [AB], 'to grow up' [CEV], 'to spring up with' [Lns; HCSB, KJV], 'to shoot up along with' [NTC], 'to shoot up' [NLT], 'to come up with' [Arn], 'to come up along with' [WBC]. The thorn plants and the grain grew up at the same time

[Crd, Gdt, WBC]. The thorn plants either came up at the same time as the grain seeds came up or shortly later while the grain was still small [TH]. The thorn roots came to life for a new season and overtook the grain in height [Kst].
  d. aorist act. indic. of ἀποπνίγω (LN **23.120**) (BAGD p. 97): 'to choke' [Arn, BAGD, BECNT, LN, WBC; all versions except NLT], 'to choke out' [NLT], 'to choke off' [AB, Lns, NTC], 'to cause to die' [**LN**]. 'To choke' is used figuratively of one type of plant causing the death of other plants by crowding them out or overshadowing them [LN]. The thorn plants outgrew the grain and choked it [NTC, TNTC].
QUESTION—Where did the thorns plants come from and how could the grain seeds fall in the midst of them?
  There are various ways to account for the presence of the thorn plants. The roots of thorn plants had been left in the ground when the field had been cleared and the roots developed new plants at the same time the grain was growing [BECNT, Kst, Lns, NIC, NIGTC, Pnt, TG]. Perhaps the seeds of the thorn plants of the previous year had had been left in the soil [Arn, NIC]. Weed seeds had fallen in the soil where the grain seeds were sown [NIGTC]. Or, the wording seems to say that the thorn plants were already above ground when the grain seeds were sown among them [EGT].

8:8a **And another (part of the seeds) fell in good^a soil and having-grown-up it-produced fruit^b a-hundredfold.**
LEXICON—a. ἀγαθός (LN **65.20**) (BAGD 1.a.b. p. 2): 'good' [AB, Arn, BAGD, BECNT, LN, Lns, NTC, WBC; all versions except NLT], 'fertile' [BAGD, **LN**; NLT]. Good soil is that soil which was not hardened by walking over it, not of shallow depth, not infested with weeds, but which was suitable for the growth of the grain [NTC, Su]. The soil is rich and fertile [TG].
  b. καρπός (LN 23.199) (BAGD 1.a. p. 404): 'fruit' [BAGD]. The phrase ἐποίησεν καρπὸν ἑκατονταπλασίονα 'produced fruit a hundredfold' [BECNT, WBC; similarly Lns, NTC; KJV] is also translated 'yielded fruit a hundredfold' [AB; similarly Arn; NRSV, REB], 'produced a hundred times (what was planted)' [**LN**], 'produced a hundred times as many seeds' [CEV], 'produced a hundred times as much grain' [NET], 'produced a hundred times as much as was planted' [GW], 'yielded a crop, a hundred times more than was sown' [NIV], 'produced a crop one hundred times as much as had been planted' [NLT; similarly HCSB], 'produced a crop: 100 times what was sown' [HCSB], 'made a hundred times more' [NCV], 'bore grain, one hundred grains each' [TEV].
QUESTION—Isn't a hundredfold too much to expect?
  It is exceptional to have a hundredfold yield [BECNT, Su]. Some think that a hundredfold is not unlikely [AB, Arn, ICC, NAC, TH].

DISCOURSE UNIT: 8:8b–10 [WBC]. The topic is knowing the secrets of the kingdom of God.

8:8b Saying these-things he was-calling-out/called-out,[a] The (one) having ears to-hear, let-him-hear.

LEXICON—a. imperf. act. indic. of φωνέω (LN 33.77) (BAGD 1.b. p. 870): 'to call out' [Arn, BAGD, LN; GW, HCSB, NASB, NCV, NET, NIV, NLT, NRSV, REB], 'to speak loudly' [BAGD, LN], 'to say with emphasis' [BAGD], 'to cry out' [BECNT, LN, Lns, WBC], 'to cry' [Lns; KJV], 'to say' [CEV]. The words 'saying...called out' are translated 'concluded' [TEV]. It means to raise one's voice [ICC, TH]. The call stresses the importance of this charge [BECNT], and its solemnity [ICC].

QUESTION—What is the significance of the imperfect tense ἐφώνει 'he was calling out'?
  1. The imperfect is iterative [AB, Arn, ICC, NTC]: he kept calling out. It means that he repeated the charge [ICC; NASB]. 'As he said these things, he would call out' [NASB].
  2. The imperfect tense is descriptive and refers to just one occasion [BECNT, Lns; all versions except NASB]: he called out. It means that Jesus proceeded to call out after a brief pause [Lns].

QUESTION—What is meant by 'the one who has ears to hear'?
In this clause, 'to hear' refers to the faculty of hearing with one's ears [TG, TH]. Some translate without a reference to hearing: 'if you have ears' [CEV], 'the one who has ears' [BECNT], 'let the person who has ears' [GW]. There is no doubt that people have ears [TG].

QUESTION—What is meant by Jesus' charge, 'let him hear'?
In the charge, 'let him hear' means to listen to what is said [TG, TH; GW, NCV, NRSV, TEV]: let him listen to my words, or, let him listen to this parable. It means to pay attention [TG; CEV], to pay close attention [NIBC], to listen and understand [NLT, Su], to discover the meaning [Lns], to take heed [AB, NAC], to listen and heed carefully [NET], to listen closely and take to heart [NTC]. It challenges the people to respond to the message [BECNT, Su], to the deeper significance of the parable [MGC, NIGTC]. This implies that there is a hidden meaning that is to be discovered and the present tense means to hear at the present time and whenever Jesus speaks [Lns].

DISCOURSE UNIT: 8:9–10 [AB, NIGTC; CEV, HCSB, NRSV, TEV]. The topic is that Jesus used parables [HCSB], the reason for speaking in parables [AB, NIGTC], the purpose of the parables [NRSV, TEV], why Jesus used stories [CEV].

8:9 And his disciples were-questioning him what this parable might-be. **8:10** And he-said, It-has-been-granted[a] to-you to-know[b] the secrets[c] of-the kingdom of-God, but to-the others (I speak) in parables so-that,[d] Seeing they-may- not -see,[e] and hearing they-may- not -understand.[f]

TEXT—In 8:9, before τίς 'what', some manuscripts add λέγοντες 'saying'. GNT does not mention this variant. Λέγοντες 'saying' is read by KJV.

LEXICON—a. perf. pass. indic. of δίδωμι (LN 13.142) (BAGD 1.b.β. p. 193): 'to be granted' [AB, BAGD, LN, NTC, WBC; NASB, REB], 'to be allowed' [LN], 'to be permitted' [NLT], 'to be given' [Arn, BECNT, Lns; HCSB, KJV, NIV, NRSV, TEV], 'to be given directly' [GW], 'to be given the opportunity' [NET], 'to be chosen' [NCV], not explicit [CEV]. The passive implies that God has granted this [AB, BECNT, Lns, MGC, NAC, NIC, NICNT, NIGTC, TG, TH; NET].
  b. aorist act. infin. of γινώσκω (LN 28.1, 32.16) (BAGD 1.a. p, 160): 'to know' [AB, BAGD, BECNT, LN (28.1), Lns, NTC, WBC; HCSB, KJV, NASB, NCV, NET, NRSV, REB], 'to understand' [Arn, LN (32.16); NLT], not explicit [CEV]. This verb is also translated as a noun: 'knowledge (about/of)' [GW, NIV, TEV].
  c. μυστήριον (LN 28.77) (BAGD p. 530): 'secret' [AB, BAGD, LN; CEV, HCSB, NCV, NET, NIV, NLT, NRSV, REB, TEV], 'mystery' [Arn, BAGD, BECNT, LN, Lns, NTC, WBC; GW, KJV, NASB].
  d. ἵνα (LN 90.49, 89.59) (BAGD II.2. p 378): 'so that' [AB, LN (89.59, 90.49), WBC; HCSB, NASB, NCV, NET, NIV, NRSV, REB, TEV], 'that' [Arn, BECNT, NTC; KJV], 'so as a result' [LN (89.59)], 'in order to' [LN (89.49)], 'in order that' [Lns], 'to' [NLT], not explicit [CEV, GW].
  e. pres. act. subj. of βλέπω (LN 32.11) (BAGD 1.d. p. 143): 'to see' [AB, Arn, BAGD, BECNT, LN, Lns, NTC, WBC; all versions except NRSV], 'to really see' [NLT], 'to look' [HCSB], 'to perceive' [NRSV], 'to understand' [LN]. In contrast to the physical act of 'seeing', it means understanding perception [TH].
  f. pres. act. subj. of συνίημι (LN 32.5) (BAGD p. 790): 'to understand' [AB, Arn, BAGD, BECNT, LN, Lns, NTC, WBC; all versions], 'to comprehend, to have insight into' [BAGD, LN]. This is a different verb than 'see' but both mean the same thing [TH].
QUESTION—Who are the disciples who questioned Jesus and when did they question him?
  This refers to the twelve apostles [Su], to the twelve apostles and the women mentioned in 8:2–3 [AB], or to a larger group of disciples than just the twelve [ICC, Lns, TH]. They were the disciples who happened to be with him at the time [NTC]. Since Jesus was speaking to 'you' in contrast to 'the others' who were not disciples, it appears that he was addressing disciples in general and not only the twelve [AB, ICC].
  1. This happened later when the disciples were alone with Jesus [Lns, MGC, NAC, NIC, NIGTC, Su]. The parallel passage in Mark 4:10 has 'when he was by himself' and although this is missing in Luke, it is assumed here [NIGTC].
  2. This happened in the hearing of the crowd that had gathered and listened to the parable [AB, WBC].

338   LUKE 8:9–10

QUESTION—What is meant by the word μυστήρια 'secrets'?

'Secret' or 'mystery' is used in Scripture to describe what can only be known when it is revealed by God or Jesus [Arn, Gdt, NIVS, TH, TNTC]. It pertains to God's secret plan [BECNT, MGC, NIGTC], to the plan of salvation [Gdt, NIGTC], and here to God's plan for the coming, establishment, and character of his kingdom [BNTC]. A mystery is a truth that would have remained unknown had not God revealed it [NTC]. The plural form 'secrets' refers to Jesus' teaching about the various aspects about the kingdom [NAC, NIGTC]. They did not come to understand all that was involved about the kingdom of God when Jesus explained the parable since after Jesus arose from the dead he further explained the kingdom (Acts 1:3) [AB]. This 'granting to know the secrets' takes place by revelation through the teaching of the gospel of the kingdom [Lns].

QUESTION—What relationship is indicated by ἵνα 'so that'?

1. It expresses the result of teaching in parables [BNTC, NAC, Su]: I speak in parables *with the result that....* When parables were used, the consequence was that others did not understand the truths that they were meant to communicate [BNTC]. Jesus used parables for the purpose of making the teaching easier to understand, but here this is about the reaction of the many people who rejected it [Su]. When the conjunction indicates the result of Jesus' preaching in parables, the failure to respond in obedience results in the fulfillment of Scripture [NAC].

2. It expresses the purpose for teaching in parables [AB, BECNT, Gdt, Hlt, ICC, Lns, MGC, NIBC, NIC, NTC, TH, TNTC, WBC; NLT]: I speak in parables *in order that....*

   2.1 The purpose is that those people will not understand [AB, BECNT, ICC, Lns, MGC, NIBC, NIC, TNTC]: so that they may not understand what they hear. Jesus did as God did when he sent prophets to harden the hearts of Israel (Isaiah 6:9–10) [AB]. Jesus used parables so that the deepest truths would not be understood by those unbelievers who brought this judgment on themselves because of their continued unwillingness to receive the truth [NIC]. Those unrepentant Pharisees refused to see and hear, so now as a punishment they are addressed in parables [Gdt, NTC, TNTC]. God hardens those who have hardened themselves [NIBC, NTC]. Their minds reject instruction and therefore they are taught in a way which deprives them of instruction [ICC]. Yet what they hear without understanding will become meaningful when their minds become fitted for it [ICC, NIC]. The parables give the disciples insight into the kingdom, but the parables are a story that prevents understanding by those who reject God's offer of revelation. Yet in spite of this statement of purpose, the opportunity for repentance was still offered [BECNT].

   2.2 The purpose is to fulfill the Scriptures that are quoted [WBC; NLT]: so that the situation depicted in Isaiah 9–10 will be fulfilled. Scripture anticipates that people do have a hardened attitude and this takes place in the plans and purposes of God [WBC].

DISCOURSE UNIT: 8:11–15 [AB, NIGTC, WBC]. The topic is the explanation of the parable of the sower [AB, NIGTC, WBC; NRSV], Jesus explains the parable of the sower [TEV], Jesus explains the story about a farmer [CEV].

8:11 And this is^a the parable. The seed is^b the word of-God.

LEXICON—a. pres. act. indic. of εἰμί (LN 13.4): 'to be' [LN]. The phrase 'this is the parable' [Arn, Lns, WBC] is also translated 'the parable is this' [KJV, NASB, NRSV], 'this is what the story means' [CEV, NCV], 'this is what the story illustrates' [GW], 'this is what the parable means' [REB, TEV], 'the parable means this' [BECNT; NET], 'this is the meaning of the parable' [AB, NTC; HCSB, NIV], 'this is the meaning of the story' [NLT]. The statement identifies the interpretation of the parable with the parable itself [AB]. The opening 'is' can be paraphrased 'it means' and the word 'this' is predicative so that the clause is 'the parable means this' [NIGTC, TH].

    b. pres. act. indic. of εἰμί (LN 58.68) (BAGD II.3. p. 224): 'to be' [AB, Arn, BECNT, Lns, NTC, WBC; all versions], 'to represent, to correspond to, to stand for, to be a figure of' [LN], 'to be a representation of, to be the equivalent of, to mean' [BAGD]. Here it means 'to stand for' [TH].

QUESTION—What is meant by the genitive construction ὁ λόγος τοῦ θεοῦ 'the word of God'?

It means the word that comes from God [BECNT, ICC, Lns, NAC, NTC, Rb, TG, TH, TNTC; CEV, GW, NCV, NIV, NLT]. The message is from God by means of Jesus' teaching [Gdt, NTC, TG, TH]. It is God's message [CEV, NCV, NLT], God's word [GW], the message God proclaims to the world [Arn]. It is the good news from God about the kingdom of God [BECNT, NTC, Su].

8:12 And the^a (ones) on/along^b the path are the (ones who) have-heard, then comes the devil^c and takes-away^d the word from their heart in-order-that-not^e having-believed they-be-saved.

TEXT—Instead of the aorist tense ἀκούσαντες 'having heard', some manuscripts read the present tense ἀκούοντες 'hearing', although GNT does not mention this variant. Ἀκούοντες 'hearing' is read by KJV.

LEXICON—a. ὁ (LN 92.11): 'the' [LN]. The pronominal use of the article is translated 'the ones' [BECNT; NRSV], 'those' [AB, Arn, Lns, WBC; KJV, NASB, NET, NIV], 'they' [Lns], 'the seeds' [CEV, HCSB], 'the seed' [REB], 'the seeds that fell' [TEV], 'the seed that fell' [NCV, NLT], '(some people are like) seeds' [GW].

    b. παρά (LN 83.25) (BAGD III.a.d. p. 611): 'on, along'. See this word at 8:5 for the interpretation of this preposition.

    c. διάβολος (LN 12.34) (BAGD 2. p. 182): 'devil'. See this word at 4:2.

d. pres. act. indic. of αἴρω (LN 15.203): 'to take away' [LN, Lns, WBC; all versions except CEV, NLT, REB], 'to take' [Arn, BECNT], 'to carry away, to remove' [LN], 'to carry off' [REB], 'to snatch' [AB; CEV], 'to snatch away' [Lns], 'to steal away' [NLT].
   e. The phrase ἵνα μή 'in order that not' is translated 'so that…(they will/may not believe)' [WBC; CEV, GW, HCSB, NASB, NET, NIV, NRSV], 'that (they may not believe)' [Arn, NTC], 'in order that (they might not believe)' [BECNT], 'in order to (keep them from believing)' [TEV], 'in order that (they may not be saved)' [Lns], 'so (they cannot believe)' [NCV], 'lest' [KJV], 'for fear that (they might/should believe)' [AB; REB], 'and prevents' [NLT].

QUESTION—Does 'the ones on (or along) the road' (where οἱ 'the ones' is masculine plural) refer to the seeds that fell there (8:5) or to the people who heard the word? This question also applies to the following illustration of 'the ones (plural) upon the rock', 'the one (singular) in the thorns', and 'the one (singular) in the good soil'.

1. The 'ones' on the road refer to seeds, and the seeds represent a class of people [Arn, BECNT, NIGTC, NTC, TNTC, WBC; all versions]: the seeds that fell on the road are the people who heard. This refers to the seeds and the masculine form refers to individual seeds or the persons represented by the seeds. A strict correspondence would have the various soils represent the different groups of people, but there is a looseness of correspondence so that the people are identified with the plants which spring from the ground as a result of sowing of the seed [NIGTC]. The people are represented by the seed that was sown [NTC].
2. The 'ones' on the road refers to the people who heard [AB, Hlt, ICC, Lns, TH, WBC]: the people on the road are those who heard. There is an abrupt transition since 'those' does not pick up the 'seeds' in 8:12 [AB]. Instead of 'seed by the wayside', this is to be taken as 'those who received seed by the wayside' [ICC]. These are the people on the road who are compared to what became of the seed that fell on the road. Another approach is 'the people who are illustrated by the seed that fell on the path' [TH]. In 8:11, the seed (singular) is the Word of God, but here 'the ones' is plural, so the comparison is between the terrain along the path and the persons in this class of people [Hlt]. The seed is the word of God, so those along the road are those who have heard the word of God and the other locations that follow will represent other groups of people who have heard [WBC]. The people fare like the good seed that fell along the path [Lns].

QUESTION—How does the devil take away the word from their hearts?
   There is no need to think that the many birds in 8:5 means that there are many devils, rather the birds refer to the different ways that Satan, the devil, takes the word from minds and hearts [Lns]. Satan prevents them from accepting the message [WBC]. They have to believe the word to be saved,

not merely hear it [NIGTC]. The part Satan plays in this does not excuse hearers who treat God's word so lightly that they do nothing with it [NTC].

8:13 And the (ones) upon the rock (are) the (ones who) when they-hear, receive[a] the word with joy,[b] and these do- not -have a-root,[c] who for a-while believe and in a-time of-testing[d] they-fall-away.[e]

LEXICON—a. pres. mid./pass. (deponent = act.) indic. of δέχομαι (LN 31.51) (BAGD 3.b. p. 177): 'to receive' [Arn, BECNT, LN, Lns, NTC, WBC; KJV, NASB, NET, NIV, NRSV, REB, TEV], 'to accept' [AB, BAGD, LN; CEV, NCV], 'to approve' [BAGD], 'to welcome' [GW, HCSB], 'to believe' [LN], not explicit [NLT].

b. χαρά (LN 25.123) (BAGD 1. p. 875): 'joy' [AB, Arn, BAGD, BECNT, LN, Lns, NTC, WBC; all versions except CEV, NCV, TEV], 'gladness' [LN]. This noun is also translated as an adverb: 'gladly (hear)' [CEV], '(accept it) gladly' [NCV], '(receive it) gladly' [TEV].

c. ῥίζα (LN 3.47) (BAGD 1.b. p. 736): 'root' [AB, Arn, BAGD, BECNT, LN, Lns, NTC, WBC; GW, HCSB, KJV, NET, NIV, NRSV, REB], 'firm root' [BAGD; NASB], 'deep roots' [CEV]. The phrase 'these do not have a root' is translated 'their roots don't go very deep' [NLT], 'it does not sink deep into them' [TEV], 'they don't allow the teaching to go deep into their lives' [NCV].

d. πειρασμός (LN 27.46) (BAGD 2.b. p. 641): 'testing' [LN; HCSB, NET, NIV, NRSV, REB, TEV], 'trouble' [NCV], 'trial' [AB, BECNT, NTC, WBC], 'temptation' [Arn, BAGD, Lns; KJV, NASB]. The phrase 'in a time of testing' is translated 'when their faith is tested' [GW, NET], 'as soon as life gets hard' [CEV], 'when the hot winds of testing blow' [NLT].

e. pres. mid. indic. of ἀφίσταμαι (L 34.26) (BAGD 2.a. p. 126): 'to fall away' [AB, Arn, BAGD, BECNT, LN, NTC; KJV, NASB, NET, NIV, NRSV, TEV], 'to stand away' [Lns], 'to give up' [CEV, NCV, REB], 'to withdraw' [WBC], 'to depart' [HCSB], 'to abandon (their faith)' [GW], 'to wilt' [NLT].

QUESTION—How could a plant not have a root?

This means that though they have a root, it is not firm [BAGD; NASB], or deep [CEV, TEV]. In this verse, 'root' should be taken metaphorically and not literally applied to seeds [NIGTC]. Applied to the people, it means that they have no depth of understanding or commitment [TG], no deep-seated convictions [NTC]. 'They don't allow the teaching to go deep into their lives' [NCV]. The meaning of having no root is described in the following clause [Lns].

QUESTION—What is involved in receiving the word?

Receiving the word includes mental consent and approval [TH]. It is responding to the preaching of the gospel with faith [WBC]. Their joy is the result the first enthusiasm of conversion [AB, TH]. Their reception is only superficial [BECNT, NIC], without deep-seated convictions [NTC].

QUESTION—How do these people believe?
They are only temporary believers [Lns], who appear to be sincere in making a real start in their faith [Rb]. They appeared to believe, but it turned out that their faith wasn't real [Su]. They were temporarily attracted to the message without really being converted [NIC]. This is not saving faith [NAC]. They never really belonged to Christ [NTC].

QUESTION—How would they be tested?
They would be tested in regard to their commitment to the word [Lns], in regard to their faith [TG, TH; NET]. In Matthew and Mark this is described as affliction or persecution, so this refers to persecution and external suffering [ICC]. It is the practical struggle of life [NIC]. This means a trial against one's faith, such as being persecuted or being taught something that draws one away from faith [BECNT]. In addition to outward trial it could include an inward lack of feeling and having doubts [EGT].

QUESTION—What is meant by the people falling away?
They lose interest, stop attending church, and drop out of sight [Rb]. They lose their faith in the word, they quit believing [TG], they abandon their faith [GW]. They are apostate [Hlt].

8:14 And the (one) having-fallen among the thorn-plants, these are the (ones who) have-heard, and (while) going-on-their-way[a] they-are-choked[b] by (the) anxieties[c] and riches[d] and pleasures[e] of-life and they do- not -bear-fruit-to-maturity.[f]

LEXICON—a. pres. mid./pass. (deponent = act.) participle of πορεύομαι (LN 41.11) (BAGD 2.d. p. 693): 'to go on their way' [HCSB, NASB, NET, NIV, NRSV], 'to go forth' [KJV], 'to pass by' [BAGD], 'to live (in a customary manner)' [LN], 'to go on' [Lns], 'to go' [BECNT], 'on the way' [WBC], 'in their pursuit of life' [AB], 'to pursue life's journey' [Arn], 'to be progressively (choked)' [NTC], '(as) life goes on' [GW], not explicit [CEV, NCV, NLT, REB, TEV]. This refers to going one's way in the course of time [TH]. In the present tense this verb indicates that the choking is a gradual process [BECNT, ICC, NTC, TH]. It refers to the gradual development of a plant that is choked on its way to bearing fruit [WBC]. It describes an active life, going and coming in the pursuit of business [Gdt]. Perhaps it refers to advancing in age [AB]. It may mean 'eventually', 'in the course of time', or 'as time goes by' [TG].

b. pres. pass. indic. of συμπνίγω (LN 23.120) (BAGD 1. p. 779): 'to be choked' [Arn, BAGD, BECNT, LN, Lns, WBC; HCSB, KJV, NASB, NET, NIV, NRSV, REB], 'to be choked off' [AB], 'to be crowded out' [NLT], not explicit [CEV]. The passive form is also translated actively: 'to choke' [GW, TEV], 'to keep from growing' [NCV]. It means to press around someone and is equivalent to ἀποπνίγω 'to choke' in 8:7 [TH].

c. μέριμνα (LN 25.224) (BAGD p. 504): 'anxiety' [AB, BAGD, LN], 'worry' [Arn, BAGD, BECNT, LN, WBC; GW, HCSB, NASB, NCV, NET, NIV, TEV], 'cares' [Lns; KJV, NLT, NRSV, REB]. This noun is

also translated as a verb: 'to be eager for (riches and pleasures)' [CEV]. This would apply to those who were poor [Gdt], but this interprets the scope too narrowly since it means excessive concern over one's welfare [BECNT]. See this word at 21:34.
  d. πλοῦτος (LN 57.30) (BAGD 1. p. 674): 'riches' [AB, Arn, BAGD, BECNT, LN, WBC; all versions except REB], 'wealth' [BAGD, LN, Lns; REB]. This would apply to those who were making their fortunes [Gdt]. It is a craving for wealth or a yearning to cling to it [NTC]. The riches themselves are a danger to faith [NIGTC]. The riches and pleasures distract one's mind from spiritual matters [TG]. It is excessive concern over one's possessions [BECNT].
  e. ἡδονή (LN 25.111) (BAGD 1. p. 344): 'pleasure' [AB, Arn, BAGD, BECNT, LN, Lns, WBC; all versions], 'enjoyment' [BAGD]. This would apply to those who were already rich [Gdt]. The pleasures may be wrong in themselves or wrong when someone overindulges in them [NTC]. The pleasures might includes those listed in 7:25, 12:19, and 16:19 [BECNT, WBC]. It is excessive concern over one's comfort [BECNT].
  f. pres. act. indic. of φορέω (LN **23.203**) (BAGD p. 810): 'to bear fruit to maturity' [BAGD], 'to produce ripe fruit, to produce mature fruit' [**LN**]. The phrase 'they do not bear fruit to maturity' is translated 'they do not bring fruit to maturity' [WBC], 'they do not produce fruit to maturity' [BECNT], 'they produce no mature fruit' [HCSB], 'they bring no fruit to maturity' [NASB], 'they bring nothing to maturity' [AB], 'their fruit does not mature' [NET, NRSV], 'their fruit never ripens' [TEV], 'they never produce anything' [CEV], 'they do not produce' [Arn], 'they don't produce anything good' [GW], 'they do not mature' [NIV], 'they never grow into maturity' [NLT], 'they bring nothing to maturity' [Lns; REB], 'they bring no fruit to perfection' [KJV], 'keep them from producing good fruit' [NCV].

QUESTION—What is the significance of beginning with 'and the one' in which το 'the one' is neuter singular?

The style has changed and the neuter form refers to a portion of the seeds [NIGTC], 'that which fell among the thorns' [ICC]. With the neuter, the figure is completely retained (fallen, choked, bring nothing to maturity). However, the neuter 'the one' refers to the persons into which the Word fell, hence it is followed by οὗτοι 'these' (masculine, plural) [Lns]. The shift is remarkable, but still does not influence the meaning of the clause since 'the one' is taken up by the masculine 'these' [TH]. The seed (singular) represents a category of people [Hlt]. It is the hearers who are choked [BECNT]. While the thorns choke the seeds in 8:7, here the anxieties and riches and pleasures choke the hearers [ICC, TH]. It is translated 'what fell among the thorn bushes represents those who listened' [AB], 'the part fallen into the thorns, these are they who heard' [Lns].

344   LUKE 8:14

QUESTION—Does the genitive phrase τοῦ βίου 'of life' go only with 'pleasures' or with all three of the preceding nouns?
1. It goes with all three of the nouns [AB, Alf, BECNT, My, NAC, NIGTC, TH, WBC; GW, NCV, NET, NIV, NLT, NRSV, TEV]: by *the* anxieties, riches, and pleasures of life. They are choked by life's worries, riches, and pleasures [NIV].
2. It goes only with 'pleasures' [REB]: with anxieties, with riches, and with *the* pleasures of life.

QUESTION—What is meant by 'they do not bear fruit to maturity'?
The faith that they have does not result in deeds [TG]. After a start in faith, there is no perseverance [NAC]. Their development is arrested and they do not reach their goal [WBC]. They do not produce good results, they do not develop fully [TH].

8:15 And the (one) in the good^a soil, these are (those) who having-heard with a-good^b and good^c heart retain^d the word and bear-fruit^e with/by endurance.^f

LEXICON—a. καλός (LN 65.22) (BAGD 2. p. 2): 'good' [AB, Arn, BAGD, BECNT, LN, NTC, WBC; all versions], 'excellent' [Lns], 'useful' [BAGD]. This refers to the quality of the soil [BAGD]. In 8:8, this soil was described as ἀγαθός 'good' and both adjectives are used in a similar sense [Lns].

b. καλός (LN 88.4) (BAGD 2.b. p. 400): 'good' [Arn, BAGD, LN; CEV, GW, NCV, NLT, REB, TEV], 'praiseworthy' [BAGD, LN], 'honest' [BECNT, NTC; HCSB, KJV, NASB, NET, NLT, NRSV], 'noble' [AB; NIV], 'excellent' [Lns], 'fine' [WBC]. This refers to the moral quality of the people [BAGD, LN]. This and the following adjective refer to an ethically good person [BECNT].

c. ἀγαθός (LN 66.1) (BAGD 1.b.β. p. 3): 'good' [BAGD, BECNT, LN, Lns, NTC, WBC; HCSB, KJV, NASB, NET, NIV, NLT, NRSV], 'honest' [CEV, GW, NCV, REB], 'obedient' [TEV], 'faithful' [Arn], 'generous' [AB].

d. pres. act. indic. of κατέχω (LN 2.49) (BAGD 1.b.β. p. 423): 'to retain' [BAGD; NIV, TEV], 'to hold something fast' [BAGD, BECNT, Lns; NASB, NRSV, REB], 'to hold onto' [AB; HCSB], 'to hold firmly onto' [WBC], 'to cling to' [Arn, NTC; NET, NLT], 'to keep' [CEV, GW, KJV], 'to continue to believe and practice' [LN], 'to obey' [NCV]. It means to keep and obey the word [TH]. Here the verb refers to clinging to the word and in effect it describes faith [BECNT].

e. pres. act. indic. of καρποφορέω (LN **23.199**) (BAGD 2. p. 405): 'to bear fruit' [Arn, BAGD, BECNT, LN, WBC; HCSB, NASB, NET, NRSV, TEV], 'to bring forth fruit' [KJV], 'to bring fruit' [Lns], 'to produce good fruit' [NCV], 'to produce a harvest' [CEV], 'to produce a huge harvest' [NLT], 'to produce a crop' [NTC; NIV], 'to produce what is good' [GW], 'to produce' [**LN**], 'to yield a harvest' [REB], 'to yield a crop' [AB], 'to

yield' [LN]. This means to produce what is planted [LN]. This is figurative for practical conduct as the fruit of the inner life [BAGD].
f. ὑπομονή (LN 25.174) (BAGD 1. p. 846): 'endurance' [BAGD, LN], 'steadfast endurance' [NET], 'perseverance' [WBC; NASB, REB], 'persistence' [AB], 'patient endurance' [NRSV], 'patience' [Arn, BAGD, BECNT, Lns; KJV]. This noun is also translated as a verb: 'to endure' [HCSB], 'to last' [CEV], 'to persevere' [NTC; NIV], 'to persist' [TEV]; and as an adverb: 'patiently' [NCV], 'steadily' [NLT]. The phrase 'with endurance' is translated 'despite what life may bring' [GW].

QUESTION—What are the differences between the descriptions καλῇ καὶ ἀγαθῇ 'good and good'?

Probably Luke used the two adjectives here because he had used both in describing the soil [NIGTC]. Both adjectives have been used to describe the soil as being good, ἀγαθός in 8:8 and καλός in the first part of this verse, and now both adjectives are combined to describe the heart [ICC, Lns]. The first adjective means excellent for its purpose and the second means good in the sense of being beneficial [Lns]. This is a pair of nearly synonymous adjectives and mean truly good, really good, and very good [TH].

QUESTION—What is being described by 'with a good and good heart'?
1. This describes the way they heard the word [BNTC, NTC, TH, TNTC, WBC; NASB, NCV, REB]: the ones who heard with a really good heart. The preposition ἐν 'with' indicates that such a heart is the means for considering what is heard [TH].
2. This describes the way they retained the word [AB, ICC, Lns, My, Rb; CEV, GW, KJV, NET, NRSV, TEV]: with a really good heart they retained the word. Like all the others, they heard the word, but the difference is that they retained the word with a good heart [Lns].
3. This describes the people [BECNT; NIV, NLT]: these are the ones with a really good heart.

QUESTION—What is the fruit they bear?

The fruit is ethical in character [NIGTC]. The fruit is faith and all that results from faith in the way of a godly life [Lns]. An example is the fruit of the Spirit in Galatians 5:22–23, with the result that they have inner joy and win souls, all to God's glory [NTC]. This involves living a life of heeding God's word [NAC].

QUESTION—What is the significance of adding the phrase ἐν ὑπομονῇ 'with/by endurance'?

This is the opposite of 'fall away' in 8:13 [BECNT, TG]. It is patiently resting in God's promises with hope so as to endure the obstacles to living faithfully [BECNT]. When the time of trial comes (8:13) these people endure [AB, BNTC]. The best fruit requires patience over the time it takes to mature [Lns].
1. Some translate the preposition ἐν as an attendant circumstance [Arn, BECNT, Lns, TH; KJV, NASB, NCV, NET, NLT, NRSV]: they bear fruit *with* endurance. This refers to the attitude of those who bear fruit [TH].

346 LUKE 8:15

This is another response to hearing the word and it is the opposite of falling away [BECNT]. This is quiet endurance under trials and this is the way spiritual fruit develops [Lns].

2. Some translate the preposition ἐν to indicate the means of bearing fruit [AB, NTC, WBC; NIV, REB, TEV]: they bear fruit *by* their endurance. They persist until they bear fruit [TEV].

QUESTION—What is the point of the parable?

The parable is allegorical and points out the importance of hearing and receiving God's word [NIGTC]. It is a parable about various responses to the God's word and it is designed to force a person to analyze how he is responding to God's message [BECNT, NAC, NTC]. The parable describes the final fate of the Word in the hearts of people: when life is finished, some show a harvest and the rest do not. The purpose of the parable is to cause us to examine ourselves as to how we are treating the word now so that we will repent and open our heart to the gospel [Lns, NTC]. The parable explains that God's word will ultimately prevail and have a great spiritual harvest [MGC, NIBC].

DISCOURSE UNIT: 8:16–21 [NASB]. The topic is the parable of the lamp.

DISCOURSE UNIT: 8:16–18 [AB, BECNT, NAC, NIGTC, Su, TNTC, WBC; CEV, HCSB, NCV, NET, NIV, NLT, NRSV, TEV]. The topic is light [CEV], the parable of the lamp [AB, NAC, NIGTC], the illustration of the lamp [NLT], a lamp on a stand [NIV], a lamp under a bowl [TEV], a lamp under a jar [NRSV], the lamp and the cover [TNTC], using your light [HCSB], a call to respond to light [BECNT], holding on to the light of revelation [NET], taking care how you hear [WBC], responsibilities in hearing and serving [Su], using what you have [NCV].

8:16 And no-one having-lit a-lamp[a] covers it with-a-bowl[b] or places (it) under a-bed,[c] but places (it) on a-lampstand,[d] in-order-that the (ones who) enter may-see the light.[e]

LEXICON—a. λύχνος (LN 6.104) (BAGD 1. p. 483): 'lamp' [AB, Arn, BAGD, BECNT, LN, Lns, NTC, WBC; all versions except KJV], 'candle' [KJV]. Since it is to be set on a stand, it refers to an oil-burning lamp and not a candlestick [BECNT]. This is a small vessel of oil which is used to produce light by burning a wick saturated with its oil [Arn, LN]. It was often a terra-cotta bowl with a handle on one side and on the other side was a nozzle-shaped extension holding a wick [NTC]. It was a shallow clay bowl of olive oil with a wick lying in it [TG, TH]. A piece of flax or cloth served as a wick [Su]. See this word at 11:33; 12:35.

b. σκεῦος (LN **6.118**) (BAGD 1.b. p. 754): 'bowl' [**LN**; CEV, GW, NCV, TEV], 'vessel' [Arn, BAGD, BECNT, LN, Lns, NTC, WBC; KJV], 'container' [LN; NASB], 'jar' [NET, NIV, NRSV], 'pot' [AB], 'basin' [REB], 'basket' [HCSB]. The phrase 'covers it with a bowl' is translated 'cover it up' [NLT]. This is a generic term for all kinds of bowls, jars, and

vases [AB, LN, TH, WBC]. The word can be used for both dry and liquid measures [Su]. It was a bowl for holding grain [TG].
  c. κλίνη (LN 6.106) (BAGD p. 436): 'bed' [AB, Arn, BAGD, BECNT, LN, Lns, NTC, WBC; all versions], 'couch, cot' [BAGD, LN]. This is a generic term for furniture that is used for reclining or lying on [LN]. This could be a bed or couch used for dining [Arn, Lns]. Beds usually were mattresses on the ground, but benches for eating at meals were raised from the floor [Gdt]. The bed would be a rolled-up mattress [NTC]. In order to place a lamp underneath a bed, it had to be a bed on four legs [TH].
  d. λυχνία (LN 6.105) (BAGD p. 483): 'lampstand' [Arn, BAGD, BECNT, LN, Lns, NTC, WBC; all versions except KJV, NIV, NLT], 'stand' [AB; NIV], 'candlestick' [KJV]. The phrase 'places it on a lampstand' is translated 'lamps are mounted in the open' [NLT]. This is a stand upon which lamps were placed, it is not a candlestick [BAGD]. It might be a stand upon which one or more lamps might be placed or hung [ICC]. It was made of metal [Lns]. It could be a shelf from a house post or wall [NTC], or a niche in the wall [TG]. See this word at 11:33.
  e. φῶς (LN 14.36) (BAGD 1.a. p. 871): 'light' [AB, Arn, BAGD, BECNT, LN, Lns, NTC, WBC; all versions except NLT]. The phrase 'in order that the ones entering may see the light' is translated 'where it can be seen by those entering the house' [NLT]. The light is what comes from the lamp [TH]. See this word at 11:33.

QUESTION—Why wouldn't someone cover a lamp with a bowl?
Most take this example and the following one of putting a lamp under a bed to conceal its light as being bizarre [WBC], ridiculous [Lns], foolish [BECNT, NIGTC], and contradictory [BECNT]. Instead of concealing the light, a few think that the purpose of covering a lamp with a bowl would be to extinguish it [AB]. However, while putting a pot over a lamp would extinguish the light, putting a lamp under a bed would only hide its light [MGC].

QUESTION—What is the point of the illustration?
This speaks about placing the lamp on a stand so people could see the light rather than so the lamp could illumine the house [Arn, WBC]. The lamp represents one who has heard God's word and responded. Having the lamp placed on the lampstand represents the person living out the word so that it is visible to others. God's purpose is that those who need to find their way may see his word coming from those already inside the kingdom [AB, WBC]. Believers must let their light shine by letting God's word control their lives so that the mystery given to them might be disclosed and not concealed [NTC]. Jesus' teaching is light and it is given in public to illuminate the way to God, and each person chooses how to respond to it [BECNT]. Jesus had kindled a light in the disciples by explaining the parable and instead of hiding it they must spread their knowledge to others [EGT, Gdt, ICC, MGC, NIC, TNTC]. As lamps are intended to give forth their light, so the disciples

are intended to spread the word [Lns]. They would proclaim to the 'others' in 8:10 what they learned [AB, NAC, NIC] after the resurrection [NAC]. How someone has heard God's word will eventually manifest itself in what they do about it [NICNT].

8:17 Because nothing is hidden that will- not -become evident[a] nor (is anything) secret[b] that will- not -be-known and come to light.[c]

LEXICON—a. φανερός (LN 28. 58) (BAGD 1. p. 852): 'evident' [BAGD, LN; NASB], 'clear' [NCV], 'plain' [NLT], 'open' [TEV], 'clearly known' [LN], 'public' [AB], 'found' [CEV], 'revealed' [GW, HCSB, NET], 'disclosed' [NTC; NIV, NRSV, REB], 'manifest' [Arn, BECNT, Lns; KJV], 'open to view' [WBC].

b. ἀπόκρυφος (LN 28.70) (BAGD p. 93): 'secret' [BECNT, LN, WBC; CEV, GW, NASB, NRSV], 'secret thing' [NCV], 'a thing secret' [Lns], 'hidden' [AB, BAGD; HCSB], 'concealed' [Arn, NTC; NET, NIV, REB], 'covered up' [TEV], 'hid' [KJV].

c. φανερός (LN 28.58) (BAGD 2. p. 852): 'light' [BAGD], 'evident' [LN]. The phrase 'to come to light' [BECNT, Lns; GW, HCSB, NASB, NRSV] is also translated 'to be brought to light' [AB; NET, NLT, TEV], 'to be brought in the open' [Arn; REB], 'to come into open view' [WBC], 'to be brought out into the open' [NIV], 'to be well known' [CEV], 'to come abroad' [KJV], not explicit [NCV].

QUESTION—What relationship is indicated by γάρ 'because'?
1. It indicates the grounds for the intended application of the preceding illustration [AB, MGC]. It is a principle that confirms the fact that the light in their hearts is to be placed on a lampstand and not to be hidden away [AB, Lns, NIGTC].
2. It explains the preceding illustration [BECNT, Lns, NIGTC]. It explains the real purpose of a lighted lamp [Lns]. The light will expose what has been hidden and this is a warning that God's standard will be one day revealed and executed [BECNT]. This indicates the significance of the parable, but it does not exactly fit the parable unless the focus is on an unkindled lamp that does not give light until it is lit since the two parallel parts of this verse state that whatever is hidden will be revealed and made known [NIGTC].
3. There is no obvious relationship with the preceding verse except both pertain to a light shining and revealing something [TG].

QUESTION—What is hidden and secret?
1. This refers to the message about the kingdom of God [AB, Lns, MGC, NAC, NIC, NIGTC, TG, TH, WBC]. This is a general saying that applies here to the kingdom of God [TH]. This principle applies to the secrets of the gospel [Lns]. Circumstances have caused Jesus to teach in secret, but before long the disciples will make known what was hidden [NIC]. Even the secrets of the kingdom must be divulged [AB]. The disciples must

proclaim the secrets of the kingdom of God which are hidden to others and then the secret will become known [NAC].
2 This refers to the lives of individuals [BECNT, NTC, Su, TNTC]. On judgment day, nothing can be concealed [TNTC]. A person may think that he can cover up evil thoughts, plans, words, and actions, but God will expose all of this [NTC]. One's true nature will be manifested [Su]. It relates to the various responses that the soils give and makes clear that God will evaluate how each person responds to his word [NIGTC].

8:18 **Therefore pay-attention-to**[a] **how you-listen.**[b] **Because whoever has,**[c] **it-will-be-given**[d] **to-him and whoever does- not -have, even what he-seems**[e] **to-have will-be-taken**[f] **from him.**

LEXICON—a. pres. act. imper. of βλέπω (LN 27.58) (BAGD 4.c. p. 143): 'to pay attention to' [LN; CEV, GW, NRSV], 'to be sure to pay attention' [NLT], 'to direct one's attention to, to consider, to note' [BAGD], 'to consider carefully' [NIV], 'to take heed' [BECNT; KJV], 'to take care' [AB, Arn, NTC, WBC; HCSB, NASB, REB], 'to be careful' [NCV, TEV], 'to see to it' [Lns]. This verb is also translated as an adverb: '(listen) carefully' [NET].

b. pres. act. indic. of ἀκούω (LN 31.56): 'to listen' [AB, BECNT, LN, NTC; all versions except KJV, NLT], 'to hear' [Arn, Lns, WBC; KJV, NLT], 'to accept, to listen and respond, to pay attention and respond, to heed' [LN].

c. pres. act. subj. of ἔχω (LN 51.1) (BAGD I.2.a. p. 332): 'to have' [BAGD, LN]. The phrase 'whoever has' [Lns, NTC, WBC; HCSB, KJV, NASB, NET, NIV] is also translated 'the one who has' [AB], 'everyone who has something' [CEV], 'those who have something' [TEV], 'him who has' [Arn], 'those who have' [NRSV, REB], 'those who have understanding' [NCV], 'those who are open to my teaching' [NLT], 'those who understand these mysteries' [GW].

d. fut. pass. indic. of δίδωμι (LN 57.71): 'to be given' [LN]. The phrase 'it will be given to him' is translated 'to him shall be given' [Arn, Lns; KJV], 'more will be given to him' [BECNT, WBC; HCSB], 'to him more shall be given' [NASB], 'will be given more' [AB; CEV, NCV, NET, NIV, REB, TEV], 'more will be given' [NTC; NRSV], 'more understanding will be given' [NLT], 'will be given more knowledge' [GW]. The passive implies that God is the one who will give this [Lns, NIGTC, TG, TH].

e. pres. act. indic. of δοκεῖ (LN 31.30) (BAGD 1.a. p. 201): 'to seem, to assume' [LN], 'to think' [BAGD, LN]. The phrase 'even what he seems to have' [Lns, WBC] is also translated 'even that which he seems to have' [KJV], 'even what they seem to have' [NRSV], 'even what he thinks he has' [AB, Arn, BECNT, NTC; HCSB, NASB, NET, NIV; similarly NCV, NLT, REB], 'even the little they think they have' [TEV], 'what little they think they have' [CEV], 'even what they think they understand' [GW].

350   LUKE 8:18

f. fut. pass. indic. of αἴρω (LN 15.203): 'to be taken' [Arn, WBC; KJV, NET, NIV], 'to be taken away' [LN, Lns, NTC; GW, HCSB, NASB, NCV, NLT, NRSV, TEV], 'to be removed' [LN]. This passive is also translated with the person as subject: 'to lose' [CEV], 'to forfeit' [REB], 'to be deprived of' [AB]. The passive implies that God is the one who takes away [Lns, TG].

QUESTION—What relationship is indicated by οὖν 'therefore'?
  1. This indicates the conclusion of the two illustrations [BECNT, ICC, Lns, NIGTC, Su, TG, TH]. This is a warning that results from the principles about secret things in 8:17 [Lns]. It is a warning to respond to Jesus' teaching [BECNT]. The parables must be heard with care and attention [NIGTC].
  2. This indicates the conclusion of the whole section 8:4–18 [MGC, NIBC, NIGTC, Su, WBC]. This pertains the two parables [MGC, Su] and Jesus' teaching in general [MGC].

QUESTION—What relationship is indicated by γάρ 'because'?
It indicates the reason one must pay attention [Lns].

QUESTION—What is it that someone has or does not have?
This is a proverb that concerns the rich becoming richer and the poor becoming poorer [AB, NAC, NIGTC], and it is applied to the way the disciples heed the word of God [NAC]. Those who pay attention to it will be given more spiritual insight, but those who do not pay attention will be deprived of even what they seem to have [NIGTC]. It refers to knowledge [NIGTC], understanding the mysteries of the kingdom [GW, TG], or insight into spiritual life and God's word [NIC]. It refers to receiving the word [AB, Lns], and Jesus' teaching [Lns; NLT]. It refers to faith (8:12–13) [TH].

QUESTION—How can those who have nothing have something taken away from them?
  1. 'To have nothing' is to be taken literally as a fact even though such a person thinks he does have it [Lns, NIGTC, NTC]. Even the false knowledge will be taken away [NIGTC]. This refers to a superficial knowledge of spiritual matters [NTC]. They think they have sufficient knowledge without Jesus' teaching, but this is valueless [Lns].
  2. 'To have nothing' is a way of speaking of a small amount [Arn, ICC, NIC, TG]. Even the little that such a person understands about the kingdom will be taken away [TG]. Whoever recognizes the truth and does not appropriate it will lose his hold of it and not be able to recognize it in the future [ICC].

DISCOURSE UNIT: 8:19–21 [AB, BECNT, NAC, NIGTC, Su, TNTC, WBC; CEV, GW, NCV, NET, NIV, NLT, NRSV, TEV]. The topic is Jesus' mother and brothers [TNTC, WBC; CEV, NIV, TEV], Jesus' true family [AB, BECNT, NAC, NIGTC; GW, NCV, NET, NLT], the true kindred of Jesus [NRSV], qualifications for kinship to Jesus [Su].

8:19 And his mother and brothers came[a] to him and they-were- not -able to-get-near[b] him because-of the crowd. **8:20** And it-was-told to-him, Your mother and your brothers have-been-standing outside wanting to-see[c] you.

LEXICON—a. aorist mid. (deponent = act.) indic. of παραγίνομαι (LN 15.86) (BAGD 1. p. 613): 'to come' [AB, Arn, BAGD, BECNT, LN, WBC; HCSB, KJV, NASB, NET, NRSV, TEV], 'to come to see' [NTC; GW, NCV, NIV, NLT], 'to come up' [Lns], 'to go to see' [CEV], 'to arrive' [LN; REB]. The singular form of the verb is accounted for by being in a construction in which a verb standing sentence-initial in the Greek, agrees with its nearer subject (mother) [ICC, NIGTC, TH].

   b. aorist act. infin. of συντυγχάνω (LN **15.76**) (BAGD p. 793): 'to get near (to)' [**LN**, NTC; CEV, NET, NIV], 'to get to' [Lns; NASB, NCV, NLT, REB], 'to come close' [AB], 'to reach' [BAGD, BECNT, LN; NRSV], 'to join' [BAGD, WBC; TEV], 'to meet with' [GW, HCSB], 'to get in touch with' [Arn], 'to come at' [KJV].

   c. aorist act. infin. of ὁράω (LN 34.50) (BAGD 6. p. 221): 'to see' [AB, Arn, BAGD, BECNT, LN, Lns, NTC, WBC; all versions], 'to visit' [BAGD, LN], 'to look after' [BAGD]. They wanted Jesus to come out from the crowd to them [NTC]. 'To see' is used in the sense of 'to visit' [NAC, NIGTC].

QUESTION—Why would Jesus' mother and brothers endeavor to see him while he was in the midst of a crowd?

They must have felt that Jesus was overtaxing himself and wanted to take him back to their home [NIC]. In Mark 3:21 the crowd thought that Jesus was working beyond his capacity like someone no longer in his rational mind [Gdt, Lns, NTC], and so out of concern and affection [NTC] Jesus' family wanted to take him away so he could rest away from the crowd [Lns, NTC]. While Mary's concern over Jesus' workload was normal, Jesus' brothers did not yet believe in him and perhaps they wanted him to stop his ministry and return to his carpenter work in Nazareth [Su].

QUESTION—Where were Jesus' mother and brothers standing outside?

Although not indicated here, from Mark 3:20–31 it appears that Jesus is inside a house [NIGTC]. Jesus' family was standing outside the house [Gdt, MGC, TG, TH]. Since no house is mentioned here, it should be taken to mean outside the crowd, on the outskirts of the crowd and Jesus would have been sitting on a raised place with the crowd sitting down and packed around him [Lns].

QUESTION—Who told Jesus about his family standing outside?

The message from Mary was passed from one another in the crowd to those sitting next to Jesus [NTC].

8:21 And answering he-said to them, My mother and my brothers are these, the (ones who) hear[a] and do[b] the word of-God.

LEXICON—a. pres. act. participle of ἀκούω (LN 36.14): 'to hear' [Arn, BECNT, Lns, WBC; all versions except NCV], 'to listen to' [AB, NTC;

NCV], 'to pay attention to and obey' [LN]. This verb is appropriate following the parable of the sower, but the stress is on the following verb, 'doing' [TNTC].
  b. pres. act. participle of ποιέω (LN 42.7): 'to do' [Arn, BECNT, LN, Lns, WBC; GW, HCSB, KJV, NASB, NET, NRSV], 'to perform' [LN], 'to obey' [CEV, NCV, NLT, TEV], 'to put into practice' [NTC; NIV], 'to act upon' [AB; REB]. To do the word includes believing it, obeying all that it says to do, and hoping in all that it promises [Lns].

QUESTION—Who did Jesus speak to?
Jesus was speaking to the people in the crowd [NAC, TG], to the ones of the crowd who informed him [TH]. By the word οὗτοί 'these' Jesus indicates the disciples sitting around him [Lns].

QUESTION—What did he mean when speaking of his mother and his brothers?
He did not use articles with the nouns ('mother of me and brothers of me') and this indicates that he was referring to a less specific group than his physical family referred to as 'the mother of his and the brothers of his' in 8:19 [NAC]. The lack of articles is primarily due to the words being the predicate [ICC, NIC, NTC, TH, WBC]: these are my mother and brothers, those who hear and do. 'These are my mother and my brothers' means 'These are mother and brothers to me' [ICC, TH]. Another view is that the nouns are a nominative absolute resumed by 'these are' [AB, BECNT]: as for my mother and brothers, these are the ones who hear and do. But this should not sound as though Jesus is contrasting this group with others, since he is focusing only on a group other than his real family [BECNT]: 'my mother and brothers—these are those who hear and do'. Jesus does not deny his family bonds, rather he affirms other bonds in which his disciples are linked together as a family with one another and with Jesus [BECNT, WBC]. The meaning is not 'my actual mother and brothers', but 'they are like my mother and brothers and just as beloved' [NIGTC]. He refers to those who are equal to his mother and brothers and as equally dear [NIGTC, Rb]. These relationships are used metaphorically and mean 'those I consider as my mother and my brothers' [TH]. He does not refer to Joseph, who was not present, because in a spiritual sense only God is Father [Gdt, ICC]. He did not intend to equate 'mother' with female disciples and 'brothers' with male disciples [Lns].

DISCOURSE UNIT: 8:22–9:17 [BECNT]. The topic is Christological authority over all.

DISCOURSE UNIT: 8:22–9:6 [AB]. The topic is the progressive revelation of Jesus' power.

DISCOURSE UNIT: 8:22–56 [NAC, NICNT, NIGTC]. The topic is the revelation of Jesus' mastery over the world, the devil, and the flesh [NAC], responding to the power of Jesus: from fear to faith [NICNT], a group of mighty works [NIGTC].

LUKE 8:22-23   353

DISCOURSE UNIT: 8:22-25 [AB, BECNT, NAC, NICNT, NIGTC, Su, TNTC, WBC; CEV, GW, HCSB, NASB, NET, NIV, NLT, NRSV, TEV]. The topic is a storm [CEV], Jesus stills the storm [AB, NICNT, Su, TNTC, WBC; NET, NIV, NLT], Jesus calms a storm [NRSV, TEV], Jesus calms the sea [NAC; GW, NASB], authority over nature: stilling of the storm [BECNT], the Master of the storm [NIGTC], winds and waves obey the Master [HCSB].

DISCOURSE UNIT: 8:22-25 [NIBC]. The topic is Jesus calming a storm.

8:22 And it-happened on one of-the days he and his disciples got-into[a] in a-boat and he-said to them, Let-us-go-over to the other-side of-the lake. And they-set-out.[b] **8:23** And (while) they-were-sailing he-fell-asleep. And a-windstorm[c] of-wind came-down[d] on the lake and they-were-being swamped[e] and were-in-danger.

LEXICON—a. aorist act. indic. of ἐμβαίνω (LN 15.95) (BAGD p. 254): 'to get into' [AB, BAGD, BECNT, LN, NTC, WBC; all versions except KJV], 'to go into' [Lns; KJV], 'to enter' [Arn], 'to embark' [BAGD, LN].
  b. aorist pass. indic. of ἀνάγομαι (LN 54.4) (BAGD 3. p 53): 'to set out' [BECNT, NTC; HCSB, NET, NIV], 'to set off' [WBC], 'to start out' [Arn; CEV, GW, NLT, TEV], 'to start across' [NCV], 'to set sail' [BAGD, LN], 'to put out' [NRSV, REB], 'to launch out' [NASB], 'to launch forth' [Lns; KJV], 'to push off' [AB]. This is a nautical term for embarking or setting sail [AB, BAGD, ICC, NAC].
  c. λαῖλαψ (LN 14.6) (BAGD p. 463): 'windstorm, squall' [LN], 'gust' [BAGD]. The phrase 'a windstorm of wind' is translated 'a storm of wind' [KJV], 'a fierce gale of wind' [NASB], 'a hurricane of wind' [Lns], 'a windstorm' [WBC; CEV, NRSV], 'a fierce windstorm' [HCSB], 'a violent windstorm' [NET], 'a fierce storm' [NLT], 'a violent storm' [GW], 'a sudden storm' [Arn], 'a squall' [NIV], 'a heavy squall' [REB], 'a furious squall' [NTC], 'a sudden squall' [AB], 'a strong wind' [TEV], 'a very strong wind' [NCV], 'a whirlwind' [BECNT]. The descriptive genitive 'of wind' is unnecessary [AB].
  d. aorist act. indic. of καταβαίνω (LN 15.107) (BAGD 1.b. p. 408): 'to come down' [BAGD, LN]. The phrase 'to come down to' is translated 'to come down on' [HCSB, KJV, NET, NIV], 'to come down upon' [AB, WBC], 'to come down into' [Lns], 'to descend on' [BECNT; NASB], 'to descend upon' [Arn, NTC], 'to sweep down on' [NRSV], 'to come across' [GW], 'to strike' [CEV, REB], 'to blow down on' [TEV], 'to blow up on' [NCV], 'to develop' [NLT]. The wind descended from the surrounding mountains [Alf, EGT, Gdt, ICC, My, TH, WBC], or from the sky [Alf].
  e. imperf. pass. indic. of συμπληρόομαι (LN **54.14**) (BAGD 1. p. 770): 'to be swamped' [AB, BAGD, **LN**, WBC; HCSB, NIV], 'to begin to be swamped' [NTC; NASB], 'to threaten to swamp' [NLT], 'to take on water' [GW], 'to fill with water' [NCV, NRSV], 'to be filled with water' [KJV], 'to begin to be filled' [Arn], 'to begin to fill with water' [TEV], 'to

start filling up with water' [NET], 'to begin to be filled up' [Lns], 'to begin to ship water' [REB], 'to start sinking' [CEV], 'to be overcome with water' [BECNT]. The imperfect tense indicates that the filling of the boat was a process, but it was not completed [ICC].

QUESTION—What is the setting?

Probably the fishing boat contained Jesus and the Twelve [AB, BECNT, NAC, NICNT, Su, WBC]. Some think that the women disciples of 8:1–3 were also in the boat [AB, BECNT, WBC]. However, the fishing boats used on the lake of Galilee were not large enough for the many women disciples referred to in 8:1–3 [NICNT]. It was a sailboat [TG] which belonged to the disciples [NIGTC, Su]. High hills surrounded the lake and they had gorges through which winds would sweep down and roar through [AB, ICC, Lns, MGC, NIGTC]. A windstorm would be caused by the cold winds descending from the mountains and striking the hot air at the surface of the lake [AB, BECNT, NTC, Su]. The other side of the lake would be the eastern shore in the Gerasene territory [Su].

QUESTION—Does the phrase 'they were being swamped' refer to the men in the boat?

This is told from the standpoint of the participants [NAC]. What happens to the boat is said to happen to the men in it [TH]. It was the boat that was filling with water, not the people in it [Arn, EGT, TG, TNTC], and the people were in danger [Arn, BECNT, NTC, TNTC]. The phrase 'they were being swamped' is translated with the boat as subject [Arn; CEV, GW, NCV, NET, NIV, NRSV, TEV].

8:24 And having-approached they-woke him saying, Master,[a] master, we-are-perishing.[b] And having-been-awakened he-rebuked[c] the wind and the wave[d] of-the water. And they-stopped[e] and it-became calm.[f]

LEXICON—a. ἐπιστάτης (LN 87.50) (BAGD p. 300): 'master'. See translations of this word at 5:5. The repetition of the noun indicates the urgency of their words [BECNT, NIGTC], their high emotion [BECNT], their uneasiness [TH], their panic [MGC], and their frantic terror [NTC]. Several were calling for Jesus' help [BECNT, Lns]. This word also occurs at 8:45; 9:33, 49; 17:13.

b. pres. mid. indic. of ἀπόλλυμαι (LN 23.106) (BAGD 2.a.α. p. 95): 'to perish' [Arn, BAGD, BECNT, LN, Lns, NTC, WBC; KJV, NASB, NRSV], 'to be lost' [AB], 'to die' [BAGD, LN], 'to be about to die' [NET, TEV], 'to be going to die' [GW, HCSB,], 'to drown' [NCV], 'to be going to drown' [NIV, NLT], 'to be about to drown' [CEV], 'to sink' [REB]. This is the inclusive use of the verb since Jesus was in the boat and he was also in danger of perishing along with them [TG, TH].

c. aorist act. indic. of ἐπιτιμάω (LN **33.331**, 33.419) (BAGD 1. p. 303): 'to rebuke' [Arn, BAGD, BECNT, LN (33.419), Lns, NTC, WBC; HCSB, KJV, NASB, NET, NIV, NLT, NRSV, REB], 'to give a command to'

[LN (33.331); NCV], 'to command' [LN (33.331)], 'to charge' [AB], 'to give an order to' [TEV], 'to order to stop' [CEV, GW].
  d. κλύδων (LN **14.25**) (BAGD p. 436): 'wave' [BAGD, **LN**], 'rough water' [BAGD]. The phrase 'the wave of the water' is translated 'the waves of water' [BECNT], 'the raging of the water' [WBC; KJV], 'the raging waters' [NIV], 'the turbulent waters' [REB], 'the rushing waters' [Arn], 'the stormy water' [TEV], 'the waves' [CEV, NCV], 'the raging waves' [HCSB, NET, NLT, NRSV], 'the surging waves' [NASB], 'the surging deep' [AB], 'the surge of the water' [Lns, NTC]. Jesus rebuked the water as well as the wind since otherwise the water would continue to be agitated after the wind stopped [Gdt].
  e. aorist mid. indic. of παύομαι (LN 68.34) (BAGD 2. p. 638): 'to stop, to cease' [BAGD, LN]. The phrase 'they stopped' [Arn, WBC; NASB, NCV] is also translated 'they ceased' [BECNT, Lns; HCSB, KJV, NRSV], 'the wind stopped' [GW], 'the storm stopped' [NLT], 'the storm subsided' [NIV, REB], 'they subsided' [AB, NTC], 'they died down' [NET], 'they quieted down' [TEV], '(ordered to stop and) they obeyed' [CEV].
  f. γαλήνη (LN 14.23) (BAGD p. 150): 'calm' [BAGD, LN]. The phrase 'it became calm' [NASB, NCV] is also translated 'it was calm' [NET], 'there was a calm' [BECNT, Lns, NTC, WBC; HCSB, KJV, NRSV, REB], 'there was a great calm' [TEV], 'a calm ensued' [AB, Arn], 'all was calm' [NIV, NLT], 'everything was calm' [CEV], 'the sea became calm' [GW].
QUESTION—The verb 'to rebuke' is applied to a fever at 4:39 and to a demon at 4:35. What is implied by using the verb 'to rebuke' in regard to the wind and the waves?
  1. This does not indicate that Jesus was speaking to a personal agent [BECNT, ICC, NAC, NTC, Su, TH, WBC]. The verb 'rebuke' represents the disciples view of what Jesus did [ICC]. This is a figurative or poetic manner of describing what Jesus said [NTC]. In this instance it means 'to cause to cease' or 'to cause to be calm' [TH]. The verb is used of rebuking any force hostile to humans, whether it be spirit, disease, or natural forces [BECNT].
  2. There is a personal agent to be rebuked in this matter [AB, Crd, NIC]. He did not think that the storm and waves were evil spirits, but by rebuking the wind and waves he actually was rebuking Satan whose power was causing the storm [NIC]. He rebuked the spirits thought to be causing the storm [AB], The wind and waves were quasi-personal powers like the devils that had to be commanded to yield [Crd].
QUESTION—What is the subject of the verbs 'they stopped' and 'it became calm'?
The subject of 'they stopped' is the wind [BECNT, TH; GW, NIV, NLT, REB]. The subject of 'became calm' is the water [TH; GW]. Instead of the water taking time to settle down, the calm was immediate [Arn, BECNT, Gdt, ICC, NIC, NTC], proving that this was a miracle [Arn, ICC, NIC].

8:25 And he-said to-them, Where[a] (is) your faith? And being-afraid[b] they-were-amazed[c] saying to one-another, Who then[d] is this that/because[e] he-commands even the winds and the water, and they-obey him?

LEXICON—a. ποῦ (LN 83.6) (BAGD 1.a. p. 696): 'where?' [BAGD, LN]. The clause 'Where is your faith?' [AB, Arn, BECNT, Lns, NTC, WBC; all versions except CEV] is also translated 'Don't you have any faith' [CEV].
  b. aorist pass. participle of φοβέομαι (LN 25.252): 'to be afraid' [BECNT, LN, WBC; KJV, NCV, NET, NRSV, TEV], 'to be frightened' [CEV, GW], 'to be fearful' [HCSB, NASB], 'to be struck with fear' [Lns], 'to be seized with fear' [Arn], 'to be filled with awe' [NLT], 'to be awestruck' [NTC]. This verb is also translated as an adverb: 'in fear (they asked)' [NIV, REB], 'in deep awe' [AB].
  c. aorist act. indic. of θαυμάζω (LN 25.213) (BAGD 1.a.α. p. 352): 'to be amazed'. See translations of this word at 1:21 and 4:22. This word also occurs at 1:63; 2:18, 33; 7:9; 11:14, 38; 20:26; 24:12, 41.
  d. ἄρα (LN 71.7, 89.46) (BAGD 2. p. 103): 'then' [BAGD, LN (89.46)]. 'Then' refers to what the disciples had experienced [Lns]. It means 'in view of all this' [NIGTC]. The clause 'who then is this' [BECNT, Lns, NTC, WBC; NASB, NET, NRSV] is also translated 'who then is this man' [Arn], 'who is this' [CEV, NCV, NIV], 'who is this man' [GW, NLT, TEV], 'what manner of man is this' [KJV], 'who can this be' [AB; HCSB, REB], 'who can this one possibly be' [LN (71.7)].
  e. ὅτι (LN 89.3, 90.21): 'that' [BECNT, LN (90.21), Lns, NTC, WBC; NASB, NCV, NLT, NRSV], 'because, in view of the fact that' [LN (89.3)], 'for' [Arn; KJV], 'since' [AB], not explicit [CEV, GW, HCSB, NET, NIV, REB, TEV].

QUESTION—Didn't Jesus know where their faith was?
  This is a rhetorical question used as a rebuke [BECNT, EGT, MGC, Su, TG, TNTC]. The question means 'you should be more trusting' [BECNT]. This does not mean they no longer had faith, but that they did not act as though they had faith to face this danger [AB, Lns]. They had enough faith to turn to Jesus for help and this situation would rouse their faith by realizing the power that Jesus possessed [AB]. They did not completely lack faith, but they lacked sufficient faith to realize that they need not fear while they were in Jesus' presence [NAC]. They had a momentary lapse of faith [NIBC]. This question shamed the disciples and also prodded what faith they had [Lns]. Their cry that they were perishing showed the inadequacy of their faith [WBC]. They had such little faith that they could not trust God to take care of them [Su]. Their lack of faith was shown by their terror [Gdt, Lns, NTC, TNTC]. The object of faith is in God [Su, WBC], in the power of God revealed in Jesus [NIGTC], in Jesus [AB, MGC, TG, TH, TNTC]. This does not refer to their initial faith, but to their faith that God was in control even while in the midst of pressure [BECNT]. The disciples were characterized by faith even if it became weak on occasion [NIGTC]. This implies that they thought their cry for help would be in vain [ICC].

QUESTION—Why were they still afraid?
They had been afraid of the storm, but now they were afraid to be in the presence of one who had stilled the storm [NTC]. This was not a cowardly fear of the storm nor were they afraid of Jesus, rather they looked on Jesus with a great awe brought about by experiencing such power [Lns]. This is the effect of seeing the miracle [AB, BECNT], encountering the presence and activity of God [BECNT, WBC], of being in the presence of the supernatural [NIGTC]. This fear was a deep reverence [NTC], an overpowering awe [AB, Lns, NTC; NLT].

QUESTION—What is the import of the disciples' question?
They do not know how Jesus had performed this miracle [TG]. The miracle performed by Jesus was the prerogative of God [WBC]. Their understanding of Jesus and his powers was imperfect and this is the first time that they had seen him control the powers of nature [ICC]. This question means 'what kind of a person is this?' as in Matthew 8:27 [Lns].

QUESTION—Does ὅτι mean 'that' or 'because' in the disciples' question about Jesus?
1. It indicates what it was about Jesus that brought on this question [BECNT, Lns, NTC, TH, WBC; NASB, NCV, NLT, NRSV]: who then is this man *that* he commands the wind and the waves? It indicates what their question refers to, not the reason for their astonishment [TH]. It means 'seeing that', not 'because' [Lns]. It emphasizes the question [NTC]. The single occurrence of commanding the winds and the water is generalized in their statement 'he commands even the winds and the water, and they obey him' [Lns, WBC].
2. It indicates the reason for their question [AB, Arn, NIGTC; KJV]: who then is this man? *We ask this because* he commands the wind and the waves. It explains their amazement [Arn]. This is similar to the question asked in 4:36 'What is this word? Because with authority and power he commands the unclean spirits and they come out' [NIGTC].

DISCOURSE UNIT: 8:26–56 [NIBC]. The topic is more acts of power.

DISCOURSE UNIT: 8:26–39 [AB, BECNT, NAC, NICNT, NIGTC, Su, TNTC, WBC; CEV, GW, HCSB, NASB, NCV, NET, NIV, NLT, NRSV, TEV]. The topic is a man with demons in him [CEV, NCV], the Gerasene demoniac [BECNT, NIGTC, TNTC], the healing of a demoniac [NET], the healing of a demon–possessed man [NIV], Jesus casts out a demon [NAC], demons driven out by the Master [HCSB], Jesus cures the Gerasene demoniac [AB, NICNT, Su, WBC; NASB, NRSV], Jesus heals a man with demons [TEV], Jesus heals a demon–possessed man [GW, NLT].

8:26 And they-sailed to the country of-the Gerasenes,[a] which is opposite[b] Galilee. **8:27** And (when) he had-gone-out upon the land a-certain man from the city met[c] (him) having demons[d] and for-a-long time was- not -dressed (in) clothing and was- not -living in a-house but among the tombs.[e]

- TEXT—In 8:26, instead of τῶν Γερασηνῶν 'of the Gerasenes', some manuscripts read τῶν Γεργεσηνῶν 'of the Gergesenes' and other manuscripts read τῶν Γαδαρηνῶν 'of the Gadarenes'. GNT reads τῶν Γερασηνῶν 'of the Gerasenes' with a C decision, indicating that the Committee had difficulty making the decision. Τῶν Γεργεσηνῶν 'of the Gergesenes' is followed by Arn, Gdt, NIC, NTC, and TH. Τῶν Γαδαρηνῶν 'of the Gadarenes' (Matthew 8:26) is read by KJV. Gerasa was about 30 miles from the lake, Gadara was about 5 miles from the lake, and Gergesa (modern Kersa or Gersa) probably was right on the lakeshore [NIGTC, TG].
- TEXT—In 8:27, instead of the dative καὶ χρόνῳ ἱκανῷ 'and for a long time' (connected to what follows, 'was not dressed in clothing'), some manuscripts read ἐκ χρόνων ἱκανῶν, καί 'from a long time, and' (connected with what precedes, 'having demons'). GNT does not mention this variant. Ἐκ χρόνων ἱκανῶν, καί 'from a long time, and' is read by Gdt. and KJV.
- LEXICON—a. Γερασηνός (LN 93.450): 'a Gerasene' [LN]. The phrase 'the country of the Geresenes' [Lns; NASB, NRSV, REB] is also translated 'the region of the Gerasenes' [AB, BECNT; GW, HCSB, NET, NIV], 'the land of the Gerasenes' [NLT], 'the district of the Gerasenes' [WBC], 'the area of the Gerasene people' [NCV], 'the territory of Gerasa' [TEV], 'near the town of Gerasa' [CEV]. A Gerasene is a person who lives in Gerasa, a city in Peraea, east of the Jordan [LN]. The city controlled the tract of land bordering on the lake of Galilee [MGC, TNTC].
  b. ἀντιπέρα (LN 83.43) (BAGD p. 75): 'opposite' [AB, Arn, BAGD, BECNT, LN, NTC, WBC; HCSB, NASB, NET, NRSV, REB], 'across from' [Lns; GW], 'across the lake from' [NIV, NLT, TEV], 'on the other side of' [LN], 'over against' [KJV], '(sailed) across' [CEV, NCV].
  c. aorist act. indic. of ὑπαντάω (LN 15.78) (BAGD p. 837): 'to meet' [AB, Arn, BAGD, BECNT, LN, Lns, NTC, WBC; GW, HCSB, KJV, NET, NLT, NRSV], 'to draw near' [LN], 'to come to' [NCV]. This active verb is also translated passively: 'to be met (by)' [CEV, NASB, NIV, REB, TEV]. The man encountered or came towards Jesus, and this was not by accident but by design [TG, TH]. The man's intention probably was to molest Jesus and the disciples [NIC]. When the man saw the boat landing, he rushed down to attack the people [NTC]. 'To meet' can also mean 'to oppose' [NIGTC].
  d. δαιμόνιον (LN 12.37) (BAGD 2. p. 169): 'demon'. See this word at 4:33. For the phrase 'to have a demon' see 7.33.
  e. μνῆμα (LN 7.75) (BAGD p. 524): 'tomb' [BAGD, LN]. The phrase 'among (ἐν) the tombs' [AB, BECNT, WBC; NET, REB] is also translated 'in the tombs' [Arn, Lns, NTC; GW, HCSB, KJV, NASB, NIV,

NRSV], 'in the burial caves' [NCV, TEV], 'in the graveyard' [CEV], 'in a cemetery;' [NLT].

QUESTION—What is modified by 'from the city'

1. The phrase 'from the city' modifies 'a certain man' [AB, Alf, Arn, BECNT, EGT, ICC, NTC, Su, TH, WBC; CEV, GW, HCSB, NASB, NCV, NIV, NRSV, REB, TEV]: a certain man from the city met him. He was not now coming from the city to meet Jesus, this simply means that he belonged to the city [Alf, EGT, WBC]. Formerly he had lived in the city [Arn, Su, TH] and belonged to the city [ICC], but now he was living among the tombs [ICC, Su]. He lived in the caves that were used as burial places [Su, TH]. He wandered among the tombs [NIC]. Probably the man had been driven out of the city and had to find refuge in a deserted tomb [WBC].
2. The phrase 'from the city' modifies the verb 'he met' [KJV]: there met him out of the city a certain man.

QUESTION—Where were the tombs?

Tombs were often built into the hillsides outside a city [Arn, BECNT, ICC]. They were openings dug into the rock with enough room to stand in [TG]. The burial chambers were hewn into the walls of the cliffs and the man lived in abandoned chambers [Lns, NTC].

QUESTION—How many demon-possessed men met Jesus?

The parallel account in Matthew 8:28 says that two demon-possessed men met Jesus. Since Mark and Luke do not say *only* one man met him, there is not a conflict with Matthew [Lns]. It may be that Luke and Mark mention only the leader and spokesman of the two [Lns, NIC].

8:28 And having-seen Jesus (and) having-cried-out[a] he-fell-down-before[b] him and in-a-loud voice said, What[c] to-me and to-you, Jesus son of-God Most-High?[d] I-beg you, do- not -torment[e] me.

LEXICON—a. aorist act. participle of ἀνακράζω (LN 33.83) (BAGD p. 56): 'to cry out' [BAGD, BECNT, NTC; HCSB, KJV, NASB, NCV, NET, NIV, REB], 'to yell out' [Lns], 'to give a loud cry' [TEV], 'to shout' [Arn, LN; GW, NRSV], 'to scream' [AB, LN; CEV], 'to scream out' [WBC], 'to shriek' [NLT]. He acted as though he were in agony or rage [Lns]. The verb can refer to other than understandable speech [TH].

b. aorist act. indic. of προσπίπτω (LN 17.22) (BAGD 1. p. 718): 'to fall down before' [Arn, BAGD, LN, NTC, WBC; HCSB, KJV, NCV, NET, NRSV], 'to fall before' [BECNT; NASB], 'to fall in front of' [GW], 'to prostrate oneself before' [LN], 'to fall to the ground before' [NLT], 'to kneel down in front of' [CEV], 'to fall at someone's feet' [NIV, REB], 'to throw oneself down at someone's feet' [TEV], 'to lunge at' [AB]. This homage was brought about by fear, not reverence [NTC]. This was an act of supplication [TH]. This was not an act of worship, rather the man went to his knees in submission to Jesus' power over him [Gdt, Lns]. This act acknowledged Jesus' authority over the demon and was also a mark of respect for Jesus' relationship to the Most High God [BECNT], One commentary differs from the others by taking this to be an act of violence [AB]. See this word at 5:8; 8:47.

c. The phrase τί ἐμοὶ καὶ σοί 'What to me and to you?' is translated 'What have I to do with you?' [BECNT, Lns; KJV], 'What have you to do with me?' [HCSB, NRSV], 'What business do we have with each other?' [NASB], 'What do you want with me?' [AB; CEV, NCV, NIV, REB, TEV], 'Why are you bothering me?' [GW, NLT], 'Why do you bother me?' [NTC], 'Why do you concern yourself with me?' [Arn], 'What good can come to me from contact with you?' [WBC], 'Leave me alone!' [NET]. He wanted Jesus to leave him alone [Lns] and not meddle with him [NIGTC]. See the similar phrase τί ἡμῖν καὶ σοί 'What to us and to you' at 4:34.

d. ὕψιστος (LN 12.4) (BAGD 2. p. 850): 'most high'. See this word at 1:32, 35, 76; 6:35. This phrase was common among the heathen nations when referring to God [BECNT, ICC].

e. aorist act. subj. of βασανίζω (LN 36.13) (BAGD2. p. 134): 'to torment' [AB, Arn, BAGD, BECNT, LN, Lns, WBC; HCSB, KJV, NASB, NET, NRSV, REB], 'to torture' [BAGD, LN, NTC; CEV, GW, NCV, NIV, NLT], 'to punish' [TEV]. This verb is used figuratively of any severe distress [BAGD].

QUESTION—What caused the demon-possessed man to cry out these words?

The sight of Jesus both attracted and repelled the man, bringing about this crisis [Gdt]. These are the words of the demons speaking through the man [AB, Arn, BECNT, Crd, Lns, MGC, NAC, NIC, NTC, Rb]. The demon expressed its distress, dread, and entreaty [WBC]. The demoniac identified himself with the demon who controlled him [ICC]. The following verse brings out the fact that Jesus had commanded the demons to leave the man [NIGTC].

QUESTION—Why did the demoniac call Jesus 'Jesus, son of God most high'?

Perhaps the man had heard talk about Jesus and instinctively recognized him, or it was the demons' supernatural knowledge [Gdt]. Demons have supernatural knowledge of Jesus' identity [Arn, MGC, NAC, NIC, WBC]. The demon was attributing deity to Jesus [Lns]. This is the same title that was given to Jesus in 1:32 [AB].

QUESTION—Why did he think Jesus would torment him?

The demon knew that he would ultimately be tormented because of his evil character and he feared that Jesus would bring this about earlier than he was due to experience it [Gdt, NAC, Su, WBC]. This is the plea of the possessed man [NIC], hence the demon was making this plea through this man [ICC, NIGTC]. It was about this time that Jesus had commanded the demon to leave the man, and the demon feared that he would be sent to the bottomless pit (8:31), the place of torture [Gdt, ICC, Lns, NAC, NTC]. The form of the torment is not known [AB], but to Luke, the demon would be afraid of being sent to hell [TH].

8:29 Because he had-commanded the unclean[a] spirit to-come-out from the man. Because many times it-had-seized[b] him and having-been-bound with chains[c] and shackles[d] and having-been-guarded[e] and (yet) breaking-apart the bonds he-was-driven[f] by the demon into the desert.

TEXT—Instead of παρήγγειλεν 'he had commanded' in the aorist tense, some manuscripts have παρήγγελλεν 'he was commanding' in the imperfect tense. GNT does not mention this variant. The imperfect tense παρήγγελλεν 'he was commanding' is followed by AB, Alf, Arn, BECNT, BNTC, Gdt, Lns, My, NIGTC, Rb; NCV, REB.

LEXICON—a. ἀκάθαρτος (LN 53.39, 12.39) (BAGD 2. p. 29): 'unclean' [AB, Arn, BAGD, BECNT, LN, Lns, NTC, WBC; HCSB, KJV, NASB, REB], 'evil' [CEV, GW, NCV, NET, NIV, NLT, TEV]. The phrases 'a spirit of an unclean demon' in 4:33, 'demon' in 4:35, and 'unclean spirit' in 4:36 and 8:29 are the equivalent of 'evil spirit' in 7:21 [Su, TG]. The phrase 'unclean spirit' refers to an evil spirit which is ritually unclean itself and which causes persons it possesses to be ritually unclean [LN (12.39)]. See this word at 4:33 and the phrase πνεῦμα ἀκάθαρτον 'unclean spirit' at 4:36.

b. pluperf. act. indic. of συναρπάζω (LN 18.5) (BAGD p. 785): 'to seize' [Arn, BAGD, BECNT, LN, Lns, NTC; HCSB, NASB, NET, NIV, REB, TEV], 'to control' [GW], 'to take control of' [NLT], 'to take hold of' [NCV], 'to overcome' [WBC], 'to catch' [KJV], 'to convulse' [AB]. The active voice is also translated passively with the man as subject: 'to be attacked' [CEV]. This refers to taking possession of the man [TH].

c. ἅλυσις (LN 6.16) (BAGD 1. p. 41): 'chain' [AB, Arn, BAGD, BECNT, LN, Lns, NTC, WBC; CEV, HCSB, KJV, NASB, NET, NRSV, REB]. The phrase 'to be bound with chains and shackles' is translated 'to be chained hand and foot' [GW, NCV, NIV], 'to be shackled with chains' [NLT], 'his hands and feet tied with chains' [TEV]. This is a chain made from metal links [LN]. This refers to the bonds which functioned as handcuffs [ICC, NIGTC].

d. πέδη (LN 6.17) (BAGD p. 638): 'shackles' [BAGD, LN, NTC; HCSB, NASB, NET, NRSV], 'fetters' [AB, Arn, BAGD, BECNT, LN, Lns, WBC; KJV, REB], 'leg irons' [CEV]. For the phrase 'to be bound with chains and shackles' see the preceding lexicon item c. The shackles were chains with special links prepared to go around the ankles [LN; NET]. They could be made of ropes or of chains [BECNT, ICC] and Mark 5:3 seems to indicate chains [BECNT]. This refers to the bonds that shackled the man's feet [BECNT, ICC, NIGTC].

e. pres. pass. participle of φυλάσσω (LN 37.120) (BAGD 1.b. p. 868): 'to be guarded' [Arn, BAGD, LN; HCSB], 'to be kept under guard' [BECNT, NTC; CEV, NASB, NCV, NET, NIV, NRSV], 'to be under guard' [Lns], 'to be closely watched' [AB], 'to be constrained' [WBC], not explicit [KJV, NLT, REB, TEV]. This passive voice is also translated actively with people as the subject: 'to keep under guard' [GW]. The purpose of

the guarding is to keep a prisoner in custody [LN] and prevent him from escaping [BAGD].
  f. imperf. pass. indic. of ἐλαύνω (LN 15.161) (BAGD p. 248): 'to be driven' [AB, Arn, BAGD, LN, Lns, NTC, WBC; HCSB, KJV, NASB, NET, NIV, NRSV, TEV], 'to be driven out' [BECNT; REB], 'to be forced out' [NCV], 'to be rushed out' [NLT]. This passive is also translated actively with the demon as subject: 'to force out' [CEV], 'to force to go' [GW]. The demons drove the man into the desert to get away from the human influence [ICC, WBC] and the desert was regarded to be the home of evil spirits [ICC].

QUESTION—What relationship is indicated by γάρ 'because' at the beginning of the verse?

This indicates the reason the demon in the demon-possessed man spoke as he did in the preceding verse [EGT, Lns, MGC, NICNT, NIGTC, TH; CEV, NCV, TEV]: the demon said this because Jesus had commanded the demon to come out from the man. This is a flashback to explain why the demon had cried out as he did [NIGTC]. This command had caused the cry of fear [EGT]. 'For he had commanded the unclean spirit' shows that this had preceded the outburst from the possessed man [TH].

QUESTION—How is the variant reading παρήγγελλεν 'he was commanding' in the imperfect tense followed by many explained?

The imperfect is explained by regarding Jesus to be commanding the unclean spirit while the man was approaching [TH]. Jesus was already commanding the unclean spirit to leave and this does not imply that the demon was resisting this command [Lns]. The imperfect tense may indicate that the action of the verb was unfulfilled or incomplete [NIGTC]. The imperfect indicates that Jesus was in the midst of ordering the unclean spirit when the possessed man cried out [Alf]. Taking this event to follow the previous verse, the imperfect is used as an inceptive aorist, 'he was about to charge the unclean spirit' [AB]. Perhaps a too abrupt change would harm the man [Arn]. The aorist tense is expected here [ICC, NIGTC] and is more logical [NTC].

QUESTION—Why is the singular 'the unclean spirit' used here (and the singular form in the preceding words spoken through the man) while the plural is used in 8:27 (demons) and 8:30 (many demons)?

With the singular forms, the demons are treated as acting in unity [NAC]. The leader of the many demons was spokesman for the demons [Arn, NTC]. The interchange between the actions and speech of the man and the demons is so rapid that it is natural to speak of the demons in the singular [ICC].

QUESTION—What relationship is indicated by γάρ 'because' at the beginning of the second sentence?

This indicates an explanation. The condition of the man explains why Jesus gave the command [My]. This explains the manner in which the demon possessed the man [Lns]. This explains the man's cry of fear upon seeing Jesus [EGT, TH]. This explains that the reason for using the imperfect 'was commanding' was because the demons had taken too deep a control of the man to instantly yield to a command [Gdt]. This develops the flash-back by explaining the details of the man's madness [NIGTC].

QUESTION—What is meant by the plural πολλοῖς χρόνοις 'many times'?
1. It means on many occasions [AB, Arn, BECNT, BNTC, EGT, ICC, Lns, MGC, NAC, NTC, TH, WBC; all versions]: many times it had seized him. Probably the man's possession (or at least its manifestation [WBC]) came and went in cycles since he was seized many times [BECNT]. Each time the demon seized the man, the man would rent the bonds [Lns].
2. It means for a long time [Alf, My; GW]: for a long time it had seized him.

QUESTION—Why was the demon-possessed man bound and guarded?
The only way the people knew to deal with such mad behavior was to restrain the man by binding him [NIGTC]. The townspeople had bound the man in order to protect themselves from him [NTC].

QUESTION—How is the participial clause 'and having been guarded' used?
1. It indicates an independent event [AB, BECNT, ICC, NTC, WBC; CEV, GW, NASB, NCV, NET, NIV]: he was bound with chains and shackles and he was guarded. During times when the man was calmer, he was guarded to prevent the demons from driving him away [ICC].
2. It indicates the purpose for which the man was bound [BNTC, TH, WBC]: he was bound with chains and shackles in order to guard him. The chains were the intended means for keeping the man under control during the manifestations of being possessed by the demons [WBC].

QUESTION—How is the participial phrase 'and breaking-apart the bonds' related to the fact that the man was bound with chains and shackles?
It indicates contra-expectation [AB, BECNT, NTC, WBC; CEV, GW, HCSB, NASB, NCV, NET, NIV, REB, TEV]: although he was bound, yet he broke apart the bonds.

8:30 And Jesus asked him, What is your name? And he-said, Legion.[a] Because many demons had-entered into him. **8:31** And they-were-begging/begged him that he- not -command them to-depart into the abyss.[b]

LEXICON—a. Λεγιών (LN 93.229) (BAGD p. 468): 'Legion' [AB, Arn, BAGD, BECNT, LN, Lns, NTC, WBC; all versions except CEV, GW, TEV], 'Legion (Six Thousand)' [GW], 'Mob' [TEV], 'Lots' [CEV]. This word is a Latin loan word for a legion or regiment of soldiers [NIGTC]. A legion consisted of 6,826 men [Lns], 6,000 men [AB, MGC, NAC, NIC, NIGTC; GW], 5,600 men [NICNT], or 4,000 to 6,000 men [TG]. This great number of demons were in this man [Alf, Lns]. Normally a legion consisted of five or six thousand soldiers, but in Mark 5:13 where 2,000 pigs were possessed by these spirits it seems to mean that there were 2,000 evil spirits [NIGTC], but we cannot know if each animal was possessed since when some pigs were set in motion, the rest would naturally follow [Gdt, ICC]. This is not to be taken literally to mean 6,000 demons but to indicate that there were a multitude of them [BECNT, NIC,

NTC, TH]. It is used figuratively and stands for a very large number [NTC].
- b. ἄβυσσος (LN 1.20) (BAGD 2. p. 2): 'abyss' [AB, Arn, BAGD, BECNT, LN, Lns, NTC, WBC; HCSB, NASB, NET, NRSV, REB, TEV], 'Abyss' [NIV], 'a very deep place' [LN], 'the deep' [KJV], 'underworld' [BAGD], 'the bottomless pit' [GW, NLT], 'the deep pit where they would be punished' [CEV], 'eternal darkness' [NCV]. It is a bottomless pit [Su, TH]. This term is used of the location of the dead and of demons [BAGD]. Although the abyss was the location of the dead in Psalm 107:26 and Romans 10:7, here it is used of the location of evil spirits as in Revelation 9:1, 11:7, 17:8, and 20:1–3 [BECNT, ICC, Lns, Su]. The abyss can be used of the home from which the demons originally came, it may be a place where rebellious spirits are imprisoned, or it may be the place of the demon's ultimate judgment [WBC]. It had been the home of demons before they had left it to dwell in the man [Gdt, NIC]. It was the place where demons were imprisoned until their final punishment [TG]. It is the place where evil powers are imprisoned and punished [NICNT, NIGTC]. It is the abyss of hell [AB, Crd, NTC], the burning pit of hell, a place of eternal torment prepared for the devil and his evil angels [Lns, MGC, NAC]. They did not want Jesus to judge them before the final judgment day [MGC].

QUESTION—Who did Jesus direct the question to and who answered?

The masculine αὐτόν 'him' shows that Jesus was addressing the man, not the unclean spirit, which would require a neuter pronoun [Arn, Lns, TH]. Jesus asked the man's name to make him realize that he had a human personality that was apart from the evil spirits that possessed him [Gdt, ICC, NIC, NTC].

1. The man himself answered with the name Legion [Gdt, NIC, NIGTC, Su, TG]. When the man said that his name was Legion, it reveals that he realized he was inhabited by a multitude of evil spirits [NIGTC, TG]. Legion was not his name, but a nickname used to describe the many demons possessing him [NIC, Su]. Also in the following request, the man speaks in the name of those who possess him [Gdt].
2. A demon answered through the man's voice [AB, Arn, BECNT, Lns, MGC, NAC, NICNT, NIVS, NTC, WBC]. Although the question was addressed to the man, it is clear that one of the demons answered, not the man [Lns]. This refers to demons speaking to Jesus as they did in 8:26 and 31 [NTC]. The demon said Legion because so many demons were in the man and the man's actual name was not important [Lns]. Instead of giving their names, the demons provided their number [MGC]. The singular form 'he said' refers to the spokesman of the demons, but beginning with 8:31 the plural form is used of the many demons [NTC].

QUESTION—What relationship is indicated by ὅτι 'because' in the clause 'because many demons had entered into him'?

This is a comment by Luke that explains why the man gave 'Legion' for his name [EGT, NAC, NICNT, WBC]. This is different from the account in Mark where the man's answer includes this explanation 'My name is Legion because we are many' (Mark 5:9) [EGT, NAC, WBC]. Translations using quotation marks do not include this explanation in the quoted reply [AB, BECNT; all versions except CEV]. Two translations enclose the clause within parenthesis marks [WBC; GW]. Two translations add the implied connection: 'This was because' [REB], 'He said this because' [CEV].

QUESTION—What is the significance of the imperfect tense παρεκάλουν 'they were begging'?

1. The imperfect tense indicates that the action was without result [TH]. This interpretation probably includes those which translate with the past tense [AB, BECNT, WBC; all versions except NASB, NET, NLT]: they begged him.
2. The imperfect tense indicates repetition [ICC, TG, TNTC; NASB, NLT]: they *kept* begging him.
3. The imperfect tense indicates inception [Lns; NET]: they *began to* beg him.

8:32 And there-was there a-herd[a] of-many pigs feeding on the mountain[b] and they-begged him that he-might-permit them to-enter into those. And he-permitted them. **8:33** And the demons having-come-out from the man entered into the pigs, and the herd rushed down the steep-bank[c] into the lake and were-drowned.

LEXICON—a. ἀγέλη (LN 4.8) (BAGD p. 8): 'herd' [BAGD, LN]. The phrase 'a herd of many pigs' [AB, NTC] is also translated 'a herd of many swine' [KJV, NASB], 'a drove of many swine' [Lns], 'a large herd of pigs' [all versions except KJV, NASB, NRSV], 'a large herd of swine' [Arn, BECNT; NRSV], 'quite a herd of pigs' [WBC]. In Mark 5:13 the number of pigs is given as about two thousand.

b. ὄρος (LN 1.46) (BAGD p. 582): 'mountain' [BAGD, LN, Lns, WBC; KJV, NASB], 'mountainside' [GW], 'hill' [Arn, BAGD; NCV], 'hillside' [AB, BECNT, NTC; CEV, HCSB, NET, NIV, NLT, NRSV, REB, TEV].

c. κρημνός (LN 1.50) (BAGD p. 581): 'steep bank' [BAGD, BECNT, Lns; CEV, HCSB, NASB, NIV], 'steep slope' [AB, LN; NET], 'steep side of a hill' [LN], 'steep hillside' [NLT], 'steep place' [KJV], 'cliff' [BAGD, NTC, WBC; GW], 'side of the cliff' [TEV], 'precipice' [Arn], 'hill' [NCV], 'edge' [REB]. This does not need to be an abrupt cliff since it could mean a steep rocky slope [ICC].

QUESTION—How did it happen there was a herd of pigs in the area?

The territory of Decapolis was predominantly Gentile in makeup and the pigs were raised to sell in the Gentile markets [WBC]. The owners were either nonpracticing Jews or they were Gentiles [Arn, BECNT]. The owners must have been Jews who were illegally raising pigs and therefore it was not wrong to destroy their herd [Lns].

QUESTION—Who begged Jesus to permit them to enter the pigs?

The demons begged Jesus [Lns, NTC, Su, TG, TH].

QUESTION—Why did the demons want to enter the pigs?

They desperately wanted to avoid being sent to the abyss [NICNT]. Since they had to leave the man, the nearby pigs could be a temporary abode [AB, BECNT, MGC, TG]. The demons preferred living in the pigs than being in the abyss [BECNT, Su]. No matter what their motive was, Jesus used it for a good end [ICC].

QUESTION—Why did the peacefully grazing pigs suddenly rush into the lake and drown?

The demonic possession of the pigs caused them to move in a mass [AB]. The same destructive power the demons had over the man were now turned on the pigs [WBC]. This was visible proof that the man had been freed of the demons [BECNT, MGC, NAC, NIGTC, TG].

8:34 And having-seen what had-happened the (ones) tending[a] fled[b] and reported[c] (it) to the city and to the farms.[d] 8:35 And they went-out to-see what had-happened and came to Jesus and they-found the man from whom the demons had-departed sitting at the feet of-Jesus having-been-dressed and being-in-his-right-mind[e] and they-were-afraid.

TEXT—In 8:34, before ἀπήγγειλαν 'they reported', some manuscripts add ἀπελθόντες 'having gone away', although GNT does not mention this variant. Ἀπελθόντες 'having gone away' is read by KJV.

LEXICON—a. pres. act. participle of βόσκω (LN 44.1) (BAGD 1. p. 855): 'to tend' [BAGD; HCSB, NIV], 'to feed' [BAGD, Lns; KJV], 'to herd' [LN], 'to take care of' [CEV, GW, TEV], 'to look after' [LN], 'to be in charge of' [NTC; REB]. The phrase 'the ones tending' is translated 'the herdsmen' [AB, Arn, BECNT, WBC; NASB, NCV, NET, NLT], 'the swineherds' [NRSV].

b. aorist act. indic. of φεύγω (LN 15.61) (BAGD 1. p. 855): 'to flee' [Arn, BAGD, BECNT, LN, Lns, NTC, WBC; KJV, NLT], 'to run away' [LN; GW, NASB, NCV], 'to run off' [AB; HCSB, NET, NIV, NRSV, TEV], 'to run' [CEV], 'to take to one's heels' [REB].

c. aorist act. indic. of ἀπαγγέλλω (LN 33.198) (BAGD 1. p. 79): 'to report' [Arn, BAGD; GW, HCSB, NASB, NIV], 'to carry the report' [Lns], 'to tell' [BAGD, BECNT, LN; NRSV], 'to tell about' [NCV], 'to tell all about' [AB], 'to go and tell' [KJV], 'to inform' [LN], 'to announce' [BAGD], 'to spread the news' [NTC; CEV, NET, NLT, TEV], 'to carry the news' [REB], 'to let it be known' [WBC].

d. ἀγρός (LN 1.93) (BAGD 3. p. 14): 'farm, settlement, hamlet' [LN], 'country' [BAGD]. The plural form refers to 'farms' [BAGD, Lns; CEV, TEV], 'the countryside' [NTC, WBC; GW, NCV, NET, NIV, REB], 'the surrounding countryside' [NLT], 'the country' [AB, Arn, BECNT; KJV,

NASB, NRSV]. This means the rural areas [TG]. They were small groups of farms in the countryside [TH, WBC] and this means 'hamlets' [TH].
e. pres. act. participle of σωφρονέω (LN **30.22**) (BAGD 1. p. 802): 'to be in one's right mind' [**LN** NTC, WBC; all versions except NLT], 'to be of sound mind' [AB, BAGD, BECNT], 'to be sane' [LN; NLT], 'to be rational' [Arn], 'to be self-controlled' [Lns]. The man was self controlled and no longer acted wild by yelling and raging about [Lns].

QUESTION—Why did the herdsmen flee and report what happened?
They ran away in fear [Su, WBC]. They ran in consternation at losing their pigs [Lns]. They ran to report to the owners who lived in the city and neighborhood [Gdt]. They had to explain the loss of the herd [BECNT] and didn't want to be blamed for the loss [Lns]. They wanted the owners and everyone else to know that Jesus was responsible for the death of pigs and not themselves [NTC].

QUESTION—In 8:35, who went out to see what had happened and why did they?
This refers to people who lived in the cities and farms [Alf, Lns, My, Su], the people to whom the herdsmen reported [TH]. The owners of the pigs lived in towns and some on farms [Lns], and they wanted to confirm the loss they had been told about [BECNT, Gdt]. It seemed incredible [Lns]. They were frightened and curious [WBC].

QUESTION—Why would the man be sitting at Jesus' feet?
This was the position taken by a disciple [AB, NICNT, NIGTC, Su, TH, WBC]. It indicates that he was being instructed by Jesus [BECNT, NIGTC]. It showed the thankfulness of the former demoniac [ICC].

QUESTION—Why were the people who saw this frightened?
They were frightened at the evident power of Jesus over demons [AB, Lns] and the presence of God's supernatural power [WBC]. They were frightened at thinking of further losses that might occur [AB].

8:36 And the (ones who) had-seen (it) reported[a] to-them how the (one who) had-been-demon-possessed[b] was-healed.[c]

TEXT—Following αὐτοῖς 'to them', some manuscripts add καί 'also', although GNT does not mention this variant. Καί 'also' is added by KJV.

LEXICON—a. aorist act. indic. of ἀπαγγέλλω (LN 33.198) (BAGD 1. p. 79): 'to report'. See this word at 8:34.
b. aorist pass. (deponent = act.) participle of δαιμονίζομαι (LN 12.41): 'to be demon possessed' [Arn, BECNT, LN, NTC, WBC; GW, NASB, NET, NIV, NLT], 'to be possessed by demons' [NRSV], 'to be possessed of the devils' [KJV], 'to be demonized' [Lns], 'to be possessed' [AB], not explicit [CEV, NCV, TEV]. The phrase 'the one having been demon possessed' is translated 'the demon-possessed man' [HCSB], 'the madman' [REB]. He was saved in the sense that he was physically delivered from the demons (although his salvation did result from this event) [BECNT].

368 LUKE 8:36

c. aorist pass. indic. of σῴζω (LN 23.136) (BAGD 1.c. p. 798): 'to be healed' [LN; CEV, KJV, NET, NLT, NRSV], 'to be cured' [Arn, LN, NTC; NIV, REB, TEV], 'to be made well' [LN; NASB, NCV], 'to be delivered' [AB, BECNT; HCSB], 'to be saved' [Lns, WBC]. This passive form is also translated actively with Jesus as the subject 'to restore to health' [GW]. The man was delivered from the evil that afflicted him [AB].

QUESTION—Who were the ones who saw the man being healed?
1. They were the herdsmen [BECNT, MGC, TG, WBC]. They would have explained that Jesus was responsible for the loss of the pigs [WBC]. Perhaps others also joined in [TG].
2. They were the herdsmen and Jesus' disciples [NTC]. This was probably the next morning and the details of the story were now given by the eyewitnesses [NTC].
3. They were the disciples [Arn, Gdt, Lns]. The herdsmen had been with the pigs at a considerable distance from Jesus and could only tell of the loss of the pigs [Gdt]. The owners already had a report from the herdsmen who might have been trying to excuse themselves. Now they went to get the true story from those who had been present with Jesus [Lns].

8:37 And all the multitude of-the surrounding-region[a] of-the Gerasenes asked him to-depart from them, because they-were-being-seized[b] with-great fear. So he having-embarked into a-boat returned.

TEXT—There are the same manuscript differences found in 8:26 for the names of the inhabitants (i.e., Γερασηνῶν 'Gerasenes', Γεργεσηνῶν 'Gergesenes', and Γαδαρηνῶν 'Gadarenes').

LEXICON—a. περίχωρος (LN **1.80**) (BAGD p. 553): 'surrounding region'. The phrase τῆς περιχώρου τῶν Γερασηνῶν 'all the multitude of the surrounding region of the Gerasenes' is translated 'all the multitude of the surrounding district of the Gadarenes' [WBC], 'all the many people of the region of the Gerasenes' [BECNT], 'the whole multitude of the country of the Gadarenes' [KJV], 'the whole multitude living in the country around the land of the Gergesenes' [Arn], 'all the people of the Gerasenes and the surrounding region' [NET], 'all the people from the surrounding region of the Gerasenes' [GW], 'all the people of the surrounding country of the Gerasenes' [NRSV], 'all the people of the country of the Gerasenes and the surrounding district' [NASB], 'the Gerasenes and the people living around them' [**LN**], 'the crowd of the neighborhood of the Gerasenes' [Lns], 'all the people of the region of the Gerasenes' [NIV], 'all the people of the Gerasene region' [HCSB], 'the entire population of the region of the Gergesenes' [NTC], 'all the people of the Gerasene country' [NCV], 'the whole population of the Gerasene district' [REB], 'the whole populace of the Gerasene countryside' [AB], 'everyone from around Gerasa' [CEV], 'all the people in that region' [NLT], 'all the people from that territory' [TEV]. See this word at 4:14.

b. imperf. pass. indic. of συνέχομαι (LN 90.65) (BAGD 5. p. 789): 'to be seized' [BAGD], 'to experience, to have' [LN]. The phrase 'to be seized with great fear' [BECNT, WBC; NET, NRSV] is also translated 'to be taken with great fear' [KJV], 'to be gripped with great fear' [NASB], 'to be gripped by a great fear' [Arn; HCSB], 'to be in the grip of great fear' [Lns], 'to be overcome with/by fear' [NIV, REB], 'to be terrified' [GW], 'to be terribly afraid' [TEV], 'to be terribly frightened' [NTC], 'to be so frightened' [CEV], 'to be very afraid' [NCV], 'a great wave of fear swept over them' [NLT], 'so great was the fear that gripped them' [AB].

QUESTION—Is 'all the multitude of the surrounding region of the Gerasenes' to be taken literally?

This is hyperbole [TG]. All of the people who had come out made this request [AB]. This does not refer to all the Gerasenes as though they belonged to the city since they were people who came from small unnamed towns nearby [Lns]. The phrase includes the town of Gergesa as well as the surrounding area and means the same as 'the country of the Gerasenes' in 8:26 [EGT, TH].

QUESTION—What was the cause of their great fear?

They might have been frightened at the supernatural power that had been displayed [AB, BECNT, Gdt, MGC, NIC, NICNT, NIGTC, Su, TG, TNTC]. This was not reverential awe, but a terror which repelled them [Su]. Or, they were afraid of further loss to themselves [AB, ICC, Lns, MGC, NIC, NIGTC, TNTC]. They feared what Jesus might do if he remained with them [Lns]

8:38 And the man from whom the demons had-gone-out was-begging him to-be with[a] him. But he-sent- him -away saying, **8:39** Return to your house and tell what God did for-you. And he-went-away throughout[b] the whole city proclaiming[c] what Jesus did for-him.

TEXT—In 8:38, following σὺν αὐτῷ 'with him', some manuscripts add ὁ Ἰησοῦς 'Jesus' as the subject of ἀπέλυσεν 'he sent away', although GNT does not mention this variant. Ὁ Ἰησοῦς is read by KJV.

LEXICON—a. σύν (LN 89.107): 'with' [LN]. The phrase 'to be with him' [Arn, BECNT, Lns, WBC; HCSB, KJV, NRSV] is also translated 'to stay with him' [AB], 'to go with him' [NTC; CEV, NCV, NET, NIV, REB], 'to accompany him' [NASB], 'to go too' [NLT]. This request is also translated as a direct quotation: 'let me go with you' [GW, TEV]. Although the Greek has '*be* with him', the fact that Jesus was traveling makes it natural to say '*go* with him' [TG, TH]. The man desired to be a disciple [AB, BECNT, ICC, NAC, NIBC, NIC], as implied by the fact that he had been sitting at Jesus' feet [AB]. The man desired to go away with Jesus since he feared the unfriendly crowd [ICC].

b. κατά (LN 84.31) (BAGD II.1.a. p. 406): 'throughout' [LN; HCSB, KJV, NASB, NET, NRSV], 'through' [AB, Arn, BAGD, Lns; GW, TEV], 'all

through' [NLT], 'all over' [NTC; CEV, NCV, NIV, REB], 'about' [WBC], 'into' [BECNT].
c. pres. act. participle of κηρύσσω (LN 33.207) (BAGD 2.a. p. 431): 'to proclaim' [AB, Arn, BAGD, BECNT, LN, Lns, NTC; HCSB, NASB, NET, NRSV, REB], 'to tell' [LN; CEV, NCV, NIV, NLT, TEV], 'to tell people' [GW], 'to publish' [KJV], 'to preach' [WBC]. The verb refers to proclaiming openly or loudly [TH]. See this word at 3:3; 4:18, 19, 44; 8:1; 9:2; 12:3; 24:47.

QUESTION—Was the man to tell only those who lived in his house?

This command was not meant to restrict him to telling only those in his own house [Arn, Lns]. Rather than focusing on the building in which he used to live, this means to return to the family he used to be a part of [TH; GW, NLT]. This means that he was to return home and tell his relatives and acquaintances [NIC], and the man more than obeyed the instructions [MGC, NIGTC]. The man did not restrict his telling to his home, but he went around the entire city [Su]. He was to witness to his community [BECNT]. The man properly interpreted Jesus' instructions to mean that from his home he was to reach out in ever-widening circles until the whole country learned about what had happened [Lns].

QUESTION—What is the significance of being commanded to tell what *God* did for him and the man's response in telling what *Jesus* did for him?

Jesus told him to attribute the healing to God [ICC]. Jesus had acted as the agent for God [AB]. What Jesus had done was what God had done working through Jesus [NICNT, NIGTC, Su]. The man could not leave out the instrument God used in healing him [BECNT, Gdt]. The change from God to Jesus does not intend to substitute Jesus for God or to identify the two, rather, in praising Jesus the man felt he was truly praising God [Lns]. It is unlikely that the man realized that Jesus was the divine Lord [BECNT], although this view is taken by some [MGC, NIC].

DISCOURSE UNIT: 8:40–56 [AB, BECNT, NAC, NICNT, NIGTC, Su, TNTC, WBC; CEV, GW, HCSB, NASB, NCV, NET, NIV, NLT, NRSV, TEV]. The topic is miracles of healing [NASB], Jesus heals in response to faith [NLT], the daughter of Jairus [TNTC], restoration and healing [NET], raising Jairus' daughter [Su], Jairus' daughter and the woman who touched Jesus' cloak [TEV], Jairus' daughter and a woman with chronic bleeding [GW], a dying girl and a sick woman [CEV], a dead girl and a sick woman [NIV], a girl restored and a woman healed [HCSB], a girl restored to life and a woman healed [NRSV], Jesus heals the hemorrhaging woman and raises Jairus' daughter [AB, NAC, NIGTC, WBC], Jesus heals a sick woman and raises a dead girl [NICNT; NCV], authority over disease and death: flow of blood and Jairus' daughter [BECNT].

8:40 And when Jesus returned the crowd welcomed[a] him because they-were all expecting[b] him.

TEXT—Some manuscripts begin with ἐγένετο 'it happened'. GNT does not mention this variant. Ἐγένετο 'it happened' is read by KJV.

LEXICON—a. aorist mid. (deponent = act.) indic. of ἀποδέχομαι (LN **34.53**) (BAGD 1. p. 90): 'to welcome' [AB, Arn, BAGD, BECNT, **LN**, Lns, WBC; all versions except KJV, NLT], 'to receive' [KJV], 'to receive with open arms' [NLT].
- b. pres. act. participle of προσδοκάω (LN 30.55) (BAGD 1. p. 712): 'to expect' [BAGD, LN, Lns; GW, HCSB, NIV, REB], 'to wait for' [Arn, BAGD, BECNT, WBC; CEV, KJV, NASB, NCV, NET, NLT, NRSV, TEV], 'to await' [AB]. They were looking forward to Jesus' coming [NTC]. They probably desired to see more healings performed by Jesus [NIGTC].

QUESTION—Where was the crowd that was expecting Jesus?
Jesus returned to the other side of the lake [TH], the west shore of Lake Galilee [AB, NIBC, TG]. Probably he returned to Capernaum which served as his headquarters [Su]. This continues a reference to the crowds as in 8:4, 19 [NAC]. It seems that the crowds Jesus left behind had not left and were awaiting his return. However in Mark's account the crowd gathered soon after it was known that Jesus had returned. In Matthew's account a paralytic was healed and Matthew was called before Jairus arrived [Gdt]. When Jesus landed, the disciples of John the Baptist were waiting to question Jesus about fasting [NTC]. The crowd was not on the shore waiting for Jesus since from Matthew we learn that Jesus went home, healed the paralytic, and called Matthew (recorded by Luke in 5:17–39) before a crowd gathered at Matthew's house near the lake [Lns].

8:41 **And behold there-came a-man named Jairus and this (man) was ruler**[a] **of-the synagogue, and having-fallen**[b] **at Jesus' feet, he-was-pleading (with) him to-come to his house, 8:42 because he had an-only daughter about twelve years-old and she was-dying. And when he went the crowds were-crowding-around**[c] **him.**

LEXICON—a. ἄρχων (LN 37.56) (BAGD 2.a. p. 113): 'ruler' [Arn, BECNT, LN, Lns, WBC; KJV, NET, NIV], 'leader' [AB; GW, HCSB, NCV, NLT, NRSV], 'authority' [BAGD], 'official' [BAGD; NASB, TEV], 'president' [REB], 'the man in charge of (the Jewish meeting place)' [CEV]. He was one of the elders who managed the services at the synagogue [Lns, NIC, NTC]. Probably he was the main elder [BECNT]. He was the official who was in charge of the arrangements for the synagogue services [BECNT, MGC, NAC, NIGTC, TNTC, WBC]. See this word at 14:1; 18:18.
- b. aorist act. participle of πίπτω (LN 17.22) (BAGD 1.b.α. p. 659): 'to fall down' [BAGD, LN], 'to prostrate oneself' [LN]. The phrase 'falling down at Jesus' feet' [Arn; KJV, NLT, TEV] is also translated 'to fall at Jesus' feet' [AB, Lns, WBC; HCSB, NASB, NCV, NET, NIV, NRSV], 'to fall before Jesus' feet' [BECNT], 'to kneel down in front of Jesus' [CEV], 'to bow down in front of Jesus' [GW], 'to throw himself down at Jesus' feet' [REB]. The man's face touched the ground in front of Jesus' feet [TH]. This is an act of supplication [LN]. It shows his respect for Jesus [NTC].

c. imperf. act. indic. of συμπνίγω (LN 19.48) (BAGD 2. p. 779): 'to crowd around' [BAGD, LN; CEV, GW, NCV], 'to crowd' [TEV], 'to closely crowd' [Lns], 'to press' [BECNT], 'to press around' [NET], 'to press against' [Arn, LN; NASB], 'to press upon' [BAGD, NTC], 'to press in on' [NRSV], 'to press closely about' [AB], 'to crush' [NIV], 'to crush in on' [WBC], 'to nearly crush' [HCSB], 'to throng' [KJV], 'to surround' [NLT], not explicit [REB].

QUESTION—When did the daughter die?

The imperfect tense 'was dying' indicates that her sickness was terminal [Su] and she was about to die [TH]. In Matthew 9:18 the ruler says that she had just now died. Luke and Mark both describe the arrival of the girl's father who says that she is at the point of dying and the arrival of messengers who bring the news that she had died. Matthew has condensed the account by leaving out the messengers and having the father report that she has died [BECNT, Gdt, ICC, TNTC].

8:43 **And a-woman being with a-flow[a] of-blood for twelve years, who having-spent all the possessions[b] on-physicians was- not -able to-be-healed by anyone.**

TEXT—Some manuscripts omit the phrase ἰατροῖς προσαναλώσασα ὅλον τὸν βίον 'on physicians having spent all the possessions', other manuscripts that include this phrase add αὐτῆς 'of her', and other manuscripts add ἑαυτῆς 'of herself' following βίον 'possessions'. GNT reads ἰατροῖς προσαναλώσασα ὅλον τὸν βίον 'on physicians having spent all the possessions' in brackets and with a C decision, indicating that the Committee had difficulty making the decision. Whether versions include αὐτῆς 'of her' probably cannot be determined, since it is implied and would generally be supplied in a translation even if it is not read in the Greek text. This clause is omitted by NAC, NTC, Su, TNTC, WBC; GW, NASB, NCV, NET, NIV, REB.

LEXICON—a. ῥύσις (LN 23.182) (BAGD p. 738): 'flow' [BAGD]. The phrase 'being with a flow of blood' is translated 'being with an issue of blood' [Lns], 'having an issue of blood' [KJV], 'had suffered from an issue of blood' [Arn], 'had a flow of blood' [BECNT, WBC], 'had a hemorrhage' [NASB, NLT], 'had been suffering from a hemorrhage' [NET], 'had been suffering from hemorrhages' [AB; NASB; similarly REB], 'had been subject to hemorrhages' [NTC], 'had been subject to bleeding' [NIC], 'had been bleeding' [CEV, NCV], 'suffering from bleeding' [HCSB], 'suffering from chronic bleeding' [GW], 'had suffered from severe bleeding' [TEV]. The phrase is an idiom for a loss of blood due to menstrual bleeding [LN].

b. βίος (LN 57.18) (BAGD 3. p. 142): 'possessions, property, livelihood' [LN], 'means of subsistence' [BAGD]. The phrase 'all the possessions' is translated 'all her livelihood' [AB], 'all her living' [BECNT, Lns; KJV], 'all her property' [Arn], 'all she had' [HCSB, NASB, TEV], 'everything she had' [CEV, NLT], not included [NTC, WBC; GW, NASB, NCV, NET, NIV, REB].

QUESTION—What was wrong with the woman?

She had a hemorrhage [BNTC, MGC, NIC, NICNT, NIGTC, TH; NASB, NET, NRSV, REB]. It could be a uterine hemorrhage [BECNT, MGC, NAC, NIGTC]. It was a menstrual disorder [TG, WBC]. It doesn't mean that the bleeding never stopped for twelve years, rather the bleeding occurred periodically throughout the twelve years [TG]. It cannot be determined what was wrong with her [Lns].

8:44 **Having-approached from-behind she-touched the edge[a] of-his garment and immediately the flow of-her blood stopped.**

TEXT—Instead ὄπισθεν ἥψατο 'from behind touched', some manuscripts read ἥψατο τοῦ κρασπέδου 'touched the fringe', and other manuscripts read ἥψατο 'touched'. GNT reads ὄπισθεν ἥψατο τοῦ κρασπέδου 'from behind touched the edge' with a B decision, indicating that the text is almost certain.

LEXICON—a. κράσπεδον (LN 6.180) (BAGD 1. p. 448): 'edge' [BAGD, WBC; GW, NCV, NET, NIV, REB, TEV], 'hem' [BAGD], 'border' [AB, BAGD; KJV], 'fringe' [BECNT, LN; NASB, NLT, NRSV], 'tassel' [Arn, Lns, NTC; HCSB], not explicit [CEV].

QUESTION—Why did the woman come up from behind Jesus?

The woman did not want to be noticed [BECNT, ICC, Lns, NTC]. She wanted to keep her ailment hidden [BECNT, Lns]. Her bleeding made her unclean [AB, BECNT, Gdt, ICC, Lns, MGC, NIBC, NICNT, NIGTC, Su, TG, TNTC, WBC], so she did not want to have her condition made public [ICC, MGC] and she knew that she shouldn't have been in the crowd [WBC]. She was ashamed and wanted to keep her ailment hidden [Lns]. She thought that Jesus would not even notice that she had approached him and thus not call attention to her [NTC]. Perhaps she thought Jesus would refuse to touch an unclean woman [BECNT].

QUESTION—What part of Jesus' garment did she touch?

The interpretation of this passage depends upon how strictly Jesus may have followed the Mosaic law in regard to what he wore [LN (6.18)].

1. She touched the edge of the garment [AB, BNTC, Su, WBC]. She touched just the extreme edge of his cloak because she thought that help would come from even this [AB].
2. She touched a tassel or the fringe of the garment [Arn, EGT, Gdt, ICC, Lns, MGC, NIBC, NIGTC, NTC, Rb, TG, TH, TNTC, WBC]. Pious Jews had tassels on the four corners of an outer garment [ICC, Lns, NIGTC] as a symbol of their devotion to God [TG]. The square upper garment would have a fringe or tassel and the garment was thrown over the shoulder so that it would have been easy to touch the tassel at the back since it did not reach the ground [Gdt, TH]. She touched the tuft that was swinging from the back of his robe [Gdt, NTC].

QUESTION—Why did she touch the garment?
She had faith, but it was mingled with superstition and she thought that Jesus' garment could heal magically [ICC]. To touch Jesus' clothes was to have access to his power, not a magical cure [BECNT]. She was so confident that God's power was working through Jesus that she thought it would heal her even if she only touched the edge of his garment [Su].

8:45 And Jesus said, Who (is) the (one) who-touched me? And everyone denying (it), Peter said, Master,[a] the crowds surround you and are-pressing against (you).

TEXT—Following ὁ Πέτρος 'Peter', some manuscripts add καὶ οἱ σὺν αὐτῷ 'and the ones with him' and other manuscripts add καὶ οἱ μετ' αὐτοῦ 'and the ones with him'. GNT reads ὁ Πέτρος 'Peter' with a B decision, indicating that the text is almost certain. The two added phrases are synonymous in meaning, so it probably cannot be determined which phrase is followed by those who include the addition. One of these additional phrases (presumably καὶ οἱ μετ' αὐτοῦ 'and the ones with him', since this is the reading of Textus Receptus) is read by Lns and KJV.

TEXT—Instead of καὶ ἀποθλίβουσιν 'and are pressing upon', some manuscripts read καὶ ἀποθλίβουσιν, καὶ λέγεις, Τίς ὁ ἁψάμενός μου; 'and press upon, and do you say, Who (is) the one having touched me?'; other manuscripts read καὶ ἀποθλίβουσιν, καὶ λέγεις, Τίς μου ἥψατο; 'press upon, and do you say, Who touched me?'; and other manuscripts read καὶ λέγεις, Τίς μου ἥψατο; 'and do you say, Who touched me?' GNT reads καὶ ἀποθλίβουσιν 'and are pressing upon' with a B decision, indicating that the text is almost certain. Καὶ ἀποθλίβουσιν, καὶ λέγεις, Τίς ὁ ἁψάμενός μου; 'and press upon, and do you say, Who (is) the one having touched me?' is probably read by KJV, since this is the reading of Textus Receptus, although the KJV is more literally a translation of καὶ ἀποθλίβουσίν, καὶ λέγεις, Τίς μου ἥψατο; 'press upon, and do you say, Who touched me?'

LEXICON—a. ἐπιστάτης (LN 87.50) (BAGD p. 300): 'master'. See translations of this word at 5:5. This word also occurs at 8:24; 9:33, 49; 17:13.

QUESTION—Did Jesus know who had touched him?
1. Jesus really did know that it was the woman [Alf, Arn, BECNT, ICC, Lns, NIC, NTC, TNTC, WBC]. He was not asking for information. He asked for the sake of the woman since she needed to admit what she had done [Alf, ICC, Lns, NIC, NTC, TNTC]. The question was asked to cause the woman to confess that she had touched him for healing [BECNT]. It was necessary that her cure be known to all her acquaintances so they would no longer regard her as unclean [TNTC]. It was also necessary to help her realize that her superstition of healing by a touch of Jesus' tassel was not the same as faith that is established by a personal relationship [TNTC]. When she touched him, Jesus supernaturally knew all about her so that his

question was asked for her sake and also for the sake of the people around him. She was not to feel that she had done something improper or magical in being healed or that she needed to be ashamed of her ailment and its removal [Lns].
2. Jesus did not know who it was [Gdt, NAC, TG]. It was not in character for Jesus to pretend to be ignorant of this [Gdt]. The reason Jesus knew that someone had touched him is given in the next verse [TG].

QUESTION—What is implied by Peter's answer?
Peter felt that Jesus' question was a bit foolish [AB, NAC]. The question was meaningless since so many people had touched Jesus [Arn, TNTC]. Being crowded by so many people made it inevitable that Jesus would be touched many times [Lns]. Peter was speaking about unintentional touching due to jostling of the crowd instead of an intentional touch that Jesus was referring to [BECNT, NTC, TH].

8:46 And Jesus said, Someone touched me, because I knew^a power having-gone-out from me.

LEXICON—a. aorist act. indic. of γινώσκω (LN 28.1) (BAGD 4.a. p. 161): 'to know' [LN], 'to perceive' [BAGD]. The clause 'I knew power having gone out from me' is translated with the object of knowing to be the release of power: 'I know power has gone out of me' [GW], 'I know that power has gone out from me' [BECNT; HCSB, NET, NIV], 'I noticed that power went forth from me' [Arn], 'I was aware that power had gone out of/from me' [NTC, WBC; NASB], 'I myself realized power having gone out from me' [Lns], 'I felt power going/go out from me' [CEV, NCV], 'I felt that power had gone out from me' [REB], 'I felt healing power go out from me' [NLT], 'I noticed that power had gone from me' [NRSV], 'I perceive virtue is gone out of me' [KJV]. The clause is translated with the object of knowing to be the touch of someone: 'I know, for power has gone forth from me' [AB], 'I knew it when power went out of me' [TEV].

QUESTION—What was the power that had gone out from Jesus?
It was Jesus' power, that is, part of his power [TH]. It was God's power which flowed from Jesus to heal the woman [BECNT, NICNT, NIGTC, TG]. Some think that the healing power drained Jesus' energy [Rb, Su]. But others think that there was no exhaustion concerned with it [Lns].
1. It was an intentional flow of power for healing [Alf, BECNT, Lns, NIC, NIGTC, TNTC, WBC]. Jesus knew that the woman had touched him in faith and therefore he caused his healing power to flow to her [NIC]. Jesus responded to the woman's touch by consciously willing his power heal her [Lns].
2. It was an unintentional flow of power for healing [Gdt, Su, TG, TH]. Jesus had no conscious participation; it was God's power working through him and this does not mean that all of Jesus' power had left him [TG].

The healing power had not been consciously used by Jesus so when he felt drained of energy he knew that someone had been healed [Su].

8:47 And the woman having-seen that she-had- not -escaped-notice, came trembling and having-fallen-down-before[a] him, she-declared before all the people for what reason she-touched him and how she-was-healed immediately.

TEXT—Following ἀπήγγειλεν 'she declared', some manuscripts add αὐτῷ 'to him', although GNT does not mention this variant. Αὐτῷ 'to him' is read by KJV.

LEXICON—a. aorist act. participle of προσπίπτω (LN 17.22) (BAGD 1. p. 718): 'to fall down before'. See this word at 5:8; 8:28.

QUESTION—Where did the woman come from and why did she tremble?

The woman may have hidden herself in the crowd [Alf]. The woman came forward to Jesus [TH]. From the words 'she came', it appears that she had already started to leave [NTC] and she came back [TNTC]. She had gone a little way from Jesus after she had been healed [ICC]. Trembling indicated her fear [BECNT, NAC, TH]. She trembled because she was nervous in having to speak about her problem before all those people [Rb, TNTC]. She feared that she had done wrong in secretly touching Jesus' robe [Gdt, ICC]. She thought she might be scolded by Jesus [AB, Arn, Lns]. She feared that her healing would be cancelled [TNTC].

QUESTION—Did the woman address the crowd?

She spoke in the presence of all the people [Arn, TNTC]. She spoke to Jesus, but loudly enough so that all the people could hear [TH].

8:48 And he-said to-her, Daughter,[a] your faith has-saved[b] you. Go in peace.[c]

TEXT—Instead of Θυγάτηρ 'Daughter', some manuscripts read Θάρσει, θυγάτηρ 'Have courage, daughter'. GNT does not mention this variant. Θάρσει, θυγάτηρ 'Have courage, daughter' is read by KJV.

LEXICON—a. θυγάτηρ (LN 9.47) (BAGD 2.a. p. 364): 'daughter' [AB, Arn, BAGD, BECNT, LN, Lns, NTC, WBC; all versions except CEV, NCV, TEV], 'my daughter' [TEV], 'lady, woman' [LN], 'dear woman' [NCV], not explicit [CEV].

b. perf. act. indic. of σῴζω (LN 23.136, 21.27) (BAGD 1.c. p. 798): 'to save' [LN (21.27)], 'to save or free from disease' [BAGD], 'to heal, to cure, to make well' [LN (13.136)]. The clause 'your faith has saved you' [BECNT, Lns, WBC] is also translated 'your faith has healed you' [Arn; NIV, REB], 'your faith has made you well' [NTC; GW, HCSB, NASB, NET, NLT, NRSV, TEV], 'you are now well because of your faith' [CEV], 'you are made well because you believed' [NCV], 'your faith has made you whole' [KJV], 'it is your faith that has brought you salvation' [AB]. Whereas most translations focus on the healing, some say that her salvation went beyond physical healing to include spiritual healing [Gdt,

NAC, WBC]. This same clause is used at 7:50 in respect to being saved spiritually. This clause is identical to the ones in 7:50; 17:19; 18:42.
  c. εἰρήνη (LN 22.42) (BAGD 2. p. 227): 'peace' [BAGD, LN]. For the words 'Go in peace' see 7:50.
QUESTION—Why did Jesus address the woman as 'daughter'?
  This is a friendly greeting used to address a woman [TH], and it shows some affectionate concern [AB, LN (9.47), NAC, NTC]. Although Jesus spoke to her as a father would speak to a daughter [NTC], she may not have been any younger than he was [NTC, TG], and possibly she was older than Jesus [BECNT].
QUESTION—In what way did the woman's faith heal her?
  The woman's faith was the channel through which Jesus healed her [NTC]. This does not mean that her faith was the direct cause, rather it was the instrument through which Jesus healed her [Lns]. Because the woman believed, Jesus could heal her [TG]. Her faith was the subjective condition that made her receptive to God's power working in her [WBC]. Her faith caused her to come to Jesus and then Jesus healed her by his power and will [Lns].

8:49 (While) he was- still -speaking, someone comes from (the house) of-the synagogue-ruler saying, Your daughter has-died. No-longer bother[a] the teacher.
TEXT—Following λέγων 'saying', some manuscripts add αὐτῷ 'to him'. GNT does not mention this variant. Αὐτῷ 'to him' is read by KJV.
TEXT—Instead of μηκέτι 'no longer', some manuscripts read μή 'not'. GNT reads μηκέτι 'no longer' with a B decision, indicating that the text is almost certain. Μή 'not' is read by KJV.
LEXICON—a. pres. act. impera. of σκύλλω (LN 22.23) (BAGD 2. p. 758): 'to bother' [BAGD, LN, NTC, WBC; CEV, GW, HCSB, NCV, NIV, TEV], 'to trouble' [AB, Arn, BAGD, BECNT, LN, Lns; KJV, NASB, NET, NLT, NRSV, REB], 'to annoy' [BAGD].
QUESTION—In what way would Jairus be bothering Jesus?
  He would be bothering Jesus if he continued to ask Jesus to come to his house [TG]. The reason for the trip was gone [WBC]. The messenger assumed that since the child has died, there was nothing that Jesus could do [Lns]. It was assumed that Jesus' power would be useless in the face of death [Lns, NAC, NTC, TNTC], and death has cancelled all hope for the girl [BECNT, NTC].

8:50 But having-heard Jesus answered[a] him, Do- not -be-afraid, only believe,[b] and she-will-be-healed.[c]
TEXT—Following αὐτῷ 'him', some manuscripts add λέγων 'saying'. GNT does not mention this variant. Λέγων 'saying' is read by KJV.
LEXICON—a. aorist pass. (deponent = act.) indic. of ἀποκρίνομαι (LN 33.28): 'to answer' [Arn, Lns; HCSB, KJV, NASB], 'to reply' [AB; NRSV], 'to respond' [WBC], 'to speak, to declare' [LN], 'to say' [BECNT, LN, NTC;

NCV, NIV, NLT, REB, TEV], 'to tell' [CEV, GW, NET]. Jesus was not answering the messenger, but speaking to Jairus [TG, TH]. In this context the verb does not mean 'to answer' but 'to respond' [WBC]. Here the answer is a response to the situation in which Jairus did not know what to do after hearing this daughter had died [Lns].
  b. aorist act. impera. of πιστεύω (LN 31.85) (BAGD 2.c. p. 662): 'to believe' [Arn, BAGD, BECNT, LN, Lns, NTC, WBC; all versions except CEV, NLT, REB], 'to trust' [BAGD, LN; NLT], 'to have faith' [AB, LN; CEV, REB].
  c. fut. pass. indic. of σῴζω (LN 23.136) (BAGD 1.c. p. 798): 'to be healed' [Arn, LN; NET, NIV], 'to be made well' [LN, NTC; HCSB, NASB], 'to be made whole' [KJV], 'to be cured' [LN], 'to be saved or freed from disease' [BAGD], 'to be saved' [AB, BECNT, Lns, WBC; NRSV]. This passive form is also translated actively with the daughter as the subject: 'to get well' [CEV, GW], 'to be well' [NCV, REB, TEV], 'to be all right' [NLT]. This refers to physical deliverance [BECNT]. This verb does not apply to the exorcism of demon possession as in 8:36 or with the healing of an illness as in 8:48, but here it is applied to death and means that she shall live again [TH]. The girl will be saved from death [AB]. She will be restored to life and to health [TG].

QUESTION—Now that the daughter had died, what was the father to believe?
  Instead of being afraid that nothing could now be done, Jairus must trust in the power of God that was in Jesus [NIGTC]. He was to trust in Jesus [NAC; NLT]. He was to believe the promise that Jesus gives here that his daughter will be saved from death [Lns, NTC]. He was to believe Jesus' promise that the child would be healed, or rather in this situation, brought back to life [NTC]. He must believe that Jesus can restore the girl to life [Su, TG]. He must have confidence in God's power and compassion to deliver the child from death [BECNT].

8:51 **And having-come into the house he-did- not -permit anyone to-enter with him except Peter and John and James and the child's father and mother.**

TEXT—Instead of τινα σὺν αὐτῷ 'anyone with him', some manuscripts read οὐδένα 'no one'. GNT does not mention this variant. Οὐδένα 'no one' is read by KJV.

QUESTION—What place didn't Jesus permit anyone to enter?
  1. Jesus permitted none of the crowd accompanying him to enter the house [Crd, NTC, TH, TNTC, WBC]: he did not permit anyone to enter the house. Probably the mother met the party outside the house [WBC]. Jesus dismissed the crowd that had accompanied him [NTC]. Mourners were already in the house [NTC].
  2. Jesus permitted none of the people already in the house to enter the room where the corpse was [Alf, Gdt, ICC, Lns, My, NIC, NIGTC, Su, TG]: he did not permit anyone to enter the room where the girl was laid out. Jesus

and his disciples had already entered the house where the mother was waiting [ICC].

8:52 And all were-weeping^a and were-mourning^b (for) her. But he-said, Do- not -weep, because she-did- not -die but is-sleeping. **8:53** And they-were-ridiculing^c him knowing that she-had-died.

LEXICON—a. imperf. act. indic. of κλαίω (LN 25.138) (BAGD 1. p. 433): 'to weep' [BAGD, BECNT, LN, NTC, WBC; KJV, NASB, NLT, NRSV, REB], 'to cry' [AB, BAGD; CEV, GW, HCSB, NCV, TEV], 'to wail' [Arn, LN, Lns; NET, NIV], 'to lament' [LN]. There is an emphasis on the noise that accompanies weeping [LN], and describes mourning for the dead [BAGD].
  b. imperf. mid. indic. of κόπτομαι (LN 52.1) (BAGD 2. p. 444): 'to mourn' [BAGD, BECNT, LN; HCSB, NET, NIV, TEV], 'to lament' [Arn, LN; NASB, REB], 'to weep' [CEV], 'to wail' [NTC; NLT, NRSV], 'to bewail' [KJV], 'to beat one's breast' [AB, BAGD, WBC], 'to beat oneself' [Lns], 'to feel sad' [NCV], 'to show how sad one is' [GW]. To beat one's breast in mourning means to wail or mourn over someone [NIGTC, NTC]. This was the Jewish way of demonstrating grief [Lns]. This verb refers more to outward behavior and gestures than to the sounds of lamentation [TH]. This expression of grief was accompanied by weeping [TG].
  c. imperf. act. indic. of καταγελάω (LN **33.410**) (BAGD p. 409): 'to ridicule' [BAGD, **LN**], 'to laugh at' [AB, Arn, BAGD, BECNT, LN, WBC; all versions except KJV, NET, TEV], 'to laugh to scorn' [Lns; KJV], 'to laugh in one's face' [NTC], 'to make fun of' [LN; NET, TEV]. This probably describes bursts of derisive laughter at Jesus' statement [NTC].

QUESTION—Who were weeping and where were they?
  This refers to the people who were already in the house [Lns, NTC, TH], but they were not in the room where the corpse was [Gdt, ICC]. According to Matthew 9:24–25 and Mark 5:40 they had been in the house and Jesus made them go outside. This refers to neighbors, relatives, and professional mourners [AB, Gdt, NAC].

QUESTION—What is meant by saying that the girl was sleeping?
  The crowd thought that Jesus, who had not seen the child, was saying that she was not dead but only sleeping. They did not recognize that Jesus used the term 'sleep' as a metaphor for death [NAC]. However, they knew that she had died and ridiculed him [NIGTC, Su, WBC]. Natural sleep is ended by awakening and the dead child was to be awakened in the sense of living again [ICC, MGC, NTC]. Death was not permanent for the girl, just a temporary rest that would last until Jesus resurrected her [AB, BECNT, NICNT].

8:54 And he having-taken her hand called-out[a] saying, Child, get-up.[b] **8:55** And her spirit returned[c] and she-got-up immediately and he-gave-orders (for something) to-be-given to-her to-eat.

TEXT—In 8:54, following αὐτὸς δέ 'and he', some manuscripts add ἐκβαλὼν ἔξω πάντας καί 'having put all outside and'. GNT does not mention this variant. Ἐκβαλὼν ἔξω πάντας καί 'having put all outside and' is read by KJV.

LEXICON—a. aorist act. indic. of φωνέω (LN 33.77) (BAGD 1.b. p. 870): 'to call out' [BAGD, BECNT, LN, NTC, WBC; GW, HCSB, NRSV, TEV], 'to call to' [NCV, REB], 'to call' [Arn, Lns; KJV, NASB], 'to speak loudly' [BAGD, LN], 'to cry out' [LN], 'to speak to' [AB], 'to say' [CEV, NET, NIV], 'to say in a loud voice' [NLT]. Raising the voice is normal in awaking someone from sleep [ICC]. It was not as though the dead have to be awakened with a loud voice, but Jesus called out to make plain to all those present that she arose at his command [Rb]. This may imply that her spirit was at a distance and had to be summoned back to her body [NIGTC].

b. aorist pass. impera. of ἐγείρω (LN 23.94) (BAGD 1.b p. 214): 'to get up' [AB, BAGD, LN, NTC; all versions except KJV, NASB, NCV], 'to rise' [WBC], 'to arise' [Arn, BECNT; KJV, NASB], 'to rise up' [Lns], 'to stand up' [NCV]. Although the verb can mean to stand up or to wake up, it also refers to rising to life [LN]. It is used of awakening someone from sleep [AB, BNTC], or from death [BAGD]. It is used here of both to arise from the dead and to sit up [NIGTC]. It is such a general word that here it probably means no more than to get up [WBC]. See this word used at 7:14 in connection with the widow's son.

c. aorist act. indic. of ἐπιστρέφω (LN 15.90) (BAGD 1.b.α. p. 301): 'to return' [BAGD, LN]. The phrase 'her spirit returned' [Arn, BECNT, Lns, NTC, WBC; HCSB, NASB, NET, NIV, NRSV, REB] is also translated 'her spirit came again' [KJV], 'her spirit came back into her' [NCV], 'her life returned' [NLT, TEV], 'her breath returned' [AB], 'she came back to life' [CEV, GW].

QUESTION—Why did Jesus take the girl's hand?
Taking the hand and speaking loudly is normal when awakening someone from sleep [ICC, Lns], and these two actions were the means of the miracle [ICC, Rb]. Touching her hand was a touch of power [Su]. Or, rather than transferring power, Jesus took her hand as a gesture that went with his command [Lns] and he did this in order to help her sit up [NIGTC]. Jesus didn't have to touch her to heal her, but he touched her to show his compassion [BECNT, MGC], and also to help her arise [BECNT].

QUESTION—Where did the girl's spirit return from?
The girl's spirit had survived death and had been separated from her body [Arn, BECNT, NAC, NIGTC], but it is of no interest to Luke as to where the girl's spirit was or what it experienced while her body was dead [NAC]. It means that the girl's breath returned as a sign that she was again alive [AB,

NIBC]. 'Spirit' may mean no more than a life force again animating the body [TH, WBC] and this means that she came back to life from death [TH; NET].

8:56 **And her parents were-astounded.**[a] **And he-ordered them to-tell no-one the (thing) having-happened.**

LEXICON—a. aorist act. indic. of ἐξίστημι (LN 25.220) (BAGD 2.b. p. 276): 'to be astounded'. See translations of this word at 2:47; 24.22.

QUESTION—Why did Jesus tell the parents not to tell anyone about the miracle?

Jesus wanted the parents to quietly remain with their daughter and worship God while the three disciples told the others [NIC]. The parents were to concentrate on their daughter's welfare [TNTC]. The appearance of the girl would make the miracle known and Jesus did not want the parents to be heralds of what Jesus had done [Lns]. Jesus didn't want the crowds to use this miracle as a reason for making him a political figure [Su, WBC].

DISCOURSE UNIT: 9:1–50 [NAC, NICNT, NIGTC; REB]. The topic is Jesus and the Twelve [NAC, NIGTC; REB], Jesus' identity and the nature of discipleship [NICNT].

DISCOURSE UNIT: 9:1–17 [NICNT]. The topic is the mission of the Twelve.

DISCOURSE UNIT: 9:1–11 [NASB]. The topic is the ministry of the Twelve.

DISCOURSE UNIT: 9:1–9 [NIV]. The topic is Jesus sends out the Twelve.

DISCOURSE UNIT: 9:1–6 [AB, BECNT, NAC, NIGTC, Su, TNTC, WBC; CEV, GW, HCSB, NCV, NET, NLT, NRSV, TEV]. The topic is Jesus sends out the twelve apostles [GW, NCV, NET, NLT], Jesus sends out the twelve disciples [TEV], the mission of the Twelve [AB, NAC, NIGTC, Su, TNTC; NRSV], instructions for the Twelve Apostles [CEV], commissioning the Twelve [HCSB], commissioned authority revealed [BECNT], sharing in Jesus' ministry [WBC].

9:1 **And having-called-together**[a] **the Twelve, he-gave them power**[b] **and authority**[c] **over all the demons and to-heal diseases**

TEXT—Instead of δώδεκα 'twelve', some manuscripts read δώδεκα μαθητὰς αὐτοῦ 'twelve disciples of him', others read μαθητὰς αὐτοῦ 'disciples of him', and still others read δώδεκα ἀποστόλους 'twelve apostles'. GNT reads δώδεκα 'twelve' with a B decision, indicating that the text is almost certain. Δώδεκα μαθητὰς αὐτοῦ 'twelve disciples of him' is read by KJV.

LEXICON—a. aorist mid. participle of συγκαλέω (LN 33.309) (BAGD 2. p. 773): 'to call together' [AB, Arn, BECNT, LN, Lns, NTC, WBC; all versions except HCSB], 'to call to one's side' [BAGD], 'to summon' [BAGD; HCSB]. He called them out from the larger company of disciples which included those mentioned in 8:1–3 [EGT]. The verb implies that he summoned some who were not then present [Lns, NIGTC, TNTC]. Some

382 LUKE 9:1

of the apostles who were fishermen had their own homes in Capernaum and may have been absent at the time [Lns, TNTC].
   b. δύναμις (LN 76.1) (BAGD 1. p. 207): 'power' [AB, Arn, BAGD, BECNT, LN, Lns, NTC, WBC; all versions except CEV]. The phrase 'power and authority' is translated 'complete power' [CEV].
   c. ἐξουσία (LN 37.35) (BAGD 3. p. 278): 'authority' [AB, Arn, BAGD, BECNT, LN, Lns, NTC, WBC; all versions except CEV]. This pertains to the right to control or govern [LN]. See this word at 10:19.
QUESTION—What is meant by giving the apostles power and authority over demons?
   This combination is also ascribed to Jesus: 'with authority and power he commands the unclean spirits and they come out' (4:36). Jesus gave them power similar to the power that was inherent in himself [Lns]. The power was the kind of power that enabled Jesus to heal (4:14, 36; 5:17; 6:19; 8:46) [NIGTC]. Some see no sharp distinction between power and authority [TG; CEV] and the two are translated 'complete power' [CEV]. Others make a distinction between the two nouns. Besides giving them power, he gave them the authority to use that power [BECNT, EGT, Gdt, ICC, NIC, NIGTC, TH, TNTC, WBC]. He gave them authority or right to cast out demons and he also gave them the power or ability to carry out that act [Arn]. The authority was both the right and the ability to use the power to continue the miracles that Jesus performed [Lns, NTC].
QUESTION—How is the grammatically awkward [AB, WBC] clause 'and to heal diseases' connected?
   1. The infinitive 'to heal' depends on 'power and authority' [AB, Arn, BECNT, EGT, ICC, Lns, NIGTC, Su, TH, WBC; CEV, GW, HCSB, NIV, NLT, REB, TEV]: and power and authority to heal diseases. He gave them power and authority to drive out all demons and to cure diseases [NIV, NLT, REB, TEV]. This does not grammatically parallel '*over* all the demons' [AB]. This clause is in a subordinate position so that 'power and authority over all demons' is the main emphasis [EGT].
   2. The infinitive 'to heal' depends on the verb 'he gave them' [Gdt; NCV]: he gave them power and authority over all the demons and he gave them the ability to heal diseases. There is no authority involved with healing diseases [Gdt]. It is implied that he gave them 'the ability' to heal sicknesses [NCV].

9:2 **and he-sent them to-preach**[a] **the kingdom of-God and to-heal the sick.**
TEXT—Instead of the adjective phrase τοὺς ἀσθενεῖς 'the sick' at the end of the verse, some manuscripts read the participial phrase τοὺς ἀσθενοῦντας 'the ones being sick', other manuscripts read πάντας τοὺς ἀσθενοῦντας 'all the ones being sick', and other manuscripts omit this phrase. GNT reads τοὺς ἀσθενεῖς 'the sick' with a C decision, indicating that the Committee had difficulty making the decision. Versions would probably not distinguish

clearly between the adjective phrase τοὺς ἀσθενεῖς 'the sick' and the participial phrase τοὺς ἀσθενοῦντας 'the ones being sick'.

LEXICON—a. pres. act. infin. of κηρύσσω (LN 33.256) (BAGD 2.b.b. p. 431): 'to preach'. See translations of this word at 3:3. This word also occurs at 4:18, 19, 44; 8:1, 39; 12:3; 24:47.

QUESTION—What was involved in preaching the kingdom of God?

They were to proclaim the coming of the kingdom [Gdt]. They were to cause the lost to realize that God is king and that he is going to establish his rule in the world through the power of the Messiah and eventually destroy all opposition [NIC]. They were to proclaim salvation by the reign of God in people's hearts [NTC].

QUESTION—What is included in the second part of the mission, 'and healing the sick'?

They were to heal the sick while preaching the kingdom of God [Gdt]. The miracles of healing were of secondary importance and served to prove the reality of God's rule [NIC]. Healing the sick includes both the curing of diseases and the expulsion of demons as mentioned in 8:1 [AB, Lns, NICNT, NTC].

9:3 And he-said to them, Take nothing for the journey, neither a-staff[a] nor a-traveler's-bag[b] nor bread[c] nor silver[d] nor have two shirts[e] apiece.

TEXT—Instead of the singular ῥάβδον 'staff', some manuscripts read the plural ῥάβδους 'staves' although GNT does not mention this variant. The plural ῥάβδους 'staves' is read by KJV.

TEXT—Some manuscripts omit ἀνά 'apiece'. GNT reads [ἀνά] 'apiece' in brackets with a C decision, indicating that the Committee had difficulty making the decision.

LEXICON—a. ῥάβδος (LN 6.218) (BAGD p. 733): 'staff' [Arn, BAGD, BECNT, Lns, NTC, WBC; KJV, NASB, NET, NIV, NRSV], 'walking stick' [AB, LN; CEV, GW, HCSB, NCV, NLT, TEV], 'stick' [REB]. This was a walking stick used as a walking aid for long journeys [MGC, NIGTC, Su, TG, WBC], not a club for protection [Su, WBC] although it could be used as a weapon [AB].

b. πήρα (LN 6.145) (BAGD p. 656): 'traveler's bag' [BAGD, LN, NTC; NLT], 'traveling bag' [CEV, GW, HCSB], 'bag' [BECNT, WBC; NASB, NCV, NET, NIV, NRSV], 'pack' [REB], 'knapsack' [AB, Arn], 'pouch' [Lns], 'scrip' [KJV], 'beggar's bag' [TEV]. It was a bag that travelers or beggars used to carry their possessions [LN]. See this word at 9:3, 10:4, 22:35.

c. ἄρτος (LN 5.8) (BAGD 1.a. p. 110): 'bread' [AB, Arn, BAGD, BECNT, Lns, NTC, WBC; HCSB, KJV, NASB, NCV, NET, NIV, NRSV, REB], 'loaf of bread' [LN], 'food' [CEV, GW, NLT, TEV]. The word is used generically for food [NTC].

d. ἀργύριον (LN 6.73) (BAGD 2.b. p. 104): 'silver' [BAGD, Lns], 'silver money, silver coin' [BAGD, LN], 'money' [AB, Arn, BECNT, NTC,

WBC; all versions]. This was the common metal for Greek coins [AB]. This refers to silver coins, that is, small change [NTC].

e. χιτών (LN 6.176) (BAGD p. 882): 'shirt'. See this word at 3:11; 6:29.

QUESTION—What was the πήρα 'bag' that they were not to take on the journey?

1. It was a traveler's bag used for carrying provisions [Arn, Lns, MGC, NAC, NIGTC, NTC, Su, TG, TH, TNTC, WBC; CEV, GW, HCSB, NLT, REB]. It was a kind of knapsack to carry supplies that would be needed while traveling [Arn, NAC, NTC]. Since they would eat in the homes where they stayed, they did not need to carry along provisions [Su]. It would normally be used to carry bread, but they were not to take bread with them [Lns, NIGTC].
2. It was a beggar's bag used for receiving hand-outs [BECNT, NIC, WBC; TEV]. The purse would hold the money they received by begging [BECNT]. Jesus was forbidding his disciples to be like representatives of other religions who begged for a living [NIC, WBC].

QUESTION—Why should they not take a staff with them and how is this reconciled with Mark's account which says they were to take a staff?

A staff would make them appear to be like other religious preachers and they should not resemble them [NIGTC]. They should avoid such encumbrances that would have to be looked after [Su]. They were to make no special preparations for the mission, but instead they were to go as they were [ICC]. Mark 6:8 has the instruction that they should take nothing on the road except a staff. Perhaps in Luke it means to take no additional staff [Gdt, NIC, NTC, TNTC; NET], although it is strange that anyone would want a spare staff [BECNT, TNTC]. They were not to buy a new staff for the journey [Arn, Lns] but could take along a staff if they already had one [Arn]. It could be that the original Aramaic command was elliptical and filled out differently by Mark and Luke [NIC, TNTC]. Perhaps Luke used a secondary source that prohibits the staff [WBC]. Perhaps Mark adapted the demands to fit in with harsher conditions of later missionary journeys [NIGTC].

QUESTION—Why were they not allowed to have two shirts?

They were not to take along a spare shirt [Arn, EGT, My, NIGTC, WBC], a change of clothes [CEV, GW], or extra clothes [NCV]. Since no traveler's bag was allowed, an extra shirt would have to be worn, explaining the command 'do not put on two shirts' in Mark 6:8 [ICC, Lns]. They are not to wear two shirts at once [Gdt, ICC, Lns, TH].

9:4 And whatever house you-may-enter into, stay there and go-out[a] from-there.

LEXICON—a. pres. mid./pass. (deponent = act.) impera. of ἐξέρχομαι (LN 15.40) (BAGD 1.a.α. p. 274): 'to go out' [BAGD, BECNT, LN], 'to go forth' [AB], 'to set out' [Arn], 'to go on' [WBC], 'to leave' [all versions except KJV, NLT], 'to depart' [KJV], 'to depart out of, to leave from within' [LN], 'to keep going out' [Lns], not explicit [NLT].

QUESTION—What is meant by the command to stay in the house they enter?
Since they took along no resources, they depended on the goodwill of those who accepted the message in each of the towns they went to [NIGTC]. Upon entering a town, they would likely be invited to stay at someone's house while they remained in that town [Lns] and no matter how poor the lodging was, they were not to seek better lodging in the town [AB, Lns, NIC, TH, WBC]. They must not be picky so that they leave one home for another that is more desirable and offers better food [Arn, Lns, NIVS, NTC]. It would create rivalry to accept hospitality from several families in succession [Gdt]. Of course this instruction does not mean that they were to stay inside the house during their entire stay in the town, rather, they were to stay as a guest in the home [TG]. This house would be their headquarters for their stay in the town [Gdt, ICC, MGC, Su].

QUESTION—What is meant by the last clause 'and go out from there'?
1. This simply enlarges on the command to stay in the house and adds that they will stay until they go out of that town to another town [Arn, BECNT, EGT, Gdt, ICC, NIC, NIGTC, NTC, TG, TH, TNTC, WBC; all versions except KJV]: stay as a guest in that house until you leave town. They should give no indication that they are making a good thing out of their missionary work by moving to different houses that offer better lodging [NIGTC].
2. This refers to using one house as a base for going out to evangelize in that town [AB, Lns]. Here 'to go out' is an iterative present tense that means to keep going out from the house day by day as long as they stay in the town [Lns]. They would go forth to preach and to heal [AB].

9:5 And as-many-as do- not -welcome[a] you, going-out from that city shake-off the dust from your feet for a-testimony[b] against them. **9:6** And going-out they-were-going-around throughout the villages announcing-the-good-news[c] and healing everywhere.

TEXT—In 9:5, before τὸν κονιορτόν 'the dust', some manuscripts add καί 'even'. GNT does not mention this variant. Καί 'even' is read by Gdt and KJV.

LEXICON—a. pres. mid./pass. (deponent = act.) subj. of δέχομαι (LN 34.53) (BAGD 1. p. 177): 'to welcome' [AB, BAGD, LN, Lns, NTC; CEV, GW, HCSB, NCV, NIV, NRSV, TEV], 'to receive' [Arn, BAGD, BECNT, LN, WBC; KJV, NASB, NET, NLT, REB], 'to have as a guest' [LN]. It refers here to rejecting the apostles and this is equivalent to not receiving the good news they preached, and it implies that that they would not receive Jesus who brought the good news [NAC]. See this word at 9:53; 10:8.
b. μαρτύριον (LN 33.264) (B 1.a. p. 493): 'testimony' [BAGD, LN], 'witness' [LN]. The phrase εἰς μαρτύριον ἐπ' αὐτούς 'for a testimony against them' [Arn, Lns] is also translated 'as a testimony against them' [AB, BECNT, NTC; HCSB, NASB, NET, NIV, NRSV], 'as a warning to them' [CEV, GW, NCV, REB, TEV], 'as an act of witness to them'

[WBC], 'it is a sign that you have abandoned that village to its fate' [NLT].

c pres. mid. participle of εὐαγγελίζω (LN 33.215) (BAGD 2.a.δ. p. 317): 'to announce good news'. See translations of this word at 1:19. This word also occurs at 2:10; 3:18: 4:18, 43; 7:22; 8:1; 16:16; 20:1.

QUESTION—Who are the referents of ὅσοι ἂν μὴ δέχωνται ὑμᾶς 'as many as do not welcome you'?

The plural is indefinite [Lns, NIGTC, WBC] and refers to the population of the city [NIGTC, WBC]. This refers indirectly to 'that city', that is, to the population of a certain town, or towns, as a whole [TH]. This pertains to the reaction of a town as a whole [NIGTC]. The whole town is described as making a corporate response to the message [WBC]. This does not refer to particular individuals in a town [NIGTC, TH].

QUESTION—What is the force of the participle ἐξερχόμενοι 'going out'?

1. This participle has the force of a command [AB, Arn, BECNT, TH, WBC; CEV, GW, TEV]: go out from that city and shake off the dust from your feet.
2. This indicates the time at which they are to shake off their feet for a testimony [BNTC, Lns, NTC; HCSB, KJV, NASB, NCV, NET, NLT, NRSV, REB]: when/as you go out from that city, shake off the dust from your feet. It is taken for granted that when the disciples are unwelcome they will leave, so here Jesus tells them what they were to do as they left the city [Lns].

QUESTION—How were they to shake off the dust from their feet?

The aorist refers to a momentary and deliberate act [Lns]. The rejected disciples were to stop outside the town, then stamp their feet as if they were removing the dust from the town [Su].

QUESTION—What is the testimony given by shaking dust off of their feet?

It was a warning and protest against the city [TH]. The act indicated that the disciples were breaking all ties with the city so completely that they did not even want to have a speck of dust from the streets left on them [NIC]. They were showing that they severed all association with the town [AB, Arn, NAC]. From then on they had nothing at all in common with the people of that town [ICC, TH]. The disciples were free of all responsibility for that town [Su]. The dust from the disciples' feet would be left as a testimony that the messengers had been in the city but their message had been rejected [AB, Lns]. This is an image of separation that threatens the towns with exclusion from what God was now doing [WBC]. Some refer this action to a Jewish custom of shaking off the dust of a Gentile city to remove what was ceremonially unclean so as not to defile their own land when they returned to it [AB, BECNT, Gdt, MGC, NICNT, NIGTC, NTC, TG, TNTC]. This act of the disciples would then imply that the Jews who rejected the kingdom of God were no better than the Gentiles [MGC, NIGTC, NTC, TNTC], that the town was ceremonially unclean and would be punished by God [NICNT, TG]. Instead of focusing on uncleanness, the main message of the act is 'good riddance' and it serves as a warning about being separated from God and experiencing the coming judgment [BECNT].

DISCOURSE UNIT: 9:7–36 [AB]. The topic is who is this?

DISCOURSE UNIT: 9:7–9 [AB, BECNT, NAC, NIGTC, Su, TNTC, WBC; CEV, GW, HCSB, NCV, NET, NLT, NRSV, TEV]. The topic is Herod the tetrarch [TNTC], Herod is worried [CEV], Herod's confusion [NLT, TEV], Herod's perplexity [NRSV], Herod's confusion about Jesus [NCV, NET], Herod's question about Jesus [BECNT, NAC, NIGTC], who then is this? [WBC], rumors about Jesus [GW], Herod's reaction to Jesus' reputation [AB], Herod's disturbance over the identity of Jesus [Su], Herod's desire to see Jesus [HCSB].

9:7 **And Herod the tetrarch heard all the (things) happening and he-was-perplexed**[a] **because it-was-said by some that John was-raised from (the) dead,**

TEXT—Following τὰ γινόμενα 'the things happening', some manuscripts add ὑπ' αὐτοῦ 'by him'. GNT does not mention this variant. Ὑπ' αὐτοῦ 'by him' is read by KJV.

TEXT—Instead of the aorist tense ἠγέρθη 'was raised', some manuscripts read the perfect tense ἐγήγερται 'is risen'. GNT does not mention this variant. The perfect tense ἐγήγερται 'is risen' is read by KJV.

LEXICON—a. imperf. act. indic. of διαπορέω (LN **32.10**) (BAGD p. 187): 'to be perplexed' [Arn, BECNT, Lns, NTC, WBC; HCSB, KJV, NIV, NRSV], 'to be thoroughly perplexed' [**LN**; NET], 'to be greatly perplexed' [BAGD; NASB], 'to be confused' [LN; NCV], 'to be very confused' [TEV], 'to not know what to make of it' [GW, REB], 'to be worried' [CEV], 'to be puzzled' [AB], 'to be worried and puzzled' [NLT]. The imperfect tense indicates that Herod continued to lack a proper explanation of all the things he heard about and all the various opinions being offered [Lns, MGC]. His question was 'Who is this about whom I hear such things?' [NICNT]. Herod was trying to sort out from the various opinions who Jesus was [BECNT, ICC].

QUESTION—Why would some think that John the Baptist had been raised to life?

Herod had imprisoned John (3:19), held him there for a while (7:16–35), and then had him beheaded (9:9). The message about the kingdom of God and the need for repentance was preached by John and now by Jesus [BECNT]. John was held in such high esteem that some attributed to him the ability to perform miracles like Jesus did [NTC]. If John had been resurrected, he might be expected to perform miracles [ICC]. People thought that the miracles of healing were being performed by the resurrected John [TG]. People said that Jesus was the resurrected John [MGC, NIBC, NIC, Su, TNTC]. Since John and Jesus were contemporaries and both had been alive at the same time, this might mean that people thought that the spirit of the now deceased John had passed on to Jesus much like when Elijah's spirit passed on to Elisha (2 Kings 2:1–15) [NAC].

QUESTION—What is meant by John being ἠγέρθη ἐκ νεκρῶν 'raised from the dead'?

1. It means to be raised from among many dead individuals [BAGD, TG, TH]. It refers to being raised from the realm of the dead [BAGD, TH]. Some translate it 'to be raised from the dead' [AB, BECNT, WBC; NET, NIV, NRSV, REB], or 'to rise from the dead' [Lns, NTC; KJV, NASB, NCV].
2. It means to be raised from death [Lns]. The absence of an article with νεκρῶν 'dead' points to the quality of being dead and there is no thought of leaving many dead persons behind [Lns]. Some translate this without the mention of other dead persons: 'to come back to life' [CEV, GW, NLT, TEV].

9:8 and by some that Elijah had-appeared,[a] but others that some prophet of-the ancients[b] has-come-back-to-life.[c]

TEXT—Instead of τις 'some (prophet)', some manuscripts read εἷς 'one'. GNT does not mention this variant. Εἷς 'one' is read by KJV. Some versions might not distinguish between these two words in their translation.

LEXICON—a. aorist pass. indic. of φαίνομαι (LN 24.18) (BAGD 2.c. p. 851): 'to appear' [AB, Arn, BAGD, BECNT, LN, Lns, NTC, WBC; all versions except CEV, NCV, NLT], 'to come' [CEV, NCV], not explicit [NLT]. Since Elijah had been taken to heaven alive (2 Kings 2:11–12), the verb refers to his return, not to being raised to life [EGT, TG, TH].

b. ἀρχαῖος (LN 67.98) (BAGDS 2. p. 111): 'ancient' [BAGD, LN], 'old' [BAGD]. The phrase 'some prophet of the ancients' is translated 'one of the prophets of/from long ago' [CEV, GW, NET, NIV, TEV], 'one of the prophets of old' [AB; NASB, REB], 'one of the prophets who lived long ago' [NCV], 'one of the old prophets' [BECNT; KJV], 'some prophet of the old ones' [Lns], 'one of the ancient prophets' [Arn, NTC; HCSB, NRSV], 'some other ancient prophet' [NLT], 'a certain prophet of the ones from ancient times' [WBC].

c. aorist act. indic. of ἀνίσταμαι (LN 23.93): 'to come back to life' [LN, NTC; CEV, GW, NIV, REB, TEV], 'to arise' [AB, Arn, Lns; NRSV], 'to rise' [BECNT, WBC; HCSB, NET], 'to rise again' [KJV, NASB], 'to rise from the dead' [NCV, NLT], 'to live again, to be resurrected' [LN].

QUESTION—Why would some think that Elijah had appeared?

Elijah was considered to be in heaven from whence he could appear without having to be resurrected [Arn, NIGTC], and Elijah had performed many miracles [Su]. Malachi 4:5 prophesied that Elijah was to appear [Arn, Lns, NIC, NTC, Su, TG, WBC]. Some might have thought that Jesus was the returned Elijah [Lns, NIC, Su], or that Jesus had taken on the role of Elijah to prepare the nation for the end times [NIGTC].

QUESTION—In what way would some ancient prophet have come back to life?
It was a common expectation among the Jews that a prophet would return, such as Moses, Jeremiah, or Isaiah [BECNT].
1. 'Arose' has the sense of coming back to life [LN, Lns, NAC, NIGTC, NTC, Su, TG, TH, WBC; CEV, GW, KJV, NASB, NCV, NIV, NLT, REB, TEV]: some prophet of the ancients arose from the dead. This is the same verb Luke uses to describe Jesus' resurrection in 16:31; 18:33; 24:7, 46 [NAC]. They had arisen from the dead [TH].
2. 'Arose' has the sense of appearing on the scene [AB, ICC, NICNT]: some prophet of the ancients appeared on the scene. This is best taken as related to the viewpoint in 7:16, 'a great prophet was raised up among us' [NICNT].

9:9 **And Herod said, I beheaded^a John. Who then is this about whom I-hear such things? And he-was-seeking^b to-see him.**
LEXICON—a. aorist act. indic. of ἀποκεφαλίζω (LN 20.80) (BAGD p. 93): 'to behead' [AB, Arn, BAGD, BECNT, LN, Lns, NTC, WBC; HCSB, KJV, NASB, NIV, NLT, NRSV, REB], 'to cut the head off' [LN; CEV, GW, NCV, TEV]. The verb means to execute by beheading [TH]. Herod initiated the action and was not the direct agent of the beheading [TG, TH]. Some translate so as to show that Herod was the cause of beheading John but did not do the deed personally: 'I had John beheaded' [NET], 'I myself had John beheaded' [NASB], 'I had John's head cut off' [CEV, GW, TEV].
b. imperf. act. indic. of ζητέω (LN 68.60) (BAGD 2,b,g, p, 339): 'to seek' [Arn, BAGD, BECNT, LN, Lns, WBC], 'to try' [LN, NTC; NASB, NCV, NIV, NLT, NRSV, TEV], 'to desire' [BAGD; KJV], 'to wish' [BAGD], 'to want' [GW, HCSB, NET], 'to be eager (to meet)' [CEV], 'to be anxious (to see)' [AB; REB].

QUESTION—Who was Herod speaking to?
After hearing what other people said about John, Herod mentally said this to himself [TH].

QUESTION—What was the logic based on the fact that John had been beheaded?
1. Herod assumed that John could not have returned to life [Arn, BECNT, BNTC, MGC, NAC, NIGTC, TH]. Herod had personally seen to the death of John, so Jesus couldn't be John [TH]. Herod assumed that John, as well as the other prophets, could not rise from the dead, so the question about the identity of Jesus remained unsolved [NIGTC]. Since it was not possible that Jesus could be John, he must be some unidentified agent of God, and so Herod desired to see Jesus in order to determine who he was [BECNT]. Perhaps Herod's thoughts that John had been raised (which are recorded in Matthew 14:2 and Mark 6:16) are edited by Luke to show how inadequate the popular statements were or else Herod's opinions vacillated [NIGTC].

2. Herod was not ruling out a return to life [EGT, ICC, Lns, NIC, NTC, Su, TNTC]. In Matthew 14:2 and Mark 6:16 Herod feared that John had arisen from the dead after he had been beheaded [NIC]. This seems to imply that Herod suspected that Jesus was John returned to life, but this had the problem of there being two such men at the same time [EGT]. Herod eventually did conclude that Jesus was John risen from the dead [NTC]. Herod personally knew John, even ordering his beheading, and the activities of Jesus did not appear to be those of a resurrected John [Lns]. Not equating John with Jesus, the thought could be 'I thought that I had got rid of this kind of trouble when I beheaded John, and here I am having it all over again'. Yet afterwards perhaps Herod did conclude that John had risen from the dead [ICC].

QUESTION—In what way did Herod seek to see Jesus?

Herod tried to find a way to meet Jesus [TH] and have a private interview with him [Gdt]. He would have Jesus brought to him [TG]. The imperfect tense 'was seeking' means that Herod continued to do this [Arn, BECNT, ICC, Rb; NASB, NCV, TEV]. Herod's motive was not faith, but curiosity or malice [AB, NAC, NIGTC]. He wanted to get to know who Jesus was and what he was doing [NET]. Perhaps he wanted to see some miracles [AB]. If Herod entertained the thought that John had returned from the dead, he wanted to meet and talk with Jesus so he could determine whether or not this was John [ICC, NIC, TNTC]. If Herod ruled out the possibility that John had returned, he wanted to see for himself who Jesus might be [MGC].

DISCOURSE UNIT: 9:10–17 [AB, BECNT, NAC, NIGTC, Su, TNTC, WBC; CEV, GW, HCSB, NCV, NET, NIV, NLT, NRSV, TEV]. The topic is the feeding of the multitudes [WBC], the feeding of the five thousand [HCSB, NET, NRSV], Jesus feeds five thousand [NAC, NIGTC, Su, TNTC; CEV, GW, NIV, NLT, TEV], more than five thousand fed [NCV], Jesus' authority to provide revealed [BECNT], the return of the apostles; the feeding of the 5,000 [AB].

9:10 **And having-returned the apostles told him what (things) they-did. And having-taken-along them he-withdrew[a] privately toward/to[b] a-city called Bethsaida.**

TEXT—Instead of εἰς πόλιν καλουμένην Βηθσαϊδά 'to a city called Bethsaida', some manuscripts read εἰς τόπον καλούμενον Βηθσαϊδά 'to a place called Bethsaida', some read εἰς τόπον πόλεως καλουμένης Βηθσαϊδά 'to a place of a city called Bethsaida', some read εἰς τόπον ἔρημον πόλεως καλουμένης Βηθσαϊδά 'to a desert place of a city called Bethsaida', some read εἰς κώμην λεγομένην Βηθσαϊδά 'to a village called Bethsaida', some read εἰς κώμην λεγομένην Βηθσαϊδά εἰς τόπον ἔρημον 'to a village called Bethsaida into a desert place', some read εἰς τόπον ἔρημον 'to a desert place', and one manuscript omits this entire phrase. GNT reads εἰς πόλιν καλουμένην Βηθσαϊδά 'to a city called Bethsaida' with a B decision, indicating that the text is almost certain. Εἰς τόπον ἔρημον πόλεως καλουμένης Βηθσαϊδά 'to a desert place of a city called Bethsaida' is read by KJV.

LEXICON—a. aorist act. indic. of ὑποχωρέω (LN 15.53) (BAGD 1. p. 848): 'to withdraw'. The phrase 'he withdrew privately' [AB, BECNT, Lns, NTC; HCSB, NRSV, REB] is also translated 'he withdrew by himself' [NASB], 'he withdrew in private' [Arn], 'he retreated privately' [WBC], 'he went aside privately' [KJV], 'he slipped quietly away with them' [NLT], 'they withdrew privately' [NET], 'they withdrew by themselves' [NIV], 'they went off by themselves' [TEV], '(took them) where they could be alone' [CEV], '(took them) where they could be alone together' [NCV], '(took them) so that they could be alone' [GW]. 'Privately' has the meaning 'all by themselves' and it includes only Jesus and the twelve apostles [NTC]. See this word at 5:16.

b. εἰς (LN 84.16): 'toward' [LN, Lns; NLT], 'in the direction of' [LN], 'to' [AB, Arn, BECNT, LN, NTC, WBC; all versions except NLT].

QUESTION—From where, to where, and how, did Jesus withdraw?

Parallel passages in Matthew 14:13 and Mark 6:32 give the information that Jesus and his apostles went by boat from the Capernaum side of Lake Galilee to a solitary place. Jesus welcomed the crowd even though this prevented the retirement he had been seeking [ICC]. Later in Luke's account at 9:12 we learn that they were in a desolate place.

1. Jesus and his apostles withdrew *toward* Bethsaida [Arn, Lns, My, Su, TG, TH, TNTC; NLT]. The clause 'he withdrew privately toward a city called Bethsaida' must be interpreted to account for this event taking place in a desolate place. In Mark 6:45 Bethsaida was the destination of the boat after feeding the crowd. This meeting with the crowd happened on the way to Bethsaida [My]. They withdrew in the direction of Bethsaida [My, TG, TH], toward Bethsaida [Arn, Lns; NLT]. It is clear from 9:12 that they did not enter Bethsaida [TG, TH].

2. Jesus and his apostles withdrew *to* Bethsaida [AB, BECNT, BNTC, ICC, MGC, NIBC, NIC, NIGTC, NTC, Su, WBC; all versions except KJV, NLT].

2.1. This implies that they arrived at the city of Bethsaida [AB, BECNT, WBC]. The town is the site of the miracle although it is peculiar that the disciples suggested sending the crowd away to villages and farms in the vicinity to get food and lodging (9:12) [AB, WBC]. Perhaps Jesus went to Bethsaida and ended up outside the city by the time the crowds arrived or perhaps by naming Bethsaida, it refers only the center of activity [BECNT].

2.2 They were headed for a secluded spot in the vicinity of Bethsaida [ICC, MGC, NIC, NIGTC, NTC, Su, TNTC]. Bethsaida is named because it was the nearest well-known town [MGC, NIGTC]. Its mention here prepares for it being addressed in 10:13 [NIGTC]. Perhaps Luke supposed the miracle took place near Bethsaida on the west shore instead of requiring a boat trip to Bethsaida Julias on the north-east end of the lake [ICC].

9:11 And the crowds having-realized (it) followed[a] him. And having-welcomed them he-was-speaking to-them about the kingdom of-God, and he-was-healing the (ones) having need of-healing.

LEXICON—a. aorist act. indic. of ἀκολουθέω (LN 15.156) (BAGD 2. p. 31): 'to follow' [AB, Arn, BAGD, BECNT, LN, Lns, NTC, WBC; all versions].

QUESTION—How could the crowd follow Jesus?
This is the crowd that was with Jesus in 6:4, 42, and 45 and Luke's account without a boat trip makes it appear that they walked along behind Jesus [WBC]. The following views take into account the parallel passages in Matthew and Mark. Since Jesus was traveling across the lake and was possibly out of sight of the crowd, this means that the crowd went to find him [TH]. The people ran around the northern edge of the lake in order to be with Jesus again [Lns, NTC, TNTC]. Another view is that this was another crowd composed of local people [NIGTC]. Perhaps Jesus was already there when the crowd arrived and he welcomed the people when they appeared [ICC, Lns, MGC, NIC, NTC, Su, TH]. Mark 6:33 indicates that some of the crowd had gone ahead and were waiting for Jesus to land [TNTC].

DISCOURSE UNIT: 9:12–27 [NASB]. The topic is five thousand fed.

9:12 And the day began to-decline.[a] And having-approached, the twelve said to-him, Send-away the crowd in-order-that having-gone into the surrounding villages and farms[b] they-may-find-lodging[c] and may-find food,[d] because here we-are in a-lonely[e] place.

LEXICON—a. pres. act. infin. of κλίνω (LN **67.118**, **68.51**) (BAGD 2. p. 436): 'to decline, to be far spent' [BAGD], 'to draw to a close' [LN (67.118)], 'to begin to end' [LN (68.51)]. The phrase 'the day began to decline' [Arn, Lns, NTC] is also translated 'the day was coming to an end' [**LN** (67.118)], 'the day was about to end' [**LN** (68.51)], 'the day was ending' [NASB], 'the day began to wear away' [BECNT, WBC; KJV], 'the day began to wear on' [AB], 'the day began to draw to a close' [NET], 'the day was drawing to a close' [NRSV], 'toward the end of the day' [GW], 'late in the afternoon' [CEV, NCV, NIV, NLT], 'late in the day' [HCSB], 'evening was drawing on' [REB], 'the sun was beginning to set' [TEV]. It was shortly after midday, so there was still time to go to the villages for food [NIC]. It was late in the afternoon [NTC, TG]. It was late in the day, the period before the end of the Jewish day at sunset, the usual time for an evening meal [NIGTC]. It was around sunset [NAC]. When the day would fully decline the people would need an evening meal and overnight hospitality [WBC].

b. ἀγρός (LN 1.95) (BAGD 3. p. 14): 'farm'. See translations of this word at 8:34.

c. aorist act. subj. of καταλύω (LN **34.61**) (BAGD 2. p. 414): 'to find lodging' [AB, Arn, BAGD, **LN**; HCSB, NASB, NET, NIV, NLT, REB, TEV], 'to get lodging' [NTC], 'to lodge' [BECNT, Lns; KJV, NRSV], 'to find a place to stay' [CEV, GW], 'to find places to sleep' [NCV], 'to get a place to rest' [WBC].

d. ἐπισιτισμός (LN 5.1) (BAGD p. 298): 'food' [AB, LN, NTC; GW, HCSB, NET, NIV, NLT, REB, TEV], 'provisions' [Arn, BAGD, BECNT, WBC; NRSV], 'supplies' [Lns], 'something to eat' [CEV, NASB, NCV], 'victuals' [KJV].

e. ἔρημος (LN 1.86) (BAGD 1.a. p. 309): 'lonely' [LN], 'desolate, empty' [BAGD]. The clause 'here we are in a lonely place' [Arn, NTC] is also translated 'here we are in a deserted place' [Lns], 'we are in a deserted place here' [HCSB; similarly NRSV], 'we are in a really deserted place here' [AB], 'we are in a deserted locale' [BECNT], 'we are in a wilderness place here' [WBC], 'here we are in a desolated place' [NASB], 'we are here in a desert place' [KJV], 'we are in an isolated place' [NET], 'we are in a remote place here' [NIV], 'this is a lonely place' [TEV], 'this is a remote place we are in' [REB], 'no one lives in this place' [NCV], 'no one lives around here' [GW], 'there is nothing in this place, it is like a desert' [CEV], 'there is nothing to eat here in this deserted place' [NLT]. See this word at 4:42.

QUESTION—Who spoke to Jesus?

The twelve apostles came as a group [Lns, NTC]. They had talked the matter over among themselves and one of them acted as a spokesman for the group [Lns]. They had realized that there was a serious problem in the matter of feeding and lodging such a large crowd and thought that it was time to finish the teaching and healing [BECNT] and hold them no longer [Lns]. They were acting as representatives of the crowd, or as observers of the situation [AB].

QUESTION—What was the reason they gave for sending the crowd away?

The reason for sending the crowd away was that they were in a desolate place and if all the people stayed there they would have no shelter for the night and no food to eat [NIGTC]. It would take time to travel to any place where they could find shelter and food [NTC]. It will turn out that the major problem of food will be met, although nothing more is said of lodging. It was impossible to find lodging for such a crowd in the surrounding villages, but perhaps many of the people lived in the area [BECNT].

9:13 **And he-said to them, Give to-them yourselves (something) to-eat. And they-said, We have no more than five loaves and two fish, unless having-gone we buy food for all these people.**

QUESTION—What is implied by the apostles' answer?

The answer showed their surprise [NIGTC] and perplexity [ICC, NIC, NTC] since they had practically no food, making it impossible for them to feed the people [Lns]. The five loaves were common flat loaves [Lns, Su] about the size of a hamburger bun [Su] and were made of barley [BECNT, MGC, TNTC], which was not well liked [BECNT]. The fish were small [Su] cooked fish [TG], dried or salted [TH] and served as a relish for the loaves, something like a sandwich filling [NIGTC].

QUESTION—Did they consider their suggestion of going to buy food for the crowd a real alternative?

They considered it to be an impossibility because they were too far from a place to buy food [Arn, TG, TNTC], and because they did not have funds with which to buy anything anyway [NIC, TNTC]. It has the force of a rhetorical question 'You don't expect us to go and buy food for this whole crowd, do you?' [TG]. The one option they did not suggest was for Jesus to provide the food [BECNT, Lns, NAC, NICNT].

9:14 Because[a] there-were about five-thousand men. And he-said to his disciples, Make them sit-down[b] (in) groups[c] of-about fifty each. **9:15** And they-did so and all sat-down.

TEXT—In 9:14, some manuscripts omit ὡσεί 'about'. GNT does not deal with this variant in the apparatus but brackets it in the text, indicating difficulty making the decision. Ὡσεί 'about' is omitted in KJV.

LEXICON—a. γάρ (LN 89.23) (BAGD 2. p. 152): 'because' [LN], 'for' [Arn, BAGD, LN, Lns, NTC, WBC; HCSB, KJV, NASB, NET, NLT, NRSV, REB], not explicit [AB, BECNT; CEV, GW, NCV, NIV, TEV].
  b. aorist act. impera. of κατακλίνω (LN **17.24**) (BAGD p. 411): 'to make someone sit down' [BECNT; KJV, NRSV, REB, TEV], 'to cause to sit down' [BAGD], 'to have someone sit down to eat' [**LN**; NASB], 'to have someone sit down' [AB; HCSB, NET, NIV], 'to have someone sit' [CEV, GW], 'to tell someone to sit' [NCV], 'to tell someone to sit down on the ground' [NLT], 'to sit someone down' [WBC], 'to have/make someone recline' [Arn, NTC], 'to cause to recline to eat' [LN], 'to make someone lie down' [Lns]. Physical force is not implied in 'making' them sit down, rather it means to order or command them to do this [TG]. Literally, the verb is 'to cause to lie down' and refers to the position of reclining at feasts, [Lns, WBC], but it came to be applied to all kinds of sitting, no matter what kind of meal [WBC]. They would recline on the green grass [NTC].
  c. κλισία (LN **11.5**) (BAGD p. 436): 'group' [AB, Arn, BAGD, BECNT, **LN**, Lns, NTC, WBC; all versions except KJV], 'company' [KJV]. This word refers to a reclining group [BECNT], and it often referred to a group that was eating together [AB, BAGD, BECNT, LN, NIGTC, Su, TH, WBC].

QUESTION—What relationship is indicated by the beginning γάρ 'because'?

It indicates an explanation [BAGD]. It explains how large a crowd 'all these people' (9:13) were [AB, NICNT, NIGTC, TH] and why the disciples were right in expressing the impossibility of feeding the crowd [Lns]. This sentence is parenthetical and supplied by Luke, not the disciples [Arn].

QUESTION—How many people were in the crowd?
 The men were roughly counted as about a hundred groups of fifty men each [BECNT, ICC, Lns, Su]. Women and children would not be as numerous as the men [Arn, ICC, TNTC] and were not counted in the reckoning (Matthew 14:21) [ICC, MGC, NIBC, NIC, NTC, TH]. According to their custom, the women and children kept themselves apart from the men [Gdt] and were not arranged in groups as were the men [Alf]. It is preferable to translate this as groups of 'fifty male persons' rather than of 'fifty persons including men, women, and children' [TH].
QUESTION—Why were the people to sit in groups?
 The spaces around the groups would make it possible for the apostles to move about as they distributed the food [Arn, BECNT, ICC, NTC, TNTC]. It also made counting easier [NTC].

9:16 And having-taken[a] the five loaves and the two fish (and) having-looked-up toward heaven he-blessed[b] them and broke-into-pieces[c] and was-giving (them) to-the disciples to-set-before[d] the crowd.
LEXICON—a. aorist act. participle of λαμβάνω (LN 18.1): 'to take' [AB, Arn, BECNT, LN, Lns, NTC, WBC; all versions], 'to take hold of' [LN].
 b. aorist act. indic. of εὐλογέω (LN 33.470) (BAGD 2.b. p. 322): 'to bless' [AB, Arn, BAGD, BECNT, LN, Lns; CEV, GW, HCSB, KJV, NASB, NRSV], 'to say the blessing (over them)' [WBC; REB], 'to give thanks' [NET, NIV], 'to thank God (for the food)' [NTC; NCV, TEV], 'to ask God's blessing (on the food)' [NLT].
 c. aorist act. indic. of κατακλάω (LN 19.38) (BAGD p. 411): 'to break into pieces' [AB, BAGD, LN; NLT], 'to break apart' [GW], 'to break' [Arn, BECNT, Lns, NTC, WBC; all versions except GW, NCV, NLT], 'to divide' [NCV]. Jesus broke the loaves of bread and also the fish [AB, NIGTC, NTC, TG, TH; CEV]. Bread was often broken during a prayer, but here it refers to breaking the food into pieces for distribution to the crowd [TNTC].
 d. aorist act. infin. of παρατίθημι (LN 57.116) (BAGD 1.a. p. 522): 'to set before' [BAGD, BECNT, NTC; HCSB, KJV, NASB, NET, NIV, NRSV], 'to place before' [Arn, Lns], 'to give food to' [LN], 'to give to' [CEV, GW, NCV, NLT], 'to distribute to' [WBC; REB, TEV], 'to pass out among' [AB]. It means 'to serve to' or 'to pass to' [TH].
QUESTION—Why did Jesus look up to heaven?
 This was the usual attitude when someone was standing in prayer [Lns, MGC, TG], and this showed his dependence on God [MGC].
QUESTION—What is meant by blessing the food?
 Some take it to mean that he consecrated the food [BAGD, Gdt]. He blessed the food so that through his power it would be increased so as to feed the crowd [EGT, NIC]. He asked God to bless the food [NLT]. Most take it to mean that Jesus offered a prayer of thanksgiving for the food [ICC, NIGTC, NTC, TH; NCV, NET]. John 6:11 defines this as giving thanks and this was

the usual thanksgiving before a meal [Lns, NTC]. When a person is the subject of the verb εὐλογέω 'to bless', it means that the person praises God for something, that is, he gives thanks for it [NIGTC, NTC], and here Jesus would include thanking God for what God was able to do with the food [NIGTC]. Jesus did not impart a blessing to the bread and fish, he said a prayer of thanksgiving that would begin with the words 'Blessed are you, O Lord' and he would mention the things for which he thanked God [MGC, TNTC]. Instead of 'he blessed them', Mark 6:41 has 'he blessed' with God as the implied object [NIBC]. Instead of taking the food as the object of the verb 'blessed', it is possible that Jesus blessed (praised) God *with respect to* the food [NIGTC, WBC].

QUESTION—When did Jesus stop breaking the bread and fish?

The imperfect tense ἐδίδου 'was giving' in the midst of the aorist verbs is significant [Gdt, ICC, Lns, MGC, NAC, NIGTC, NTC, TH, WBC]. Jesus kept giving broken pieces to the disciples [Arn, Gdt, Lns, MGC, NTC, WBC; GW, NASB, NLT]. It indicates successive acts of breaking and handing out [NIGTC]. There were miraculously more and more pieces to break off [Arn, Lns] and Jesus kept giving them to the disciples for distribution [NTC]. The text does not suggest that the crowd was aware of where all the food was coming from, so perhaps the miracle was known only to Jesus and the twelve disciples [WBC].

9:17 **And all ate and were-satisfied,ᵃ and the (food) having-been-left-over by-them was-picked-up, twelve baskets of-pieces.ᵇ**

LEXICON—a. aorist pass. indic. of χορτάζω (LN 23.16) (BAGD 2.a. p. 884): 'to be satisfied' [Arn, BAGD, LN, WBC; NASB, NCV, NET, NIV, REB], 'to eat one's fill' [BAGD, LN], 'to be filled' [AB, BECNT, Lns, NTC; HCSB, KJV, NRSV, TEV], '(to eat) all one wants' [CEV, GW], '(to eat) as much as one wants' [NLT]. This pertains to being satisfied with food [LN]. The two verbs emphasize the climax, 'they ate (and not only that) they were satisfied, all of them' [TH].

b. κλάσμα (LN 19.40) (BAGD p. 433): 'piece' [BAGD, LN, Lns, NTC; GW], 'broken piece' [BECNT; NASB, NET, NIV, NRSV], 'fragment' [AB, Arn, BAGD, LN, WBC; KJV], 'scrap' [REB], 'leftover' [NLT], 'what (was left over)' [CEV, NCV, NET, TEV]. These were the pieces resulting from breaking the food [TH].

QUESTION—Who took up what was left over and what was it they took up?

The disciples picked up what was left over [BNTC, Lns, MGC, NAC, TG, TH, TNTC; TEV]. They picked up pieces of bread and fish that had not been eaten, not the crumbs and bits of food that had fallen to the ground [TG]. This refers to unused broken pieces that were not eaten by the crowd [NIC]. The people took more of the bread and fish than they could eat and this food was not to be wasted [Lns].

DISCOURSE UNIT: 9:18–50 [BECNT]. The topic is a Christological confession and instruction about discipleship.

DISCOURSE UNIT: 9:18–27 [NAC, NICNT, TNTC; NIV]. The topic is Peter's confession of Christ [NIV], Peter's confession and teachings on the passion and discipleship [NAC], Peter's confession and the nature of discipleship [NICNT], discipleship [TNTC].

DISCOURSE UNIT: 9:18–22 [NET]. The topic is Peter's confession.

DISCOURSE UNIT: 9:18–21 [AB, Su; CEV, GW, NCV]. The topic is Peter's confession [AB, Su], Peter declares his belief about Jesus [GW], who is Jesus? [CEV], Jesus is the Christ [NCV].

DISCOURSE UNIT: 9:18–20 [BECNT, NIGTC, TNTC, WBC; HCSB, NLT, NRSV, TEV]. The topic is Peter's confession [BECNT, NIGTC, TNTC], Peter's confession of the Messiah [HCSB], Peter's declaration about Jesus [NLT, NRSV, TEV], we say you are the Christ of God [WBC].

9:18 And it-happened while he is praying alone[a] the disciples were-with him, and he-questioned them saying, Whom (do) the crowds[b] say me to-be?
LEXICON—a. μόνος (LN **58.51**) (BAGDS 3. p. 528): 'alone' [AB, BAGD, LN]. The idiom κατὰ μόνας 'according to that which is private' is translated 'alone' [**LN**, Lns, WBC; CEV, KJV, NASB, NCV, NLT, NRSV, TEV], 'in a lonely place' [Arn], 'privately' [GW], 'in private' [NTC; HCSB, NIV], 'by himself' [BECNT; NET, REB].
  b. ὄχλος (LN 11.1): 'crowd' [AB, BECNT, LN, WBC; HCSB, NET, NIV, NRSV, TEV], 'multitude' [LN, Lns], 'people' [Arn, NTC; CEV, GW, KJV, NASB, NCV, NLT, REB]. There is a continuity in the narrative brought about by this reference to the crowds who had been around Jesus in this section [WBC]. This does not refer just to the crowds mentioned 9:11, but to people in general [TH]. It refers to the people the apostles met in their mission throughout the area [Gdt].
QUESTION—How could the disciples be with Jesus while he was praying alone?
  It seems to be an inconsistency [AB]. The word 'alone' refers to Jesus being in a solitary place and although his disciples were with him, Jesus was the only one who prayed [ICC]. Jesus was away from the crowds, not from his disciples [Arn, Gdt, NIC]. Jesus was praying by himself and the disciples were nearby [Lns, TH; NET, NRSV]. He was praying alone when the disciples came to him [TG; TEV]. In Mark 4:10, the same phrase κατὰ μόνας 'alone' is used of Jesus although it is clear that his disciples were with him [NIGTC].

9:19 And answering they-said, John the Baptist, and others (say) Elijah, and others that some prophet of-the ancients[a] has-come-back-to-life.[b] **9:20** And he-said to-them, And you (plural), whom do-you-say me to-be? And answering Peter said, 'The Messiah[c] of-God'.
LEXICON—a. ἀρχαῖος (LN 67.98) (BAGDS 2. p. 111): 'ancient'. See this word and the phrase 'some prophet of the ancients' at 9:8.

b. aorist act. indic. of ἀνίσταμαι (LN **23.93**): 'to come back to life'. See this word at 9:8.
c. Χριστός (LN 53.82): 'Messiah, Christ' [LN]. This word is literally 'one who has been anointed' [LN]. The phrase 'the Messiah of God' [NRSV] is also translated 'the Christ of God' [BECNT, Lns, NTC, WBC; KJV, NASB, NCV, NET, NIV], 'God's Messiah' [AB; HCSB, REB, TEV], 'the Messiah sent from God' [CEV, NLT], 'the Messiah whom God has sent' [GW], 'the Anointed of God' [Arn].

QUESTION—What is meant by the title 'the Messiah of God'?

The title 'Messiah' was used by the angels at 2:11, by Luke at 2:26, and indirectly by Jesus at 4:18. It is similar to the phrase 'the Messiah of the Lord' in 2:26, but in the body of his narrative, Luke reserves 'Lord' to refer to Jesus [WBC]. By adding 'of God' it emphasizes that Jesus is the one anointed by God to serve him [NIGTC]. God both anointed Jesus and sent him [ICC]. The Messiah belongs to God and has been sent by him [Gdt]. Jesus was the Messiah whom God had promised to send [NAC, Su, TG]. It was a settled conviction of the disciples that Jesus was the Messiah of Jewish hope and prophecy [Rb]. He was God's agent whom God anointed and sent in the Davidic or political tradition [AB].

QUESTION—Why is Peter's answer different in the parallel passages?

In Matthew 16:16 Peter says, 'You are the Messiah, the Son of the living God' and in Mark 8:29 Peter says, 'You are the Messiah.' Mark's statement seems to be the most likely one uttered by Jesus, with Matthew and Luke giving interpretive variations [Su]. Or, Luke has abbreviated the answer given in Matthew's account [Lns].

DISCOURSE UNIT: 9:21–50 [WBC]. The topic is making ready for the trip to Jerusalem.

DISCOURSE UNIT: 9:21–27 [NLT, NRSV, TEV]. The topic is Jesus' prediction of his death [NLT], Jesus speaks about his suffering and death [TEV], Jesus foretells his death and resurrection [NRSV].

DISCOURSE UNIT: 9:21–22 [BECNT, NIGTC, TNTC, WBC; HCSB]. The topic is Jesus' prediction of his suffering [BECNT, TNTC], his death and resurrection predicted [HCSB], the reply of Jesus [NIGTC], the command to tell no one because the Son of Man must suffer [WBC].

9:21 And commanding/warning/rebuking[a] he-ordered[b] them to-tell no-one this

LEXICON—a. aorist act. participle of ἐπιτιμάω (LN 33.331, 33.419) (BAGD 1. p. 303): 'to command' [LN (33.331)], 'to rebuke' [BAGD, LN (33.419)], 'to reprove' [BAGD]. The phrase 'commanding/warning/rebuking he ordered' is translated 'he commanded and charged' [BECNT], 'he sternly ordered and commanded' [NRSV], 'he ordered' [GW], 'he forcefully commanded' [NET], 'he strictly charged' [KJV], 'he gave strict orders' [AB; REB, TEV], 'he warned and commanded' [NTC],

'he warned and he instructed' [NASB], 'he strictly warned and instructed' [HCSB], 'he warned' [NCV, NLT], 'he strictly warned' [CEV, NIV], 'he sternly urged them' [Arn], 'with a rebuke he commanded' [WBC], 'with rebuking he charged' [Lns].
  b. aorist act. indic. of παραγγέλλω (LN 33.327) (BAGD P. 613): 'to order, to command' [LN], 'to give orders, to command, to instruct, to direct' [BAGD]. See above for how the two verbs are translated together.

QUESTION—What is the force of the two verbs ἐπιτιμήσας…παρήγγειλεν 'commanding/warning/ rebuking…he ordered'?
  1. Both verbs refer to giving a command to the disciples [AB, BECNT, ICC, NIGTC, TH; GW, KJV, NET, NRSV, REB, TEV]. The verbs reinforce each other [NIGTC, TH; NET] and the two verbs could be rendered by one verb phrase 'he commanded them strictly' or 'he commanded then in a severe tone' [TH]. Usually this verb means 'to rebuke' as in 4:35, but here it means 'to charge, to speak seriously' [NIGTC].
  2. The first verb includes an element of warning [NTC; CEV, HCSB, NASB, NCV, NIV, NLT]. There is an impliction of a threat in the verb ἐπιτιμήσας 'commanding' [LN]. They were warned because if they proclaimed that Jesus was the Messiah this might cause the people to consider him to be the one who would deliver them from subjection to Rome and then authorities would try to bring Jesus' ministry to an end [NTC]. See the next question for various reasons for not telling anyone.
  3. The first verb includes an element of rebuke [Lns, WBC]. The participle 'rebuking' indicates an action that is simultaneous with the main verb 'he ordered' and he rebuked them about the false conclusions they were inclined to draw from their vain Jewish hopes in regard to the role of the Messiah [Lns]. This verb is subordinated to the other verb παρήγγειλεν 'he ordered' and probably the idea of rebuke is present, pertaining to the disciples not understanding the fact that the path of service involved suffering [WBC].

QUESTION—What shouldn't the disciples tell anyone about and why shouldn't they?
  'This' refers to the fact that Jesus was the Messiah [NIGTC, TG, TH]. The prohibition was for the time of Jesus' ministry, but after the resurrection they would tell about the crucified and risen Messiah [AB]. If this fact was proclaimed publicly it would bring about an immediate confrontation with Roman authorities [NAC]. The disciples were not to tell because of the erroneous ideas about the Messiah held by people in general [Gdt, ICC, Lns, NIVS; NET]. The expected Messiah was thought to be a political figure who would deliver the people from Roman rule [AB, Arn, Lns, MGC, NAC, NTC, Rb, TNTC, WBC] and therefore people would not understand what Jesus was teaching them [TNTC]. Their false ideas of a Messiah would lead to the revolution the people desired [Su]. The Messiah was yet to suffer before his greatness would be fully manifest and the disciples still had to learn the kind of Messiah Jesus would be [BECNT].

DISCOURSE UNIT: 9:22–27 [Su; CEV]. The topic is the prediction of the passion [Su], Jesus speaks about his suffering and death [CEV].

DISCOURSE UNIT: 9:22 [AB; GW]. The topic is the first announcement of the passion [AB], Jesus foretells that he will die and come back to life [GW].

9:22 having-said, It-is-necessary (for) the Son of-Man[a] to-suffer[b] much and to-be-rejected[c] by the elders[d] and chief-priests and scribes and to-be-killed and to-be-raised[e] on-the third day.

LEXICON—a. υἱὸς τοῦ ἀνθρώπου 'Son of Man'. This title for Christ occurs at 5:24; 6:5, 22; 7:34; 9:22, 26, 44; 11:30; 12:8, 40; 17:22, 24, 26; 18:8, 31; 19:10; 21:27, 36; 22:22, 48, 69; 24:7. See the discussions of this title at 5:24, 6:5, and 9:22.
- b. aorist act. infin. of πάσχω (LN 24.78) (BAGD 3.b. p. 634): 'to suffer' [BAGD, LN], 'to endure' [BAGD]. The phrase 'to suffer much' [BECNT; TEV] is also translated 'to suffer terribly' [CEV], 'to suffer a lot' [GW], 'to undergo great suffering' [NRSV], 'to endure great sufferings' [REB], 'to suffer many things' [AB, Arn, Lns, NTC, WBC; HCSB, KJV, NASB, NCV, NET, NIV], 'to suffer many terrible things' [NLT]. It refers to physical suffering that is caused by violence [TH]. See this word at 17:25.
- c. aorist pass. infin. of ἀποδοκιμάζω (LN 30.117) (BAGD 2. p. 91): 'to be rejected' [Arn, BAGD, BECNT, LN, Lns, NTC, WBC; all versions except CEV], 'to be repudiated' [AB], 'to be regarded as not worthy' [LN]. This passive is also translated actively with the three groups of men as actors: 'to reject' [CEV]. It implies that after considering Jesus' claims, they would decide against him [ICC, TH, TNTC]. See this word at 17:25.
- d. πρεσβύτερος (LN 53.77) (BAGD 2.a.b. p. 700): 'elder' [AB, Arn, BAGD, BECNT, LN, Lns, NTC, WBC; HCSB, KJV, NASB, NET, NIV, REB, TEV], 'leader' [GW, NLT], 'older Jewish leader' [NCV], 'the nation's leaders' [CEV].
- e. aorist pass. infin. of ἐγείρω (LN 23.94): 'to be raised' [AB, Arn, BECNT, WBC; HCSB, KJV, NET, NRSV], 'to be raised up' [Lns, NTC; NASB], 'to be raised to life' [LN; NIV, TEV], 'to be made to live again' [LN], 'to be raised from the dead' [NCV, NLT], 'to be raised again' [REB]. This passive voice is also translated actively: 'to rise to life' [CEV], 'to come back to life' [GW]. The passive implies that God will raise him [AB, BECNT, Lns, NIGTC, TG].

QUESTION—How is the aorist participle 'having said' related to the previous verse?

This participle modifies the main verb 'he ordered' in the previous verse [AB]. Here Jesus gives the reason he did not want them to tell anyone about his identity [BECNT, EGT, NICNT, TH]. Many translate this verse as a new sentence: 'Then he said' [AB], 'And he said' [NTC; NIV, REB], 'Jesus said' [GW, NCV], 'He also told them' [TEV], 'Jesus told his disciples' [CEV], 'For' [NLT].

LUKE 9:22

QUESTION—Why did Jesus refer to himself as the Son of Man at this point?
He has already referred to himself as the Son of Man in 5:24, 6:5, and 6:22. The titles Messiah and Son of Man should not be confused, and here Jesus used the title 'Son of Man' as a corrective to the messianic title [AB].

QUESTION—What is the necessity for the Son of Man to suffer?
The verb δεῖ 'it is necessary' is an impersonal verb and refers to what is necessary to reach a desired end [Su]. It is a logical necessity [ICC, WBC] and moral necessity [WBC] for Christ to fulfill God's purposes revealed in Scripture [WBC]. It is necessary because it is God's will and plan [AB, BECNT, Gdt, ICC, Lns, MGC, NAC, NIC, NICNT, NIGTC, TG, TH, TNTC, WBC]. It is necessary to fulfill God's plan of salvation and because it is prophesied in the Scriptures [NIC]. The necessity involves all of the verbs in this sentence [NTC, TG]. Jesus also wills this since it is necessary in order to ransom the world [Lns].

QUESTION—What is meant by suffering much?
1. It means to suffer very much [TH; CEV, GW, NRSV, REB, TEV]. This adverbial sense is slightly preferable [TH].
2. It means to suffer many things [AB, BECNT, Lns, NIGTC, NTC, Su, TNTC, WBC; HCSB, KJV, NASB, NCV, NET, NIV, NLT]. This refers to all that is involved in being rejected and persecuted since the rejection and crucifixion follow after this [BECNT, NIGTC, WBC]. Jesus only specifies his final rejection in regard to the many things he must suffer [TNTC].

QUESTION—Who were the elders, chief priests, and scribes and how were they involved with the preceding verbs?
The three groups of men constituted the Sanhedrin which had a total of 71 men [AB, Arn, BECNT, Gdt, ICC, Lns, MGC, NICNT, NIGTC, WBC]. By omitting the article with the second and third nouns, the three groups are treated as a unity [AB, ICC, NAC, NIGTC, TH, TNTC, WBC]. They formed the whole group that composed the Sanhedrin [TNTC]. They were united in their plans and purposes [NAC]. The elders were presidents of synagogues [Gdt], or men who were experienced judges in the lower courts and had been advanced to membership in the Sanhedrin [Lns]. They were the lay members of the Sanhedrin and were from highly privileged families [NTC]. The chief priests were heads of the twenty-four orders of Jewish priests who served in the temple [TG, WBC], and others of them were priests belonging to the family of the high priest, Caiaphas [Lns, TG]. They came from priestly families [AB, NTC], controlled the temple activities, and were members of the Sanhedrin [AB]. The scribes were the experts in the interpretation of the Jewish law and rabbinical tradition [Lns, NTC]. Both of the preceding infinitives are connected: it is necessary for the Son of Man *to suffer* at the hands of the Sanhedrin and *to be rejected* by it [NIGTC, TH; CEV]. The rejection by the Sanhedrin includes the trial that resulted in Jesus being killed, although the verb for 'to kill' refers to murder with no thought of justice being done [Lns].

QUESTION—What is meant by 'on the third day'?
The numbering includes the day that the numbering starts [TG] and the phrase 'on the third day' includes both the first and last of the three days [TH]. It means the second day afterwards [BNTC]. In Semitic idiom it can refer to the two nights Jesus was in the grave [WBC], allowing for a Friday crucifixion and a Sunday resurrection [NAC].

DISCOURSE UNIT: 9:23–27 [AB, BECNT, NIGTC, TNTC, WBC; GW, HCSB, NET]. The topic is the new way of suffering [BECNT], a call to discipleship [NET], implications for the disciples [NIGTC], following Jesus [AB], what it means to follow Jesus [GW], to follow me, you must give away your life [WBC], taking up the cross [TNTC], take up your cross [HCSB].

9:23 And he-was-saying to all, If anyone wants[a] to-come after[b] me, let-him-deny[c] himself and take-up[d] his cross daily and let-him-follow[e] me.

LEXICON—a. pres. act. subj. of θέλω (LN 25.1): 'to want' [LN, WBC; all versions except KJV, NASB, NIV], 'to desire' [Arn, LN], 'to wish' [AB, BECNT, LN, NTC; NASB], 'to will' [Lns]. The phrase 'wants to come' is translated 'would come' [NIV], 'will come' [KJV].
  b. ὀπίσω (LN 36.35) (BAGD 2.a.β. p. 575): 'after' [BAGD, LN]. The phrase 'to come after me' [Arn, BECNT, Lns, WBC; KJV, NASB, NIV] is also translated 'to come with me' [AB; GW, HCSB, TEV], 'to come behind me' [NTC], 'to follow me' [NCV], 'to be my follower' [CEV, NLT], 'to be a follower of mine' [REB], 'to become my follower' [NET, NRSV].
  c. aorist mid. (deponent = act.) impera. of ἀρνέομαι (LN **30.52**) (BAGD 4. p. 108): 'to deny' [Arn, BAGD, BECNT, Lns, NTC, WBC; HCSB, KJV, NASB, NET, NIV, NRSV], 'to renounce' [REB], 'to disregard' [AB, BAGD, LN], 'to forget' [TEV], 'to pay no attention to' [LN], 'to say No to' [**LN**], 'to say no to the things one wants' [GW], 'to give up the things one wants' [NCV], 'to put aside one's selfish ambition' [NLT], 'to forget about oneself' [CEV]. It can be expressed 'to refuse to pay attention to what one's own desires are saying', 'to refuse to think about what one just wants for oneself', or 'to put oneself at the end of the line' [LN].
  d. aorist act. impera. of αἴρω (LN 15.203, 24.83) (BAGD 2. p. 24): 'to take up' [AB, Arn, BECNT, Lns, NTC, WBC; all versions except GW, NCV, NLT], 'to pick up' [GW], 'to shoulder' [NLT], 'to lift up and carry away' [BAGD, LN (15.203)]. The clause is translated 'they must be willing to give up their lives daily' [NCV].
  e. pres. act. impera. of ἀκολουθέω (LN 36.31): 'to follow' [AB, Arn, BECNT, LN, Lns, NTC, WBC; all versions], 'to be a disciple of' [LN]. It means to accompany, to go the same way [TH].

QUESTION—Who are now being addressed by 'he was saying to all'?
The imperfect 'was saying' indicates a continuation of Jesus' discourse, but there is a break because this is no longer a private teaching for the disciples since Jesus is now addressing all who contemplate following him, as is seen

in Mark 9:34 where he calls together the crowd [Arn, NIGTC, NTC]. 'All' includes the disciples and the crowd now present [AB, Alf, Crd, EGT, Gdt, Lns, MGC, NIGTC, NTC, Rb, TG, TH]. This is not restricted to a special group of disciples but it is a general call for discipleship [WBC].

QUESTION—Is there a difference between 'come after me' and 'follow me'?
Both verbs mean much the same thing [Lns, NAC, NIGTC, TG; CEV, NCV, NET, NLT, NRSV, REB]. However, many take the desire to come after Christ to focus on the initial decision to be a disciple, and following him to be a continued life of discipleship. *To come after Jesus* refers to becoming his disciple [AB, Arn, ICC, NAC, NIC, NICNT]. It refers to outward adherence to Jesus [Gdt, Lns]. *To follow Jesus* refers to faithfulness in fulfilling the consequences of a commitment [Gdt, NICNT], being loyal to him [ICC], continually obeying him [BECNT, NTC]. It means to accompany Jesus, walking along behind him on the path [Arn]. Discipleship involves self-denial, bearing one's cross, and accompanying Jesus [NICNT].

QUESTION—What is involved in denying oneself?
The disciple must deny anything that would prevent his complete commitment to Jesus [Su]. He must put his own interests and wishes in the background [NIC]. He must deny self-interest and concern for his own well-being [WBC]. This means to reject a life based on self-interest and self-fulfillment in order to seek to fulfill the will of Christ [NAC]. This refers to conversion in which a person disowns the natural sinful self and he enters into a new relationship with Christ [Lns]. Self-denial is recognizing that a person cannot save himself and must give his life over to God's care and protection, deciding that God must direct him [BECNT]. It involves a renunciation of self, not merely of one's sinful conduct [AB].

QUESTION—What is meant by taking up one's cross?
Taking up a cross refers to the Roman form of crucifixion in which the condemned man carries the cross or its cross-bar to the place of execution [BECNT, NICNT, TG, WBC]. The phrase αἴρω τὸν σταυρόν 'to take up one's cross' is an idiomatic expression meaning to be prepared to endure severe suffering, even to the point of death [LN (24.83)]. This is a commitment to suffer martyrdom if need be [NAC, NIGTC]. Jesus' follower must be like Jesus in being prepared to be persecuted and even die [Su, TG]. This is being ready for martyrdom and also being ready to suffer persecution and opposition every day [AB]. Jesus chose this metaphor because he himself would bear his cross to be crucified. Each disciple was to bear the particular cross they would be allotted as a result of their faithful connection to Christ [Lns]. The cross was a symbol for suffering and a person's cross was his particular burden of sorrow [Arn]. The addition 'daily' means that this must be a daily resolve [NAC, TG, WBC], a continual commitment [Su]. 'Daily' indicates that this demand is not so much a literal martyrdom as a continuing attitude of self-denial and dying to self and sin [AB, MGC, NICNT, NIGTC, TH, WBC]. The cross does not refer to ordinary trials and suffering but to that which must be suffered in serving Christ [Lns, NIC].

The disciple accepts pain, shame, and persecution for the sake of Christ [NTC]. Carrying the cross signifies that the condemned man is submitting to the authority of the government. The disciple is to submit to the authority of God and live a life of self-denial and submission to him [BECNT].

9:24 **Because whoever wants to-save^a his life will-lose it.^b But whoever loses^c his life on-account-of^d me, this (one) will-save it.**

LEXICON—a. aorist act. infin. of σῴζω (LN 21.18, 21.27) (BAGD 3. p. 798): 'to save' [Arn, BAGD, BECNT, Lns, NTC, WBC; all versions except NLT], 'to preserve' [AB], 'to rescue (from danger)' [LN (21.18)], 'to save (to experience divine salvation)' [LN (21.27)]. The phrase 'to save his life' is translated 'to keep your life for yourself' [NLT].
  b. fut. act. indic. of ἀπόλλυμι (LN 27.29) (BAGD 1.b. p. 95): 'to lose' [AB, Arn, BAGD, BECNT, LN, NTC, WBC; all versions except CEV, NCV], 'to destroy' [CEV], 'to give up' [NCV].
  c. aorist act. subj. of ἀπόλλυμι (LN 23.114) (BAGD 1.b. p. 95): 'to lose' [BAGD]. The phrase ἀπόλλυμι τὴν ψυχήν 'to lose one's life' is an idiom [LN] and is translated 'to experience the loss of life, to die' [LN], 'to lose one's life' [AB, Arn, BECNT, Lns, NTC, WBC; GW, HCSB, KJV, NASB, NET, NIV, NRSV, REB, TEV], 'to give up one's life' [CEV, NCV, NLT].
  d. ἕνεκεν (LN 90.43) (BAGD p. 264): 'on account of' [BAGD, Lns], 'because of' [BAGD, LN; HCSB], 'for (my) sake' [AB, BAGD, BECNT, LN, NTC, WBC; KJV, NASB, NET, NRSV, REB, TEV], 'on (my) account' [Arn], 'for' [CEV, GW, NCV, NIV, NLT]. It means on account of one's faith in Christ and one's faithfulness to him [Lns]. It refers to doing this because of loyalty to Jesus [NIGTC].

QUESTION—What relationship is indicated by γάρ 'because'?
  It is the reason for the preceding commands [Lns], particularly for taking up one's cross [Gdt]. It explains the images of the previous verse [Arn, BECNT, NIC]. It indicate the reason for an implied clause [BAGD (1.e. p. 152), NTC]: *let him not refuse,* because, etc. This serves as both a warning and a promise [Lns].

QUESTION—What is meant by the first occurrence of the verb σῴζω 'to save' in the clause 'wants to save his life'?
  1. This refers to saving one's life from physical death [Arn, BAGD, BNTC, TG, TH]. The clause 'whoever wants to save his life' refers to rescuing himself from natural dangers and afflictions [BAGD (3)]. It means to keep oneself from danger and death [Arn, TH]. To save his life he would reject the Messiah if that meant he would escape crucifixion by the Romans [BNTC].
  2. This refers to keeping one's way of life [AB, BECNT, Lns, NAC, NIC, NIGTC, NTC, Su, WBC]. Saving one's life is the opposite of taking up one's cross and means to refuse to be identified with Jesus [WBC]. It refers to a person who seeks to preserve his own way of life by not

denying himself, not taking up his cross, and not following Jesus [Lns, NAC, NIGTC, Su]. It refers to wanting to get the best out of life [TNTC]. It means keeping control of one's life, to seek to be accepted by the world and therefore not submit to God's way [BECNT]. Such a one wants to hold on to his present sinful life along with its material possessions, pleasures, and prestige [NTC].

QUESTION—What is meant by the first occurrence of the verb ἀπόλλυμι 'to lose' in the clause 'will lose it'?
1. This refers to the final judgment [BNTC, NAC, NIGTC]. He will lose his life at the final judgment and thus not enjoy eternal life in the age to come [NIGTC]. He will suffer the judgment of hell [NAC].
2. This refers to the person's present existence [AB, Arn, BECNT, NIC, NICNT, NTC, Su, TG]. His life is doomed to be a failure, never finding real joy or a full life [NIC]. This is worse than physical death since his life will be without meaning [Su]. He will lose whatever remnant of the higher life that was left in him at the beginning [NTC]. His life will be an unprofitable waste [AB]. He will not have true or eternal life [TG].

QUESTION—What is meant by the second occurrence of the verb ἀπόλλυμι 'to lose' in the clause 'whoever loses his life on account of me'?
1. This refers to physically dying [AB, Arn, Lns]. It refers to the loss of life [AB].
2. This refers figuratively to dying to self [BECNT, NAC, NIC, NICNT, NIGTC, NTC, Su, TNTC, WBC]. This refers to self denial in general [NIGTC]. He loses his life by devoting himself to serving Christ, others, and the gospel [NTC]. The person lays his life on the altar to serve Christ [NIC]. Here it means that he gives his spiritual and physical welfare over to Christ, although in other applications of this proverbial saying it could include martyrdom [BECNT].

QUESTION—What is meant by the second occurrence of the verb σῴζω 'to save' in the clause 'loses his life will save it'?
1. This refers to the salvation of the soul and receiving eternal life [AB, BAGD, Lns, NAC, TG]. The clause 'whoever loses his life will save it' refers to being saved from eternal death [BAGD]. He will be safe and blessed with Christ and God [Lns].
2. This refers to a full life as a believer [BECNT, NIC, NICNT, NIGTC, NTC, Su, TNTC]. He will find true life and joy both before death and hereafter [NIC]. Life will be filled with peace, assurance, and joy [NTC].

9:25 Because what (is) a-man benefited[a] having-gained[b] the whole world but having-lost[c] himself or having-been-forfeited[d]?

LEXICON—a. pres. pass. indic. of ὠφελέω (LN 35.2) (BAGD 1.a. p. 900): 'to be benefited' [BAGD], 'to be helped' [BAGD, LN]. The phrase 'what is a man benefited' [Arn, Lns; HCSB; similarly WBC; NET, NLT] is also translated 'what is a man advantaged' [KJV], 'what does it profit a man' [BECNT; similarly NASB, NRSV], 'what good does it do a man/person'

[BECNT, NTC; similarly AB, BAGD; GW, NIV], 'what does anyone gain' [REB; similarly CEV, TEV]. The rhetorical question is also translated as a statement: 'it is worth nothing for them' [NCV].
  b. aorist act. participle of κερδαίνω (LN 57.189) (BAGD 1.a. p. 429): 'to gain' [Arn, BAGD, BECNT, LN, Lns, NTC, WBC; HCSB, KJV, NASB, NET, NIV, NLT, NRSV], 'to acquire' [AB], 'to win' [GW, REB, TEV], 'to own' [CEV], 'to have' [NCV]. This verb is usually used in connection with the pursuit of wealth and business success [AB].
  c. aorist act. participle of ἀπόλλυμι (LN 57.68) (BAGD 1.b. p. 95): 'to lose' [AB, Arn, BAGD, BECNT, LN, Lns, NTC, WBC; HCSB, KJV, NASB, NET, NIV, NLT, NRSV], 'to destroy' [CEV], 'to be destroyed' [NCV], 'to be lost' [TEV]. The phrase 'having lost or having been forfeited' is translated 'at the cost of destroying' [REB].
  d. aorist pass. participle of ζημιόομαι (LN 57.69) (BAGD 1. p. 338): 'to forfeit' [AB, Arn, BAGD, BECNT, LN, Lns, NTC, WBC; HCSB, NASB, NET, NIV, NLT, NRSV], 'to suffer loss' [BAGD, LN], 'to destroy' [GW], 'to waste (your life)' [CEV], 'to be cast away' [KJV], 'to be lost' [NCV], 'to be defeated' [TEV], not explicit [REB]. This verb is usually used in documents relating to business transactions [AB].

QUESTION—What relationship is indicated by γάρ 'because'?

It indicates that verses 9:25–26 are the grounds for making the statement in the first clause of 9:24 [Gdt, WBC]. It explains the previous images [BECNT]. It explains the paradox expressed in 9:24 so that to save one's life means to obtain as much as the world offers and to lose one's life is to forgo what the world offers [Lns]. It gives the reason for following Jesus [Lns]. It stresses the urgency of choosing between the two ways to life in 9:24 [NIGTC].

QUESTION—What is the purpose of this rhetorical question?

It implies that a man is not profited in doing this [NIGTC, Su, TG], it is useless and senseless [AB, Lns]. There is nothing material that is worth the loss of the self [TNTC]. It is implied that the answer is that there is no good whatever, just evil [NTC].

QUESTION—What is meant by gaining the whole world?

It means to gain everything there is or anything the person wants [TG]. Although it is impossible for any human being to gain the whole world, this is the absolute limit that one could possess of the world's wealth, power, pleasures, and glory [Lns]. For the sake of the argument, it is assumed that one could gain the whole world in regard to its wealth, pleasure, and position [Su].

QUESTION—In the clause ἑαυτὸν ἀπολέσας ἢ ζημιωθείς 'himself having lost or having been forfeited' does ἑαυτόν 'himself' go with both verbs?

1. 'Himself' goes with both verbs [AB, Arn, BECNT, BNTC, EGT, Lns, NIGTC, NTC, WBC; HCSB, NASB, NCV, NET, NIV, NLT, NRSV, TEV]: he loses or forfeits himself.

2. 'Himself' goes with only the first verb [TH; CEV, GW, KJV, REB]: he loses himself or is forfeited. He destroys himself or wastes his life [CEV]. He loses his life by destroying it [GW]. He does so at the cost of destroying himself [REB].

QUESTION—What is the difference between losing oneself and forfeiting oneself?

1. The two participles are equivalent in meaning [My, NIGTC, NTC, WBC]. 'Losing oneself' explains what is meant by 'forfeiting oneself' [NIGTC]. These are not two ways of losing one's true life but there are two ways of expressing the loss and a translation does not have to use two different words to express the meaning [TG]. By adding the synonym 'losing oneself' to 'forfeiting oneself' the link to 9:24 is made explicit [NIGTC]. Such a person loses the right to possess his own higher life [NTC].
2. The two participles have different aspects of meaning [EGT, Gdt, TH; CEV, GW]. The conjunction ἤ 'or' suggests that the verbs are to be differentiated so that 'to lose oneself' contrasts with 'to gain the whole world' and refers to dying, while being forfeited refers to punishment after death [TH]. They lose their lives by destroying them [GW]. They destroy themselves and waste their lives [CEV].

9:26 Because whoever is-ashamed-of[a] me and my words, the Son of Man will-be-ashamed-of this (one) when he-comes in the glory[b] of-him and of-the Father and of-the holy angels.

TEXT—Instead of τοὺς ἐμοὺς λόγους 'my words', some manuscripts read τοὺς ἐμούς, giving the sense, 'my people'. GNT reads τοὺς ἐμοὺς λόγους 'my words' with an A decision, indicating that the text is certain.

LEXICON—a. aorist pass. (deponent = act.) subj. of ἐπαισχύνομαι (LN 25.193) (BAGD 1. p. 282): 'to be ashamed of' [AB, Arn, BAGD, BECNT, LN, Lns, NTC, WBC; all versions].

b. δόξα (LN 14.49, 79.18) (BAGD 1.a. p. 203): 'glory' [AB, Arn, BECNT, LN (79.18), Lns, NTC, WBC; all versions], 'brightness, radiance' [BAGD, LN (14.49)], 'splendor' [BAGD, LN 79.18)]. See this word at 9:31.

QUESTION—What relationship is indicated by γάρ 'because'?

This introduces a reason [Lns] why the warning in 9:25 must not be ignored [NIGTC, NTC]. It explains that losing oneself (9:25) consists of being denied by Jesus [Gdt]. It explains the reality of the danger of gaining the world and losing one's spiritual life [BECNT].

QUESTION—In what way could people be ashamed of Jesus and his words?

The disciples could fail to be faithful in the face of ridicule or violence [Gdt]. The opposition by people could cause someone to shrink from identifying himself with Jesus or his teaching [NIGTC, WBC]. Peter, in 22:56–60, is an example of being ashamed of being identified with Jesus [AB, WBC], but Peter moved on from his failure [WBC]. It is being so proud that one does not want to have anything to do with Jesus [NTC]. It is refusal to confess Jesus publicly [BECNT]. It means to deny Jesus [Lns, NAC].

QUESTION—What coming of the Son of Man is referred to here?

This refers to the second coming of Christ [Arn, BECNT, BNTC, Gdt, ICC, Lns, MGC, NIC, NICNT, NIGTC, NTC, Su, TG, TH, TNTC]: when he comes in glory from heaven. He will come to execute judgment [BECNT, Lns, NIC, NIGTC, Su]. It does not tell what he will do when he comes, but that Christ will be ashamed of such a person implies that Christ will act as judge [NICNT].

QUESTION—What is meant by the Son of Man coming in the glory *of* him and *of* the Father and *of* the holy angels?

This does not specifically indicate that the Father in his glory and the holy angels in their glory will accompany the Son of Man when he comes in his glory [AB, BECNT, EGT, My, TG, TH, WBC; GW]. In Mark 8:38 it says that the angels will accompany Jesus, but here it refers to Jesus coming in the glory that the Father and the angels also manifest [AB]. Jesus will appear in glory, bearing the glory of God and the glory of heavenly realm signified by 'the glory of angels' [WBC]. Jesus will have the heavenly glory of the visible majesty possessed by the Father and the heavenly host [BECNT]. It means that Jesus will come from heaven surrounded by the heavenly glory in which the Father and the angels live and in which Jesus will live after the resurrection [TH]. Jesus will come as a shining figure, with the same kind of bright light that the Father and angels have [TG]. It is the glory that Jesus shares with the Father and the angels [GW]. It is not clear whether Jesus will be accompanied by the angles, but the point is that the Son will come with the glory associated with the Father and the angels [NIGTC]. Some understand this to mean that the angels in their glory will accompany the Son of Man when he comes [Alf, Arn, Gdt, Lns]. The three genitives are added to the one word 'glory' and this means that the presence of the Father's glory will also accompany Jesus as he comes surrounded by the glory of the angels who will assist him [Lns]. The angels will accompany Jesus and surround him with their brightness [Alf].

9:27 **And I-say to-you truly,[a] there-are some of-the (ones) standing here who by-no-means[b] will-taste[c] death until[d] they-have-seen[e] the kingdom of-God.**

LEXICON—a. ἀληθῶς (LN 70.3) (BAGD 1. p. 37): 'truly' [AB, BAGD, BECNT, LN, NTC, WBC; NRSV], 'truthfully' [Arn; NASB], 'in truth' [BAGD; REB], 'of a truth' [Lns; KJV], 'most certainly' [NET]. The phrase 'I say to you truly' is translated 'you can be sure that' [CEV], 'I can guarantee this truth' [GW], 'I tell you the truth' [HCSB, NCV, NIV], 'I assure you that' [NLT, TEV]. This word makes the saying particularly solemn [NIGTC]. See this word at 12:44.

b. οὐ μή (LN 70.3): The two negatives are translated 'by no means' [LN], 'in no way' [Lns], 'certainly not' [WBC], or as a simple negation of the

verb: 'not' [AB, Arn, BECNT, NTC; all versions except NCV], not explicit [NCV].
c. aorist mid. (deponent = act) subj. of γεύομαι (LN 24.72, 90.78) (BAGD 2. p. 157): 'to taste' [AB, Arn, BAGD, BECNT, LN (24.72), Lns, NTC, WBC; HCSB, KJV, NASB, NET, NIV, NRSV, REB]. This word has a figurative extension that means 'to experience' [ICC, LN (90.78), NIGTC]. The phrase 'to taste death' is translated 'to die' [CEV, GW, NCV, NLT, TEV].
d. ἕως (LN 67.119): 'until' [Arn, BECNT, LN, Lns, NTC; GW, HCSB, KJV, NASB, TEV], 'before' [AB, WBC; CEV, NCV, NET, NIV, NLT, NRSV, REB]. It can be translated positively, 'I assure you that some of you here will live to see the kingdom of God' [TG].
e. aorist act subj. of ὁράω (LN 24.1, 90.79): 'to see' [AB, Arn, BECNT, LN (24.1), Lns, NTC, WBC; all versions]. This word has a figurative extension that means 'to experience' [LN (90.79)].

QUESTION—What is meant by some seeing the kingdom of God?
1. This refers to the transfiguration that was seen by Peter, John, and James [BNTC, MGC, My, NAC, NICNT, WBC]. The transfiguration was proof that the kingdom of God had entered history through Christ and it was a preview of the Second Coming [MGC].
2. This refers to the resurrection, the events of Pentecost, and the extension of the church [AB, Arn, EGT, Gdt, NIGTC, NTC]. The disciples will come to understand the mysteries of the kingdom in a new way after the resurrection [AB]. The disciples will come to realize that the kingdom is already present when they see its power in the events of the resurrection and Pentecost [NIGTC]. At Pentecost some of those present would receive the Holy Spirit and understand the wonderful works of God, which Jesus called the kingdom of God [Gdt]. This refers to the power shown in Christ's resurrection, his return in the Spirit at Pentecost (which was connected with Christ's coronation in heaven), and all the momentous events involved with the age of the church, such as conversions of thousands, the presence of charismatic gifts, and the extension of the church among the Gentiles [NTC]. A new understanding of the kingdom will be gained when the disciples obtain a fuller revelation of the mysteries of the kingdom [AB].
3. This refers to the destruction of Jerusalem [Alf, Lns, NIC]. The King would come in power with judgment on the nation of Israel [Lns]. Those still alive in A.D. 70 would see God reveal his kingly rule in the history of mankind when he executed his judgment on the Jewish nation, showing that the ceremonial temple religion had been replaced by the new people of God, the church of Christ [NIC].
4. This refers to the second coming of Christ [Su, TG]. In the last day God will manifest his complete power as King and all people will acknowledge that he is ruler and judge [TG]. Jesus referred to his coming in glory at the end of the present world [Su].

5. This refers to entering the kingdom as disciples and seeing a preview of the revelation of the fully glorified Jesus [BECNT].

DISCOURSE UNIT: 9:28–45 [NASB]. The topic is the transfiguration.

DISCOURSE UNIT: 9:28–36 [AB, BECNT, NAC, NICNT, NIGTC, Su, TNTC, WBC; CEV, GW, HCSB, NCV, NET, NIV, NLT, NRSV, TEV]. The topic is the transfiguration [AB, BECNT, NAC, NICNT, NIGTC, Su, TNTC; HCSB, NET, NIV, NLT, NRSV, TEV], a foretaste of Jesus' future glory [WBC], the true glory of Jesus [CEV], Moses and Elijah appear to Jesus [GW], Jesus talks with Moses and Elijah [NCV].

9:28 And it-happened about eight days after these words, and having-taken Peter and John and James he-went-up to the mountain to-pray. **9:29** And it-happened while he was-praying the appearance[a] of-his face (became) different[b] and his clothing (became) dazzling[c] white.

TEXT—In 9:28, before παραλαβών 'having taken', some manuscripts omit καί 'and'. GNT does not deal with this variant in the apparatus but brackets it in the text, indicating difficulty in making the decision. Καί 'and' is omitted in KJV.

LEXICON—a. εἶδος (LN **58.14**) (BAGD 1. p. 221): 'appearance' [BAGD, LN]. The clause 'the appearance of his face' [AB, BECNT; GW, HCSB, NASB, NCV, NET, NIV, NLT, NRSV, REB] is also translated 'the appearance of his countenance' [Arn, Lns, NTC], 'the fashion of his countenance' [KJV], 'the form of his face' [WBC], 'his face' [CEV], 'his face (changed) its appearance' [TEV].

b. ἕτερος (LN 58.36) (BAGD 2. p. 315): 'different' [BAGD, LN]. The phrase 'became different' [AB, Arn, Lns, WBC; NASB] is also translated 'changed' [BECNT, NTC; CEV, GW, HCSB, NCV, NIV, NLT, NRSV, REB, TEV], 'altered' [KJV], 'was transformed' [NET].

c. ἐξαστράπτω (LN 14.47) (BAGD p. 273): 'dazzling' [AB, Arn, BECNT, LN, Lns, WBC; GW, HCSB, NET, NLT, NRSV, REB], 'shining' [CEV, NCV], 'gleaming' [NASB], 'glistering' [KJV], 'flash or gleam like lightening' [BAGD], 'flashing like lightning' [NTC], 'as bright as a flash of lightning' [NIC]. This verb indicates an intense brilliance [TG].

QUESTION—What period of time is indicated by the phrase 'about eight days'?

In Matthew 17:1 and Mark 9:2 the time is given as 'after six days', which was the exact interval [BECNT, Lns] and this agrees with 'about' eight days [ICC]. 'Eight days' may be a rounded-off number and mean 'about a week later' [AB, NIC, TG, TH, WBC] while Matthew and Mark give the exact time [NIC]. Perhaps Luke included the day of Peter's confession and the day of the transfiguration while Matthew and Mark referred to only the intervening days [Alf, Crd, NIC, NIGTC, NTC].

QUESTION—How did the appearance of Jesus' face become different?

In 9:32 it says that the disciples saw his glory, his 'bright splendor' [TH]. In Matthew 17:2 it says that Jesus' face shone like the sun [Lns, NTC]. This is comparable with Moses' face being radiant when he came down from talking with God on Mount Sinai (Exodus 34:29) [BECNT, MGC, NAC, NIBC, NICNT, NIGTC, WBC]. One explanation is that as Jesus prayed in God's presence, he reflected God's glory [NIGTC]. Another explanation is that it was different from Moses' glory which came from the outside and here it refers to Jesus' own future glory being revealed [NAC, WBC]. Perhaps Jesus' whole body shone with the light and splendor of his heavenly divinity, as in Revelation 1:13–15 [Lns]. Jesus' inward glory transformed his natural body into brilliant light [MGC].

QUESTION—What happened to Jesus' clothing?
1. The clothing changed to a brilliant white color [Arn, Lns, WBC]. His clothing was transfigured as well as his features [Lns].
2. The light came from Jesus [Gdt, Su]. Jesus' glorified body shone through his clothing [Gdt]. The light from his face reflected on his originally white clothing [Su].

9:30 And behold two men were-conversing[a] with-him, who were Moses and Elijah,

LEXICON—a. imperf. act. indic. of συλλαλέω (LN 33.157) (BAGD p. 776): 'to converse with' [AB, BAGD, LN], 'to talk with' [BAGD, LN, Lns, NTC, WBC; all versions except CEV], 'to speak with' [Arn, BECNT, LN; CEV]. This verb refers to the act of talking [Lns]. The imperfect tense is translated 'began talking with him' [NET, NLT]. The imperfect tense indicates that the conversation had already lasted for some time when the disciples awoke and saw what was taking place [Gdt].

QUESTION—What is the function of ἰδού 'behold'?
1. It has the usual function of focusing attention on what follows [TH; NET]. The word adds interest and emphasis [NET].
2. It expresses the suddenness of the appearing of Moses and Elijah [Gdt; CEV, GW, REB, TEV]: and suddenly Moses and Elijah were conversing with Jesus.

QUESTION—Why did Moses and Elijah appear?

Moses represented the Law and Elijah represented the prophets [ICC, Lns, MGC, NAC, NIC, NIGTC, NTC, Su, TNTC, WBC; NET]. That they came to speak with Jesus indicates the continuity between their work and the work of Jesus [NICNT].

9:31 who having-appeared[a] in glory[b] were-speaking-of[c] his departure,[d] which he-was-about to-fulfill[e] in Jerusalem.

LEXICON—a. aorist pass. participle of ὁράω (LN 33.69) (BAGD 1.a.δ. p. 578): 'to appear' [AB, Arn, BAGD, BECNT, Lns, NTC, WBC; all versions except NLT], 'to be seen' [LN; NLT], 'to become visible' [BAGD].

b. δόξα (LN 14.49, 79.18) (BAGD 1.a. p. 203): 'glory' [AB, Arn, BAGD, BECNT, LN, Lns, WBC; HCSB, KJV, NASB, NRSV, REB], 'heavenly glory' [CEV, GW, NCV, TEV], 'glorious splendor' [NTC; NET, NIV]. This noun is also translated as an adjective: '(they were) glorious' [NLT]. They were surrounded with a heavenly brightness or radiance [Lns, NTC]. See this word at 9:26.

c. imperf. act. indic. of λέγω (LN 33.69) (BAGD II.2. p. 470): 'to speak of' [AB, BAGD, BECNT, LN, Lns; HCSB, KJV, NASB, NLT, NRSV, REB], 'to speak about' [Arn, WBC; NET, NIV, NLT], 'to talk about' [LN; CEV, NCV, TEV], 'to discuss' [GW]. This verb refers to the contents of their talking [Lns].

d. ἔξοδος (LN 23.101) (BAGD 2. p. 276): 'departure' [AB, Arn, BAGD, LN, Lns, NTC; NASB, NCV, NET, NIV, NRSV, REB], 'exodus' [BECNT, WBC], 'death' [CEV, GW, HCSB], 'decease' [KJV]. This noun is also translated as a verb: 'to die' [NLT, TEV]. This verb is used as a euphemism for 'departing from life' and refers to dying [BAGD, LN].

e. pres. act. infin. of πληρόω (LN 13.106) (BAGD 4.a. p. 671): 'to fulfill' [Arn, BAGD, BECNT, LN; GW, NLT, REB, TEV], 'to bring to fulfillment' [NIV], 'to accomplish' [Lns, NTC, WBC; HCSB, KJV, NASB, NLT, NRSV], 'to bring about' [NCV], 'to carry out' [NET], 'to complete' [AB]. The phrase 'which he was about to fulfill' is translated 'all that (Jesus' death) would mean' [CEV].

QUESTION—What is indicated by Moses and Elijah appearing in glory?

That they appeared in glory indicated that they were heavenly persons, since glory usually refers to the radiance or splendor associated with God's presence [AB, Lns, MGC, NAC, NIGTC]. They appeared in glory like all of the inhabitants of heaven do [Lns, TG, WBC].

QUESTION—What was the departure they were speaking about?

They were talking about Jesus' death [Alf, Arn, Crd, Rb, Su, TH, WBC; CEV, GW, HCSB, KJV, NLT, TEV]. 'Departure' or 'exodus' refers to more than his death [Lns]. They were talking about Jesus' approaching suffering, death, resurrection, and ascension [AB, BECNT, EGT, Gdt, ICC, Lns, MGC, My, NAC, NIBC, NICNT, NIGTC, NTC]. It was a departure from earth to heaven [Rb]. In Jerusalem Jesus was not only going to complete his death but also his ascension [AB]. Moses and Elijah were not informing Jesus that he was going to die, since Jesus had already had told the Twelve about this [AB, Gdt]. Perhaps they would be relating Jesus' departure to their own prophetic roles in the OT, that is, about what Moses and the prophets have said about him [AB].

QUESTION—What was Jesus going to fulfill in Jerusalem?

1. This refers to completing the task he had to do [AB, ICC, Lns, NAC, NIGTC, TG, TH; NLT, TEV]. He would fulfill God's plan/purpose [TG; NLT, TEV]. Jesus' death would be a fulfillment of his mission that was ordained by God [TH]. This refers to fulfilling the actual event that was

ordained, not to fulfilling the Scriptures [NIGTC]. He would fulfill the foreordained plan of God for salvation [AB].
2. This refers to fulfilling the OT prophecies about his destiny [TNTC].

9:32 **And Peter and the (ones) with him had-been weighed-down**[a] **with-sleep. And having-awakened they-saw the glory of-him and the two men, (who) stood with-him.**
LEXICON—a. perf. pass. participle of βαρέομαι (LN **23.71**) (BAGD p. 133): 'to be weighed down' [BAGD]. The phrase βαρέομαι ὕπνῳ 'to be weighed down with sleep' is an idiom for being in a state of deep sleep and is translated 'to be weighed down with sleep' [BECNT, Lns, NTC, WBC; NRSV], 'to be burdened with sleep' [Arn], 'to be sound asleep' [**LN**; CEV, TEV], 'to sleep soundly' [GW], 'to be completely asleep' [LN], 'to be overcome with/by sleep' [NASB, REB], 'to be heavy with sleep' [BAGD; KJV], 'to be very sleepy' [NCV, NIV], 'to be quite sleepy' [NET], 'to be in deep sleep' [HCSB], 'to be drowsy with sleep' [AB], 'to be very drowsy and fall asleep' [NLT].
QUESTION—Were the three disciples asleep or only sleepy?
1. They were asleep and had to wake up from their sleep [Arn, BECNT, Crd, EGT, Gdt, LN (23.71), Lns, MGC, NIC, NIGTC, NTC, Rb, Su, TG, TH, TNTC; CEV, GW, HCSB, NLT, REB, TEV]. While Jesus was praying they fell asleep and were awakened by the bright light [NIC, TNTC]. Either the light or the sound of the conversation awakened them [Arn, TG]. The transfiguration of Jesus and the arrival of Moses and Elijah took place while they were asleep [Lns]. They missed most of the conversation [BECNT]. The disciples did not hear the conversation [NIGTC, Su] and Jesus must have told them about it later [NIGTC].
2. They were awake but sleepy and had to become fully awake [Alf, My, NICNT, WBC; NASB, NCV, NET, NIV, NRSV]. They were drowsy but were not actually asleep [My]. They were barely awake, yet aware of what was happening [NICNT]. They kept awake [Alf, WBC], so it was clear that this event was not merely a vision seen in sleep [Alf].

9:33 **And it-happened in their parting**[a] **from him Peter said to Jesus, Master,**[b] **it-is good**[c] **for-us to-be here. And, Let-us-make three shelters,**[d] **one for-you and one for-Moses and one for-Elijah, not knowing**[e] **what he-says.**
LEXICON—a. pres. pass. infin. of διαχωρίζομαι (LN **15.50**) (BAGD p. 191): 'to part from' [BAGD, **LN**], 'to depart from' [LN], 'to go away' [BAGD]. The phrase 'in their parting' is translated 'they were about to leave' [CEV], 'when they were about to leave' [NCV], 'as they were about to depart' [WBC], 'when they were withdrawing' [Arn], 'as they were starting to leave' [NTC; NET, NLT], 'as they were moving away' [REB], 'as they gradually withdrew' [AB], 'as they were leaving' [GW, NASB, NIV, NRSV, TEV], 'as they were departing' [BECNT; HCSB; similarly Lns; KJV]. They were leaving to go back to heaven [TG]. The present infinitive suggests a gradual withdrawal [AB], they were *beginning* to go

away [MGC, NIGTC, TNTC]. They were preparing to part from Jesus [Gdt]. They hadn't yet left and Peter's remark was an impulse to prevent them from leaving [ICC].
  b. ἐπιστάτης (LN 87.50) (BAGD p. 300): 'master'. See translations of this word at 5:5. This word also occurs at 8:24, 45; 9:49; 17:13.
  c. καλός (LN 66.2) (BAGD 3.a. p. 400): 'good' [AB, Arn, BAGD, BECNT, LN, NTC, WBC; all versions except NLT], 'wonderful' [NLT], 'excellent' [Lns].
  d. σκηνή (LN 7.9) (BAGD p. 754): 'shelter' [NTC; CEV, NET, NIV, REB], 'tent' [Arn, BAGD, LN; GW, NCV, TEV], 'booth' [BAGD, BECNT, Lns, WBC], 'hut' [AB], 'tabernacle' [HCSB, KJV, NASB], 'dwelling' [BAGD; NRSV].
  e. perf. act. participle of οἶδα (LN 32.4): 'to know' [AB, Arn, BECNT, Lns, WBC; all versions except NASB, TEV], 'to understand, to comprehend' [LN], 'to really know' [TEV], 'to realize' [NTC; NASB].

QUESTION—How did the disciples know that Moses and Elijah were the men talking with Jesus?

There are various possibilities: the heavenly beings introduced themselves, the disciples knew by intuition, they deduced this by what was being said, or God revealed it to them [NTC]. Perhaps they heard Jesus speak to them by name or perhaps those who are glorified bear the impress of their identity [Gdt]. The disciples were given the ability to know who they were [ICC, NIC]. God causes people to know by intuition the identity of the saints in heaven when they see them [Lns].

QUESTION—What did Peter mean when he said 'it is good for us to be here' and 'let us make three tents'?

By 'it is good for us' the 'us' meant the three disciples [ICC, TG, TH]. Another view is that since Peter was speaking to Jesus, Jesus was included in the 'us' being there [Lns]. In the offer 'let us make three tents' the 'us' refers only to the three disciples [Lns, TH].
  1. It was a good thing for the disciples to enjoy this experience [Lns, NAC, NIC, NIGTC, NTC, Su, WBC]. It was a privilege for the disciples to be there [WBC]. They were filled with awe to be in the presence of the glorified Jesus and the heavenly visitors and wanted to prolong the presence of the Moses and Elijah [Lns].
  2. It was a good thing that the disciples were there to be of service to Jesus and the heavenly visitors by building the tents [AB, Arn, MGC, TG, TH]. Because the disciples were there, they could perhaps prevent the departure of Moses and Elijah [AB, Arn].

QUESTION—What kind of shelters was Peter talking about?

The shelters would have to be constructed from what was at hand on the mountain [WBC]. Here 'shelters' would refer to leafy shelters or huts [TNTC]. It would be just a temporary shelter [Alf, Crd, Gdt, ICC, Lns, My, NIC, NTC, TNTC, WBC]. Peter said this because he thought that all of them would be there for a while [TG]. This offer to build shelters was made to

LUKE 9:33   415

encourage Moses and Elijah to prolong their visit [Alf, EGT, Gdt, NIGTC, NTC, WBC]. The time was near for the Feast of the Tabernacles in which Jews lived in temporary shelters along the roads into Jerusalem, on the streets, and on the flat roof tops, so Peter suggested that they spend the time where they were instead of going to Jerusalem [BECNT, Rb, Su]. Peter wanted to delay their departure by suggesting that they celebrate the Feast of Tabernacles there on the mountain [BECNT]. Peter didn't say anything about shelters for the disciples since he felt so humble that he planned to sleep out in the open [Lns].

QUESTION—What didn't Peter know when he said this?

Peter of course knew the words he spoke, but he didn't understand the situation and that his proposal was out of place [TH]. Peter didn't understand he was attempting to stand in the way of God's purpose [WBC]. He didn't understand the implication of his words, since the Lord had chosen the way of suffering and was not going to continue to live in his divine glory [NIC]. It was foolish to think that men in a glorified state would remain on earth and need shelters like ordinary men [AB, Arn, Lns, NTC]. It was foolish to think that branches and shrubbery would be adequate to provide shelter had it been needed [NTC]. Peter didn't know that the heavenly visitors had not come to stay [NIC, NIGTC] and his proposal was meaningless [TG]. He was wrong in equating God's Son, Jesus, with God's servants, Moses and Elijah, but the voice from heaven would correct his understanding [NAC].

9:34 **And (while) he was-saying these (things) a-cloud came and was-overshadowing^a them. And they-were-afraid while they entered^b into the cloud.**

LEXICON—a. imperf. act. indic. of ἐπισκιάζω (LN 14.62) (BAGD 2. p. 298): 'to overshadow, to cast a shadow on' [BAGD, LN], 'to cover' [BAGD]. The phrase 'a cloud came and was overshadowing them' is translated 'a cloud came and overshadowed them' [Arn, BECNT; NET, NRSV; similarly Lns; KJV], 'a cloud came and covered them' [NCV], 'a cloud overshadowed them' [GW], 'a cloud came over them' [NLT], 'a cloud formed and began to overshadow them' [NASB], 'there came a cloud which cast its shadow over them' [REB], 'a cloud formed and cast its shadow over them' [AB], 'a shadow from a cloud passed over them' [CEV], 'a cloud appeared and covered them with its shadow' [TEV], 'a cloud appeared and overshadowed them' [HCSB], 'a cloud appeared and enveloped them' [NIV], 'a cloud came and enveloped those men' [NTC, WBC].

b. aorist act. infin. of εἰσέρχομαι (LN 15.93) (BAGD 1.a.β. p. 232): 'to enter' [BAGD, LN]. The phrase 'they entered into the cloud' [KJV] is also translated 'they entered the cloud' [BECNT, WBC; HCSB, NASB, NET, NIV, NRSV, REB], 'they went into the cloud' [Arn, Lns; GW], 'they passed into the cloud' [AB], 'the cloud covered them' [CEV, NCV, NLT], 'the cloud came over them' [TEV].

QUESTION—How did the cloud come and overshadow them?

The aorist tense 'the cloud came' refers to the fact of the appearance of the cloud [TH]. It came suddenly [Lns]. The imperfect 'was overshadowing them' refers to the continuing situation that followed the appearance of the cloud [TH]. The cloud began to overshadow them [Rb]. It overshadowed them by enveloping them [NTC, WBC; NIV]. The cloud was not an ordinary cloud [Gdt]. In Matthew 17:5 it is called 'a bright cloud'. The cloud was bright, luminous, or white [ICC, Lns, NTC]. It was a sign of God's presence [AB, Gdt, MGC, NAC, NIC, NICNT, NIGTC, TG, TNTC, WBC] and at the same time hid him from the sight of men [NIGTC]. The cloud was the Shekinah glory [NIC, WBC]. Strictly speaking, a luminous cloud does not overshadow, but it may veil [ICC]. The brightness of a central light came through the cloud which had cast a shadow on the ground [Gdt].

QUESTION—Who were overshadowed, who were afraid, and who entered into the cloud?

1. The cloud came, overshadowed, and enveloped all those present and the disciples were afraid as they themselves entered the cloud with the others [AB, EGT, Lns, MGC, NAC, NICNT, Rb, TG, WBC]. Entering the cloud means that the cloud was moving, not the disciples [TG]. The cloud overshadowed them by enveloping them all and the disciples were afraid of the supernatural character of the cloud and became even more afraid as its white film hid everything [Lns]. All six entered the cloud but only the disciples were afraid [Rb].

2. The cloud came, overshadowed all, and the disciples were afraid when Jesus, Moses, and Elijah entered the cloud [Crd, Gdt, ICC, NIGTC, NTC, TNTC]. Since the voice came to the disciples from out of the cloud, the disciples had not entered it [Gdt, NTC, TNTC]. Since Jesus was conversing with Moses and Elijah, he entered the cloud with them [NTC]. The disciples were frightened as they saw the others disappear in the cloud [NIGTC].

3. The cloud came and overshadowed all, and the disciples were afraid as Moses and Elijah entered the cloud [Arn, My, NIC, TH]. Moses and Elijah were parting from Jesus, so when Peter was speaking to Jesus, the cloud appeared and overshadowed Moses and Elijah who continued their departure by entering into the cloud [My].

9:35 And a-voice came from the cloud saying, This is my Son the (one) having-been-chosen,[a] listen-to[b] him.

TEXT—Instead of ἐκλελεγμένος 'chosen', some manuscripts read ἀγαπητός 'beloved' and some manuscripts read ἀγαπητὸς ἐν ᾧ εὐδόκησα 'beloved in whom I am well-pleased'. GNT reads ἐκλελεγμένος 'chosen' with a B decision, indicating that the text is almost certain. Ἀγαπητός 'beloved' is read by KJV.

LEXICON—a. perf. pass. participle of ἐκλέγομαι (LN **30.92**) (BAGD 4. p. 242): 'to be chosen' [BAGD, **LN**, Lns; CEV, NCV, NIV], 'my Chosen

One' [AB; NASB, NET], 'my Chosen' [NRSV, REB], 'the Chosen One' [AB, WBC; HCSB], 'the Elect One' [Arn]. This passive verb is also translated actively with God as the speaker: 'whom I have chosen' [GW, TEV].

b. pres. act. impera. of ἀκούω (LN 36.14) (BAGD 4. p. 32): 'to listen to' [AB, Arn, BAGD, BECNT, WBC; all versions except KJV], 'to hear' [Lns; KJV], 'to pay attention to and obey' [LN], 'to follow' [BAGD]. The present imperative indicates a continuous action, to keep on listening to him [Su], to be constantly listening [Lns]. They were to pay attention to what Jesus says [NIC, TG], with faith [NIC], and obedience [NIC, NIGTC, TG]. The present imperative means to be constantly hearing him [Lns] and not be concerned about hearing the words of Moses and Elijah [NIBC]. It implies that Jesus has more authority than Moses and Elijah [AB].

QUESTION—In what respect was Jesus chosen?

'Chosen' is equivalent to the title ὁ ἐκλεκτός 'the Chosen One', which is a Messianic title used in 23:35 [AB, TG, TH]. God chose Jesus for his ministry [Lns, TNTC] of redeeming the world [Lns]. Since Jesus is called 'the Chosen One' at 23:35, it refers to God's choice of his Son to take the path of suffering that leads to glory [NIGTC]. God chose Jesus for the great work that had to be accomplished [Arn].

9:36 And after the voice came,ª Jesus was-foundᵇ alone. And they were-silentᶜ and toldᵈ no-one in those days anything of-what they-had-seen.

LEXICON—a. aorist mid. (deponent = act.) infin. of γίνομαι (LN 13.48): 'to become' [LN]. The phrase 'after the voice came' is translated 'when the voice came' [Arn, Lns; similarly WBC], 'when the voice had spoken' [BECNT; NASB, NIV, NRSV], 'after the voice had spoken' [CEV, GW, HCSB, NET, REB], 'when the voice finished speaking' [NCV], 'once that voice had spoken' [AB], 'when the voice died away' [NLT], 'when the voice stopped' [TEV], 'when the voice ceased' [NTC], 'when the voice was past' [KJV]. 'After the voice had come' means when it had ceased [ICC].

b. aorist pass. indic. of εὑρίσκω (LN 27.27) (BAGD 1.c.α. p. 325): 'to be found' [BAGD, LN; KJV, NASB, NET, NRSV]. The phrase 'Jesus was found alone' [Arn, BECNT, Lns, NTC] is also translated 'Jesus was found to be alone' [AB, WBC], 'they found that Jesus was alone' [NIV], 'they saw that Jesus was alone' [GW], 'Jesus was seen to be alone' [REB], 'they saw only Jesus' [CEV], 'only Jesus was found' [HCSB], 'only Jesus was there' [NCV], 'Jesus was there alone' [NLT], 'there was Jesus all alone' [TEV]. That Jesus was found does not mean that someone was searching for him, rather it is an idiomatic way of saying that the disciple saw only Jesus there [TG], and it implies that Moses and Elijah were gone [TH].

c. aorist act. indic. of σιγάω (LN **33.121**) (BAGD 1.c. p. 749): 'to be silent' [Arn, BAGD, Lns, WBC], 'to keep silent' [AB, BAGD, BECNT, NTC; HCSB, NASB, NET, NRSV], 'to keep silence' [REB], 'to keep quiet' [**LN**; CEV, TEV], 'to keep it close' [KJV], 'to keep this to themselves' [NIV], 'to say nothing' [LN; GW, NCV], not explicit [NLT].

d. aorist act. indic. of ἀπαγγέλλω (LN 33.198): 'to tell, to inform' [LN]. The phrase 'to tell no one' [AB, BECNT, NTC; GW, HCSB, KJV, NCV, NET, NIV, NRSV, TEV] is also translated 'to tell nobody' [WBC], 'to report to no one' [Lns; NASB], 'to not say a word to anyone' [REB], 'to not tell anyone' [NLT], 'to not say anything' [CEV], 'to announce to no one' [Arn].

QUESTION—In what way was Jesus found alone?

Jesus was alone in the sense that he was no longer accompanied by Moses and Elijah [AB, Arn, TH]. We are to understand that the cloud had disappeared and also the glory that had surrounded Jesus [Arn, Lns, NIC, NICNT, WBC]. Upon hearing God's voice the disciples prostrated themselves in worship and when the voice ceased speaking, they looked up and saw that Jesus stood there alone [Lns, NIC, NTC].

QUESTION—Why did the disciples not tell anyone of what they had seen?

Many of the commentaries point out that in Matthew 17:9 and Mark 9:9 that as they came down the mountain, Jesus ordered his three disciples to tell no one about what they had seen until he had been raised from death. The words 'in those days' refers to the time of Jesus' ministry [AB, EGT, Gdt, Lns, MGC, NIBC, NIGTC, Su], in contrast with the days after the resurrection [AB]. They had seen something that required reflection, not making it public [BECNT].

DISCOURSE UNIT: 9:37–50 [AB, BECNT, NICNT, TNTC]. The topic is the misunderstanding of the disciples [NICNT], the disciples' failure and Jesus' instruction [BECNT], further miracles and sayings of Jesus [AB], Jesus and the disciples [TNTC].

DISCOURSE UNIT: 9:37–45 [NIV]. The topic is the healing of a boy with an evil spirit.

DISCOURSE UNIT: 9:37–43a [AB, BECNT, NAC, NIGTC, Su, TNTC, WBC; CEV, GW, HCSB, NCV, NET, NLT, NRSV, TEV]. The topic is the demon–possessed boy [TNTC], the healing of the boy with an unclean spirit [NAC, NIGTC, WBC], Jesus heals a boy [CEV], Jesus heals a sick boy [NCV], Jesus heals a demon–possessed boy [GW, NLT, NRSV], Jesus heals a boy with an evil spirit [TEV], healing an epileptic boy [NET], the cure of the epileptic boy [AB, Su], the power of faith over a demon [HCSB], the disciples' failure and Jesus' reversal [BECNT].

9:37 And it-happened on-the following day (when) they had-come-down from the mountain, a-large crowd met[a] him. **9:38** And behold a-man from the crowd shouted saying, Teacher, I-beg you to-look[b] at my son, because[c] he-is my only (child),

TEXT—In 9:38, instead of ἐβόησεν 'shouted' some manuscripts read ἀνεβόησεν 'cried out'. GNT does not mention this variant. Ἀνεβόησεν 'cried out' is read by KJV.

LEXICON—a. aorist act. indic. of συναντάω (LN 15.78) (BAGD 1. p. 784): 'to meet' [AB, Arn, BAGD, BECNT, LN, Lns, NTC, WBC; all versions except CEV, REB], 'to come to meet' [REB], 'to draw near' [LN]. This active voice is also translated with the passive voice, keeping Jesus as the subject: 'to be met by' [CEV]. The crowd came to meet Jesus [TH].
   b. aorist act. infin. of ἐπιβλέπω (LN 30.45, 35.8) (BAGD p. 290): 'to look at' [BAGD], 'to take note of' [LN (30.45)], 'to be concerned with, to look upon and help, to help' [LN (35.8)]. The phrase ἐπιβλέψαι ἐπί 'to look at' [AB; all versions except CEV, KJV] is also translated 'to look upon' [BECNT, Lns, NTC; KJV], 'to look with pity on' [WBC], 'to do something for' [CEV], 'to give one's concern to' [Arn]. It means to take an interest in someone [BAGD], to take special notice of someone [LN (35.8)], to regard with pity [EGT, ICC, Lns, WBC]. It means to look upon the boy with favor and compassion, and this a request for help [NTC].
   c. ὅτι (LN 89.33): 'because' [Arn, LN, Lns, NTC; HCSB, NCV], 'for' [BECNT; KJV, NASB, NIV], not explicit [AB; CEV, GW, NET, NLT, NRSV, REB, TEV].

QUESTION—Where did the crowd come from?

Apparently the crowd was awaiting Jesus since his other nine disciples were with the crowd [AB, ICC, Lns, MGC, NIGTC, TG]. The crowd was so eager to meet Jesus that they ran up to welcome him (Mark 9:15) [NTC].

QUESTION—What relationship is indicated by ὅτι 'because'?

It indicates the reason that Jesus should look at the boy and help him [Lns, Su]. The reason was that the boy was the father's only son [Lns, Su] and was the only hope the father had to continue his family line [NICNT, Su]. Another reason is added in the next verse where the condition of the boy is explained [BECNT].

9:39 and behold a-spirit[a] seizes[b] him and suddenly he-screams[c] and (it) convulses[d] him with foam[e] and hardly[f] departs from him crushing[g] him. **9:40** And I-begged your disciples that they-might-cast- it -out, and they-were- not -able.

LEXICON—a. πνεῦμα (LN 12.37) (BAGD 4.a. p. 676): 'spirit' [AB, Arn, BAGD, BECNT, Lns, NTC, WBC; all versions except CEV, NCV, NLT], 'evil spirit' [BAGD, LN; NCV, NLT], 'demon' [BAGD, LN; CEV]. In 9:42 this spirit is referred to as τὸ δαιμόνιον 'the demon' and τῷ πνεύματι τῷ ἀκαθάρτῳ 'the unclean spirit'.
   b. pres. act. indic. of λαμβάνω (LN 18.1) (BAGD 1.c. p. 464): 'to seize' [AB, Arn, BAGD, BECNT, NTC, WBC; HCSB, NASB, NCV, NET, NIV, NLT, NRSV, REB], 'to take hold of, to grab' [LN], 'to take control

of' [GW], 'to attack' [CEV, TEV], 'to take' [Lns; KJV]. The present tenses in this verse make this a vivid experience that repeatedly occurred [Lns; NLT]. It occurred from time to time [TG, TH; REB].
c. pres. act. indic. of κράζω (LN 33.83) (BAGD 1. p. 447): 'to scream' [AB, BAGD, LN, NTC; CEV, NASB, NCV, NET, NIV, NLT, REB], 'to shriek' [BAGD, Lns; GW, HCSB, NRSV], 'to cry out' [BAGD, BECNT, WBC; KJV], 'to cry' [Arn]. This verb is also translated as a noun: '(with) a shout' [TEV].
d. pres. act. indic. of σπαράσσω (LN **23.167**) (BAGD p. 760): 'to convulse' [AB, Arn, BAGD, BECNT, Lns, WBC; NRSV], 'to throw into a convulsion' [**LN**; NASB], 'to throw into convulsions' [HCSB, NET, NIV, NLT, REB], 'to throw into a fit' [LN; TEV], 'to shake' [CEV], 'to tear' [KJV], 'to cause (him) to lose control of himself' [NCV]. This is also translated with the boy as the subject: 'to go into convulsions' [GW].
e. ἀφρός (LN **14.27**) (BAGD p. 12): 'foam' [BAGD, LN]. This refers to frothy saliva coming from the boy's mouth, something that is typical of epileptic seizures [LN]. The phrase μετὰ ἀφροῦ 'with foam' is translated 'with foaming' [Lns], 'with foaming at the mouth' [NASB], 'so that he foams' [Arn, BECNT], 'so that he foams at the mouth' [NIV, NLT, REB, TEV], 'so that he froths at the mouth' [AB], 'and causes him to foam at the mouth' [**LN**; NET], 'and produces foaming' [WBC], 'and foam at the mouth' [NCV; similarly GW], 'until he foams at the mouth' [CEV, HCSB, NRSV], 'that he foams again' [KJV].
f. μόλις (LN **78.41**) (BAGD 1. p. 526): 'hardly' [LN; KJV, REB], 'hardly ever' [HCSB, NET, NLT], 'scarcely' [**LN**, NTC; NRSV], 'scarcely ever' [NIV], 'with difficulty' [BAGD, BECNT, Lns], 'with reluctance' [Arn], 'only with difficulty' [WBC; NASB], 'only after a struggle' [AB], 'almost never (leaves)' [NCV], not explicit [CEV, GW].
g. pres. act. participle of συντρίβω (LN **19.46**) (BAGD 1.b. p. 793): 'to crush' [BAGD, **LN**], 'to smash, to shatter' [BAGD], 'to bruise' [BECNT, LN, Lns; KJV], 'to bruise badly' [AB], 'to maul' [NTC; NASB, NRSV], 'to wound' [HCSB], 'to keep hurting' [NCV, TEV], 'to hit and to injure' [NLT], 'to maltreat' [Arn], 'to torture severely' [NET], 'to torment' [REB], 'to destroy' [NIV], 'to devastate' [WBC]. This is also translated with the boy as the subject: 'to be worn out' [GW], 'to be completely worn out' [CEV].

QUESTION—Who screamed when the spirit seized the boy?
1. The boy screamed [Alf, BECNT, EGT, Lns, MGC, My, TG; all versions except REB, TEV]. There is a rapid change of subject at this point [EGT]. When the demon has seized the boy, the boy suddenly screams because of the seizure produced by the spirit [TG]. The demon makes the boy scream [CEV, NLT].
2. The spirit screamed [NIGTC, TH, WBC; REB, TEV]. The spirit shouted out through the boy's voice [TH]. It cried out inarticulately [NIGTC].

QUESTION—Can this affliction be identified?
The description corresponds to epilepsy [AB, Arn, BNTC, Gdt, Lns, MGC, NAC, NIGTC, NTC, Su, TG, WBC; NET]. In Matthew 17:15 the father says that his son σεληνιάζεται 'suffers epileptic seizures, is an epileptic' [LN (23.169)]. However, this seizure was due to demon possession [MGC, TNTC, WBC], so it was not just ordinary epilepsy [Lns, TNTC].
QUESTION—What is meant by μόγις ἀποχωρεῖ ἀπ' αὐτοῦ 'hardly departs from him'?
The adverb 'hardly' indicates that the demon reluctantly gives up its control of the boy [AB]. The convulsions lasted a long time [Su] and the attacks subsided slowly [Lns]. The demon 'won't leave him until it has completely worn the boy out' [CEV]. 'After a struggle the spirit goes away' [GW]. The spirit almost never leaves the boy [NAC; NCV, NET, NIV, NLT].
QUESTION—What is meant by the last phrase of 9:39, συντρῖβον αὐτόν 'crushing him'?
1. This is connected with the demon leaving the boy. [AB, MGC, NIGTC, NTC, TH, WBC; GW, KJV, NASB]. It is an act simultaneous with leaving and means that after a struggle it leaves the boy badly bruised [TH]. The spirit mauls the boy as it leaves [Arn, MGC; NASB]. It scarcely leaves the boy alone while it continues to wear him out [NIGTC]. 'While mauling him it will scarcely let him go' [NTC]. 'Even after devastating the boy, it can only with difficulty be got to leave him' [WBC].
2. This is another description of the seizures [BECNT, Lns, TG; CEV, HCSB, NCV, NIV, NLT, NRSV, REB, TEV]. The boy is bruised by falling down during the seizures [BECNT, Lns]. The spirit is always hitting and injuring the boy [NLT].

9:41 And answering Jesus said, O unbelieving[a] and being-perverted[b] generation,[c] until[d] when will-I-be with you and will-I-put-up-with[e] you? Bring your son here.
LEXICON—a. ἄπιστος (LN 31.98) (BAGD 2. p. 85): 'unbelieving' [AB, Arn, BAGD, LN, Lns, WBC; GW, HCSB, NASB, NET, NIV, REB, TEV], 'faithless' [BAGD, BECNT, NTC; KJV, NLT, NRSV], 'lacking in trust' [LN]. This adjective is also translated as a verb phrase: 'you don't have faith' [CEV], 'you have no faith' [NCV]. This adjective can indicates both unbelief and faithlessness [Lns, NIC]. It means to have no faith, to be without faith [TG]. They refused to trust when they ought to trust [Lns]. It was because of the disciples' lack of faith that the boy had not been healed [BECNT].
b. perf. pass. participle of διαστρέφω (LN 88.264) (BAGD 1.b. p. 189): 'to be perverted' [BAGD, LN, Lns], 'to be depraved' [BAGD], 'to be misled' [LN], 'to be wrong' [TEV], 'to be stubborn' [CEV]. This participle is also translated as an adjective: 'perverted' [NTC; NASB], 'perverse' [AB, Arn, BECNT, WBC; KJV, NET, NIV, NRSV, REB], 'corrupt' [GW],

'stubborn' [NLT], 'rebellious' [HCSB]; as a clause: 'your lives are all wrong' [NCV]. This refers to those who have strayed from walking the right path [BECNT]. The verb 'to be turned around' has a moral meaning here of being sinful [TG].
- c. γενεά (LN 11.4) (BAGD 2. p. 154): 'generation' [AB, Arn, BAGD, BECNT, LN, Lns, NTC, WBC; GW, HCSB, KJV, NASB, NET, NIV, NRSV, REB], 'you people' [CEV, NCV, NLT, TEV]. This refers to the people of Jesus' time as a whole, although there were a few exceptions [Lns]. See this word at 1:48, 50; 7:31; 11:29, 50; 16:8; 17:25; 21:32.
- d. ἕως (LN 67.119): 'until' [LN]. The phrase ἕως ὅτου 'until when' [WBC] is also translated 'how long' [AB, Arn, BECNT, Lns, NTC; all versions except CEV, NET, NRSV], 'how much longer' [CEV, NET, NRSV].
- e. fut. mid. indic. of ἀνέχομαι, ἀνέχω (LN 25.171) (BAGD 1.a. p. 65): 'to put up with' [AB, BAGD, NTC, WBC; CEV, GW, HCSB, NASB, NCV, NIV, NLT, TEV], 'to bear with' [Arn, BAGD, BECNT; NRSV], 'to endure someone' [BAGD, Lns; NET, REB], 'to be patient with' [LN], 'to suffer someone' [KJV].

QUESTION—What is the function of the participle διεστραμμένη 'being perverted'?

This gives the reason for the people being unbelieving [Lns]. Most translate this as an added attribute of this generation.

QUESTION—Who was Jesus rebuking?
1. Jesus was rebuking the father and also the entire group of people assembled [AB, Arn, BECNT, Gdt, ICC, MGC, NAC, NIBC, NIGTC, NTC, TH]. The rebuke was addressed to the father, but it includes the crowd [ICC]. It was addressed to the father, although it described the crowd and the disciples since they were all members of the unbelieving generation [NIGTC]. The father acknowledged his lack of belief in Mark 9:24, the scribes did not believe (Mark 9:14), the people in general were influenced by the scribes, and the disciples were unable to heal the boy because of their unbelief [Gdt]. The father, the scribes, the crowd in general, and the disciples to some extent were faithless [Arn, NTC]. Jesus addressed them all, but especially the disciples [BECNT].
2. Jesus was rebuking the crowd in general, not the father [TNTC]. The father wouldn't be addressed as a generation, and he did have enough faith to bring his son. The crowd in general had assembled merely to see what the disciples could or could not do [TNTC].
3. Jesus was rebuking the nine disciples [BNTC, Lns, My, NIC, WBC]. The disciples had been given authority to cast out demons, and their inability to do so was due to their lack of faith [NICNT]. The disciples did not have faith to drive out the demon and they exhibited the unbelief characteristic of the whole generation [Lns]. Although not directly addressed to the disciples, the words were about them [BNTC]. Jesus addressed the disciples as being representatives of the generation [WBC].

QUESTION—What is meant by the question 'until when will I be with you and put up with you'?

The future tense of 'will be' implies compulsion, with the idea 'must I be with you' [TH]. With this rhetorical question Jesus expressed his pain and disappointment that after such a long time of being with the disciples they were like this generation in their unbelief [Lns]. It shows his concern about their lack of faith [TNTC]. It indicates Jesus' impatience with their continuing lack of faith [Gdt, NIGTC]. In view of Jesus' own trust in the Father, it was painful to put up with those who lacked faith [NTC]. It expresses Jesus' hope that that he would not be with them much longer and have to endure them [MGC, TG]. Jesus anticipated his execution and was disappointed with the disciples' lack of readiness to take up the ministry he planned for them [NICNT].

9:42 **And (while) still approaching him the demon threw- him -down^a and convulsed^b (him). And Jesus rebuked the unclean spirit and healed the child and returned^c him to-his father. 9:43a And all were-astonished^d at the mighty-power^e of-God.**

LEXICON—a. aorist act. indic. of ῥήγνυμι (LN **23.168**) (BAGD 2.a. p. 735): 'to throw someone down' [Arn, BAGD, WBC; KJV], 'to throw down to the ground' [**LN**], 'to throw on the ground' [NCV], 'to throw to the ground' [BECNT; NET, NIV], 'to knock to the ground' [GW, NLT, TEV], 'to knock down' [HCSB], 'to slam to the ground' [NASB], 'to dash to the ground' [AB, NTC; NRSV, REB], 'to attack' [CEV], 'to tear' [Lns]. In the aorist tense, the verb forms are the same for 'to throw down' and for 'to tear' [AB, BECNT, TG, TH], but 'to tear' does not fit the context [TG, TH]. This would be the first stage in the process of throwing the boy into convulsions [LN].

b. aorist act. indic. of συσπαράσσω (LN **23.167**) (BAGD p. 794): 'to convulse' [Arn, BAGD, **LN**, Lns, WBC], 'to throw down in convulsions' [LN], 'to throw into convulsions' [GW, REB], 'to throw into a convulsion' [AB, NTC; NASB], 'to throw into a violent convulsion' [NLT], 'to throw into severe convulsions' [HCSB], 'to throw into a fit' [TEV], 'to cause to go into convulsions' [BECNT], 'to shake someone with convulsions' [NET], 'to make to shake all over' [CEV], 'to make someone lose control of himself' [NCV], 'to tear' [KJV], 'in a convulsion' [NIV], 'in convulsions' [NRSV].

c. aorist act. indic. of ἀποδίδωμι (LN 57.151) (BAGD 2. p. 90): 'to return' [AB, BAGD], 'to give back' [Arn, BAGD, BECNT, LN, Lns, NTC; all versions except KJV], 'to give' [WBC], 'to deliver again' [KJV]. This refers to turning the boy back to his father's care [TG, TH].

d. imperf. pass. indic. of ἐκπλήσσομαι (ἐκπλήσσω) (LN 25.219) (BAGD 2. p. 244): 'to be astonished'. See translations of this word at 2:48 and 4:32.

e. μεγαλειότης (LN **76.2**) (BAGD p. 496): 'mighty power' [**LN**; KJV, NET, TEV], 'great power' [CEV, NCV], 'wonderful power' [GW], 'majestic power' [AB], 'display of power' [NLT], 'majesty' [Arn, BAGD, BECNT, Lns, NTC], 'magnificence' [WBC], 'greatness' [HCSB, NASB, NIV, NRSV, REB]. This is a rare word that is equivalent to 'glory' [TH]. It was a demonstration of God's great power [TG].

QUESTION—Who was approaching Jesus?

There is a rapid change of subject and this refers to the boy approaching Jesus [AB, Alf, BECNT, EGT, ICC, NTC, Rb, TH, TNTC, WBC; CEV, NCV, NET, NIV, NLT, REB, TEV]. The boy was being brought to Jesus [CEV]. However, the demon attacked before the boy could reach Jesus [REB].

QUESTION—In what way did Jesus rebuke the unclean spirit?

The rebuke was a command for the demon to leave the boy [TG]. 'Jesus ordered the evil spirit to leave' [GW]. Jesus' word was sufficient to cause the demon to depart from the boy [NICNT].

QUESTION—In what way did Jesus heal the boy?

1. This refers to casting out the demon [AB, BECNT, Lns, MGC, My, NICNT, NTC, Su, TG, TH]. In most cases, 'heal' is used of healing diseases, but here it is used of exorcism, maybe because the demon was using a physical ailment in its attack [AB, BECNT]. Healing is the result of rebuking the demon [Lns, NTC, TH]. Jesus healed the boy by ordering the evil spirit to go out of him [TG].
2. Healing was a separate act from casting out the demon [BNTC, ICC, NIBC, NIC]. After rebuking the unclean spirit and casting it out, the boy was left in a condition that required healing [ICC]. After the demon had left the boy, the boy needed physical healing, so had Jesus accomplished two miracles [NIC].

QUESTION—How did the people recognize the mighty power of God

The people recognized the majesty of God in the healing of the boy [NTC]. They recognized that Jesus had healed the boy as God's agent so that God's majesty was manifested through him [AB, Lns, NAC]. In Jesus' mighty works, God was at work [WBC].

DISCOURSE UNIT: 9:43b–45 [AB, BECNT, NAC, NIGTC, Su, TNTC, WBC; CEV, GW, HCSB, NCV, NET, NLT, NRSV, TEV]. The topic is Jesus talks about his death [NCV], Jesus again speaks about his death [CEV, TEV], the second passion announcement [AB, NAC, Su, TNTC], another prediction of Jesus' suffering [NET], a prediction of betrayal [BECNT, NIGTC, WBC; GW], Jesus again predicts his death [NLT, NRSV], the second prediction of his death [HCSB].

9:43b And (while) all were-amazed[a] at everything which he-was-doing he-said to his disciples, 9:44 You put[b] into your ears these words,[c] namely/because[d] the Son of-Man[e] is-about to-be-delivered[f] into (the) hands of-men.

TEXT—In 9:43, instead of ἐποίει 'he was doing', some manuscripts read ἐποίησεν ὁ Ἰησοῦς 'Jesus did'. GNT does not mention this variant. Ἐποίησεν ὁ Ἰησοῦς 'Jesus did' is read by KJV.

LEXICON—a. pres. act. participle of θαυμάζω (LN 25.213) (BAGD 1.a.β. p. 352): 'to be amazed'. See this word at 1:21, 63; 2:18, 33; 4:22; 7:9; 8:25; 11:14, 38; 20:26; 24:12, 41.

b. aorist mid. impera. of τίθημι (LN **24.64, 29.5**) (BAGD II.1.c. p. 816): 'to put, to place' [BAGD]. The idiom τίθεμαι εἰς τὰ ὦταα 'to put into the ears' has the meaning of listening carefully, and it implies that the person is not to forget what he hears [LN (24.64)]. The phrase is translated 'to put into one's ears' [Lns, WBC], 'to let sink into one's ears' [BECNT, NTC; HCSB, NASB, NRSV; similarly KJV], 'to give ear to' [Arn], 'to lay up deep within one' [AB], 'to pay close attention to' [CEV], 'to listen carefully to' [GW], 'to take to heart' [NET], 'to listen to' [REB], 'to listen carefully to' [**LN** (24.64); NIV], 'to listen to and remember' [NLT], 'to remember well' [LN (29.5)], 'to not forget' [LN (29.5); NCV, TEV], 'to bear in mind' [**LN** (29.5)],

c. λόγος (LN 33.98): 'word' [LN (33.98)], 'saying' [LN (13.98)]. The phrase λόγους τούτους 'these words' [BECNT, Lns, NTC, WBC; HCSB, NASB, NET, NRSV] is also translated 'these words of mine' [AB], 'these sayings' [KJV], 'these remarks' [Arn], 'what I say' [GW, NLT], 'what I am telling you' [CEV], 'what I tell you now' [NCV], 'what I have to tell you' [REB], 'what I am about to tell you' [NIV, TEV].

d. γάρ (LN 89.23): 'namely' [BECNT], 'because' [LN], 'for' [Arn, LN, Lns, WBC; KJV, NASB], not explicit [CEV, GW, HCSB, NLT, REB, TEV]. The function of the conjunction is signaled by a colon which implies the meaning 'namely' [AB, NTC; NCV, NIV, NRSV].

e. υἱὸς τοῦ ἀνθρώπου 'Son of Man'. This title for Christ occurs at 5:24; 6:5, 22; 7:34; 9:22, 26, 44; 11:30; 12:8, 40; 17:22, 24, 26; 18:8, 31; 19:10; 21:27, 36; 22:22, 48, 69; 24:7. See the discussions of this title at 5:24, 6:5, and 9:22.

f. pres. pass. indic. of παραδίδωμι (LN 37.12) (BAGD 1.b. p. 614): 'to be delivered, to be handed over' [BAGD]. The idiom παραδίδωμι εἰς χεῖρας 'to give into the hands' means to hand someone over into the control of others [LN]. The phrase 'to be delivered into the hands of men' [BECNT, Lns; KJV, NASB] is also translated 'to be delivered up into the hands of men' [Arn, WBC], 'to be handed over into the hands of men' [AB], 'to be handed over to people' [NCV], 'to be handed over to his enemies' [CEV], 'to be handed over to the power of human beings' [TEV], 'to be given up into the power of men' [REB], 'to be betrayed into the hands of men' [NTC; HCSB, NET, NIV], 'to be betrayed into human hands' [NRSV], 'to be betrayed and handed over to people' [GW]. The verb refers to being given over in some way, and can mean handing Jesus over to be arrested or it can mean betraying Jesus [NIGTC]. It means to be handed over to the custody of men [TH], to be handed over to the authorities, to be arrested [TG]. See this word at 21:12.

QUESTION—In what way were the disciples to put the words into their ears?

They were to listen carefully to Jesus' words [LN, TH; CEV, GW, NIV, REB]. They were to keep his words in their minds and remember them [Arn, Gdt, ICC, LN; NCV, TEV]. They were to pay attention to the words, store them in their memories, and meditate on them [NTC; NLT].

QUESTION—What words were they to put in their ears and how does the conjunction γάρ 'namely, because' connect with that?

1. The words are those in the following statement [AB, BECNT, Crd, Gdt, ICC, NAC, NICNT, NIGTC, NTC, TG, TH, TNTC, WBC; NCV, NIV, NRSV, REB, TEV]: put into your ears these words I am going to tell you, *namely that* the Son of Man is about to be delivered into the hands of men. The conjunction γάρ indicates the words that are referred to [NIGTC]. It explains why such a solemn warning was given and it makes clear what he wants them to hear [BECNT, WBC].
2. The words refer to the several announcements of Jesus' death [Alf]: put into your ears the words I keep telling you about my death, *specifically that* the Son of Man is about to be delivered into the hands of men. It does not mean 'what I am about to tell you', but refers to the statements of his death that he makes from time to time, of which the following words are the second of such statements [Alf].
3. The words refer to the expressions of amazement by all the people in 9:43 [My]: put into your ears these words of amazement you have heard, *because* the Son of Man is about to be delivered into the hands of men. The disciples needed to remember the events that brought on such amazement because of the contrast in the events that would soon happen to Jesus [My].
4. The words are not recorded by Luke [Lns]: put into your ears those words I have already told you, *because* the Son of Man is about to be delivered into the hands of men. They are the words quoted by Matthew 17:22 and Mark 9:31 about Jesus being killed and rising again, but in Luke the words are only implied by the conjunction 'because' [Lns].

QUESTION—Who would hand over or betray Jesus?

1. God would hand over Jesus [Gdt, ICC, NAC, NIGTC, TH]. The passive is often used to indicate God's action and this agrees with the phrases 'it is necessary' and 'as it is written' [NIGTC]. Jesus would be handed over according to God's plan [AB, Gdt]. The meaning 'betray' would not be intended here [NAC].
2. Some people would hand over Jesus [TG], or people would betray him [BECNT].
3. Judas would hand over Jesus to men [EGT, Lns, Su; GW] or betray Jesus to men [GW, NET, NIV]. The verb παραδίδωμι is used of Judas betraying Jesus at 22:4 and he would deliver Jesus in the sense of formally

identifying him so that a legal arrest could be made [Su]. The passive form keeps from naming Judas at this time [Lns].

QUESTION—Who are the men that Jesus would be handed over to?
There is a play on words: the 'Son of Man' and 'the hands of men' [NAC].
1. The men were the Jewish religious leaders [MGC, Su]. The elders, chief priests, and scribes are specified in 9:22 [Su].
2. The men were the authorities [Lns, TG]. They would include the Sanhedrin and Pilate [Lns].

9:45 But they-were-not-understanding this word and it-had-been hidden[a] from them so-that[b] they-did- not -understand it, and they-were-afraid to-ask him about this word.

LEXICON—a. perf. pass. participle of παρακαλύπτω (LN **28.82**) (BAGD p. 617): 'to be hidden' [AB, Arn, BAGD, **LN**, Lns, NTC; CEV, GW, NCV, NIV, NLT, REB, TEV], 'to be hid' [KJV], 'to be concealed' [BAGD, BECNT, WBC; HCSB, NET, NRSV].
b. ἵνα (LN 89.49, 89.59): 'so that' [AB, Arn, LN, Lns, WBC; GW, HCSB, NET, NIV, NRSV, REB, TEV], 'that' [BECNT, NTC; KJV], 'as a result' [LN (89.49)], 'so' [NCV, NLT], 'in order that' [LN (89.59)], not explicit [CEV].

QUESTION—In what way didn't they understand the word?
It does not mean that the words themselves were unintelligible [BECNT; NET]. They did not get the point of what Jesus said [NET] and did not see how it could fit into God's plan [BECNT; NET].

QUESTION—How could the significance of this word be hidden from them?
1. God hid the significance of Jesus' words from them [AB, Alf, BECNT, Gdt, ICC, MGC, My, NIBC, NIC, NIGTC, NTC, TG, TH]. The passive voice again points to God's action [NIGTC]. It was God's purpose that they not understand it at that time [NIGTC]. Perhaps without experiencing the resurrection and ascension of Jesus and the coming of the Holy Spirit the disciples were not prepared to realize the significance of these words [NTC].
2. Their own ideas hid it from them [Lns, NAC, NICNT, Su]. Their preconceived ideas about Jesus' victory and reign as Messiah prevented them from understanding the true meaning of Jesus' words [Lns]. Since Jesus wanted them to understand, it was not God who hid it from them, rather it was their unwillingness to accept the necessity of Jesus' death [Su].
3. The devil hid it from them [TNTC, WBC]. Since the statement in the preceding verse was not very specific, that could be the reason they did not understand, but more importantly, there was opposition from the forces of evil [TNTC].

QUESTION—Does ἵνα 'that' indicate the result or purpose for the meaning being hidden from them?
    1. It indicates the result [AB, BECNT, Lns, NAC, Su, TH; GW, NCV, NIV, NLT]: it had been hidden from them *and so* they did not understand it. Interpreting the fact that it was hidden from them was due to their own slowness to catch on requires that ἵνα be taken as result [NAC].
    2. It indicates purpose [Alf, Gdt, ICC, MGC, My, NIGTC, Rb]: it had been hidden from them *in order that* they not understand it. This was God's purpose for hiding the meaning from the disciples [Rb]. They were not allowed to understand at the time, but understanding would come afterwards when they realized that Jesus had met his sufferings with full knowledge and free will [ICC].

QUESTION—Why would they be afraid to ask Jesus?
They may have been embarrassed that they did not understand [BECNT] and they may have been afraid of what the answer might be [BECNT, TG]. They were afraid that it might be true that Jesus was going to die [Lns]. They might be realizing that Jesus' destiny might have implications for them [AB]. They may be afraid after witnessing the mighty power of God [NAC].

DISCOURSE UNIT: 9:46–56 [NASB]. The topic is the test of greatness.

DISCOURSE UNIT: 9:46–50 [BECNT, NAC; NIV]. The topic is humility and openness [NAC], greatness and cooperation [BECNT], who will be the greatest? [NIV].

DISCOURSE UNIT: 9:46–48 [AB, NIGTC, Su, TNTC, WBC; CEV, GW, HCSB, NCV, NET, NLT, NRSV, TEV]. The topic is the strife among the disciples [NIGTC], the rivalry of the disciples [AB], who is the greatest? [WBC; CEV, HCSB, NCV, TEV], true greatness [NRSV], concerning the greatest [NET], the greatest in the kingdom [GW, NLT], the disciples' pride [TNTC], teaching on humility [Su].

9:46 And a-reasoning[a] arose among them, as-to who might-be (the) greatest[b] of-them.

LEXICON—a. διαλογισμός (LN 30.16, **33.446**) (BAGD 2. p. 186): 'reasoning' [LN (30.16), Lns; KJV], 'discussion' [GW], 'inquiry' [Arn], 'argument' [AB, BAGD, BECNT, LN (33.446); HCSB, NASB, NET, NIV, NLT, NRSV, REB, TEV], 'dispute' [NTC, WBC]. The phrase 'a reasoning arose among them' is translated 'they argued' [**LN**], 'they were arguing' [CEV], 'they began to have an argument' [NCV].
    b. μέγας (LN 87.22, 87.28) (BAGD 2.b.α. p. 498): 'greater' [LN, Lns], 'greatest' [AB, Arn, BECNT, LN, NTC, WBC; all versions]. Although it is grammatically in the comparative degree 'greater', it is used here as a superlative, the 'greatest' [AB, Crd, NAC, NIGTC, NTC, TH]. See this word at 1:15, 32; 7:28; 22:24.

QUESTION—Was the reasoning that arose among the disciples outward or inward?
1. The reasoning was an outward argument [AB, Alf, BNTC, Gdt, ICC, LN, Lns, NIC, NTC, Rb, TG, TH, WBC; CEV, GW, HCSB, NASB, NCV, NET, NIV, NLT, NRSV, REB, TEV]: an argument arose among them. The phrase ἐν αὐτοῖς 'among them' indicates that this was an argument that had taken place among the disciples [BECNT, Gdt]. It is not necessary to confine this to their thoughts, which would make this different from Mark 9:33. Possibly their inward desires to be considered superior were not expressed out loud in the argument and Jesus rebuked such thoughts in the next verse although 'among them' implies that they expressed such desires [ICC].
2. The reasoning was an inward thought [Arn, EGT, My]: a thought entered their minds. This was a thought in their hearts as described in the next verse and it is not an open argument as Mark 9:33 has it [EGT, My].

QUESTION—What is meant by being the greatest?

It means to be greatest in the matter of rank, position, and prestige [NIGTC]. 'Greatest' could mean having the most authority, receiving the most preferential treatment, being the most valuable, or being the most favored by God [NAC]. It is being the most important, having the highest standing in the group of disciples [TG]. It could refer to the ranking of the group of disciples as they accompanied Jesus [Su]. It probably refers to being the greatest in the future kingdom [BECNT, Crd, ICC], and refers to the one nearest to Christ [ICC]. Some indicate that the status of a single one of them was the point of the argument: 'which one of them was the greatest' [BECNT, Lns; CEV, NCV, NRSV, REB, TEV]. Although most take the superlative sense of the word, two take it as a comparative so that the question is which ones will be greater than the others. All twelve would be great in the coming kingdom, but they were arguing about which ones of them would outrank others [Lns], or which would be the highest ranking officials in the kingdom of God [MGC].

9:47 **And Jesus knowing the reasoning[a] of their heart(s), having-taken[b] a-child stood[c] it beside himself,**

TEXT—Instead of εἰδώς 'knowing', some manuscripts read γνούς 'having known' and some manuscripts read ἰδών 'having seen'. GNT reads εἰδώς 'knowing' with a C decision, indicating that the Committee had difficulty making the decision.

LEXICON—a. διαλογισμός (LN 30.16) (BAGD 1. p. 186): 'reasoning' [BAGD, LN, Lns], 'thought' [BAGD, BECNT; HCSB, KJV], 'inquiry' [Arn], 'what they were thinking' [NTC; NASB, TEV], 'contentious thoughts' [WBC]. The phrase 'the reasoning of their hearts' is translated as a verb phrase 'what they were thinking' [CEV, GW, NCV], 'what was going on in their minds' [REB], 'their innermost thoughts' [NET], 'their

430   LUKE 9:47

inner thoughts' [NRSV], 'the thoughts that were in their minds' [AB], 'their thoughts' [NIV, NLT].
   b. aorist mid. (deponent = act.) participle of ἐπιλαμβάνομαι (LN 18.2) (BAGD 1. p. 295): 'to take' [AB, Arn, BECNT, NTC, WBC; all versions except CEV, NLT], 'to take up' [Lns], 'to take hold of' [BAGD, LN], 'to grasp' [BAGD, LN], not explicit [CEV, NLT]. This means that Jesus drew the child to himself [TH]. It was a sign that the child belonged to him as the humblest of his followers [ICC, NIC].
   c. aorist act. indic. of ἵστημι (LN 85.40) (BAGD I.1.a. p. 382): 'to place' [BAGD, LN, WBC], 'to make to stand' [LN], 'to stand (him)' [AB, Lns; NASB, NCV, REB, TEV], 'to have him stand' [NTC; GW, NET, NIV], 'to set' [BAGD; KJV], 'to put' [BECNT, LN; NRSV], 'to place' [Arn]. The phrase 'having taken a child stood it beside himself' is translated 'he had a child stand there beside him' [CEV], 'had him stand next to him' [HCSB], 'he brought a little child to his side' [NLT]. The child stood at his side so that all attention would be focused on the child [TH]. To be at Jesus' side was a place of honor [EGT, ICC, NICNT, NIGTC].

QUESTION—What relationship is indicated by the use of the participle εἰδώς 'knowing'?
   1. It is temporal [AB, BECNT, Su; NET]: *when* Jesus knew the reasoning of their hearts, he stood a child beside him.
   2. It indicates a coordinate circumstance in relation to the main verb 'to stand' [Arn, Lns, NTC, WBC; CEV, GW, KJV, NASB, NCV, NIV, NRSV, REB]: Jesus, knowing the reasoning of their hearts, stood a child beside him.
   3. It indicates reason [NLT, TEV]: *because* Jesus knew the reasoning of their hearts, he stood a child beside him.

QUESTION—Why did Jesus have to know their thoughts if they had just been arguing?
   Perhaps Jesus had been far enough away from the disciples that he could not hear what they were arguing about [NTC, TG, WBC]. In Mark 9:33, Jesus asked them what they were arguing about on the way, and in shame they kept silent, so intuitively he knew their thoughts which were still present [Crd, NIGTC]. He didn't need to hear what they had said to know their thoughts, it was a supernatural knowledge [NAC, NTC, TH]. It was Jesus' supernatural knowledge of the thoughts still going on in their hearts [Lns, NIGTC]. The discussion had been about who was the greatest and in their hearts was the thought 'I am the greatest' [ICC].

9:48 and he-said to-them, Whoever receives[a] this child in[b] my name, receives me. And whoever receives me, receives the (one) having-sent me. Because the (one who) is least[c] among all of-you, this (one) is great/ greatest.[d]

LEXICON—a. aorist mid. (deponent = act.) subj. of δέχομαι (LN 34.53) (BAGD 1. p. 177): 'to receive' [AB, Arn, BAGD, BECNT, LN, Lns,

WBC; KJV, NASB, REB], 'to welcome' [BAGD, LN, NTC; CEV, GW, HCSB, NET, NIV, NLT, NRSV, TEV], 'to accept' [LN; NCV].
- b. ἐπί (LN 90.23) (BAGD II.3. p. 288). This preposition ἐπί (with the genitive) and also the prepositions εἰς (with the accusative) and ἐν (with the dative) are markers of content as a means of specifying a particular referent: 'concerning, with respect to, with reference to, about, in' [LN (90.23)]. The formula ἐπὶ τῷ ὀνόματί μου 'in my name' [AB, BECNT, NTC; all versions except CEV, NLT] is also translated 'on my name' [Lns], 'on account of my name' [Arn], 'because of me' [CEV], 'on my behalf' [NLT], 'as though he were me' [WBC].
- c. μικρός (LN 87.58) (BAGD 1.c. p. 521): 'least' [AB, BAGD, BECNT, LN, NTC, WBC; all versions except CEV], 'lesser' [Lns], 'unimportant' [LN], 'most humble' [CEV]. This pertains to a person's esteem, importance, influence, and power [BAGD].
- d. μέγας (LN 87.22) (BAGD 2.b.α. p. 498): 'great' [AB, BECNT, Lns, NTC, WBC; HCSB, KJV, NASB, NET], 'greatest' [LN; CEV, GW, NCV, NIV, NLT, NRSV, REB, TEV]. This noun pertains to being great in terms of status and means 'important' [BECNT, LN, TG]. It refers to rank and dignity [TH]. See this word at 9:46.

QUESTION—What child was to be received and how is he to be received?

When Jesus referred to τοῦτο παιδίον 'this child', he used that particular child as an example [EGT, Lns, NTC, TG, TH]. Mark 9:36 indicates that Jesus meant 'one such child', that is, this child or any similar child [ICC]. Instead of referring to the child as an individual, Jesus refers to the child as a representative of unimportant people in general [NICNT, TG], those of the lowest social status, the poor, and even this child [NICNT]. It means such a *person* as this child [AB]. To receive such a person is to welcome Jesus [NICNT, NIGTC, NTC; CEV, GW, NET, NIV, NLT, NRSV, TEV]. Receiving a person refers to hospitality in the form of welcoming someone [BECNT]. It includes caring for his needs [Arn, Lns, NIGTC, Su]. It means to accept and esteem him [AB]. It is to be kind to him and ignore whatever status he has [BECNT].

QUESTION—What is meant by the phrase ἐπὶ τῷ ὀνόματί μου 'in my name'?
1. This phrase modifies the verb 'receives'.
    1.1 It means to receive 'on the basis of my name', 'because of my name', or 'for my sake' [ICC, NAC, NIC, NICNT, NIGTC, TH]. A disciple is to do this because he follows Jesus [NIGTC], and wants to do the same as Jesus does [NIGTC]. A disciple does this as a follower of Jesus [TH]. The disciple knows that the child belongs to Christ, so he receives the child for Christ's sake [ICC]. He does this for Christ's sake because he loves Christ [NIC].
    1.2 It means to receive 'on the basis of my will and teaching' [Lns, NTC]. The disciple will receive the child as Jesus' teaching requires [Lns]. Christ's name refers to Christ and his self-revelation, so the disciple will

welcome such a child and care for it with love and consideration as Jesus told his followers to do [NTC].

1.3 It means to receive 'as my representative' [Su]. The disciple acts in Jesus' place and receives the child in the manner Jesus would receive him [Su].

2. This phrase modifies the noun 'child' and describes how the child relates to Jesus [AB, Arn, My, NAC, TG, WBC]. The child is to be received because he belongs to Jesus [Arn, My]. The child is Jesus' follower, his disciple [TG]. The child is to be received as being a representative of Jesus [AB, TG, WBC]. It can be stated 'receive this child as though he were me' [WBC]. As the child is received as being a representative of Jesus, so Jesus is received as being a representative of the Father [NAC].

QUESTION—What is meant by receiving Jesus?

Most seem to take the verb in the same way as it is used in receiving a child, so that the action done to the child is regarded as being done to Christ. The relation between the child and Jesus is so very close that what is done for Jesus' sake to the child is done to Jesus, and also to the Father who sent him [NTC]. To receive a child in the name of Christ is like receiving Christ himself [Lns]. However, some think that 'to receive Christ' has a different meaning from that of receiving a child [NIGTC, TH]. It now refers to obedient acceptance of Christ as Lord [NIGTC]. It means to acknowledge Christ and obey him [TH]. Behind the imagery of hospitality in receiving Jesus and the Father, there is a sense of having fellowship with Jesus and the Father when one extends hospitality to the least [WBC].

QUESTION—What relationship is indicated by γάρ 'because' in the last clause?

1. This gives the answer to the question that was debated in 9:46 about who was the greatest [AB]. It corresponds to Jesus' answer in Mark 9:35 where it precedes the episode with the child [AB].

2. This gives the reason why one should receive even the least [BECNT]. One must love all because even the least are great [BECNT].

3. This gives the conclusion to the episode with the child [Gdt, Lns]. To do a service that is considered to be unimportant and which others decline to do is great in Jesus' estimation [Lns].

QUESTION—What is meant by the one who is least?

1. This refers to the person who is least important [AB, BECNT, Gdt, ICC, Lns, NAC, NIC, Su, TG]. The disciple who is least is the one who is least important or considers himself to be least important [TG]. He is prepared to identify himself with the lowly by receiving them [NTC, WBC]. Such a person does a service that others decline to do because they consider it to be least [Lns]. He is willing to humble himself in order to serve others [NAC]. All of the disciples are important and not one of them should be comparing himself with the others [BECNT].

2. This refers to the child standing there with Jesus [NIGTC]. This child is the least among them, yet he is great in God's estimation, so the disciples should not desire to be pre-eminent [NIGTC].

QUESTION—Is μέγας the positive term 'great' or does it have the superlative force 'greatest'?
   1. It has the superlative force of 'greatest' [Arn, Crd, NAC, Su, TG; CEV, GW, NCV, NIV, NLT, NRSV, REB, TEV]: the one being the least among all of you, this one is really the greatest among you. It has the superlative force here because it is contrasted with the superlative force of 'least' [NAC, TG].
   2. It has the positive meaning of being great [AB, BECNT, BNTC, ICC, Lns, My, NIBC, NIC, NIGTC, NTC, TH, TNTC; HCSB, KJV, NASB, NET]: the one being the least among you, this one is really great. 'Great' is the goal that all disciples should attain, so this is not a matter of just one being greater than the rest [Lns]. The act itself is greatness [ICC, NTC]. He is not encouraging the disciples to seek to be above the others [ICC, TNTC]. By speaking of greatness, Jesus indicates that comparisons are not to be made between the disciples and if the least is great, greatness is found in all [BECNT].

DISCOURSE UNIT: 9:49–50 [AB, NIGTC, Su, TNTC, WBC; CEV, GW, HCSB, NCV, NET, NLT, NRSV, TEV]. The topic is using the name of Jesus [GW, NLT], in his name [HCSB], another exorcist [NRSV], the strange exorcist [NIGTC, TNTC, WBC], the exorcist who was an outsider [AB], on working together [Su], being for or against Jesus [CEV], anyone not against us is for us [NCV], whoever is not against you is for you [TEV], on the right side [NET].

9:49 And answering John said, Master,[a] we-saw someone casting-out demons in[b] your name and we tried-to-stop[c] him, because he-is- not -following[d] with us.

TEXT—Instead of the imperfect ἐκωλύομεν 'we tried to stop', some manuscripts read the aorist ἐκωλύσαμεν 'we stopped'. GNT reads the imperfect ἐκωλύομεν 'we tried to stop' with a B decision, indicating that the text is almost certain. The aorist ἐκωλύσαμεν 'we stopped' is read by KJV.

LEXICON—a. ἐπιστάτης (LN 87.50) (BAGD p. 300): 'master'. See translations of this word at 5:5. This word also occurs at 8:24, 45; 9:33; 17:13.
   b. ἐν with dative object (LN 89.76, 90.23): The formula ἐν τῷ ὀνόματί σου 'in your name' [Arn, BECNT, Lns, NTC, WBC; HCSB, KJV, NASB, NET, NIV, NRSV, REB, TEV] is also translated 'using your name' [AB; CEV, NCV, NLT], 'by using the power and authority of your name' [GW]. This preposition ἐν (with the dative) and also the prepositions ἐπί (with the genitive) and εἰς (with the accusative) are markers of content as a means of specifying a particular referent: 'concerning, with respect to, with reference to, about, in' [LN (90.23)] or it indicates means [LN (89.76)].

c. imperf. act. indic. of κωλύω (LN 13.146) (BAGD 1. p. 461): 'to try to stop' [AB, NTC, WBC; GW, HCSB, NET, NIV, NLT, NRSV, REB], 'to try to keep (him) from it' [Arn], 'to forbid' [BAGD, BECNT; KJV], 'to hinder' [BAGD, LN], 'to prevent' [BAGD, LN], 'to try to prevent' [Lns; NASB], 'to tell to stop' [CEV, NCV, TEV].
d. pres. act. indic. of ἀκολουθέω (LN 15.156) (BAGD 2. p. 31): 'to follow' [BAGD, LN], 'to accompany as a follower' [LN], 'to go along with' [BAGD, LN]. The phrase 'he is not following with us' [BECNT; similarly Lns; KJV, NRSV] is also translated 'he is not following along with us' [NTC; similarly AB; NASB], 'he does not belong to our group' [NCV], 'he was not a follower like us' [Arn], 'he is not a disciple with us' [NET], 'he is not one of us' [CEV, NIV, REB; similarly GW], 'he isn't in our group' [NLT], 'he doesn't belong to our group' [TEV], 'he doesn't follow you with us' [WBC]. It means that 'he is not together with us in following you' [TH], 'he does not follow as we do' [NICNT], 'he does not follow us' [HCSB]. He did not follow Jesus [Crd, Lns, NIGTC, TH] along with the Twelve [NIGTC] and the other regular disciples [Lns].

QUESTION—What was John answering to?

'Answer' is used in the sense of responding to Jesus' words in 9:48 [AB, Lns, NICNT, NIGTC, Su, TNTC, WBC]. The link is the 'name of Jesus' [Gdt, MGC, Su]. After hearing Jesus say that a good act done in Jesus' name pleases Jesus and the Father, John may have had doubts about whether he had acted rightly when he interfered with the man who was acting in Jesus' name [Gdt, Lns]. Here the disciples' desire to have exclusive claim to the powers of the new age is part of their desire for greatness [WBC]. Perhaps John meant, 'But surely it would not apply to this situation' or perhaps his conscience was troubled about what he relates here [TNTC]. Perhaps John told this incident with the implicit question, 'What do we do about this?' [AB]. John may have been embarrassed at the rebuke concerning arguing about who was greatest and wanted to change the subject [Rb]. The verb 'answering' is omitted by the following translations: NTC; CEV, NIV, NLT, REB, and TEV.

QUESTION—Where was the man who was casting out demons and who was he?

When John said 'we saw' it was an exclusive 'we' [TH], probably referring to the disciples who went out on the recent preaching and healing trip described in 9:1–6 [Su]. 'We' could refer to all of the disciples or part of them and from 9:51–56 we might assume that it was John and James who had stopped the man who was healing [Su]. From 11:19 we learn that other people than Jesus' disciples were casting out demons. Since Jesus had cast out demons from many people, it may be that others attempted to do so in Jesus' name [TNTC]. The man succeeded in casting out demons by invoking the power associated with Jesus' name [AB]. The man must have believed that there was power in Jesus' name and spoke Jesus' name to do the good work of casting out demons [ICC]. The man probably was a true believer in

Jesus but had not established a close relationship with the other disciples [NICNT, NTC]. The man was working as a follower of Jesus and doing his work as Jesus' representative [Su].

QUESTION—Does the imperfect tense ἐκωλύομεν 'we tried to stop him' indicate that the man stopped?

The imperfect means they tried to stop him [Lns, MGC, NIGTC, NTC, Rb, TG, TH], but probably the attempt did not succeed [Lns, NTC]. The imperfect tense may mean 'we tried to stop him' or 'we kept stopping him' [ICC, TNTC]. They repeatedly tried to get the man to stop [BECNT]. They wanted to stop him because they thought that he could not really be acting in Jesus' name since he was not in fellowship with the group of disciples [Su].

9:50 And Jesus said to him, You(plural)-must- not -stop (him) because (he who) is not against[a] you(plural) is for[b] you(plural).

LEXICON—a. κατά with genitive object (LN 90.31): 'against' [AB, Arn, BECNT, LN, Lns, NTC, WBC; all versions], 'in opposition to' [LN].

b. ὑπέρ with genitive object (LN 90.36): 'for' [AB, Arn, BECNT, LN, Lns, NTC, WBC; all versions except REB], 'on (your) side' [REB].

QUESTION—What relationship is indicated by γάρ 'because'?

This conjunction indicates the reason they are not to stop the man [BECNT, Lns, NAC]. The reason is given by using a proverb [AB, BECNT, MGC, NIGTC]. Here the proverb was used in reference to their attitude to someone who was an outsider [AB, MGC]. In 11:23 the reverse of this proverb says 'he who is not with me is against me' and that is used as a warning against being neutral [AB, MGC], or functions as a test to examine oneself [AB, ICC, NIBC, TNTC].

QUESTION—Why did Jesus use 'you' instead of 'us' when he said 'he who is not against you is for you'?

1. Jesus included himself [Lns]. The 'you' refers to them as the disciples of Jesus and involves Jesus as much as 'us' does in Mark 9:40, where it says 'whoever is not against us, is for us' [Lns].
2. Jesus did not include himself [Gdt, NIGTC]. Jesus was not involved in the conflict since the man cast out demons in Jesus' name, so this concerns the group of Jesus' followers and the man who had not joined that group [Gdt]. The man may not have been authorized by Jesus to cast out demons, but since he was not opposed to the disciples, he was on their side [NIGTC]. That man was on the right side and should be welcomed, not opposed [TNTC].

DISCOURSE UNIT: 9:51–19:48 [NICNT]. The topic is being on the way to Jerusalem.

DISCOURSE UNIT: 9:51–19:44 [BECNT, TNTC]. The topic is the Jerusalem journey: Jewish rejection and the new way [BECNT], from Galilee to Jerusalem [TNTC].

436   LUKE 9:51

DISCOURSE UNIT: 9:51–19:27 [AB, NAC, Su]. The topic is Jesus' journey to Jerusalem.

DISCOURSE UNIT: 9:51–19:10 [NIGTC]. The topic is progress towards Jerusalem.

DISCOURSE UNIT: 9:51–18:14 [AB]. The topic is Luke's travel account.

DISCOURSE UNIT: 9:51–13:21 [AB, NAC]. The topic is the first mention of the journey to Jerusalem [NAC], from the first to the second mention of Jerusalem as Jesus' destination [AB].

DISCOURSE UNIT: 9:51–11:13 [REB]. The topic is the journey to Jerusalem.

DISCOURSE UNIT: 9:51–10:42 [NICNT, NIGTC]. The topic is discipleship, hearing and doing the word [NICNT], duties and privileges of discipleship [NIGTC].

DISCOURSE UNIT: 9:51–10:24 [WBC]. The topic is accompanying Jesus to Jerusalem.

DISCOURSE UNIT: 9:51–62 [NICNT, TNTC]. The topic is the departure to Jerusalem [NICNT], more lessons in discipleship [TNTC].

DISCOURSE UNIT: 9:51–56 [AB, BECNT, NAC, NIGTC, TNTC, WBC; CEV, GW, HCSB, NCV, NET, NIV, NLT, NRSV, TEV]. The topic is the mission to Samaria [NAC], Samaritan opposition [NIV, NLT], rejection in Samaria [BECNT, TNTC, WBC; NET], a town rejects Jesus [NCV], people from a Samaritan village reject Jesus [GW], a Samaritan village refuses to receive Jesus [CEV, NRSV, TEV], Jesus and the Samaritan village [NIGTC], the journey to Jerusalem [HCSB], the departure for Jerusalem and a Samaritan reception [AB].

DISCOURSE UNIT: 9:51 [Su]. The topic is the departure from Galilee.

9:51 And it-happened while the days were-being completed[a] of-his ascension[b] and he set[c] (his) face to-go to Jerusalem.

LEXICON—a. pres. pass. infin. of συμπληρόομαι, συμπληρόω (LN 15.103) (BAGD 2. p. 779): 'to be completed, to come to an end' [LN], 'to approach, to be fulfilled' [BAGD]. The phrase 'while the days were being completed' is translated 'when the days were approaching' [NASB], 'when the days drew near' [BECNT; NET, NRSV], 'when the time was come' [KJV], 'when the time was coming near' [NCV], 'as the time drew near' [NLT, TEV], 'as the days were drawing near' [AB], 'when the days were coming to a close' [HCSB], 'the days were drawing to a close' [WBC], 'the time was coming closer' [GW], 'as the time approached' [NIV, REB], 'not long before it was time' [CEV], 'when the days were being completely filled' [Lns], 'when the days were being fulfilled' [Arn], 'as the predetermined days were running out' [NTC].

b. ἀνάλημψις (LM **15.103**) (BAGD p. 57): 'ascension' [BAGD, LN, NTC; KJV], 'his return to heaven' [NLT]. This noun is also translated as a verb: 'to be taken up' [Arn, **LN**, Lns, WBC; HCSB, NET, NRSV], 'to be received up' [BECNT, **LN**; KJV], 'to depart' [NCV], 'to be taken up to heaven' [AB; CEV, NIV, REB, TEV], 'to be taken to heaven' [GW].
c. aorist act. indic. of στηρίζω (LN **30.80**) (BAGD 1. p. 768): 'to set' [BAGD], 'to fix' [LN] The phrase αὐτὸς τὸ πρόσωπον ἐστήρισεν 'he set his face' [AB, Arn, BECNT, WBC; NRSV] is also translated 'he set his face resolutely (towards)' [REB], 'he set his face firmly' [Lns], 'he set out resolutely' [NET], 'he resolutely set out' [NIV, NLT], 'he steadfastly set his face' [KJV], 'he was determined' [GW, NASB, NCV], 'he determined (to journey)' [HCSB], 'he made up his mind' [**LN**; CEV, TEV], 'he resolutely (set out)' [NTC]. This is a Semitic idiom that emphases finality and means 'to decide firmly, to resolve, to make up one's mind definitely' [LN]. The phrase means to determine to do something [NIGTC].

QUESTION—What is meant by 'while the days were being completed'?

1. This refers to the nearing of the time that Jesus would ascend [Lns, TH, WBC; CEV, GW, KJV, NASB, NCV, NLT, TEV]: the time was approaching for his ascension. This refers to the period that was to elapse before the ascension could take place [TH]. The days were being completed for his ascension to heaven [Lns].
2. This focuses on the fulfillment of something that had been determined [AB, Alf, Arn, BECNT, Gdt, ICC, MGC, NAC, NIGTC, NTC, WBC]: while the days leading to his ascension were being fulfilled. It refers to the fulfillment of God's plan and the plural 'days' and present tense 'were fulfilling' means the completion of the period before the ascension would take place [NIGTC]. The 'days' were the days of Jesus' earthly life [Gdt, WBC]. The days were approaching their fulfillment [Alf]. The days that had been allotted to the interval before his ascension were coming to a close [ICC]. Nothing would happen by accident [BECNT]. In accordance with God's plan, the predetermined days before his ascension were coming to an end [NTC]. God's plan had reached a new stage in being realized [AB].

QUESTION—What is meant by Jesus' ascension?

It means Jesus' ascension into heaven [Alf, EGT, ICC, Lns, MGC, My, NAC, NIC, NICNT, NTC, Rb, TG, TNTC]. The noun can also refer to his death and the primary meaning is Jesus' death, although there must be an allusion to being taken up to God in the ascension [NIGTC]. The word combines both the ideas of his death and his ascension since together they are the consummation of Jesus' return to the Father [Gdt]. This does not say 'his death', because his crucifixion was a stepping stone to his crown [NTC]. The use of the plural 'days' indicates that not only the ascension is in mind but also Jesus' suffering, death, and resurrection that would precede his ascension [NIC, TNTC]. The days include the time from his birth to his ascension to heaven [NAC]. With the words 'he set his face to go to Jerusalem', Luke has in mind the consummation of Jesus' work by his crucifixion, and then his resurrection and ascension [TNTC].

QUESTION—What is implied by Jesus setting his face to go to Jerusalem?
1. It means that he was determined to face something difficult or dangerous [AB, Arn, BECNT, EGT, ICC, NAC, NIC, Rb; NET]. It is the cross that is in view rather than what lay beyond [EGT]. He was aware of the suffering that awaited him in Jerusalem, but with set purpose he went there [NIC]. Jesus was determined to face opposition and accomplish his work [BECNT]. Jesus was determined to face his destiny and whatever opposition that was related to it [AB].
2. It means that he fixed his attention on his ascension [Lns]. Rather than facing death bravely, it means that Jesus looked forward to his return to his Father [Lns].

DISCOURSE UNIT: 9:52–56 [Su]. The topic is the journey into Samaria.

9:52 And he-sent messengers[a] before his face.[b] And having-gone they-entered into a-village of-Samaritans in-order to-make-preparations[c] for-him.

LEXICON—a. ἄγγελος (LN 33.195) (BAGD 1.a. p. 7): 'messenger' [AB, Arn, BAGD, BECNT, LN, Lns, NTC, WBC; all versions except NCV], 'man' [NCV].

b. πρόσωπον (LN 67.19) (BAGD 1.c.ζ. p. 721): 'face' [BAGD, LN]. The phrase 'before his face' [Arn, Lns, WBC; KJV] is also translated 'ahead of him' [BECNT; HCSB, NCV, NRSV, TEV], 'on ahead of him' [AB; NASB, NET], 'on ahead' [NTC; CEV, NIV], 'ahead' [NLT, REB]. The phrase means 'before him' or 'ahead of him' [TH; GW].

c. aorist act. infin. of ἑτοιμάζω (LN 77.3) (BAGD 1. p. 316): 'to make preparations for someone' [BAGD], 'to prepare, to make ready' [LN]. The phrase 'to make preparations for him' [NTC; HCSB] is also translated 'to make arrangements for him' [AB; NASB, REB], 'to get things ready for him' [CEV, NIV], 'to make ready for him' [BECNT, Lns; KJV, NRSV], 'to make everything ready for him' [NCV], 'to get everything ready for him' [TEV], 'to make things ready in advance for him' [NET], 'to arrange a place for him to stay' [GW], 'to prepare for his arrival' [NLT], 'in order to prepare for him' [WBC], 'to prepare quarters' [Arn].

QUESTION—Who were the messengers and what was their mission?
It cannot be known who they were [Alf, ICC]. Probably they were some of the twelve disciples [NIBC, TG]. The preparation could refer to preparing the people for Jesus' arrival [NIGTC], either the preparation for lodging or for mass preaching [BECNT, Crd]. Because there was a large group of people accompanying Jesus, he would not want to stop in a village without making preparations for hospitality [Lns, NIGTC, NTC]. They would make arrangement for overnight lodging [AB, Crd, EGT, Lns, MGC, NAC, NIC,

NIGTC, NTC, Su, TG] and food [NIC, NTC]. It would have meant more than arranging for food and lodging, it must have been that the messengers were to preach [BECNT] and announce that the Messiah was coming [Alf].

9:53 And they-did- not -welcome[a] him, because his face[b] was going toward Jerusalem.

LEXICON—a. aorist mid. (deponent = act.) indic. of δέχομαι (LN 34.53) (BAGD 1. p. 177): 'to welcome'. The phrase 'they did not welcome him' [BECNT; GW, HCSB, NIV] is also translated 'they would not welcome him' [AB; NCV], 'they refused to welcome him' [NTC; CEV, NET], 'they did not receive him' [Arn, Lns; KJV, NASB, NRSV], 'they would not receive him' [WBC; REB, TEV], 'but they were turned away, the people of the village refused to have anything to do with Jesus' [NLT]. They would not receive Jesus when he would arrive [TH]. They would not welcome the messengers, and indirectly Jesus [MGC]. Probably this was the indirect refusal to welcome Jesus that was reported back to Jesus by the messengers [NIGTC]. See this word at 9:5; 10:8.

b. πρόσωπον (LN 9.9) (BAGD 1.b. p. 721): 'face' [BAGD], 'person, individual' [LN]. The phrase 'his face was going' [WBC] is also translated 'his face was set' [BECNT; NRSV], 'his face was as though he would go' [KJV], 'his face was as proceeding to' [Lns], 'he was facing toward' [Arn], 'he was on the way' [CEV, GW, REB], 'it was clear he was on his way' [TEV], 'he was traveling' [NASB], 'he was heading for' [NIV], 'he was headed for' [NTC], 'he was set on going' [NCV], 'he was determined to go' [NET], 'he determined (to journey)' [HCSB], 'his intention was to proceed to' [AB].

QUESTION—What is meant by the phrase 'because his face was going to Jerusalem'?

Some simply treat it as a Hebrew phrase that is equivalent to the third person pronoun [TH; CEV]: he was going to Jerusalem. Others find nuances in the use of this phrase: his intention was to proceed to Jerusalem [AB], he was set on going [NCV], 'he was determined to go' [NET]. The direction that Jesus was going indicated that he was going to worship in Jerusalem [Arn, Su]. The conjunction ὅτι 'because' gives the reason the Samaritans would not welcome Jesus [BECNT, EGT]. The reason was Jesus' destination [AB, MGC, NAC, TNTC]. Samaritans were hostile to all Jews and therefore they would not help anyone who was traveling to worship in Jerusalem [Alf, NIC, TNTC]. The Samaritans had their own place of worship on Mount Gerizim and they were hostile to Jews who were on their way to worship in Jerusalem [ICC, NIC, TG]. This reason excuses the Samaritans to some degree [WBC]. A few give other reasons. Perhaps the reason was that Jesus was being proclaimed as Messiah and they wouldn't believe that a real Messiah would pass them up to go on to Jerusalem [My]. They had heard about Jesus' miracles and were put out that he was passing right through their land, acting as though their worship amounted to nothing [Lns].

9:54 And having-learned-about/having-seen[a] (this) the disciples James and John said, Lord, do-you-want (that) we-should-call[b] fire to-come-down from heaven and to-destroy[c] them?

TEXT—Instead of οἱ μαθηταί 'the disciples', some manuscripts read οἱ μαθηταὶ αὐτοῦ 'his disciples'. GNT does not mention this variant. Οἱ μαθηταὶ αὐτοῦ 'his disciples' is read by KJV.

TEXT—Following the last word αὐτούς 'them', some manuscripts add ὡς Ἠλίας ἐποίησεν 'as Elijah did', and some manuscripts read ὡς καὶ Ἠλίας ἐποίησεν 'as Elijah also did'. GNT rejects both of these additions with a B decision, indicating that the text is almost certain. Ὡς καὶ Ἠλίας ἐποίησεν 'as Elijah also did' is read by KJV.

LEXICON—a. aorist act. participle of ὁράω (LN 27.5): 'to learn about, to find out about' [LN], 'to hear about' [NLT], 'to see' [AB, Arn, BECNT, Lns, NTC, WBC; all versions except NLT].
  b. aorist act. subj. of λέγω (LN 33.69): 'to call' [AB; CEV, GW, HCSB, NCV, NET, NIV, REB, TEV], 'to tell' [LN, WBC], 'to say' [Lns], 'to command' [KJV, NASB, NRSV], 'to order' [NLT], 'to bid' [BECNT, NTC], 'to speak the word (to let fire come down)' [Arn]. Here the verb means 'to command' [NIGTC].
  c. aorist act. infin. of ἀναλίσκω (LN **20.47**) (BAGD p. 57): 'to destroy' [Arn, BAGD, **LN**, WBC; CEV, NCV, NIV, TEV], 'to consume' [AB, BAGD, BECNT, Lns, NTC; HCSB, KJV, NASB, NET, NRSV, REB], 'to burn up' [GW, NLT].

QUESTION—When did James and John learn about the Samaritans refusing to welcome Jesus?
  1. The verb ἰδόντες means 'having learned about' [ICC, TG, TH; NLT]. James and John learned about this when the messengers returned from the village [ICC, TH]. Not having witnessed the Samaritans' refusal, the verb has the meaning 'they became aware of, heard about, learned about' this [TG, TH; NLT].
  2. The verb ἰδόντες means 'having seen' [AB, BECNT, Lns, NTC, WBC; all versions except NLT]. They saw the messengers returning [ICC, My, Rb] and recognized that the messengers would not have returned if the villagers were disposed to welcome Jesus [My]. The disciples were watching the interview and saw that the Samaritans' attitude indicated their refusal [NIGTC]. Peter and John must have been the messengers since they were the ones who saw the refusal of the Samaritans, while the rest of the disciples only heard their report [Lns].

QUESTION—What made James and John think of calling down fire on the Samaritans?
  They were thinking of what Elijah did to the hostile soldiers in 2 Kings 1:10–12 [AB, Alf, Gdt, ICC, Lns, MGC, My, NAC, NIC, NICNT, NIGTC, NTC, Rb, Su, WBC]. Perhaps it was the recent visit of Elijah with Jesus that brought this to mind [Alf, Gdt, ICC, Lns, NTC, Rb]. They thought that the

power Jesus had previously granted the disciples would enable them to do this [BECNT, NAC, NICNT].

9:55 And having-turned he-rebuked[a] them. **9:56** And they-went to another village.

TEXT—Following αὐτοῖς 'them', some manuscripts add καὶ εἶπεν, Οὐκ οἴδατε ποίου πνεύματός ἐστε 'and said you do not know of what spirit you are', other manuscripts add καὶ εἶπεν, Οὐκ οἴδατε οἵου πνεύματός ἐστε ὑμεῖς. ὁ γὰρ υἱὸς τοῦ ἀνθρώπου οὐκ ἦλθεν ψυχὰς ἀνθρώπων ἀπολέσαι ἀλλὰ σῶσαι 'and he said, You do not know of what sort of spirit you are. For the Son of Man did not come to destroy souls of men but to save'. GNT rejects these additions with an A decision, indicating that the text is certain. Καὶ εἶπεν, Οὐκ οἴδατε οἵου πνεύματός ἐστε ὑμεῖς. ὁ γὰρ υἱὸς τοῦ ἀνθρώπου οὐκ ἦλθεν ψυχὰς ἀνθρώπων ἀπολέσαι ἀλλὰ σῶσαι 'and he said, You do not know of what sort of spirit you are. (56) For the Son of Man did not come to destroy souls of men but to save' is read by My, WBC; KJV.

LEXICON—a. aorist act. indic. of ἐπιτιμάω (LN 33.419) (BAGD 1. p. 303): 'to rebuke' [AB, Arn, BAGD, BECNT, LN, Lns, NTC, WBC; all versions except CEV, GW, NCV], 'to reprove' [BAGD], 'to scold' [NCV], 'to correct' [CEV, GW]. See this word at 4:35.

QUESTION—Why did Jesus turn before rebuking them and why did he rebuke them?

The disciples were following Jesus, so he had to turn around to speak to them [AB, Gdt, ICC]. Jesus needed to face them directly in order to make his words more effective [Arn, Lns]. The disciples still did not understand what Jesus' mission was about [AB]. Their zeal for Jesus' honor was misguided and they proposed misusing the authority that had been granted them [BECNT, NAC].

QUESTION—What village did they then go to?

The village was probably not a Samaritan village, but a Jewish village at the border of Galilee so that they could travel around Samaria [EGT, Gdt, Lns, NIC, NTC]. Another view is that it was another Samaritan village that would welcome Jesus [BECNT, ICC, Su, TH] since Jesus had planned to pass through Samaria [ICC].

DISCOURSE UNIT: 9:57–62 [AB, BECNT, NAC, NIGTC, Su, TNTC, WBC; CEV, GW, HCSB, NASB, NCV, NET, NIV, NLT, NRSV, TEV]. The topic is teachings on discipleship [NAC], what it takes to be a disciple [GW], warnings about discipleship [BECNT], following Jesus [HCSB, NCV], the cost of following Jesus [NIV, NLT], exacting discipleship [NASB], readiness for discipleship [NIGTC], challenging professed followers [NET], counseling and calling disciples [Su], following Jesus without qualification [WBC], the would–be followers of Jesus [NRSV, TEV], three people who wanted to be followers [CEV], three would–be followers of Jesus [AB], whole heartedness [TNTC].

9:57 And (as) they-were-going on the road a-certain (man) said to him, I-will-follow[a] you wherever you-go.

TEXT—Instead of καί 'and' at the beginning of the verse, some manuscripts read ἐγένετο δέ 'and it happened'. GNT does not mention this variant. Ἐγένετο δέ 'and it happened' is read by KJV.

TEXT—Following ἀπέρχῃ 'you go' some manuscripts add κύριε 'Lord'. GNT does not mention this variant. Κύριε 'Lord' is read by KJV.

LEXICON—a. fut. act. indic. of ἀκολουθέω (LN 36.31) (BAGD 3. p. 31): 'to follow'. See translations of this word at 5:11. This word also occurs at 5:27; 18:43.

QUESTION—What did the man propose to do?

The man wanted to become a permanent disciple [ICC, Lns] and wanted to accompany Jesus wherever Jesus may lead him [Arn, ICC, Lns, NIGTC]. He wanted to belong to the closer group of disciples that went along with Jesus to Jerusalem [WBC], and all his travels [NIGTC]. This does not apply only to the journey in progress to Jerusalem [ICC].

9:58 And Jesus said to-him, The foxes have dens and the birds[a] of-the sky nests, but the Son of-Man does- not -have (a place) where he-may-lay-down[b] (his) head.

LEXICON—a. πετεινόν (LN 4.41) (BAGD p. 654): 'bird' [BAGD]. For the phrase πετεινὰ τοῦ οὐρανοῦ 'birds of the sky' see 8:5.
  b. aorist act. subj. of κλίνω (LN 23.83) (BAGD 1.b. p. 436): 'to lay down' [BAGD, LN]. The idiom τὴν κεφαλὴν κλίνω 'to lay down the head' refers to experiencing the rest which comes from sleep and means 'to lie down to rest, to lie down to sleep' [LN, TH]. The phrase 'he doesn't have a place where he may lay down his head' is translated 'he has not where he may lay his head' [Arn, Lns], 'he has nowhere to lay his head' [AB, BECNT, NTC, WBC; KJV, NASB, NRSV, REB], 'he has no place to lay his head' [HCSB, NET, NIV], 'he has no place to rest his head' [NCV], 'he has no place to lie down and rest' [TEV], 'he has nowhere to sleep' [GW], 'he doesn't have a place to call his own' [CEV], 'I have no home of my own, not even a place to lay my head' [NLT]. It implies that Jesus possessed no permanent home [LN].

QUESTION—What was the implication of Jesus' response?

This man is called a scribe in Matthew 8:19. Luke does not identify the man as a scribe since Jesus' words were relevant for anyone [BECNT]. The man thought it would be good to be associated with Jesus who was so popular at this point, but he did not understand that discipleship meant self-denial, sacrifice, service, and suffering [NTC]. Perhaps Jesus detected an overzealous spirit in the man [ICC, Su]. Jesus wanted the man to count the cost [Lns, MGC, NIC, NIGTC]. Jesus had no fixed place to stay at night, and any follower had to be willing to share Jesus' homelessness [TG]. The example of homelessness was merely an illustration of the need for Jesus' followers to choose a life with eternal purposes and heavenly treasures instead of a life of temporal purposes and earthly wealth and this man did not realize the life of privation that discipleship would involve [Lns], a life of extreme privation [NIC]. Jesus did not indicate whether he accepted or rejected the man's offer to follow him [Lns].

QUESTION—Didn't Jesus ever have an opportunity to sleep?

Jesus had no place that he could call his home and now that he had entered public ministry he slept wherever he found a welcome [Su]. Jesus was constantly on the move and had no fixed place to call home [Lns, NTC]. Jesus was dependent on others offering him hospitality and he was homeless without it [NICNT]. Nazareth had cast him out, he had chosen to leave Capernaum for a wandering life, and the Samaritans had not offered hospitality, so when he needed intervals of rest he had no place to call home [ICC]. Although Jesus was offered hospitality at various places in his travels, the basic point is the rejection that Jesus faced [NIGTC], or it was simply the general lack of physical comforts [NAC].

9:59 **And he-said to another, Follow me. But he-said, Lord, allow me first to-go to-bury^a my father.**

TEXT—Some manuscripts omit Κύριε 'Lord'. GNT includes Κύριε 'Lord' in brackets with a C decision, indicating that the Committee had difficulty making the decision. Κύριε 'Lord' is omitted by AB and REB.

LEXICON—a. aorist act. infin. of θάπτω (LN 52.4, **35.46**) (BAGD p. 351): 'to bury' [AB, Arn, BAGD, BECNT, LN (52.4), Lns, NTC; all versions]. The verb means to dispose of a dead body by putting it into the earth [TH]. The phrase θάπτω τὸν πατέρα μου 'to bury my father' may be an idiom meaning to take care of one's father until his death [**LN** (35.46)].

QUESTION—Was this man already a disciple?

This man was already a disciple [EGT, Gdt, ICC, Lns, NIGTC, NTC, Su] and this is made explicit in Matthew 8:21 [Gdt, NIGTC]. The man was a disciple in the broad sense of the word and Jesus asked him to become a permanent follower in Jesus' company [ICC, Lns, NIGTC, NTC], to have a ministry as one of Jesus' associates [Su]. This disciple had enough instruction to be able to proclaim the kingdom of God [Lns].

QUESTION—Was the man's father already dead?

1. The man's father had just died [Gdt, ICC, Lns, NAC, NIGTC, NTC, TG, TH, TNTC]. Since the father either had just died or was at the point of death, the funeral would be taking place at once and the man wanted to be allowed to follow later after the burial [ICC, WBC]. He had just received word of his father's death and was asking for a delay of a day or two [Lns].
2. The man's father was not at that time near death [NIC, NIVS, Rb, Su, WBC]. The father was not dead since if he was dead, the man would have been at home making preparations for the burial. Perhaps the father was old or ill and the disciple did not want to desert his father at the present

time and would join Jesus after his father had died some time in the future [NIC]. The man may have been offering an excuse for delaying [Su].

9:60 **And he-said to-him, Let the dead (ones) bury their-own dead (ones), but you having left^a proclaim^b the kingdom of-God.**

TEXT—Following αὐτῷ 'to him', some manuscripts evidently add ὁ Ἰησοῦς 'Jesus', although GNT does not mention this variant. Ὁ Ἰησοῦς 'Jesus' is read by KJV.

LEXICON—a. aorist act. participle of ἀπέρχομαι (LN 15.37): 'to leave, to depart' [LN], 'to go away' [LN, Lns], 'to go' [AB, Arn, BECNT, NTC, WBC; all versions]. This action is probably connected with the sending out of the seventy disciples in 10:1 [Alf].
  b. pres. act. impera. of διαγγέλλω (LN 33.207) (BAGD 1. p. 182): 'to proclaim' [Arn, BAGD, BECNT, LN; NASB, NET, NIV, NRSV, TEV], 'to proclaim abroad' [Lns], 'to announce' [AB; REB], 'to preach' [KJV, NLT], 'to tell about' [LN; CEV, NCV], 'to tell everywhere' [GW], 'to spread the news' [HCSB].

QUESTION—Who are the dead when Jesus said to let the dead bury the dead and what did he mean?
  1. The first reference to 'the dead' is metaphorical and means the spiritually dead while the second reference is to the ones that are to be buried in a grave and means those who have died physically [AB, Arn, BECNT, Crd, ICC, Lns, MGC, NAC, NIBC, NIC, NIGTC, NTC, Rb, Su, TNTC]: let the spiritually dead people bury the physically dead people. The first noun, 'the dead', refers to people who have not followed Jesus and this disciple has to realize the urgency to follow Jesus has priority over filial obligations [AB]. This reasonable excuse was rejected by Jesus because nothing was to postpone the start of discipleship. The coming of the kingdom of God requires such priorities [BECNT]. There were plenty of people who were spiritually dead to tend to ordinary family duties and by the time the funeral rites and the ceremonial cleansing from pollution were completed, Jesus would be far away [ICC]. People who are devoted to secular affairs could attend to the burial, but the disciple had a greater obligation to preach the kingdom [Lns]. Possible reasons for Jesus' command are that Jesus was about ready to embark (Matthew 8:18) and the man had to join him at once, or Jesus wanted to impress on the man that following him meant doing whatever he commanded without qualification or conditions, or the ties of earthly families are superceded by those of the spiritual family [NTC].
  2. The first reference to 'the dead' does not refer to spiritually dead people but is simply applied to disciples who postpone answering Jesus' call while the second reference to the dead who are to be buried are the physically dead who have died [TH].
  3. Both references to 'the dead' refer to the physically dead [WBC]. The dead belonged to the underworld, a different realm from the living and

those who are already in the underworld must take the responsibility of receiving this newcomer. Of course the words were not to be taken literally, and the harsh words were meant to impress on the disciple that some other arrangements must be made for his father's burial since he had more pressing responsibilities [WBC].

9:61 And also another said, I-will-follow you, Lord. But first allow me to-say-goodbye[a] to-the (ones) in my house. **9:62** And Jesus said to him, No-one having-put the hand upon a-plow[b] and looking to the (things) behind[c] is fit[d] for-the kingdom of-God.

TEXT—In 9:62, instead of εἶπεν δὲ πρὸς αὐτὸν ὁ Ἰησοῦς 'and said to him Jesus', some manuscripts read εἶπεν δὲ ὁ Ἰησοῦς πρὸς αὐτὸν 'and said Jesus to him', some manuscripts read ὁ δὲ Ἰησοῦς εἶπεν αὐτῷ 'and Jesus said to him', and some manuscripts read εἶπεν δὲ ὁ Ἰησοῦς 'and said Jesus'. GNT reads εἶπεν δὲ πρὸς αὐτὸν ὁ Ἰησοῦς 'and said to him Jesus' with a C decision and places πρὸς αὐτὸν 'to him' in brackets, indicating that the Committee had difficulty making the decision. Most versions would probably not distinguish between the first three of these variants. Εἶπεν δὲ ὁ Ἰησοῦς 'and said Jesus' is evidently read by NIV.

LEXICON—a. aorist mid. infin. of ἀποτάσσομαι (LN **33.23**) (BAGD 1. p. 100): 'to say goodbye' [**LN**], 'to say farewell, to take leave of' [BAGD]. The phrase 'to say goodbye to the (ones) in my house' is translated 'to say goodbye to those at my house' [HCSB], 'to say goodbye to those at home' [NASB], 'to say goodbye to my people at home' [AB; REB], 'to say goodbye to the folks at home' [NTC], 'to say goodbye to the members of my household' [WBC], 'to say goodbye to my family' [NET, NLT], 'to go and say goodbye to my family' [NCV, TEV], 'to go back and say goodbye to my family' [NIV], 'to tell my family goodbye' [GW], 'to say farewell to those in my house' [BECNT], 'to say farewell to those at my home' [NRSV], 'to bid farewell to the people in my house' [Arn, Lns], 'to go bid them farewell which are at home in my house' [KJV], 'to go back and take care of things at home' [CEV].

b. ἄροτρον (LN **6.4**, **68.6**) (BAGD p. 108): 'plow' [BAGD, **LN** (6.4)]. The phrase ἐπιβάλλω τὴν χεῖρα ἐπ' ἄροτρον 'having put the hand upon a plow' is translated 'after putting his hand to the plow' [NASB; similarly KJV], 'having just put his hand to a plow' [Lns; similarly NTC], 'who has placed his hand upon a plow' [Arn], 'puts his hand to the plow' [AB, BECNT, **LN** (68.6), WBC; HCSB, NET, NIV; similarly NLT, NRSV], 'sets his hand to the plough' [REB], 'starts to plow' [GW, TEV], 'starts plowing' [CEV].

c. ὀπίσω (LN 83.40) (BAGD 1.a. p. 575): 'behind' [LN], 'backwards' [BAGD]. The phrase βλέπων εἰς τὰ ὀπίσω 'looking to the (things) behind' is translated 'looking back' [KJV, NASB], 'looks back' [Arn, BECNT, WBC; GW, HCSB, NET, NIV, NLT, NRSV, REB], 'keeps looking back' [AB, LN (68.6); CEV, TEV], 'continues to look back'

[NTC], 'continuing to look to the rear' [Lns], 'then has second thoughts' [LN (68.6)]. Here the application is looking back on the things that are abandoned in order to follow Jesus, specifically the man's family relationships [NAC].

d. εὔθετος (LN **66.3**) (BAGD p. 320): 'fit' [BAGD, BECNT, **LN**, Lns, NTC, WBC; GW, HCSB, KJV, NASB, NET, NLT, NRSV, REB], 'fitted' [Arn], 'fit for service' [NIV], 'suitable, usable' [BAGD, LN], 'suited' [AB], '(to be) of use' [TEV], '(to be) worth something' [CEV].

QUESTION—What is the meaning of the metaphor about putting the hand to a plow and looking behind?

The *image* is of an animal pulling a plow, the plow point being guided to make a straight furrow by a man holding the handle. If the man keeps looking backwards he cannot do a good job of plowing [TG]. In order to plow a straight furrow, the plowman must look forward to where he is going and not backward [AB, Alf, EGT, Gdt, Lns, NICNT, MGC, NIGTC, NTC, Rb, TG, WBC]. Just as the persons who plows must look forward and devote full attention to the work, so also he who wants to be a follower of Christ must not allow other matters to distract his attention from his calling [NIC]. In this context, family ties represent a looking back [NIGTC]. The claims of the kingdom make family ties a part of the things that are behind [AB]. Another view is also suggested: As the man who toils in plowing but looks back to the comforts of house and town with the result that he will gather no crop at harvest time, so is the man who wants to commit himself to Jesus but looks longingly back to what he has left behind with the result that he is not fit for the kingdom of God [Su]. The clause ἐπιβάλλω τὴν χεῖρα ἐπ' ἄροτρον καὶ βλέπω εἰς τὰ ὀπίσω: 'one who puts his hand to the plow and looks back' is a Semitic idiom meaning to begin some activity requiring close attention but then to change one's mind about proceeding, 'to start to do something and then to hesitate, to begin but have second thoughts about continuing' [LN (68.6)]. This describes a person who has made a decision ('having put' in the punctiliar aorist tense) but does not live up to it ('looking behind' in the durative present tense) [NTC, TH]. Rather than being a refusal, this is a warning not to initially follow Jesus but then long for the old life later [BECNT].

QUESTION—What is meant by being fit for the kingdom of God?

Fit means to measure up to the requirement of single-minded devotion to the task, of not being distracted by other matters [TG]. The emphasis of the word 'fit' is not on moral or spiritual fitness but on practical usefulness [BECNT, Lns, Su, TH]. It does not mean to be fit to enter the kingdom of God, but to be fit to work in the kingdom as a useful disciple [Arn, ICC]. The focus is on how one serves and follows Jesus effectively [BECNT]. A true follower of Jesus has complete devotion to serving him and unconditional faithfulness to the task he is called to [NIC].

LUKE 10:1

DISCOURSE UNIT: 10:1–24 [BECNT, TNTC; GW, NIV]. The topic is the mission of the seventy(–two) [BECNT, TNTC], Jesus sends out the seventy–two [NIV], Jesus sends disciples to do mission work [GW].

DISCOURSE UNIT: 10:1–20 [NICNT, Su; NLT]. The topic is the mission of the seventy–two [NICNT], Jesus sends out his disciples [NLT], the appointment and mission of the Seventy [Su].

DISCOURSE UNIT: 10:1–16 [NAC, NIGTC, WBC; NASB, NET]. The topic is the mission of the seventy(–two) [NAC; NET], the seventy sent out [NASB], the mission charge of the seventy who are sent ahead [WBC], the Second Mission [NIGTC].

DISCOURSE UNIT: 10:1–12 [AB, TNTC; CEV, HCSB, NCV, NRSV, TEV]. The topic is the mission of the seventy(–two) [AB; NRSV], Jesus sends out the seventy(–two) [HCSB, NCV, TEV], the work of the seventy–two followers [CEV], the mission and the message [TNTC].

10:1 **And after these (things) the Lord appointed[a] seventy-[two] others and he-sent them two by two before his face[b] into every city and place[c] where he-was-about to-come.**

TEXT—Before ἑτέρους 'others', some manuscripts add καί 'also'. GNT does not mention this variant. Καί 'also' is read by KJV.

TEXT—Instead of ἑβδομήκοντα δύο 'seventy two', some manuscripts read ἑβδομήκοντα 'seventy'. GNT reads ἑβδομήκοντα δύο 'seventy two' with a C decision, placing δύο 'two' in brackets, indicating that the Committee had difficulty making the decision. Ἑβδομήκοντα 'seventy' is read by BNTC, EGT, Gdt, ICC, Lns, NIC, Su; GW, HCSB, KJV, NASB, and NRSV.

TEXT—Instead of ἀνὰ δύο δύο 'by two two', some manuscripts read ἀνὰ δύο 'by two'. GNT reads ἀνὰ δύο δύο 'by two two' with a C decision, placing the second δύο 'two' in brackets, indicating that the Committee had difficulty making the decision. Most versions probably do not distinguish between these variants.

LEXICON—a. aorist act. indic. of ἀναδείκνυμι (LN **37.96**) (BAGD 2. p. 53): 'to appoint' [AB, Arn, BAGD, BECNT, **LN**, Lns, NTC, WBC; GW, HCSB, KJV, NASB, NET, NIV, NRSV, REB], 'to commission' [BAGD], 'to choose' [CEV, NCV, NLT, TEV], 'to designate, to assign, to give a task to' [LN]. The disciples were appointed to a special mission [Lns].

b. πρόσωπον (LN 67.19) (BAGD 1.c.ζ. p. 721): 'face' [BAGD, LN]. See the idiom πρὸ προσώπου 'before the face,' at 9:52.

c. τόπος (LN 80.1) (BAGD 1.a. p. 822): 'place' [AB, Arn, BAGD, BECNT, LN, Lns, NTC, WBC; all versions except CEV, NLT], 'village' [CEV, NLT]. The word means an inhabited place and is less specific than 'city' [BAGD, TH].

QUESTION—Who were the seventy-two (or seventy) others?

They were part of a large number of followers Jesus had accumulated by now [Lns]. The disciples he now appointed were other than the Twelve apostles [AB, Alf, Arn, BECNT, EGT, Gdt, ICC, Lns, MGC, NAC, NICNT, NIGTC, NTC, Rb, Su, TG, TH, WBC] and possibly other than the messengers in 9:52 [AB]. This implies that the Twelve remained with Jesus while the others went out [NAC]. In 10:9 it appears that Jesus gave them power and authority to preach about the kingdom and to cure the sick [AB, NICNT].

QUESTION—How could Jesus go to all the places the thirty-six pairs of disciples went to?

Jesus wanted this mission accomplished quickly and all these disciples went as advance messengers along the route Jesus would be taking [Lns]. They prepared the towns for Jesus' arrival [Arn, MGC]. They went to the places Jesus wished to visit during the few months before his crucifixion [NIC], and this indicates the busy itinerary Jesus had ahead of him [TNTC]. Since Jesus had little time to spend in each place, these messengers would prepare the people so that the people would be expectant and eager for his only visit to them [Gdt]. On the other hand, it does not seem possible that Jesus could go to all the places visited by these disciples and there is no evidence that he did so. Possibly this refers to a spiritual coming after the resurrection since these disciples are told in 10:16 that they would be taking the place of Jesus [NIGTC]. This does not indicate that Jesus would take a circuitous route to pass through thirty-two villages on his trip to Jerusalem, so these messengers were preparing for Jesus' spiritual coming after the resurrection [NAC].

10:2 And he-was-saying to them, Indeed the harvest[a] (is) much,[b] but the workers[c] (are) few. Therefore ask the Lord of-the harvest that he-might-send-out workers into his harvest.

TEXT—Instead of ἔλεγεν δέ 'and he was saying', some manuscripts read ἔλεγεν οὖν 'therefore he was saying', although GNT does not mention this variant. Ἔλεγεν οὖν 'therefore he was saying' is read by KJV.

LEXICON—a. θερισμός (LN **43.15**) (BAGD 2.a. p. 359): 'harvest' [AB, Arn, BAGD, BECNT, **LN**, Lns, NTC, WBC; all versions except CEV, NCV, REB], 'crop' [LN; CEV, REB], 'grain' [LN], 'people to harvest' [NCV]. It refers to a ripe field of grain ready to be harvested [Lns, Su]. The harvest refers to what results from the process of harvesting [TH].

b. πολύς (LN 59.11) (BAGD I.1.b.a. p. 688): 'much' [BAGD, LN], 'great' [BAGD, LN, Lns; KJV], 'so great' [NLT], 'large' [BAGD, WBC; CEV, GW, TEV], 'plentiful' [BECNT, NTC; NASB, NET, NIV, NRSV], 'abundant' [AB, Arn; HCSB], 'heavy' [REB], 'a great many (people)' [NCV].

c. ἐργάτης (LN 42.43) (BAGD 1.a. p. 307): 'worker' [Arn, LN, Lns, WBC; CEV, GW, HCSB, NCV, NET, NIV, NLT, TEV], 'workman' [BAGD], 'laborer' [AB, BAGD, BECNT, NTC; KJV, NASB, NRSV, REB].

QUESTION—What is meant by the metaphor about harvest and workers?

The *image* is a large field of grain ready to be harvested, but there are only a few workers to do the harvesting, so more workers are needed. The harvest has already been produced [Lns], and the harvest is ready to be gathered into a barn [TG]. The *topic* concerns the many people who are ready to be persuaded to enter the kingdom by accepting Jesus' message [TG]. They are the many people in whom God's grace worked [Lns]. The plentiful harvest indicates that in spite of rejection there will be a positive response from many [BECNT].

QUESTION—Who are the referents of the two occurrences of 'Lord' in these two verses?

In 10:1, as in 7:13, Luke calls Jesus Lord [EGT, Lns, WBC]. However, in 10:2 Jesus spoke of God as the Lord of the harvest [Arn, Lns, NIGTC, WBC; NCV].

QUESTION—How is the Lord related to the harvest in the genitive construction τοῦ κυρίου τοῦ θερισμοῦ 'the Lord of the harvest'?

The Lord is the owner of the crop [AB, Lns, TG, TH, WBC; NCV, REB, TEV], and is responsible for and controls the harvesting of it [Lns, Su, TH]. The Lord is in charge of the crop or harvest [CEV, NLT]. The Lord gives the harvest [GW].

QUESTION—What does the prayer ask for?

There were already a few workers, so the prayer is for *more* workers to go to the field [TG; NCV]. The seventy-two disciples were considered to be too few to meet the needs of the harvest [My]. If people accept the message, they should also help deliver it, so the disciples must ask God for his help and then rely on his sovereign provision [BECNT]. It is not the messengers' work to get workers, they are to ask God to find and send out the workers [Lns].

10:3 Go.[a] Behold I-send you like lambs in (the) midst-of[b] wolves.

LEXICON—a. pres. act. impera. of ὑπάγω (LN 15.35) (BAGD 2. p. 836): 'to go' [Arn, BAGD, LN], 'to depart' [LN]. The command is translated 'Go!' [BECNT, NTC, WBC; GW, NASB, NET, NIV, TEV], 'Now go' [AB; CEV, HCSB], 'Go now' [NCV, NLT], 'Go on your way' [NRSV], 'Be going!' [Lns], 'Be on your way' [REB], 'Go your ways' [KJV]. They are to go to where he told them to go [TH].

b. μέσος (LN 83.9) (BAGD 2. p. 507): 'the midst of' [BECNT, Lns, NTC, WBC; NASB, NRSV], 'among' [AB, Arn, LN; GW, HCSB, KJV, NCV, NIV, NLT, REB, TEV], 'middle' [BAGD], 'surrounded by' [NET]. The phrase ἐν μέσῳ 'in the midst' is translated 'into a pack (of wolves)' [CEV].

QUESTION—What is the application of the metaphor of lambs in the midst of wolves?

The *image* is of lambs being sent to go into the midst of wolves. The *topic* is the disciples being sent to go into the midst of dangerous opponents. The disciples are like lambs in the sense of being helpless to defend themselves [AB, EGT, Lns, NIC, NIGTC, NTC, TG, TH, TNTC], or of being vulnerable [BECNT, WBC]. They have lost all the viciousness associated with sin and wickedness [Lns]. Their opponents are like wolves in the sense of being dangerous [NIC, TH, TNTC] and vicious in their opposition [TNTC]. They are wicked because of being filled and animated with sin [Lns]. Wolves suggest perils, opposition, and hostility that they will meet on the way [AB]. The image of sheep brings with it the idea of being protected by God, the Great Shepherd [BECNT, MGC, NIGTC]. With the emphatic 'Behold I send you' they don't have to fear danger from the wolves since they have a protector [Lns].

10:4 **Do- not -carry a-purse,[a] nor a traveler's-bag,[b] nor sandals, and greet[c] no-one along the way.**
LEXICON—a. βαλλάντιον (LN **6.144**) (BAGD p. 130): 'purse' [AB, Arn, BAGD, BECNT, **LN**, Lns, NTC, WBC; KJV, NCV, NIV, NRSV, REB, TEV], 'money bag' [BAGD, LN; CEV, HCSB, NET], 'wallet' [GW], 'money belt' [NASB], 'any money' [NLT]. They were not to take any money for buying food and necessities [Lns]. See this word at 12:33, 22:35.
  b. πήρα (LN 6.145) (BAGD p. 656): 'traveler's bag' [BAGD, LN, NTC; NET, NLT], 'traveling bag' [CEV, GW, HCSB], 'bag' [BECNT, WBC; NASB, NCV, NIV, NRSV], 'knapsack' [AB, Arn], 'pack' [REB], 'pouch' [Lns], 'scrip' [KJV], 'beggar's bag' [TEV]. This was a larger bag than the purse and was used for carrying food or clothes [Lns, NIGTC, Su]. It held supplies and gave the impression of independence [BECNT]. The context seems to rule out the alternate meaning of beggar's bag and besides they had never been out begging [Lns]. Or, it refers to a beggar's bag [TEV]. See this word at 9:3, 22:35.
  c. aorist mid. (deponent = act.) subj. of ἀσπάζομαι (LN 33.20) (BAGD 1.a. p. 116): 'to greet' [Arn, BAGD, LN, NTC, WBC; HCSB, NASB, NET, NIV, NRSV], 'to salute' [BECNT, Lns; KJV]. The phrase 'greet no one' is translated 'exchange no greeting' [REB], 'do not exchange greetings with anyone' [AB], 'don't stop to greet anyone' [GW, NLT, TEV], 'don't waste time greeting people' [CEV], 'don't waste time talking with people' [NCV].
QUESTION—Why is the list of preparations only about the things they should not take?
  These are practically the same instructions given to the messengers who were sent out in 9:3. The list is suggestive, not exhaustive [WBC] and the statement about sandals would apply to other clothing [Lns]. The disciples must have faith in God to provide for their needs [Arn, ICC, MGC, NIC, NIGTC, NTC]. The work was too urgent for delay and there was no time for preparation, so they had to go as they were [NIC, Su, WBC]. They were not to bother with needless baggage because this is a mission of haste and dedication [WBC]. This verse gives the same instructions as given to Jews who went to the Temple Mount and the disciples were to go in the same spirit as they would go to temple services [ICC].

QUESTION—What is meant by forbidding the disciples to carry sandals?
1. This permits the wearing of sandals but forbids carrying an extra pair [Arn, BECNT, Gdt, ICC, Lns, NIC, NIVS, NTC, Su, TH, TNTC, WBC; NLT]. They were not to carry sandals in addition to what they wore [ICC, TNTC].
2. This forbids even the wearing of sandals [ICC, TG; REB]. They are to travel barefoot [REB].

QUESTION—Why should they not greet anyone as they were on their way?
To greet someone can mean to pay one's respects in the sense of visiting with someone [WBC]. This does not mean to be impolite, it refers to greetings that functioned as introductions to conversations and there was to be no delay because of that [Lns]. They must not waste time in the Eastern time-consuming greeting along the way [Arn, MGC, NAC, NIVS, NTC, Su, TNTC]. They were to hurry to their destinations without wasting any time [Gdt, TG, TH]. This emphasizes the urgency of their mission [NIC, NICNT, NIGTC]. Of course when they arrived at their destination they would give a greeting [ICC]. This instruction was given as hyperbole in order to emphasis the need for a spirit of urgency and it was not necessarily to be taken literally [EGT].

10:5 **And into whatever house you-enter,**[a] **first say, Peace**[b] **to-this house.**

LEXICON—a. aorist act. subj. of εἰσέρχομαι (LN 15.93): 'to enter' [AB, Arn, BECNT, LN, Lns, NTC, WBC; CEV, HCSB, KJV, NASB, NET, NIV, NLT, NRSV], 'to go into' [LN; GW, NCV, REB, TEV]. Here this has the idea of entering a house in order to take up lodging [BECNT, Lns, TNTC]. It would be a house in which they were invited to stay while in town [Lns]. Others seem to take this to refer to any house that they approached [ICC, MGC, Su, WBC] and obtained admission [ICC].
b. εἰρήνη (LN 22.42) (BAGD 2. p. 227): 'peace' [BAGD, LN]. The greeting 'Peace to this house' [Lns, NTC, WBC; NIV, NRSV, REB] is also translated 'Peace be to this house' [AB; KJV, NASB] 'Peace be with this house' [NCV, TEV], 'Peace on this house' [BECNT], 'May peace be on this house' [NET], 'Peace to this household' [HCSB], 'May there be peace in this house' [GW], 'May peace come to this house' [Arn], 'God bless this home with peace' [CEV]. The clause 'say, Peace to this house' is translated 'give it your blessing' [NLT]. See this noun at 7:50.

QUESTION—What was the significance of saying 'Peace to this house'?
This phrase was a standard Hebrew greeting [BECNT, BNTC, Lns, NAC, NIC, NICNT, NIGTC, NTC, TG, TH, WBC]. 'House' is used as a metonymy for the people in it [AB, BECNT, NIGTC, TG]. Wishing peace was a form of a blessing [NAC, Su, TH]. Peace means to be in a condition of well-being, health, and prosperity [TG]. It refers to the Hebrew *Shalom* [AB, Su]. It is equivalent to saying 'May God be with you' [BECNT]. However, there was a deeper significance when used by the disciples [AB, BECNT, Lns, NIBC, NIC, NICNT, NIGTC, NTC, WBC] in view of speaking of the

peace remaining or returning [Lns]. It describes the Messianic kingdom [TH, WBC], the Messianic salvation and the blessings associated with it [NAC]. It offers them God's goodwill which can be either received or rejected [BECNT]. It refers to a deeper peace resulting from God's salvation [MGC, NIC, NIGTC]. It is the peace produced by the gospel in which God is our friend and Father so that all is well with us and it includes the subjective feeling of enjoying that peace [Lns]. It offers them the peace that salvation brings [AB, NIBC]. The disciples were actually bringing this peace on behalf of the one who sent them [NTC].

10:6 **And if a-son[a] of-peace is there, your peace will-rest[b] upon him. But if not, it-will-return[c] upon you.**

LEXICON—a. υἱός (LN 9.4) (BAGD 1.c.δ. p. 834): 'son' [BAGD, LN]. The phrase 'a son of peace' [Arn, BECNT, Lns, WBC; HCSB, KJV, NET] is also translated 'a man of peace' [NASB, NIV, REB], 'a peaceful person' [AB; GW], 'peaceful people' [NCV], 'the people are peace-loving' [CEV], 'someone who is peace-loving' [TEV], 'a lover of peace' [NTC], 'anyone who shares in peace' [NRSV], 'those who are worthy' [NLT].

b. fut. pass. (deponent = act.) indic. of ἐπαναπαύομαι (LN **13.25**) (BAGD 1. p. 282): 'to rest' [BAGD], 'to remain' [**LN**], 'to continue to be on' [LN]. The phrase 'your peace will rest upon/on him' [AB, Arn, Lns, NTC; HCSB, NASB, NIV, REB; similarly NRSV] is also translated 'your peace will rest upon it (the house)' [KJV], 'it will rest upon him' [WBC], 'your peace will remain on him' [NET], 'your blessing of peace will stay with them' [NCV], 'your greeting shall rest on him' [BECNT], 'your greeting will be accepted' [GW], 'your prayer for peace will bless them' [CEV], 'the blessing will stand' [NLT], 'let your greeting of peace remain on that person' [TEV].

c. fut. act. indic. of ἀνακάμπτω (LN 15.89) (BAGD 1.b. p. 55): 'to return' [BAGD, LN]. The phrase 'it will return upon you' is translated 'it will return to you' [Arn, BECNT, NTC, WBC; HCSB, NASB, NET, NIV, NRSV, REB], 'it shall turn to you again' [KJV], 'it will come back to you' [AB], 'it will come back upon you' [Lns], 'your blessing will come back to you' [NCV], 'your prayer will return to you' [CEV], 'the blessing will return to you' [NLT], 'take back your greeting of peace' [TEV], 'your greeting will be rejected' [GW].

QUESTION—What is meant by the idiom 'son of peace'?

This refers to a person belonging to the class or kind that is specified by the genitive construction [LN (9.4), NTC]. This refers to the head of the household [Rb]. In Matthew 10:13 the instructions were to look for a worthy person's house to stay at while in the town and the instructions about a 'son of peace' mean essentially the same thing [My, TH; NLT].

1. It means a person who is characterized by peace [ICC, Rb, Su, TG, TNTC, WBC; CEV, GW, NCV, TEV]. This means a peaceful man [WBC], a peace-loving person [TG; CEV]. He is one who is inclined

towards peace [ICC, Rb]. A peace-loving man would be friendly and hospitable [TG]. A man who has a peaceful character or nature would accept the blessing and be blessed by it [Su].
2. Here it means a person who is ready for or destined to peace [AB, Alf, BECNT, BNTC, Lns, NIBC, NIGTC, TH, WBC]. It does not mean a person who was already a disciple, but one who was ready to receive the message of the peace of salvation [MGC, NIGTC, WBC]. He is looking for God's peace [BNTC] and desires the peace that Jesus offers through his messengers [Lns]. Or, the person already has this peace as a believer [NIBC].

QUESTION—How could the disciple's peace rest upon a man of peace?

The man would receive the blessing offered by the disciples [NIGTC, TH]. The greeting would be effective with the power to save the person [AB]. If the person was already a believer, he would be strengthened in his possession of peace, but if the person was not a believer and did not reject the spoken blessing, his heart would be opened to lead him to true happiness [Arn]. 'Your peace' means the peace you have wished for the person [TH].

QUESTION—What is meant by the peace returning upon the disciples?
1. It simply means that this peace will not be given to the unworthy person [Arn, MGC, NAC, NIBC, NIC, NIGTC, NTC, TG, TNTC; GW]. The prayer for peace will not be effective when faith is not present [NAC]. It does not mean that the disciples will get the blessing instead of the man of the house [NIGTC]. The blessing will be of no use to man of the house [NIC]. The greeting will be rejected [GW]. The intended recipient forfeits the blessing of peace by having it withdrawn [NIBC, NIGTC] and this is equivalent to being cursed [NIGTC]. It means to cancel the blessing [TG]. This is figurative speech to reassure the disciples that they need not fear pronouncing blessings upon an unworthy person [Arn].
2. It means the disciples will receive the peace instead of the unworthy person [AB, EGT, Gdt, ICC, Lns, Rb, Su, WBC]. It will not be lost [AB]. It will return for reallocation [Lns, WBC]. The prayer for God's peace is not wasted, it will return to bless the one who offered it [Su]. It will be as though the prayer had been spoken to the disciple instead of by the disciple [ICC]. The blessing that is not received by the unworthy man will return with redoubled force on the disciple who spoke it [Gdt]

10:7 And stay in the same[a] house eating and drinking the (things) from/with[b] them, because the worker (is) worthy of-his wages. Do- not -move[c] from house to house.

LEXICON—a. αὐτός (LN 58.31): 'same' [Arn, BECNT, LN; CEV, HCSB, KJV, NET, NRSV], 'that' [Lns, WBC; NASB, NIV, REB], 'that same' [TEV], 'that one' [AB], 'that very' [NTC]. The phrase 'the same house' is translated 'one place' [NLT], 'the family that accepts you' [GW], 'the peaceful house' [NCV].

b. παρά (LN 90.4, 89.111) (BAGD I.4.b.α. p. 610): 'from' [BAGD, LN (90.4)], 'with' [LN (89.111)]. The prepositional phrase 'the (things) from/with them' is translated 'the things from them' [Lns], 'what they give you' [NASB, NET], 'whatever they give you' [NTC; CEV, NIV], 'what the people there give you' [NCV], 'what they offer' [Arn; HCSB], 'whatever they offer you' [GW, TEV], 'what they provide' [BECNT], 'what they provide you' [NLT], 'whatever they provide' [NRSV], 'such things as they give' [KJV], 'what they have' [AB, WBC], 'sharing (their food and drink)' [REB].

c. pres. act. impera. of μεταβαίνω (LN 15.2) (BAGD 1.b. p. 510): 'to move' [AB, BAGD, LN; NCV], 'to keep moving' [NASB], 'to move around' [CEV, GW, NET, NIV, NLT, REB, TEV], 'to move about' [WBC; NRSV], 'to keep moving about' [NTC], 'to be moving' [HCSB], 'to go' [BAGD, BECNT; KJV], 'to be changing' [Lns], 'to change' [Arn].

QUESTION—What is meant by the command to stay in the same house?

See the discussion of this question at 9:4 where the twelve apostles were told to stay in one house during the time they remained in any village. That house was to serve as their base of operations for that town [Su, WBC]. It was that house in which a 'son of peace' had invited them to stay [Lns, WBC].

QUESTION—Are they to eat and drink the things from or with the people in the house?

1. The things are provided by the people of the house [Alf, Arn, BECNT, ICC, Lns, NIGTC, TH; all versions except REB]: eat and drink the things you receive from them. They are the things that are offered to them [TH]. They are things the people have and give to the disciples [NIGTC].

2. The things are shared with the people of the house [REB]: eat and drink with them.

QUESTION—What relationship is indicated by γάρ 'because' which introduces the proverbial saying?

It introduces the reason the disciples are to eat and drink what they are offered [Crd, EGT, MGC, TNTC, WBC]. The wage consists of the hospitality and the food they are given [BECNT]. They are entitled to their food and drink in return for their spiritual ministry [NIC, NIGTC]. The food is to be regarded as their salary, not alms [NIC, NIGTC], and they are not to feel guilty about living on the generosity of others [Arn, My, NTC, TNTC]. This justifies the instructions they received about not taking provisions with them and about expecting free hospitality [TG].

QUESTION—What is the purpose of instructing the disciples not to move from house to house?

This is a negative counterpart to the preceding command to stay in the same house [TH]. They are not to fear that they are being burdensome to their host [ICC, NIC]. They are not to seek better quarters [ICC, Lns, TG, WBC]. Perhaps this also is a warning against wasting time by responding to numerous invitations for social events [ICC, Rb, TNTC].

10:8 And into whichever city you-enter and they-welcome[a] you, eat the (things) being-set-before you **10:9** and heal the (ones) in it (who are) sick and say to-them, The kingdom of-God has-come-near[b] to you.

LEXICON—a. pres. mid./pass. (deponent = act.) subj. of δέχομαι (LN 34.53) (BAGD 1. p. 177): 'to welcome'. See translations of this word at 9:5 and 9:53.

b. perf. act. indic. of ἐγγίζω (LN 67.21) (BAGD 5.b. p. 213): 'to come near' [Arn, BAGD, LN, NTC; HCSB, KJV, NASB, NRSV, TEV], 'to be near' [GW, NCV, NIV, NLT], 'to draw near' [AB, WBC], 'to approach' [BAGD, LN]. The clause 'the kingdom of God has come near to you' is translated 'the kingdom of God has come on/upon you' [BECNT; NET, REB], 'you can be sure that God's kingdom will soon be here' [CEV].

QUESTION—What is the connection between 10:7 and 10:8?

While the instructions in 10:5–7 apply to the single home in which they lodge, now instructions are given concerning towns in which the townspeople welcome them [Arn, BECNT, Gdt, ICC, MGC, NAC, NIGTC, NTC]. The instructions about eating are not a repetition of 10:7 since they now concern eating individual meals at whatever house [BECNT]. In 10:7, 'the things from them' means from the people who live in the house they would stay in, while in 10:8 'they welcome you' refers to various people in the town [TH]. Or, the instructions about eating in 10:8 are merely emphasizing the same instructions given in 10:7 [Arn].

QUESTION—In 10:8, what is the intent of the command to eat the things set before them?

They are to be content with whatever they get [BECNT, EGT, TG]. They should not demand more or anything different [ICC]. They must not be fussy about the ceremonial purity of food that Gentiles might offer them [Lns, NIC, NTC, Su, TNTC]. However, they were in Jewish and Samaritan country and the Gentile issue probably is not addressed [BECNT, Gdt, NAC, WBC]. The issue is about the quality of the food [NAC].

QUESTION—In 10:9, who are the referents in the command 'and say to them'?

This does not mean that the disciples were to speak only to the sick people, rather it means that they were to speak to all of the people in the town [ICC, TG, TH].

QUESTION—Is the kingdom of God near in the sense that it was already among them or near in the sense that it would not be long until it arrived?

1. The kingdom of God was already there among them [Arn, Crd, Gdt, Lns, MGC, NIC, NICNT, NIGTC, NTC, TH; NET, REB]. The perfect tense indicates that it was a present reality [TH]. It is already present 'to you', that is, among those to whom the kingdom is preached [Crd]. In the presence of Jesus and his commissioned disciples the kingdom was then present in time and it was near in space to those who would be reached by their ministry [NIGTC]. This refers to God's saving activity in the ministry of Jesus and the disciples he sends [NICNT]. This focuses on the kingdom's saving power and not on the glorious manifestation to come

later [NIGTC]. The kingdom is spiritual in nature [MGC]. The miraculous healings would prove that God's sovereignty was exercised through Christ and his disciples [NIC]. God's kingship and rule is in the hearts and lives of his people [NTC]. It had come from heaven and had come near so that it was then present [Lns].
2. The kingdom of God was near in time, but not yet present with them [AB, NAC; CEV]. The full arrival of the kingdom was still in the future [AB]. Perhaps it means that it was near because Jesus would soon be entering the town [AB, NAC].
3. Both meanings are included [BECNT, ICC, Su, WBC]. The kingdom had begun with Jesus' presence and ministry, but awaited a future consummation [ICC, WBC]. The acts of healing signaled the coming of the kingdom in the beginning of a new divine age [BECNT].

10:10 And into whatever city you-enter and they-do- not -welcome you, having-gone-out into its streets say, 10:11 Even the dust clinging^a to-us from your city, to the feet, we-wipe-off^b (against) you. Nevertheless^c know this that the kingdom of-God has-come-near.

TEXT—In 10:11, some manuscripts omit εἰς τοὺς πόδας 'to the feet'. GNT does not mention this variant.

TEXT—At the end of 10:11, following ἤγγικεν 'has come near', some manuscripts add ἐφ' ὑμᾶς 'to you'. GNT does not mention this variant. Ἐφ' ὑμᾶς 'to you' is read by KJV.

LEXICON—a. aorist pass. participle of κολλάομαι, κολλάω (LN 18.21) (BAGD 2.a.α. p. 441): 'to cling to' [AB, Arn, BAGD, BECNT, LN, WBC; HCSB, NASB, NET, NRSV, REB], 'to stick to' [LN, Lns, NTC; NCV, NIV, TEV], 'to cleave to' [KJV], not explicit [CEV, GW, NLT].
  b. pres. mid. indic. of ἀπομάσσομαι, ἀπομάσσω (LN **16.9**) (BAGD p. 97): 'to wipe off' [AB, Arn, BAGD, BECNT, **LN**, Lns, NTC, WBC; all versions except CEV, GW, NLT], 'to wipe from' [GW, NLT], 'to shake from' [CEV].
  c. πλήν (LN 89.130) (BAGD 1.b. p. 669): 'nevertheless' [BAGD, BECNT, LN, Lns, NTC; NET], 'notwithstanding' [KJV], 'however' [Arn], 'yet' [NASB, NIV, NRSV], 'but' [BAGD, LN, WBC; GW, NCV, TEV], 'only' [REB], 'rather' [AB], 'and' [CEV, NLT], not explicit [HCSB].

QUESTION—In 10:10, what are they to go out of when they go out into its streets?

They were to go out of a house into the city streets [EGT, ICC, My, Rb, TH], the street being something like the city's main street [Arn]. They must go out of the house that they had entered [My]. They will go out of inhospitable houses [EGT, Rb]. They are to go out of the house in which they were lodging [ICC, TH]. They might be received into one house, yet the town as a whole might reject them [ICC]. As they pass through the streets they will give this message [TH] as a public warning [ICC]. The similar instruction in 9:5, 'going out from that city shake-off the dust from your feet' suggests that this is the same [NIGTC]. Or, they are to go out of the city into the roads leading from the city [NIGTC].

QUESTION—What are they to do with the dust and what is the significance of this act?

In 9:5 they were to shake off the dust, but here they are to wipe it off by removing their sandals and wiping off the dust [TG]. Wiping is a more thorough way of getting rid of dust than shaking [EGT]. In this way they will show that they will take nothing from that city with them, not even the dust they got on their feet from walking through the streets [Lns]. They even return the dust on their feet, and in this way break every bond of connection with the town [Gdt]. This act is done against the inhabitants, meaning the same as 'for a testimony against them' in 9:5 [NAC, NIGTC]. This is a symbolic act to signify God's displeasure with them because they rejected the gospel [NTC]. It indicates God's rejection of the people [BECNT]. It is the fault of the citizens of the town that the kingdom of God and its blessing came to them in vain [EGT]. The dust is a testimony that the messengers of the kingdom had been there and had to leave because their message was rejected [Lns].

QUESTION—In 10:11, what relationship is indicated by πλήν 'nevertheless'?

It indicates contrast while implying the validity of something irrespective of other considerations [LN (89.130)]. This indicates a restriction with the sense 'Further, we have nothing else to announce to you, excepting that…' [Gdt]. This points out the grievous character of what they did in rejecting the message of Christ's messengers [NTC]. They have no excuse for not partaking in the kingdom [NIC]. The kingdom comes in spite of their refusal to accept the message [BECNT]. In spite of wiping off the dust in an act against the inhabitants, they must remember that the kingdom had come near and perhaps some may come to realize this and repent of their action and accept the kingdom [Lns].

10:12 I say to-you that it-will-be more-bearable[a] for-Sodom in that day than for-that city.

TEXT—Instead of λέγω 'I say', some manuscripts read λέγω δέ 'But I say'. GNT does not mention this variant. Λέγω δέ 'But I say' is read by KJV.

LEXICON—a. ἀνεκτός (LN 25.172) (BAGD p. 64): 'more bearable' [BAGD, LN; NET, NIV, REB], 'more endurable' [BAGD, LN, Lns], 'more tolerable' [AB, Arn, LN, NTC, WBC; HCSB, KJV, NASB, NRSV], 'easier' [GW], 'better' [BECNT; NCV], 'better off' [NLT]. The phrase 'it will be more bearable' is translated 'will get off easier' [CEV], 'God will show more mercy (to Sodom)' [TEV].

QUESTION—What day is 'that day'?

It is the coming day of judgment [BECNT, BNTC, ICC, NAC, NIVS, NTC, TG, TH, TNTC, WBC; CEV, GW, NCV, NLT, REB, TEV].

QUESTION—Why is Sodom mentioned?
Genesis 19 tells about the terrible sins of the people of Sodom and their fate. Later this city had become proverbial as representing sin and devastating judgment [NIGTC]. There was no hope for Sodom and there is even less hope for a city that commits the greatest sin of all, that of rejecting the gospel [NIGTC]. The people of Sodom did not have the opportunities that the present city had, so judgment will be severer for the ones who had the greater opportunities [NIC].

DISCOURSE UNIT: 10:13–16 [TNTC; CEV, HCSB, NCV, NRSV, TEV]. The topic is the unbelieving towns [CEV, TEV], the unrepentant towns [HCSB], Jesus warns unbelievers [NCV], woe to unrepentant cities [NRSV], the doom of the Galilean cities [TNTC].

DISCOURSE UNIT: 10:13–15 [AB]. The topic is the woes uttered against the towns of Galilee.

10:13 Woe[a] to-you, Chorazin, woe to-you, Bethsaida. Because if the miracles[b] having-happened in you had-occurred in Tyre and Sidon, they (would have) repented[c] long-ago, sitting in sackcloth[d] and ashes. **10:14** Nevertheless it-will-be more-bearable for-Tyre and Sidon in the judgment than for-you.

LEXICON—a. οὐαί (LN **22.9**) (BAGD 1.a. p. 591): 'woe, alas' [BAGD], 'disaster, horror' [LN]. The phrase 'woe to you' [AB, Arn, BECNT, Lns, NTC, WBC; HCSB, KJV, NASB, NET, NIV, NRSV] is also translated 'alas for you' [REB], 'how terrible for you' [NCV], 'how terrible it will be for you' [TEV], 'how disastrous it will be for you' [**LN**], 'how horrible it will be for you' [GW], 'what horrors await you' [NLT], 'you people are in for trouble' [CEV]. See this word at 6:24; 11:42; 17:1; 21:23; 22:22.

b. δύναμις (LN 76.7) (BAGD 4. p. 208): 'miracle' [AB, BAGD, LN, WBC; all versions except KJV, NRSV], 'mighty deed' [LN], 'mighty work' [BECNT, NTC; KJV], 'deed of power' [Arn, BAGD; NRSV], 'work of power' [Lns], 'wonder' [BAGD]. See this word at 19:37.

c. aorist act. indic. of μετανοέω (LN 41.52) (BAGD p. 512): 'to repent' [AB, Arn, BAGD, LN; HCSB, KJV, NASB, NET, NIV, NLT, NRSV, REB], 'to turn to God' [CEV], 'to turn from one's sins' [TEV], 'to change one's life' [NCV], 'to change the way one thought and acted' [GW]. See this word at 11:32; 13:3, 5; 15:7, 10; 16:30; 17:3, 4.

d. σάκκος (LN 6.164) (BAGD p. 740): 'sackcloth' [AB, Arn, BAGD, BECNT, LN, Lns, NTC, WBC; all versions except NCV], 'rough cloth' [NCV]. This was a heavy material normally used for making sacks [BAGD, LN]. The material was made from the hair of goats [AB, BECNT, NAC, NIGTC, TH, WBC], or of other animals [BECNT, ICC, TH]. Being dark in color it was suitable for use in mourning [BAGD, NTC, TG]. Although this material was used for making sacks, it was also used for making clothing and here the people would be wearing the sackcloth [ICC]. It was a kind of a shirt, slit down the front and covering the loins [NTC]. It was worn as a loin covering over the naked body [AB].

QUESTION—What is meant by 'woe to you'?

This is an expression of sorrow [NIGTC], or deep regret [TNTC] for the fate that is to be theirs. He was speaking of being punished by God [TG]. The woes here function as a verdict pronounced in advance by the Judge with deep pathos [Lns]. This is a figure of speech called apostrophe in which Jesus addressed the populace in general of the two cities as though they were present, and this does not imply that not a single individual in those cities had been converted [Arn]. The following clause beginning with ὅτι 'because' gives the reason for pronouncing woe on the two cities [Lns].

QUESTION—Where were Chorazin and Bethsaida?

Capernaum was Jesus' headquarters for a long time and he did miracles not only in Capernaum but in the near-by towns of Chorazin and Bethsaida. The site of Chorazin is not known [AB, BECNT, MGC, NAC, NIGTC, WBC]. It is often identified with the modern town of Kerazeh, about two miles northeast of Capernaum [AB, BNTC, ICC, MGC, NIC, NIGTC, NTC, WBC]. Bethsaida was a town about five miles east of Capernaum and was the home of Andrew, Peter, and Philip [Su].

QUESTION—Why are Tyre and Sidon mentioned and how could cities repent and sit in sackcloth and ashes?

They were Gentile cities in Phoenecia on the Mediterranean coast and were notorious for their wickedness. Tyre was about thirty miles from Capernaum and Sidon was twenty miles further away [Su]. The two cities are personified [Gdt] and it means that the inhabitants would have repented and be sitting in sackcloth and ashes [My]. In mourning, a person would wear the dark rough garment next to the skin as a symbol of remorse and humiliation [Lns], self-humiliation and grief [BECNT]. Another symbol of mourning was either throwing ashes over themselves [BECNT, Gdt, NAC, NIGTC, TG, WBC; CEV, NCV, NLT, TEV] or sitting on ashes [NAC, NIGTC, WBC; GW]. People would sit in the ashes and cover their heads and shoulders with ashes as a sign of mourning [Lns]. Here it is a sign of remorse rather than mourning [TH].

QUESTION—How could miracles cause people to repent?

Miracles by themselves could not produce faith, but the evidence of the power of a mighty God would bring about contrition and terror so that the people would cease their outward sins and crimes [Lns]. Tyre and Sidon had once been destroyed because of their wickedness (Isa. 23:1–8) [MGC]. If the miracles had been performed long ago in those ancient cities, they would have repented long ago [BECNT]. Since Jesus' miracles in Chorazin and Bethsaida had not been performed long ago, saying that if they had had occurred in Tyre and Sidon the people would have repented 'long ago' is a hyperbole and means that they would have repented immediately or would not have waited long to do so [TG].

460   LUKE 10:13–14

QUESTION—In 10:14, what relationship is indicated by πλήν 'nevertheless'?
It means 'yet, in spite of the fact that Tyre and Sidon have not repented' [TH], or 'but, guilty as they are' [ICC]. The fact is that the miracles were not done in Tyre and Sidon, so those people did not repent and they will be judged. However, God will sentence them with a lighter punishment than those in the Jewish cities [Gdt, Lns, NIGTC, TH].

10:15 And you, Capernaum, you-will-be-exalted[a] up to-(the)-heaven[b] will you? You-shall-go-down[c] to Hades.[d]

TEXT—Instead of μὴ ἕως οὐρανοῦ ὑψωθήσῃ; 'not will you be exalted up to heaven? (expecting the reply 'No')', some manuscripts read ἡ ἕως τοῦ οὐρανοῦ ὑψωθεῖσα 'the one having been exalted up to heaven'. GNT does not mention this variant. Ἡ ἕως τοῦ οὐρανοῦ ὑψωθεῖσα 'the one having been exalted up to heaven' is read by KJV.

TEXT—Instead of καταβήσῃ 'you shall go down', some manuscripts read καταβιβασθήσῃ 'you shall be brought down'. GNT reads καταβήσῃ 'you shall go down' with a C decision, indicating that the Committee had difficulty making the decision. Καταβιβασθήσῃ 'you shall be brought down' is read by BECNT, Lns, NTC; KJV, NASB, NCV, NET, NLT, NRSV, REB, TEV.

LEXICON—a. fut. pass. indic. of ὑψόω (LN 87.20) (BAGD 1. p. 851): 'to be exalted' [AB, Arn, BECNT, LN, Lns, NTC, WBC; HCSB, KJV, NASB, NET, NLT, NRSV, REB], 'to be lifted up' [BAGD; GW, NCV, NIV], 'to be raised high' [BAGD], 'to be honored' [CEV], 'to lift yourself up' [TEV]. This symbol means to be crowned with the highest honors [BAGD].
  b. οὐρανός (LN 1.5) (BAGD 1.b. p. 594): 'heaven' [Arn, BECNT, Lns, NTC, WBC; all versions except NIV], 'sky' [AB, BAGD, LN; NIV]. The phrase ἕως οὐρανοῦ 'to the sky' expresses a great height [BAGD].
  c. fut. mid. (deponent = act.) indic. of καταβαίνω (LN 15.107) (BAGD 2. p. 408): 'to go down' [AB, BAGD, LN, WBC; CEV, HCSB, NIV], 'to descend' [Arn], 'to go' [GW], 'to be brought down' [BECNT; NASB, NLT, NRSV, REB], 'to be thrown down' [NCV, NET, TEV], 'to be thrust down' [NTC; KJV], 'to be cast down' [Lns].
  d. ᾅδης (LN 1.19) (BAGD 1. p. 17): 'Hades' [Arn, BAGD, BECNT, LN, Lns, NTC, WBC; HCSB, NASB, NET, NRSV, REB], 'the underworld' [BAGD], 'the world of the dead' [LN], 'the place of the dead' [NLT], 'death's abode' [AB], 'the depths' [NCV, NIV], 'hell' [CEV, GW, KJV, TEV]. See this word at 16:23.

QUESTION—What is the intent of the question 'you will be exalted up to heaven, will you?'
The question is introduced with the negative particle μή 'not' and assumes a negative answer [AB, Arn, BECNT, Lns, NTC, Su, TH, TNTC, WBC; NET]. It can be translated 'you surely don't expect to be exalted to heaven, do you?' [NTC]. This is asked in irony since Capernaum does expect to be

exalted [Lns, NTC]. The people of Capernaum might expect to be exalted because of the many cures performed by Jesus in that city [AB, NAC, NIGTC]. The taunt recorded in Isaiah 14:15 against the king of Babylon is applied to the people of Capernaum [BNTC, MGC].

QUESTION—What is meant by being exalted to 'heaven'?
1. Heaven refers to where God is [BECNT, Gdt]. Heaven represents God's highest favors [Gdt]. Instead of heaven, the destination is Hades [BECNT, Lns].
2. 'Heaven' is used to refer to the highest location possible [AB, ICC, TG, TH, TNTC; NIV], and the sky is the highest location [AB; NIV]. This refers to their desire to receive the highest place of honor [TH]. It means the height of glory [ICC, TNTC]. It means to become the greatest and most powerful of all the towns [TG].

QUESTION—What is meant by going down to 'Hades'?
1. Hades refers to a place of punishment, to hell [BECNT, Lns, NAC, NIGTC, NTC; CEV, GW, KJV, TEV]. Hades is a place of torment and flame (16:23–24) and this is a prediction of being punished in hell [NTC]. It is the place of the damned [Lns], the place where the unrighteous reside after judgment [BECNT, NAC]. It is the opposite of heaven and the thought is of humiliation and perhaps punishment [NIGTC].
2. Hades means the place of the dead [AB, MGC, Su, TG, WBC; NLT]. This refers to the town experiencing the doom of death and extinction [Su]. God will completely destroy them [TG]. In Hades the proud are stripped of their power and humbled in death [WBC].
3. Hades is used to signify the lowest place in contrast with the highest place [Gdt, ICC, NIGTC, TH, TNTC; NCV, NIV]. Heaven and Hades are the highest and lowest points in the universe [TH]. This refers to the depth of shame [ICC], and degradation [TNTC]. It signifies humiliation, but perhaps the use of 'Hades' also includes punishment [NIGTC]. It means deepest abasement [Gdt].

DISCOURSE UNIT: 10:16 [AB]. The topic is the disciples as representatives.

10:16 **The (one) listening-to**[a] **you listens-to me, and the (one) rejecting**[b] **you rejects me. And the (one) rejecting me rejects the (one) having-sent me.**

LEXICON—a. pres. act. participle of ἀκούω (LN 31.56): 'to listen to' [AB, LN, NTC, WBC; CEV, HCSB, NASB, NCV, NET, NIV, NRSV, REB, TEV], 'to hear' [Arn, BECNT, Lns; GW, KJV], 'to listen and respond, to pay attention and respond, to heed' [LN], 'to accept (the message)' [LN; NLT]. Since this verse deals with positive and negative responses, this verb includes both hearing and accepting [AB, NIGTC]. It means to accept what one hears [TH]. Or, 'to listen' does not imply acceptance and it means that when the disciples speak, Jesus is speaking [Arn].
b. pres. act. participle of ἀθετέω (LN 31.100) (BAGD 1.b. p. 21): 'to reject' [AB, BAGD, BECNT, LN, NTC, WBC; all versions except CEV, KJV,

462　　　　　　　　　　　　　LUKE 10:16

NCV], 'to say No to' [CEV], 'to refuse to accept' [NCV], 'to set aside' [Lns], 'to despise' [Arn; KJV].

QUESTION—Who is Jesus speaking to now?

It is clear that Jesus has stopped addressing the inhabitants of the three cities and now addresses the seventy two disciples he was sending out [Arn, Crd, NAC]. This is made explicit in some translations: 'Then he said to the disciples…' [NLT], 'Jesus said to his disciples…' [TEV], 'My followers, whoever listens to you…' [CEV]. This emphasizes their authority as messengers and the importance of their message [BECNT, TNTC]. It authorizes the disciples to act in the name of Jesus [NIGTC]. The disciples must do all that is possible to have their message accepted [ICC].

QUESTION—In what way were the messengers rejected?

Rejecting the messenger is accomplished by rejecting his message, and here to do so is to reject Jesus who sent the messengers [NIGTC]. The people rejected the call to faith in Jesus and allegiance to him [TH]. A person would refuse to accept the disciples' message as coming from Jesus and ultimately from God [AB]. The logic is that since the messengers say what Jesus told them to say, people reject Jesus when they reject what the messengers say [Lns].

QUESTION—Who is the one who sent Jesus and how is this one rejected?

The one who sent Jesus is God [Arn, MGC, NIGTC, TG, TH; NET, NLT]. Jesus applied to himself what he has told his disciples [TH]. In the act of rejecting Jesus, the person rejects God who sent Jesus [TNTC]. The messengers proclaimed the message given them by Jesus, and Jesus proclaimed the message God directed him to proclaim [Crd]. It is implied that accepting the message of the disciples is to accept what Jesus says and thus to accept what his Father says [Lns]. The emphasis is on the seriousness of rejecting the message [Lns, NTC].

DISCOURSE UNIT: 10:17–29 [NASB]. The topic is the happy results.

DISCOURSE UNIT: 10:17–20 [AB, NAC, NIGTC, TNTC, WBC; CEV, HCSB, NCV, TEV]. The topic is the return of the seventy(–two) [AB, NAC, TNTC, WBC; CEV, HCSB, TEV], the return of the missionaries [NIGTC], Satan falls [NCV].

10:17 **And the seventy-[two] returned with joy[a] saying, Lord, even[b] the demons submit[c] to-us in[d] your name.**

TEXT—Some manuscripts omit δύο 'two' so that this refers to only seventy. GNT includes this word with a C decision and brackets it in the text, indicating that the Committee had difficulty making the decision. Δύο 'two' is omitted by BNTC, EGT, Gdt, ICC, Lns, NIC, Su; GW, KJV, NASB, NRSV.

LEXICON—a. χαρά (LN 25.123) (BAGD 1. p. 875): 'joy' [Arn, BAGD, BECNT, LN, Lns, NTC, WBC; HCSB, KJV, NASB, NET, NIV, NRSV], 'great joy' [TEV], 'gladness, great happiness' [LN]. The phrase μετά χαρᾶς 'with joy' is translated 'full of joy' [AB], '(were) very happy' [NCV], '(were) excited' [CEV], '(came back) jubilant' [REB], '(came back) very happy' [GW], 'joyfully (reported)' [NLT]. They were full of joy over the success of their mission [AB, TNTC]. They were excited and happy that they had authority even over demons [Alf, BECNT, Lns, NTC].

b. καί (LN 89.93) (BAGD II.2. p. 393): 'even' [AB, Arn, BAGD, BECNT, LN, Lns, NTC, WBC; all versions].

c. pres. pass. indic. of ὑποτάσσομαι (ὑποτάσσω) (LN 36.18) (BAGD 1.b.β. p. 848): 'to submit' [AB, Arn, LN, Lns; HCSB, NET, NIV, NRSV, REB], 'to obey' [LN; CEV, GW, NCV, NLT, TEV], 'to be subject to' [BAGD, BECNT, NTC, WBC; KJV, NASB]. The present tense indicates repetition [Rb].

d. ἐν with dative object (LN 89.76, 90.23): 'by means of' [LN (89.76)]. This preposition ἐν (with the dative) and also the prepositions ἐπί (with the genitive) and εἰς (with the accusative) are markers of content as a means of specifying a particular referent: 'concerning, with respect to, with reference to, about, in' [LN (90.23)]. The formula ἐν τῷ ὀνόματί σου 'in your name' [Arn, BECNT, Lns, NTC, WBC; HCSB, NASB, NET, NIV, NRSV, REB] is also translated 'through thy name' [KJV], 'when we used/use your name' [NCV, NLT], 'when we spoke in your name' [CEV], 'when we gave them a command in your name' [TEV], 'when we use the power and authority of your name' [GW], 'with the use of your name' [AB].

QUESTION—How long were the disciples gone?

Luke does not say how long the disciples were away or where it was that they reported back to Jesus [Arn, TNTC]. This must have occurred after a period of some weeks [TH] or several months [Arn]. It probably was not a long time [Alf, Lns] since there were thirty-five (or thirty-six) pairs going throughout the territory [Lns]. Jesus must have arranged with them both the time and place to meet after the mission [Gdt, Lns, NIC] and they all gathered at that time [Lns]. Or, they would not have all returned at the same time, so perhaps they returned to Jesus at different points along his route as he traveled along after them [ICC, My].

QUESTION—What is the force of καί 'even (the demons submit)'?

They were especially glad that the demons were submitting to them even though Jesus had not laid stress on casting out demons in 10:9 [EGT, Lns]. 'Even' is added since they had not explicitly been sent to cast out demons [TH]. It was more than they had expected [AB, Alf, Arn, EGT, ICC]. It expresses their surprise [NIGTC].

QUESTION—What did the disciples mean by the demons submitting to them 'in your name'?

The disciples commanded the demons with the authority Jesus had given them [WBC]. The disciples functioned as Jesus' representatives [Su, TG]. They spoke Jesus' name in casting out demons [Arn, My, TG, TH]. They invoked Jesus' name [AB], they invoked his power and authority [TG; NET]. The power in connected with the person of Jesus became effective through invoking his name [AB]. Jesus' name was not used as a charm [Lns, NAC], and this means 'in connection with the revelation of Jesus' [Lns], by the power of Jesus [NAC]. They acted in Jesus' name [NIC], in his stead as his representatives [Su].

10:18 **And he-said to-them, I-was-seeing Satan like lightning from heaven having-fallen.**[a]

LEXICON—a. aorist act. participle of πίπτω (LN 15.118) (BAGD 1.a. p. 659): 'to fall' [AB, Arn, BAGD, BECNT, LN, Lns, NTC, WBC; all versions].

QUESTION—How is this verse connected with 10:17?

It explains why the disciples' mission was so successful [WBC]. Jesus explained why the demons had submitted to the disciples [NIC]. He described what the disciples' authority meant [BECNT]. This gives the reason the demons had to leave when the disciples commanded them to [Lns]. It explains the significance of the power of Jesus' name over the demons [NIGTC].

QUESTION—What is the significance of the use of the imperfect tense ἐθεώρουν 'I was seeing'?

1. The imperfect 'I was seeing' indicates a continuing experience [AB, Crd, EGT, Gdt, NAC, NIC, NTC, Su, TG, TH, TNTC; GW, NASB, NRSV]: I was seeing Satan fall. This is translated 'I watched' [GW, NRSV], 'I was watching' [AB, NTC; NASB], 'I was beholding' [Lns]. It means 'I was watching and saw Satan fall' [TG]. Throughout the mission of the disciples and as a result of it, Jesus was watching Satan fall [EGT, NAC, NIC, TNTC].
2. The imperfect refers to one event [Arn, BECNT, Lns, NIGTC, WBC; CEV, HCSB, KJV, NCV, NET, NIV, NLT, REB, TEV]: I saw Satan fall. This timeless imperfect is descriptive and dramatic so that Jesus was not watching the progress of Satan's falling, but saw the fall as an instantaneous fall like a flash of lightning [Lns]. This refers to the fact of the fall, not the process of how it was accomplished [WBC].

QUESTION—How did Jesus see Satan fall?

1. This refers to what Jesus literally saw either in his pre-incarnation state or in a vision [Alf, Crd, NICNT, WBC].
    1.1 This refers to the original fall of Satan before the foundation of the world, but Satan had been in the process of falling ever since and it would finally be accomplished when all things were to be put under Jesus' feet [Alf].
    1.2 This describes a vision [Crd, NICNT, WBC]. Perhaps he saw this vision during the time the seventy-two were on their mission [Crd]. This refers to a vision that revealed Jesus' own mission of bringing about the triumph of God's kingdom over the rule of Satan, and at this time Jesus' ministry was being extended through his disciples [WBC]. This was a

LUKE 10:18

prophetic vision of Satan's ultimate downfall at the time of judgment [NICNT].
2. This refers to Jesus' interpretation of events in a symbolical description of the defeat of Satan [Arn, Gdt, ICC, Lns, My, NAC, NIC, NIGTC, NTC, Su, TNTC].
2.1 This describes the result of the mission of the disciples [Arn, Gdt, ICC, NIC, NTC, Su]. While the disciples were expelling Satan's subordinates, Jesus was contemplating the fall of the demon's master and in this way the complete destruction of Satan's kingdom had begun with the successes of the disciples [Gdt, NTC]. This also refers to all similar events that would take place in the future [NTC]. Jesus regarded the defeat of the demons by the disciples as a symbol and token of the future complete overthrow of Satan [ICC]. Casting out demons was a sign of the defeat of Satan [NIGTC]. Satan's kingdom was being overcome as the disciples exercised their authority over demons and ultimately the defeat would be total [Su].
2.2 This describes the defeat of Satan at the time of Jesus' temptation in the wilderness [Lns].

QUESTION—What is meant by Σατανᾶν ὡς ἀστραπὴν ἐκ τοῦ οὐρανοῦ πεσόντα 'Satan like lightning from heaven having fallen'?

The phrase 'from heaven' modifies the verb 'having fallen' [AB, Alf, Arn, BECNT, ICC, My, NAC, NIC, NIGTC, NTC, TG, TH, WBC; CEV, GW, KJV, NASB, NLT, NRSV, REB]: I saw Satan fall from heaven like lightning falls.
1. Heaven is where God is [AB, Alf, BECNT, TG, TH; NET]. This reflects the symbolism of Isaiah 14:12 where the king of Babylonia falls from heaven and is cast down to earth [BECNT, TG; NET]. Satan had a role in heaven as an accuser of God's people (Job 1–2; Zechariah 3:1–2) [AB, BECNT]. This implies that God cast Satan out of heaven and this was a current defeat [BECNT].
2. This is a figurative use of heaven [Arn, Gdt, ICC, Lns, My, NIGTC, TNTC]. This does not mean that Satan was living in heaven at the time, but it refers to Satan's exalted power [My]. Heaven is a symbol of height, prosperity, and power [ICC, TNTC], and of supernatural power [Lns]. Satan's fall from heaven meant that he had lost his power to act upon human consciousness [Gdt]. Satan was conquered and could not rule as he pleased [Lns].

QUESTION—Why is Satan's fall compared with lightning?

The point of similarity is its suddenness [Arn, My, NAC, NIGTC, NTC, TG], swiftness [My, NIGTC, TG], being visible and unmistakable [ICC], and startling [NTC]. Not only is the comparison with the suddenness, but also with the brightness of lightning [Alf].

10:19 **Behold I-have-given you the authority[a] to-tread on snakes and scorpions, and over all the power[b] of-the enemy, and nothing may-injure[c] you in-any-way.**

TEXT—Instead of the perfect tense δέδωκα 'I have given', some manuscripts read the present tense δίδωμι 'I give'. GNT does not mention this variant. Δίδωμι 'I give' is read by KJV.

LEXICON—a. ἐξουσία (LN 37.35) (BAGD 2. p. 278): 'authority' [AB, BAGD, BECNT, LN, Lns, NTC, WBC; GW, HCSB, NASB, NET, NIV, NLT, NRSV, TEV], 'right to control' [LN], 'absolute power' [BAGD], 'power' [Arn; CEV, KJV, NCV, REB]. This noun includes the power and the right to exercise that power [Lns, TNTC, WBC]. Here, it means that Jesus has enabled or empowered them to do this [TH]. See this word at 9:1.

  b. δύναμις (LN 76.1): 'power' [AB, BECNT, LN, Lns, NTC, WBC; all versions except NET, REB], 'full force' [NET], 'the forces' [REB]. The phrase 'and over all the power of the enemy' is translated 'and authority over all the power of the enemy' [WBC], 'and over every might of the Evil One' [Arn], 'and to overcome all the power of the enemy' [NIV, TEV], 'and to defeat the power of your enemy Satan' [CEV], 'and to destroy the enemy's power' [GW], 'power that is greater than the enemy has' [NCV].

  c. aorist act. subj. of ἀδικέω (LN 20.25) (BAGD 2.b. p. 17): 'to injure' [BAGD; NASB, NLT], 'to harm' [AB, Arn, LN, Lns, WBC; CEV, HCSB, NIV, REB], 'to hurt' [BECNT, LN, NTC; GW, KJV, NCV, NET, NRSV, TEV]. This is figurative language which means that all the forces of evil could not defeat them [Su].

QUESTION—Is treading on the snakes and scorpions to be taken literally?

  1. This statement is to be taken literally [BECNT, Gdt; NET]. It is given as an example of the hostility that is in the creation that is defeated by Jesus [BECNT; NET], and of all the physical evils used by Satan [Gdt]. In Acts 28:3–6 Paul was unaffected by a snake bite. This is not telling the disciples to handle such dangerous creatures, rather they are to know that forces like these and those they represent can be opposed and crushed [BECNT].

  2. This is to be taken figuratively or symbolically [AB, ICC, Lns, My, NIC, NIGTC, NTC, Su, TG, TNTC]. There is no record of the disciples treading on snakes or scorpions without suffering harm [Lns, NTC, TNTC]. Snakes and scorpions are OT symbols of all kinds of evil [AB]. The snakes and scorpions describe the evil spirits [NIGTC]. These dangerous creatures were fit symbols of the Satanic forces that would oppose Jesus [My, Su]. They are used as symbols for cunning and dangerous spiritual enemies [NIC], evil spirits [NIGTC], physical evils used by Satan [Gdt], fraud and treachery [ICC], deadly delusions, deceptions, and falsehoods by Satan [Lns]. The next clause explains the symbolism [AB, ICC, NTC].

QUESTION—What is the power of the enemy?

It is the power of their enemy, Satan himself [AB, BECNT, EGT, ICC, Lns, My, NAC, NIGTC, Rb, TG, TH, TNTC, WBC; CEV, NET]. This power includes all agencies of nature, human society, and spiritual powers that Satan could use to oppose the work of Jesus [NIC]. This refers to victory over spiritual forces, but may include protection from physical harm [ICC].

10:20 Nevertheless (do) not rejoice in this, that the spirits[a] submit[b] to-you, but rejoice that your names are-written[c] in the heavens.

TEXT—Following χαίρετε δέ 'but rejoice', some manuscripts add μᾶλλον 'rather', although GNT does not mention this variant. Μᾶλλον 'rather' is read by KJV.

TEXT—Instead of the perfect tense compound verb ἐγγέγραπται 'have been written', some manuscripts read the aorist tense of the simple verb ἐγράφη 'were written'. GNT does not mention this variant. Some versions would probably not distinguish clearly between these two verb forms.

LEXICON—a. πνεῦμα (LN 12.37) (BAGD 4.c. p. 676): 'spirit' [AB, Arn, BAGD, BECNT, Lns, NTC, WBC; HCSB, KJV, NASB, NCV, NET, NIV, NRSV, REB], 'evil spirit' [BAGD, LN; CEV, GW, NLT, TEV], 'demon' [BAGD, LN]. In a Hebrew context the unqualified noun 'spirit' means 'evil spirit' [NIGTC].

b. pres. pass. indic. of ὑποτάσσομαι, ὑποτάσσω (LN 36.18) (BAGD 1.b.β. p. 848): 'to submit'. See translations of this word at 10:17.

c. perf. pass. indic. of ἐγγράφω (LN 33.62) (BAGD 1. p. 214): 'to be recorded' [BAGD, LN, NTC, WBC; NASB], 'to be written' [BAGD, LN; CEV, GW, HCSB, KJV, NCV, NIV, NRSV, TEV], 'to stand written' [AB, BECNT; NET], 'to be inscribed' [Arn], 'to be enrolled' [Lns; REB], 'to be registered as citizens' [NLT].

QUESTION—Should the disciples rejoice that the spirits submit to them?

1. It was proper for the disciples to rejoice in their power over demons [NIC, NIGTC, NTC, Su, TG, TH]. When they cast out evil spirits it brought glory to God and delivered men from the powers of darkness [NTC]. This negative command is used in conjunction with the following positive command to indicate comparison [EGT, TG], preference [TH], and importance [NIGTC, NTC, Su]. They are not to rejoice just because of that [NLT]. They are not to rejoice primarily over this, rather they are to rejoice even more over the fact that their names are recorded in heaven [NIGTC].

2. The disciples were not to rejoice in their power over demons [ICC, Lns]. They are to stop rejoicing in their power over demons and to continue to rejoice in something better [ICC]. It would be dangerous to rejoice about this because it could lead to pride about something that they are not doing by themselves but by Jesus' power [Lns].

QUESTION—What is meant by having their names written in heaven? This implies that God did the writing [Lns, NIGTC, TH]. It gives a picture of a written roll containing the names of all those who are redeemed by God [Su]. It is a roll listing the names of all those who are citizens or members of heaven [ICC, MGC, NIGTC, TH, WBC; NLT]. The roll is like the genealogical records of the Jews and lists all those who are accepted by God as his children [Lns]. This roll is the book of life [AB, Arn, BECNT, BNTC, NIGTC, NTC], listing all who belong to God [AB]. This means that there is an assured place in the kingdom of God for them [BECNT, WBC].

DISCOURSE UNIT: 10:21–24 [AB, NAC, NICNT, NIGTC, Su, TNTC, WBC; CEV, HCSB, NCV, NLT, NRSV, TEV]. The topic is the blessedness of the disciples [NAC, NICNT], Jesus' joy [TNTC], Jesus rejoices [NRSV, TEV], Jesus prays to the Father [NCV], Jesus thanks his Father [NIGTC; CEV, NLT], Jesus rejoices at what God has now been pleased to reveal [WBC], rejoicing at certain victory [Su], Jesus' praise of the Father; the blessedness of the disciples [AB], the Son reveals the Father [HCSB].

10:21 In the same hour he-rejoiced[a] in the Holy Spirit and he-said, I-thank[b] you, Father, Lord of-heaven and earth, that/because you-hid[c] these (things) from (the) wise[d] and intelligent[e] and you-revealed them to-little-children.[f] Yes[g] Father, that/because thus it-was well-pleasing[h] before you.

TEXT—Instead of ἠγαλλιάσατο ἐν τῷ πνεύματι τῷ ἁγίῳ 'he rejoiced in the Holy Spirit', some manuscripts read ἠγαλλιάσατο ἐν τῷ πνεύματι 'he rejoiced in the (*i.e.*, his) spirit/in the Spirit', some manuscripts read ἠγαλλιάσατο τῷ πνεύματι ὁ Ἰησοῦς 'Jesus rejoiced in the spirit/Spirit', some manuscripts read ἠγαλλιάσατο τῷ πνεύματι τῷ ἁγίῳ ὁ Ἰησοῦς 'Jesus rejoiced in the Holy Spirit', and some manuscripts read ἠγαλλιάσατο ὁ Ἰησοῦς τῷ πνεύματι τῷ ἁγίῳ 'Jesus rejoiced in the Holy Spirit'. GNT reads ἠγαλλιάσατο ἐν τῷ πνεύματι τῷ ἁγίῳ 'he rejoiced in the Holy Spirit' with a C decision and places ἐν 'in' in brackets in the text, indicating that the Committee had difficulty making the decision. Ἠγαλλιάσατο τῷ πνεύματι ὁ Ἰησοῦς 'Jesus rejoiced in the spirit' is read by Gdt, My, and KJV.

LEXICON—a. aorist mid. indic. of ἀγαλλιάω (LN 25.133) (BAGD p. 4): 'to rejoice'. The phrase ἠγαλλιάσατο ἐν τῷ πνεύματι τῷ ἁγίῳ 'he/Jesus rejoiced in the Holy Spirit' [BECNT, WBC; HCSB, NCV, NET, NRSV] is also translated 'he/Jesus rejoiced greatly in the Holy Spirit' [NTC; NASB], 'Jesus felt the joy that comes from the Holy Spirit' [CEV], 'the Holy Spirit filled Jesus with joy' [GW], 'Jesus rejoiced through the Holy Spirit' [Arn], 'Jesus, full of joy through the Holy Spirit' [NIV], 'Jesus was filled with the joy of the Holy Spirit' [NLT], 'Jesus was filled with joy by the Holy Spirit' [TEV], 'he/Jesus exulted in the Holy Spirit' [Lns; REB], 'Jesus found delight in the Holy Spirit' [AB]. One takes another reading of the text: 'Jesus rejoiced in spirit' [KJV]. See this word at 1:47.

b. pres. mid. indic. of ἐξομολογέομαι, ἐξομολογέω (LN 33.351) (BAGD 2.c. p. 277): 'to thank' [LN], 'to praise' [BAGD]. The phrase ἐξομολογοῦμαί σοι ὅτι 'I thank you that' [BECNT, WBC; KJV] is also translated 'I thank you for' [NLT, REB], 'I am grateful that' [CEV], 'I praise you that' [Arn, NTC; NASB], 'I praise you for' [GW], 'I openly confess to thy honor that' [Lns], 'I praise you because' [AB; HCSB, NCV, NET, NIV], 'I thank you because' [NRSV, TEV]. Jesus praised God for what God has done [NIGTC]. Or, he praised God because of what he himself had done [TH].
c. aorist act. indic. of ἀποκρύπτω (LN 28.80) (BAGD p. 93): 'to hide' [AB, Arn, BAGD, BECNT, NTC, WBC; all versions], 'to conceal' [BAGD, LN, Lns], 'to keep secret' [LN]. This is similar to God hardening the heart of Pharaoh in Exodus 7:3 [AB].
d. σοφός (LN 32.35) (BAGD 2. p. 760): 'the wise' [AB, BAGD, BECNT, LN, Lns, NTC, WBC; all versions except NLT], 'wise people' [Arn], 'intelligent, sagacious' [BAGD], 'one who thinks himself so wise' [NLT]. This refers to a man who is regarded to be especially able to understand the philosophical aspects of knowledge and experience [LN].
e. συνετός (LN 32.27) (BAGD p. 788): 'the intelligent' [AB, BAGD, LN; GW, NASB, NET, NRSV], 'the intellectual' [Lns], 'the educated' [CEV], 'the learned' [NTC; HCSB, NIV, REB, TEV], 'the insightful' [LN], 'the understanding' [Arn, BECNT, LN, WBC], 'the smart' [NCV], 'the prudent' [KJV], 'one who thinks himself so clever' [NLT], 'sagacious, wise' [BAGD].
f. νήπιος (LN 9.43) (BAGD 1.b.β. p. 537): 'little child' [GW, NET, NIV], 'small child' [AB, LN], 'infant' [Arn, BAGD; HCSB, NASB, NRSV], 'baby' [BECNT, WBC], 'babe' [Lns, NTC; KJV], 'those who are like little children' [NCV], 'ordinary person' [CEV], 'the childlike' [NLT], 'the simple' [REB], 'the unlearned' [TEV].
g. ναί (LN 69.1) (BAGD 3. p. 533): 'yes' [Arn, BAGD, BECNT, LN, Lns, NTC, WBC; all versions except KJV], 'indeed' [AB], 'even so' [KJV]. This emphatically affirms what Jesus has just said [Lns]. It expresses agreement in the sense 'Yes, you have done this because it was your will and I agree with what you have done' or 'Yes, I praise you that this was your will' [NIGTC]. It strongly indicates Jesus' acceptance of this paradoxical course [Gdt].
h. εὐδοκία (LN 25.88) (BAGD 2. p. 319): 'what pleases' [LN], 'good pleasure' [BAGD]. The phrase οὕτως εὐδοκία ἐγένετο ἔμπροσθέν σου 'thus it was well-pleasing before you' is translated 'thus it was good pleasure before thee' [Lns], 'such was your good pleasure' [NTC, WBC], 'such was pleasing to you' [BECNT], 'that/this is what pleased you' [CEV, GW], 'this was your gracious will' [NET], 'such was your gracious will' [NRSV], 'such was your choice' [REB], 'this is what you decided upon' [Arn], 'this is what you really want' [NCV], 'this way was well-pleasing in your sight' [NASB], 'this was your good pleasure' [HCSB,

NIV], 'this has been your good pleasure' [AB], 'so it seemed good in your sight' [KJV], 'it pleased you to do it this way' [NLT], 'this was how you were pleased to have it happen' [TEV].

QUESTION—What was the same hour that Jesus rejoiced?

It was the time the messengers returned and reported to him [AB, Arn, ICC, My, NIC, NTC, Su] and Jesus commented on their mission [AB]. It was when Jesus told the messengers what they should really rejoice about [Lns]. This temporal phrase refers back to what precedes it [NIGTC]. It appears to refer to what has just preceded, but it probably is used in a vague and general way [TG].

QUESTION—What did Jesus rejoice about?

Jesus rejoiced over the disciples' report [NTC]. He rejoiced over the successful mission completed by his disciples and their victory over Satan [Rb, WBC]. He rejoiced that God had arranged things so that insight was given into the truths of the kingdom [NIC]. He rejoiced that his disciples were saved and their position in heaven was secure [BECNT].

QUESTION—What is meant by rejoicing ἐν 'in' the Holy Spirit?

The Holy Spirit caused this joy [AB, Lns, NTC, Rb, Su, WBC]. The joy Jesus experienced and the words he now spoke were inspired by the Holy Spirit [Arn, ICC, NICNT, NIGTC]. Jesus was filled with the Holy Spirit who caused both this joy and the expression of it [Arn]. Jesus rejoiced through, because of, and under the influence of the Holy Spirit [TH]. Jesus rejoiced because he was experiencing the Holy Spirit's power or influence [TG].

QUESTION—What were ταῦτα 'the things' that were concealed and revealed?

There is no clear antecedent to 'these things' [AB, Crd, NIGTC]. It is probably the gospel of the kingdom [NIGTC], the mysteries of the kingdom [Arn]. They are the facts about God's kingdom that the messengers had made known in their mission [ICC]. They are the knowledge about the presence of God's kingdom and the fall of Satan [MGC, NAC]. They are things Jesus spoke about in 10:18–20, they concern the gospel by which names are recorded in heaven [Lns]. They concern the knowledge of God's will [Crd]. They are the experiences of the messengers in having power over demons [TH].

QUESTION—Did Jesus rejoice that God had concealed these things?

1. Concealing these things is one of the things that Jesus thanked God for [Gdt, ICC, Lns, NICNT, NTC, TH; TEV]: I thank you that you concealed these things from the wise and that you revealed them to the childlike. God had proved that he was independent of human intellect [ICC]. Jesus thanked God for revealing to the children what he had concealed from the wise [TEV]. By rejecting the wise, people who were considered to be wiser were humbled when they realized that they were not needed for God's work [Gdt].

2. Jesus was not thanking God for concealing these things [MGC, NIGTC, Su]: I thank you that although you have concealed these things from the wise, you have nevertheless revealed them to the childlike. The first

clause about concealing things is unstressed [NIGTC]. The concealing was not due to God failing to reveal these things but was the result of the wise failing to understand [Su].

QUESTION—Is there a difference intended between σοφός 'wise' and συνετός 'intelligent'?

The two words mean the same and if there are no synonyms available, one word may be used in a translation [TG]. Some find a difference. The noun 'wise' refers to one's intellectual capacities while 'intelligence' refers to the knowledge and insight obtained by learning and experience [TH]. These people were wise in their own conceits in contrast with the humble [NTC]. They considered themselves to be wise and sensible and wanted to test the truth of the gospel by their own intellect [NIC]. This description is aimed especially at the leaders of the scribes and Pharisees [BECNT, ICC, Lns, NIC, NIGTC, Su].

QUESTION—Who were the little children?

This designation is used figuratively of people who were unsophisticated, inexperienced, immature [TG], humble [NIC, Su], childlike [NIGTC; NCV, NLT], ordinary [CEV], common [Su], and simple [AB, Su, TH, WBC; REB]. They were unlearned and thus free from the prejudices of the scholars who were trained in Rabbinical schools [ICC]. They accepted the truths revealed by God without intellectual arrogance [ICC]. They were the disciples in contrast with the scribes and others who would not listen to Jesus [AB]. They were the seventy-two messengers [NAC].

QUESTION—In the last sentence, does ὅτι mean 'that' or 'because'?

1. It means 'that' [ICC, TG, TH; CEV, GW, NCV]. It repeats the ὅτι 'that' in the previous statement and depends on 'I thank you' [ICC, TG, TH]: I thank you that you concealed…and revealed…. Yes, Father, I thank you that thus it was well pleasing before you.
2. It means 'because' [Arn, Gdt, TH, WBC; HCSB, KJV, NASB, NET, NIV, NRSV]. It indicates the reason Jesus thanked the Father [Gdt]: Yes, Father, I praise you because thus it was well pleasing before you. Or, it gives the reason that God concealed and revealed as he did [Lns]: Yes, Father, it was thus because it was well pleasing before you. However, it makes little difference whether it is stated why he praised God or what he praised God for since the thing about which we praise God is the reason we praise him [Lns].
3. Many translate this so that it is just a statement of fact [CEV, GW, NCV, NLT, REB, TEV]: Yes, Father that is well pleasing before you.

10:22 Everything was-handed-over[a] to-me by my Father, and no-one knows who the Son[b] is except the Father, and who is the Father except the Son and to-whomever the Son wishes[c] to-reveal[d] (him).

TEXT—Before πάντα 'everything', some manuscripts read καὶ στραφεὶς πρὸς τοὺς μαθητὰς εἶπεν, 'and having turned to the disciples he said'.

472   LUKE 10:22

GNT rejects this addition with an A decision, indicating that the text is certain.

LEXICON—a. aorist pass. indic. of παραδίδωμι (LN 57.77) (BAGD 3. p. 615): 'to be handed over' [Arn, LN, NTC; NASB, NRSV], 'to be passed on' [BAGD, WBC], 'to be transmitted, to be taught' [BAGD], 'to be given' [Lns; NET], 'to be delivered' [BECNT; KJV], 'to be entrusted' [AB; HCSB, REB], 'to be committed' [NIV]. This passive is translated actively with the Father as subject: 'to give' [CEV, NCV, NLT, TEV], 'to turn over' [GW]. The verb can be used of handing down knowledge such as a tradition handed down by a teacher or it can be used of transferring power or authority [NIGTC].

  b. υἱός (LN 12.15) (BAGD 2.b. p. 834): This noun is capitalized: 'Son' [AB, Arn, BAGD, BECNT, LN, Lns, NTC, WBC; all versions]. This is used as a title for the Son of God [BAGD, LN]. Here Jesus refers to himself in an absolute sense as 'the Son' [AB, MGC, NAC]. Here and in Mark 13:32 are the only places in the synoptic Gospels where Jesus referred to himself as 'the Son' [NAC, TNTC]. Both 'the Son' and 'the Father' are used as titles [TH].

  c. pres. mid./pass. (deponent = act.) subj. of ἀποκαλύπτω (LN 25.3) (BAGD 2.b. p. 146): 'to wish' [Arn, BAGD, WBC], 'to desire' [BAGD, LN; HCSB], 'to want' [BAGD, LN; CEV], 'to decide' [NET], 'to will' [Lns; KJV, NASB], 'to be willing' [GW], 'to choose' [AB, BECNT, NTC; NCV, NIV, NLT, NRSV, REB, TEV].

  d. aorist act. infin. of ἀποκαλύπτω (LN 28.38) (BAGD 2. p. 92): 'to reveal' [AB, Arn, BAGD, BECNT, LN, Lns, NTC, WBC; all versions except CEV, NCV], 'to disclose' [BAGD, LN], 'to tell' [NCV], 'to tell others about the Father, so that they can know him too' [CEV].

QUESTION—Whom was Jesus speaking to now?

  1. Jesus was speaking in prayer to the Father in the presence of his disciples [Arn, Gdt, Lns, NIGTC, Rb, WBC; NET]. It is a continuation of Jesus' prayer although the context becomes didactic; the disciples are not addressed until the next verse which begins 'and having turned to the disciples' [NIGTC, WBC]. Jesus' adoration turns to mediation and when Jesus prayed 'and to whomever the Son wishes to reveal him' his thoughts turned to the disciples and so he addressed them in the next verse [Gdt].

  2. Jesus was no longer speaking to God but to his disciples [TG, TH]. Jesus is speaking to the seventy and other people who are present [TH].

QUESTION—What were all the things handed over to Jesus by his Father?

  1. 'Everything' refers to knowledge [AB, Crd, TG, TH]: all knowledge has been handed over to me by my Father. It is the knowledge of Jesus' mutual relation with God [AB].

  2. 'Everything' refers to power and authority [Gdt, ICC; NLT]: all authority has been handed over to me by my Father. Christ has the power to reveal and conceal in executing God's decrees [ICC]. This refers to authority over everything [NLT].

3. 'Everything' refers to both knowledge and authority [BECNT, Lns, MGC, NAC, NIGTC, NTC, Su, WBC]. In relation to what follows, this refers to both the Son's knowledge and his authority to reveal the Father [NIGTC]. The Son has total authority over salvation and over imparting knowledge of the Father [BECNT]. This refers to all that God has given Jesus in the realms of wisdom and power [Su]. Jesus is the Son and heir and has been given all that God disposes as an inheritance [WBC]. All that was necessary to carry out his task as mediator had been entrusted to Jesus [NTC]. As the Son of God, Christ was equal to the Father but when he became man, God gave Christ all the divine power and majesty that he used as needed in his ministry and would fully enter into when he arose from death [Lns].

QUESTION—What doesn't anyone know about the Son?

This refers to knowing about the Son's divine nature as it was joined to his human nature [Lns]. It refers to his supreme position [TNTC]. It refers to his nature, counsel, and will [ICC].

QUESTION—What is the intent of the two clauses about knowing the Son and the Father?

The two clauses are stated as a basis for the final clause of the verse and the point is that Jesus' intimacy with the Father enabled him to reveal God to his disciples [WBC]. The clauses are to be taken together to refer to the mutual knowledge of the Father and the Son so that the meaning is that only a father and a son know each other, and therefore only the Son can reveal the Father [NIGTC]. The Father and the Son know each other's will, mind, and thought as they pertain to us [Lns].

10:23 And having-turned to the disciples privately[a] he-said, Blessed[d] (are) the eyes seeing the (things) you-see. **10:24** Because I-say to-you that many prophets and kings wanted to-see the (things) you see and they-did- not -see (them), and to-hear the (things) you-hear and they-did- not -hear (them).

LEXICON—a. κατ' ἰδίαν (LN 28.67) (BAGD 4. p. 370): The idiom κατ' ἰδίαν 'according to that which is private' is translated 'privately' [AB, Arn, BAGD, BECNT, LN, NTC, WBC; HCSB, KJV, NASB, NCV, NET, NIV, NRSV, TEV], 'in private' [Lns; CEV, GW], 'when they were alone' [NLT], 'when he was alone with this disciples' [REB]. The phrase pertains to something that occurs in a private setting and is not made known publicly [LN].

b. μακάριος (LN 25.119) (BAGD 3.a. p. 487): 'blessed'. See translations of this word at 1:45 and 6:20. This word also occurs at 1:45; 6:20; 7:23; 11:27; 12:37, 43; 14:14; 23:29.

QUESTION—In what way was this said privately?

In speaking privately to his disciples, it is implied that the previous words were spoken in the hearing of more people than the disciples [Lns, TNTC]. After speaking the words recorded in 10:22 in the hearing of a multitude of people, Jesus turned around and addressed these words especially to the disciples [NIC]. By turning to the disciples, Jesus excluded the other people who were present [My]. Although many others were present, this beatitude applied only to the disciples [Lns]. This beatitude is only applicable to the disciples because they have seen to some degree the events surrounding Jesus [WBC]. Or, Jesus waited until he was alone with the disciples [ICC, TH; NLT, REB], thus making an interval between 10:22 and this verse [ICC]. These words were not addressed to the seventy, but primarily to the twelve disciples [BNTC]. In Matthew 13:16–17 similar words were spoken to the Twelve, but here 10:17 indicates that Jesus was speaking to the seventy–two messengers [Lns].

QUESTION—Who's eyes were blessed?

This personification of the eyes stresses personal experience [NIGTC, WBC].

1. It refers to the disciples' own eyes [CEV, GW, NCV, NLT, TEV] and is translated 'you are really blessed to see what you see' [CEV], 'how blessed you are to see what you've seen' [GW], 'you are blessed to see what you now see' [NCV], 'how privileged you are to see what you have seen' [NLT], 'how fortunate you are to see the things you see' [TEV].
2. It refers to more than the disciples he was speaking to [BECNT, Lns, NIGTC, TH]. All who see what the seventy are seeing are blessed [Lns, NIGTC]. This includes disciples outside the group of seventy-two messengers and even includes Luke's readers [BECNT, NAC].

QUESTION—What had the disciples seen and heard?

It refers to what the disciples had seen on their mission trip [NAC]. They had seen the kingdom being manifested in Jesus' ministry [NIBC, NICNT]. The disciples had seen Jesus' work and had seen God's power work in their own ministry [Su]. They had seen mighty works done by Jesus and the signs of the coming of the era of salvation [NIGTC]. They had seen the incarnate Christ and his miracles [NTC]. Probably 'to see' means more than physical sight and refers to perceiving the truths about God and about his kingdom [TG]. It implies that they perceived the significance of what is happening [NIGTC].

DISCOURSE UNIT: 10:25–11:13 [BECNT, NIGTC]. The topic is discipleship: looking to one's neighbor, Jesus, and God [BECNT], the characteristics of disciples [NIGTC].

DISCOURSE UNIT: 10:25–42 [WBC]. The topic is the love of God and love of neighbor.

DISCOURSE UNIT: 10:25–37 [BECNT, NAC, NICNT, Su, TNTC; CEV, GW, HCSB, NCV, NET, NIV, NRSV, TEV]. The topic is the good Samaritan [CEV, NCV], the parable of the good Samaritan [BECNT, NAC, Su, TNTC; GW, HCSB, NET, NIV, NRSV, TEV], the parable of the compassionate Samaritan [NICNT].

DISCOURSE UNIT: 10:25–29 [NLT]. The topic is the most important commandment.

DISCOURSE UNIT: 10:25–28 [AB, NIGTC, WBC]. The topic is the lawyer's question [NIGTC], what shall I do to inherit eternal life? [WBC], the commandment for eternal life [AB].

10:25 And behold a-certain lawyer[a] stood-up testing[b] him saying, Teacher, by-having-done what will-I-receive[c] eternal life?
LEXICON—a. νομικός (LN **33.338**) (BAGD 2. p. 541): 'lawyer'. See translations of this word at 7:30. This word also occurs at 11:45, 46, 52; 14:3.
   b. pres. act. participle of ἐκπειράζω (LN 27.31) (BAGD p. 243): 'to test' [NTC, WBC; GW, HCSB, NCV, NET, NIV, NLT, NRSV, REB], 'to put to the test' [BAGD, BECNT; NASB], 'to ask a question to see what he would say' [CEV], 'to try to test' [AB], 'to try to trap' [LN; TEV], 'to attempt to catch in a mistake' [LN], 'to tempt' [Arn, Lns; KJV]. The participle indicates purpose [BECNT].
   c. fut. act. indic. of κληρονομέω (LN 57.131) (BAGD 2. p. 434): 'to receive' [BAGD, LN; NLT, TEV], 'to be given' [LN], 'to gain possession of' [BAGD, LN], 'to get' [NCV], 'to have' [CEV], 'to inherit' [AB, Arn, BECNT, Lns, NTC, WBC; GW, HCSB, KJV, NASB, NET, NIV, NRSV, REB]. See this same question asked by a ruler at 18:18.
QUESTION—What was the lawyer's motive in testing Jesus?
   He was testing Jesus' wisdom and teaching [TH], his ability as a teacher [ICC, NIC], his orthodoxy or theological knowledge [Gdt]. The lawyer was an authority on the interpretation of the law and he was testing an unofficial teacher to see if he would give the correct answers [NIGTC]. Some think that this testing did not imply that he had a sinister motive to entrap Jesus [Alf, ICC, NIBC]. Others think that the lawyer had a hostile attitude and was trying to trap him [AB, BECNT, NAC, NICNT, Su; TEV]. The present tense is conative, he was *trying* to tempt Jesus [Rb]. The lawyer may have hoped that Jesus would do badly so that he could show him up [TNTC] and embarrass him [NTC]. He wanted to defeat Jesus in theological discussion [Su]. He expected an answer that he could challenge [Lns].
QUESTION—What is meant by 'eternal life'?
   Eternal life refers mainly to salvation as a life with God after death [NIGTC]. It is a life that will never end and a life of such a quality that that it is suited for the age to come [TNTC]. Receiving this life is regeneration and that life goes on forever with temporal death only transferring it to the heavenly world [Lns]. It is the life in the future age [MGC, TG]. Eternal life refers to the eschatological blessing of the righteous and the question amounts to, 'What must I do to share in the resurrection of the righteous at the end?' or 'How can I be sure I'll be saved at the final resurrection?' [BECNT].

10:26 And he-said to him, In the law[a] what has-been-written? How do-you-read[b] (it)?

LEXICON—a. νόμος (LN 33.56) (BAGD 4.b. p. 543): 'Law' [AB, Arn, WBC; NASB, NIV], 'law' [BAGD, BECNT, Lns, NTC; HCSB, KJV, NCV, NRSV, REB], 'holy writings' [LN], 'Scriptures' [LN; CEV, TEV], 'the law of Moses' [NLT]. The 'law' refers to the first five books of the OT, the Torah [TG].
  b. pres. act. indic. of ἀναγινώσκω (LN 33.68) (BAGD 1. p. 51): 'to read' [BAGD, LN]. The question πῶς ἀναγινώσκεις; 'How do you read' [BECNT, Lns; KJV] is also translated 'How do you read it?' [AB, NTC, WBC; HCSB, NIV, NLT], 'How does it read to you?' [NASB], 'How do you understand it?' [NET], 'How do you understand them?' [CEV], 'How do you interpret them?' [TEV], 'What do you read in it?' [Arn], 'What is your reading of it?' [REB], 'What do you read there?' [GW, NCV, NRSV].

QUESTION—What is meant by Jesus' question, Πῶς ἀναγινώσκεις; 'How do you read it?'
  1. The question asks how the lawyer interprets the law [Alf, Arn, BECNT, ICC, My, NICNT, TG, WBC; CEV, NET, TEV]. He wants to know how the lawyer understands it [CEV]. Scripture evidence is wanted [ICC]. Here, this does not refer to the act of reading, but perceiving the meaning of what has been read [WBC]. Jesus asked what the lawyer had learned from reading the Law [TG]. This asks for a summary of what the lawyer read in the Law [Alf]. It is equivalent of asking him 'How is the way of salvation outlined in what you read?' [Arn].
  2. The question asks how the lawyer recites it in worship [Lns, MGC, NIGTC, TH; NCV, NRSV]. 'How' refers to the content of what he reads in a synagogue service [TH]. This asks the lawyer to quote the words that are written in the law [Lns]. Probably he was asking what was the law the lawyer recited at worship, although this interpretation has a problem in that the lawyer recited more than the contents of the Shema that was recited in regular worship [NIGTC].
  3. The question merely restates the previous question, 'what has been written in the law?' [BECNT, ICC, Lns; probably GW, NCV, NRSV which translate it as 'what do you read there?']. He merely asked the lawyer to quote the words [Lns]. Although Jesus might refer to reciting the Shema, it is more likely that he is asking the lawyer to give Scriptural support, not an appeal to tradition [BECNT]. This was a rabbinical formula for asking for scriptural evidence [ICC].

10:27 And answering he-said, You-will-love[a] (the) Lord your God from all your heart[b] and with all your soul[c] and with all your strength[d] and with all your mind,[e] and (you-will-love) your neighbor[f] as (you love) yourself.

LEXICON—a. fut. act. indic. of ἀγαπάω (LN 25.43) (BAGD 1.a.β. p. 4): 'to love' [AB, Arn, BAGD, BECNT, LN, Lns, NTC, WBC; all versions]. The future tense has the force of an imperative [Arn, Lns, TH]. The lawyer's use of 'you' is not addressing Jesus alone since he is quoting the singular form of this verb and the following singular pronouns σου 'your' from the OT command which is addressed to Israel as a whole [TG].

b. καρδία (LN 26.3) (BAGD 1.b.ζ. p. 404): 'heart' [BAGD, LN], 'inner self, mind' [LN], 'inner life' [BAGD]. The phrase ἐξ ὅλης τῆς καρδίας σου 'from all your heart' is translated 'with all your heart' [AB, BECNT, NTC; all versions], 'with your whole heart' [Arn, WBC], 'out of thy whole heart' [Lns]. The heart refers to the inner life [WBC], one's vitality [NICNT], the center of one's being [Lns, WBC]. It concerns a person's emotional response [AB, Arn, BECNT, NAC, NICNT].

c. ψυχή (LN 26.4) (BAGD 1.b.γ. p. 893): 'soul' [BAGD], 'inner self, mind, thoughts, feelings, heart, being' [LN]. The phrase ἐν ὅλῃ τῇ ψυχῇ σου 'with all your soul' [AB, BECNT, NTC; all versions] is also translated 'with your whole soul' [Arn], 'with your whole life' [WBC], 'in thy whole soul' [Lns]. The soul is the life force that animates the body [Lns, WBC]. It is one's personality, one's conscious being [WBC], the inner life in general [Arn]. It is a person's consciousness [AB, BECNT, NAC], and vitality [AB, NICNT].

d. ἰσχύς (LN 74.8) (BAGD p. 383): 'strength' [BAGD, LN], 'power, might' [BAGD], 'capability' [LN]. The phrase ἐν ὅλῃ τῇ ἰσχύϊ σου 'with all your strength' [Arn, BECNT, NTC; all versions] is also translated 'with your whole strength' [WBC], 'in thy whole strength' [Lns], 'with all your might' [AB]. This is physical strength [WBC]. It is the person's powerful and instinctive drive [AB, BECNT]. It is one's drive and energy [NICNT], the ability to do given tasks [Arn]. It is a person's motivation [NAC].

e. διάνοια (LN 26.14) (BAGD 1. p. 187): 'mind' [BAGD, LN], 'understanding, intelligence' [BAGD]. The phrase ἐν ὅλῃ τῇ διανοίᾳ σου 'with all your mind' [AB, BECNT, NTC; all versions] is also translated 'with your whole mind' [WBC], 'in thy whole mind' [Lns], 'with all your understanding' [Arn]. It is the capacity to think [WBC]. It is the thinking and planning processes [WBC]. It is one's reason along with its thoughts, ideas, and convictions [Lns]. It is a person's intelligence [AB, Arn, BECNT, NAC], and planning qualities [AB]. It is one's understanding and disposition [NICNT].

f. πλησίον (LN 11.89) (BAGD 1.b. p. 672): 'neighbor' [AB, Arn, BAGD, BECNT, LN, Lns, NTC, WBC; all versions], 'one who is near or close by, fellow man' [BAGD]. This refers to someone who is near us [Lns, NIGTC], one with whom we come in contact [Lns]. It refers to someone of the same country or race, and means 'fellow countryman' or 'fellow Jew' [TG]. The Jews understood this to refer to members of the same religious community, that is, fellow Jews and this is how the lawyer would understand it [NIGTC]. The point of the following story is the definition of 'neighbor' and Jesus will redefine the word more broadly [NIGTC, TG].

QUESTION—Did the lawyer quote from the OT?

The lawyer quoted from Deuteronomy 6:5 (part of the *Shema* which was recited daily in synagogue services) and Leviticus 19:18. The hundreds of laws in the Torah are summarized in the Ten Commandments which has two sections, one dealing with our relationship to God and one dealing with our relationships with people. The lawyer astutely included both relationships in his answer [Su]. The passage in Deuteronomy lists three faculties with which we are to love God (heart, soul, and strength), while the lawyer lists four (heart, soul, strength, and mind). The word for 'mind' is an alternate translation of the Hebrew word for 'heart' [BNTC, WBC].

QUESTION—What is the significance of the preposition ἐξ (ἐκ) 'from' being connected with 'heart' and the preposition ἐν 'with' being connected with 'soul', 'strength', and 'mind'?

In Mark and in the Septuagint ἐξ 'from' is used throughout, but in Matthew ἐν 'in' is used throughout.

1. There is no significant difference [Lns, TH]. The preposition ἐξ 'from' was commonly used with reference to the heart [Lns]. Both ἐξ 'from' and ἐν 'with' have instrumental force [TH]. Most translations use the preposition 'with' in relation to all four of the faculties [AB, BECNT, NTC, WBC; all versions].
2. There is a distinction with ἐξ 'from' indicating the source and ἐν 'with' indicating the means or manner [Arn]. The moral life comes 'from' the heart and manifests itself 'in' or 'with' three forms of activity [Gdt].

QUESTION—What is the effect of listing the four faculties for loving God?

They function together rather than separately to denote a person in his totality [NICNT, TG, TH]. They cover a person's physical, intellectual, and moral activity [ICC]. Together they mean that we are to love God with all that we are [TNTC]. The entire person must respond [BECNT]. There are no clear distinctions between these different aspects of personality [NIGTC].

QUESTION—What is meant by loving your neighbor as yourself?

This means to love your neighbor just as much as you love yourself [TG]. Or, this does not commend self-love and it does not mean 'as much as you love yourself'. It means to behave towards others as though you were on the receiving end and would want kindly and considerate behavior [WBC].

10:28 And he-said to-him, You-have-answered correctly. Do this and you-will-live.[a]

LEXICON—a. fut. mid. indic. of ζάω (LN 23.88) (BAGD 2.b.α. p. 336): 'to live' [BAGD, LN]. The verb 'you will live' [Arn, BECNT; HCSB, NASB, NCV, NET, NIV, NRSV, TEV] is also translated 'you shall live' [AB, Lns, NTC, WBC; KJV], 'you will have life' [REB], 'life will be yours' [GW], 'you will have eternal life' [CEV].

QUESTION—How would the lawyer live?

He would live in reference to 'eternal life' and this means 'do this and you will have or acquire eternal life' [AB, Arn, Lns, TH]. He would live in the fullest sense of the word for time and eternity [NIC]. The present imperative ποίει 'do' means to continually do the commandments quoted in the previous verse [Arn, BECNT, ICC, Lns, NAC, NIC, NTC, Rb, TH]. The imperative 'do this' functions as a conditional clause, meaning 'if you do this, then you will live' [NIGTC, TH]. This does not imply that it is possible to obey the commandment perfectly and this fact should make the lawyer realize his guilt [NIV]. People are incapable of complete obedience to the law [Su].

DISCOURSE UNIT: 10:29–37 [AB, NIGTC, WBC]. The topic is the good Samaritan [AB, NIGTC], who is my neighbor? [WBC].

10:29 And wanting to-justify[a] himself he-said to Jesus, And who is my neighbor?

LEXICON—a. aorist act. infin. of δικαιόω (LN 88.16) (BAGD 2. p. 197): 'to justify, to vindicate' [BAGD], 'to show to be right, to prove to be right' [LN]. The phrase 'to justify himself' [AB, Arn, BECNT, Lns, NTC, WBC; HCSB, KJV, NASB, NET, NIV, NRSV, TEV] is also translated 'to justify his question' [GW, REB], 'to justify his actions' [NLT], 'to show that he knew what he was talking about' [CEV], 'to show the importance of his question' [NCV].

QUESTION—What was it that the lawyer wanted to justify?

1. He wanted to justify the validity of his former question about what he must do to obtain eternal life [AB, Arn, Lns, My, NIGTC, Rb, TG; GW, NCV, REB]. He wanted to show that he was right to ask his initial question even though it proved to have such a simple answer [AB]. If the answer was as simple as Jesus had made it appear, a lawyer should have known the answer himself, so he wanted to show that it was not so simple after all [Arn, Lns]. The lawyer had been forced to answer his own question, so he asked another question to show that his first question had some point to it [Rb] and that he asked it for a good reason [My].
2. He wanted to justify his failure to love some people [BECNT, EGT, MGC, NIBC, NIC, NICNT, NTC, Su, WBC]. The lawyer felt that he was justified in deciding who his neighbor was and therefore who he was to love [Su], Since the lawyer realized that his own words indicated that he had not kept the law, he began to quibble over the definition of neighbor [WBC]. He was looking for an excuse for not having to treat all people alike with love and wanted to prove that not all people were his neighbors and therefore the law did not demand that he love all people [NIC]. He wanted to seek to be confident in his position by softening the demand [BECNT]. He wanted to quiet his conscience and also embarrass Jesus [NTC].

QUESTION—Why did the lawyer begin his question with καί 'and'?
   This introduces another question in the discussion [TH]. The lawyer accepted Jesus' answer and that led him to ask this question [Arn, Gdt, ICC].
QUESTION—Didn't the lawyer know who his neighbor was?
   He recognized that 'neighbor' must mean more than just the person next door, but he was puzzled about how many more people it included [TNTC]. His question implied that there was a problem in drawing the line in deciding who a person's neighbor was [AB, Arn, BECNT, ICC, WBC]. The definition of the neighbor we are commanded to love was not clear [TG]. There must be someone who was not a neighbor and therefore did not have to be loved, so he wanted to know the limits of the duty to show love for others [NIGTC].

DISCOURSE UNIT: 10:30–37 [NASB, NLT]. The topic is the story of the good Samaritan.

10:30 Replying Jesus said, A-certain man was-coming-down from Jerusalem to Jericho and he-fell-among[a] robbers, who also/both[b] having-stripped[c] him and having-inflicted[d] blows went-away leaving (him) half-dead.[e]

TEXT—Following ἡμιθανῆ 'half dead' some manuscripts add τυγχάνοντα 'finding himself' or 'as indeed he was' [BAGD]. GNT does not mention this variant.

LEXICON—a. aorist act. indic. of περιπίπτω (LN **37.11**) (BAGD 1. p. 649): 'to fall among' [Arn, BECNT, Lns, NTC, WBC; KJV, NASB], 'to fall into the hands of' [BAGD, **LN**; HCSB, NET, NIV, NRSV], 'to fall in with' [AB], 'to be seized by' [LN], 'to be attacked by' [NLT], 'to be set upon' [REB], not explicit [GW]. This is also translated with the robbers as subject: 'to attack' [CEV, NCV, TEV]. The man fell among the robbers because they surrounded him [Gdt]. Or, the verb simply means that he encountered them [EGT].

b. καί (LN 89.93, 89.102) (BAGD II.6. p. 393): 'also' [BAGD, LN (89.93)], 'both (...and...)' [LN (89.102), Lns], not explicit [AB, Arn, BECNT, NTC, WBC; all versions]. Following the relative pronoun 'who', καί focuses attention on the following events [TH]. This conjunction means that in addition to mistreating him, they took his clothing [Arn].

c. aorist act. participle of ἐκδύω (LN 49.18) (BAGD 1. p. 239): 'to strip' [AB, Arn, BAGD, BECNT, LN, Lns, NTC, WBC; GW, HCSB, NASB, NET, NRSV, REB, TEV], 'to take off clothes' [LN], 'to strip of raiment' [KJV], 'to strip him of his clothes' [NIV, NLT], 'to tear off his clothes' [NCV], 'to grab everything he had' [CEV].

d. aorist act. participle of ἐπιτίθημι (LN **90.87**) (BAGD 1.a.β. p. 303): 'to inflict' [BAGD], 'to subject to' [LN]. The phrase 'to inflict blows' is translated 'to lay blows on' [Lns], 'to strike him blow upon blow' [NTC], 'to beat' [AB, Arn, BECNT, **LN**; GW, NASB, NCV, NIV, NRSV, REB], 'to beat up' [WBC; CEV, HCSB, NET, NLT, TEV], 'to wound' [KJV].

This implies that the man resisted the robbers, who then beat him up [Bai, ICC, Lns, My], probably using clubs or sticks [TG, TH].
- e. ἡμιθανής (LN **23.122**) (BAGD p. 348): 'half dead' [AB, Arn, BAGD, BECNT, **LN**, Lns, NTC, WBC; all versions except GW, NCV], 'nearly dead' [LN], 'almost dead' [NCV]. The phrase 'leaving him half dead' is translated 'left him for dead' [GW]. Having been left unconscious [AB, Bai], he appeared to be dead [AB]. He would die if someone did not come to his aid [EGT]. He was injured to the extent that that his life was in peril, but the Samaritan will be able to recognize that he is still alive [Hlt].

QUESTION—Did this event actually happen?

It is a parable [Arn, BECNT, Blm, ICC, NIBC, NICNT, NTC, Pnt, Su, WBC], but the events were taken from real life situations [ICC, NICNT]. The characters in this story are fictional [NAC]. The main characters represent classes of people similar to them [Blm]. This is an illustration, not a parable, of what might occur on such a road [Lns].

QUESTION—What was the man stripped of?
1. He was stripped of his clothes [AB, Arn, Crd, ICC, Lns, MGC, My, NICNT, NIGTC, TNTC; KJV, NCV, NIV, NLT]. The preceding conjunction καί means 'also' and supposes that first the robbers took the man's purse and then also took his clothes [Gdt]. In addition to other violence, they stripped him, something that did not always happen [ICC]. It is understood that they robbed the man and taking his clothes highlights the violent ill-treatment they then inflicted [TNTC].
2. This refers to taking all of the man's possessions [Alf, Gdt, NTC, Rb, TG; CEV]. They stripped him of his clothing and all that he had [Alf]. They took his clothing, money, and if he had been riding on a donkey, they took that also [NTC].

10:31 **And by chance**[a] **a-certain priest was-coming-down by that way and having-seen him he-passed-by-on-the-other-side.**[b]

LEXICON—a. συγκυρία (LN **13.116**) (BAGD p. 775): 'chance, coincidence' [BAGD, LN]. The phrase κατὰ συγκυρίαν 'by chance' [Arn, BECNT, WBC; GW, KJV, NASB, NET, NLT, NRSV] is also translated 'by coincidence' [AB, Lns], 'it so happened that' [**LN**; NCV, REB, TEV], 'to happen' [NTC; CEV, HCSB, NIV].

- b. aorist act. indic. of ἀντιπαρέρχομαι (LN **15.30**) (BAGD p. 75): 'to pass by on the other side' [AB, Arn, BECNT; HCSB, KJV, NASB, NET, NIV, NRSV], 'to pass by on the opposite side' [BAGD, LN, NTC], 'to go by on the other side' [**LN**, Lns, WBC], 'to go past on the other side' [REB], 'to walk by on the other side' [Lns; CEV, NCV, TEV], 'to go around and continue on his way' [GW], 'to cross to the other side of the road and pass him by' [NLT]. The priest was walking [Lns; CEV, NCV, TEV]. Or, being of the upper-class, the priest would have been riding on an animal and could have really helped the man like the Samaritan does later in the story, but the Levite that came next probably was walking [Bai].

QUESTION—What is the import of beginning 10:31 with κατὰ συγκυρίαν 'by chance'?

It introduces another event that was going to happen at the same place and about the same time [TG]. It was not to be expected that the possibility of help would soon come by [EGT, Lns]. The coming of the priest at first appeared to be a fortunate means of help [BECNT].

QUESTION—What is the significance of the priest passing by on the other side of the road?

The priest did not want to be ceremonially defiled by any contact with the man who appeared to be dead [AB, MGC, NIBC, Su, TG, TNTC]. The priest recognized that the man was still alive and had no excuse for not helping him, [Hlt]. The priest had no desire to help the man [Lns] and did not want to get involved [NTC]. Perhaps the priest feared ambush by the robbers [MGC, NIGTC, WBC]. The priest is a fictional character and Jesus would have made explicit the thoughts in the priest's mind if it were important to the story [NAC].

10:32 And likewise[a] also a-Levite having-come upon the place, having-come and having-seen, he-passed-by-on-the-other-side.

TEXT—Some manuscripts omit γενόμενος 'having come'. GNT does not mention this variant in the apparatus but brackets it in the text, indicating difficulty in making the decision. Most versions probably would not distinguish between the presence and absence of γενόμενος 'having come' in their translations.

LEXICON—a. ὁμοίως (LN 64.1) (BAGD p. 568): 'likewise' [BAGD, LN]. The phrase ὁμοίως καί 'likewise also' [BECNT; NASB] is also translated 'so likewise' [NRSV], 'likewise moreover' [Lns], 'likewise' [KJV], 'similarly' [AB, WBC], 'so too' [NTC; NET, NIV, REB], 'in the same way' [HCSB, TEV], 'in a similar way' [Arn], '(he) too' [GW], '(he) also' [CEV], not explicit [NCV, NLT].

QUESTION—What position did Levites have among the Jews?

Levites were descendents of Levi, but not of Levi's descendent Aaron from whom the priests were descended [BECNT, Hlt]. While priests offered sacrifices at the temple, the Levites cared for lesser temple duties such as cleaning the buildings and utensils, maintaining the lamps, and carrying out the musical liturgy [Su]. 'Levite' is also translated 'temple helper' [CEV], 'temple assistant' [NLT].

10:33 But a-certain Samaritan traveling[a] came upon him and having-seen (him), he-was-moved-with-compassion.[b]

LEXICON—a. pres. act. participle of ὁδεύω (LN 15.19) (BAGD p. 553): 'to travel' [Arn, BAGD, LN, NTC; NIV, NRSV], 'to be traveling' [NET], 'to be traveling that way' [TEV], 'to travel along' [GW], 'to travel down/along the road' [CEV, NCV], 'to be on a journey' [AB, BAGD, LN, Lns, WBC; HCSB, NASB], 'to journey' [BECNT; KJV], 'to be going that way' [REB], 'to come along' [NLT].

b. aorist pass. (deponent = act.) indic. of σπλαγχνίζομαι (LN 25.49) (BAGD p. 762): 'to be moved with compassion' [Lns] 'to feel compassion (for)' [LN; NASB, NET], 'to have compassion (on)' [BECNT, WBC; HCSB, KJV], 'to have pity, to feel sympathy' [BAGD], 'to take pity (on)' [NIV], 'to pity' [Arn], 'to be moved with pity' [NRSV], 'to be moved to pity' [AB; REB], 'to feel deep pity' [NLT], 'to feel sorry (for)' [CEV, GW, NCV], 'his heart was filled with pity' [TEV], 'his heart went out to him' [NTC]. See this word at 7:13; 15:20.

QUESTION—What is significant about the third man to come along being a Samaritan?

That the Samaritan was traveling suggests that he was a foreigner and although there is no indication of his destination, from 10:35 it appears that he was not on his way home [TH]. He was probably a businessman [Arn], a traveling merchant [NICNT]. Jews had no respect for the people of the neighboring country of Samaria, whom they considered to be unclean [BECNT]. The hostility between Jews and Samaritans was mutual [Lns, NAC, NTC, Su, WBC]. A Samaritan would be the last person the lawyer would expect to illustrate the actions of a neighbor [BECNT, TNTC].

10:34 And having-approached he-bandaged his wounds pouring-over (them) oil and wine, and having-mounted[a] him upon (his) own animal[b] he-brought him to an-inn and cared-for[c] him. **10:35** And on the next-day having-taken-out he-gave two denarii to-the inn-keeper and said, Care-for him, and whatever you-spend-in-addition I will-repay you when I return.

TEXT—In 10:35, following αὔριον 'next day', some manuscripts add ἐξελθών 'having departed'. GNT does not mention this variant. Ἐξελθών 'having departed' is added by KJV.

TEXT—In 10:35, following εἶπεν 'he said', some manuscripts add αὐτῷ 'to him'. GNT does not mention this variant. Αὐτῷ 'to him' is read by KJV.

LEXICON—a. aorist act. participle of ἐπιβιβάζω (LN **15.98**) (BAGD p. 290): 'to cause to mount' [BAGD, LN]. The phrase 'having mounted him upon' is translated 'he mounted him on' [NTC, WBC], 'he put him on' [all versions except KJV, REB], 'he placed him upon' [Arn], 'he lifted him on' [REB], 'he set him on' [AB, BECNT, Lns; KJV]. The Samaritan would then have walked alongside [Alf, Arn, BECNT, NTC, TNTC] in order to hold the man on and guide the animal [Lns].

b. κτῆνος (LN **4.6**) (BAGD p. 455): 'animal' [BAGD; GW, HCSB, NET, NRSV, TEV], 'beast' [Lns, WBC; KJV, NASB, REB], 'riding animal' [**LN**], 'mount' [AB], 'mule' [Arn], 'donkey' [CEV, NCV, NIV, NLT]. This is a generic term for large types of domesticated animals used for riding or carrying loads [LN]. This was an animal used for riding, and probably it was a mule [Arn, TG, TH], or a donkey [Bai, TG; CEV, NCV, NIV, NLT].

c. aorist pass. (deponent = act.) indic. of ἐπιμελέομαι (LN **35.44**) (BAGD p. 296): 'to care for' [BAGD, **LN**; NCV], 'to take care of' [Arn, BAGD,

BECNT, LN, Lns, WBC; all versions except NCV, REB], 'to look after' [REB], 'to provide whatever is needed' [LN], 'made provision for' [AB]. This term covers providing for the man's need in way of clothing and whatever else was needed [Lns].

QUESTION—What is the actual order of the Samaritan's actions when 'he bandaged his wounds, pouring over them oil and wine'?

The act of 'pouring' came before bandaging [TH; CEV, GW, NCV, NLT, NRSV, TEV], or during the process of bandaging [BECNT, ICC, NIGTC]. The oil was olive oil used to sooth the pain [Lns, MGC, NTC, Su, TG, TH, TNTC], to soften the wound [AB, Hlt, WBC], or to cleanse the wound [Bai]. The alcoholic content of the wine was used as a disinfectant [AB, Arn, Bai, Hlt, Lns, MGC, NTC, Su, TG, TH, TNTC, WBC]. He probably bandaged him with cloth torn from his head cloth or linen undergarment [BECNT]. The bandages would stop further bleeding [MGC].

1. The order was: he poured on wine to disinfect the wounds, then he poured on olive oil to sooth them, and finally he bandaged the wounds [NTC]. He cleansed the wound with the wine and then used oil as a kind of soothing salve [Lns].
2. The order was: he poured on olive oil to cleanse and soften the wounds, then he poured on wine to disinfect them, and finally he bandaged them [Bai].
3. The order was: he poured on a mixture of oil and wine, then he bandaged them [AB, BNTC, EGT]. Both Greek and Jews used a mixture of oil and wine as an ointment [BNTC].
4. The order was: during the process of bandaging, he poured on the oil and wine as needed [BECNT, ICC, NIGTC].

10:36 Who of-these three seems[a] to-you to–have-become[b] a-neighbor to-the (one) having-fallen[c] among the robbers?

TEXT—Following τίς 'who', some manuscripts add οὖν 'therefore'. GNT does not mention this variant. Οὖν 'therefore' is read by KJV.

LEXICON—a. pres. act. indic. of δοκεῖ (LN **31.30**) (BAGD 2.a. p. 202): 'to seem' [BAGD, **LN**]. The phrase 'seems to you' [AB, Arn, Lns, WBC] is also translated 'do you think' [BECNT, NTC; GW, HCSB, KJV, NASB, NCV, NET, NIV, NRSV, REB], 'would you say' [NLT], 'in your opinion' [TEV], not explicit [CEV].

b. perf. act. infin. of γίνομαι (LN 13.3): 'to have become' [Arn, Lns, WBC], 'became' [BECNT; NET], 'proved to be' [NTC; HCSB, NASB], 'to have been' [AB], 'was' [LN; CEV, GW, KJV, NCV, NIV, NLT, NRSV, REB], 'acted like' [TEV]. He became a neighbor by what he did [My, WBC]. It asks which became a neighbor by performing a neighborly action [EGT]. He became an example of a neighbor [BECNT].

c. aorist act. participle of ἐμπίπτω (LN **90.71**) (BAGD 2. p. 256): 'to fall' [BAGD], 'to be beset by' [**LN**]. The phrase τοῦ ἐμπεσόντος εἰς τοὺς λῃστάς 'the one having fallen among the robbers' is translated 'the one who fell among the robbers' [Arn, BECNT, Lns, WBC], 'him that fell among the thieves' [KJV], 'the man who fell into the hands of the robbers' [AB, NTC; HCSB, NET, NIV, NRSV, REB], 'the man who fell into the robbers' hands' [NASB], 'the man who was beaten up by robbers' [CEV], 'the man who was attacked by the robbers/bandits' [GW, NCV, NLT, TEV]. This phrase ἐμπεσόντος εἰς 'having fallen among' is equivalent to the phrase περιέπεσεν 'he fell among' with the dative in 10:30 [TH].

QUESTION—How does Jesus' question correspond with the lawyer's original question 'Who is my neighbor?' in 10:29?

The lawyer's question is turned around so that instead of seeking the answer for who his neighbor is, he is to consider who acted as a neighbor [Alf, Arn, Gdt, Hlt, ICC, Lns, MGC, NAC, NIC, NICNT, NIGTC, NTC, TNTC]. The real question is 'To whom must you become a neighbor?' [Bai]. There are no restrictions to be made for determining the scope of neighbor [WBC]. The lawyer's first question is indirectly answered 'Your neighbor is anyone in need with whom you are thrown into contact' [Hlt, NIC, Pnt]. The parable has addressed the meaning of love rather than the meaning of neighbor [NIGTC].

10:37 And he-said, The (one) having-shown mercy[d] on him. And Jesus said to-him, Go and you do likewise.

TEXT—Instead of εἶπεν δέ 'and he said', some manuscripts read εἶπεν οὖν 'then he said'. GNT does not mention this variant. Εἶπεν οὖν 'then he said' is read by KJV.

    d. ἔλεος (LN 88.76) (BAGD 1. p. 250): 'mercy' [Arn, BAGD, BECNT, LN, Lns, WBC; HCSB, KJV, NASB, NCV, NET, NIV, NLT, NRSV], 'pity' [NTC; CEV], 'kindness' [AB; REB]. This noun is also translated as an adjective: '(was) kind' [TEV]. '(was) kind enough to help' [GW].

QUESTION—What is the significance of the form of the lawyer's answer?

The lawyer may have wanted to avoid using the despised name 'Samaritan', so he used the description 'the one having shown mercy on him' [Alf, BECNT, Crd, Hlt, ICC, MGC, NAC, NIC, NIGTC, Rb]. The lawyer had seen the point of the question, but could not bring himself to say 'The Samaritan' [BECNT]. However, by using a description, the answer serves to give more credit to the Samaritan than had he just named him [Lns]. Describing what kind of a person had come to the man's aid is even a better answer than simply saying 'the Samaritan' [NTC, WBC]. The answer indicates both who was a neighbor and why he is to be considered a neighbor [EGT].

DISCOURSE UNIT: 10:38–42 [AB, BECNT, NAC, NICNT, NIGTC, Su, TNTC, WBC; CEV, HCSB, NASB, NCV, NET, NIV, NLT, NRSV, TEV]. The topic is Martha and Mary [AB, BECNT, NAC, TNTC; CEV, HCSB, NASB, NCV], Jesus and Martha [NET], Jesus visits Martha and Mary [NLT, NRSV, TEV], at the home of Martha and Mary [NIV], visiting the home of Martha and

Mary [Su], how to welcome Jesus [NICNT], serving Jesus [NIGTC], the one necessary thing [WBC], Mary listens to Jesus [GW]

10:38 **And while they traveled he entered into a-certain village. And a-certain woman by-name Martha welcomed^a him.**

TEXT—Some manuscripts begin the verse with ἐγένετο 'it happened'. GNT does not mention this variant. Ἐγένετο 'it happened' is read by KJV.

TEXT—Following αὐτόν 'him', some manuscripts add εἰς τὴν οἰκίαν 'into the house' and some manuscripts add εἰς τὴν οἰκίαν αὐτῆς 'into her house'. GNT rejects both of these additions with a B decision, indicating that the text is almost certain. Some versions would not distinguish between these two additions. Εἰς τὴν οἰκίαν αὐτῆς 'into her house' is read by KJV (since 'her' is not italicized in the KJV). Either εἰς τὴν οἰκίαν 'into the house' or εἰς τὴν οἰκίαν αὐτῆς 'into her house' is read by AB, Arn, ICC, Lns, NTC, WBC; CEV, GW, HCSB, NASB, NCV, NIV, NLT, NRSV, and TEV.

LEXICON—a. aorist mid. (deponent = act.) indic. of ὑποδέχομαι (LN **34.53**) (BAGD p. 844): 'to welcome' [AB, BAGD, **LN**, NTC, WBC; CEV, GW, HCSB, NASB, NLT, NRSV, TEV], 'to welcome as a guest' [NET], 'to make welcome' [REB], 'to receive' [Arn, BAGD, BECNT, LN; KJV], 'to have as a guest' [LN], 'to entertain as a guest' [BAGD], 'to invite (into her home)' [Lns], 'to open her home (to him)' [NIV], 'to let (Jesus) stay' [NCV].

QUESTION—Who are included in the group that went as they traveled?

'They' refers to Jesus and his twelve disciples [NTC]. It refers to Jesus, the twelve disciples, and more of his disciples [Su, TH].

QUESTION—Who entered the village where Martha welcomed Jesus?

1. Only Jesus entered the village and was welcomed by Martha while his disciples went on to Jerusalem [Lns, My, Su]. The phrase αὐτὸς εἰσῆλθεν 'he entered' emphasizes 'he' and makes a contrast with the previous πορεύεσθα αὐτούς 'they went' [Lns, Su].
2. The disciples entered the village with Jesus [BECNT, EGT, NICNT, NTC, TG, TH; NLT]. The singular 'he' and 'him' does not mean that the disciples were not there also. The singular is used because Jesus was the leader of the group [NTC].

10:39 **And to-this (one) was a-sister called Mary, who also^a having-sat-down at the feet of-the Lord was-listening to his word.^b**

TEXT—Instead of τοῦ κυρίου 'of the Lord', some manuscripts read τοῦ Ἰησοῦ 'of Jesus'. GNT does not mention this variant. Τοῦ Ἰησοῦ 'of Jesus' is read by KJV.

LEXICON—a. καί (LN 89.93): 'also' [LN, Lns; HCSB, KJV], not explicit [AB, Arn, BECNT, NTC, WBC; all versions except KJV].

b. λόγος (LN 33.98) (BAGD 1.a.b. p. 477): 'word' [LN, Lns, WBC; KJV, NASB], 'words' [REB], 'message' [BAGD, LN], 'instruction' [BAGD], 'teaching' [BAGD, BECNT; TEV], 'discourse' [Arn], 'what he taught' [NLT], 'what he said' [CEV, NET, NIV], 'what he was saying' [AB;

NRSV]. This noun is also translated as a verb: 'to talk' [GW], 'to teach' [NCV].

QUESTION—What is meant by καί 'also' in the phrase 'who also having sat down at the feet of the Lord'?

The meaning of καί is not clear [ICC]. What Mary did was in addition to what Martha did [WBC]. Besides whatever Mary had done in welcoming Jesus at the time of his arrival, she also sat his feet [Arn, Lns, My]. Perhaps she had begun serving as did Martha and after finishing her task, she sat at Jesus' feet [Gdt]. Perhaps it merely emphasizes the relative pronoun 'who' [NIC]. After the relative pronoun, it focuses attention on what follows [TH].

QUESTION—What was Jesus' word that Mary listened to?

Perhaps this singular form, λόγον 'word', means that Mary listened as Jesus spoke about his work or the journey that had just ended [Su]. Sitting at Jesus' feet may merely describe where she was located as Jesus reclined at the table and Mary was listening to what he said [Gdt, TH]. Or, while the meal was being prepared, Jesus would have been sitting cross-legged on a couch while Mary sat on a rug on the floor before him as she listened [Lns]. Sitting at Jesus' feet probably indicates that she was like a pupil or disciple listening to what Jesus was teaching [AB, Alf, Crd, ICC, Lns, MGC, My, NICNT, NIGTC, Su, TG, WBC]. Some translations specify his word to be what he was teaching [BECNT; NCV, NLT, TEV]. Jesus' message was about the kingdom of God [WBC].

10:40 But Martha was-worried/overburdened[a] about much serving.[b] And having-approached[c] she-said, Lord, is-it-of- no -concern[d] to-you that my sister left me alone to-serve?[e] Then speak to-her that she-may-help me.

LEXICON—a. imperf. act. indic. of περισπάομαι, περισπάω (LN **25.238**) (BAGD 2. p. 650): 'to be worried' [Lns; CEV], 'to worry' [NLT], 'to be upset' [GW, TEV], 'to be preoccupied' [AB], 'to be distracted' [BAGD, BECNT, NTC, WBC; HCSB, NASB, NET, NIV, NRSV, REB], 'to be distracted and anxious' [LN], 'to be in a state of distraction' [Arn], 'to be overburdened' [BAGD], 'to be overburdened and worried' [**LN**], 'to be busy' [NCV], 'to be cumbered' [KJV].

b. διακονία (LN **46.13**) (BAGD 2. p. 184): 'serving' [**LN**, Lns], 'service' [BAGD, BECNT], 'preparations' [BAGD; NASB, NET, NIV], 'work' [GW, NCV, TEV], 'domestic work' [WBC], 'tasks' [HCSB, NRSV, REB], 'all that had to be done' [NTC; CEV], 'the details of serving' [AB], 'the big dinner she was preparing' [NLT]. This noun is also translated as a verb phrase: 'to try to render many services' [Arn]. This pertains to serving food and drink to those who are eating [LN]. It relates to the service connected with preparing a meal [BAGD].

c. aorist act. participle of ἐφίσταμαι (LN15.75) (BAGD 1.a. p. 330): 'to approach' [BAGD, LN], 'to draw near, to come near' [LN], 'to go in' [NCV], 'to go to' [BECNT; CEV], 'to come up to' [WBC; HCSB, NASB,

NET], 'to come to' [AB, NTC; KJV, NIV, NLT, NRSV, REB, TEV], 'to step up' [Arn, Lns], not explicit [GW].
   d. pres. act. indic. of μέλει (LN 25.223) (BAGD 3. p. 500): 'to be of concern' [LN], 'to be a concern' [BAGD]. The phrase 'is it of no concern to you' is translated 'are you not concerned' [AB], 'doesn't it bother you' [CEV], 'don't you care' [Arn, BECNT, Lns, NTC, WBC; all versions except CEV, NLT], 'doesn't it seem unfair to you' [NLT].
   e. pres. act. infin. of διακονέω (LN 35.19) (BAGD 1. p. 184): 'to serve' [Arn, BECNT, LN, Lns; HCSB], 'to wait on someone at table' [BAGD], 'to do the work' [NTC; CEV, GW, NCV, NET, NIV, NLT, NRSV, TEV], 'to do the domestic work' [WBC], 'to do the serving' [AB; NASB], 'to get on with the work' [REB].

QUESTION—What was the matter with Martha?

She was worried and distracted [EGT, Lns, NTC, Su, TH, TNTC]. She was drawn away in different directions by her elaborate plans for the meal [AB]. The appearance of a number of guests must have been unexpected. She was concerned about the many things that needed to be done for the guests. Probably she wanted to do something special for Jesus and was involved in elaborate preparations [Lns, TNTC]. Martha was trying to listen to Jesus but couldn't because of her work [Arn, BECNT, MGC, NAC, NIGTC]. She was feeling very busy [TH]. She was overburdened [NIGTC]. There was too much to do in preparing the meal [CEV].

QUESTION—What is implied when Martha asked Jesus 'is it of no concern to you'?

This implies reproach [BECNT, EGT, Gdt, ICC, NTC, Rb, TG, TNTC]. She thought that Jesus was monopolizing Mary at Martha's expense [Rb]. Martha was angry and exasperated and was finding fault with Jesus for allowing Mary to just sit there [NTC]. She was exasperated with both Mary and Jesus [NTC]. She couldn't understand how Jesus could condone Mary's failure to help in a crisis situation [Su]. Another view is that she was not finding fault with Jesus, but assumed that Jesus must have thought as she did [Lns]. A 'yes' answer is expected by the use of οὐ 'no' [BECNT, TH], so Martha expected that Jesus would say that he was concerned and would do something about it [BECNT].

QUESTION—What relationship is indicated by οὖν 'then' in the last sentence?

It indicates the consequence to the implied condition '*If you really care,* then speak to her...' [MGC, TH]. It indicates the conclusion of an implied grounds '*Because leaving me thus to serve alone is evidently wrong,* tell her...' [Lns].

10:41 And answering the Lord said to-her, Martha, Martha, you-are-worried[a] and troubled[b] about many (things), **10:42** but one is necessary.[c] Because[d] Mary chose the good portion[e] which will- not -be-taken-away from-her.

TEXT—Instead of ὁ κύριος 'the Lord', some manuscripts read ὁ Ἰησοῦς 'Jesus'. GNT does not mention this variant. Ὁ Ἰησοῦς 'Jesus' is read by KJV.

TEXT— In 10:41-42, instead of μεριμνᾷς καὶ θορυβάζῃ περὶ πολλά, ἑνὸς δέ ἐστιν χρεία 'you are anxious and troubled about many things, but one thing is necessary', some manuscripts read μεριμνᾷς καὶ τυρβάζῃ περὶ πολλά, ἑνὸς δέ ἐστιν χρεία 'you are anxious and troubled about many things, but one thing is necessary', some manuscripts read μεριμνᾷς καὶ θορυβάζῃ περὶ πολλά, ὀλίγων δέ ἐστιν χρεία ἢ ἑνός 'you are anxious and troubled about many things, but few things are necessary', one important Greek and Latin manuscript reads only θορυβάζῃ 'you are troubled', and some manuscripts omit this entire phrase. GNT reads μεριμνᾷς καὶ θορυβάζῃ περὶ πολλά, ἑνὸς δέ ἐστιν χρεία 'you are anxious and troubled about many things, but one thing is necessary' with a C decision, indicating that the Committee had difficulty making the decision. The versions would probably not distinguish between the first two variant readings in their translations.

LEXICON—a. pres. act. indic. of μεριμνάω (LN 25.225) (BAGD 1. p. 505): 'to be worried' [LN, NTC, WBC; CEV, HCSB, NASB, NCV, NET, NIV, NRSV, TEV], 'to worry' [Arn; GW], 'to be anxious' [BAGD, BECNT, LN], 'to fret' [AB; REB], 'to be unduly concerned' [BAGD], 'to be distracted' [Lns], 'to be careful' [KJV]. The phrase 'are worried and troubled' is translated 'are so upset over all these details' [NLT]. See this word at 12:11, 22, 25, 26.

b. pres. pass. indic. of θορυβάζομαι (LN **25.234**) (BAGD p. 362): 'to be troubled' [BAGD, BECNT, **LN**, Lns, WBC; KJV, NET, TEV], 'to be distressed' [LN], 'to be distracted' [NRSV], 'to be upset' [LN, NTC; CEV, HCSB, NCV, NIV], 'to be agitated' [Arn], 'to be bothered' [NASB], 'to fuss' [GW, REB], 'to be disturbed' [AB].

c. χρεία (LN 57.40) (BAGD 1. p. 231): 'necessary' [NTC, WBC; CEV, HCSB, NASB, REB], 'needed' [Arn, BAGD, LN; NET, NIV, TEV], 'needful' [BECNT, Lns; KJV], 'important' [NCV], not explicit [NLT]. The phrase ἐστιν χρεία 'is necessary' is translated 'you need' [GW], 'there is need of' [AB; NRSV]. This refers to Martha's personal need [NIGTC].

d. γάρ (LN 89.23): 'because' [LN], 'for' [AB, Lns, WBC; NASB], not explicit [Arn, BECNT, NTC; all versions except NASB].

e. μερίς (LN 63.13) (BAGD 2. p. 505): 'portion' [BAGD, LN]. The phrase τὴν ἀγαθὴν μερίδα 'the good portion' [BECNT, WBC] is also translated 'that good portion' [NTC], 'the good part' [Lns; NASB], 'that good part' [KJV], 'the good role' [Arn], 'what is best' [CEV, REB], 'what is better'

[NIV], 'the best part' [AB; NET], 'the better part' [NRSV], 'the better thing' [NCV], 'the right thing' [TEV], 'the right choice' [GW, HCSB], 'one thing worth being concerned about' [NLT].

QUESTION—What is the implication of the repetition, 'Martha, Martha'?

It expresses Jesus' affection and concern [ICC, NIC], his love [NTC]. It indicates a gentle and tender reproof [AB, Alf, Gdt, Lns, MGC, NTC, Su, WBC]. Jesus appreciated Martha's desire to be a good hostess but he felt it caused her to miss what was important [NTC, Su]. It indicates that Jesus had something important to tell her [Arn].

QUESTION—What is the difference between μεριμνάω 'to be worried' and θορυβάζομαι 'to be troubled'?

'Worried' refers to mental anxiety, while 'troubled' refers to outward agitation [Alf, ICC, NIC, Rb]. The two verbs reinforce each other [LN (25.234)].

QUESTION—What relationship is indicated by γάρ 'because'?

The conjunction indicates an illustration [TH] or explanation [ICC] of what the one necessary thing is.

QUESTION—What is the one thing that is necessary?

The one thing that Martha lacked was the 'good thing' that Mary had chosen [Lns, NICNT, NIGTC]. The good part was the Word of God [BECNT, Lns]. It is spiritual nourishment from the word [Gdt]. The good portion is expressed by Mary learning at the feet of Jesus in an attitude of dependence on him [TNTC]. It refers to listening to Jesus [Arn, Lns, MGC, NAC, NICNT, NTC, Su, TH, TNTC] and in a general sense to have faith in him [TH]. This implies that Mary should not be deprived of this good thing by helping Martha [MGC, NIGTC], and that Martha should curtail her preparations for the meal so as to be able to do the one thing that matters [NIGTC]. Martha's company meant more to Jesus than her cooking [WBC]. It could refer to what Mary was doing, but it could refer to just one dish or a simple meal instead of the feast Martha was preparing [TG].

QUESTION—In what sense will the good portion not be taken away from Mary?

Jesus will not tell Mary to leave her place at his feet to go and help Martha prepare the meal [MGC, NAC, NIGTC, WBC], although it may also include her heavenly reward in the future or that she will be remembered in history for this [NAC]. Mary's devotion will last forever [NTC]. Her spiritual attitude would never be lost [TNTC]. In future days, Martha would remember her distraction and the meal she prepared, but Mary would cherish the time she sat at Jesus' feet and heard his words [Su]. Mary's portion that she received by God's grace will not be taken away from her at the day of judgment [TH].

DISCOURSE UNIT: 11:1–13 [BECNT, NAC, NICNT, Su, TNTC, WBC; CEV, NASB, NET, NIV, NLT, TEV]. The topic is prayer [CEV], instructions on prayer [NET], Jesus' teaching about prayer [NAC, Su, TNTC; NASB, NIV,

NLT, TEV], a call to prayer [BECNT], a confident prayer to the Father [WBC], the fatherhood of God [NICNT].

DISCOURSE UNIT: 11:1–4 [AB, NIGTC, TNTC, WBC; GW, HCSB, NCV, NRSV]. The topic is the Lord's prayer [NIGTC, TNTC; GW, NRSV], the model prayer [HCSB], praying like Jesus [WBC], Jesus teaches about prayer [NCV], the Our Father [AB].

11:1 **And it-happened while he was in a-certain place praying, as he-finished, a-certain (one) of-his disciples said to him, Lord, teach us to-pray, just-as also John taught his disciples.**
QUESTION—What did the disciple ask Jesus to do in regard to prayer?
  The disciple may have wanted to learn the words to use in prayer, or a pattern on which to model his prayers, or some general instruction on the subject of prayer [TNTC]. The disciple wanted Jesus to teach the disciples the words to say when they prayed [Arn, TG, TH]. He wanted a model prayer [NIC]. From Jesus' answer, it appeared that he wanted both the form for prayer and general instructions about the way to pray [Lns].

11:2 **And he-said to-them, When you(plural)-pray say, Father, let-be-held-in-reverence^a your name. Let come^b your kingdom.**
TEXT—Instead of πάτερ 'Father', some manuscripts read πάτερ ἡμῶν ὁ ἐν τοῖς οὐρανοῖς 'our Father the one in the heavens'. GNT reads πάτερ 'Father' with an A decision, indicating that the text is certain. Πάτερ ἡμῶν ὁ ἐν τοῖς οὐρανοῖς 'our Father the one in the heavens' is read by KJV.
TEXT—Instead of ἐλθέτω ἡ βασιλεία σου 'may your kingdom come', some manuscripts read ἐλθέτω τὸ πνεῦμά σου τὸ ἅγιον ἐφ' ἡμᾶς καὶ καθαρισάτω ἡμᾶς 'may your Holy Spirit come upon us and cleanse us', some manuscripts read ἐφ' ἡμᾶς ἐλθέτω σου ἡ βασιλεία 'may your kingdom come upon us', and one Church Father source reads ἐλθάτω τὸ ἅγιον πνεῦμά σου, ἐλθάτω ἡ βασιλεία σου 'may your Holy Spirit come, may your kingdom come'. GNT reads ἐλθέτω ἡ βασιλεία σου 'may your kingdom come' with an A decision, indicating that the text is certain.
TEXT—Following ἡ βασιλεία σου 'your kingdom', some manuscripts add γενηθήτω τὸ θέλημά σου 'may your will come to pass', and some manuscripts add γενηθήτω τὸ θέλημά σου ὡς ἐν οὐρανῷ καὶ ἐπὶ τῆς γῆς 'may your will come to pass as in heaven also upon the earth', and one manuscript reads γενηθήτω τὸ θέλημά σου ὡς ἐν οὐρανῷ καὶ ἐπὶ τῆς γῆς ἀλλὰ ῥῦσαι ἡμᾶς ἀπὸ τοῦ πονηροῦ 'may your will come to pass as in heaven also upon the earth but deliver us from the evil one/from evil'. GNT rejects these additions with an A decision, indicating that the text is certain. Γενηθήτω τὸ θέλημά σου ὡς ἐν οὐρανῷ καὶ ἐπὶ τῆς γῆς 'may your will come to pass as in heaven also upon the earth' is read by KJV.
LEXICON—a. aorist pass. impera. of ἁγιάζω (LN 88.27) (BAGD 3. p. 9): 'to be held in reverence' [BAGD], 'to be honored as holy, to be regarded as holy, to be hallowed' [LN]. The clause 'let be held in reverence your

name' is translated 'let your name be kept holy' [GW], 'may your name be sanctified' [AB, WBC], 'let your name be sanctified' [BECNT], 'may your name always be kept holy' [NCV], 'hallowed be your name' [Arn, Lns, NTC; KJV, NASB, NIV, NRSV], 'may your name be hallowed' [REB], 'may your name be honored' [NET, NLT], 'may your holy name be honored' [TEV], 'your name be honored as holy' [HCSB], 'help us to honor your name' [CEV].

b. aorist act. impera. of ἔρχομαι (LN 15.81) (BAGD I.2.b. p. 311): 'to come' [AB, Arn, BAGD, BECNT, LN, Lns, NTC, WBC; all versions except CEV], 'to appear' [BAGD]. This verb is also translated with God as the subject: 'to come and set up (his kingdom)' [CEV].

QUESTION—What did Jesus mean by saying 'when you pray say…'?

Jesus intended the prayer to be said with these words [TNTC, WBC]. Since the form of the prayer here in Luke is slightly condensed from that in Matthew 6:9–13, it appears that Christ never intended that exactly the same words be always recited, rather this is a pattern or model for prayer [My, NTC]. It is not implied that the disciples were to regularly repeat this prayer word for word [Arn, EGT]. This is a model prayer for constant use [NIC, WBC]. It is a model for one's attitudes rather than a prayer to be prayed [Su]. The model was not to be prayed on every occasion of prayer, but Jesus gave it to characterize the kind of prayer that is given in a free and varied manner [Gdt].

QUESTION—What is meant by 'let your name be held in reverence'?

In Jewish usage, a person's name was thought to stand for the person himself [Su]. A person's name was the person as he has revealed himself [ICC, NTC, TH, TNTC]. People in general are the agents who are to hold God's name in reverence [TH]. He asks that people acknowledge and treat God's name to be holy [ICC]. He asks God to bring about a situation in which people will reverence and worship him [NIC, NIGTC, NTC, TG, WBC]. This request looks forward to the establishment of the kingdom at the final day when God will receive the honor due him [NAC]. God is to manifest his rule so that his glory is evident to all [BECNT].

QUESTION—In what way will God's kingdom come?

This is asking God to set up his rule [NIGTC], so that he will rule over all humanity [TG], and remove the wickedness of Satan's rule [ICC, NIGTC]. God's rule is realized at the present time as he rules in the hearts of people who subject themselves to his will, but in another sense it will not come until his will is fully obeyed throughout the world [NICNT, TG]. He asks that God's rule will be established more and more [Arn, NIC, NTC]. It expresses the submission of the individual praying [Su]. The coming of God's kingdom refers to the inauguration of the Messianic age [MGC, TH]. It refers to the full realization of God's promised rule [BECNT, NAC]. It looks forward to God's coming with judgment and salvation [WBC].

11:3 **Our daily^a bread give to-us each day.**

LEXICON—a. ἐπιούσιος (LN 67.183, 67.206) (BAGD p. 297): 'daily' [LN], 'necessary for existence, for today, for the following day, for the future, that belongs to it' [BAGD]. The phrase 'our daily bread' [BECNT, NTC; HCSB, KJV, NASB, NET, NIV, NRSV, REB] is also translated 'the daily bread we need' [Arn], 'our bread for the day' [WBC], 'the food we need' [CEV, NCV, TEV], 'our needful bread' [Lns], 'our bread for subsistence' [AB]. The whole sentence is translated 'give us our bread day by day' [GW], 'give us our food day by day' [NLT].

QUESTION—What is meant by ἄρτος 'bread'?

'Bread' is to be taken in the broader sense of 'food' and is not limited to just a loaf of bread [NAC, NICNT, NIGTC, TG, TH; CEV, NCV, NLT, TEV]. It stands for everything that is necessary to sustain one's physical life [NTC]. It stands for everything that a person needs for earthly existence [NIC]. It refers to the bare necessities of life and not to luxuries [NAC].

QUESTION—What is meant by ἐπιούσιος 'daily'?

1. It means bread that is needed daily, that is, for this day [Alf, BECNT, EGT, NAC, NIC, NTC, Su, TH, TNTC, WBC]. It is a request for daily provision of food [BECNT].
2. It means bread that is needed for the coming day [BNTC, Crd, ICC, My, NICNT]. One day in advance of today is meant [ICC].
3. It means bread that is needed for existence [AB, Lns; CEV]. It is bread for subsistence, that which is essential for existence [AB].
4. It means bread belonging to the age to come [MGC, NIGTC]. It refers to both the physical and spiritual food which belongs to the God's kingdom in the age to come, but which believers can enjoy in the present time [MGC]. God provides for body and soul as a foretaste of his provision in the coming kingdom of God [NIGTC].

11:4 **And forgive us our sins, because indeed we-are-forgiving everyone being-indebted-to^a us. And may-you- not -lead^b us into temptation/testing.^c**

TEXT—Following πειρασμόν 'temptation', some manuscripts add ἀλλὰ ῥῦσαι ἡμᾶς ἀπὸ τοῦ πονηροῦ 'but deliver us from the evil one/from evil'. GNT rejects this addition with an A decision, indicating that the text is certain. Ἀλλὰ ῥῦσαι ἡμᾶς ἀπὸ τοῦ πονηροῦ 'but deliver us from the evil one/from evil' is read by KJV.

LEXICON—a. pres. act. participle of ὀφείλω (LN **88.298**) (BAGD 2.b.β. p. 599): 'to be indebted to' [BAGD, BECNT, NTC, WBC; KJV, NASB, NRSV], 'to be in debt to' [HCSB], 'to owe' [Lns], 'to commit sin against' [BAGD], 'to sin against' [**LN**; NET, NIV, NLT], 'to wrong' [Arn], 'to do wrong to' [AB; CEV, NCV, REB, TEV], not explicit [GW]. The Aramaic word behind both 'sins' and 'debt' is the one word *hobha* [BNTC, NIGTC, TH]. Sin is regarded as a debt [TNTC].

b. aorist act. subj. of εἰσφέρω (LN 90.93) (BAGD 90.93 p. 233): 'to lead into' [BAGD, BECNT, LN, NTC, WBC; KJV, NASB, NET, NIV], 'to take into' [Arn], 'to bring into' [AB, BAGD, LN, Lns; HCSB], 'to bring to' [NRSV, TEV], 'to cause' [LN]. The clause 'do not lead us into temptation' is translated 'do not cause us to be tempted' [NCV], 'keep us from being tempted' [CEV], 'don't allow us to be tempted' [GW], 'don't let us yield to temptation' [NLT], 'do not put us to the test' [REB].

c. πειρασμός (LN 27.46, 88.308) (BAGD 2.b. p. 640): 'temptation' [AB, Arn, BAGD, BECNT, LN (88.308), Lns, NTC; HCSB, KJV, NASB, NET, NIV, NLT], 'testing' [LN (27.46)], 'hard testing' [TEV], 'the test' [REB], 'what is a trial' [WBC], 'the time of trial' [NRSV]. This noun is also translated as a verb: 'to be tempted' [CEV, GW, NCV].

QUESTION—What are the sins God is asked to forgive?

Probably these sins are offenses against other people [Su]. The forgiveness is an ongoing need of daily forgiveness for daily sins [NIVS, WBC]. Another view is that the aorist tense of ἄφες 'forgive' probably refers to forgiveness at the final judgment [TH].

QUESTION—What relationship is indicated by γάρ 'because'?

It states the reason we can *ask* God to forgive our sins [NIC, NIGTC]. Since even sinful persons like us forgive others, we can confidently approach our merciful God to forgive us [Arn, NIC, TNTC]. Forgiving others is a prerequisite or condition for asking God to forgive us [NIC, NIGTC, Su]. What we ask of God, we should be ready to do as well [BECNT, NAC]. There is no thought of our good works being the ground for being forgiven [Arn, Lns, MGC, NAC, NIC, NICNT, NIGTC, NTC, TNTC], since the grace of God is the reason that he forgives us [Arn, Lns, NIC, TNTC] and forgiveness is based on the application of Christ's merits [NTC].

QUESTION—What is meant by God leading us into temptation or testing?

1. The meaning is 'lead us not into temptation' [Arn, BAGD, BECNT, BNTC, ICC, Lns, NAC, NIC, NIGTC, NTC, Su, TG, TNTC; CEV, GW, KJV, NASB, NCV, NET, NIV, NLT]. It implies that God governs everything that happens in our lives and may or may not allow the devil to tempt us to sin [TG]. We are to ask God to guide our lives away from circumstances that expose us to temptations [Arn, NIC, NTC, Su]. It does not mean 'do not cause us to succumb to temptation' but 'cause us not to succumb to temptation' [NIGTC; NLT], 'do not permit us to enter into temptation' [NAC]. God does not want us to fall into sin and he can prevent sin from overwhelming us when we ask for his aid [BECNT]. It is a request that God will not permit such weak disciples as we are to enter into situations where we would be exposed to temptation that would bring about a possible fall [NTC, TNTC]. Because of our weaknesses, we want to be preserved from internal solicitations to sin from the devil [ICC].

2. The meaning is 'lead us not into testing' [AB, NICNT, TH, WBC; NRSV, REB, TEV]. Some take the testing to be the difficulties of persecutions and tribulations in the last times [AB, TH] and the sin would be apostasy [AB]. The trial is not a test that shows the true state of affairs, but it is the pressures on our loyalty that we might not be able to withstand [WBC].

DISCOURSE UNIT: 11:5–13 [GW, HCSB, NCV, NRSV]. The topic is the power of prayer [GW], perseverance in prayer [NRSV], continue to ask [NCV], keep asking, searching, knocking [HCSB].

DISCOURSE UNIT: 11:5–8 [AB, NIGTC, TNTC, WBC]. The topic is the friend at midnight [NIGTC, TNTC], help from a friend [WBC], the parable of the persistent friend [AB].

11:5 And he-said to them, Who among you will-have a-friend and will-go to him at-midnight and say to-him, Friend, lend me three loaves-of-bread,^a **11:6** because a-friend of-mine has-come to me from a-journey and I-do-not -have what I-will-set-before him. **11:7** And-that (one) answering from-within says, (Do) not cause me troubles.^b The door already has-been-shut and my children are with me in the bed. I-am- not -able having-arisen to-give you (anything).

LEXICON—a. ἄρτος (LN 5.8) (BAGD 1.a. p. 110): 'loaf of bread' [AB, BAGD, LN, Lns; CEV, GW, HCSB, NCV, NET, NIV, NLT, NRSV, TEV], 'loaf' [Arn, BECNT, WBC; KJV, NASB, REB], 'bread-cake' [NTC]. Some take the loaves to be small, something like rolls or buns [AB, LN], or flat cakes [Lns], and one man could eat three of them [AB, Lns, NIGTC, Su, TNTC]. The bread could have been thin, flat loaves of bread nearly two feet across or it could have been round and raised, but it was larger than buns and just one would be enough for a man [Bai]. One loaf would be for the guest, one for the host who would eat with him, and one would be their reserve [Gdt].

b. κόπος (LN 22.7) (BAGD 1. p. 443): 'trouble' [BAGD, LN], 'difficulty' [BAGD]. The phrase 'do not cause me troubles' is translated 'do not cause me trouble' [Arn], 'stop furnishing me troubles' [Lns], 'do not bother me' [AB, BECNT, NTC, WBC; all versions except KJV], 'trouble me not' [KJV].

QUESTION—Where is the end of this question?

'Who among you' is the beginning of a rhetorical question with the implied answer, 'nobody' [Bai, NICNT, TH]. The illustration begins as a question, but 11:5–7 in the Greek text is one long sentence in which the question is never ended nor is an answer given [EGT, NTC, TH]. The question is lost in the prolongation of the sentence [BNTC, ICC]. Some put a question mark at the end of 11:6 [My; KJV]. Others regard 11:6–7 to be a unit and place a question mark at the end of 11:7 [Alf, Bai, BECNT, Blm, Hlt, Lns, NIGTC, WBC]. Some avoid using a question and begin the story with 'suppose' [AB, NTC; all versions except KJV].

QUESTION—Where does the phrase 'my children are with me in the bed' locate the children?

1. The children were in the same bed or sleeping area as their father [AB, BECNT, Hlt, MGC, NICNT, NIGTC, Su, TG, WBC; probably NET, NIV, NRSV]. 'My children are with me in bed' [BECNT, WBC; NIV, NRSV]. Evidently this was a one-room house and the whole family would

be sleeping together on a mat [AB, Hlt, MGC, NICNT, NIGTC, TG], or on a raised platform at one end of the house [TNTC]. The father could not get up to answer the door or get bread without disturbing the whole family [AB, MGC, Su, TNTC, WBC].
2. The children were in their own bed apart from their father's bed [Arn, Lns, NAC, NTC; possibly CEV, GW, HCSB, NASB, NCV, NET, NLT, REB, TEV]. All were not sleeping in the same bed since μετ' ἐμοῦ 'with me' means 'in company with me', the father also being in bed [Lns]. The children were in bed as he too was in bed [Arn]. Often all of the individual beds were in one room, so the singular 'bed' may be used as a collective singular instead of meaning they were all in a common bed [NET]. The children were lying on their own mats on the floor [NAC, NTC]. 'My children and I are in bed' [CEV, NASB, NCV, TEV]. 'my children are in bed' [GW], 'we are all in bed' [NLT], 'my children and I have gone to bed' [HCSB, REB].

QUESTION—What did the man mean when he said 'I am not able to give you anything'?

It was not a matter of inability but of unwillingness. He was not willing to do this [Rb]. He meant 'I won't give you anything' [NIGTC]. It is the effort that he objects to, not lending the bread [ICC]. It would be inconvenient [Su]. This was a selfish and unfriendly excuse [Lns].

11:8 **I-say to-you, even if (he will) not arise (and) give to-him because he-is his friend, yet because-of his shamelessness/persistence[a] he will arise and give to-him as-much-as he-needs.**

LEXICON—a. ἀναίδεια (LN **66.12**) (BAGD p. 54): 'shamelessness' [LN, Lns], 'insolence' [BAGD, **LN**], 'impudence' [BAGD, LN], 'boldness' [NCV, NIV], 'bold shamelessness' [BECNT], 'audacity' [LN], 'shameless importunity' [Arn], 'persistence' [AB, BAGD, NTC; HCSB, NASB, NRSV, REB], 'sheer persistence' [NET], 'importunity' [KJV]. The clause 'yet because of his shamelessness/persistence' is translated 'because you are not ashamed to keep on asking' [TEV], 'simply because you are not ashamed to keep on asking' [CEV], 'and because you were so bold' [GW], 'because of the prospect of him being shamed' [WBC], 'so his reputation won't be damaged' [NLT].

QUESTION—Who is the man that is described as being shameless or persistent?
1. This describes the man standing outside the door [AB, Alf, Arn, BECNT, BNTC, EGT, Gdt, Hlt, ICC, Lns, MGC, My, NAC, NIC, NTC, Pnt, Rb, Su, TG, TH, TNTC; all versions except NLT].
   1.1 It refers to his shamelessness in coming to the house at midnight in order to waken his neighbor and make his request [BECNT, Hlt, Lns, MGC, My, NIC, NTC]. This story is not given to illustrate persistence in prayer, rather it about showing no shame in bothering a friend [BECNT, Lns]. That he came at an inconvenient time shows his

shamelessness [NIC]. That he repeats the request that was first refused shows his shamelessness [NTC]. It is understood that God's response is in contrast with the neighbor's reluctant response, but the point of the parable is the comparison between the man in need and the disciples who are to approach God boldly with their requests [BECNT].
- 1.2 It refers to his persistence in requesting bread in spite of the first refusal [AB, Alf, Arn, BNTC, EGT, Gdt, ICC, Lns, NAC, NTC, Pnt, TG, TH, TNTC; CEV, HCSB, NASB, NET, NRSV, TEV]. It is assumed that the man at the door kept on knocking at the door and asking for bread [EGT, Gdt, NTC, TH]. The teaching of the parable is about persistence [ICC; NET], about shameless insistence, bold persistence [TG].
- 2 This describes the man in the house who shamelessly refused to comply with the requests of the man standing outside [Bai, NICNT, NIGTC, WBC; NLT]. This story does not illustrate the human attitude that gains a hearing from God, rather it illustrates the contrast between God's character and the attitude of the man inside the house [NIGTC]. No friend would behave like this [WBC]. If the man outside has to go to another house, the story of the refusal would spread all over the village to his shame [Bai]. The threat of dishonor causes him to grant his assistance [NICNT, WBC; NLT].

DISCOURSE UNIT: 11:9–13 [AB, NIGTC, TNTC]. The topic is encouragement to pray [NIGTC], asking as a son of the Father [WBC], the efficacy of prayer [AB], asking and giving [TNTC].

11:9 **And-I tell you, ask and it-will-be-given to-you, seek**[a] **and you-will-find, knock and it-will-be-opened to-you.** **11:10** **Because everyone asking receives and the (one) seeking finds and to-the (one) knocking it-will-be-opened.**

TEXT—In 11:10, instead of the future middle ἀνοιγήσεται 'it will open itself' (evidently translated by many as a passive 'it will be opened'), some manuscripts read the future passive ἀνοιχθήσεται 'it will be opened', and some manuscripts read the present passive ἀνοίγεται 'it is opened'. GNT follows the reading ἀνοι[γή]σεται, indicating doubt between the future middle ἀνοιγήσεται 'it will open itself' (probably read as a passive 'it will be opened') and the present passive ἀνοίγεται 'it is opened'.

LEXICON—a. pres. act. impera. of ζητέω (LN 57.59) (BAGD 1.a.β. p. 338): 'to seek' [Arn, BAGD, BECNT, LN, Lns, NTC, WBC; KJV, NASB, NET, NIV, REB, TEV], 'to search' [AB; CEV, GW, HCSB, NCV, NRSV], 'to look' [NLT], 'to try to obtain, to attempt to get' [LN].

QUESTION—How is this connected with the preceding illustration?
- 1. This is the application of the preceding illustration [Arn, BECNT, Gdt, NIBC, NICNT, TH]. The connection is translated 'so I tell you' [CEV, GW, NET], 'and so I tell you' [NLT], 'so I say to you' [NTC; NASB, NIV, NRSV, REB], 'so to you I say' [WBC], 'and so I say to you' [TEV]. It is the moral of the story [EGT], it gives the inferences to be drawn from

the story [TH]. If one's friend would finally help, whatever his motive might be, then our heavenly Father who has the purest motives will surely help us when we ask [NTC, Pnt].
2. This adds to the point of the preceding illustration [AB, ICC, Lns]. The connection is translated 'besides, I myself to you declare' [Lns], 'and I say to you' [AB]. The illustration teaches that if a man so succeeds with such a friend, then we will surely succeed with our heavenly Father, thus encouraging us to pray and now besides that illustration, the Lord adds this strong declaration about prayer [Lns]. The parable has a lesson for them and now Jesus adds to that teaching [ICC].

QUESTION—What is the significance of the order of the verbs asking, seeking, and knocking?

This section uses a vocabulary in keeping with the preceding story [Alf, Arn, Gdt, ICC]: 'ask' alludes to the request of the friend in need, 'seek' alludes to finding the friend's house in the dark of night, 'knock' alludes to arriving at the door of the friend's house [Gdt]. On the other hand, Jesus used none of the three verbs in the illustration [Lns]. The three verbs refer to prayer [NIGTC]. It does not mean that sometimes they just need to ask, but at other times what is needed is seeking, and at other times nothing less than knocking is needed. Rather, asking should also be a seeking and at the same time those verbs may be described as knocking. The three terms are synonymous, yet each verb is more intense than the one it follows [Lns]. The order shows an increasing earnestness [ICC], an increasing energy to cope with different obstacles [Gdt]. The three pairs indicate persistence in prayer [AB, EGT, Hlt] and the unresponsive neighbor represents God as he might appear to be [EGT, Hlt]. To *'ask'* is used of prayer [BECNT, NAC, NIGTC, TH] and the one who gives is God [AB, BECNT, MGC, NAC, NIGTC, TG, TH; NCV]. One asks for what he does not possess but needs [TG, WBC]. To *seek* refers to seeking God's face [NAC]. The person with a need asks and seeks the answer [BECNT]. He seeks something from God [Lns, TG]. He seeks what brings righteousness and advances God's plan [BECNT]. Along with asking, this is actively endeavoring to obtain the fulfillment of what is needed [NIC, NTC], such as examining the Scriptures and trying to obey God's will [NTC]. While waiting for God to answer what is asked, the person must do all that is necessary on his part [NIC]. Again, it is by God's help they will find [AB, MGC]. The verb is commonly used of seeking after God and indicates here that God is waiting to be found [NIGTC]. To *knock* relates to prayer [NIGTC]. It means to come into God's presence, so that when asking and seeking the answer, the disciple brings his request directly to God [BECNT]. Right asking and seeking constitute knocking to enter the heavenly house of God where God will open the door by favorably receiving the petition [Lns]. This adds perseverance to asking and acting [NTC]. Diligence is required [MGC]. It represents urgent sincerity in asking and seeking [NIC].

QUESTION—What is the significance of the three verbs being in the present imperative?

The present imperative indicates that they are to continue to ask, seek, and knock [Bai, BECNT, ICC, Lns, MGC, NIC, NTC, TNTC, WBC; NLT]. It refers to actions that are habitual [Su], and persistent [TNTC]. Every time they have a need they are to pray [Lns]. Every appeal to God will have results [WBC]. They combine to indicate perseverance [ICC, MGC, NTC]. The imperative functions as a condition, not a command: 'if you ask, you will receive' [NAC].

QUESTION—How certain are the results of asking, seeking, and knocking?

It is implied that God is willing to respond to prayer [NIGTC]. Requests are sure to be answered [NIGTC, TNTC] and sometimes the answer is 'No' if God thinks that is best [TNTC]. No prayer is spoken in vain, but not every prayer will be answered in the way the person desires [Arn]. It is stated as an exaggeration, since not all prayers are answered; a believer must pray in accordance with God's will [NAC]. God always hears believing prayers, but a true disciple prays for nothing that is not according the will of God [Lns]. It is understood that requests for real needs are offered by believers who are in a right relationship with God [NIC].

11:11 **And what father among you (if) the son will-ask-for a-fish, and instead of-a-fish will-he-give him a-snake? 11:12 Or (if) he-will-ask-for an-egg, will-he-give him a-scorpion?**

TEXT—In 11:11, instead of ἰχθύν 'a fish', some manuscripts read ἄρτον μὴ λίθον ἐπιδώσει αὐτῷ; ἢ καὶ ἰχθύν 'bread, will he give him a stone (expecting the response 'No')? or even a fish', and some manuscripts read ἄρτον μὴ λίθον ἐπιδώσει αὐτῷ; ἢ ἰχθύν 'bread, will he give him a stone (expecting the response 'No')? or a fish'. GNT reads ἰχθύν 'a fish' with a B decision, indicating that the text is almost certain. Ἄρτον μὴ λίθον ἐπιδώσει αὐτῷ; ἢ καὶ ἰχθύν 'bread, will he give him a stone (expecting the response 'No')? or even a fish' is probably read by KJV, since this is the reading of Textus Receptus, although KJV does not translate καί 'even'.

TEXT—In 11:11, instead of καί 'and' after 'fish', some manuscripts read μή (expecting the response 'No' to the question). GNT reads καί 'and' with a C decision, indicating that the Committee had difficulty making the decision. Μή (expecting the response 'No' to the question) is read by KJV.

TEXT—In 11:12, before ἐπιδώσει 'will he give', some manuscripts add μή (expecting the response 'No' to the question). GNT rejects this addition with a C decision, indicating that the Committee had difficulty making the decision. The addition of μή is read by Hlt, Lns.

QUESTION—What are the answers to the questions in 11:11 and 11:12?

These two verses are rhetorical questions that expect a negative answer [AB, Arn, BECNT, MGC, NICNT, NTC, TG, TH, WBC], such as 'Not one of us would do this' [BECNT]. When asked for essential things, no father would supply dangerous things [AB, BECNT, NTC].

11:13 Therefore if you being evil[a] know-how[b] to-give good gifts to your children, how-much more the Father the (one) from[c] heaven will-give (the) Holy Spirit to-the-ones asking him.

TEXT—Instead of ὁ πατὴρ ὁ ἐξ οὐρανοῦ 'the Father the (one) from heaven', some manuscripts read ὁ πατὴρ ὑμῶν ὁ ἐξ οὐρανοῦ 'your Father the (one) from heaven', some manuscripts read ὁ πατὴρ ἐξ οὐρανοῦ 'the Father from heaven', some manuscripts read ὁ πατὴρ ὁ ἐν τοῖς οὐρανοῖς 'the Father the (one) in the heavens', and some manuscripts read ὁ πατὴρ ὑμῶν ὁ οὐράνιος 'your heavenly Father'. GNT reads ὁ πατὴρ ὁ ἐξ οὐρανοῦ 'the Father the (one) from heaven' with a C decision and places the second ὁ 'the' in brackets in the text, indicating that the Committee had difficulty making the decision. Various versions would probably not distinguish clearly between some of these readings. The reading ὁ πατὴρ ἐξ οὐρανοῦ 'the Father from heaven' is taken by Hlt and WBC which translate it 'how much more will the Father give (the) Holy Spirit from heaven'.

TEXT—Instead of πνεῦμα ἅγιον '(the) Holy Spirit' some manuscripts read πνεῦμα ἀγαθόν 'good spirit/Spirit', some manuscripts read ἀγαθὸν δόμα '(a) good gift', some manuscripts read δόματα ἀγαθά 'good gifts', and some manuscripts read ἀγαθά 'good things'. GNT reads πνεῦμα ἅγιον '(the) Holy Spirit' with a B decision, indicating that the text is almost certain.

LEXICON—a. πονηρός (LN 88.110) (BAGD 1.b.α. p. 690): 'evil' [AB, Arn, BAGD, BECNT, LN, NTC, WBC; GW, HCSB, KJV, NASB, NET, NIV, NRSV], 'wicked' [BAGD, LN, Lns], 'sinful' [NLT], 'bad' [CEV, NCV, REB, TEV].
   b. perf. act. indic. of οἶδα (LN 28.7) (BAGD 3. p. 556): 'to know how' [AB, BAGD, BECNT, LN, Lns, NTC, WBC; all versions], 'to know' [Arn]. This is used in the sense of having practical experience in doing this [TH].
   c. ἐκ (LN 90.16) (BAGD 6.a. p. 236): 'from' [BAGD, LN]. The phrase ὁ πατὴρ ὁ ἐξ οὐρανοῦ 'the father the one from heaven' is translated 'the Father in heaven' [Arn; TEV], 'your Father in heaven' [GW, NIV], 'the heavenly Father' [AB, BECNT; HCSB, NET, NRSV, REB], 'your heavenly Father' [NTC; CEV, KJV, NASB, NCV, NLT], 'the Father (will give the Holy Spirit) from heaven' [WBC]. The article ὁ 'the' with 'Father' has the force of the possessive pronoun 'your Father' [TH]. The preposition ἐκ 'from' indicates that God gives from heaven [TH]. The phrase is a contraction meaning 'the Father in heaven will give from heaven' [Arn]. The Father is in heaven and from there he gives his blessings [Gdt, NIGTC, NTC].

QUESTION—Who are the people Jesus called evil?
   1. He calls all of his audience evil [AB, Hlt, Lns, MGC, NAC, NIGTC, Su, TG, WBC]. This is a statement of a fact because all human beings are evil [NAC, TG]. This implies an appeal to experience [AB]. They are evil by nature [MGC]. This humbles his disciples by reminding them of all their sins in contrast with their holy Father in heaven [Lns]. This is not a

criticism of any particular people, rather it assumes the limitations of all earthly fathers [WBC]. Here 'evil' refers to 'grasping', pointing out that they all are inclined to keep rather than to give [Su]. God is absolutely good while they are not and 'wicked' is used as a comparative term [Hlt].
2. He calls the Pharisees evil [Bai]. The same phrase is used in Matthew 12:34 and there the question was addressed to the Pharisees, so here too he is addressing his opponents [Bai].

QUESTION—What is the argument indicated by πόσῳ μᾶλλον 'how much more'?

It is an argument from the lesser to the greater [Alf, Arn, BECNT, Gdt, Hlt, Lns, MGC, NAC, NICNT] to assure them that the heavenly Father will surely answer their prayers [Lns]. There is a comparison of the heavenly Father with earthly fathers [AB, Arn, MGC, NICNT, NIGTC, Su] in regard to providing for their children [MGC]. An earthly father with all his limitations is contrasted with God who is completely good [WBC].

QUESTION—Why does the argument not conclude with 'how much more will your Father in heaven give *good things*' (Matthew 7:11) instead of 'how much more will your Father in heaven give you *the Holy Spirit*'?

Most commentators think that 'good things' was in the original teaching and Luke worded it as 'Holy Spirit' to indicate that good gifts were to be understood in a spiritual sense, but Matthew might have written 'good things' in order to generalize the gift so that the second part of the saying better matched the first part [NIGTC]. God will not only give the good things that are needed, but even the supreme gift of the Holy Spirit [AB]. The Holy Spirit is the most important and greatest gift that the heavenly Father can give [Alf, Lns, NAC, NIC, NICNT, NIVS, Su, TG] and this gift also includes every needed temporal gift [Alf, Lns, NIC]. The Holy Spirit is the supreme object desired by all true disciples [EGT], God's gifts apply not just to physical needs as seen in the Lord's prayer, but apply to the greatest possible gift [WBC]. The good gift God gives is not left in general terms, but is specified as the Holy Spirit who is the gift for our highest good and this involves the Spirit's work in our lives in general [TNTC]. The Holy Spirit is the source of all that is good [NTC]. Since it is a prayer of a disciple, the disciple is requesting God's presence, guidance, and intimacy [BECNT]. This looks forward to God's gift of the Holy Spirit at Pentecost and indicates that the messianic age has begun in Christ [MGC].

DISCOURSE UNIT: 11:14–14:34 [REB]. The topic is opposition and questioning.

DISCOURSE UNIT: 11:14–54 [BECNT, NICNT, NIGTC, WBC]. The topic is Jesus' behavior questioned [NICNT], controversies, corrections, and calls to trust [BECNT], controversy with the Pharisees [NIGTC], conflict and contrast [WBC].

502　LUKE 11:14

DISCOURSE UNIT: 11:14–36 [NICNT]. The topic is Jesus' response to the crowds.

DISCOURSE UNIT: 11:14–28 [NASB, NIV, NLT]. The topic is Jesus and Beelzebub [NIV], Jesus and the prince of demons [NLT], the Pharisees' blasphemy [NASB].

DISCOURSE UNIT: 11:14–26 [NIGTC, Su, TNTC; GW]. The topic is the Beelzebul controversy [NIGTC, Su], Jesus and the evil spirits [TNTC], Jesus is accused of working with Beelzebul [GW].

DISCOURSE UNIT: 11:14–23 [AB, BECNT, NAC, TNTC, WBC; CEV, HCSB, NCV, NET, NRSV, TEV]. The topic is Jesus and the ruler of demons [CEV], Jesus and Beelzebul [NET, NRSV, TEV], the Beelzebul controversy [AB, NAC, TNTC], controversy: what do healings mean? [BECNT], casting out demons by the finger of God [WBC], Jesus' power is from God [NCV], a house divided [HCSB].

11:14 And he-was casting-out a-demon[a] and it was mute.[b] And it-happened (when) the demon had-come-out the mute spoke and the crowds were-amazed.[c]

TEXT—Instead of δαιμόνιον καὶ αὐτὸ ἦν κωφόν '(a) demon and it was mute' some manuscripts read δαιμόνιον κωφόν '(a) mute demon'. GNT reads δαιμόνιον καὶ αὐτὸ ἦν κωφόν '(a) demon and it was mute' with a C decision and places καὶ αὐτὸ ἦν 'and it was' in brackets in the text, indicating that the Committee had difficulty in making the decision.

LEXICON—a. δαιμόνιον (LN 12.37): 'demon'. See translations and discussion of this word at 4:33.

    b. κωφός (LN 33.106) (BAGD 1. p. 462): 'mute' [AB, BAGD, BECNT, LN, WBC; HCSB, NASB, NET, NIV, NRSV], 'dumb' [Arn, BAGD, LN, Lns; KJV, REB], 'unable to speak' [LN]. The phrase 'and it was mute' is translated 'that could not talk' [NCV, TEV]. The clause 'he was casting out a demon and it was mute' is translated so as to show that the man was a mute: 'cast a demon out of a man who couldn't speak' [NLT], 'forced a demon out of a man who could not talk' [CEV], 'was expelling a demon who had deprived a man of the power of speech' [NTC], 'was forcing a demon out of a man. The demon had made the man unable to talk' [GW].

    c. aorist act. indic. of θαυμάζω (LN 25.213) (BAGD 1.a.α. p. 352): 'to be amazed'. See translations of this word at 1:21 and 4:22. This word also occurs at 1:63; 2:18, 33; 7:9; 8:25; 11:38; 20:26; 24:12, 41.

QUESTION—What is a demon who was mute?

The characteristic a demon causes in its victim is ascribed to the demon [NIGTC]. The demon is called mute because it made the man mute [Arn, ICC, MGC, NIC, NIVS, NTC; CEV, GW, NET, NLT]. As long as the demon possessed the man, the man was mute [NIC]. Or, the demon itself was mute and because of that, the man who is possessed by the mute demon is also mute [TH]. Some translations are worded so as to indicate that the demon was mute [AB, BECNT, Lns, WBC; KJV, NASB, NCV, NET, NIV, NRSV, REB, TEV], although one has a footnote that says that the demon caused the man to be mute [NET]. The possessed man was mute, so people concluded that the demon itself was mute [TG].

11:15 **But some of them said, By^a Beelzebul^b the ruler of-the demons he-casts-out the demons. 11:16 And testing^c (him) others were-demanding^d a-sign^e from heaven from him.**

LEXICON—a. ἐν (LN 90.6): 'by' [AB, LN, NTC, WBC; HCSB, NASB, NIV, NRSV, REB], 'through' [Arn; KJV], 'in' [BECNT], 'in conjunction with' [Lns], 'by the power of' [CEV, NET], 'with the help of' [GW], 'uses the power of' [NCV], '(he) gets his power from' [NLT], '(who) gives (him) the power to' [TEV]. It means 'through' or 'with the help of' [TH]. It expresses agency [AB], or instrument [NTC]. It has the meaning 'in the name of', indicating that Jesus was acting as a subordinate of Beelzebul [TG].

b. Βεελζεβούλ (LN 93.68) (BAGD p. 139): 'Beelzebul' [AB, Arn, BECNT, LN, Lns, NTC, WBC; all versions except KJV, NIV, NLT], 'Beelzebub' [BAGD; KJV, NIV], 'Satan' [NLT]. The Latin Vulgate altered the word to Beelzebub to conform to 2 Kings 1 [ICC, NIGTC, TNTC].

c. pres. act. participle of πειράζω (LN 27.31) (BAGD 2.c. p. 640): 'to test' [Arn, BECNT, WBC; GW, NASB, NCV, NET, NIV, NRSV], 'to put to the test' [AB, BAGD; CEV], 'to try to test' [NLT], 'to try to trap' [LN], 'to want to trap' [TEV], 'to tempt' [NTC; KJV], 'by way of a test' [REB], 'as a test' [HCSB]. See this word at 10:25.

d. imperf. act. indic. of ζητέω (LN 33.167) (BAGD 2.a. p. 339): 'to demand' [AB, BAGD, LN, NTC; GW, HCSB, NASB, NRSV, REB], 'to ask for' [BAGD; NET, NIV, NLT], 'to request' [BAGD], 'to ask' [CEV, NCV, TEV], 'to seek' [Arn, BECNT; KJV], 'to want' [WBC]. The imperfect tense means that they *began* to do this [NET], or that they *kept on* doing this [AB, Rb, WBC; NASB, NRSV], or that they *tried* to get him to do this [TH].

e. σημεῖον (LN 33.477) (BAGD 2.a. p. 748): 'sign' [AB, Arn, BAGD, BECNT, LN, NTC, WBC; all versions except GW, NLT, TEV], 'miracle' [TEV], 'miraculous sign' [GW, NLT]. The phrase 'were demanding a sign' is translated 'asked him to show them a sign' [CEV], 'asked him to give them a sign' [NCV], 'asked him to perform a miracle' [TEV], 'demanded that he show them some miraculous sign' [GW]. They wanted a sign that consisted of a miracle [BAGD, WBC]. See this word at 11:29; 23:8.

QUESTION—In 11:15, who were the people who said this?

Although the people in general were amazed, Jesus' opponents, the Pharisees among the crowd, were not [Lns, NIGTC]. They were scribes from Jerusalem (Mark 3:22) who came to prove their theory that Jesus' powers were not from God [NTC]. They were the ones who would not acknowledge

Jesus to be the Messiah under any circumstances [NIC]. These people had probably come to watch Jesus and oppose him [ICC]. Matthew identifies them as the Pharisees, Mark as scribes, or this could be an unspecified 'they' to be identified with the crowds [WBC].

QUESTION—Who was Beelzebul?

Beelzebul is derived from the word 'Baalzebul', the chief god of the pagan 'baals' [Su]. It is a transliteration into Greek of a Canaanite god [WBC]. It is not known if the Jews thought Beelzebul was Satan himself or a subordinate to Satan [ICC]. Although the derivation of the name is disputed, it was used as a popular name for the ruler of the demons [NIGTC]. Luke was not interested in the word's origin or in any wordplay involved with it, rather he used it as a title used for Satan [BECNT]. In the NT, Beelzebul is used as a name for Satan [AB, Arn, BECNT, Gdt, Lns, MGC, NAC, NIBC, NIC, NICNT, NTC, Rb, TG, TNTC, WBC; NET] as indicated by the article τῷ ἄρχοντι 'the ruler' [AB]. From Jesus' reply in 11:18, it is seen that he understood it to refer to Satan [AB, NAC, NICNT, NIGTC, TNTC].

QUESTION—What was the purpose of their test?

It is not clear what the people wanted Jesus to prove, perhaps his messiahship, or his authority, or his prophetic office [BECNT]. They wanted to know if Jesus had the proper credentials for his ministry [NIGTC]. They wanted to know the nature of Jesus' power [Arn]. Their purpose was evil, so they were trying to trap Jesus [TG]. A sign from heaven was a sign from God [CEV]. A sign from heaven would signify that God's power was working through Jesus [Su, TG]. It would be a sign that he truly was the Messiah [NIC, TH]. It is hard to know what sign they desired since Jesus had already performed many healings [BECNT]. Perhaps they expected a spectacular display of power as the devil had suggested he do in 4:3–11 [Rb], or perhaps they wanted him to make fire come down from heaven [NTC].

11:17 **And having-known their thoughts he said to-them, Every kingdom being-divided^a against itself is-destroyed^b and house^c against house falls.^d**

LEXICON—a. aorist pass. participle of διαμερίζω (LN 39.14, 63.23) (BAGD 2. p. 186): 'to be divided' [BAGD, LN (39.14, 63.23)], 'to be against, to be opposed to' [LN (39.14)], 'to be disunited' [LN (63.23)]. The phrase 'every/any kingdom divided against itself' [AB, Arn, BECNT, Lns, NTC, WBC; all versions except CEV, NLT, TEV] is also translated 'any kingdom at war with itself' [NLT], 'a kingdom where people fight each other' [CEV], 'any country that divides itself into groups which fight each other' [TEV].

   b. pres. pass. indic. of ἐρημόομαι, ἐρημόω (LN 20.41) (BAGD p. 309): 'to be destroyed' [LN; NCV, NET], 'to be headed for destruction' [HCSB], 'to be laid waste' [BAGD, BECNT; NASB, REB], 'to become waste' [Lns], 'to be depopulated (by civil war)' [BAGD], 'to be ruined' [GW, NIV], 'to be on the way to ruin' [NTC], 'to end up in ruin' [CEV], 'to end

in ruins' [AB], 'to become desolate' [Arn], 'to be desolated' [WBC], 'to be brought to desolation' [KJV], 'to become a desert' [NRSV], 'to be doomed' [NLT], 'will not last very long' [TEV].
  c. οἶκος (LN 7.2, 10.8) (BAGD 1.a.α. p. 560): 'house' [BAGD, LN (7.2)], 'family' [LN (10.8)]. The phrase 'a house against a house' is translated 'house falls against house' [Lns], 'house falls on house' [NRSV], 'house falls upon house' [Arn], 'one house falls upon another' [AB], 'a house divided against a house' [NTC, WBC; KJV], 'a house divided against itself' [GW, HCSB, NASB, NIV], 'a family that is divided against itself' [NCV, TEV], 'a divided house' [BECNT; NLT], 'a divided household' [NET, REB], 'a family that fights' [CEV].
  d. pres. act. indic. of πίπτω (LN 15.119) (BAGD 1.b.b. p. 659): 'to fall' [AB, Arn, BAGD, BECNT, LN, Lns, WBC; GW, HCSB, KJV, NASB, NET, NIV, NRSV, REB], 'to fall apart' [TEV], 'to break up' [CEV], 'to not continue' [NCV], 'to be doomed' [NLT], 'to fail' [NTC].
QUESTION—Was Jesus aware of what the people were saying?
  1. Jesus knew what was really behind the words they spoke to him in 11:15–16 [Arn, BECNT, Gdt, Lns, MGC, TH]. Jesus knew their secret reasons for saying what they did [Lns]. He knew that their thoughts were hostile [BECNT]. He knew that the people were suspicious of the source of his power [MGC].
  2. The crowd's comments were made among themselves and not to Jesus [NIC, TG, TNTC, WBC]. They did not dare utter their accusations directly to Jesus [NIC]. The men spoke to those around themselves and could not be overheard by Jesus [WBC].
QUESTION—How can a kingdom be divided against itself?
  The kingdom or country has factions in it fighting each other so that the kingdom loses its unity [Su]. Different parts of the kingdom are divided against one another, not that they are all against the kingdom as a whole [TH]. The two clauses describe a civil war [AB, BAGD, Lns, WBC], with the resulting desolation [NIGTC, WBC] and depopulation [BAGD, NIGTC]. It implies that if Satan's kingdom of evil is divided by having Satan take sides against his subordinates, then his kingdom would not be able to stand [NIGTC].
QUESTION—What is meant by 'house against house'?
  1. This gives a further statement about the results of a divided kingdom [AB, Arn, BECNT, BNTC, EGT, Gdt, ICC, Lns, MGC, My, NIC, NIGTC, TH, TNTC; NRSV]. Luke presents just one example, that of a divided kingdom, different from the three examples of a kingdom, a city, and a house in Matthew 12:25 [ICC].
    1.1 Houses fall down upon each other [AB, Arn, BNTC, EGT, Lns, My, TH]: the kingdom is laid waste and one house falls against another house. This describes the desolation indicated by 'laid waste' in which a building falling into ruin strikes an adjoining house [EGT, My].

1.2 One household in the kingdom falls upon (attacks) another household [BECNT, Gdt, ICC, MGC, NIC, NIGTC, TNTC; NRSV]: the kingdom is laid waste and household falls upon household. This refers to the internal conflict in a divided community [BECNT] during a civil war [MGC, NIGTC]. This is the ruin of families resulting from civil discord [Gdt].
2. This is a second example and describes a household with divided family members [Alf, Crd, NTC, TG, WBC; GW, KJV, NASB, NCV, NET, NIV, NLT, REB, TEV]. The verb 'divided' is implied from the previous clause [BECNT; GW, KJV, NASB, NCV, NET, NIV, NLT, REB, TEV]: and house divided against house falls. The illustration applied to a kingdom is now applied to a household [WBC]. If Satan is casting out his own demons, he has a divided house [BECNT].

11:18 **And if also Satan was-divided against himself, how will his kingdom stand?**[a] **Because you-say by Beelzebul I cast-out the demons.**
LEXICON—a. fut. pass. indic. of ἵσταμαι (LN 13.29, 13.90) (BAGD II.1.d. p. 382): 'to stand' [AB, Arn, BECNT, Lns, NTC, WBC; HCSB, KJV, NASB, NET, NIV, NRSV, REB], 'to stand firm' [BAGD], 'to firmly remain' [LN (13.29)], 'to continue' [LN (13.90); NCV], 'to last' [CEV, GW, TEV], 'to survive' [NLT].
QUESTION—How can Satan be divided against himself?
This is the application to the general truth of a kingdom being divided against itself in 11:17 [MGC, NIGTC, TH], and by metonymy 'Satan' is now used for the kingdom of Satan [NIGTC]. Satan would be fighting against himself by empowering Jesus to cast out demons [MGC; NLT]. Satan would be destroying his own work [NTC]. If Satan is casting out his own demons, his kingdom will not stand. However, Satan's power is real and therefore the opponents' conclusions about Jesus are wrong [BECNT]. The question is rhetorical and means that then Satan's kingdom would not stand [Lns, TH]. It shows the error in the accusers' logic [NIBC, NICNT]. Since it is absurd to think that Satan would destroy his own kingdom, the people are wrong in saying that it is by Satan that Jesus casts out demons [Lns, Su].
QUESTION—What relationship is indicated by ὅτι 'because' in the last sentence?
This indicates the reason Jesus asked the preceding rhetorical question [ICC, My; GW, NET, NIV]. The implied beginning of the sentence is 'I say this because' [Arn, NTC; GW, NIV], 'I ask you this because' [NET]. What they have said about Jesus implies that Satan is divided against himself and this explains Jesus' question [Lns, TH].

11:19 **And if I by Beelzebul cast-out the demons, by whom do your sons**[a] **cast-out (demons)? Because-of this they will-be your judges.**[b]
LEXICON—a. υἱός (LN 36.39) (BAGD 1.c.a. p. 833): 'son' [Arn, BAGD, BECNT, Lns, NTC, WBC; HCSB, KJV, NASB, NET], 'follower'

[BAGD, LN; CEV, GW, NIV, NLT, TEV], '(your) people' [NCV], '(your) own people' [AB; REB], '(your) exorcists' [NRSV].
  b. κριτής (LN 56.28) (BAGD 1.b. p. 453): 'judge' [BAGD, LN]. The phrase 'they will be your judges' [Arn, BECNT, Lns, NTC, WBC; GW, HCSB, KJV, NASB, NCV, NET, NIV, NRSV] is also translated 'they are the ones who will judge you' [CEV], 'they will sit in judgment over you' [AB], 'they will judge you for what you have said' [NLT], 'they themselves will refute you' [REB], 'your own followers prove that you are wrong' [TEV]. It means that their own followers will convict them of wrongdoing [BAGD].

QUESTION—Did Jesus admit that he cast out demons by Beelzebul?

It is just for the sake of argument that Jesus assumed that he did this [Rb]. Jesus stated his opponents' position in order to take it to a logical dead end [BECNT].

QUESTION—Who were the sons of Jesus' accusers and did they really cast out demons?

1. This refers to people associated with the accusers [AB, Arn, BNTC, Gdt, Lns, MGC, NAC, NIC, NICNT, NIGTC, NTC, Su, TG, TH, TNTC, WBC]. Their 'sons' may be their actual sons or it may mean 'your own people' [TNTC]. It means their own people who cast out demons [Arn, TH], the people who belonged to their group [TG], their countrymen [Gdt]. It means their disciples [NAC], pupils [BNTC, NIGTC], who used the exorcisms that they were taught by those whom Jesus addressed [BNTC]. It is used like the 'sons of prophets' [Lns, My], that is, disciples of the prophets, men who were experts of their own guild [Lns]. Jesus assumed that they really did cast out demons by the power of God [Gdt, Lns, NICNT, NIGTC, TNTC] and Acts 19:13 refers to some Jews who went around driving out evil spirits [Gdt]. They must not have been very successful, because there were many demoniacs who came to Jesus for healing [Lns].

2. This refers to Jesus' disciples who were the accusers' sons in the sense that they were also Jewish [BECNT, My; NET]. The disciples had really cast out demons in the ministry Jesus had given them [NET].

QUESTION—What relation is indicated by διὰ τοῦτο 'because of this' in 11:19?

'This' refers to the fact there actually were Jewish exorcists and the people would know that they did not cast out demons by the power of Beelzebul [TH]. God used them as his instruments to cast out demons [Arn].

QUESTION—In what way would their sons who cast out demons be their judges?

The existence of Jewish exorcists proved that the accusers were wrong [TG, TH; TEV]. That Jewish exorcists will be their judges is not to be taken literally and it simply means that such people will not agree with the accusation [WBC]. Such exorcists knew that it was God, not Beelzebul, who gave them the power to cast out demons, so they would judge the accusation that Jesus cast out demons by the power of Beelzebul to be untrue and as a result the accusers would stand condemned [TH]. God will let the Pharisaic exorcists pronounce the sentence on the Pharisees who accused Jesus [Lns]. The accusations against Jesus were implicitly made against the Jewish exorcists also and in the final judgment God will support the exorcists who acted by his power and they will judge against the critics [MGC, NIGTC]. Or, if the 'sons' are Jesus' disciples, they will have a role in the final judgment [BECNT].

11:20 **But if by (the) finger[a] of-God I cast-out the demons, then the kingdom of-God came[b] upon you.**

TEXT—Some manuscripts omit ἐγώ 'I'. GNT does not deal with this variant in the apparatus, but places it in brackets in the text, indicating difficulty in making the decision. Most versions would not distinguish between the presence and absence of this emphatic pronoun.

LEXICON—a. δάκτυλος (LN 76.3) (BAGD p. 170): 'finger' [BAGD], 'power' [**LN**]. The phrase 'by the finger of God' [AB, BECNT, NTC, WBC; HCSB, NASB, NET, NIV, NRSV, REB] is also translated 'with the finger of God' [KJV], 'through the finger of God' [Arn], 'with God's finger' [Lns], 'by the power of God' [NLT], 'by means of God's power' [TEV], 'with the help of God's power' [GW], 'I use God's power' [CEV], 'I use the power of God' [NCV]. This phrase is an OT expression [NIC] and denotes God's power [AB, BECNT, ICC, LN, NAC, NIC, NTC; NET]. This anthropomorphism expresses the ease with which Jesus cast out the demons [AB, Lns] (or, this is unlikely [ICC]). It took only a small motion of God's finger to cause the demons to flee [Lns].

b. aorist act. indic. of φθάνω (LN 13.123) (BAGD 2. p. 856): 'to come' [BAGD, LN]. The phrase 'came upon you' is translated 'is come upon you' [KJV], 'has come upon you' [BECNT, NTC, WBC; NASB], 'has already come upon you' [REB], 'has come on you' [NET], 'has come to you' [Arn; GW, HCSB, NCV, NIV, NRSV], 'has already come to you' [CEV, TEV], 'has arrived among you' [NLT], 'has already reached you' [AB], 'did already reach to you' [Lns].

QUESTION—What relationship is indicated by εἰ δέ 'but if' at the beginning of the verse?

The conditional sentence assumes that the condition is true [Arn, MGC, TG]. It assumes that the opponents' accusation has to be rejected and gives this alternative to 11:19 [Lns, NIGTC]. This is Jesus' interpretation of his success in casting out demons [Crd, NICNT]. It is Jesus' own claim, but it is not presented as the only logical alternative to the view criticized in the previous verses [WBC].

QUESTION—What relationship is indicated by ἄρα 'then' in the last sentence of the verse?

The conjunction indicates the conclusion [Gdt], or the consequences [NIGTC] of the preceding statement.

QUESTION—If Jewish exorcists had already been casting out demons, how did the fact that Jesus also cast out the demon from the mute man show that God's kingdom had come?

Wherever God's power is demonstrated, God's kingly rule is evident [NICNT, NIGTC]. However, the coming of the kingdom of God is not linked only to the fact of casting out demons, but it involves the role of Jesus himself in which the presence and power of God were with him in some distinctive manner [WBC]. The exorcisms of Jesus must be connected with his overall teachings and claims [NAC].

QUESTION—In what sense did the kingdom of God come upon them?

The aorist tense indicates that casting out demons showed that the kingdom was already in their midst [Lns, MGC, TG] and they should welcome it [Lns]. The kingdom arrived when Jesus came [NAC]. The kingdom had come in its initial form, the first phase of the kingdom in which God's rule is emphasized [BECNT]. The proof that God's rule was near to the hearers was that its power had been seen in the lives of the exorcised people and God's rule was there for them to accept [NIGTC]. God's dominion had come upon earth and it was active in Christ [NIC], in his preaching and activity [AB]. God was exercising his rule through the activity of Jesus [WBC]. God's kingdom is still to come, yet it was already active when Jesus acted [Crd]. Its presence was seen in the power that casts out the forces of evil [TNTC].

11:21 **When the strong (man) having-been-fully-armed[a] guards[b] his-own dwelling,[c] his possessions[d] are in peace.[e]**

LEXICON—a. perf. act. participle of καθοπλίζω (LN **55.1**) (BAGD 1. p. 391): 'to be fully armed' [AB, Arn, BAGD, BECNT, **LN**, WBC; GW, HCSB, NASB, NET, NIV, NRSV, REB], 'to be completely armed' [Lns; NLT], 'to be armed to the teeth' [NTC], 'to be armed' [KJV], 'to arm one's self' [CEV], 'to be equipped' [BAGD]. This verb is also translated as a prepositional phrase: 'with many weapons' [NCV], 'with all his weapons ready' [TEV].

b. pres. act. subj. of φυλάσσω (LN 37.120) (BAGD 1.c. p. 868): 'to guard' [Arn, BAGD, BECNT, Lns, NTC; all versions except KJV, REB], 'to guard closely' [LN], 'to be on guard over' [REB], 'to keep guard over' [WBC], 'to stand guard over' [AB], 'to protect' [BAGD], 'to keep' [KJV].

c. αὐλή (LN **7.6**) (BAGD 2., 4. p. 121): 'dwelling' [**LN**], 'house' [BAGD (2.), BECNT, NTC; NASB, NCV, NIV, TEV], 'home' [CEV], 'mansion' [GW], 'estate' [HCSB], 'palace' [Arn, BAGD (4.); KJV, NET, NLT, REB], 'castle' [WBC; NRSV], 'court' [Lns], 'courtyard' [AB]. In the NT the noun is used in different senses: the courtyard in front of a house, the court around a house, or the house as a whole [Rb]. Here it refers to a courtyard [Lns, MGC], palace [NIGTC], castle [NICNT], fortress [Gdt], premises [My], homestead [ICC], dwelling or house [TH]. The noun refers here to a secure abode [BECNT].

d. pres. act. participle of ὑπάρχω (LN 57.16) (BAGD 1. p. 838): 'to belong to' [BAGD, LN]. The phrase τὰ ὑπάρχοντα 'possessions' [Arn, BAGD, BECNT, LN, Lns, NTC; HCSB, NASB, NCV, NET, NIV, REB] is also translated 'belongings' [AB; TEV], 'goods' [WBC; KJV], 'property' [BAGD, LN; GW, NRSV], 'everything he owns' [CEV], 'it (the palace)' [NLT].

e. εἰρήνη (LN 22.42) (BAGD 1.a. p. 227): 'peace' [BAGD, LN]. The phrase 'are in peace' [Arn, Lns; KJV] is also translated 'are/is safe' [all versions except KJV, NASB], 'are safe and sound' [AB], 'are secure' [BECNT, NTC; HCSB], 'are secured' [WBC], 'are undisturbed' [NASB]. It means that they are kept safe [TH], or undisturbed [Lns]. His belongings are in a situation without war [AB].

QUESTION—What relationship is indicated by ὅταν 'when'?

The conjunction ὅταν 'when, whenever' generalizes an illustration [Lns]. This is an illustration of the point he wanted to make [BECNT, Gdt]. It is an allegory [Su], a similitude [WBC], or a brief parable [EGT, ICC, NIGTC, TG, WBC].

QUESTION—Who is the strong man?

The strong man represents Satan [AB, Alf, Arn, BECNT, BNTC, EGT, Gdt, ICC, Lns, MGC, My, NIBC, NIC, NIGTC, NTC, Rb, Su, TG, TH, TNTC, WBC; NET, NLT]. The strong man is Satan who is represented by the demonic agent who possessed the man healed by Jesus [NICNT]. This strong man is not an ordinary householder, but a lord of a castle [AB]. The man's weapons represent Satan's power and the courtyard represents the world under Satan's sway [Lns].

QUESTION—What do the strong man's possessions represent?

The possessions that the strong man is guarding represent the people under his control [NTC], the demon-possessed people [Lns, NTC]. The castle and the property represent the demonized person [NICNT].

11:22 But when a-stronger (man) (than) he having-attacked[a] conquers[b] him, he-takes his armor on which he-had-depended[c] and he distributes the spoils[d] of-him.

TEXT—Instead of ἰσχυρότερος '(a) stronger', some manuscripts read ὁ ἰσχυρότερος 'the stronger'. GNT does not mention this variant.

LEXICON—a. aorist act. participle of ἐπέρχομαι (LN **39.47**) (BAGD 2.b. p. 285): 'to attack' [AB, BAGD, **LN**; all versions except CEV, KJV, NCV], 'to assault' [LN], 'to come' [Arn, BECNT, NTC; CEV, NCV] 'to come upon' [Lns, WBC; KJV]. The verb 'come upon' is used in a hostile sense here [NIGTC].

b. aorist act. subj. of νικάω (LN 39.57) (BAGD 2.a. p. 539): 'to conquer' [Arn, BAGD, LN, Lns, WBC; NET], 'to overpower' [AB, NTC; HCSB, NASB, NIV, NLT, NRSV, REB], 'to overwhelm' [BECNT], 'to overcome' [BAGD; KJV], 'to be victorious over' [LN], 'to defeat' [CEV, GW, NCV, TEV].

c. pluperf. act. indic. of πείθω (LN 31.82) (BAGD 2.a. p. 639): 'to depend on' [BAGD, LN; TEV], 'to trust in' [BAGD, BECNT, LN, NTC; CEV, GW, HCSB, KJV, NCV, NIV, NRSV], 'to put trust in' [WBC], 'to rely on' [AB, Arn, LN, Lns; NASB, NET, REB], not explicit [NLT].

d. σκῦλα (LN 57.243) (BAGD p. 758): 'spoils' [BAGD, LN], 'booty' [BAGD, LN], 'plunder' [LN]. The phrase 'he distributes the spoils of him' is translated 'he distributes his spoils' [Arn, Lns; NASB], 'he distributes the spoil' [REB], 'he divides his spoils' [BECNT; KJV], 'he divides up the spoils' [NIV], 'he divides his plunder' [NRSV], 'he will divide the loot' [GW], 'he divides up his plunder' [HCSB, NET], 'he divides up his booty' [AB], 'he distributes the booty' [WBC], 'he distributes his goods as spoils' [NTC], 'he will divide with others what he has taken' [CEV], 'he divides up what he stole' [TEV], 'will give away the possessions' [NCV], 'he carries off his belongings' [NLT]. He divides his spoil among his companions or followers [TG, TH], his friends [EGT].

QUESTION—Who does the stronger man represent?

The stronger man represents Jesus [AB, Alf, Arn, BECNT, BNTC, EGT, Gdt, ICC, Lns, MGC, My, NAC, NIBC, NIC, NICNT, NIGTC, NIVS, NTC, Rb, Su, TG, TH, TNTC; NET]. Or, taking into account the phrase 'by the finger of God' and the 'kingdom of God' in 11:2, the stronger man represents the mighty God who was with Jesus [WBC].

QUESTION—What is meant by the stronger man conquering the strong man?

Jesus, the stronger man, has already bound Satan, the strong man [NIC]. The temptation in the wilderness proved that Jesus was stronger than Satan [NTC]. Jesus overcame Satan at the temptation in the wilderness [Gdt]. Or, Jesus had just overcome Satan by casting out the demon [TNTC]. The taking of the armor indicates that full victory has been accomplished and Satan was no longer in control [BECNT], and from then on was helpless [NIGTC]. Or, the defeat of Satan had not yet occurred and the issue was only the exorcism of the demon possessed man [NICNT]. When Jesus healed the demoniac, it indicated that the war was being won and the kingdom was coming [NET]. It is not clear whether the conquering of Satan refers to the wilderness experience, the crucifixion and resurrection, or is deliberately vague [NIGTC].

QUESTION—In the phrase τὰ σκῦλα αὐτοῦ 'the spoils of him', whose spoils are distributed by the stronger man?

1. 'Him' refers to the strong man of 11:21 and 'his spoils' means the spoils the strong man had previously taken from someone else and which has now been taken from him by the stronger man [Gdt, NIBC, TG, TH]. This is another way of referring to 'his possessions' in 11:21 [NIGTC, TH]. The stronger man not only captures the strong man's weapons, he also distributes what the strong man has amassed [NIGTC]. The booty consists of the demon-possessed person and in a wider sense all humans who bear the chains of sin [Gdt]. This refers to what Jesus did by freeing those possessed by Satan's agents, the demons [NIBC].

2. 'Him' refers to the stronger man of 11:22 and 'his spoils' means the things the stronger man has taken from the strong man [Arn, BECNT, EGT, Lns, NTC, Su]. He plunders his goods, but we cannot determine whether the spoil refers to sinful men who are regenerated or to the dead taken from Satan by resurrection [Su]. He distributes Satan's goods as spoils and this refers to the demon-possessed man who was included among Satan's goods but now belongs to Christ as his spoils [NTC]. The distributed spoils refer to the benefits of salvation such as forgiveness, the Holy Spirit and his gifts, and eternal life [BECNT, WBC]. This would refer to Jesus' extensive healing ministry among demoniacs [EGT]. Or, the spoils are only part of the illustration and have no allegorical meaning [Arn].

11:23 The (one) not being with[a] me is against[b] me, and the (one) not gathering[c] with me scatters.[d]

LEXICON—a. μετά (LN 90.42) (BAGD A.II.1.c.δ. p. 509): 'with' [AB, Arn, BAGD, BECNT, LN, Lns, NTC, WBC; all versions except CEV, NLT, TEV], 'on the same side' [LN]. The phrase 'not being with me' is translated 'are not on my side' [CEV], 'is not for me' [TEV], 'isn't helping me' [NLT].
  b. κατά (LN 90.31) (BAGD I.2.b.γ. p. 406): 'against' [AB, Arn, BAGD, BECNT, LN, Lns, NTC, WBC; all versions except NLT], 'in opposition to, in conflict with' [LN]. The phrase 'is against me' is translated 'opposes me' [NLT].
  c. pres. act. participle of συνάγω (LN 15.125) (BAGD 1. p. 782): 'to gather' [AB, Arn, BECNT, Lns, NTC, WBC; GW, HCSB, KJV, NASB, NET, NIV, NRSV, REB], 'to gather in' [BAGD], 'to gather together' [LN]. The phrase 'not gathering with me' is translated 'does not help me gather' [TEV], 'don't gather in the crop with me' [CEV], 'does not work with me' [NCV], 'isn't working with me' [NLT].
  d. pres. act. indic. of σκορπίζω (LN 15.135) (BAGD 1. p. 757): 'to scatter' [AB, Arn, BAGD, BECNT, LN, Lns, NTC, WBC; all versions except NCV, NLT], 'to cause to disperse' [LN], 'to disperse' [BAGD]. The verb 'scatters' is translated 'is working against me' [NCV, NLT].
QUESTION—What is meant be being with Jesus or against him?
This is a metaphor about taking sides in war [AB, BECNT, Gdt, Lns, NAC, NICNT, NTC, TG, TH, TNTC, WBC]. The choice is siding with Jesus or aligning with the forces of Satan [NIGTC, WBC]. This strife between Jesus and Satan was made clear in the preceding verses [NIGTC]. It is not possible to be neutral in the conflict between Christ and Satan [BECNT, ICC, Lns, NIGTC, NTC, Su, TG, TH, TNTC]. The fight is between the forces of the kingdom of God and the forces of Satan [TG]. When the Pharisees decided that they would not be on Jesus' side, they had gone to the opposing side so that they were with Satan and against Jesus [Lns]. To be with Jesus is to believe in him and to be against him is to reject him [NIBC].

QUESTION—What is meant by gathering with Jesus or scattering?
1. The object to be supplied in this metaphor is a flock of sheep [ICC, Lns, MGC, NIGTC, NTC, TH, TNTC, WBC]. The metaphor refers to a band of followers [ICC]. Jesus' work was to gather the sheep, while Satan's work was scattering them like a wolf would scatter sheep [Lns].
2. The object to be supplied is a crop to be harvested [BECNT, NAC, NICNT, TG; CEV]. Gathering in the harvest refers to gathering in people, bringing people to Jesus [TG]. Jesus' followers do not join Jesus in shepherding people, they join him in bringing others into the kingdom and if they don't, then they influence them not to come into the kingdom [BECNT]. Even with the alternative figure of a flock of sheep where a shepherd tries to keep the sheep together, the point of the saying is the same [TG].

QUESTION—Does this contradict Jesus' words 'he who is not against you is for you' in 9:50?

Both statements are true in their contexts [NIGTC]. In 9:50 the reference is to an exorcist who unconsciously cooperated with Jesus, while here the reference is to those who consciously opposed him [WBC]. In 9:50, the emphasis is on serving Christ and means that his followers should not have a spirit of exclusivity. Here the emphasis is on accepting Christ and means that non-Christians cannot hide behind a claim of neutrality [MGC]. Doing a miracle or kind deed in Jesus' name is neither neutral nor hostile to Jesus [Lns].

DISCOURSE UNIT: 11:24–36 [BECNT]. The topic is warnings about response.

DISCOURSE UNIT: 11:24–28 [NAC; NET]. The topic is the return of the unclean spirit and true blessedness [NAC], the response to Jesus' work [NET].

DISCOURSE UNIT: 11:24–26 [AB, BECNT, TNTC, WBC; CEV, HCSB, NCV, NRSV, TEV]. The topic is the empty person [NCV], the return of the unclean spirit [HCSB, NRSV], the return of an evil spirit [AB; CEV, TEV], the parable of the returning spirits [BECNT, TNTC], the false hope of a temporary benefit [WBC].

11:24 When the unclean spirit goes-out[a] from the man, it-goes through waterless[b] places seeking a-resting-place[c] and not finding (it). Then it-says, I-will-return to my house[d] from-where I-came-out.

TEXT—Instead of τότε λέγει 'then it says', some manuscripts read λέγει 'it says'. GNT reads τότε λέγει 'then it says' with a C decision and places τότε 'then' in brackets in the text, indicating that the Committee had difficulty making the decision.

LEXICON—a. aorist act. subj. of ἐξέρχομαι (LN 14.40) (BAGD 1.a.δ. p. 274): 'to go out of' [BAGD, LN], 'to depart out of' [LN]. The phrase 'to go out from' [Lns] is also translated 'to go out of' [Arn, NTC; NASB, NET, NRSV, TEV], 'to come out from' [BECNT], 'to come out of' [AB; GW,

HCSB, NCV, NIV, REB], 'to leave' [CEV, NLT], 'to depart from' [WBC], 'to be gone out of' [KJV].
- b. ἄνυδρος (LN 2.8) (BAGD p. 76): 'waterless' [Arn, BAGD, BECNT, LN, Lns, NTC, WBC; HCSB, NASB, NET], 'dry' [BAGD, LN; GW, KJV, NCV], 'arid' [NIV]. The phrase 'waterless places' is translated 'waterless regions' [NRSV], 'areas without water' [AB], 'dry country' [TEV], 'the desert' [CEV, NLT], 'the desert sands' [REB].
- c. ἀνάπαυσις (LN 23.87) (BAGD 3. p. 58): 'a resting place' [AB, BAGD, WBC; NRSV, REB], 'a place to rest' [LN; CEV, GW, NCV, TEV], 'a state of rest' [LN], 'rest' [BECNT, Lns, NTC; HCSB, KJV, NASB, NET, NIV, NLT], 'refreshment' [Arn]. It portrays the demon as being homeless like a nomad [AB].
- d. οἶκος (LN 7.2) (BAGD 1.b.β. p. 560): 'house' [AB, Arn, BECNT, LN, Lns, NTC, WBC; HCSB, KJV, NASB, NCV, NIV, NRSV, TEV], 'dwelling, habitation' [BAGD], 'home' [CEV, GW, NET, REB], 'person' [NLT]. 'House' is a metaphor for the person possessed by the demon [TH]. It is 'my house' because the demon considered the man he had possessed to still belong to him [TG, TH]. It was the home it had left [GW]. No other demon had taken possession of the man [ICC].

QUESTION—What is the setting of this account?

The story is about the exit of a demon and does not say anything about whether the demon left by its own volition or was cast out of the possessed man [Su]. The conjunction ὅταν 'when' describes a general case [NIGTC] and the articles in 'the unclean spirit' and 'the man' have generic force [NIGTC, TH]. Or, the articles refer to a specific case and do not mean that all healed demon-possessed men become demon-possessed again [Lns]. 'The man' means the man who has been possessed by the demon [ICC].

QUESTION—What caused the demon to depart from the man?
1. The demon was cast out of the man [AB, BECNT, Gdt, MGC, NAC, NIBC, NIC, NICNT, NIGTC, TG, TH]. This could be the result of the demon being expelled by the finger of God, by Jesus' power, or by Jewish exorcists [AB], by Jesus, one of his disciples, or even by a Jewish exorcist [MGC]. This refers to an evil spirit cast out by the 'sons' of Jesus' accusers, a temporary victory [NIBC]. An exorcist has cast out a demon, but it had not been conquered and sent to prison [Gdt].
2. The demon itself chose to leave the man in order to explore [ICC, Su, TNTC, WBC]. There is no mention of the demon being cast out of the house and later the demon still speaks of 'my house' [ICC, TNTC]. The demon left the man to seek another place to live, but did not find any more desirable place [Su].

QUESTION—What is the significance of passing through waterless places?

This refers to the wilderness, a natural abode of demons [AB, ICC, NAC, NTC, Su, TG, TH, TNTC, WBC]. All dangerous forms of non-human life live in the wilderness, but there was no desirable place for the demon to dwell outside of a human being [Su]. The point is that the absence of humans in the wilderness was the reason the demon could not find a resting place [MGC, NIGTC]. It needs a soul in which to rest [ICC].

QUESTION—With what is the phrase μὴ εὑρίσκον 'not finding one' connected?

    1. It is connected with the preceding clause [GW, NET, NIV]: it goes through waterless places seeking a resting place and not finding it. Then it says....

    2. It is connected with the following clause [AB, BECNT, ICC, Lns, WBC; CEV, KJV, NASB, NCV, NLT, NRSV, REB, TEV]: it goes through waterless places seeking a resting place. Not finding one, it then says....

11:25 **And having-come it-finds (it) having-been-swept and having-been-put-in-order.**[a]

TEXT—Following εὑρίσκει 'it finds (it)', some manuscripts add σχολαζοντα 'being empty'. GNT reads εὑρίσκει 'it finds (it)' with a B decision, indicating that the text is almost certain.

LEXICON—a. perf. pass. participle of κοσμέω (LN 79.12) (BAGD 1, 2.a.β. p. 445): 'to be put in order' [BAGD (1.), BECNT, NTC; HCSB, NASB, NET, NIV, NRSV], 'to be set in order' [AB, Lns], 'to be in order' [GW], 'to be in good order' [Arn], 'to be clean' [NLT], 'to be made neat' [NCV], '(to be swept clean) and tidy' [REB], 'to be beautified' [LN], 'to be decorated' [BAGD (2.a.β.), WBC], 'to be fixed up' [CEV, TEV], 'to be garnished' [KJV]. The house was tidied up [NIGTC].

QUESTION—What is the significance of finding the house swept and put in order?

It means that the house was unoccupied [ICC, MGC, Su, TH]. It was cleaned out so as to be ready for occupancy [BECNT, Su]. It was refurbished into an attractive place in which to live [WBC]. It was ready to attract any passer-by [AB, ICC], or prepared to receive a guest [AB, Lns]. It describes a moral cleaning up by the man [TNTC]. The man is spiritually empty and ready to receive some spiritual guest [BECNT]. No other spirit had taken the demon's place in the man [Su]. Although the man was leading an outwardly undisturbed life, the Holy Spirit was not dwelling in the man [Lns, TNTC]. The Holy Spirit had not been made a guest in place of the demon [Gdt, ICC].

11:26 **Then it-goes and takes-along**[a] **seven other spirits more-evil (than) itself and they-having-entered it-dwells**[b] **there. And the last (condition) of-that man becomes worse (than) the first.**

LEXICON—a. pres. act. indic. of παραλαμβάνω (LN 15.168) (BAGD 1. p. 619): 'to take along' [BAGD, LN, WBC; NASB], 'to take with' [Arn, Lns], 'to take' [KJV, NIV], 'to bring along' [AB, BAGD, LN; GW], 'to bring' [BECNT; HCSB, NCV, NET, NRSV, TEV], 'to fetch' [NTC], 'to collect' [REB], 'to find' [CEV, NLT].

    b. pres. act. indic. of κατοικέω (LN 85.69) (BAGD 1.b. p. 424): 'to dwell' [AB, Arn, BAGD, BECNT, LN, Lns; KJV], 'to live' [BAGD, LN, NTC; NASB, NCV, NET, NIV, NLT, NRSV, TEV], 'to reside' [BAGD, LN],

516   LUKE 11:26

'to settle down' [BAGD; HCSB], 'to settle' [REB], 'to make (their) home' [CEV], 'to take up residence' [WBC], 'to take up permanent residence' [GW]. This singular verb is translated as plural so as to include all eight demons [AB, BECNT, Lns, NTC, WBC; all versions]. The demons settle down to live there permanently [TH, TNTC].

QUESTION—Why would the demon go and get seven more evil spirits?
The house was so fixed up that that the demon can now have the company that it wants since there is room for eight [Lns, NIGTC]. The presence of eight demons indicates a greater ability to resist exorcism a second time [AB, Arn, BECNT, NIBC]. The number seven symbolizes completeness [Su], the totality of evil or uncleanness [AB, NAC], the severity of the possession [NIBC]. However, the number of demons present in the house is now eight, not seven [BECNT].

QUESTION—What is the point of this story?
There is a danger of having a demon cast out of a person if that person does not follow it up with faith [BECNT, Crd]. It is a warning to the person who has had a demon cast out that he should not fail to fill the empty house with a new inhabitant, or it may be a criticism of the Jewish exorcists who do not take Jesus' side and thus make the situation worse [NIGTC]. Neutrality is impossible, either the heart is filled with Christ or with Satan and it cannot remain empty [NIC]. The point of the story is the deceptiveness of apparent improvement as long as the 'strong man' is still in control and warns against a false hope that is placed in other than the kingdom of God or in Jesus [NIGTC].

DISCOURSE UNIT: 11:27–12:59 [TNTC]. The topic is Jesus teaching the people.

DISCOURSE UNIT: 11:27–36 [Su]. The topic is a collection of short teachings.

DISCOURSE UNIT: 11:27–32 [GW]. The topic is the sign of Jonah.

DISCOURSE UNIT: 11:27–28 [AB, BECNT, NIGTC, TNTC, WBC; CEV, HCSB, NCV, NRSV, TEV]. The topic is the blessing for keeping God's word [BECNT], true blessedness [HCSB, NIGTC, TNTC; NRSV], being really blessed [CEV], who is blessed? [AB, WBC], true happiness [TEV], people who are truly happy [NCV].

11:27 And it-happened while he says these (things) a-certain woman from the crowd having-raised[a] (her) voice said to-him, Blessed[b] (is) the womb[c] having-carried you and (the) breasts[d] which you-sucked. **11:28** And he said, On-the-contrary,[e] blessed (are) the (ones who) hear the word of-God and keep[f] (it).

LEXICON—a. aorist act. participle of ἐπαίρω (LN **33.78**) (BAGD 1. p. 282): 'to raise' [AB, Arn, BAGD, BECNT, **LN**, Lns, WBC; HCSB, NASB, NRSV], 'to lift up' [NTC; KJV], 'to cry out' [LN]. The phrase 'having

lifted up her voice said' is translated 'spoke up' [CEV, TEV], 'spoke out' [NET], 'called out' [NCV, NIV, NLT, REB], 'shouted' [GW].
b. μακάριος (LN 25.119) (BAGD 3.a. p. 487): 'blessed'. See translations of this word at 1:45 and 6:20. This word also occurs at 7:23; 10:23; 12:37, 43; 14:14; 23:29.
c. κοιλία (LN 8.69) (BAGD 2. p. 437): 'womb' [AB, BAGD, BECNT, LN, Lns, NTC, WBC; KJV, NASB, NRSV]. The phrase 'blessed is the womb having carried you' is translated 'happy the womb that carried you' [REB], 'blessed is the womb that bore you' [Arn; HCSB, NET], 'how happy is the woman who bore you' [TEV], 'the woman who gave birth to you is blessed' [CEV], 'blessed is the mother who gave you birth' [NIV], 'how blessed is the mother who gave birth to you' [GW], 'happy is the mother who gave birth to you' [NCV], 'God bless your mother—the womb from which you came' [NLT].
d. μαστός (LN **8.37**) (BAGD 2. p. 495): 'breast' [BAGD, BECNT, **LN**, Lns, NTC, WBC], 'pap' [KJV]. The phrase 'the breasts which you sucked' [Arn] is also translated 'the breasts that suckled you' [REB], 'the breasts that nursed you' [GW, NLT, NRSV], 'the breasts at which you nursed' [NASB, NET], 'the breasts that you fed on' [AB], 'the woman/one who nursed you' [CEV, HCSB, TEV], 'the mother who nursed you' [NCV, NLT]. The womb and the breasts are cases of synecdoche where parts are used for the whole and therefore the woman was praising Mary [MGC, TH; NET] in connection with her being Jesus' mother, so that this simply means 'Happy is the mother of such a son' [NIGTC].
e. μενοῦν, μενοῦνγε (LN 89.128) (BAGD p. 503): 'on the contrary' [BAGD, LN; NASB], 'no' [NCV, REB], 'rather' [AB, BAGD, BECNT; GW, NET, NIV, NRSV, TEV], 'yea rather' [Lns; KJV], 'but' [LN], 'but even more blessed' [NLT], 'on the other hand' [LN], 'yes, but' [Arn, WBC], 'yes, but better still' [NTC], 'even more' [HCSB], 'that's true, but' [CEV].
f. pres. act. participle of φυλάσσω (LN 36.19) (BAGD 1.f. p. 868): 'to keep' [Arn, BAGD, BECNT, LN, WBC; HCSB, KJV, REB], 'to obey' [CEV, GW, NCV, NET, NIV, NRSV, TEV], 'to observe' [AB, NTC; NASB], 'to put into practice' [NET], 'to guard' [Lns].

QUESTION—Why would the woman bless Jesus' mother instead of Jesus himself?

By blessing Jesus' mother, she was complimenting Jesus himself [Arn, WBC]. It is implied that the woman wished that she could have such a son as Jesus [Lns, NIGTC]. The woman was fulfilling the prophecy in 1:48 where Mary said, 'From now on all generations will regard me as blessed' [Lns, NTC, WBC].

QUESTION—Did Jesus rebuke the woman when he said, 'On the contrary'?

There are three possible meanings for the particle μενοῦνχαν [AB, MGC, NAC, WBC]. It can introduce a contradiction ('no, rather' [AB, BAGD, BECNT, ICC; GW, NASB, NCV, NET, NIV, NRSV, REB, TEV]), an affirmation ('yes, indeed'), or a correction or modification ('yes, but') [AB, Alf, Arn, Lns, MGC, NAC, NTC, TH, WBC; CEV, KJV, NLT]. Jesus was not criticizing the woman for blessing Mary [Alf, BECNT, ICC, Lns, MGC, My, NIC, NTC, TNTC, WBC]. The word μενοῦν 'on the contrary' does not deny the truth of what the woman said, but Jesus was emphasizing the greater relevance of what he was to say [TH, TNTC]. He broadened the scope of blessedness to include all believers [NTC]. It has the meaning 'yes, but happier are those who...' [Alf, TH]. Jesus was pointing out that there was something more important than being his mother [NIC, TG]. 'Blessed' did apply to Mary's being the mother of Jesus, but much higher is the blessedness resulting from the spiritual connection with Jesus [Lns, NIC]. Mary's blessedness was not so much in being Jesus' mother as in her keeping the word Jesus had spoken to her [Alf]. The woman's statement was inadequate because she had missed the main point [ICC] and Jesus here corrected her statement [Alf, EGT, NICNT, NIGTC].

DISCOURSE UNIT: 11:29–36 [NASB]. The topic is the sign of Jonah.

DISCOURSE UNIT: 11:29–32 [AB, BECNT, NAC, NIGTC, TNTC, WBC; CEV, HCSB, NCV, NET, NIV, NLT, NRSV, TEV]. The topic is a sign from God [CEV], the sign of Jonah [AB, NAC, NIGTC, TNTC; HCSB, NET, NIV, NLT, NRSV], no sign except Jonah [BECNT, WBC], the demand for a miracle [TEV], the people want a miracle [NCV].

11:29 And (as) the crowds were-gathering-even-more[a] he-began[b] to-say, This generation[c] is an-evil generation. It-is-seeking a-sign[d] and a-sign will-not -be-given to-it except the sign of-Jonah. **11:30** Because just-as Jonah became a-sign to-the Ninevites, so will-be also the Son of-Man[e] to-this generation.

TEXT—In 11:29, instead of γενεὰ πονηρά '(an) evil generation', some manuscripts read πονηρά 'evil'. GNT does not mention this variant. Πονηρά 'evil' is read by KJV.

TEXT—In 11:29, following Ἰωνᾶ 'Jonah', some manuscripts add τοῦ προφήτου 'the prophet'. GNT does not mention this variant. Τοῦ προφήτου 'the prophet' is read by KJV.

LEXICON—a. pres. pass. participle of ἐπαθροίζομαι, ἐπαθροίζω (LN **15.132**) (BAGD p. 281): 'to gather even more' [BAGD], 'to gather more' [**LN**], 'to gather' [Arn], 'to increase' [NTC; HCSB, NIV, NRSV], 'to be increasing' [BECNT; NASB, NET], 'to grow larger' [NCV], 'to gather around' [CEV, GW], 'to crowd around' [TEV], 'to swarm round' [REB], 'to throng about' [Lns], 'to collect' [LN], 'to be gathered thick together' [KJV], 'to press in' [NLT], 'to press closely about' [AB, WBC].

b. aorist mid. indic. of ἄρχομαι (LN 68.1): 'to begin, to commence' [LN]. The phrase 'he began to say' [BECNT, Lns, WBC; KJV, NASB, NET, NRSV] is also translated 'he began saying' [HCSB], 'Jesus started to say'

[AB], 'he went on to say' [REB, TEV], 'he/Jesus said' [Arn, NTC; CEV, GW, NCV, NIV, NLT].
  c. γενεά (LN 11.4) (BAGD 2. p. 154): 'generation'. The phrase 'an evil generation' [AB, Arn, BECNT, WBC; HCSB, KJV, NLT, NRSV] is also translated 'a wicked generation' [Lns, NTC; NASB, NET, NIV, REB], 'the people living today are evil' [GW], 'the people who live today are evil' [NCV], 'how evil are the people of this day' [TEV], 'you people of today are evil' [CEV]. See this noun at 1:48, 50; 7:31; 9:41; 11:50; 16:8; 17:25; 21:32.
  d. σημεῖον (LN 33.477) (BAGD 2.a. p. 748): 'sign'. The phrase 'the sign of Jonah' [AB, Arn, BECNT, Lns, NTC, WBC; all versions except CEV, TEV] is also translated 'what happened to Jonah is the only sign' [CEV], 'the miracle of Jonah' [TEV]. It means the sign like the one that Jonah showed or produced [TH]. It means the sign that consists in Jonah [NIC, NIGTC, NTC, TNTC]. See this word at 11:16; 23:8.
  e. υἱὸς τοῦ ἀνθρώπου 'Son of Man'. This title for Christ occurs at 5:24; 6:5, 22; 7:34; 9:22, 26, 44; 11:30; 12:8, 40; 17:22, 24, 26; 18:8, 31; 19:10; 21:27, 36; 22:22, 48, 69; 24:7. See the discussions of this title at 5:24, 6:5, and 9:22.

QUESTION—What is meant by the crowds gathering even more?
  1. It means that there was an increase in the numbers present in the crowd [BECNT, Gdt, MGC, My, NIC, NTC; HCSB, NASB, NCV, NET, NIV, NRSV]: the crowd was growing larger. He began this part of his teaching while the crowd was still assembling in greater numbers [My]. The people continued to gather in order to see the healed person (11:14) and listen to the conversations [NIC].
  2. It means that the people were crowding together without implying that there were more people [AB, Lns, TH, WBC; CEV, GW, KJV, NLT, REB, TEV]: the people were crowding together around Jesus. The people were anxious to hear Jesus and they surrounded him in a compact body [Lns].

QUESTION—Why was this generation called an evil generation?
  They were evil in not only committing open crimes, but in rejecting God's word, his grace, and the Savior he sent [Lns]. The Jews of that time were spiritually corrupt [NIC]. The entire generation had lost contact with God [Lns]. The crowds sympathized with the religious characteristics of its leaders [EGT]. That they were evil was shown because they were seeking a sign [AB, BECNT, MGC, NAC, NIBC, NICNT, NIGTC, NTC, TNTC, WBC]. In spite of many signs already given, they still sought for a sign [BECNT]. When they requested a sign, it showed their unbelief and unwillingness to become fully persuaded [NIBC]. Their demand for a sign was insulting and impudent, and also hypocritical because they thought they were asking for something Jesus could not do [NTC]. Their demand for a sign showed their refusal to hear and obey the word of God announced by Jesus [NIGTC].

QUESTION—What kind of a sign did they demand?

They dismissed the exorcisms as being the work of Satan and wanted something that could not be doubted [NIGTC]. Their demand indicated that they thought all that Jesus had done was insufficient and wanted a sign in the heavens [AB, Lns] that affected the movements of the heavenly bodies, or the appearance of angel armies [Lns]. They wanted something from heaven, such as God's voice or a pillar of fire [ICC].

QUESTION—What would be Jesus' sign to his generation that was like Jonah's sign to the Ninevites?

1. The sign would be his preaching [AB, Alf, BECNT, BNTC, MGC, Su, TG, TH, WBC; NET]. The sign that Jesus was the Messiah would be like the sign of Jonah and it is specified in 11:32 that the sign of Jonah was his preaching [BNTC, TH]. The Ninevites did not witness Jonah's adventure with the great fish, but only heard his preaching [BNTC]. Jesus had said that he was not going to give them a miraculous sign, so with reference to Jonah's preaching in 11:32, Jesus must have meant that they both preached the message of repentance [MGC]. Both Jonah and Jesus proclaimed God's message with a demand for repentance in order to escape God's judgment [Su]. The future tense 'will be' is a reference to Jesus' ministry in progress [BECNT].

2. The sign would be his resurrection [Arn, EGT, Gdt, ICC, Lns, My, NAC, NIBC, NIC, NIGTC, NTC, Rb, TNTC]. The sign was not preaching, since Jesus had already been preaching many times and the sign was to be given in the future [EGT, Gdt, ICC, NIC, TNTC]. Jonah and Jesus were themselves the signs, not their words [NTC, TNTC]. The outstanding feature in the OT story of Jonah that would immediately be thought of was his miraculous deliverance from death [NIGTC]. Jesus was referring to his future resurrection with Jonah as a type of the future burial and resurrection of Christ [ICC, NTC]. Jonah was miraculously saved from the belly of the huge fish as proof that he was sent from God and Jesus' resurrection in the future will prove to his generation that he was sent by God to be the Messiah [NIC]. Matthew has made the sign explicit: 'As Jonah was three days and three nights in the belly of the huge fish, so the Son of Man will be three days and three nights in the heart of the earth' (Matt. 12:40 NIV) [Lns, NIC, TNTC].

11:31 (The) queen[a] of-(the) south will-rise-up[b] at the judgment[c] with the men/people[d] of-this generation and she-will-condemn[e] them, because she-came from the ends[f] of-the earth to-hear the wisdom of-Solomon, and behold (someone/something) greater (than) Solomon (is) here.

LEXICON—a. βασίλισσα (LN 37.68) (BAGD p. 137): 'queen' [BAGD, LN]. The phrase 'the queen of the south' [AB, Arn, BECNT, NTC, WBC; all versions except GW, NLT, TEV] is also translated 'a queen of the south' [Lns], 'the queen from the south' [GW], 'the queen of Sheba' [NLT, TEV]. This refers to the queen of Sheba (1 Kings 10:1–13) [AB, Arn,

BECNT, EGT, MGC, NAC, NICNT, NIGTC, Su, TG, TH, TNTC, WBC]. The south refers to southern Arabia [AB, ICC, TNTC, WBC], more specifically it refers to Yemen [Arn, ICC, NIGTC, TNTC].
- b. fut. pass. indic. of ἐγείρω (LN 56.8) (BAGD 2.e. p. 215): 'to rise up' [HCSB, KJV, NASB, NET], 'to rise' [Arn, WBC; NIV, NRSV], 'to arise' [AB, BECNT, Lns, NTC], 'to rise up (against)' [NLT] 'to stand up' [GW, NCV], 'to stand there' [CEV], 'to stand up (and accuse)' [TEV], 'to appear' [BAGD], 'to appear in court' [REB], 'to bring charges, to accuse formally' [LN].
- c. κρίσις (LN 30.110) (BAGD 1.a.α. p. 452): 'the judgment' [AB, Arn, BAGD, BECNT, LN, Lns, NTC, WBC; HCSB, KJV, NASB, NET, NIV, NRSV], 'the time of judgment' [GW], 'when the judgment comes' [CEV], 'the Judgment Day' [NCV, TEV], 'on judgment day' [NLT], 'when (the men of this generation) are on trial' [REB]. This is the eschatological judgment as in 10:13–15 [WBC], the final judgment day [AB, ICC, NAC, NIC, NTC, Su, TNTC].
- d. ἀνήρ (LN 9.1): 'people' [LN; NCV, NET, NRSV], 'human being' [LN], 'man' [AB, Arn, BECNT, Lns, NTC, WBC; GW, HCSB, KJV, NASB, NIV], 'you' [CEV], not explicit [NLT]. This noun usually refers to males, but here it is used in a generic sense of people [AB, NAC; NCV, NET, NRSV]. She was a woman while they were men in the days of male supremacy [Gdt, Lns, TNTC, WBC].
- e. fut. act. indic. of κατακρίνω (LN 56.31) (BAGD p. 412): 'to condemn' [AB, Arn, BAGD, BECNT, LN, Lns, NTC, WBC; all versions except NCV, REB, TEV], 'to accuse' [TEV], 'to ensure their condemnation' [REB], 'to show they are guilty' [NCV].
- f. ἔρας (LN 80.6) (BAGD 1. p. 644): 'end, limit' [BAGD, LN]. The phrase 'the ends of the earth' [AB, Arn, BECNT, Lns, NTC, WBC; GW, HCSB, NASB, NET, NIV, NRSV, REB] is also translated 'the utmost parts of the earth' [KJV], 'a distant land' [NLT], 'far away' [NCV], 'a long way' [CEV], 'all the way from her country' [TEV]. Her kingdom was in the southern part of Arabia, a thousand miles away [Lns], near the limits of the known world at that time [ICC, Lns, NIC, TH]. This is a form of hyperbole [WBC].

QUESTION—What is the meaning of 'will rise up at the judgment with the men of this generation' and the similar phrase 'will stand up at the judgment with this generation' in 11:32?
- 1. This refers to standing before the judgment bar of God and does not explicitly refer to the act of arising from death [Lns, NIGTC, TG, TH; CEV, GW, NCV, NLT, REB, TEV]. The queen will appear in court [TH]. The queen will be standing side by side with the Jews when they appear before God [Lns]. The queen will act as a witness against these men [TG]. The sense of 'accuse' connects better with the following words 'at the judgment', but of course this presupposes the resurrection and the last judgment [NIGTC].

2. This describes the event of rising up from death, at which time all will appear at the place of the final judgment [Arn, Gdt, NAC, NICNT, Su]. It refers to the resurrection and the day of judgment [Su]. The queen will be raised from the grave and stand at God's judgment bar together with all of Jesus' contemporaries [Arn]. God will raise the queen from death at the same time he raises the Jews [Gdt].

QUESTION—How will the queen of the south condemn the men of this generation?

The queen is not the one who judges the men, but she will accuse them or show that they are guilty [TH]. Here 'condemn' means to bring a charge rather than to pronounce judgment [NIGTC]. The queen will be their accuser [WBC]. The queen's case will serve as a condemnation in the case of the Jews [Lns]. The men will be condemned by such an example of the queen's actions [TNTC]. The queen's good example will cause the wickedness of the men to be more evident and worthy of condemnation [Arn, NIC]. The contrast between the response of the queen and the response of the men of this generation will put them on opposite sides at the judgment when the queen is vindicated and the men will be condemned [NICNT].

QUESTION—What relationship is indicated by ὅτι 'because'?

This indicates the reason that the men of this generation will be condemned [MGC]. The queen went to hear the wisdom of Solomon in spite of the danger, hardships, and expense of travel, but the men of this generation ignored Jesus, who was greater than Solomon and was right among them [Lns]. The queen responded to the wisdom of Solomon, and the Jews should have responded to Jesus who is the bearer of greater wisdom from God [BECNT]. Since some people of the heathen world responded to the message God's messengers, the conduct of the enlightened Jews will be condemned because of their rejection of Jesus and his message [Su].

QUESTION—What is meant by the use of the neuter adjective πλεῖον 'greater' both here and in 11:32?

1. This is an indirect reference to the person of Jesus himself [TH; GW, NCV, NIV, NLT]: *someone* greater than Solomon is here. Here this word refers to a person [TH].
2. The neuter does not refer directly to the person Jesus but to something concerning Jesus [AB, BECNT, ICC, Lns, NAC, NIGTC, NTC, TG, TNTC, WBC; CEV, NASB, NET, NRSV, REB, TEV]: *something* greater than Solomon is here. Instead of comparing Solomon and Jesus, it is a comparison between the wisdom of Solomon, and the greater wisdom of Jesus [NAC]. It is used of the quality of wisdom spoken by Solomon and by Jesus [NIGTC, TG]. Jesus' message was greater than what Solomon offered [BECNT; NET], and the time Jesus represented was greater than Solomon's [BECNT]. It means that God's actions in the coming of Jesus and the inauguration of the kingdom were mightier than what God had done in Solomon [TNTC]. What God offered in Solomon did not compare

with what he offered in Jesus [WBC]. The neuter stands for all that is embodied in Jesus [Lns].

11:32 **The Ninevite men will-stand-up^a at the judgment with this generation and will-condemn it, because they repented^b at the preaching of-Jonah, and behold (something, someone) greater (than) Jonah (is) here.**

LEXICON—a. fut. mid. indic. of ἀνίστημι (LN 17.7) (BAGD 2.c. p. 70): 'to stand up' [AB, BAGD, LN, Lns, NTC; GW, NASB, NCV, NET, NIV], 'to stand up (and accuse)' [TEV], 'to rise' [Arn, WBC], 'to rise up' [BAGD, BECNT, LN; HCSB, KJV, NRSV], 'to rise up (against)' [NLT], 'to stand there' [CEV], 'to appear in court' [REB]. This verb is synonymous with ἐγείρω 'to rise up' in 11:31 [NIGTC] and like that verb it can mean either to appear in court or to arise from the dead [TH].
  b. aorist act. indic. of μετανοέω (LN 41.52) (BAGD p. 512): 'to repent'. See translations of this word at 10:13. This word also occurs at 13:3, 5; 15:7, 10; 16:30; 17:3, 4.

DISCOURSE UNIT: 11:33–36 [AB, BECNT, NAC, NIGTC, TNTC, WBC; CEV, GW, HCSB, NCV, NET, NIV, NLT, NRSV, TEV]. The topic is light [CEV], internal light [NET], the light of the body [NRSV, TEV], the lamp of the body [HCSB, NIV], sayings about light [AB, NAC], two sayings about light [BECNT], Jesus talks about light [GW], light and darkness [NIGTC], make good use of the lamps [WBC], receiving the light [NLT], the light that is in you [TNTC], be a light for the world [NCV].

11:33 **No-one having-lit a-lamp^a puts (it) in a-hidden-place^b nor under the bowl,^c but on the lampstand,^d in-order-that the (ones who) enter may-see the light.^e**

TEXT—Some manuscripts omit οὐδὲ ὑπὸ τὸν μόδιον 'nor under the bowl'. GNT reads οὐδὲ ὑπὸ τὸν μόδιον 'nor under the bowl' with a C decision and places this phrase in brackets in the text, indicating that the Committee had difficulty making the decision. It is omitted by WBC; NRSV, REB.
LEXICON—a. λύχνος (LN 6.104) (BAGD 1. p. 483): 'lamp'. See translations of this word at 8:16 and 12:35.
  b. κρύπτη (LN **28.78**) (BAGD p. 454): 'hidden place' [Arn, LN; NET], 'secret place' [**LN**; KJV, NCV], 'a dark and hidden place' [BAGD], 'a place where it will be hidden' [NIV], 'cellar' [BAGD, BECNT, Lns, NTC; HCSB, NASB, NRSV, REB], 'crypt' [WBC], 'crevice' [AB]. The phrase 'puts it in a hidden place' is translated 'and hides it' [CEV, GW, NLT, TEV]. This is probably some kind of recess in the wall [WBC]. The noun means a dark and hidden place [BAGD, BECNT, NIGTC] and in a house this would describe the cellar [BECNT]. A cellar might be found in a wealthy Greek house, but not in a one-roomed Galilean cottage, so this means a hidden location [NIGTC].
  c. μόδιος (LN 6.151) (BAGD p. 525): 'bowl' [NCV, NIV, TEV], 'basket' [LN; GW, HCSB, NASB, NET, NLT], 'box' [LN], 'clay pot' [CEV].

'peck-measure' [BAGD, Lns, NTC], 'bushel' [AB, Arn, BECNT; KJV]. It is a container with a capacity of about two gallons of dry ingredients [LN, TG]. With the article, τὸν μόδιον 'the bushel' means the one in the room [Gdt, ICC].
    d. λυχνία (LN 6.105) (BAGD p. 483): 'lampstand'. See translations of this word at 8:16.
    e. φῶς (LN 14.36) (BAGD 1.a. p. 871): 'light'. See translations of this word at 8.16.

QUESTION—In the illustration, why would someone want to see the light?

Most translations speak of seeing the light and this is important for the application when the light represents Jesus or his teaching. Some, however, take it to mean that the people entering the room would use the light to see [NCV], 'it is put on a lampstand to give light to all who enter the room' [NLT].

QUESTION—What is the application of this illustration?

This has a different application from the similar saying in 8:16 [BECNT, NIGTC, NTC, WBC]. Instead of the application that they were to be witnesses found in 8:16, here it means that they were to let the light of Jesus shine into their own hearts [NTC]. The lamp is a metaphor for Jesus [NAC]. The light represents Jesus' message [BECNT]. It represents Jesus and his preaching [AB, NIBC, NIGTC]. God has given light in the person of Jesus and it is not hidden [MGC, NIGTC] and therefore a sign would not be needed for confirmation [ICC, NIGTC]. It was not because Jesus wished to hide the light of his self-revelation that he refused to give a sign, rather, he refused because the Jews' spiritual vision was obscured by their unbelief when they demanded a sign [NIC]. People are responsible if they do not allow the light of Jesus' ministry to enter the whole of their lives [WBC].

11:34 **The lamp[a] of-the body[b] is your eye. When your eye is sound,[c] then your entire body is full-of-light.[d] But when it-is diseased,[e] then your body (is) full-of-darkness.[f]** **11:35** **Therefore see-to-it (that) the light in you is not darkness.**

TEXT—In 11:34, instead of ὁ ὀφθαλμός σου 'your eye', some manuscripts read ὁ ὀφθαλμός 'the eye'. GNT does not mention this variant. Ὁ ὀφθαλμός 'the eye' is read by KJV.

TEXT—In 11:34, following ὅταν 'when', some manuscripts add οὖν 'therefore'. GNT does not mention this variant. Οὖν 'therefore' is read by KJV.

LEXICON—a. λύχνος (LN 6.104) (BAGD 1. p. 483): 'lamp'. See translations of this word at 8:16 and 12:35.
    b. σῶμα (LN 8.1) (BAGD 1.b. p. 799): 'body' [BAGD, LN]. The phrase 'the lamp of the body' [AB, Arn, Lns, WBC; HCSB] is also translated 'the lamp of your body' [BECNT; GW, NASB, NET, NIV, NRSV, REB], 'the/a lamp for your body' [CEV, NLT], 'like a lamp for the body' [TEV],

'your body's lamp' [NTC], 'the light of the body' [KJV], 'a light for the body' [NCV].

c. ἁπλοῦς (LN **23.132**) (BAGD p. 86): 'sound' [BAGD, **LN**, NTC; REB, TEV], 'healthy' [BAGD, BECNT, LN; NET, NRSV], 'clear' [BAGD, WBC; NASB], 'clear-sighted' [AB], 'unclouded' [GW], 'good' [CEV, HCSB, NCV, NIV], 'pure' [NLT], 'single' [Arn, Lns; KJV]. The noun 'single' means in moral contexts 'sincerity', 'wholeheartedness', 'guilelessness', and 'generosity', but in connection with eyes it means 'clear', 'sound', or 'healthy' [WBC].

d. φωτεινός (LN 14.51) (BAGD p. 872): 'full of light' [BAGD, BECNT, LN, Lns; GW, HCSB, KJV, NASB, NCV, NET, NIV, NRSV, TEV], 'light' [Arn], 'illuminated' [BAGD, NTC, WBC], 'well lighted' [LN]. The phrase 'your body is full of light' is translated 'you have light for your whole body' [REB], 'your whole body has light' [AB], 'you have all the light you need' [CEV], 'lets sunshine into your soul' [NLT].

e. πονηρός (LN 23.149) (BAGD 1.a.α. p. 690): 'diseased' [WBC; NET], 'sick' [BAGD, LN], 'not healthy' [BECNT; NRSV], 'ill' [Arn], 'no good' [TEV], 'in poor condition' [NTC], 'bad' [AB; CEV, HCSB, NASB, NIV, REB], 'evil' [GW, KJV, NCV, NLT], 'wicked' [Lns]. This noun usually means 'evil' or 'wicked', but in connection with eyes it means 'diseased' [WBC].

f. σκοτεινός (LN 14.54) (BAGD p. 757): 'full of darkness' [Lns; GW, HCSB, KJV, NASB, NCV, NET, NIV, NRSV], 'dark' [Arn, LN], 'darkened' [WBC], 'in darkness' [AB, BECNT, LN; REB, TEV], 'darkness' [BAGD]. The phrase 'your body is full of darkness' is translated 'your body also will be darkened' [NTC], 'everything is dark' [CEV], 'plunges you into darkness' [NLT].

QUESTION—What is the significance of addressing the crowd with the singular forms of 'you' and 'your'?

Jesus had been using the plural forms in 11:19–20, but now he addresses each individually so that each will consider his own heart [NIC, NTC]. The singular forms refer to anyone in general [TG, TH].

QUESTION—In what way is the eye a lamp of the body?

One's eye is the organ by which one perceives light [AB, BECNT, NIC, NIGTC, TNTC] and thus the eye acts as a lamp to the interior of the body [NIGTC]. The singular form, 'your eye', signifies both eyes [NTC, TG] and is translated 'your eyes' [CEV, TEV]. A healthy eye enables one to make use of the light that comes to it from the outside, but a diseased eye does not make use of it [NIC]. A person with good eyesight can see the light and he may be said to be illumined within, while a person with bad sight cannot see light and so is dark within [AB]. It implies that if a person has good eyes, he will see the light offered by Jesus, but someone with an eye that is not sound will not be able to see that light [BECNT]. The descriptions of the eyes are both medical (either sick or healthy) and ethical (either selfish, covetous, and rebellious or generous and sincere) and both types of meanings are involved

[NICNT]. The eye is a metaphor for one's moral disposition [NIBC]. A diseased eye still has sight, so this is speaking of spiritual conditions and the one eye in the illustration refers to the heart that draws the whole body into the light to follow Jesus or into the dark to oppose Jesus [Lns]. When a person's inner disposition is illumined, he will truly know God and experience peace of mind, but when his heart is not right with God, he will experience the darkness of stubborn unbelief [NTC]. In 11:33 the lamp is a metaphor for Jesus, but here it is a metaphor for a person's reaction to Jesus [NAC].

QUESTION—What is meant by the application 'see to it that the light in you is not darkness'?

1. This is a paradox since light cannot be darkness at the same time [Lns, NAC, TG]. A person should consider whether what he thinks is light could in fact be darkness [NIBC, NIGTC, NTC]. They must make sure that what directs their lives is really the true light [NAC]. It means to make sure that they have light in themselves and not darkness [TG]. It is translated 'be sure that your light isn't darkness' [CEV], 'make sure that the light you think you have is not really darkness' [NLT].
2. The invitation is to check whether any light is getting in [WBC]. They were to make sure that what entered into them was light and not darkness, and in reference to spiritual matters Jesus offered them light and the Jewish leaders were offering them darkness [Su]. If they do not believe in Jesus, the light of the world, then their unbelief will make them spiritually blind [MGC]. A person's inner attitude must not hinder the light of Christ from shining into his life [NIC].
3. This is a caution to make sure that the light in them does not become darkness [EGT]. This is translated 'be careful not to let the light in you become darkness' [NCV].

11:36 Therefore if your whole body (is) full-of-light, not having any part[a] dark, it-will-be wholly full-of-light as when the lamp shines-on you with (its) light.

LEXICON—a. μέρος (LN 63.14) (BAGD 1.a. p. 505): 'part' [BAGD, LN]. The clause 'not having any part dark' is translated 'having no portion that is dark' [BECNT], 'and no part of it dark' [NIV], 'having no part dark' [Arn; KJV], 'not having any part full of darkness' [Lns], 'with no part in the dark' [NET], 'with no part of it in darkness' [AB; HCSB, NRSV, TEV], 'no part of it being darkened' [NTC], 'without any part darkened' [WBC], 'with no dark part in it' [NASB], 'and not darkness' [GW], 'and none of it is dark' [NCV], 'nothing is dark' [CEV], 'with no trace of darkness' [REB], 'with no dark corners' [NLT]. This clause emphasizes 'whole' in the first clause, 'your whole body is full of light' [TH].

QUESTION—What relationship is indicated by οὖν 'therefore'?

This indicates a conclusion to 11:34 where it says 'when your eye is sound, then your entire body is full of light' [Alf, Crd, Gdt, ICC, Lns, NIGTC,

NTC, TH; NET]: therefore, if it be true that your body is full of light, then it will be wholly full of light. The emphasis here is on ὅλον 'whole': if your *whole* body is full of light, it will be *wholly* full of light [Gdt, ICC, My], and therefore such a person will not need a sign from heaven to recognize the truth [ICC]. The result is emphasized by giving a comparison: your entire person will be full of light, in fact it will be as bright as when a lamp is shining on you with its full brilliance [Alf, Gdt, Lns, NTC]. The main point is the reference to the light from the outside: when the body is full of light, then the body will also enjoy the light from the outside [Arn, TH]. At first glance it appears to be a mere platitude that repeats 11:34 [Crd, EGT, NTC], but probably it is a conclusion taking in both 11:33 and 34: 'if the heart is truly receptive of light, it will receive light from the true light, that is from Christ' [AB, BECNT, Crd, Lns, MGC, WBC]. This describes a body that is totally lit and refers to a spiritually healthy person who takes in the light offered by Jesus so as to shine brightly and give off light, reflecting the rays of God's truth by the way he lives [BECNT]. This verse also presents the alternative to 11:35 [NIGTC].

DISCOURSE UNIT: 11:37–54 [AB, BECNT, NAC, NICNT, NIGTC, WBC; CEV, GW, HCSB, NASB, NET, NIV, NLT, NRSV, TEV]. The topic is a denunciation of the Pharisees and Scribes [AB, BECNT, NAC, WBC], Jesus denounces Pharisees and lawyers [NRSV], six woes [NIV], woes upon the Pharisees [NASB], rebuking the Pharisees and Experts in the Law [NET], Jesus condemns the Pharisees and teachers of the Law of Moses [CEV], Jesus criticizes the religious leaders [GW, NLT], Jesus accuses the Pharisees and the teachers of the law [TEV], Jesus responds to the Pharisees and teachers [NICNT], the hypocrisy of the Pharisees and scribes [NIGTC], religious hypocrisy denounced [HCSB].

DISCOURSE UNIT: 11:37–52 [Su]. The topic is genuine versus spurious religious practice.

DISCOURSE UNIT: 11:37–44 [NCV]. The topic is Jesus' accusation of the Pharisees.

DISCOURSE UNIT: 11:37–41 [TNTC]. The topic is true cleansing.

11:37 And while/after[a] he-spoke a-Pharisee asks him that he-have-a-meal[b] with him. And having-entered he-reclined[c] (at a table). **11:38** And the Pharisee was-amazed[d] having-seen that he-did- not -wash[e] first before the meal.

TEXT—In 11:37, instead of Φαρισαῖος '(a) Pharisee', some manuscripts read Φαρισαῖός τις '(a) certain Pharisee'. GNT does not mention this variant. Φαρισαῖός τις '(a) certain Pharisee' is read by KJV.

LEXICON—a. ἐν (LN 67.136): 'while' [NRSV], 'during, in the course of' [LN], 'as' [Lns; HCSB, KJV, NET, NLT], 'after' [BECNT, NTC; GW, NCV]. The phrase ἐν τῷ λαλῆσαι 'in the to speak' is translated 'when

528   LUKE 11:37–38

(Jesus) finished speaking' [CEV, TEV], 'when (Jesus) had finished speaking' [WBC; NIV, REB], 'when he spoke' [Arn], 'when he had spoken' [NASB], 'when he had said this' [AB].
b. aorist act. subj. of ἀριστάω (LN **23.20**) (BAGD 2. p. 106): 'to have a meal' [**LN**; NCV], 'to eat a meal' [BAGD, LN], 'to eat a morning meal' [Lns], 'to have breakfast' [Arn], 'to have lunch' [GW, NASB], 'to eat' [NTC; NCV, NIV, TEV], 'to dine' [AB, BECNT, WBC; HCSB, KJV, NRSV]. The phrase 'that he have a meal' is translated 'for a meal' [CEV, NLT], '(invited him) to a meal' [REB].
c. aorist act. indic. of ἀναπίπτω (LN 17.23) (BAGD 1. p. 59): 'to recline' [BECNT, LN, Lns], 'to recline at the table' [AB, Arn, NTC; HCSB, NASB, NIV], 'to sit at the table' [NCV], 'to eat a meal' [BAGD], 'to sit down' [WBC; REB], 'to sit down to eat' [LN; CEV, TEV], 'to sit down to meat' [KJV], 'to take one's place at the table' [NET, NLT, NRSV], not explicit [GW].
d. aorist act. indic. of θαυμάζω (LN 25.213) (BAGD 1.b.γ. p. 352): 'to be amazed'. See translations of this word at 1:21 and 4:22. The Pharisee must have expressed his amazement in some manner, perhaps by words, because Jesus addressed the Pharisees about this matter [Alf]. Jesus was answering the Pharisee's thoughts [AB, BECNT, ICC, My, NTC]. This word also occurs at 1:63; 2:18, 33; 7:9; 8:25; 11:14; 20:26; 24:12, 41.
e. aorist pass. indic. of βαπτίζω (LN 53.31) (BAGD 1. p. 131): 'to wash' [AB, BAGD, BECNT, LN; GW, KJV, NIV, NRSV, REB, TEV], 'to get washed' [WBC], 'to wash his hands' [CEV, NCV, NET], 'to purify' [LN], 'to ceremonially wash' [NTC; NASB], 'to perform the ritual washing' [Arn; HCSB], 'to perform the ceremonial washing required by Jewish custom' [NLT].

QUESTION—When did the Pharisee ask Jesus to have a meal with him?
1. This was done while Jesus was speaking [EGT, Lns, Rb; HCSB, KJV, NET, NLT, NRSV]: *while* Jesus was speaking, a Pharisee asked him to dinner. The aorist infinitive 'to speak' indicates the fact of speaking but not the time and here the setting indicates that it was as Jesus was speaking [Lns].
2. This was done after Jesus had finished speaking [AB, BECNT, Crd, ICC, MGC, NAC, NIC, NIGTC, NTC, TG, TH, TNTC, WBC; CEV, GW, NASB, NCV, NIV, REB, TEV]: *after* Jesus was finished speaking, a Pharisee asked him to dinner. It is natural to suppose that the Pharisee would wait until Jesus had finished speaking [NTC, TNTC]. This event was closely linked to the previous one [BECNT, NAC, NIC, NIGTC]. Or, there may have been a considerable interval between 11:36 and 11:37 [ICC].

QUESTION—What kind of a meal was this?
It may have been a light meal in the morning [Alf, EGT, Gdt, ICC, MGC, NIGTC], perhaps breakfast [Arn, EGT, My], a morning meal [Alf], lunch [NIC, NTC, TH, TNTC; GW, NASB], a noonday meal [AB]. Perhaps it was

the main meal of the day [TG]. Reclining was usual for Sabbath meals [NAC]. It was not a breakfast, but a meal around noon after returning from synagogue prayers [Lns]. It was a Sabbath meal [NIGTC]. Or, it was not a Sabbath meal [BECNT]. Others had been invited also, as indicated by the following verses [BECNT, Gdt, Lns, NTC] and they were probably Jewish leaders [BECNT]. The disciples were not present [Lns].

QUESTION—What was involved in washing before a meal?

This washing did not have the purpose of removing dirt, but had a ceremonial purpose of washing off contamination from touching some religiously unclean object [NICNT, Su, TNTC]. Dipping the hands in water was both a hygienic matter to get rid of dirt and a ritual to get rid of religious defilement caused by contact with Gentiles or with ritually unclean objects [TG]. The ritual was not demanded by the Law of Moses, but it was a rule decreed by the Pharisees [Arn, ICC, Lns, MGC, NAC, NIGTC, NTC, Su]. This ceremonial ritual was especially needed in the Pharisee's estimation since Jesus had been in contact with the crowd and had been casting out demons [AB, ICC]. Before eating, a Pharisee would have water poured over his hands [NTC, TNTC] to remove the defilement that had occurred by his contact with the sinful world [TNTC]. The Pharisees dipped their hands in water before eating and sometimes between courses for ceremonial purification [Rb]. The amount of water and the manner of washing were prescribed in detail in the regulations of the Pharisees [TNTC]. Either Jesus had not washed before he reclined at the table or had refused the water servants offered him at the table in protest against the burdens the Pharisees bound on men [ICC]. Jesus was snubbing his host by failing to wash before the meal [NICNT]. The Pharisee was amazed because he assumed that Jesus would have thought this practice to be binding [Lns]. His amazement implies criticism [BECNT].

11:39 And the Lord said to him, Now[a] you Pharisees clean[b] the outside of-the cup and the dish, but the inside of-you is-full of-greed[c] and wickedness.[d] **11:40** Fools,[e] (did) not (the one) having–made the outside also make the inside?

LEXICON—a. νῦν (LN 67.38): 'now' [BECNT, LN, Lns, WBC; KJV, NASB, NET, NRSV], 'now then' [NTC; HCSB, NIV, TEV], not explicit [AB; CEV, GW, NCV, NLT, REB].
 b. pres. act. indic. of καθαρίζω (LN 79.49) (BAGD 1.a. p. 387): 'to clean' [AB, LN, Lns, NTC, WBC; all versions except KJV], 'to make clean' [BAGD, LN; KJV], 'to cleanse' [Arn, BAGD, BECNT, LN], 'to purify' [BAGD].
 c. ἁρπαγή (LN **25.24**) (BAGD 3. p. 108): 'greed' [AB, BAGD, WBC; GW, HCSB, NCV, NET, NIV, NLT, NRSV, REB], 'violence' [BAGD; TEV], 'violent greed' [**LN**], 'rapacity' [WBC], 'pillage' [Lns], 'extortion' [Arn, BECNT, NTC], 'robbery' [NASB], 'ravening' [KJV]. The phrase 'to be full of greed' is translated 'to be greedy' [CEV]. This word refers to

robbery or to the abstract meanings of greed or rapacity [BECNT, NIGTC]. It describes a person who is governed by a desire to plunder [NICNT], a desire for robbery or dishonesty [Su].
  d. πονηρία (LN 88.108) (BAGD p. 690): 'wickedness' [AB, Arn, BAGD, BECNT, LN, Lns, NTC; KJV, NASB, NET, NIV, NLT, NRSV, REB], 'evil' [WBC; GW, HCSB, NCV, TEV], 'maliciousness, sinfulness' [BAGD]. The phrase 'to be full of wickedness' is translated 'to be evil' [CEV]. This is the inner corruption that is the source of their greed [Gdt]. To be full of violence and evil means to have ideas of violence and evil in their hearts [TG]. This describes their moral corruption [NICNT].
  e. ἄφρων (LN 32.52) (BAGD p. 127): 'foolish' [BAGD, LN], 'ignorant' [BAGD], 'senseless, unwise' [LN]. As a substantive, it is translated 'fools' [Arn, BECNT, Lns, WBC; HCSB, NLT, TEV], 'foolish people' [AB], 'you fools' [NTC; CEV, GW, KJV, NET, NRSV, REB], 'you foolish ones' [NASB], 'you foolish people' [NCV, NIV]. They were responsible for their ignorance and the word is a strong reproach [TH]. They were foolish in cleaning the outside of the dishes and not the inside [MGC]. They had a false piety [NIGTC]. They were foolish to think that God would accept their external cleanliness when they were internally corrupt [Su].

QUESTION—What is the meaning of νῦν 'now' in 11:39?
  1. It has a temporal meaning [Alf, ICC, My, Rb]. This refers to their present conduct [Alf]. It was not so in past times, but this is a fact now [ICC]. Or, they are doing now what they had formerly done [Rb].
  2. It has a non-temporal meaning [Arn, EGT, Gdt, Lns, NIGTC, NTC, TH; NIV, TEV]. It means 'Well now, there you are, you Pharisees, I have you in the act' [Gdt]. It has the sense of 'indeed' and serves to emphasize what follows [TH].

QUESTION—In what sense did the Pharisees clean the cup and the dish?
  'Clean' is used of making something physically clean [BAGD, Gdt]. However, physically cleansing the vessels was involved in making them ceremonially clean [BECNT, NIC, NIGTC, TG]. The Pharisees were so careful in their ceremonial cleansing that they even cleaned the outsides of their cups and dishes to avoid ceremonial uncleanness [NIC].

QUESTION—How are the outsides of cups and dishes connected with the insides of the Pharisees?
  The stated *image* of the metaphor is about cleansing only the outsides of cups and dishes and the unstated *topic* is the external ritual cleansing of the Pharisees. But instead of the image continuing with a description of the insides of the cups and dishes being filthy, the image is left unstated and the *topic* is stated, that the hearts of the Pharisees are full of greed and wickedness [Alf, BECNT, Gdt, Lns, MGC, NIGTC]. This does not imply that the usual Pharisaic ritual only involved washing the outsides of their vessels, rather it implies that only cleansing the outside of a man is as foolish as only cleansing the outside of a dirty vessel [NIGTC]. By abandoning the

metaphor, a contrast is made between the outsides of the cup and dish with the inward nature of the Pharisees [ICC, My, WBC].

QUESTION—Does the metaphor concerning the cup and dish continue in 11:40?

1. The apparent reference is to a cup maker who made the vessel spoken of in 11:39, but with the vocative 'Foolish people' the further meaning of God being the Maker is implied [AB]. Verse 40 refers to both the potter and to God [MGC, NIGTC]. The one who made both the outside and the inside refers first of all to the human who made the vessel to be clean on the outside and the inside, and secondly to God who made humans to be clean physically and spiritually [MGC].
2. The reference is to God who made both the outside and inside of people [Alf, BECNT, Gdt, ICC, Lns, NAC, NIBC, NIC, Su, TH, WBC]. God made the universe and he also made men's souls [ICC]. God made both the body and the soul and the purification of the body cannot be a substitute for the purification of the soul [Gdt]. The point is that God is as much concerned for the inside as for the outside [WBC]. God made both, but the Pharisees were acting as though God made their hands to be ceremonially washed and didn't make their hearts to be kept clean of wickedness [Lns].

11:41 But the (things) being-inside^a give (as) alms,^b and behold all (things) are clean^c for-you.

LEXICON—a. pres. act. participle of ἔνειμι (LN **85.19**) (BAGD p. 264): 'to be inside' [BAGD, LN]. The phrase 'the things being inside' is translated 'what is inside' [GW, REB], 'what is within' [HCSB, NASB], 'those/the things that are within' [BECNT, Lns; NRSV], 'in connection with what is inside' [WBC], 'what is in your cups and plates' [**LN**; TEV], 'what is in your dishes' [NCV], 'its contents' [AB], 'what you have' [CEV], 'such things as ye have' [KJV], 'what you greedily possess' [NLT], 'what is in you' [Arn], 'your inner self' [NTC], '(give) from your heart' [NET].

b. ἐλεημοσύνη (LN 57.112) (BAGD p. 250): 'alms' [AB, Arn, BAGD, BECNT, Lns, WBC; KJV, NRSV], 'charitable giving' [BAGD], 'charity' [HCSB, NASB, REB], 'gift, money given to the needy, charity donation' [LN], 'a gift to the poor' [GW]. The phrase 'to give as alms' is translated 'to give to the poor' [CEV, NCV, TEV], 'to help the poor' [NTC], 'to give to those in need' [NET], 'to give to the needy' [NLT]. This is the act of giving money or food to the poor in order to relieve their destitute condition [BECNT]. See this word at 12:33.

c. καθαρός (LN 79.48) (BAGD 4. p. 388): 'clean' [BAGD, LN]. The phrase 'all things are clean for you' [NASB] is also translated 'all things will be clean for you' [Arn], 'all things are clean to you' [Lns], 'everything is clean for you' [WBC; HCSB], 'all things are clean' [BECNT], 'everything will be clean for you' [NTC; GW, NET, NRSV], 'all will be clean for you' [AB], 'everything will be ritually clean for you' [TEV], 'all things are clean unto you' [KJV], 'all is clean' [REB], 'you will be fully clean' [NCV], 'you will be clean all over' [NLT], 'everything you do would please God' [CEV].

QUESTION—What relationship is indicated by πλήν 'but'?

The conjunction indicates a strong contrast [Lns, TH]. Rather than the outside, they are to devote attention to the inside [EGT, Rb]. It expands the thought with 'only' [ICC]. It is translated 'nevertheless' [BECNT], 'so' [NCV, NLT].

QUESTION—What are the things inside?

1. This refers to the things within cups and dishes or the things that are represented by them [BNTC, EGT, Gdt, ICC, LN (85.19), MGC, My, NAC, NIC, TG, TH, WBC; CEV, NCV, NLT]. It refers to the contents of cups [NIC, TH]. They should give what remains in the vessels at the close of a feast to the poor [Gdt]. The things in the vessels also stand for the things that are given as alms [NIC, Rb]. The things in the vessels stand for all of a person's possessions and they should be available to use in charitable service to others [BNTC, NIC].

2. This refers to the things within a person [Arn, BECNT, Lns, NIGTC, NTC, Rb, Su, TNTC; NET]. This refers to one's inner self and they must give themselves to help the poor [NTC]. The inward state of a person is right when he gives alms [TNTC]. The illustration in 11:39 hasn't referred to the contents of the vessels so this must refer to the things people have; they are to give alms from what is inside them, that is, from their hearts filled with love and charity [Lns]. The things are those connected with their character and spirituality and their caring for others [BECNT]. This means that the offering they should give to God is their very selves [Su]. They are to give from the heart [TNTC; NET].

QUESTION—What becomes clean by giving alms?

1. The cups and dishes become clean [ICC, My, TG, TH; probably GW, KJV, NASB, NET which translate with 'things']. In saying 'all things are clean for you', this means all the things considered by the Pharisees to need cleansing, such as the vessels which must be ceremonially cleansed [TH]. The vessels would not defile them when they themselves are benevolent [ICC]. In this context these things are the cups and plates, and in a broader sense, everything they have [TG]. The contents of the vessels stand for all the things the Pharisees think to be in need of cleansing [My, TH].

2. The person becomes clean [Arn, BECNT, MGC, NAC, NIC, NIGTC, NTC, Rb, Su; CEV, NCV, NLT]. The inward righteousness of giving alms makes them clean [Rb]. Giving alms will purify and cleanse their motives from within [MGC]. A man's inner life is purified when he gives alms and in this manner he will become clean before God and have no need for ceremonial purifications [NIC]. When one's inner self is expressed by giving alms, God's approval rest on that person [NTC]. In the context of greed this refers to the cleansing of the heart [NAC]. When

a Pharisee overcomes his greed by giving alms, then instead of being inwardly unclean, he will be clean and as a result any ritual washing will be unnecessary [NIGTC]. When their motives are right they are clean inside and they will not be defiled by touching objects that were considered religiously unclean [Su]. This implies repentance [BECNT].

DISCOURSE UNIT: 11:42–44 [TNTC]. The topic is woe to the Pharisees.

11:42 But woe[a] to-you Pharisees, because you-tithe[b] the mint[c] and the rue[d] and every herb[e] and you neglect[f] the justice[g] and the love of-God. And it-was-necessary to-do these (things) and not to-overlook[h] those (things).

TEXT—Instead of ταῦτα δὲ ἔδει ποιῆσαι κἀκεῖνα μὴ παρεῖναι 'and these things it was necessary to do and those things not to overlook', some manuscripts read ταῦτα ἔδει ποιῆσαι κἀκεῖνα μὴ ἀφιέναι 'these things it was necessary to do and those things not to pass by', some manuscripts read ταῦτα δὲ ἔδει ποιῆσαι κἀκεῖνα μὴ ἀφιέναι 'and these things it was necessary to do and those things not to pass by', and one Greek-Latin manuscript omits this clause. GNT reads ταῦτα δὲ ἔδει ποιῆσαι κἀκεῖνα μὴ παρεῖναι 'and these things it was necessary to do and those things not to overlook' with a B decision, indicating that the text is almost certain. Various versions would probably not distinguish clearly between these three wordings.

LEXICON—a. οὐαί (LN 22.9) (BAGD 1.a. p. 591): 'woe'. See this word at 6:24; 10:13; 17:1; 21:23; 22:22.
   b. pres. act. indic. of ἀποδεκατόω (Ln **57.114**) (BAGD 1. p. 89): 'to tithe' [AB, Arn, BAGD, BECNT, LN, Lns, NTC, WBC; KJV, NLT, NRSV], 'to pay tithes' [NASB, REB], 'to give a tenth' [**LN**; HCSB, NET], 'to give one tenth' [BAGD; NCV] 'to give God a tenth' [CEV, NIV], 'to give God one-tenth' [GW, TEV].
   c. ἡδύοσμον (LN 3.23) (BAGD p. 344): 'mint' [AB, Arn, BAGD, BECNT, LN, Lns, NTC, WBC; all versions except NLT]. The phrase 'the mint and the rue and every herb' is translated 'even the tiniest part of your income' [NLT]. The leaves of the mint were aromatic [TH] and were used for seasoning [Su; TEV]. The stems and leaves were sprinkled on food [TG].
   d. πήγανον (LN 3.22) (BAGD p. 655): 'rue' [AB, Arn, BAGD, BECNT, Lns, NTC, WBC; all versions except GW, NLT], 'spices' [GW]. The plant was about three feet high and had gray-green leaves and yellow flowers [NIGTC]. The leaves were sprinkled on food [TG]. It was a seasoning herb [TEV]. Its bitter leaves were used for medicine [Su].
   e. λάχανον (LN 3.29) (BAGD p. 467): 'herb' [Arn, BAGD, LN; HCSB, KJV, NET, NRSV, TEV], 'garden herb' [Lns, NTC; GW, NASB, NIV, REB], 'edible herb' [AB, BECNT], 'edible plant' [WBC], 'spices from the garden' [CEV], 'every other plant in your garden' [NCV]. This is a generic word for all types of garden vegetables [MGC, NIGTC] used for their leaves, roots, or seeds [Su]. The mint and rue were examples of the kinds of the spices in the garden [CEV].

f. pres. mid./pass. (deponent = act.) indic. of παρέρχομαι (LN **36.28**) (BAGD 1.b.β. p. 626): 'to neglect' [Arn, BAGD; NET, NIV, NRSV, REB, TEV], 'to disregard' [AB, BECNT; NASB], 'to ignore' [GW], 'to completely forget about' [NLT], 'to bypass' [HCSB, NLT], 'to pass by' [Lns, WBC], 'to pass over' [KJV], 'to transgress' [BAGD, **LN**], 'to disobey' [BAGD, LN], 'to break the law' [LN], 'to fail to be' [NCV]. The phrase 'you neglect the justice and the love of God' is translated 'you cheat people and you don't love God' [CEV]. The verb literally means 'to go or pass by' and figuratively it means 'to neglect' [ICC, NIGTC, TH], 'to disregard' [TH].

g. κρίσις (LN 56.25) (BAGD 3. p. 453): 'justice' [AB, BAGD, BECNT, LN, Lns, NTC, WBC; GW, HCSB, NASB, NET, NIV, NLT, NRSV, REB], 'judgment' [KJV], 'the proper distinctions' [Arn]. The phrase 'you neglect the justice' is translated 'you fail to be fair to others' [NCV], 'you cheat people' [CEV]. Here the word is to be understood as being concerned with social relationships [NAC, NIGTC, NTC]. It refers to having a sense of justice [AB] towards others [MGC]. It means to judge a person righteously [Lns]. It is the discernment of what is just [Gdt]. It refers to the proper distinctions between right and wrong [Arn]. It means to do the right thing to others [TG], to deal justly with all, especially with the needy [NIC], and to be just to people and treat them fairly and equitably [TH]. Instead, the Pharisees were indifferent to the poor [NAC].

h. aorist act. infin. of παρίημι (LN **13.145**) (BAGD 1. p. 627): 'to overlook' [**LN**; REB], 'to neglect' [AB, Arn, BECNT, NTC; HCSB, NASB], 'to leave undone' [BAGD, WBC; KJV, NIV, NLT], 'to avoid' [LN], 'to dismiss' [Lns], not explicit [CEV]. Some translate this verb the same as they translate παρέρχομαι above at f.: 'to neglect' [BAGD; NET, NRSV, TEV], 'to ignore' [GW]. The phrase 'and not to overlook' is translated 'while continuing to do' [NCV].

QUESTION—What relationship is indicated by the initial conjunction ἀλλά 'but'?

1. It indicates a contrast [BECNT, Gdt, ICC, NIGTC, NTC; KJV, NASB, NET, NRSV]. It is a contrast between what 11:41 says the Pharisees ought to do and what they actually did [Gdt, ICC, NIGTC]. Instead of acting as indicated in 11:41 and receiving the blessing, they receive a curse [ICC].

2. It marks a transition [Lns, TH]. No contrast is being made by this transitional conjunction [TH]. It merely indicates the breaking off of the previous line of thought as another is begun [Lns].

QUESTION—Why did the Pharisees tithe these plants?

The OT Law in Deut. 14:22–29, 26:12–14, Lev. 27:30–33, and Mal. 3:8–10 required the tithing of farm and garden produce [NIGTC]. The Law was concerned with the products of the field, that of grain, wine, and oil, but the Pharisees overextended the Law and included the aromatic herbs of the gardens [MGC, NTC, TG]. This type of detail was not actually required by the Law, so the Pharisees were going beyond the Law's requirements [NAC, TH, TNTC].

QUESTION—What is meant by the genitive construction τὴν ἀγάπην τοῦ θεοῦ 'the love of God'?

It means love for God [BECNT, Lns, NAC, Su, TG, TH; CEV, NCV, NET, TEV]. It means to obey the commandment to love God [TG]. It means either to love God or to have the love demanded by God [NIGTC].

QUESTION—What things were necessary to do and what things were not to be neglected?

1. Justice and love for God were necessary to do and the tithing of herbs should not be neglected [AB, BECNT, BNTC, ICC, Lns, NIC, NIGTC, Su, TG, TH, WBC; CEV, NIV]. Justice and love for God were the really important things to be done, but people were not to neglect doing the less important things concerning tithing [TG]. Neither in Luke nor in Matthew can the necessary things refer to tithing because meeting God's requirements is not possible if justice and love for God are neglected [Su].
2. Tithing herbs was necessary to do and the duties of justice and love for God should not be neglected [NAC, NTC; NLT]. Jesus was not endorsing the requirement to tithe every garden herb. He was saying that God's ordinances with respect to tithing should be observed, but of course without neglecting the weightier matters of the law [NAC, NTC].

11:43 **Woe to-you Pharisees, because you-love^a the place-of-honor^b in the synagogues and the greetings^c in the marketplaces.^d 11:44 Woe to-you, because you-are like unmarked graves,^e and the (ones) walking over (them) have- not -known (it).**

TEXT—In 11:44, following ὑμῖν 'to you', some manuscripts add γραμματεῖς καὶ Φαρισαῖοι, ὑποκριταί 'scribes and Pharisees, hypocrites'. GNT does not mention this variant. Γραμματεῖς καὶ Φαρισαῖοι, ὑποκριταί 'scribes and Pharisees, hypocrites' is read by KJV.

TEXT—In 11:44, instead of οἱ περιπατοῦντες 'the ones walking', some manuscripts read περιπατοῦντες 'walking'. GNT does not mention this variant but places οἱ 'the ones' in brackets in the text, indicating doubt about including it.

LEXICON—a. pres. act. indic. of ἀγαπάω (LN 25.104) (BAGD 2. p. 5): 'to love' [AB, Arn, BAGD, BECNT, LN, Lns, NTC, WBC; all versions], 'to take pleasure in, to like' [LN]. This means to like something because of having a high regard for its value or importance [LN]. It means to highly value something [ICC, My]. This is what they wanted, liked to have, or desired [TH]. They enjoyed doing this [NICNT].

b. πρωτοκαθεδρία (LN 87.18) (BAGD p. 725): 'place of honor' [BAGD, LN], 'seat of honor' [LN; NLT, NRSV], 'best seat' [BAGD, LN; NET], 'chief seat' [Arn, Lns, NTC, WBC; NASB, REB], 'most important seat' [NCV, NIV], 'front seat' [AB, BECNT; CEV, GW, HCSB], 'reserved seat' [TEV], 'uppermost seat' [KJV]. Literally 'first seat' [WBC], the seat was at the front of the synagogue and it faced the congregation [ICC, NTC, Su, TNTC]. Such a seat was reserved for important men [TG] and was a place of honor [AB, MGC]. It was a circular bench at the front [ICC, Su]. Anyone who was seated there was in view of the congregation and was regarded as being a prominent man [Lns, TNTC].

c. ἀσπασμός (LN 33.20) (BAGD 1. p. 117): 'greeting' [Arn, BAGD, BECNT, LN; HCSB, KJV, NIV], 'respectful greeting' [NASB, NLT], 'greeting of respect' [AB], 'elaborate greeting' [NET], 'salutation' [Lns], 'formal salutation' [NTC]. This noun is also translated as a verb phrase: 'to be greeted' [WBC; GW], 'to be greeted with honor' [CEV], 'to be greeted with respect' [NCV, NRSV, TEV], 'to be greeted respectfully' [REB]. This refers to formal greetings [BAGD, NTC]. It is implied that these were greetings to someone who was especially honored [WBC]. It was a sign of respect to a superior [NIGTC]. Elaborate greetings in public places indicated that the person being greeted was an important man worthy of respect [Arn, NTC]. It was an effusive greeting with words of honor and repeated bows [Lns, Su]. The Pharisees' love of receiving such greetings was due to their pride [BECNT, Lns] and self-centeredness [Su]. See this word at 20:46.

d. ἀγορά (LN 57.207) (BAGD p. 12): 'marketplace'. See translations of this word at 7:32.

e. μνημεῖον (LN7.75) (BAGD 2. p. 524): 'grave, tomb' [BAGD, LN]. The phrase 'unmarked graves' [AB, BECNT, NTC; CEV, GW, HCSB, NET, NIV, NRSV, REB, TEV] is also translated 'unseen tombs' [WBC], 'graves which appear not' [KJV], 'hidden graves' [Arn; NCV, NLT], 'concealed tombs' [NASB]. It describes an old, forgotten tomb that no longer had the appearance of a tomb [Lns]. It was a burial cave [Su]. It was a grave dug in the ground and filled with the bones of those who had died [AB].

QUESTION—What is the teaching of the simile about an unmarked grave?

Contact with corpses, human bones, or graves would make a person ceremonially unclean for seven days (Num. 19:16), and so Jews often whitewashed graves (Matthew 23:27) in order to avoid contact with them [ICC, MGC, NAC, NIC, NTC]. Coming in contact with an unmarked grave would defile a person without their knowing it [BECNT, Crd, Gdt, ICC, NTC, Su, TH, TNTC]. Outwardly Pharisees appeared to be religious, righteous, and good, but inwardly they were morally unclean [TNTC], corrupt [NIGTC], evil [TH], and hypocritical [Gdt].

1. The point is that the unrighteous character of the Pharisees is not outwardly apparent [Arn, Crd, EGT, NIBC, NIGTC, TH]: like the outward appearance of an unmarked grave hides the existence of the corruption inside, so the outward appearance of the Pharisees hides their inward corruption. Like the defiling contents of an unmarked grave is not suspected, so the evil moral interior of the Pharisees is not suspected [Crd]. In Matthew 23:7, the whitewashed tombs are obvious, but here they

are hidden, but in both descriptions, the point is that what looks all right on the outside is evil on the inside [NIGTC].
2. The point is that an unsuspecting person becomes defiled by the concealed depravity of the Pharisees [BECNT, ICC, Lns, MGC, NAC, NIC, NICNT, NTC, Su, TG, TNTC, WBC]: like a person is unknowingly defiled by coming into contact with an unmarked grave, so a person is unknowingly defiled by coming into contact with the outwardly righteous Pharisees. Contact with the Pharisees is an unwitting exposure to their moral contamination [WBC]. The people who followed the Pharisees were being spiritually contaminated without knowing it [MGC]. The teachings of the Pharisees lead their people to death [BECNT]. The Pharisees contaminate all who come in contact with them [Lns]. Like becoming defiled by coming in contact with an unrecognized grave, so people become defiled by the externally religious Pharisees [Su, TG]. Like becoming ceremonially unclean by walking over an unmarked grave, people become morally unclean by walking in the teachings and ways of the Pharisees [NTC, TNTC].

DISCOURSE UNIT: 11:45–54 [TNTC; NCV]. The topic is Jesus talks with the experts on the Law [NCV], woe to the lawyers [TNTC].

11:45 And answering one of-the lawyers[a] says to-him, Teacher, (by) saying these (things) you-insult[b] us also. **11:46** And he-said, Woe to-you lawyers also, because you-burden[c] people (with) burdens difficult-to-bear,[d] and you-yourselves do- not -touch[e] the burdens (with) one of-your fingers.

LEXICON—a. νομικός (LN 33.338) (BAGD 2. p. 541): 'lawyer'. See translations of this word at 7:30. This word also occurs at 10:25, 11:46, 52; 14:3.
  b. pres. act. indic. of ὑβρίζω (LN **33.390**) (BAGD p. 831): 'to insult' [AB, Arn, BAGD, BECNT, **LN**, Lns, NTC, WBC; all versions except CEV, KJV], 'to reproach' [KJV], 'to say cruel things about' [CEV].
  c. pres. act. indic. of φορτίζω (LN **15.207**) (BAGD p. 865): 'to burden' [BAGD, NTC; GW], 'to put burdens on' [Arn], 'to load' [Lns; CEV, HCSB, NRSV, REB], 'to cause to bear a load' [**LN**], 'to cause to carry' [BAGD, LN], 'to load down' [NET, NIV], 'to load up' [WBC], 'to lade' [KJV], 'to weigh down' [AB; NASB], 'to put on people's backs' [TEV], 'to crush beneath' [NLT], 'to make (strict rules)' [NCV]. This refers to the religious duties which they added to the law with the result that these burdened the people [BECNT].
  d. δυσβάστακτος (LN **22.34**) (BAGD p. 209): 'difficult to bear' [**LN**], 'hard to bear' [Arn, BAGD, LN]. The phrase 'burdens difficult to bear' [NET] is also translated 'loads which are difficult to carry' [WBC], 'burdens that are hard to bear' [NTC; NASB, NRSV], 'loads that are hard to carry' [Lns; GW, HCSB, TEV], 'burdens grievous to be borne' [KJV], 'burdens they can hardly carry' [NIV], 'burdens they can scarcely bear' [AB], 'heavy burdens' [CEV], 'intolerable burdens' [REB], 'strict rules that are

very hard for people to obey' [NCV], 'impossible religious demands' [NLT].

e. pres. act. indic. of προσψαύω (LN **18.11, 24.75**) (BAGD p. 720): 'to touch' [Arn, BAGD, **LN** (24.74)], 'to touch to help' [**LN** (18.11)]. The clause is translated 'you will not lift a finger to lighten the load' [REB], 'you will not lift one finger to help them' [NIV], 'you won't lift a finger to help them carry the loads' [CEV], 'you will not stretch out a finger to help them carry those loads' [TEV], 'you won't lift a finger to carry any of these loads' [GW], 'you never lift a finger to help ease the burden' [NLT], 'you do not lift a finger to ease them' [NRSV], 'you will/do not even touch the burdens with one of your fingers' [NTC; HCSB, KJV, NASB; similarly Lns, WBC], 'you will not lift a single finger to the burdens' [AB], 'you refuse to touch the burdens with even one of your fingers' [NET], 'you don't even try to follow those rules' [NCV].

QUESTION—In 11:45 what is the meaning of καί 'also' when the lawyer said 'you insult us also'?

Most of the lawyers were Pharisees [ICC, Lns, MGC, My, NAC, NIGTC, NTC, Rb, Su, TH, WBC]. They were the better instructed men among the Pharisees [ICC]. They were the legal specialists among the Pharisees [AB]. They sometimes scoffed at much of what the Pharisee's did and taught and here the lawyer understood that Jesus was condemning the lawyers' legalism as well [Su]. He thought that Jesus was speaking against the whole class of men who made a profession of studying the OT and rabbinical traditions [Lns]. He realized that his profession of codifying the law was being condemned as well as those who carefully observed those laws [NIGTC]. Men of his profession were responsible for the details of the laws practiced by the Pharisees [AB, Arn, WBC].

QUESTION—What is meant by the metaphor of burdening people with burdens?

The 'burden' was the burden of obeying the law as interpreted by the lawyers [TH]. The burdens refer to interpretations which augmented the OT law [AB, ICC, NIC, NTC, Rb, TNTC]. They made the Law more severe than it was intended to be and promoted rigorous ritualism [ICC]. Their interpretations caused people to suffer under laws that were exceedingly hard to accomplish [Su]. They had added many regulations to the Law of Moses and these had deprived the people of their liberty and peace of mind [NTC]. They imposed heavy obligations that were difficult to obey [TG] The traditions they added to the Law made it impossible for the average person to keep them all [NAC].

QUESTION—What is meant by the criticism 'you yourselves do not touch the burdens with one of your fingers'?

1. They did not help lighten the burdens of the people [AB, Arn, BECNT, ICC, MGC, NAC, NIBC, NICNT, Rb, Su, TG, WBC; CEV, NIV, NLT, NRSV, REB, TEV]. They were unconcerned when the people felt that it was impossible to fulfill the requirements and they would not remove or

change such laws [Su]. They had no compassion on the people when they interpreted the OT Law and imposed their laws on the people [TG]. They did not interpret the Law properly or sanely [Arn, ICC]. This refers to the initial burdening when they laid the burden of the law upon the people and they did not support and encourage the people afterwards [WBC].
  2. They did not bear the burdens that others were required to bear [Crd, Gdt, Lns, NIC, NIGTC, NTC, TH, TNTC; GW, NCV]. The lawyers knew how to evade the burdens they placed on others [Crd]. They did not live up to all the laws they imposed on others [Lns]. They do not touch them in order to carry them their selves, rather they had learned to avoid the burdens, as it is said in Matthew 23:3, 'they say things but do not do them' [NTC].

11:47 Woe to-you, because you-build^a the memorials^b of-the prophets, and your ancestors^c killed them.

LEXICON—a. pres. act. indic. of οἰκοδομέω (LN 45.1) (BAGD 1.a. p. 558) 'to build' [AB, Arn, BAGD, BECNT, LN, Lns, NTC, WBC; all versions except TEV], 'to construct' [LN], 'to make' [TEV]. The present tense is to be understood as a habitual action [TH]. The lawyers were building or rebuilding the tombs of the prophets and probably redecorating them as well [NTC]. There were many tombs of the prophets, and perhaps they were then building such structures [Gdt].
  b. μνημεῖον (LN **7.76**) (BAGD 1. p. 524): 'memorial' [BAGD, **LN**], 'monument' [BAGD, LN; CEV, GW, HCSB, REB], 'tomb' [AB, Arn, BECNT, Lns, NTC, WBC; NASB, NCV, NET, NIV, NLT, NRSV], 'fine tomb' [TEV], 'sepulcher' [KJV]. The phrase 'you build the memorials of the prophets' is translated 'you build monuments to honor the prophets' [CEV].
  c. πατήρ (LN 10.20) (BAGD 1.b. p. 635): 'ancestor' [BAGD, LN; GW, NCV, NET, NLT, NRSV, TEV], 'forefather' [BAGD, LN; NIV], '(your) own people' [CEV], 'fathers' [AB, Arn, BECNT, Lns, NTC, WBC; HCSB, KJV, NASB, REB].

11:48 Therefore you-are witnesses^a and you-approve-of^b the deeds of your ancestors, because they killed them, and you build (the memorials).

TEXT—Instead of μάρτυρές ἐστε 'you are witnesses', some manuscripts read μαρτυρεῖτε 'you testify'. GNT does not mention this variant.

TEXT—Following οἰκοδομεῖτε 'you build', some manuscripts add αὐτῶν τὰ μνημεῖα 'their tombs' and some manuscripts add τοὺς τάφους αὐτῶν 'their tombs'. GNT rejects both of these additions with a B decision, indicating that the text is almost certain. One of these additions is read by KJV.

LEXICON—a. μάρτυς (LN 33.270) (BAGD 2.b. p. 494): 'witness' [Arn, BAGD, BECNT, LN, Lns, WBC; GW, HCSB, NASB, NRSV], 'one who testifies' [LN], not explicit [CEV, NLT]. The phrase 'you are witnesses' is translated as a verb phrase: 'you testify' [NTC; NET, NIV, REB], 'you

give testimony' [AB], 'you bear witness' [KJV], 'you admit' [TEV], 'you show that' [NCV].
   b. pres. act. indic. of συνευδοκέω (LN 31.17) (BAGD p. 788): 'to approve of' [AB, Arn, BAGD, Lns, NTC; GW, HCSB, NASB, NCV, NET, NIV, NRSV, REB, TEV], 'to give approval' [WBC], 'to consent to' [BAGD, LN], 'to agree to' [BECNT, LN], 'to allow' [KJV]. The phrase 'you are witnesses and you approve of the deeds of your ancestors' is translated 'you must think that was the right thing for your people to do' [CEV], 'You agree with your ancestors that what they did was right. You would have done the same yourselves' [NLT].

QUESTION—How are the verbs related in the clause 'you are witnesses and you approve of the deeds of your ancestors'?
   1. They were witnesses to the fact that their ancestors had killed the prophets and they approved of their ancestors' actions [ICC, My, NTC, TG, TH; probably BECNT, Lns; GW, NASB, NRSV which connect the verbs with 'and'].
   2. They testified that they approved of what their ancestors did in killing the prophets [AB, Arn, Lns, NIGTC, NTC; KJV, NCV, NET, NIV, REB, TEV].

QUESTION—How did building memorial tombs lead to the conclusion that they were witnesses?

Normally, memorial tombs are built to honor the lives of the deceased [BECNT, MGC, NTC, TNTC, WBC]. Luke uses irony [BECNT, NICNT, WBC] to portray the building of monuments to be an act of celebrating the deaths of the prophets and it means 'your ancestors committed the murder of the prophets and you are celebrating this' [WBC]. Since their testimony was given not by what they said but by what they did, they showed or proved by their actions that they knew what their fathers did [TG, TH]. By building tombs for the prophets they witnessed to the fact that they approved of killing the prophets [Lns, My, NIGTC] and were associated in the guilt of their ancestors [AB, NIBC]. If it is ironic, it means 'your fathers killed the prophets, and you make sure they that stay dead' or it means 'you are no better than your fathers who refused to hear the prophets and killed them. You, to be sure, build their tombs, but you are equally unwilling to hear them' [NIGTC]. They wanted people to think that they were honoring the prophets by building the tombs, but since they did not live according to the teaching of the prophets, they proved that they were no better than their ancestors who killed the prophets [NTC]. The tombs they built were memorials of rejection that reflect their agreement with their ancestors [BECNT]. Although they outwardly honored the prophets, the building of the monuments simply served to draw attention to the fact that they were the children of the people who had murdered the prophets [NIC]. By building memorials for the prophets it appeared that they disapproved of what their ancestors did, but they really opposed the teachings of the prophets just as their ancestors did and so they were witnesses against themselves [Rb]. By building the memorials, they kept alive the view that the prophets deserved to die [Su]. The Pharisees only honored the prophets who were dead [Crd; NET] and they killed the prophets whom God sends to them [Crd]. Or, 'witness' is used as a technical Jewish term for the part played by witnesses that were required in carrying out a punishment such as stoning, and here it means that they took the part of witnesses of the killing of the prophets by their ancestors [Gdt].

QUESTION—What is being confirmed in the last clause, 'because they killed them, and you build the memorials'?

This emphasizes the lawyers' partnership with their ancestors and it comes out that the tombs are celebrating not the lives of the prophets but their extermination [WBC]. They were only completing the work of those who killed the prophets [TNTC]. Their ancestors killed the prophets and the Pharisees buried them, thus finishing their work [Gdt]. The lawyers are no better than their ancestors who killed the prophets [MGC]. Although outwardly the Pharisees were honoring the prophets, they were dishonoring them as much as their ancestors did because they did not obey the teachings of the prophets and ignored their testimony to Christ [ICC].

11:49 **Because-of this also the wisdom[a] of-God said, I-will-send to them prophets and apostles, and (some) of them they-will-kill and (some) they-will-persecute,[b]**

LEXICON—a. σοφία (LN **32.41**) (BAGD 4. p. 760): 'wisdom' [BAGD, **LN**]. Here wisdom is personified [BAGD]. The phrase 'the wisdom of God said' [Arn, BECNT; HCSB, KJV, NASB, NET] is also translated 'the Wisdom of God said' [Lns, NTC, WBC; CEV, GW, NRSV, REB, TEV], 'God's wisdom has said' [AB], 'in his wisdom God said' [NCV], 'God in his wisdom said' [NIV, NLT].

b. fut. act. indic. of διώκω (LN 39.45) (BAGD 2. p. 201): 'to persecute' [AB, Arn, BAGD, BECNT, LN, Lns, NTC, WBC; all versions except CEV, NCV], 'to mistreat' [CEV], 'to treat cruelly' [NCV]. See this word at 21:12.

QUESTION—What is the reference of 'this' in the opening phrase διὰ τοῦτο 'because of this'?

It is because they are like the people described in 11:47–48 [WBC]. It is because of their complicity in the murder of the prophets by their ancestors [ICC]. Their ancestors killed prophets and the Pharisees were in agreement with them [NTC]. It is because of the Pharisees' attitude about the OT prophets [NIGTC]. It is because of their evil deeds [CEV]. They had perverted the teaching of the prophets and hypocritically built tombs for the prophets [Lns].

QUESTION—What is meant by 'the wisdom of God said'?

1. This means God, in his wisdom, said [Arn, BECNT, BNTC, Crd, ICC, Lns, NIC, NTC; NCV, NIV, NLT]. It refers to God and his will [BECNT]. It means 'the wise God said' [Arn]. Although this quote can be

found in substance in various places in the OT, the exact quotation is not there and therefore this quotation is what Jesus in his supernatural knowledge of God understood [Lns].
2. This is a self-designation of Jesus as the Wisdom of God [MGC, My, Su]. This is a roundabout way in which Jesus referred to himself and this is supported in the parallel passage at Matthew 23:34 where Jesus states that he was the one who would send out prophets and others who would be killed or persecuted [Su].
3. This is a personification of the Wisdom of God [BAGD, BECNT, NIBC, NIGTC, TG, WBC; CEV, GW, NET, NRSV, REB, TEV]. It is a personification of God's attribute of wisdom [WBC], of his wise will [NET]. This is the Jewish personification of Wisdom (as in Prov. 9) and Jesus has been informed by Wisdom of her intention [WBC].

QUESTION—Where does the quotation from the wisdom of God end?
1. The quotation ends at the end of 11:49 [BECNT; GW, NCV, NET, NIV, NLT, REB, TEV].
2. The quotation ends after the word 'sanctuary' in the middle of 11:51 [Arn, Lns, NIGTC, TH, WBC]. After reporting what Wisdom said, Jesus added 'Yes, I say to you it will be required of this generation' [WBC].
3. The quotation ends at the end of 11:51 [CEV, NASB].

QUESTION—Who were the prophets and apostles who would be killed or persecuted?
1. The words 'I will send to them' indicate that this will happen in the time of the present generation [Arn, BECNT, Gdt, Lns, NAC, NIC, Su, WBC]. Speaking of the Wisdom of God is a graphic way of portraying God's plan by expressing it as a saying that was written in the past, but this refers to God's current representatives [BECNT]. The apostles were Christian apostles and therefore the prophets were Christian prophets [NAC]. Adding 'prophets' to the designation 'apostles' indicates that the apostles are in the same class as the OT prophets [Lns]. The sending of the emissaries is future to the prophetic activity in 11:50–51 and the phrase 'prophets and apostles (emissaries)' designates God's messengers, including John, Jesus, and those who will act in Jesus' name [Arn, NIC, WBC]. Jesus' apostles were the new prophets [Gdt]. The apostles were the Twelve and those associated with them [Lns, WBC]. By sending this new batch of prophets and emissaries, Wisdom will provoke a repetition of the murderous actions of the ancestors and expose the true nature of those who were building the tombs [WBC].
2. The words 'I will send to them' include the whole history of God's sending prophets and apostles [ICC, MGC, NIGTC, NTC]. God sent prophets to the Jews and apostles to the Christians and by joining the apostles with the prophets of the OT the solidarity of the Pharisees with their murderous ancestors is indicated [ICC]. In light of 11:47 and 11:50–51, the prophets certainly refer to the OT prophets, but 'prophets' may also include the early Christian prophets since the word 'apostles'

refer to the apostles of Jesus [MGC]. The prophets and apostles are the same group of emissaries viewed from different angles: the emissaries are called prophets because they convey God's message and they are called apostles because they are officially sent and commissioned. This refers to the OT prophets and to the NT prophets and apostles, some examples being the murder of Jesus, John, James, and Peter and the persecution of Paul and his helpers [NTC].

11:50 in-order-that[a] the blood of-all the prophets having-been-poured-out[b] from the creation[c] of-(the)-world may-be-required[d] from this generation,

LEXICON—a. ἵνα (LN 89.59, 89.49) (BAGD II.2. p. 378): 'in order that' [Arn, BAGD, BECNT, LN (89.59), Lns], 'that' [NTC; KJV], 'so that' [BAGD, LN (89.49), WBC; HCSB, NASB, NET, NIV, NRSV, REB], 'so' [GW, NCV, TEV], 'therefore' [NIV], 'consequently' [AB], 'and' [NLT], not explicit [CEV]. Purpose and result are identical in declarations of God's will [BAGD].

  b. perf. pass. participle of ἐκχύννομαι (LN 23.112) (BAGD 1. p. 247): 'to be poured out, to be shed' [BAGD]. The phrase 'the blood having been poured out' is translated 'the blood poured out' [WBC], 'the blood shed' [Lns; HCSB, NASB, NRSV, REB], 'the blood that was shed' [Arn, BECNT; KJV], 'the blood that has been shed' [AB; NET, NIV], 'the blood that is being shed' [Lns], 'the murder of' [GW, NLT, TEV], 'who have been murdered' [CEV], 'the deaths (of all who) were killed' [NCV]. Blood is a metaphor for death [NAC, NIGTC]. To shed a person's blood means to kill him [LN, TH].

  c. καταβολή (LN 42.37) (BAGD 1. p. 409): 'creation' [LN; NLT, TEV], 'foundation' [AB, BAGD, Lns, WBC; HCSB, KJV, NASB, NRSV, REB], 'the beginning' [BECNT; CEV, NCV, NET, NIV], 'the founding' [Arn, NTC]. The phrase 'from the creation of the world' is translated 'since the world was made' [GW].

  d. aorist pass. subj. of ἐκζητέω (LN **56.9**) (BAGD 4. p. 240): 'to be required' [AB, Arn, BAGD, BECNT, Lns, WBC; KJV], 'to be charged' [BAGD, **LN**; GW, NASB, NRSV], 'to be exacted' [NTC], 'to be held accountable' [NET], 'to be held responsible' [HCSB, NIV, NLT], 'to have to answer for' [REB], 'to be punished' [CEV, NCV, TEV]. This speaks of avenging their deaths [AB]. God is the one who will charge them [TG, TH].

QUESTION—What is the relationship of the initial conjunction ἵνα?
  1. It indicates purpose [Arn, BECNT, Lns; KJV]: I will send them in order that.... This is God's purpose [Lns].
  2. It indicates result [BECNT, ICC, MGC, TH; GW, NASB, NCV, NET, NIV, REB, TEV]: I will send them and the result will be this.

QUESTION—Why would this generation be responsible for all the murders of the prophets since the creation of the world?

Every new generation that does not learn from the preceding generation is adding to its own guilt and to the severity of its punishment [Lns, NTC]. By aligning themselves with the people of all the former generations who killed the prophets, the people of the present generation will be punished for the deaths of all the prophets [TNTC]. Guilt and punishment are cumulative so that the last acts approve all the former acts of the same type and they involve the guiltiness for all the acts [Lns]. Failure to heed the lessons of the preceding generation adds to the guilt and severity of punishment of the present generation [NTC]. The wickedness of previous generations has accumulated and finally brought about God's judgment on the present generation [Gdt, WBC] which has both personal responsibility and inherited guilt [WBC]. Since the OT prophets prophesied of the time of the current generation, the rejection of God's current messengers was also a rejection of the whole line of prophets [BECNT]. The present Jewish generation was especially guilty by rejecting and killing the Son of God and persecuting his followers [NIC]. This does not mean that the present generation was to be punished for the sins of the previous generations. When the present generation rejected Jesus, the Son of God, and the ones he sent out, it was the climax of the long history of rejection and murder [NIC, Su] and being the generation in which all that guilt culminated they would experience the culmination of retribution [Su]. This was the generation that would be punished by the terrible destruction of Jerusalem in A.D. 70, and there would also be the ultimate judgment at the final judgment at the end of the age [NAC, Su].

11:51 from (the) blood of-Abel to (the) blood of Zechariah, the (one) having-perished[a] between the altar and the sanctuary.[b] Yes, I say to-you, it-will-be-required[c] from this generation.

LEXICON—a. aorist mid. participle of ἀπόλλυμι (LN 20.31): 'to perish' [AB, Arn, BECNT, Lns, NTC, WBC; HCSB, KJV, NRSV], 'to die' [NCV], 'to be destroyed' [LN], 'to be murdered' [CEV, GW], 'to be killed' [GW, NASB, NET, NIV, NLT, TEV], 'to meet one's death' [REB].

b. οἶκος (LN **7.2**) (BAGD 1.a.β. p. 560): 'sanctuary' [AB, BECNT, NTC, WBC; HCSB, NET, NIV, NLT, NRSV, REB], 'the Holy Place' [TEV], 'temple' [**LN**; CEV, GW, KJV, NCV], 'temple building' [BAGD], 'house' [Arn, BAGD], 'the House' [Lns], 'house of God' [NASB]. 'House' is any large building [BAGD] and it became a designation for the temple because the temple was spoken of as God's dwelling place [LN]. In the parallel passage at Matt. 23:35 the word used is ναός 'sanctuary' or 'temple' and that must be what the word οἶκος 'house' refers here to [Alf, EGT, ICC].

c. fut. pass. indic. of ἐκζητέω (LN 56.9) (BAGD 4. p. 240): 'to be required' See this word at 11:50.

QUESTION—Why is Abel mentioned?
　　The murder of Abel is the first murder recorded in the OT (Gen. 4:8) [Arn, BECNT, Gdt, ICC, Lns, MGC, NAC, NIC, NICNT, NIGTC, NTC, Rb, Su, TG, TH, TNTC, WBC]. He is classed with the prophets in a broad sense [BECNT, My, NIGTC] as being a righteous man [BECNT, My, NAC], as being one who testified to God's way of righteousness [Lns], as being like other prophets who suffered for righteousness' sake [MGC]. This mention of Abel explains 'the blood of all the prophets, having been poured out from the beginning of the world' in the previous verse [BECNT].

QUESTION—Why is Zechariah mentioned?
　　The murder of Zechariah is the last person who was murdered in the arrangement of the books in the Hebrew Bible [Arn, Gdt, ICC, Lns, NAC, NIBC, NIC, NICNT, NTC, Rb, Su, TG, TH, TNTC, WBC]. This is recorded in 2 Chronicles 24:20–21, the last book in the Jewish canon [ICC, Lns]. Although historically the prophet Urijah was killed 200 years later (Jer. 26:23), Jesus confined his examples to the first and last books of the Jewish Scriptures [ICC, Lns]. Zechariah was killed in the courtyard between the altar of burnt sacrifices in the priest's court and the Sanctuary building that contained the Holy Place and the Holy of Holies [Lns]. He was not ordinarily considered to be a prophet, but he prophesied when the Spirit of God inspired him to announce to the people that God had forsaken the people because they had forsaken God, and it was because of that they stoned him to death in the courtyard [AB]. Many commentaries discuss problems in identifying Zechariah [AB, BECNT, BNTC, Crd, Gdt, MGC, NAC, NICNT, NIGTC, WBC]. One of the problems is that in 2 Chronicles 24:20–25 the father of Zechariah is named Jehoiada, but Matthew says that Zechariah's father was Berekiah (Matt. 23:35) [MGC, NIGTC].

QUESTION—Who is the speaker of 'Yes, I say to you'?
　　1. This is still the Wisdom of God being quoted [CEV, NASB].
　　2. This is now Jesus who is directly speaking [BECNT, NIGTC, TH; GW, NCV, NET, NIV, NLT, REB, TEV].

11:52 Woe to-you lawyers, because you-took-away[a] the key of-knowledge. You-yourselves did- not -enter-in[b] and you-hindered[c] the (ones) entering-in.

LEXICON—a. aorist act. indic. of αἴρω (LN 15.203): 'to take away' [LN]. The phrase 'you took away the key of knowledge' [Arn, Lns; similarly BECNT, WBC; HCSB, KJV, NASB, NRSV, REB] is also translated 'you have taken away the key to knowledge' [NTC; NET, NIV], 'you have taken away the key that unlocks knowledge' [GW], 'you have taken away the key to learning about God' [NCV], 'you carry the keys to the door of knowledge about God' [CEV], 'you have carried off the key of knowledge' [AB], 'you hide the key to knowledge from the people' [NLT], 'you have kept the key that opens the door to the house of knowledge' [TEV]. Here the verb means to take away from its proper place so that it cannot be used [TH].

b. aorist act. indic. of εἰσέρχομαι (LN 15.93, 90.70) (BAGD 2.a. p. 233): 'to enter in' [BAGD, LN; KJV], 'to enter' [AB, Arn, BECNT, NTC, WBC; NASB, NIV, NLT, NRSV], 'to go in' [BAGD, LN (15.93), Lns; CEV, HCSB, NET, REB, TEV], 'to gain entrance' [GW], 'to experience, to attain' [LN (90.70)], 'to learn' [NCV].
c. aorist act. indic. of κωλύω (LN 13.146) (BAGD 1. p. 461): 'to hinder' [BAGD, LN], 'to prevent' [LN]. The phrase 'you hindered the ones entering in' is translated 'you hindered those who were entering' [BECNT, NTC; NASB, NIV, NRSV; similarly KJV], 'you hindered those who wanted to enter' [WBC], 'you have hindered those who would enter' [AB], 'those who tried to enter you hindered' [Arn], 'those who were trying to go in you prevented' [REB], 'you stop those who are trying to go in' [TEV], 'you hindered those who were going in' [HCSB, NET], 'you keep others from going in' [CEV], 'you prevent others from entering' [NLT], 'you've kept out those who wanted to enter' [GW], 'those trying to go in you effectively hindered' [Lns], 'you stopped others from learning' [NCV].

QUESTION—What is meant by the genitive construction τὴν κλεῖδα τῆς γνώσεως 'the key of knowledge'?
1. The key opens the way to knowledge [AB, Arn, BECNT, Gdt, ICC, My, NAC, NIC, NTC, Su, TH, TNTC, WBC; CEV, GW, NCV, NET, NIV, NLT, TEV]. The key unlocks the meaning of Scripture [TNTC]. They took away the key that opens the treasures of knowledge by their wrong interpretations of the OT [Arn].
2. The key consists of knowledge [Alf, EGT, Lns]. The key is the correct knowledge of the Scriptures [Alf].

QUESTION—What is the knowledge about?
It is the knowledge about Wisdom [BECNT], the truth [BECNT], God [Gdt, MGC, NIGTC, TNTC; CEV, NCV], both God and his will [AB, Su, TG], the Messiah [Lns], the Law [Alf, TG], the Scriptures [Alf, ICC, My, NAC, NIC, NTC, TH, TNTC], especially the Scriptures concerning salvation [ICC, My, NAC, NIC, NTC, TH]. The key unlocked the meaning of Scripture that leads to a true knowledge of God [TNTC].

QUESTION—In what way did they take away the key of knowledge?
They treated Scripture as nothing but Law with terrible legal burdens [Lns]. The lawyers wrongly interpreted the OT [Arn, ICC, NIC, Su, TH], making it impossible for them to teach others [ICC, TNTC] about how they could obtain salvation [Su, TH]. They added a great number of rigid provisions to the Law and taught salvation by works [NTC]. They took the key away from others when they held the people in contempt as being incapable of receiving knowledge [ICC]. They took away the key when their teaching opposed the saving truth of Scriptures and rendered people incapable of recognizing the truth [My]. They blocked access to knowledge [WBC].

QUESTION—What is indicated by the present tense in the phrase τοὺς εἰσερχομένους 'the ones entering in'?
They were in the process of entering [Gdt, My, NTC, TNTC; KJV, NASB, NET, NIV, NRSV]: you hindered the ones who were entering in. The people intended to enter [My] and if they hadn't been hindered they would have entered [NTC]. They were ready for this knowledge but lacked the correct interpretation of Scripture [Gdt]. They were on their way to this knowledge but were turned away by their teachers [TNTC]. The present participle of εἰσερχομένους 'entering in' is conative [BECNT, ICC, Lns, TH, WBC; REB, TEV]: you hindered the ones who were *trying* to enter in. Some translate so as to indicate the result of hindering others [CEV, GW, NCV, NLT]: you prevented others from entering.

DISCOURSE UNIT: 11:53–54 [Su]. The topic is the hostility of Jewish religious leaders.

11:53 **And-from-there he having-gone-out[a] the scribes and the Pharisees began terribly to-be-hostile[b] and to-closely-question him about many (things), 11:54 plotting[c] to-catch[d] him (in) something from his mouth.**
TEXT—In 11:53, instead of κἀκεῖθεν ἐξελθόντος αὐτοῦ 'and from there he having gone out', some manuscripts read λέγοντος δὲ αὐτοῦ ταῦτα πρὸς αὐτούς 'and he saying these things to them'. GNT does not mention this variant. Λέγοντος δὲ αὐτοῦ ταῦτα πρὸς αὐτούς 'and he saying these things to them' is read by KJV.
TEXT—In 11:54, following αὐτόν 'him', some manuscripts add ζητοῦντες 'seeking' and some manuscripts evidently add καὶ ζητοῦντες 'and seeking', although GNT does not mention καί 'and'. Καὶ ζητοῦντες 'and seeking' is read by KJV.
TEXT—In 11:54, following τοῦ στόματος αὐτοῦ 'his mouth' some manuscripts add ἵνα κατηγορήσωσιν αὐτοῦ 'in order that they might accuse him'. GNT does not mention this variant. Ἵνα κατηγορήσωσιν αὐτοῦ 'in order that they might accuse him' is read by KJV.
LEXICON—a. aorist act. participle of ἐξέρχομαι (LN 15.40): 'to go out of, to depart out of' [LN]. The phrase 'and from there he having gone out' is translated 'Jesus was about to leave' [CEV], 'as Jesus finished speaking' [NLT], 'when he went outside' [NRSV], 'after he had left the house' [REB], 'and as he was going away from there' [BECNT], 'when Jesus left that place' [TEV], 'when Jesus had gone out of there' [AB], 'when he had gone out from there' [Arn, WBC], 'when he went out from there' [NET], 'when he left there' [NTC; HCSB, NASB, NIV], 'and having gone out thence' [Lns], 'when Jesus left' [GW, NCV]. He went out of the Pharisee's house that he had entered in 11:37 [AB, My, NIC, Rb, TH].
  b. pres. act. infin. of ἐνέχω (LN **39.4**) (BAGD 1. p. 265): 'to be hostile towards' [BAGD, LN]. The phrase 'began terribly to be hostile' is translated 'began to be very hostile' [**LN**; NASB], 'began to be very hostile toward him' [NRSV], 'began to oppose him fiercely' [HCSB,

NIV], 'began to oppose him violently' [WBC], 'began to oppose him bitterly' [NET], 'began to criticize him bitterly' [TEV], 'began to assail him fiercely' [REB], 'began to give him trouble' [NCV], 'held a terrible grudge against him' [GW], 'began to be violently enraged against him' [NTC], 'wanted to get even with him' [CEV], 'were furious' [NLT], 'began to react violently against him' [AB], 'began to set themselves vehemently against him' [Lns], 'began to press him' [BECNT], 'began to press upon him vehemently' [Arn].

c. pres. act. participle of ἐνεδρεύω (LN **30.70**, 39.51) (BAGD p. 264): 'to plot' [BAGD, **LN** (30.70)], 'to make plans against' [LN (30.70)], 'to be in ambush, to make plans for a secret attack' [LN (39.51)]. See the next item for the translation of the phrase.

d. aorist act. infin. of θηρεύω (LN 27.30) (BAGD p. 360): 'to catch' [BAGD, LN], 'to trap' [LN]. The phrase 'plotting to catch him in something from his mouth' is translated 'plotting to catch him in something he might say' [AB; NASB], 'plotting against him, to catch him in something he might say' [NET], 'they were plotting against him to catch him in something (wrong) he might say' [**LN**], 'trying to catch him saying something wrong' [NCV], 'and watched him closely to trap him in something he might say' [GW], 'waiting to catch him in something he might say' [NIV], 'so that they could catch him saying something wrong' [CEV], 'plotting as if in ambush to catch him with respect to something that might fall from his lips' [NTC], 'trying to lay traps for him and catch him saying something wrong' [TEV], 'laying snares to catch something out of his mouth' [Arn], 'laying snares to catch him with his own words' [REB], 'trying to trap him into saying something they could use against him' [NLT], 'lying in ambush for him, to capture something out of his mouth' [Lns], 'lying in ambush to catch at something from his mouth' [WBC], 'lying in wait for him to trap him in something he said' [HCSB], 'lying in wait for him to catch him in something he might say' [NRSV], 'lying in wait for him to catch something he might say' [BECNT], 'laying wait for him to catch something out of his mouth' [KJV].

QUESTION—When did the scribes and Pharisees question Jesus?

1. It was when Jesus was about to leave the house [CEV].
2. It was as soon as Jesus went out of the house [AB, BECNT, Gdt, ICC; NRSV]. This was the house he had entered in 11:37 [AB]. The scribes and the Pharisees had attended the meal and now they left the house with Jesus [BECNT, ICC] and crowded around him [BECNT].
3. It was after Jesus had left the house [Lns, MGC, NICNT, Su; NLT, REB]. 'Began' indicates a new course of action and the following happened during the next days [Lns]. It was from that time on [NLT]. This covers the period up to the time of Jesus' death [Su].

QUESTION—Why did they question Jesus?

Jesus had accused them of a lack of knowledge and so they wanted to dishonor him by their questions, hoping that Jesus would make a blunder in his answers [BECNT]. They tried to get him to say something on the spur of the moment that they could use against him when accusing him before the authorities [Lns]. They wanted to get Jesus to say something for which they could accuse him of disobeying the Law or offending God [TG]. They wanted Jesus to say something that would be a reason for his execution [Su].

www.ingramcontent.com/pod-product-compliance
Lightning Source LLC
Chambersburg PA
CBHW071218290426
44108CB00013B/1217